ALSO BY AMERICA'S TEST KITCHEN

THE COOK'S ILLUSTRATED ALL-TIME BEST SERIES

COOK'S COUNTRY TITLES

FOR A FULL LISTING OF ALL OUR BOOKS

CooksIllustrated.com

AmericasTestKitchen.com

PRAISE FOR AMERICA'S TEST KITCHEN TITLES

"America's Test Kitchen diligently digs into red-sauce favorites in this fun and flavorful collection. . . . This is an exercise in nostalgia, but a successful one."
Publishers Weekly on *Big Flavors from Italian America*

"If there's room in the budget for one multicooker/Instant Pot cookbook, make it this one."
Booklist on *Multicooker Perfection*

"*The Perfect Cookie* . . . is, in a word, perfect. This is an important and substantial cookbook. . . . If you love cookies, but have been a tad shy to bake on your own, all your fears will be dissipated. This is one book you can use for years with magnificently happy results."
The Huffington Post on *The Perfect Cookie*

"Use this charming, focused title to set a showstopping table for special occasions."
Library Journal on *All-Time Best Holiday Entertaining*

"Another winning cookbook from ATK. . . . The folks at America's Test Kitchen apply their rigorous experiments to determine the facts about these pans."
Booklist on *Cook It in Cast Iron*

"A one-volume kitchen seminar, addressing in one smart chapter after another the sometimes surprising whys behind a cook's best practices. . . . You get the myth, the theory, the science, and the proof, all rigorously interrogated as only America's Test Kitchen can do."
NPR on *The Science of Good Cooking*

"This is a wonderful, useful guide to healthy eating."
Publishers Weekly on *Nutritious Delicious*

Selected as the Cookbook Award Winner of 2019 in the Health and Special Diet Category
International Association of Culinary Professionals (IACP) on *The Complete Diabetes Cookbook*

"If you're a home cook who loves long introductions that tell you why a dish works followed by lots of step-by-step hand holding, then you'll love *Vegetables Illustrated*."
The Wall Street Journal on *Vegetables Illustrated*

"This book upgrades slow cooking for discriminating, 21st-century palates—that is indeed revolutionary."
The Dallas Morning News on *Slow Cooker Revolution*

"The 21st-century *Fannie Farmer Cookbook* or *The Joy of Cooking*. If you had to have one cookbook and that's all you could have, this one would do it."
CBS San Francisco on *The New Family Cookbook*

"The sum total of exhaustive experimentation . . . anyone interested in gluten-free cookery simply shouldn't be without it."
Nigella Lawson on *The How Can It Be Gluten-Free Cookbook*

"The go-to gift book for newlyweds, small families, or empty nesters."
Orlando Sentinel on *The Complete Cooking for Two Cookbook*

"Some 2,500 photos walk readers through 600 painstakingly tested recipes, leaving little room for error."
Associated Press on *The America's Test Kitchen Cooking School Cookbook*

"An exceptional resource for novice canners, though preserving veterans will find plenty here to love as well."
Library Journal (starred review) on *Foolproof Preserving*

"This book is a comprehensive, no-nonsense guide . . . a well-thought-out, clearly explained primer for every aspect of home baking."
The Wall Street Journal on *The Cook's Illustrated Baking Book*

The Complete

Cook's Country

TV Show Cookbook

Every Recipe and Every Review
from All Fourteen Seasons

AMERICA'S TEST KITCHEN

Photo of Toni Tipton-Martin on the back cover courtesy of Toni Tipton-Martin

Photo of Toni Tipton-Martin on page ix by Pableaux Johnson

Photo of Edna Lewis on page 7 by John T. Hill

Photo of Colonel Sanders on p. 28: Bettmann/Getty

Image of Count Pavel Stroganov on p. 50: Asar Studios/Alamy Stock Photo

Photo of common fennel, far right on page 401: Shutterstock

America's Test Kitchen
21 Drydock Avenue
Boston, MA 02210

The Complete Cook's Country TV Show Cookbook
Every Recipe and Every Review from All Fourteen Seasons

ISBN 978-1-948703-72-7
ISSN 2330-5726

Printed in Canada

10 9 8 7 6 5 4 3 2

Distributed by Penguin Random House Publisher Services
Tel: 800-733-3000

facebook.com/americastestkitchen

twitter.com/TestKitchen

youtube.com/AmericasTestKitchen

instagram.com/TestKitchen

pinterest.com/TestKitchen

Editor in Chief, Cook's Country Toni Tipton-Martin
Executive Food Editor, Cook's Country Bryan Roof
Executive Editor, Cook's Country Scott Kathan
Deputy Editor, Cook's Country Megan Ginsberg
Deputy Food Editor, Cook's Country Morgan Bolling
Senior Editors, Cook's Country Matthew Fairman and Lawman Johnson
Associate Editor, Cook's Country Jessica Rudolph
Test Cooks, Cook's Country Mark Huxsoll and Amanda Luchtel

Editorial Director, Books Adam Kowit
Executive Managing Editor, Books Debra Hudak
Assistant Editor, Books Emily Rahravan
Design Director, Books Lindsey Timko Chandler
Deputy Art Director, Books Janet Taylor
Photography Director Julie Bozzo Cote
Photography Producer Meredith Mulcahy
Feature Photography Joseph Keller
Senior Staff Photographers Steve Klise and Daniel J. van Ackere
Additional Photography Carl Tremblay
Staff Photographer Kevin White
Featured Food Stylist Catrine Kelty
Food Stylists Tara Busa, Chantal Lambeth, Ashley Moore, Marie Piraino, Elle Simone Scott, and Sally Staub
Photo Team and Special Events Manager Alli Berkey
Photoshoot Kitchen Team
    Lead Test Cook Eric Haessler
    Test Cooks Hannah Fenton, Jacqueline Gochenouer, and Gina McCreadie
    Assistant Test Cook Christa West
Senior Manager, Publishing Operations Taylor Argenzio
Imaging Manager Lauren Robbins
Production and Imaging Specialists Tricia Neumyer, Dennis Noble, and Amanda Yong
Historical Researcher Meg Ragland
Copyeditors Christine Campbell, April Poole, Cheryl Redmond, and Rachel Schowalter
Proofreaders Christine Corcoran Cox, Amanda Poulsen Dix, Kelly Gauthier, and Patricia Jalbert-Levine
Indexer Elizabeth Parson

Chief Creative Officer Jack Bishop
Executive Editorial Directors Julia Collin Davison and Bridget Lancaster

CooksCountry.com
AmericasTestKitchen.com

contents

welcome to cook's country

"Tell me what you eat: I will tell you what you are."

Over the years this insightful sentiment by French gastronome Jean Anthelme Brillat-Savarin has encouraged everything from eating a healthy diet to socially conscious cooking based on local ingredients. The philosophy invites you to remember where your people came from and to reflect on your kitchen style and what you value. It even encourages you to explore the ways our food traditions reveal another truism: we are different, yet alike.

"What you eat" recalls a time when the food on your table was part of a long, rich heritage started by your great grandparents, carried on through generations. The dishes your family enjoyed were similar to those your neighbors ate, but they were different, too. Everyone had a turkey on the Thanksgiving table, but a family's cultural tastes determined the way it was prepared and served. In your home, a toasted bread stuffing accompanied the holiday bird, while your next-door neighbor preferred cornbread dressing. Around the corner, a cook with coastal roots tossed oysters into the mix; farm cooks stirred in country sausage.

Thinking about "what you eat" also considers the cultural influences in a single dish. Peek into a pot of the American classic gumbo, for instance, and you'll see vestiges of the many groups who have settled in New Orleans. The base, a roux, arrived with the French; smoked sausage was brought by Germans and Acadians (from northeastern Canada); the okra came from Africa (as does its name: Gombo is the West African word for okra), and ground sassafras (filé powder) was used by Native Americans. Many Louisiana natives fondly remember waking up to the smell of cooking roux, which Mom would stir for hours over low heat until it was chocolate-colored. Aromatic vegetables were stirred in, then homemade stock, and finally the meat: Poultry, sausage, game, and seafood are all traditional, depending upon her taste preferences.

Or consider the nuances of pizza beyond the boundaries of New York and Chicago. Connie Piccinato created Detroit-style pizza by adapting a classic formula with locally produced brick cheese to satisfy a craving for the pies of her youth, while St. Louis–style pizza is made without yeast, has a wafer-thin crust, and gets a flavorful lift from another regional ingredient—Provel cheese. Here, the ingredients available to the cook are what give the dish character.

How closely do these Americanized versions resemble the original dishes brought to this country by first-generation immigrants? Not much. But adaptations of home-cooking, family histories and immigrant tastes paint a rich and broad portrait of the American culinary landscape. From coast to coast, to the city and the country, through the suburbs, and down back roads, they tell us something hopeful about American cooking today.

It is true that fewer and fewer of us live as adults in the same town where we were born and raised. We are a mobile, peripatetic people. As each generation reaches farther afield, its tether to its roots frays a little. We pass on fewer traditions. We carry less of our history into the future. Our children know little about our own childhoods.

It is also true that all this moving from house to house, and city to city encourages us to connect with new traditions. We exchange ideas with our neighbors and mix some of their way of doing things with ours. We learn to appreciate bold tastes and

alluring aromas. Our family favorites grow beyond the borders of our old neighborhoods and our way of doing things.

Consider the young woman who moves from the Carolina Lowcountry to New York and longs for the taste of her grandmother's shrimp gravy. She samples recipes for shrimp and grits in restaurants, but fancy creations just don't compare to the comforting dish of tender shrimp, silky sauce and creamy grits she remembers from childhood. She sends up a flare for the family recipe, then adapts it according to the ingredients she can source in her new hometown. She gets the taste just right and shares the recipe with new friends. Soon, one of the friends is inspired to make the dish her own too. To honor the origin story of the dish, she places a special order for stone-ground grits from a miller of heirloom grains located near the Sea Islands of Carolina. She makes the dish her own. When asked about her recipe, the cook tells the story behind her version. It is a tribute to the original, she says.

This action captures something special about American food: traditional dishes that are ethnically and regionally diverse are evolving, and that encourages a return to the simple pleasures of the table and inspires cooking with love. Here, at *Cook's Country*, we celebrate them all. We look at rural foods, from low country grits to high desert tacos. We look at city foods, from New Orleans gumbo to New York cheesecake. We search high, low, and in between for recipes from every community in the country, the old ones and the new, from centuries-old switchel to modern-day monkey bread.

It's been 13 years since *Cook's Country* presented its first recipe. Since then, our hard-working crew of test cooks, editors, and instructors have carried on the mission to find these recipes and work hard to perfect

them. We look for ways to refine the ingredients and techniques to jibe with contemporary cooking habits, while zealously maintaining the integrity and spirit of the originals. It can take weeks of experimentation, tinkering with seasoning amounts and cooking times until we get things just right. And we don't stop there. These recipes inspire brand-new ideas for simple, straightforward, easy meals that mix time-tested knowledge with fresh discoveries.

Our goal is to produce recipes that are easy, clear, and rewarding enough that you'll want to make them, too. We work to clarify concepts, streamline processes, and shorten the distance from hunger pang to dinner time. Over the past 14 years, we've been proud to share thousands of recipes with you. And as we work into our second decade, we've added to our cast of characters. These new faces, in our test kitchen and on our TV show and website, represent a whole new set of cooking traditions to explore.

It can take us weeks, or maybe months, to produce even a simple, two-step recipe. But it's worth it. Because by getting these dishes from our kitchens to your table, we believe we're helping to preserve, and expand, our shared American recipe book.

It's a big country, Cook's Country, and there's no better time to celebrate America's incredibly

rich, incredibly broad, and incredibly deep cooking traditions. There's plenty of room in the kitchen, no matter where you're from.

Welcome home. Now, grab an apron. Let's cook.

Toni Tipton-Martin
Editor in Chief
Cook's Country magazine

This book has been tested, written, and edited by the folks at America's Test Kitchen. Located in Boston's Seaport District in the historic Innovation and Design Building, it features 15,000 square feet of kitchen space including multiple photography and video studios. It is the home of *Cook's Country* and *Cook's Illustrated* magazines and is the workday destination for more than 60 test cooks, editors, and cookware specialists. The test kitchen tests recipes over and over again until we understand how and why they work and until we arrive at the best version.

Cook's Country celebrates cooking in America. Our mission is to seek out America's best cooking ideas and create easy-to-follow recipes for bringing people together.

Bridget Lancaster and Julia Collin Davison are the hosts of the show and have the answers to the questions you might ask. It's the job of our chefs, Morgan Bolling, Lawman Johnson, Ashley Moore, Christie Morrison, and Bryan Roof, to demonstrate our recipes. Editor in Chief Toni Tipton-Martin gives viewers historical and cultural context for our recipes. Jack Bishop shares helpful information about kitchen staples like herbs, broths, and thickening agents, while Adam Ried reveals the test kitchen's top choices for equipment, including wooden spoons, oven mitts, and 12-inch nonstick skillets.

Although only a handful of cooks appear on the television show, dozens more worked to make the show a reality. Executive Producer Kaitlin Keleher conceived and developed each episode along with Producer Caroline Rickert with support from Line Producer Diane Knox. Special thanks to Director Herb Sevush and Director of Photography Dan Anderson.

Along with the on-air crew, Culinary Producers Morgan Bolling and Stephanie Pixley helped plan and organize the 13 television episodes shot in April 2021 and ran the "back kitchen," cooking all the food that appeared on camera. Carolyn Grillo, Chase Brightwell, and Miye Bromberg organized the ingredient and equipment segments.

Test Kitchen Director Erin McMurrer, Assistant Test Kitchen Director Alexxa Benson, Test Kitchen Manager Meri Lippard, Test Kitchen Facilities Coordinator Kasjah Scarlett, Test Kitchen Shopping and Receiving Lead Heather Tolmie, and Senior Kitchen Assistant Shopper Avery Lowe were charged with making sure all the ingredients and kitchen equipment we needed were on hand. We also appreciate the hard work of the television crew—which was smaller than normal this year—including Mikaela Bloomberg, Mike Duca, Eric Fisher, Victor Fink, Shawn Gauvain, Eric Goddard, Josh Land, Jay Maurer, Lisa Roche, Alec Roy, Jennifer Tawa, Amanda Wayman, and Fred Young.

Additional thanks to our Editors, Pete Hyzak, Hamilton Jones, Sean Sandefur, and Herb Sevush; our Post-Production Supervisor, Chen Margolis; and Assistant Editors Yiorgos Tsivranidis and Jennifer Cuciti. Cara Eisenpress assisted with all the historical recipe research and Lisa Abitbol assisted with the historical photography research. We also would like to thank Judy Barlow at American Public Television, which presents the show. Sub-Zero, Wolf, and Cove; Kohler; Acorn TV; and Valley Fig Growers sponsored the show, and we thank them for their support. We also thank Sara Domville and Meredith Taylor for serving our sponsors.

as good as grandma's

OLD-FASHIONED CHICKEN NOODLE SOUP

SERVES 4 TO 6

If you prefer, 4 ounces (2 cups) of egg noodles can be substituted for the spaghetti. Fresh dill can be substituted for the parsley.

1½ pounds bone-in chicken breasts and/or thighs, trimmed
    Salt and pepper
1 tablespoon vegetable oil
8 cups chicken broth
1 onion, chopped
1 carrot, peeled and cut into ½-inch pieces
1 celery rib, cut into ½-inch pieces
2 sprigs fresh thyme
1 bay leaf
5 ounces spaghetti, broken into 1-inch pieces (1½ cups)
1 tablespoon minced fresh parsley

1. Pat chicken dry with paper towels and sprinkle with ¼ teaspoon salt and ¼ teaspoon pepper. Heat oil in Dutch oven over medium-high heat until shimmering. Cook chicken until well browned all over, 8 to 10 minutes.

2. Add broth, onion, carrot, celery, thyme sprigs, bay leaf, and ¼ teaspoon salt, scraping up any browned bits. Bring to boil, cover, and reduce heat to low. Simmer until breasts register 160 degrees and/or thighs register at least 175 degrees, 14 to 17 minutes.

3. Remove pot from heat; discard thyme sprigs and bay leaf. Transfer chicken to plate and let cool slightly. Using 2 forks, shred chicken into bite-size pieces; discard skin and bones.

4. Return soup to boil over medium-high heat and add pasta. Cook, uncovered, until pasta is tender, 9 to 11 minutes, stirring often. Add chicken and parsley and cook until chicken is warmed through, about 2 minutes. Season with salt and pepper to taste. Serve.

The American Table: Campbell's Noodle with Chicken Soup

Time was, radio advertisements weren't prerecorded interruptions; rather, a host would simply take a moment out of the show to read some copy prepared by the sponsor. What could go wrong? A misreading of the product name, that's what. So it went in 1938, when a radio host misread his script touting "Campbell's Noodle with Chicken Soup," instead calling it "Chicken Noodle Soup." Campbell's wasn't happy, but consumers loved the catchy name: Thousands thought this was a new product and soon started asking for it at local grocers. What could have been a disaster quickly became a boon—rather than fight the tide, Campbell's changed the product name and the packaging, and sales took off. Today, Campbell's sells nearly 200 million cans of the stuff each year, and its iconic label remains one of the most recognizable in American supermarkets. And while the name may have changed, the company's slogan has remained the same since the product was introduced in 1934: "M'm! M'm! Good!"

Why This Recipe Works There's nothing more comforting when you're feeling under the weather than a warm bowl of chicken noodle soup. This easy recipe is deeply flavorful and starts by browning bone-in chicken parts then simmering them in store-bought chicken broth, which created an intensely savory base. A standard mix of onion, celery, and carrot simmered with the chicken enhanced the broth's richness. Though egg noodles are common in homemade chicken noodle soup, we preferred spaghetti broken into bite-size pieces that cooked right in the soup. The final product gave a nostalgic nod to canned versions but had loads more flavor.

Why This Recipe Works Homemade stock tastes a lot better than even the best store-bought broths. While it's not complicated to make, it does require some babysitting on the stovetop, so instead, we turned to our slow cooker. We piled vegetables and leftover cooked chicken bones in cold water, added seasonings, and set it on high. The slow cooker prevented evaporation, so the bones remained submerged, which is often a challenge with stovetop stock recipes. Refrigerating the strained stock allowed the fat to rise to the top and solidify, making it easy to discard. This rich, savory stock is remarkably easy—and thrifty too.

SLOW-COOKER CHICKEN STOCK

MAKES ABOUT 3 QUARTS

This stock is great to use in any of our recipes calling for chicken broth. You can freeze chicken carcasses one at a time until you have the 2½ pounds needed for this recipe; three to four rotisserie chicken carcasses or one 6-pound roaster carcass will weigh about 2½ pounds. This recipe was developed using bones from cooked chicken.

3	quarts water
2½	pounds roasted chicken bones
1	onion, chopped
2	carrots, peeled and cut into 1-inch chunks
2	celery ribs, chopped
1	teaspoon black peppercorns
1	teaspoon salt
1	bay leaf

1. Place all ingredients in slow cooker. Cover and cook on high for 8 to 10 hours.

2. Let stock cool slightly, then strain through fine-mesh strainer set over large bowl. Use immediately or let cool completely, then refrigerate until cold. (When cold, surface fat will solidify and can be easily removed with spoon. Stock will keep, refrigerated, for up to 5 days, or frozen for up to 2 months.)

Stock Storage

Frozen homemade chicken stock lasts for up to two months. Freeze small and medium amounts in ice cube trays or muffin tins; once frozen, pop out the stock blocks and keep them in zipper-lock bags for easy access when making pan sauces or gravy. Freeze larger amounts in plastic quart containers or zipper-lock bags, which are easy to stack in crowded freezers.

SMALL	MEDIUM	LARGE
AMOUNTS	AMOUNTS	AMOUNTS

Celery

Buy loose celery heads, not bagged celery heads (with clipped leaves) or bagged celery hearts. Loose celery heads tend to be fuller and fresher. Look for glossy green stalks without brown edges or yellowing leaves. Revive limp celery stalks by cutting off about 1 inch from both ends and submerging the stalks in a bowl of ice water for 30 minutes. The best way to store celery is to wrap it in foil and store it in the refrigerator. It will keep for several weeks.

Carrots

Buy fresh carrots with greens attached for the best flavor. If buying bagged carrots, check that they are evenly sized and firm (they shouldn't bend). Don't buy extra-large carrots, which are often woody and bitter. To prevent shriveling, store carrots in the crisper drawer in a partially open zipper-lock bag or in their original plastic bag. Before storing green-topped carrots, remove and discard the greens or the carrots will become limp. Both bagged and fresh carrots will keep for several weeks.

Why This Recipe Works We first ate "Chicken and Pastry" at Red's Little Schoolhouse in Grady, Alabama. It features tender shreds of chicken and chewy bites of pastry in an ultrasavory stock. To prepare a flavorful base, we browned chicken thighs before pouring in store-bought broth and water. We opted for bone-in thighs over lean breasts because they stayed tender. For the soup's trademark pastry dumplings, we took a cue from Edna Lewis's recipe and cut the dough into diamond shapes to give this homey dish a touch of style. Once stirred in and simmered, the pastry became tender and its starch thickened the soup, making it rich and velvety.

CHICKEN AND PASTRY

SERVES 4 TO 6

Keep the root ends of the onion halves intact so the petals don't separate during cooking and the onion is easy to remove from the pot.

1½ cups (7½ ounces) all-purpose flour
 2 teaspoons baking powder
   Salt and pepper
 ½ cup milk
 2 tablespoons unsalted butter, melted, plus
   1 tablespoon unsalted butter
 2 pounds bone-in chicken thighs, trimmed
 4 cups chicken broth
 1 cup water
 1 onion, peeled and halved through root end
 1 celery rib, halved crosswise

1. Combine flour, baking powder, ½ teaspoon salt, and ½ teaspoon pepper in large bowl. Combine milk and melted butter in second bowl (butter may form clumps). Using rubber spatula, stir milk mixture into flour mixture until just incorporated. Turn dough out onto lightly floured counter and knead until no flour streaks remain, about 1 minute. Return dough to large bowl, cover with plastic wrap, and set aside.

2. Pat chicken dry with paper towels and season with pepper. Melt remaining 1 tablespoon butter in Dutch oven over medium-high heat. Add chicken, skin side down, and cook until golden brown, 3 to 5 minutes. Flip chicken and continue to cook until golden brown on second side, 3 to 5 minutes longer.

3. Add broth and water, scraping up any browned bits. Nestle onion and celery into pot and bring to boil. Reduce heat to low, cover, and simmer for 25 minutes.

4. Meanwhile, roll dough into 12-inch square, about ⅛ inch thick. Using pizza cutter or knife, cut dough lengthwise into 1-inch-wide strips, then cut diagonally into 1-inch-wide strips to form diamonds (pieces around edges will not be diamonds; this is OK).

5. Remove pot from heat. Transfer chicken to plate and let cool slightly. Discard onion and celery. Return broth to boil over medium-high heat and add pastry. Reduce heat to low, cover, and simmer, stirring occasionally, until pastry is tender and puffed, about 15 minutes. While pastry cooks, shred chicken into bite-size pieces, discarding skin and bones.

6. Stir chicken into stew and cook, uncovered, until warmed through and stew has thickened slightly, 2 to 4 minutes. Season with salt and pepper to taste. Serve.

The American Table: Southern Cooking with Style

A descendant of freed slaves, Edna Lewis grew up on a subsistence farm in rural Virginia and had made a life as a farmer, a seamstress, and a celebrated New York City chef before legendary cookbook editor Judith Jones convinced  her to compile her recipes and share her wisdom. That book, *The Taste of Country Cooking* (1976), became a cornerstone of the American cookbook shelf; Julia Child, Alice Waters, and Craig Claiborne praised its pure recipes and intimate tone.

At Café Nicholson in New York, where she cooked in the 1950s, Lewis was known for comforting meals (roast chicken was a specialty) presented with a chic flourish (cheese soufflé on the side). It was this sense of style that inspired her to cut her dumplings into diamond shapes, as we do in our Chicken and Pastry; it's a bit of elegance in a dish whose mission is to deliver deep homespun flavor.

Edna Lewis died in 2006, having emphatically accomplished the goal she articulated to the *New York Times* in 1989: "As a child in Virginia, I thought all food tasted delicious. After growing up, I didn't think food tasted the same, so it has been my lifelong effort to try and recapture those good flavors of the past."

CLASSIC TOMATO SOUP

SERVES 6 TO 8

Use unseasoned canned tomatoes.

  2 (28-ounce) cans diced tomatoes
  ¾ cup low-sodium chicken broth
  3 tablespoons unsalted butter
  1 onion, chopped
  1 bay leaf
  1 teaspoon brown sugar
  2 tablespoons tomato paste
  2 tablespoons all-purpose flour
  ½ teaspoon baking soda
     Salt and pepper
  ½ cup heavy cream

1. Drain tomatoes in colander set over large bowl, pressing lightly to release juices. Transfer tomato juice and chicken broth to large measuring cup (mixture should measure about 4 cups); reserve.

2. Melt butter in Dutch oven over medium heat. Add onion and cook until softened, about 5 minutes. Add two-thirds of drained tomatoes, bay leaf, and brown sugar and cook, stirring occasionally, until tomatoes begin to brown, about 15 minutes.

3. Add tomato paste and flour to pot and cook, stirring frequently, until paste begins to darken, 1 to 2 minutes. Slowly stir in reserved tomato juice–broth mixture, remaining tomatoes, baking soda, and ½ teaspoon salt and bring to boil. Reduce heat to medium-low and simmer until slightly thickened, about 5 minutes. Remove from heat.

4. Discard bay leaf. Puree soup in batches. Return pureed soup to pot and stir in cream. Season with salt and pepper. Serve. (Soup can be refrigerated for 3 days.)

Are You Kidding Me?

You can use it to brush your teeth, scrub your counters, or make your refrigerator smell better. Still, we were shocked at the difference that a mere ½ teaspoon of baking soda made in our Classic Tomato Soup. It neutralized some of the acid in the tomatoes for a perfect sweet-tart balance. And its sodium ions weakened the pectin in the cells of the tomatoes, allowing them to puree into a silken soup.

Bay Leaves

Bay leaves are a standard addition to soups, stews, and bean dishes. We prefer dried bay leaves to fresh; they work just as well in long-cooked recipes, are cheaper, and will keep for months in the freezer. We prefer Turkish bay leaves to those from California. The California bay leaf has a medicinal and potent flavor, like something you'd put in a cough drop. The Turkish bay leaf has a mild, green, and slightly clove-like flavor.

Why This Recipe Works We were shocked that the key to a satiny, well-balanced classic tomato soup turned out to be just ½ teaspoon of baking soda, which also helped neutralize the metallic taste and acidity of the canned tomatoes. To enhance the tomatoes' complexity, we browned most of them in a Dutch oven to concentrate their flavor—and saved some to add at the end of cooking to keep the soup fresh. We were tempted to add a variety of classic seasonings—but found that they made the soup taste like marinara sauce. Tasters were most satisfied with a single bay leaf, chicken broth, and the richness of heavy cream.

BEST POTLUCK MACARONI AND CHEESE

SERVES 8 TO 10

Block American cheese from the deli counter is best here, as prewrapped singles result in a drier macaroni and cheese.

- 4 slices hearty white sandwich bread, torn into quarters
- 4 tablespoons unsalted butter, melted, plus 4 tablespoons unsalted butter
- ¼ cup grated Parmesan cheese
- 1 pound elbow macaroni
  Salt
- 5 tablespoons all-purpose flour
- 3 (12-ounce) cans evaporated milk
- 2 teaspoons hot sauce
- 1 teaspoon dry mustard
- ⅛ teaspoon ground nutmeg
- 8 ounces extra-sharp cheddar cheese, shredded (2 cups)
- 5 ounces American cheese, shredded (1¼ cups)
- 3 ounces Monterey Jack cheese, shredded (¾ cup)

1. Adjust oven rack to middle position and heat oven to 350 degrees. Pulse bread, melted butter, and Parmesan in food processor until ground to coarse crumbs, about 8 pulses. Transfer to bowl.

2. Bring 4 quarts water to boil in large pot. Add macaroni and 1 tablespoon salt and cook, stirring often, until just al dente, about 6 minutes. Reserve ½ cup macaroni cooking water, then drain and rinse macaroni in colander under cold running water. Set aside.

3. Melt remaining 4 tablespoons butter in now-empty pot over medium-high heat. Stir in flour and cook, stirring constantly, until mixture turns light brown, about 1 minute. Slowly whisk in evaporated milk, hot sauce, mustard, nutmeg, and 2 teaspoons salt and cook until mixture begins to simmer and is slightly thickened, about 4 minutes. Off heat, whisk in cheeses and reserved cooking water until cheese melts. Stir in macaroni until completely coated.

4. Transfer mixture to 13 by 9-inch baking dish and top evenly with bread-crumb mixture. Bake until cheese is bubbling around edges and top is golden brown, 20 to 25 minutes. Let sit for 5 to 10 minutes before serving.

To Make Ahead The macaroni and cheese can be made in advance through step 3. Increase amount of reserved macaroni cooking water to 1 cup. Scrape mixture into 13 by 9-inch baking dish, cool, lay plastic wrap directly on surface of pasta, and refrigerate for up to 1 day. Bread-crumb mixture may be refrigerated for up to 2 days. When ready to bake, remove plastic, cover with aluminum foil, and bake for 30 minutes. Uncover, sprinkle bread crumbs over top, and bake until topping is golden brown, about 20 minutes longer. Let sit before serving.

Keeping It Together

Using already stabilized ingredients like American cheese and evaporated milk ensures that this cheesy sauce doesn't break in the oven.

Why This Recipe Works We can thank James Hemings, the enslaved French-trained chef of Thomas Jefferson, for helping to make macaroni and cheese so popular today. At the time, recipes consisted of just pasta, cheese, and butter but Hemings added cream to his version turning it into a rich baked casserole that was served at the White House. Our Best Potluck Macaroni and Cheese follows the creamy tradition incorporating evaporated milk and American cheese; the stabilizers in these ingredients kept the sauce from breaking, so it emerged from the oven satiny smooth.

Why This Recipe Works To pack our mac and cheese with bright tomato flavor, we discovered that undercooking the pasta and adding petite canned diced tomatoes with their juices to the drained macaroni allowed the macaroni to soak up more of the tomato flavor. Returning the pasta to the heat afterward allowed the noodles to absorb some of the tomato juice. Finally, to avoid a curdled sauce, we added fat in the form of half-and-half (cut with some chicken broth) and a mix of sharp and mild cheddar cheeses.

MACARONI AND CHEESE WITH TOMATOES

SERVES 8 TO 10

Let the finished dish rest for 10 to 15 minutes before you serve it; otherwise, it will be soupy.

- 1 pound elbow macaroni
  Salt and pepper
- 1 (28-ounce) can petite diced tomatoes
- 6 tablespoons unsalted butter
- ½ cup all-purpose flour
- ¼ teaspoon cayenne pepper
- 4 cups half-and-half
- 1 cup chicken broth
- 1 pound mild cheddar cheese, shredded (4 cups)
- 8 ounces sharp cheddar cheese, shredded (2 cups)

1. Adjust oven rack to middle position and heat oven to 400 degrees. Bring 4 quarts water to boil in large Dutch oven. Add macaroni and 1 tablespoon salt and cook, stirring often, until just al dente, about 6 minutes. Drain pasta and return to pot. Pour diced tomatoes with their juices over pasta and stir to coat. Cook over medium-high heat, stirring occasionally, until most of liquid is absorbed, about 5 minutes. Set aside.

2. Meanwhile, melt butter in medium saucepan over medium heat. Stir in flour and cayenne and cook until golden, about 1 minute. Slowly whisk in half-and-half and broth until smooth. Bring to boil, reduce heat to medium, and simmer, stirring occasionally, until mixture is slightly thickened, about 15 minutes. Off heat, whisk in cheeses, 1 teaspoon salt, and 1 teaspoon pepper until cheeses melt. Pour sauce over macaroni and stir to combine.

3. Scrape mixture into 13 by 9-inch baking dish set in rimmed baking sheet and bake until top begins to brown, 15 to 20 minutes. Let sit for 10 to 15 minutes before serving.

To Make Ahead The macaroni and cheese can be made in advance through step 2. Scrape mixture into 13 by 9-inch baking dish, cool, lay plastic wrap directly on surface of pasta, and refrigerate for up to 2 days. When ready to bake, remove plastic, cover with aluminum foil, and bake for 30 minutes. Uncover and bake until top is golden brown, about 15 minutes. Let sit for 10 to 15 minutes before serving.

An Automat Classic

Home cooks have long put their stamp on plain-Jane macaroni and cheese, stirring in such items as hot dogs or diced ham and peas. One appealing, old-fashioned variation, however, is practically endangered: baked macaroni and cheese with tomatoes. The genius in the recipe is that the bright acid of the tomato cuts the richness of the cheese. Today, people of a certain age remember tomato mac and cheese fondly from Horn and Hardart's automats.

Automats started in Germany in 1896 as a way to quickly feed hundreds of thousands of workers during their lunch hour. The idea was very much like a vending machine. Rather than ordering their meals through a server, patrons would drop coins into a slot to open a glass door in front of a compartment holding a menu item. Frank Hardart brought back the automat idea after a visit to Germany. Hardart, along with his partner, Joseph B. Horn, hired an engineer to further simplify the German system so they could transform their traditional lunch counter into an automat in 1902.

As for one of their most popular menu items, macaroni and cheese with tomatoes, most of us have never heard of it, much less tasted it. Automats may be a thing of the past, but a good recipe for macaroni and cheese shouldn't be.

Why This Recipe Works Grits are a Southern staple, but their appeal can be lost in bland, gluey incarnations. To take this down-home dish from dull to delicious, we needed to work on both texture and flavor. Replacing some of the cooking water with milk gave a creamy sweetness to the unadorned grits. As for the cheese, we found that a combination of Monterey Jack and sharp cheddar lent both smoothness and pronounced cheesy flavor. To give the dish more depth, we sautéed scallion whites and added real pureed corn for an extra boost of corn flavor.

CREAMY CHEESE GRITS

SERVES 4 TO 6

The grits are ready when they are mostly creamy but still retain a little bite. If the grits get too thick, whisk in a little water. If you are using frozen corn, thaw it first.

- ½ cup fresh or frozen corn kernels
- 3½ cups water
- 4 tablespoons unsalted butter
- 4 scallions, white parts minced, green parts sliced thin
- 1 cup milk
- ½ teaspoon hot sauce
- Salt and pepper
- 1 cup old-fashioned grits
- 4 ounces Monterey Jack cheese, shredded (1 cup)
- 4 ounces sharp cheddar cheese, shredded (1 cup)

1. Puree corn and ¼ cup water in blender until smooth, about 1 minute; set aside. Melt 2 tablespoons butter in medium saucepan over medium heat. Add scallion whites and cook until softened, about 2 minutes. Stir in remaining 3¼ cups water, milk, hot sauce, ½ teaspoon salt, and ½ teaspoon pepper and bring to boil.

2. Slowly whisk grits into saucepan until no lumps remain. Reduce heat to low and cook, stirring frequently, until thick and creamy, about 15 minutes.

3. Off heat, stir in Monterey Jack, cheddar, pureed corn, and remaining 2 tablespoons butter until incorporated. Season with salt and pepper to taste. Serve sprinkled with scallion greens.

Know Your Corn

Cornmeal Cornmeal is corn kernels that are dried and ground to a powder.

Grits Grits are cornmeal, but the name also refers to the cooked porridge popular in the South.

Hominy Grits Hominy grits are corn kernels with the hull and bran removed before grinding.

Polenta Polenta is cornmeal, but the name also refers to the cooked Italian porridge, which is traditionally enriched with butter and Parmesan.

Weighing Cheese

Our recipes specify cup amounts of cheese to reflect the habits of the typical home cook. But cheese is sold by weight, so it can be hard to determine how much to buy. Also, one person's measure may not precisely equal another's. To complicate matters, we classify cheese into three categories: hard, such as Parmesan and Pecorino Romano; semisoft, such as cheddar and Monterey Jack; and soft, such as feta, blue, and fresh goat cheeses. Each packs into cup measures differently. To develop a standard weight for each cheese category, we gathered 10 test cooks and had each weigh out 1-cup samples of each type. We averaged the weights to account for the heavy and light hands of different individuals. We found that 1 cup of grated hard cheese equals about 2 ounces, while the same measure of soft and semisoft is about 4 ounces. And remember, when measuring cheese, lightly pack measuring cups meant for dry ingredients; don't use liquid measuring cups, which will give you an inaccurate measurement for dry ingredients.

STRAWBERRY PRETZEL SALAD

SERVES 10 TO 12

For a sturdier crust, use (thinner) pretzel sticks, not (fatter) rods. Thaw the strawberries in the refrigerator the night before you begin the recipe. You'll puree 2 pounds of the strawberries and slice the remaining 1 pound.

6½   ounces pretzel sticks
2¼   cups (15¾ ounces) sugar
12   tablespoons unsalted butter,
        melted and cooled
8   ounces cream cheese
1   cup heavy cream
3   pounds (10½ cups) frozen strawberries,
        thawed
¼   teaspoon salt
4½   teaspoons unflavored gelatin
½   cup cold water

1. Adjust oven rack to middle position and heat oven to 400 degrees. Spray 13 by 9-inch baking pan with vegetable oil spray. Pulse pretzels and ¼ cup sugar in food processor until coarsely ground, about 15 pulses. Add melted butter and pulse until combined, about 10 pulses. Transfer pretzel mixture to prepared pan. Using bottom of measuring cup, press crumbs into bottom of pan. Bake until crust is fragrant and beginning to brown, about 10 minutes, rotating pan halfway through baking. Set aside crust, letting it cool slightly, about 20 minutes.

2. Using stand mixer fitted with whisk, whip cream cheese and ½ cup sugar on medium speed until light and fluffy, about 2 minutes. Increase speed to medium-high and, with mixer still running, slowly add cream in steady stream. Continue to whip until soft peaks form, scraping down bowl as needed, about 1 minute longer. Spread whipped cream cheese mixture evenly over cooled crust. Refrigerate until set, about 30 minutes.

3. Meanwhile, process 2 pounds strawberries in now-empty food processor until pureed, about 30 seconds. Strain mixture through fine-mesh strainer set over medium saucepan, using underside of small ladle to push puree through strainer. Add remaining 1½ cups sugar and salt to strawberry puree in saucepan and cook over medium-high heat, whisking occasionally, until bubbles begin to appear around sides of pan and sugar is dissolved, about 5 minutes; remove from heat.

4. Sprinkle gelatin over water in large bowl and let sit until gelatin softens, about 5 minutes. Whisk strawberry puree into gelatin. Slice remaining strawberries and stir into strawberry-gelatin mixture. Refrigerate until gelatin thickens slightly and starts to cling to sides of bowl, about 30 minutes. Carefully pour gelatin mixture evenly over whipped cream cheese layer. Refrigerate salad until gelatin is fully set, at least 4 hours or up to 24 hours. Serve.

The American Table: Salad Days

Baked beans, marshmallows, fruit cocktail, flavored gelatin, grated American cheese, ginger ale, sauerkraut . . . Do the words "salad fixings" spring to mind? Probably not, but then you aren't a well-bred, middle-class lady living in the first half of the 20th century. Had you been reared on the tenets of the domestic science movement that dominated American cooking at that time, such a list would indeed have suggested salad. As a "progressive housekeeper," you would have cringed at the very idea of what we call salad today. As culinary historian Laura Shapiro has detailed in *Perfection Salad: Women and Cooking at the Turn of the Century*, vegetables had to be tamed, and the very best way to render untidy raw vegetables harmless was to encase them in gelatin. After molding and chilling her salad, she could gild the lily with a few stuffed prunes, rococo swirls of thinned mayonnaise, and a carved tomato tulip. Pretzel salad is a direct descendent of such "Festive for Special Occasions Salads," as Betty Crocker's *New Picture Cook Book* grouped similar concoctions as late as 1961. Even today, despite the Cool Whip and the strawberry Jell-O, pretzel salad is not dessert—it's a salad.

Why This Recipe Works This tri-layer Midwestern specialty doesn't much resemble salad, but the sweet-salty, creamy-crunchy combination grabbed our attention. We knew we could make this slightly offbeat potluck favorite shine with some home-made elements. We replaced the "whipped topping" with real cream, which we whipped into softened cream cheese with some sugar for a tangy, not-too-sweet middle layer. The top layer, traditionally made from boxed Jell-O, got an upgrade to plain gelatin flavored with real pureed strawberry juice and sliced frozen berries. The time it took to make these elements from scratch was well worth the extra effort.

ROASTED GREEN BEANS WITH GOAT CHEESE AND HAZELNUTS

SERVES 4 TO 6

To trim green beans quickly, line up a handful so the stem ends are even and then cut off the stems with one swipe of the knife.

1½ pounds green beans, trimmed
5½ tablespoons extra-virgin olive oil
 ¾ teaspoon sugar
   Kosher salt and pepper
 2 garlic cloves, minced
 1 teaspoon grated orange zest
   plus 2 teaspoons juice
 2 teaspoons lemon juice
 1 teaspoon Dijon mustard
 2 tablespoons minced fresh chives
 2 ounces goat cheese, crumbled (½ cup)
 ¼ cup hazelnuts, toasted, skinned, and chopped

1. Adjust oven rack to lowest position and heat oven to 475 degrees. Combine green beans, 1½ tablespoons oil, sugar, ¾ teaspoon salt, and ½ teaspoon pepper in bowl. Evenly distribute green beans on rimmed baking sheet.

2. Cover sheet tightly with aluminum foil and roast for 10 minutes. Remove foil and continue to roast until green beans are spotty brown, about 10 minutes longer, stirring halfway through roasting.

3. Meanwhile, combine garlic, orange zest, and remaining ¼ cup oil in medium bowl and microwave until bubbling, about 1 minute; let steep for 1 minute. Whisk orange juice, lemon juice, mustard, ¼ teaspoon salt, and ¼ teaspoon pepper into garlic mixture.

4. Transfer green beans to bowl with dressing, add chives, and toss to combine. Transfer to serving platter and sprinkle with goat cheese and hazelnuts. Serve.

ROASTED GREEN BEANS WITH ALMONDS AND MINT

Omit orange zest and juice, substitute with 1 teaspoon grated lime zest and 4 teaspoons lime juice; ¼ cup torn fresh mint leaves for chives; and ¼ cup whole blanched almonds, toasted and chopped, for hazelnuts. Omit goat cheese.

ROASTED GREEN BEANS WITH PECORINO AND PINE NUTS

Omit orange zest and juice, substitute with 1 teaspoon grated lemon zest and 4 teaspoons lemon juice; 2 tablespoons chopped fresh basil for chives; 1½ ounces Pecorino Romano cheese, shredded, for goat cheese; and ¼ cup pine nuts, toasted, for hazelnuts.

Steam and Then Roast Uncovered

For tender green beans with a hint of flavorful browning, we found that a hybrid moist-then-dry roasting method worked best. First we roast the beans covered with foil, which traps steam and helps them cook through quickly. Then we remove the foil to allow the beans to brown in the dry heat.

Why This Recipe Works For tender green beans with a hint of flavorful browning, we developed a hybrid method—first steaming the beans under a foil cover and then removing the foil and allowing them to roast. Adding a bit of sugar to the beans promoted the browning and blistering we wanted in the oven's high heat. Tossing the beans with a light citrus dressing and goat cheese brightened their flavor, while toasted hazelnuts provided a welcome crunch.

CLASSIC TUNA SALAD

MAKES 2 CUPS; ENOUGH FOR 4 SANDWICHES

For slightly milder salads, use an equal amount of shallot instead of onion.

¼ cup finely chopped onion
2 tablespoons olive oil
3 (5-ounce) cans solid white tuna in water
½ cup plus 2 tablespoons mayonnaise
1 celery rib, minced
2 teaspoons lemon juice
½ teaspoon sugar
  Salt and pepper

1. Combine onion and oil in small bowl and microwave until onion begins to soften, about 2 minutes. Let onion mixture cool for 5 minutes. Place tuna in fine-mesh strainer and press dry with paper towels. Transfer tuna to medium bowl and mash with fork until finely flaked.

2. Stir mayonnaise, celery, lemon juice, sugar, ½ teaspoon salt, ½ teaspoon pepper, and onion mixture into tuna until well combined. Season with salt and pepper to taste. Serve. (Salad can be refrigerated for up to 24 hours.)

TUNA SALAD WITH HARD-COOKED EGGS, RADISHES, AND CAPERS

Substitute 2 tablespoons extra-virgin olive oil for olive oil and 6 tablespoons extra-virgin olive oil for mayonnaise. Add 2 thinly sliced hard-cooked eggs; 2 trimmed, halved, and thinly sliced radishes; and ¼ cup capers, minced, to salad.

TUNA SALAD WITH APPLE, WALNUTS, AND TARRAGON

Add 1 apple, cored and cut into ½-inch pieces; ½ cup walnuts, toasted and chopped coarse; and 1 tablespoon minced fresh tarragon to salad.

TUNA SALAD WITH CORNICHONS AND WHOLE-GRAIN MUSTARD

Add ¼ cup finely chopped cornichons, 1 tablespoon minced fresh chives, and 1 tablespoon whole-grain mustard to salad.

TUNA SALAD WITH CURRY AND GRAPES

Add 1 teaspoon curry powder to bowl with onion and oil before microwaving. Add 1 cup green grapes, halved, to salad.

Draining Tuna

Place tuna in fine-mesh strainer and press dry with paper towels to remove excess moisture and prevent watery tuna salad. Once drained, transfer to medium bowl and mash with fork until finely flaked.

Why This Recipe Works A classic lunch box staple, tuna salad too often turns out watery, chalky, and/or bland. It may sound odd, but the key to great tuna salad is to first thoroughly drain chunked tuna and dry it with paper towels. Mashing the dried tuna with a fork made for a nice, uniform consistency. To moisten the salad, we quickly infused olive oil with chopped onion in the microwave and added it to the tuna, along with a bit of sugar, lemon juice, and mayo to round out the flavor. We tasted every variety of canned tuna and the runaway winner was solid white tuna packed in water.

Why This Recipe Works Too often a bright, crisp romaine salad is weighed down by an overly heavy dressing, so we set out to make a light and flavorful green goddess dressing. We achieved this by using three kinds of herbs: tarragon, parsley, and chives. To discreetly add depth, we used a single anchovy fillet, and for the creamiest texture, we used mayo and sour cream and prepared the dressing in a blender. While modern versions of green goddess dressing often contain avocado, the original version, credited to chef Philip Roemer of the Palace Hotel in San Francisco in the 1920s, does not, so we skipped it.

GREEN GODDESS DRESSING

MAKES 1¼ CUPS; ENOUGH FOR 6 WEDGES OF LETTUCE

To appreciate the full flavor of this rich dressing, drizzle it over chilled wedges of mild iceberg lettuce or romaine lettuce leaves. A blender yields a brighter, slightly more flavorful dressing, but a food processor will work, too.

2	teaspoons dried tarragon
1	tablespoon lemon juice
1	tablespoon water
¾	cup mayonnaise
¼	cup sour cream
¼	cup coarsely chopped fresh parsley
1	garlic clove, chopped
1	anchovy fillet, rinsed and dried
¼	cup chopped chives
	Salt and pepper

1. Combine tarragon, lemon juice, and water in small bowl and let sit for 15 minutes.

2. Blend tarragon mixture, mayonnaise, sour cream, parsley, garlic, and anchovy in blender until smooth, scraping down sides as necessary. Transfer to medium bowl, stir in chives, and season with salt and pepper. Chill until flavors meld, about 1 hour. (Dressing can be covered and refrigerated for up to 1 day.)

Don't Fear the Fish

The single anchovy fillet we call for in this recipe may seem superfluous, but it adds savory depth to the dressing (without tasting like fish). Try adding a minced anchovy to your next batch of beef stew or tomato sauce—it will boost the flavor considerably. Anchovies are sold jarred or canned. Extra jarred anchovies can be refrigerated right in the jar according to package directions. But extra canned anchovies should be transferred to a nonreactive airtight container, covered with oil, and refrigerated for up to 2 weeks.

Juicing Lemons

We squeezed a dozen lemons—cold, rolled, and warm—and found that each yielded the same amount of juice. The only difference was that warm and room-temperature lemons were softer and therefore easier to squeeze than the cold lemons. When you use a tool like a reamer or juicer, this doesn't come into play as much, but if you're juicing by hand, we recommend room-temperature lemons. To quickly warm a cold lemon, you can heat it in the microwave until it is warm to the touch.

To quickly juice a lemon, we prefer a wooden reamer with a sharp tip that can easily pierce the flesh. Plastic reamers with rounded tips didn't work as well in our tests. Plastic and glass juicers (which sit on the counter and collect juice) are better suited to oranges and grapefruits than lemons. When purchasing lemons at the supermarket, choose large ones that give to gentle pressure; hard lemons have thicker skin and yield less juice.

Why This Recipe Works Made with fresh herbs and rich mayonnaise, green goddess dressing is usually a creamy complement to salads and crudités. We thought it might make a flavorful marinade for chicken with one key change. We used buttermilk in the marinade instead of mayo to provide deeper seasoning and tangy flavor. Before marinating the chicken, we reserved some of the mixture to use as a sauce for the roasted chicken. To give our herby sauce more creamy richness, we reintroduced some mayo and a splash more buttermilk. Roasting the chicken at high heat for just 25 minutes yielded nicely browned skin and juicy meat.

GREEN GODDESS ROAST CHICKEN

SERVES 4 TO 6

Don't spend a lot of time chopping the herbs and garlic. Chop them just enough to measure them, and then let the blender do the bulk of the work.

½ cup chopped fresh chives
½ cup chopped fresh parsley
¼ cup plus 1 tablespoon buttermilk
2 tablespoons lemon juice
4 teaspoons chopped fresh tarragon
2 garlic cloves, chopped
2 anchovy fillets, rinsed
¼ cup mayonnaise
1½ teaspoons salt
3 pounds bone-in chicken pieces (2 split breasts cut in half crosswise, 2 drumsticks, and 2 thighs), trimmed

1. Process chives, parsley, ¼ cup buttermilk, lemon juice, tarragon, garlic, and anchovies in blender until smooth, about 30 seconds, scraping down sides of blender jar as needed.

2. Transfer 2 tablespoons herb mixture to bowl; add mayonnaise and remaining 1 tablespoon buttermilk and stir to combine. Cover and set aside until ready to serve.

3. Combine salt and remaining herb mixture in 1-gallon zipper-lock bag. Add chicken to bag, press out air, seal bag, and turn to coat chicken in marinade. Refrigerate for at least 2 hours or up to 24 hours.

4. Adjust oven rack to middle position and heat oven to 475 degrees. Line rimmed baking sheet with aluminum foil. Place chicken, skin side up, on prepared sheet (do not brush off marinade that sticks to chicken). Make sure skin is not bunched up on chicken. Roast until breasts register 160 degrees and drumsticks/thighs register 175 degrees, 25 to 30 minutes.

5. Transfer chicken to platter, tent with foil, and let rest for 10 minutes. Serve chicken with sauce.

CAST IRON BAKED CHICKEN

SERVES 4

Our favorite cast-iron skillet is the Lodge Classic Cast Iron Skillet, 12". Note that the cast-iron skillet should be preheated along with the oven; this is key to getting crispy, well-browned skin. You will not achieve the same type of browning with a conventional skillet. A 4-pound whole chicken will yield the 3 pounds of parts called for in the recipe. Our favorite paprika is The Spice House Hungarian Sweet Paprika.

- 2 teaspoons paprika
- 2 teaspoons salt
- 1 teaspoon pepper
- ½ teaspoon onion powder
- ½ teaspoon granulated garlic
- 3 pounds bone-in chicken pieces (2 split breasts, 2 drumsticks, 2 thighs, and 2 wings with wingtips discarded), trimmed
- 2 tablespoons unsalted butter
- 6 sprigs fresh thyme

1. Adjust oven rack to middle position, place 12-inch cast-iron skillet on rack, and heat oven to 450 degrees. Combine paprika, salt, pepper, onion powder, and granulated garlic in bowl. Pat chicken dry with paper towels and sprinkle all over with spice mixture.

2. When oven is heated, carefully remove hot skillet. Add butter, let it melt, and add thyme sprigs. Place chicken in skillet skin side down, pushing thyme sprigs aside as needed. Transfer skillet to oven and bake for 15 minutes.

3. Remove skillet from oven and flip chicken. Return skillet to oven and bake until breasts register 160 degrees and drumsticks/thighs register at least 175 degrees, about 15 minutes longer.

4. Let chicken rest in skillet for 10 minutes. Transfer chicken to platter and spoon pan juices over top. Serve.

Success Starts with a Hot Skillet

Get Skillet Ripping Hot
Cast iron preheats evenly in the oven.

Start Chicken Skin Side Down
This initial browning imparts deep flavor.

Why This Recipe Works For baked chicken with the crispiest possible skin, we turned to kitchen workhorse and heat-retainer extraordinaire: a cast-iron skillet. We carefully placed colorful paprika-seasoned chicken pieces skin side down into the preheated skillet to get an instant sizzle, achieving that trademark rendered skin. After a quick flip halfway through, our chicken emerged from the oven with an evenly browned exterior that crunched faintly against the juicy meat. Sprigs of thyme and some butter mingled together with the pan juices to create a silky sauce that we spooned over the top for an herby finish.

ONE-BATCH FRIED CHICKEN

SERVES 4

Use a Dutch oven that holds 6 quarts or more. To take the temperature of the chicken pieces, take them out of the oil and place them on a plate; this is the safest way and provides the most accurate reading.

Brine and Chicken

- 2 cups buttermilk
- 1 tablespoon salt
- 3 pounds bone-in chicken pieces (2 split breasts cut in half crosswise, 2 drumsticks, and 2 thighs), trimmed
- 1½ quarts peanut or vegetable oil

Coating

- 3 cups all-purpose flour
- 3 tablespoons white pepper
- 1 tablespoon pepper
- 1 tablespoon celery salt
- 1 tablespoon granulated garlic
- 1 tablespoon ground ginger
- 1 tablespoon Italian seasoning
- 1 tablespoon baking powder
- ½ teaspoon salt
- 6 tablespoons buttermilk

1. For the Brine and Chicken Whisk buttermilk and salt in large bowl until salt is dissolved. Submerge chicken in buttermilk mixture. Cover with plastic wrap and refrigerate for at least 1 hour or up to 24 hours.

2. For the Coating Whisk flour, white pepper, pepper, celery salt, granulated garlic, ginger, Italian seasoning, baking powder, and salt together in large bowl. Add buttermilk and, using your fingers, rub flour mixture and buttermilk together until craggy bits form throughout.

3. Set wire rack in rimmed baking sheet. Working with 2 pieces of chicken at a time, remove from buttermilk mixture, allowing excess to drip off, then drop into flour mixture, turning to thoroughly coat and pressing to adhere. Transfer to prepared rack, skin side up. Refrigerate, uncovered, for at least 1 hour or up to 2 hours.

4. Set second wire rack in second rimmed baking sheet and line with triple layer of paper towels. Add oil to large Dutch oven until it measures about 1 inch deep and heat over medium-high heat to 350 degrees. Add all chicken to oil, skin side down in single layer (some slight overlap is OK) so that pieces are mostly submerged. Cover and fry for 10 minutes, rotating pot after 5 minutes. Adjust burner, if necessary, to maintain oil temperature around 300 degrees.

5. Uncover pot (chicken will be golden on sides and bottom but unset and gray on top) and carefully flip chicken. Continue to fry, uncovered, until chicken is golden brown and breasts register 160 degrees and drumsticks/thighs register 175 degrees, 7 to 9 minutes longer. Transfer chicken to paper towel—lined rack and let cool for 10 minutes. Serve.

The American Table: The Colonel

His iconic white suit is part of what makes Harland Sanders's image an indelible one in the American food landscape, but according to Josh Ozersky's biography *Colonel Sanders and the American Dream* (2012), the Colonel's original suit was black. "It came with a string tie and was distinctive enough in its way, but something about it lacked oomph, panache."

Eventually, in a bid to portray the image of a "paternal-looking Southern gentleman," Sanders bleached his beard and changed up the suit; as Ozersky tells it, "television producers told him the white suit made him stand out, giving him a visual signature."

Why This Recipe Works Inspired by the covered pressure-frying machine in which Colonel Sanders created his famous fried chicken, we set out to find a faster way to fry that would get a full cut-up chicken on the table in one batch. To fit all the chicken into a Dutch oven, we had to decrease the amount of oil. Covering the pot for the first half of cooking allowed the oil, which dropped in temperature when we added the chicken, to quickly heat up again. We let the pieces fry undisturbed, so the coating set almost entirely around each piece before flipping and frying the chicken uncovered to allow excess moisture to escape.

Why This Recipe Works Our take on smothered chicken had two goals: big chicken flavor and weeknight ease. For perfectly tender, evenly cooked Southern-style smothered chicken, we started with chicken parts rather than a whole bird. We browned the pieces and then shallow-braised them in a savory gravy built from pantry ingredients: chicken broth, flour, sautéed onions, celery, garlic, and dried sage. We found that we needed just 2 tablespoons of flour to thicken the gravy to a rich—but not stodgy—consistency. A splash of cider vinegar brightened the sauce and helped the chicken's flavor shine.

SOUTHERN-STYLE SMOTHERED CHICKEN

SERVES 4

This dish is best served with rice, but it's also good with potatoes. You may substitute ground sage for the dried sage leaves, but decrease the amount to ¼ teaspoon.

- 3 pounds bone-in chicken pieces (split breasts cut in half crosswise, drumsticks, and/or thighs), trimmed
  Salt and pepper
- ½ cup plus 2 tablespoons all-purpose flour
- ¼ cup vegetable oil
- 2 onions, chopped fine
- 2 celery ribs, chopped fine
- 3 garlic cloves, minced
- 1 teaspoon dried sage leaves
- 2 cups chicken broth
- 1 tablespoon cider vinegar
- 2 tablespoons minced fresh parsley

1. Pat chicken dry with paper towels and season with salt and pepper. Spread ½ cup flour in shallow dish. Working with 1 piece at a time, dredge chicken in flour, shaking off excess, and transfer to plate.

2. Heat oil in Dutch oven over medium-high heat. Add half of chicken to pot, skin side down, and cook until deep golden brown, 4 to 6 minutes per side; transfer to plate. Repeat with remaining chicken, adjusting heat if flour begins to burn.

3. Pour off all but 2 tablespoons fat and return pot to medium heat. Add onions, celery, 1 teaspoon salt, and ½ teaspoon pepper and cook until softened, 6 to 8 minutes. Stir in garlic, sage, and remaining 2 tablespoons flour and cook until vegetables are well coated with flour and garlic is fragrant, about 1 minute. Whisk in broth, scraping up any browned bits.

4. Nestle chicken into sauce, add any accumulated juices from plate, and bring to boil. Reduce heat to low, cover, and simmer until breasts register 160 degrees and drumsticks/thighs register 175 degrees, 30 to 40 minutes.

5. Transfer chicken to serving dish. Stir vinegar into sauce and season with salt and pepper to taste. Pour sauce over chicken, sprinkle with parsley, and serve.

How to Split and Trim Breasts

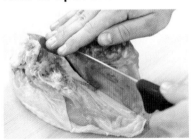  

1. With whole breast skin side down on cutting board, center knife on breastbone, then apply pressure to cut through and separate breast into two halves.

2. Using kitchen shears, trim off rib section from each breast, following vertical line of fat from tapered end of breast up to socket.

3. Using chef's knife or kitchen shears, trim excess fat and skin from breasts.

CHICKEN PAPRIKASH AND BUTTERED SPAETZLE

SERVES 4 TO 6

We call for removing the skin from bone-in chicken thighs here. Rather than discarding the skin, try crisping it in a skillet in a little oil set over medium-high heat and setting it aside for a snack. Be sure to use sweet Hungarian paprika here, not hot or smoked, and make sure it's fresh (once opened, paprika loses its flavor quickly). Serve with Buttered Spaetzle (recipe follows) or buttered egg noodles.

- ¼ cup extra-virgin olive oil
- 1 large onion, halved and sliced thin
- 1 red bell pepper, stemmed, seeded, and sliced thin
- 1 (14.5-ounce) can diced tomatoes, drained
- 5 garlic cloves, chopped fine
- 2 teaspoons table salt, divided
- 8 (5- to 7-ounce) bone-in chicken thighs, skin removed, trimmed
- ¾ teaspoon pepper
- 2½ cups chicken broth
- 2 tablespoons paprika, plus extra for serving
- ¼ teaspoon cayenne pepper
- ⅓ cup sour cream, plus extra for serving
- 3 tablespoons all-purpose flour
- 2 tablespoons chopped fresh parsley

1. Heat oil in Dutch oven over medium-high heat until shimmering. Add onion, bell pepper, tomatoes, garlic, and 1 teaspoon salt and cook, stirring often, until vegetables are softened and fond begins to develop on bottom of pot, about 10 minutes.

2. Sprinkle chicken with pepper and remaining 1 teaspoon salt. Stir broth, paprika, and cayenne into pot, scraping up any browned bits. Submerge chicken in broth mixture and bring to simmer. Reduce heat to medium-low, cover, and simmer until chicken is very tender and registers at least 195 degrees, about 30 minutes, stirring and flipping chicken halfway through simmering.

3. Whisk sour cream and flour together in bowl. Slowly whisk ½ cup cooking liquid into sour cream mixture. Stir sour cream mixture into pot until fully incorporated. Continue to simmer, uncovered, until thickened, about 5 minutes longer. Off heat, season with salt and pepper to taste. Let stand for 5 minutes. Sprinkle with parsley and serve with extra paprika and extra sour cream.

BUTTERED SPAETZLE
SERVES 6 TO 8
The 13 by 9-inch disposable aluminum pan serves as a makeshift sieve for portioning the batter.

- 2 cups all-purpose flour
- ¾ teaspoon table salt, plus salt for cooking spaetzle
- ½ teaspoon pepper
- ¼ teaspoon ground nutmeg
- ¾ cup whole milk
- 3 large eggs
- 1 (13 by 9-inch) disposable aluminum pan
- 2 tablespoons unsalted butter, melted

1. Whisk flour, salt, pepper, and nutmeg together in large bowl. Whisk milk and eggs together in second bowl. Slowly whisk milk mixture into flour mixture until smooth. Cover and let rest for 15 to 30 minutes.

2. While batter rests, use scissors to poke about forty ¼-inch holes in bottom of disposable pan. Bring 4 quarts water to boil in Dutch oven.

3. Add 1 tablespoon salt to boiling water and set prepared disposable pan on top of Dutch oven. Transfer half of batter to disposable pan. Use spatula to scrape batter across holes, letting batter fall into water. Boil until spaetzle float, about 1 minute. Using spider skimmer or slotted spoon, transfer spaetzle to colander set in large bowl to drain. Repeat with remaining batter.

4. Discard any accumulated water in bowl beneath colander. Pour spaetzle into now-empty bowl. Add melted butter and toss to combine. Serve.

Why This Recipe Works We learned a lot about paprika from visiting Balaton in Cleveland, Ohio. Chicken paprikash is a Hungarian stew that sings of the toasty flavor of paprika, but paprika is sensitive to heat. To prevent it from burning and tasting bitter, we added it to the pot with chicken broth rather than blooming it in oil. Cayenne provided balanced warmth, and red bell pepper and onion lent sweetness. Bone-in chicken thighs turned tender in the stew—removing their skin prevented greasiness. We like to serve paprikash with spaetzle, a homey cross between egg noodles and dumplings, which we made using a makeshift spaetzle press.

Why This Recipe Works Once-trendy chicken Divan's original recipe calls for many different components and even more cooking steps. We wanted to stay true to the original flavor of the dish but streamline the cooking process. To do this, we batch-cooked the broccoli first, then the chicken. While the broccoli and chicken rested, we used the same pan to prepare our sauce. And instead of making a separate hollandaise sauce, like the traditional chicken Divan recipes demand, we whisked egg yolks and lemon juice together, tempered the mixture with the hot pan sauce, and whisked in butter at the end.

CHICKEN DIVAN

SERVES 4

Use one small onion instead of the shallots, if desired.

3 tablespoons vegetable oil
1 pound broccoli florets, cut into 1-inch pieces
2½ cups chicken broth
¼ cup all-purpose flour
4 (6-ounce) boneless, skinless chicken breasts, trimmed
Salt and pepper
2 shallots, minced
1 cup heavy cream
½ cup dry sherry
2 teaspoons Worcestershire sauce
3 ounces Parmesan cheese, grated (1½ cups)
3 large egg yolks
1 tablespoon lemon juice
3 tablespoons unsalted butter

1. Adjust oven rack to lower-middle position and heat broiler. Heat 1 tablespoon oil in large skillet over medium-high heat until just smoking. Add broccoli and cook until spotty brown, about 1 minute. Add ½ cup broth, cover, and steam until just tender, about 1½ minutes. Remove lid and cook until liquid has evaporated, about 1 minute. Transfer broccoli to plate lined with paper towels; rinse and wipe out skillet.

2. Heat remaining 2 tablespoons oil in now-empty skillet over medium-high heat until smoking. Meanwhile, place flour in shallow dish. Season chicken with salt and pepper and dredge in flour to coat. Cook chicken until golden brown on both sides, 4 to 6 minutes. Transfer chicken to plate.

3. Add shallots to skillet and cook until just softened, about 1 minute. Add remaining 2 cups broth and cream and scrape browned bits from bottom of pan. Return chicken to skillet and simmer over medium-high heat until cooked through, about 10 minutes. Transfer chicken to clean plate and continue to simmer sauce until reduced to 1 cup, about 10 minutes. Add sherry and Worcestershire and simmer until reduced again to 1 cup, about 3 minutes. Stir in 1 cup Parmesan.

4. Whisk egg yolks and lemon juice in small bowl, then whisk in about ¼ cup sauce. Off heat, whisk egg yolk mixture into sauce in skillet, then whisk in butter.

5. Cut chicken into ½-inch-thick slices and arrange on broiler-safe platter. Scatter broccoli over chicken and pour sauce over broccoli. Sprinkle with remaining ½ cup Parmesan and broil until golden brown, 3 to 5 minutes. Serve.

Broccoli Makes It to the Big Time

It can seem hard to believe today, but broccoli, a key ingredient in chicken Divan, an elegant chicken dish from Manhattan's Divan Parisien restaurant (see page 36), was a relative latecomer to the American diet. This headline from *The New York Times* in 1926 attests to its arrival on the scene: "New Vegetables Vary our Menus: Broccoli, Artichoke, and Avocado Naturalized, and Fennel Enters Under Foreign Name—Homely Carrot Is Still in Demand." Broccoli aside, the restaurant's recipe required a whole poached chicken and a sauce made with béchamel, hollandaise, Parmesan cheese, and whipped cream. The ingredients were combined à la minute (just before being plated) and broiled to perfection. Sounds good, but if we're counting right, that's at least five pots, four recipes, and more time than we'd care to spend in the kitchen. No wonder most "modern" recipes rely on canned soup. We wanted to bring Divan into the 21st century without compromising the flavors of the original dish.

CHICKEN FLORENTINE

SERVES 4 TO 6

We like tender, quick-cooking bagged baby spinach here; if using curly-leaf spinach, chop it before cooking.

    2   tablespoons vegetable oil
   12   ounces (12 cups) baby spinach
    4   (6-ounce) boneless, skinless chicken
        breasts, trimmed
        Salt and pepper
    1   shallot, minced
    2   garlic cloves, minced
 1¼   cups chicken broth
 1¼   cups water
    1   cup heavy cream
    6   tablespoons grated Parmesan cheese
    1   teaspoon grated lemon zest
        plus 1 teaspoon juice

1. Adjust oven rack to upper-middle position and heat broiler. Heat 1 tablespoon oil in 12-inch skillet over medium-high heat until shimmering. Add spinach and cook, stirring occasionally until wilted, 1 to 2 minutes. Transfer spinach to colander set over bowl and press with spoon to release excess liquid. Discard liquid.

2. Pat chicken dry with paper towels and season with salt and pepper. Wipe out pan and heat remaining 1 tablespoon oil over medium-high heat until just smoking. Cook chicken on both sides until golden, 4 to 6 minutes. Add shallot and garlic to skillet and cook until fragrant, about 30 seconds. Stir in broth, water, and cream and bring to boil.

3. Reduce heat to medium-low and simmer until chicken is cooked through, about 10 minutes; transfer chicken to plate and tent with aluminum foil. Continue to simmer sauce until reduced to 1 cup, about 10 minutes. Off heat, stir in 4 tablespoons Parmesan and lemon zest and juice.

4. Cut chicken crosswise into ½-inch-thick slices and arrange on broiler-safe platter. Scatter spinach over chicken and pour sauce over spinach. Sprinkle with remaining Parmesan and broil until golden brown, 3 to 5 minutes. Serve.

Draining Spinach

As it cooks, spinach releases a lot of moisture, which can make dishes like our Chicken Florentine watery. To prevent that, we transferred the spinach to a colander and pressed the leaves with a spoon to force the liquid out. We drained nearly ¼ cup of liquid from the 12 ounces of spinach used in this recipe.

Enchanting Chicken—Without a Wand

The idea of chicken Florentine as a dish made from chicken, spinach, and a cheesy cream sauce appeared in print as early as 1931, when *The Lowell (Mass.) Sun* breathlessly described Chicken Mornay Florentine as served at the Manhattan restaurant, Divan Parisien: "They make magic passes over spinach, then cover it with breasts of chicken and a Mornay sauce." In the "Tables for Two" column of *The New Yorker*, April 25, 1931, the Divan Parisien was described as "a quiet and extremely civilized restaurant with an assorted clientele. . . ." What a shame then, that one of their most popular dishes morphed into a 1960s casserole (made with frozen spinach, margarine, packaged bread crumbs, and condensed soups) and then into wedding banquet fare in the 1970s and '80s (breasts stuffed with spinach, rolled, fried, and served with a cheesy sauce). We wanted to deconstruct the casserole, unroll the spirals, and return chicken Florentine to its earliest version: a bright, elegant, streamlined sauté with a pan sauce. No magic passes involved.

Why This Recipe Works To restore chicken Florentine to its elegant roots, we started with fresh spinach. To prevent the water from the spinach from washing out the other flavors in the dish, we drained excess liquid from the cooked spinach by pressing the leaves with the back of a spoon in a colander. For flavor, we seared the chicken breasts first and then poached them in the sauce before broiling. We used cream to make the sauce silky and built volume with equal amounts of chicken broth and water. We also added a squeeze of lemon juice and a hit of zest, along with Parmesan cheese for its nutty, savory punch.

ONE-POT CHICKEN JARDINIÈRE

SERVES 4 TO 6

Buy a 4-ounce hunk of pancetta from the deli counter. Try to buy potatoes with a 1-inch diameter. If you can find only slightly larger potatoes, up to 2 inches in diameter, cut them in half. Do not substitute russet potatoes for Yukon Gold potatoes. Note that the dark and white meat are added to the pot at different times in step 3.

- 3 pounds bone-in chicken pieces (split breasts cut in half, drumsticks, and/or thighs), trimmed
- ¾ teaspoon table salt, divided
- ¾ teaspoon pepper, divided
- 1 teaspoon vegetable oil
- 4 ounces pancetta, cut into ½-inch pieces
- 1 onion, chopped fine
- 3 garlic cloves, minced
- 2 teaspoons minced fresh thyme
- 3 tablespoons all-purpose flour
- 2 cups chicken broth
- ¾ cup dry white wine
- 12 ounces small Yukon Gold potatoes, unpeeled
- 8 ounces small white mushrooms, trimmed and halved
- 4 carrots, cut into 1-inch chunks
- ½ cup frozen peas
- 1 tablespoon chopped fresh tarragon or parsley
  Lemon wedges

1. Pat chicken dry with paper towels and sprinkle with ¼ teaspoon salt and ¼ teaspoon pepper. Heat oil in Dutch oven over medium-high heat until shimmering. Add chicken, skin side down, and cook until well browned on both sides, about 3 minutes per side. Transfer chicken to plate.

2. Reduce heat to medium. Add pancetta, onion, garlic, thyme, and remaining ½ teaspoon salt to now-empty pot and cook until onion just begins to soften, about 4 minutes. Stir in flour and cook for 1 minute. Slowly whisk in broth and wine. Stir in potatoes, mushrooms, carrots, chicken drumsticks and thighs, and remaining ½ teaspoon pepper and bring to simmer. Cover and simmer for 25 minutes.

3. Uncover and stir. Add chicken breasts and any accumulated juices to pot; return to simmer. Cover and continue to cook until breasts register 160 degrees and drumsticks/thighs register at least 175 degrees, about 20 minutes longer. Off heat, stir in peas and let sit uncovered for 5 minutes. Stir in tarragon and season with salt and pepper to taste. Serve with lemon wedges.

Building the Braise Is a Simple Process

1. Brown all chicken pieces and remove from pot.

2. Add pancetta, onion, garlic, and thyme to pot and sauté until starting to soften.

3. Add flour, broth, wine, vegetables, and chicken and simmer before adding peas.

Why This Recipe Works "Gardener's Stew" doesn't cut it in English, but borrow a French word and you've got Chicken Jardinière, an elegant braise of bone-in chicken parts and vegetables flavored with garlic, herbs, and wine. This streamlined version can be prepared in just one pot. We started by browning the chicken to build a rich base for the sauce. Sautéing the carrots and mushrooms proved unnecessary, so we stirred them directly into the sauce. Simmering the dark meat in the sauce before adding the white meat ensured that all the chicken was done at the same time. Frozen peas and fresh tarragon finished our stew with color and brightness.

Why This Recipe Works With a flaky crust topping savory chicken and vegetables suspended in a velvety cream gravy, it's hard to imagine anything more comforting than a traditional pot pie, but we upped the ante by adding a second buttery crust underneath. Incorporating sour cream and egg into the dough made it easy to handle after an hour-long rest in the fridge, and using rotisserie chicken streamlined the process (and cut down on dirty dishes). Letting the pie cool on a wire rack for 45 minutes gave the filling time to firm up, producing a pie that was satisfyingly sliceable.

DOUBLE-CRUST CHICKEN POT PIE

SERVES 6 TO 8

The pie may seem loose when it comes out of the oven; it will set up as it cools. You can substitute 3 cups of turkey meat for the chicken, if desired.

Crust

- ½ cup sour cream, chilled
- 1 large egg, lightly beaten
- 2½ cups (12½ ounces) all-purpose flour
- 1½ teaspoons salt
- 12 tablespoons unsalted butter, cut into ½-inch pieces and chilled

Filling

- 4 tablespoons unsalted butter
- 1 onion, chopped fine
- 2 carrots, peeled and cut into ¼-inch pieces (⅔ cup)
- 2 celery ribs, cut into ¼-inch pieces (½ cup)
- ½ teaspoon salt
- ½ teaspoon pepper
- 6 tablespoons all-purpose flour
- 2¼ cups chicken broth
- ½ cup half-and-half
- 1 small russet potato (6 ounces), peeled and cut into ¼-inch pieces (1 cup)
- 1 teaspoon minced fresh thyme
- 1 (2½-pound) rotisserie chicken, skin and bones discarded, meat shredded into bite-size pieces (3 cups)
- ¾ cup frozen peas
- 1 large egg, lightly beaten

1. For the Crust Combine sour cream and egg in bowl. Process flour and salt in food processor until combined, about 3 seconds. Add butter and pulse until only pea-size pieces remain, about 10 pulses. Add half of sour cream mixture and pulse until combined, 5 pulses. Add remaining sour cream mixture and pulse until dough begins to form, about 10 pulses.

2. Transfer mixture to lightly floured counter and knead briefly until dough comes together. Divide dough in half and form each half into 4-inch disk.

Wrap disks tightly in plastic wrap and refrigerate for 1 hour. (Wrapped dough can be refrigerated for up to 2 days or frozen for up to 2 months. If frozen, let dough thaw completely on counter before rolling.)

3. Let chilled dough sit on counter to soften slightly, about 10 minutes, before rolling. Roll 1 disk of dough into 12-inch circle on lightly floured counter. Loosely roll dough around rolling pin and gently unroll it onto 9-inch pie plate, letting excess dough hang over edge. Ease dough into plate by gently lifting edge of dough with your hand while pressing into plate bottom with your other hand.

4. Roll other disk of dough into 12-inch circle on lightly floured counter, then transfer to parchment paper–lined baking sheet; cover with plastic. Refrigerate both doughs for 30 minutes.

5. For the Filling Meanwhile, adjust oven rack to lowest position and heat oven to 450 degrees. Melt butter in large saucepan over medium heat. Add onion, carrots, celery, salt, and pepper and cook until vegetables begin to soften, about 6 minutes. Add flour and cook, stirring constantly, until golden, 1 to 2 minutes. Slowly stir in broth and half-and-half and bring to boil over medium-high heat.

6. Stir in potato and thyme. Reduce heat to medium and simmer until sauce is thickened and potato is tender, about 8 minutes. Off heat, stir in chicken and peas.

7. Transfer filling to dough-lined pie plate. Loosely roll remaining dough round around rolling pin and gently unroll it onto filling. Trim overhang to ½ inch beyond lip of plate. Pinch edges of top and bottom crusts firmly together. Tuck overhang under itself; folded edge should be flush with edge of plate. Crimp dough evenly around edge of plate using your fingers. Cut four 2-inch slits in top of dough.

8. Brush top of pie with egg. Place pie on rimmed baking sheet. Bake until top is light golden brown, 18 to 20 minutes. Reduce oven temperature to 375 degrees, rotate sheet, and continue to bake until crust is deep golden brown, 12 to 15 minutes longer. Let pie cool on wire rack for at least 45 minutes. Serve.

GLAZED MEATLOAF

SERVES 6 TO 8

*Both ground sirloin and ground chuck work well
here, but avoid ground round—it is gristly and bland.*

Glaze

  1   cup ketchup
 ¼   cup packed brown sugar
 2½ tablespoons cider vinegar
 ½   teaspoon hot sauce

Meatloaf

  2   teaspoons vegetable oil
  1   onion, chopped fine
  2   garlic cloves, minced
 17   square or 19 round saltines
 ⅓   cup whole milk
  1   pound 90 percent lean ground beef
  1   pound ground pork
  2   large eggs plus 1 large yolk
 ⅓   cup finely chopped fresh parsley
  2   teaspoons Dijon mustard
  2   teaspoons Worcestershire sauce
 ½   teaspoon dried thyme
      Salt and pepper

1. For the Glaze Whisk all ingredients in saucepan
until sugar dissolves. Reserve ¼ cup glaze mixture,
then simmer remaining glaze over medium heat
until slightly thickened, about 5 minutes. Cover and
keep warm.

2. For the Meatloaf Line rimmed baking sheet
with aluminum foil and coat lightly with vegetable
oil spray. Heat oil in nonstick skillet over medium
heat until shimmering. Cook onion until golden, about
8 minutes. Add garlic and cook until fragrant,
about 30 seconds. Transfer to large bowl.

3. Process saltines and milk in food processor until
smooth, about 30 seconds. Add beef and pork and
pulse until well combined, about 10 pulses. Transfer
meat mixture to bowl with cooled onion mixture.
Add eggs and yolk, parsley, mustard, Worcestershire,
thyme, 1 teaspoon salt, and ¾ teaspoon pepper to
bowl and mix with hands until combined.

4. Adjust 1 oven rack to middle position and second
rack 4 inches from broiler element; heat broiler.
Transfer meat mixture to prepared baking sheet and
shape into 9 by 5-inch loaf. Broil on upper rack
until well browned, about 5 minutes. Brush 2 tablespoons unreduced glaze over top and sides of loaf
and then return to oven and broil until glaze begins
to brown, about 2 minutes.

5. Transfer meatloaf to lower rack and brush with
remaining unreduced glaze. Reduce oven temperature to 350 degrees and bake until meatloaf registers
160 degrees, 40 to 45 minutes. Transfer to cutting
board, tent with foil, and let rest for 20 minutes. Slice
and serve, passing remaining reduced glaze at table.

Ketchup—The Truffle Oil of the '20s?

Say "meatloaf" and many Americans think
1950s comfort food and Mom, but this humble
recipe has surprisingly elegant roots in a
now-forgotten dish called "cannelon." A typical
cannelon recipe from the original *Boston
Cooking-School Cookbook* calls for chopping
and seasoning beef, shaping it into a log, and
basting it with melted butter as it bakes. The
wide availability of meat grinders and the advent
of reliable refrigeration made ground beef a
household staple in the early 20th century and
meatloaf recipes gained wide circulation. As
a topping, butter was usurped by tomato sauce
until ketchup became popular in the 1920s.
The Heinz company created a "House of Heinz"
campaign to tout the gourmet appeal their
products gave to everyday dishes such as meatloaf. Along with their ketchup, Heinz suggested
incorporating other Heinz products, such as
beefsteak sauce, chili sauce, and olives into
meatloaf, or serving cubes of meatloaf with
pickle slices for an easy hors d'oeuvre. For our
meatloaf, we skipped the gourmet aspirations
and unnecessary mix-ins for a stellar version
of the 1950s favorite.

Why This Recipe Works For our old-fashioned meatloaf, we cut ground beef with an equal portion of sweet ground pork for better flavor. As for seasoning, we stuck with tradition: salt, pepper, Dijon mustard, Worcestershire sauce, thyme, parsley, sautéed onion, and garlic. To add moisture and structure, we used a panade (paste) of milk and saltines. Combining the panade in a food processor and then pulsing it with the meat gave the loaf the most cohesive, tender structure. To evaporate the surface moisture that was inhibiting the formation of a crust, we broiled the loaf prior to baking and glazing.

FROSTED MEATLOAF

SERVES 6 TO 8

If you don't have a ricer or a food mill, just mash the potatoes thoroughly.

- ¼ cup ketchup
- 1 tablespoon packed light brown sugar
- 1 tablespoon cider vinegar
- ½ teaspoon hot sauce
- 8 tablespoons unsalted butter
- 1 onion, chopped fine
- 3 garlic cloves, minced
- 17 square or 19 round saltines, crushed (⅔ cup)
- 1 cup whole milk
- 1 pound ground pork
- 2 large eggs plus 1 large yolk
- ⅓ cup minced fresh parsley
- 2 teaspoons Dijon mustard
- 2 teaspoons Worcestershire sauce
  Salt and pepper
- ½ teaspoon dried thyme
- 1 pound 90 percent lean ground beef
- 2 pounds russet potatoes, peeled and cut into 1-inch pieces

1. Adjust oven racks to upper-middle and lower-middle positions and heat broiler. Line rimmed baking sheet with aluminum foil, set wire rack in sheet, and place 14 by 6-inch piece of foil in center of rack. Whisk ketchup, sugar, vinegar, and hot sauce together in bowl; set aside glaze.

2. Melt 2 tablespoons butter in 10-inch skillet over medium heat. Add onion and cook until just softened, 3 to 5 minutes. Add garlic and cook until fragrant, about 30 seconds. Set aside off heat.

3. Combine saltines and ⅓ cup milk in large bowl and mash with fork until chunky paste forms. Add pork, eggs and yolk, parsley, mustard, Worcestershire, 1 teaspoon salt, ¾ teaspoon pepper, thyme, and onion mixture and knead with your hands until mostly combined. Add beef and knead until combined.

4. Transfer meat mixture to foil rectangle on wire rack and form into 9 by 6-inch loaf. Broil on upper-middle oven rack until well browned, 5 to 7 minutes. Brush glaze over top and sides of meatloaf, return to upper-middle rack, and broil until glaze begins to brown, 3 to 5 minutes. Move meatloaf to lower-middle oven rack, adjust oven temperature to 350 degrees, and bake until meatloaf registers 160 degrees, 40 to 45 minutes. Remove from oven.

5. Meanwhile, bring potatoes and 2 quarts water to boil in Dutch oven over high heat. Reduce heat to medium-low and simmer until potatoes are tender, 20 to 25 minutes; drain potatoes thoroughly in colander. Set ricer or food mill over now-empty pot and press or mill potatoes into pot. Stir 1 teaspoon salt, remaining 6 tablespoons butter, and remaining ⅔ cup milk into potatoes until combined.

6. Using offset spatula, spread mashed potatoes evenly over top and sides of meatloaf. Heat broiler and return meatloaf to lower-middle oven rack. Broil until potatoes are browned, about 15 minutes. Using foil as sling, transfer meatloaf to carving board and let rest for 15 minutes. Slice and serve.

Reviving Comfort Food

During World War II, meat was rationed. Americans were encouraged to extend short supplies through many means, boosting meatloaf's popularity. In the '50s, this classic was reinvented as a centerpiece for entertaining, topped with garnishes, glazes, sauces, and, of course, mashed potatoes.

Why This Recipe Works Meatloaf and potatoes are an unbeatable combination, so frosted meatloaf—meatloaf coated in a layer of mashed potatoes—was an idea we could get behind. To perfect this nearly forgotten 1950s classic, we found that we had to broil the meatloaf in stages to keep the potatoes from slipping off: First, it was broiled to create a crust and then coated with a tangy, ketchup-based glaze for flavor and broiled again. After cooking through, the meatloaf was frosted with creamy mashed potatoes and broiled for a final stint to turn the fluffy crown of potatoes beautifully brown.

Why This Recipe Works As much as we love classic meatloaf, a recipe for a rustic meatloaf with a deep-brown crust and hearty mushroom gravy piqued our interest. Sliced button mushrooms plus minced porcini gave the gravy an earthy richness. To further boost the flavor of the meatloaf itself, we added the porcini soaking liquid and more button mushrooms, which we ground in a food processor and sautéed. To keep the procedure simple, we baked the meatloaf in the same skillet. Then, while the loaf was resting, we used the skillet and the meat drippings to build our gravy.

MEATLOAF WITH MUSHROOM GRAVY

SERVES 8

If you're short the 2 tablespoons of meatloaf drippings needed to make the gravy, supplement the drippings with melted butter or vegetable oil.

- 1 cup water
- ¼ ounce dried porcini mushrooms, rinsed
- 16 square or 18 round saltines
- 10 ounces white mushrooms, trimmed
- 1 tablespoon vegetable oil
- 1 onion, chopped fine
  Salt and pepper
- 4 garlic cloves, minced
- 1 pound ground pork
- 2 large eggs
- 1 tablespoon plus ¾ teaspoon Worcestershire sauce
- 1 pound 85 percent lean ground beef
- ¾ teaspoon minced fresh thyme
- ¼ cup all-purpose flour
- 2½ cups chicken broth

1. Adjust oven rack to middle position and heat oven to 375 degrees. Microwave water and porcini in covered bowl until steaming, about 1 minute. Let sit until softened, about 5 minutes. Strain porcini through fine-mesh strainer lined with coffee filter, reserving liquid. Mince and reserve porcini.

2. Process saltines in food processor until finely ground, about 30 seconds; transfer to large bowl and reserve. Pulse 5 ounces of white mushrooms in processor until finely ground, 8 to 10 pulses.

3. Heat oil in 12-inch nonstick oven-safe skillet over medium-high heat until shimmering. Add onion and cook until browned, 6 to 8 minutes. Stir in processed mushrooms and ¼ teaspoon salt and cook until liquid evaporates and mushrooms begin to brown, about 5 minutes. Add garlic and cook until fragrant, about 30 seconds. Transfer to bowl with saltines and let cool to room temperature, about 15 minutes. Wipe out skillet with paper towels.

4. Add pork, ¼ cup reserved porcini liquid, eggs, 1 tablespoon Worcestershire, 1 teaspoon salt, and ¾ teaspoon pepper to cooled mushroom-saltine mixture and knead gently until nearly combined. Add beef and knead until well combined. Transfer meat mixture to now-empty skillet and shape into 10 by 6-inch loaf. Bake until meatloaf registers 160 degrees, 45 to 55 minutes. Transfer meatloaf to carving board and tent loosely with aluminum foil.

5. Slice remaining 5 ounces white mushrooms. Discard any solids in skillet and pour off all but 2 tablespoons fat. Heat fat over medium-high heat until shimmering. Add sliced mushrooms and reserved porcini and cook, stirring occasionally, until deep golden brown, 6 to 8 minutes. Stir in thyme and ¼ teaspoon salt and cook until fragrant, about 30 seconds. Add flour and cook, stirring frequently, until golden, about 2 minutes. Slowly whisk in broth, ½ cup reserved porcini liquid, and remaining ¾ teaspoon Worcestershire, scraping up any browned bits, and bring to boil. Reduce heat to medium and simmer, whisking occasionally, until thickened, 10 to 15 minutes. Season with salt and pepper to taste. Slice meatloaf and serve with gravy.

One Skillet, Start to Finish

ON THE STOVE
We brown the onion and ground mushrooms for robust flavor.

INTO THE OVEN
We shape and bake the meatloaf in the same skillet.

BACK TO THE STOVE
While the meatloaf rests, we use its drippings to make the gravy.

BACON-WRAPPED MEATLOAF

SERVES 6 TO 8

Bull's-Eye Original is our favorite barbecue sauce. Do not use thick-cut bacon for this recipe, as the package will yield fewer strips for wrapping the meatloaf. Oscar Mayer Naturally Hardwood Smoked Bacon is our favorite thin-sliced bacon.

¼ cup barbecue sauce, plus extra for serving
1 tablespoon cider vinegar
1 tablespoon Worcestershire sauce
1 tablespoon spicy brown mustard
17 square or 19 round saltines, crushed (⅔ cup)
4 slices coarsely chopped bacon,
   plus 8 whole slices
1 onion, chopped coarse
3 garlic cloves, minced
⅓ cup whole milk
2 large eggs plus 1 large yolk
⅓ cup minced fresh parsley
¾ teaspoon salt
½ teaspoon pepper
1½ pounds 90 percent lean ground beef

1. Adjust oven rack to upper-middle position and heat oven to 375 degrees. Line rimmed baking sheet with aluminum foil and set wire rack in sheet. Whisk barbecue sauce, vinegar, Worcestershire, and mustard together in bowl; set glaze aside.

2. Process saltines in food processor until finely ground, about 30 seconds; transfer to large bowl. Pulse chopped bacon and onion in now-empty processor until coarsely ground, about 10 pulses. Transfer bacon mixture to 10-inch nonstick skillet and cook over medium heat until onion is soft and translucent, about 5 minutes. Add garlic and cook until fragrant, about 30 seconds. Set aside off heat.

3. Add milk, eggs and yolk, parsley, salt, pepper, and 2 tablespoons glaze to saltines and mash with fork until chunky paste forms. Stir in bacon mixture until combined. Add the beef and knead with your hands until combined.

4. Lightly spray 8½ by 4½-inch loaf pan with vegetable oil spray. Line pan with large sheet of plastic wrap, with extra plastic hanging over edges of pan. Push plastic into corners and up sides of pan. Line pan crosswise with remaining 8 bacon slices, overlapping them slightly and letting excess hang over edges of pan (you should have at least ½ inch of overhanging bacon). Brush bacon with 3 tablespoons glaze. Transfer meatloaf mixture to bacon-lined pan and press mixture firmly into pan. Fold bacon slices over mixture.

5. Using metal skewer or tip of paring knife, poke 15 holes in one 14 by 3-inch piece of foil. Center foil rectangle on top of meatloaf. Carefully flip meatloaf onto wire rack so foil is on bottom and bacon is on top. Gripping plastic, gently lift and remove pan from meatloaf. Discard plastic. Gently press meatloaf into 9 by 5-inch rectangle.

6. Bake until bacon is browned and meatloaf registers 150 degrees, about 1 hour. Remove from oven and heat broiler. Brush top and sides of meatloaf with remaining 2 tablespoons glaze. Broil meatloaf until glaze begins to char and meatloaf registers 160 degrees, 3 to 5 minutes. Using foil as sling, transfer meatloaf to carving board and let rest for 15 minutes. Slice and serve, passing extra barbecue sauce.

That's a Wrap

Invert the foil-topped loaf, bacon and all, onto a wire rack set in a baking sheet, remove the loaf pan and plastic, press the meatloaf into shape, and bake.

Why This Recipe Works What's even better than a bacon-wrapped meatloaf? A bacon-wrapped meatloaf that also has chopped bacon added to the ground beef inside. To make shaping easy, we lined a loaf pan with plastic wrap and then shingled slices of bacon in the pan. After pressing the meatloaf mixture into the pan, we turned it out onto a piece of foil set on a wire rack inside a rimmed baking sheet. This allowed the fat from the meat to drain away from the loaf as it cooked. A pass under the broiler ensured that the bacon was crisp and that the spicy-sweet glaze caramelized to perfection.

GROUND BEEF STROGANOFF

SERVES 4

Pennsylvania Dutch Wide Egg Noodles are our favorite.

2 tablespoons vegetable oil
8 ounces white mushrooms, trimmed and
   sliced thin
   Salt and pepper
1 onion, chopped fine
2 garlic cloves, minced
1 pound 85 percent lean ground beef
3 tablespoons all-purpose flour
4 cups chicken broth
¼ cup dry white wine
8 ounces (4 cups) egg noodles
½ cup sour cream, plus extra for serving
2 tablespoons minced fresh chives

1. Heat 1 tablespoon oil in Dutch oven over medium-high heat until shimmering. Add mushrooms and ¼ teaspoon salt and cook until liquid has evaporated and mushrooms begin to brown, 5 to 7 minutes; transfer to bowl.

2. Add remaining 1 tablespoon oil to now-empty pot and return to medium-high heat until shimmering. Add onion, garlic, ½ teaspoon salt, and ½ teaspoon pepper and cook, stirring occasionally, until onion begins to soften, about 5 minutes. Add beef, ¼ teaspoon salt, and ¼ teaspoon pepper and cook, breaking up meat with spoon, until no longer pink, 5 to 7 minutes.

3. Add flour and stir until beef is well coated; cook for 1 minute. Stir in broth and wine and bring to simmer, scraping up any browned bits. Cook until mixture is slightly thickened, about 3 minutes. Stir in noodles; reduce heat to medium; and cook, uncovered, until noodles are tender, 10 to 12 minutes, stirring occasionally.

4. Off heat, stir in sour cream and mushrooms until fully combined. Season with salt and pepper to taste. Transfer to shallow platter and sprinkle with chives. Serve, passing extra sour cream separately.

The Namesake of a Favorite Noodle Dish

Picture him with his knee-high riding boots, tousled hair, and piercing eyes: Count Pavel Stroganov cut a striking figure in 18th-century Russia. At that time, members of the Russian court were Francophiles, speaking French and turning to Paris for cultural inspiration. Beef Stroganoff was likely created by a French chef in honor of the Count. As was often the case when cooking for a patron, the dish was named for him, and the name stuck even as it reached American shores a century after his death. In the 1950s, the dish enjoyed a minor vogue in fancy stateside restaurants; after a few decades in obscurity, it's seen a revival in recent years.

Why This Recipe Works Many upscale versions of beef Stroganoff call for pricey beef tenderloin, while the weeknight version of this recipe features ground beef with canned cream of mushroom soup. We set out to create an easy and comforting Stroganoff that kicked the can to the curb while remaining quick and inexpensive. For the sauce, we used a combination of chicken broth and white wine. Increasing the amounts of each allowed us to cook the egg noodles right in the sauce. Sautéed fresh mushrooms boosted the dish's meatiness, and sour cream added tang and richness. To finish, we sprinkled the dish with bright-green chives for, oniony bite.

Why This Recipe Works We wanted to rescue this American classic from the frozen foods aisle for a great weeknight option. We started by mixing a panade (a milk and bread paste) into ground beef to help bind the meat and preserve moisture, but this trick made the dish taste too much like meatloaf. On a lark, we added mashed potatoes as seen in one recipe and were impressed with the silky texture and great flavor of the patties. To make the dish easier, we swapped in instant potato flakes. We browned the patties on both sides and let them finish cooking in the extra-rich mushroom and onion sauce, which kept the beef tender.

SALISBURY STEAK

SERVES 4

When shaping the patties in step 1, be sure to wet your hands to prevent sticking. Tawny port or dry sherry can be substituted for the ruby port. Do not use potato granules, which add an off-flavor.

½ cup milk
7 tablespoons instant potato flakes
1 pound 90 percent lean ground beef
  Salt and pepper
4 tablespoons unsalted butter
1 onion, halved and sliced thin
1 pound white mushrooms, trimmed and
  sliced thin
1 tablespoon tomato paste
2 tablespoons all-purpose flour
1¾ cups beef broth
¼ cup ruby port

1. Whisk milk and potato flakes in large bowl. Add beef, ½ teaspoon salt, and ½ teaspoon pepper and knead until combined. Shape into four ½-inch-thick oval patties and transfer to parchment paper–lined plate. Refrigerate for at least 30 minutes or up to 4 hours.

2. Melt 1 tablespoon butter in 12-inch nonstick skillet over medium-high heat. Cook patties until well browned on each side, about 10 minutes. Transfer to plate.

3. Add onion and remaining 3 tablespoons butter to now-empty skillet and cook until onion is softened, about 5 minutes. Add mushrooms and ½ teaspoon salt and cook until liquid has evaporated, 5 to 7 minutes. Stir in tomato paste and flour and cook until browned, about 2 minutes. Slowly stir in broth and port and bring to simmer. Return patties to skillet, cover, and simmer over medium-low heat until cooked through, 12 to 15 minutes. Season sauce with salt and pepper to taste. Serve.

The American Table: Take 2 Aspirin— or Have Some Salisbury Steak

It's hard to imagine that chopped steak could be considered health food, but that's just what Dr. James Henry Salisbury had in mind when he invented his eponymous dish as a "meat cure" for wounded and ill Civil War soldiers (who were instructed to eat it three times a day—with no vegetables allowed). Some 60 years later, during the period of World War I food rations, restaurateurs ground up their lean beef scraps, shaped them into patties, dressed the cooked patties with a rich mushroom cream sauce, and called it Salisbury steak. Around this time, recipes for Salisbury steak began showing up in cookbooks, but with a nod toward the original recipe, instructions indicated that the ill or injured should skip the sauce. During World War II, Salisbury steak again enjoyed popularity because it was a great way to stretch meat: cream of wheat, oats, and soy grits were common fillers. And in 1965, Salisbury steak really hit the big time when Swanson introduced it in a special three-course TV dinner. Impressed by its storied past, we couldn't resist resurrecting this American classic.

Why This Recipe Works The point of Swiss steak is to transform a tough, inexpensive cut of meat into a delicate meal so tender you can almost eat it with a spoon. Many recipes called for tenderizing the meat by pounding it before cooking, but we know from experience that pounding meat does nothing to tenderize it. Instead we relied on a slow braise to create the ideal texture. To flavor the Swiss steak gravy, we found a combination of sautéed onion, diced tomatoes, and sun-dried tomatoes was ideal.

SWISS STEAK WITH TOMATO GRAVY

SERVES 6 TO 8

Top blade roast may also be labeled chuck roast first cut, top chuck roast, flat iron roast, or simply blade roast.

- 1 (3½- to 4-pound) boneless top blade roast, trimmed
  Salt and pepper
- 2 tablespoons vegetable oil
- 1 onion, halved and sliced thin
- 2 tablespoons tomato paste
- 1 tablespoon all-purpose flour
- 3 garlic cloves, minced
- ½ teaspoon dried thyme
- 1 (14.5-ounce) can diced tomatoes
- 1½ cups chicken broth
- 1 tablespoon sun-dried tomatoes packed in oil, rinsed, patted dry, and minced
- 1 tablespoon minced fresh parsley

1. Adjust oven rack to middle position and heat oven to 300 degrees. Cut roast crosswise into quarters and remove center line of gristle from each quarter to yield 8 steaks.

2. Pat steaks dry with paper towels and season lightly with salt and pepper. Heat 1 tablespoon oil in Dutch oven over medium-high heat just until smoking. Brown 4 steaks on both sides, about 6 minutes. Transfer to plate and repeat with remaining oil and steaks.

3. Add onion to empty pot and cook until softened, about 5 minutes. Add tomato paste, flour, garlic, and thyme and cook until fragrant, about 1 minute. Stir in diced tomatoes and broth and bring to boil.

4. Return steaks and any accumulated juices to pan. Cover, transfer to oven and cook until steaks are fork-tender, about 2 hours. Transfer steaks to platter, tent with aluminum foil, and let rest for 5 minutes. Skim fat from sauce. Stir in sun-dried tomatoes and parsley. Season with salt and pepper to taste. Pour sauce over steaks. Serve.

Preparing Blade Roast for Swiss Steak

Top blade roast, a shoulder cut with great flavor, has a pesky line of gristle that runs horizontally through its center. Follow these simple steps to remove it and cut perfect Swiss steaks.

1. Place roast on cutting board and cut crosswise into 4 even pieces.

2. One piece at a time, turn meat on its side to expose line of gristle that runs through its center.

3. Remove by slicing through meat on either side of gristle to yield 2 "steaks."

MILK-CAN SUPPER

SERVES 6 TO 8

If your Dutch oven is slightly smaller than 8 quarts, the lid may not close all the way when you start cooking. But as the contents of the pot cook, they will decrease in volume, so you'll soon be able to clamp on the lid. Use small red potatoes, measuring 1 to 2 inches in diameter. Light-bodied American lagers, such as Budweiser, work best in this recipe.

  1 tablespoon vegetable oil
2½ pounds bratwurst (10 sausages)
  2 pounds small red potatoes, unpeeled
  1 head green cabbage (2 pounds),
     cored and cut into 8 wedges
  3 ears corn, husks and silk removed,
     ears cut into 3 pieces
  6 carrots, peeled and cut into 2-inch pieces
  1 onion, halved and cut through root end
     into 8 wedges
  4 garlic cloves, peeled and smashed
10 sprigs fresh thyme
  2 bay leaves
     Salt and pepper
1½ cups beer
  2 green bell peppers, stemmed, seeded,
     and cut into 1-inch-wide strips

1. Heat oil in 8-quart Dutch oven over medium heat until shimmering. Add bratwurst and cook until browned all over, 6 to 8 minutes. Remove pot from heat. Transfer bratwurst to cutting board and halve crosswise.

2. Place potatoes in single layer in now-empty Dutch oven. Arrange cabbage wedges in single layer on top of potatoes. Layer corn, carrots, onion, garlic, thyme, bay leaves, 1 teaspoon salt, and ½ teaspoon pepper over cabbage. Pour beer over vegetables and arrange browned bratwursts on top.

3. Bring to boil over medium-high heat (wisps of steam will be visible). Cover, reduce heat to medium, and simmer for 15 minutes. Add bell peppers and continue to simmer, covered, until potatoes are tender, about 15 minutes. (Use long skewer to test potatoes for doneness.)

4. Transfer bratwurst and vegetables to large serving platter (or roasting pan, if your platter isn't large enough); discard thyme sprigs and bay leaves. Pour 1 cup cooking liquid over platter. Season with salt and pepper to taste. Serve, passing remaining cooking liquid separately.

The American Table: Trail Talk

Food often outlasts the culture that created it. Milk-can supper, for example, originated as a way of feeding cowhands after a long day of work. It is still popular in parts of the West and upper Midwest, but the food lingo of the cowboys who once ate this dish has faded away. Some names for individual dishes, such as calf slobber (for meringue), reflected the coarseness of trail language. Perhaps most revealing was the name for the 5- or 10-gallon can that served as an all-purpose cooking utensil throughout a thousand-mile cattle drive: It was called the squirrel can, the uncomplimentary moniker coming from the idea that it was never emptied during the course of the entire drive but instead became the receptacle for whatever the cook found to add to it. In her 1933 article "Ranch Diction of the Texas Panhandle," author Mary Dale Buckner declared, "It is true that when a spoon, cup, dipper or some small object was dropped into [the squirrel can], usually no one bothered to remove it." We'll stick with the milk can.

Why This Recipe Works Traditionally, cowboys layered vegetables and meat (usually sausage) into a giant milk can, then cooked it over an open fire to feed large groups of cowhands. To bring this all-in-one dish into the home kitchen, we opted to use a Dutch oven but keep the basic technique of layering ingredients according to cooking time. Browning the Bratwurst first created flavorful fond. We lined the bottom of the pot with sturdy red potatoes to protect the other vegetables from burning, and we added the quick-cooking green bell peppers halfway through cooking. Traditional lager as a cooking liquid gave our meat-and-potatoes meal toasty depth.

PAN-FRIED PORK CHOPS

SERVES 4

Chops between ¾ and 1 inch thick will work in this recipe.

> 1 teaspoon garlic powder
> ½ teaspoon paprika
> ½ teaspoon salt
> ½ teaspoon pepper
> ¼ teaspoon cayenne pepper
> 1 cup all-purpose flour
> 4 (8- to 10-ounce) bone-in pork rib or center-cut chops, about ¾ inch thick, trimmed
> 3 slices bacon, chopped
> ½ cup vegetable oil

1. Combine garlic powder, paprika, salt, pepper, and cayenne in bowl. Place flour in shallow dish. Pat chops dry with paper towels. Cut 2 slits about 2 inches apart through fat and connective tissue on edge of each chop. Season both sides of chops with spice mixture, then dredge chops lightly in flour (do not discard flour). Transfer to plate and let rest for 10 minutes.

2. Meanwhile, cook bacon in 12-inch nonstick skillet over medium heat until fat renders and bacon is crisp, 5 to 7 minutes. Using slotted spoon, transfer bacon to paper towel–lined plate and reserve for another use. Do not wipe out pan.

3. Add oil to fat in pan and heat over medium-high heat until just smoking. Return chops to flour dish and turn to coat chops again. Cook chops until well browned on each side, 6 to 8 minutes. Serve.

BBQ PAN-FRIED PORK CHOPS

Replace first 5 ingredients with 3 tablespoons light brown sugar, 1 teaspoon chili powder, 1 teaspoon paprika, ½ teaspoon salt, ½ teaspoon dry mustard, ¼ teaspoon ground cumin, and ¼ teaspoon cayenne pepper.

HERBED PAN-FRIED PORK CHOPS

Replace first 5 ingredients with ½ teaspoon dried marjoram, ½ teaspoon dried thyme, ¼ teaspoon dried basil, ¼ teaspoon dried rosemary (crumbled), ¼ teaspoon dried sage, pinch ground fennel, and ½ teaspoon salt.

Preventing Curly Chops

Pork chops—especially thin-cut chops—have a tendency to curl as they cook. When exposed to the high heat of the pan, the ring of fat and connective tissue that surrounds the exterior tightens, causing the meat to buckle and curl. To prevent it, we cut two slits about 2 inches apart through the fat and connective tissue on each chop.

BUCKLED CHOP
No slits

FLAT CHOP
Slits cut

Why This Recipe Works Not all pork chops are created alike—for pan-frying, we found that center-cut or bone-in pork chops worked best. The bone added valuable flavor to the meat and prevented it from drying out. Simply dredging the pork chops in flour, as most recipes instructed, produced a spotty, insubstantial crust that wouldn't stay put. We have had success letting floured chicken rest before re-dredging and frying, and we wondered if the same treatment would work for pork. Sure enough, our double-dipped chops emerged from the pan with a hefty, crisp, golden-brown crust.

Why This Recipe Works Bone-in chops were a must for smothered pork chops, because the bone kept the meat moist and added flavor to the sauce. Caramelizing the onions made the sauce too sweet and took almost an hour. We had better luck cooking them in butter until they were lightly browned. We swapped out chicken broth in favor of meatier beef broth, which greatly improved the flavor of our sauce. Adding dried thyme, a bay leaf, and cider vinegar bumped up the flavor even more. To thicken our broth, we made a cornstarch-and-broth slurry. The results? A silky sauce that clung to our chops.

SMOTHERED PORK CHOPS

SERVES 4

Chops thicker than ½ inch won't be fully tender in the allotted cooking time.

- 1 teaspoon onion powder
- ½ teaspoon paprika
  Salt and pepper
- ¼ teaspoon cayenne pepper
- 4 (8- to 10-ounce) bone-in blade-cut pork chops, about ½ inch thick, trimmed
- 1½ tablespoons vegetable oil
- 1 tablespoon unsalted butter
- 2 onions, halved and sliced ¼ inch thick
- 2 garlic cloves, minced
- ¼ teaspoon dried thyme
- ¾ cup plus 1 tablespoon beef broth
- 1 bay leaf
- 1 teaspoon cornstarch
- 1 teaspoon cider vinegar

1. Adjust oven rack to middle position and heat oven to 300 degrees. Combine onion powder, paprika, ½ teaspoon salt, ½ teaspoon pepper, and cayenne in small bowl. Pat chops dry with paper towels. Cut 2 slits about 2 inches apart through fat and connective tissue on edge of each chop. Rub chops with spice mixture.

2. Heat oil in large skillet over medium-high heat until just smoking. Brown chops on both sides, 6 to 8 minutes, and transfer to plate. Melt butter in now-empty skillet over medium heat. Cook onions until browned, 8 to 10 minutes. Add garlic and thyme and cook until fragrant, about 30 seconds. Stir in ¾ cup broth and bay leaf, scraping up any browned bits, and bring to boil. Return chops and any accumulated juices to pan, cover, and transfer to oven. Cook until chops are completely tender, about 1½ hours.

3. Transfer chops to platter and tent with aluminum foil. Discard bay leaf. Strain contents of skillet through fine-mesh strainer into large liquid measuring cup; reserve onions. Let liquid settle, then skim fat. Return 1½ cups defatted pan juices to now-empty skillet and bring to boil. Reduce heat to medium and simmer until sauce is reduced to 1 cup, about 5 minutes.

4. Whisk remaining 1 tablespoon broth and cornstarch in bowl until no lumps remain. Whisk cornstarch mixture into sauce and simmer until thickened, 1 to 2 minutes. Stir in reserved onions and vinegar. Season with salt and pepper to taste. Serve.

Pork Chop Perfection

You might think smothered pork chops were born in a diner somewhere. You'd be wrong. "Smother" is an English term that refers to a method of cooking meat, poultry, or game slowly in a covered vessel. This method, essentially a braise, goes back at least to the 16th century. Recipes for smothers first came to the United States from England during the Revolutionary War. Amelia Simmons's *American Cookery*, written in 1796, includes a recipe for smothering a chicken with oysters, though onions are the most common smothering agent. It is believed onions in smothers were used to tone down the gaminess of meat or hide off-flavors. Sailors smothered their salt beef and salt pork rations with onions and potatoes when out to sea. Regional variations soon developed throughout the country: New Englanders often made smothers with fresh pork; in the South, Creole cooking advised against smothering pork, but recommended it for beef, chicken, and veal; and while other traditions in the Deep South did smother pork, it was more typically tails, chitterlings, or other tough or gamy parts—the parts of the pig most available to enslaved African Americans. Eventually, pork chops did make it into the pot, and we're glad they did.

Why This Recipe Works The apple flavor in cider-braised pork chops can be fleeting. We wanted tender, juicy chops infused with deep, rich cider flavor. Tasters preferred 1-inch blade chops for their heft, silky meat, and rich taste. Patting the chops dry before adding them to the heated Dutch oven helped them develop a flavorful crust. Apple cider lent both sweetness and tartness to the braising mixture and sauce, while a bit of fresh thyme provided a heady herbal component. Jarred apple butter added further apple flavor, and its natural pectin gave the sauce a thick, glossy consistency. A splash of cider vinegar provided brightness.

CIDER-BRAISED PORK CHOPS

SERVES 6

Do not use chops thinner than 1 inch. In step 3, a fat separator makes quick work of defatting the sauce.

6   (8- to 10-ounce) bone-in blade-cut pork chops, about 1 inch thick, trimmed
    Salt and pepper
2   tablespoons vegetable oil
1   onion, chopped
¼   cup apple butter
2   tablespoons all-purpose flour
3   garlic cloves, minced
1   cup apple cider
1   sprig fresh thyme
1   teaspoon cider vinegar
1   tablespoon finely chopped fresh parsley

1. Adjust oven rack to lower-middle position and heat oven to 300 degrees. Pat chops dry with paper towels. Cut 2 slits about 2 inches apart through fat and connective tissue on edge of each chop. Season chops with salt and pepper. Heat oil in Dutch oven over medium-high heat until just smoking. Brown 3 chops on each side, about 8 minutes; transfer to plate, and then repeat with remaining 3 chops.

2. Pour off all but 1 tablespoon fat from pot and cook onion over medium heat until softened, about 5 minutes. Stir in 2 tablespoons apple butter, flour, and garlic and cook until onion is coated and mixture is fragrant, about 1 minute. Stir in cider and thyme, scraping up any browned bits with wooden spoon, and bring to boil. Add browned chops and any accumulated juices to pot, cover, and transfer to oven. Braise until chops are completely tender, about 1½ hours.

3. Transfer chops to serving platter. Strain sauce, then skim off fat. Whisk in vinegar, parsley, and remaining 2 tablespoons apple butter. Season with salt and pepper to taste. Serve, passing sauce at table. (Pork chops and sauce can be refrigerated separately for up to 2 days. To serve, reheat sauce and chops together over medium heat until chops are warmed through.)

Three Keys to Better Apple Flavor

Cider alone won't provide much apple flavor. To pack the taste of apples into our pork chops, we settled on a triple helping of apple products.

APPLE BUTTER
Apple butter provides intense apple and warm spice flavor. It also helps thicken the sauce.

CIDER VINEGAR
Finishing with a splash of cider vinegar adds brightness and complexity to the sauce.

CIDER
Sweet-tart cider provides most of the liquid for the braising mixture and sauce.

CRISPY FISH STICKS WITH TARTAR SAUCE

SERVES 4

Be sure to rinse the capers, otherwise the tartar sauce will be too salty. Halibut, haddock, or catfish can be substituted for the cod.

  4 slices hearty white sandwich bread,
      torn into quarters
 16 square or 18 round saltines
 ½ cup all-purpose flour
  2 large eggs
  1 cup mayonnaise
  2 pounds skinless cod, cut into 1-inch-thick strips
      Salt and pepper
 ¼ cup finely chopped dill pickles,
      plus 1 tablespoon pickle juice
  1 tablespoon capers, rinsed and minced
  1 cup vegetable oil

1. Adjust oven rack to middle position and heat oven to 200 degrees. Pulse bread and saltines in food processor to fine crumbs, about 15 pulses; transfer to shallow dish. Place flour in second shallow dish. Beat eggs with ¼ cup mayonnaise in third shallow dish.

2. Pat fish dry with paper towels and season with salt and pepper. One at a time, coat fish strips lightly with flour, dip in egg mixture, and then dredge in crumbs, pressing on both sides to adhere. Transfer breaded fish to plate. Combine remaining ¾ cup mayonnaise, pickles, pickle juice, and capers in small bowl and set aside.

3. Heat ½ cup oil in large 12-inch nonstick skillet over medium heat until just smoking. Fry half of fish strips until deep golden and crisp on both sides, about 4 minutes. Drain on paper towel–lined plate and transfer to oven to keep warm. Discard oil, wipe out skillet, and repeat with remaining ½ cup oil and remaining fish. Serve with tartar sauce.

Fish Sticks—Pioneering the Frozen Food Landscape

Commercial freezing brought fish to the people, but it was the fish stick, introduced in 1953 by Birds Eye, that got them interested in eating fish. Why? Fish sticks have always appealed on a few levels. The breading helps prevent the fish from sticking to the pan; their mild flavor and crunchy crust appeal to children; and conveniently, fish sticks require minimal cleanup. Over the years, neither the expanded market created by freezing nor the wild popularity of fish sticks did much to boost the nation's overall fish consumption. But fish sticks did fire up the frozen foods market, both in terms of the creativity of producers and the enthusiasm of consumers for new, convenient heat-and-eat food products. Before fish sticks went commercial in the frozen foods industry, they were found at fish markets and delis along the East Coast. And of course, they were made at home. Homemade might not be as convenient as the frozen type, but we still aimed for a recipe that was easy enough for a weeknight.

Why This Recipe Works Forget the boxed varieties in the frozen foods aisle—our homemade fish sticks are fresh and crisp, and fry up in just minutes. Our recipe calls for cod, but halibut, haddock, and catfish are all worthy substitutes. Eggs beaten with mayonnaise helped our coating of crisp saltines and fresh bread crumbs adhere to the fish. We pan-fried the fish in two batches to ensure they cooked up even and crisp.

fork-in-the-road favorites

Why This Recipe Works The old-fashioned method of batter-fried chicken calls for dipping chicken parts in a batter not unlike pancake batter before frying. For juicy meat, we brined our chicken. To ensure a crisp crust, we replaced the milk in our initial batters with plain old water. With milk, the sugars in the milk solids browned too fast and produced a soft crust. Using equal parts cornstarch and flour in the batter also helped ensure a crisp crust on the chicken. And baking powder added lift and lightness without doughiness.

BATTER-FRIED CHICKEN

SERVES 4 TO 6

Use a Dutch oven that holds 6 quarts or more for this recipe.

Brine and Chicken
- ¼ cup salt
- ¼ cup sugar
- 4 pounds bone-in chicken pieces (breasts halved crosswise and leg quarters separated into drumsticks and thighs), trimmed

Batter
- 1 cup all-purpose flour
- 1 cup cornstarch
- 5 teaspoons pepper
- 2 teaspoons baking powder
- 1 teaspoon salt
- 1 teaspoon paprika
- ½ teaspoon cayenne pepper
- 1¾ cups cold water
- 3 quarts peanut or vegetable oil

1. For the Brine and Chicken Dissolve salt and sugar in 1 quart cold water in large container. Submerge chicken in brine, cover, and refrigerate for 30 minutes or up to 1 hour.

2. For the Batter Meanwhile, combine flour, cornstarch, pepper, baking powder, salt, paprika, and cayenne in large bowl, add water, and whisk until smooth. Refrigerate batter while chicken is brining.

3. Set wire rack in rimmed baking sheet. Add oil to large Dutch oven until it measures about 2 inches deep and heat over medium-high heat to 350 degrees. Using tongs, remove chicken from brine and pat dry with paper towels. Rewhisk batter. Transfer half of chicken to batter and turn to coat. Remove chicken from batter, 1 piece at a time, allowing excess to drip back into bowl, and transfer to oil. Fry chicken, adjusting burner as necessary to maintain oil temperature between 300 and 325 degrees, until deep golden brown and breasts register 160 degrees and thighs and drumsticks register 175 degrees, 12 to 15 minutes. Drain chicken on prepared baking sheet. Return oil to 350 degrees and repeat with remaining chicken. Serve.

Keys to Best Batter-Fried Chicken

1. Whisk together flour, cornstarch, baking powder, spices, and water to make thin batter for crisp crust.

2. After dipping chicken in batter, let excess drip off (back into bowl) to avoid doughy coating.

3. To prevent chicken pieces from sticking together in oil, don't crowd pot. Fry chicken in 2 batches.

Why This Recipe Works This crispy fried chicken is seasoned with the bold flavors of Creole cuisine of the Gulf South. We built our own Creole seasoning based on its three traditional ground peppers: three parts black, two parts cayenne, and one part white. One of the hallmarks of Creole cooking is its layering of flavors, so we took a three-step approach: After brining the chicken, we sprinkled the raw pieces with our homemade seasoning for added flavor. We also added seasoning to the chicken's flour coating to lend a potent punch. And for a peppery finish, we sprinkled the hot chicken with more seasoning when it came out of the oil.

CREOLE FRIED CHICKEN

SERVES 4 TO 6

In step 1, do not soak the chicken longer than 8 hours, or it will be too salty. Use a Dutch oven that holds 6 quarts or more for this recipe.

Seasoned Brine and Chicken

- ¼ cup sugar
- 3 tablespoons Worcestershire sauce
- 3 tablespoons hot sauce
- 2 tablespoons salt
- 1 tablespoon garlic powder
- 4 pounds bone-in chicken pieces (breasts halved crosswise and leg quarters separated into drumsticks and thighs), trimmed

Creole Seasoning

- 1 tablespoon pepper
- 1 tablespoon dried oregano
- 1 tablespoon garlic powder
- 2 teaspoons onion powder
- 2 teaspoons cayenne pepper
- 1 teaspoon white pepper
- 1 teaspoon celery salt
- 2 cups all-purpose flour
- 3 quarts peanut or vegetable oil

1. For the Seasoned Brine and Chicken Dissolve sugar, Worcestershire, hot sauce, salt, and garlic powder in 1 quart cold water in large container. Submerge chicken in brine, cover, and refrigerate for 1 hour or up to 8 hours.

2. For the Creole Seasoning Combine pepper, oregano, garlic powder, onion powder, cayenne, white pepper, and celery salt in large bowl; reserve ¼ cup spice mixture. Add flour to bowl with remaining spice mixture and stir to combine. Set wire rack in rimmed baking sheet.

3. Remove chicken from brine and pat dry with paper towels. Sprinkle chicken with 3 tablespoons reserved spice mixture and toss to coat. Dredge chicken pieces in flour mixture. Shake excess flour from chicken and transfer to wire rack. (Do not discard flour mixture.)

4. Adjust oven rack to middle position and heat oven to 200 degrees. Set second wire rack in second rimmed baking sheet. Add oil to large Dutch oven until it measures about 2 inches deep and heat over medium-high heat to 375 degrees. Return chicken pieces to flour mixture and turn to coat. Fry half of chicken, adjusting burner as necessary to maintain oil temperature between 300 and 325 degrees, until deep golden brown and breasts register 160 degrees and thighs and drumsticks register 175 degrees, 10 to 12 minutes. Transfer chicken to prepared baking sheet and place in oven. Return oil to 375 degrees and repeat with remaining chicken. Sprinkle crisp chicken with remaining 1 tablespoon spice mixture. Serve.

Secrets to Boldly Flavored Creole Fried Chicken

1. Soaking chicken in brine of sugar, Worcestershire, hot sauce, salt, and garlic powder seasons chicken fully.

2. After brining, a homemade Creole seasoning adds flavor without dusty saltiness of packaged spice blends.

3. The homemade Creole seasoning also lends potent punch to chicken's flour coating.

4. For peppery finish, sprinkle hot chicken with more homemade Creole seasoning when it comes out of oil.

EXTRA-CRUNCHY FRIED CHICKEN

SERVES 4

Keeping the oil at the correct temperature is essential to producing crunchy fried chicken that is neither too brown nor too greasy. Use a Dutch oven that holds 6 quarts or more for this recipe. If you want to produce a slightly lighter version of this recipe, you can remove the skin from the chicken before soaking it in the buttermilk. The chicken will be slightly less crunchy.

- 2 tablespoons salt
- 2 cups plus 6 tablespoons buttermilk
- 1 (3½-pound) whole chicken, cut into 8 pieces and trimmed (4 breast pieces, 2 drumsticks, 2 thighs), wings discarded
- 3 cups all-purpose flour
- 2 teaspoons baking powder
- ¾ teaspoon dried thyme
- ½ teaspoon pepper
- ¼ teaspoon garlic powder
- 1 quart peanut or vegetable oil

1. Dissolve salt in 2 cups buttermilk in large container. Submerge chicken in brine, cover, and refrigerate for 1 hour.

2. Whisk flour, baking powder, thyme, pepper, and garlic powder together in large bowl. Add remaining 6 tablespoons buttermilk; with your fingers rub flour and buttermilk together until buttermilk is evenly incorporated into flour and mixture resembles coarse, wet sand. Set wire rack inside rimmed baking sheet.

3. Dredge chicken pieces in flour mixture and turn to coat thoroughly, gently pressing flour mixture onto chicken. Shake excess flour from each piece of chicken and transfer to prepared baking sheet.

4. Line platter with triple layer of paper towels. Add oil to large Dutch oven until it measures about ¾ inch deep and heat over medium-high heat to 375 degrees. Place chicken pieces skin side down in oil, cover, and fry until deep golden brown, 8 to 10 minutes. Remove lid after 4 minutes and lift chicken pieces to check for even browning; rearrange if some pieces are browning faster than others. Adjust burner, if necessary, to maintain oil temperature between 300 and 315 degrees. Turn chicken pieces over and continue to fry, uncovered, until chicken pieces are deep golden brown on second side and breasts register 160 degrees and thighs and drumsticks register 175 degrees, 6 to 8 minutes. Using tongs, transfer chicken to prepared platter; let stand for 5 minutes. Serve.

EXTRA-SPICY, EXTRA-CRUNCHY FRIED CHICKEN

Add ¼ cup hot sauce to buttermilk-salt mixture in step 1. Replace dried thyme and garlic powder with 2 tablespoons cayenne pepper and 2 teaspoons chili powder in step 2.

Steps to an Extra-Crunchy Coating

1. Soak chicken in buttermilk-salt mixture.

2. Coat chicken with buttermilk-moistened flour.

3. Add chicken to hot oil and cover pot to capture steam.

4. Use tongs to flip chicken and finish cooking with cover off.

Why This Recipe Works For well-seasoned, extra-crunchy fried chicken we started by brining the chicken in heavily salted buttermilk. For the crunchy coating, we combined flour with a little baking powder, then added buttermilk to make a thick slurry, which clung tightly to the meat. Frying the chicken with the lid on the pot for half the cooking time contained the spatter-prone oil and kept it hot.

NASHVILLE HOT FRIED CHICKEN

SERVES 4 TO 6

Chicken quarters take longer to cook than smaller pieces. To ensure that the exterior doesn't burn before the inside cooks through, keep the oil temperature between 300 and 325 degrees while the chicken is frying. Use a Dutch oven that holds 6 quarts or more for this recipe. Serve the chicken as they do in Nashville, on white bread with pickles.

Brine and Chicken
½ cup hot sauce
½ cup salt
½ cup sugar
1 (3½- to 4-pound) whole chicken, quartered

Coating
3 quarts peanut or vegetable oil
1 tablespoon cayenne pepper
½ teaspoon paprika
½ teaspoon sugar
¼ teaspoon garlic powder
Salt and pepper
2 cups all-purpose flour

1. For the Brine and Chicken Dissolve hot sauce, salt, and sugar in 2 quarts cold water in large container. Submerge chicken in brine, cover, and refrigerate for 30 minutes or up to 1 hour.

2. For the Coating Heat 3 tablespoons oil in small saucepan over medium heat until shimmering. Add cayenne, paprika, sugar, garlic powder, and ½ teaspoon salt and cook until fragrant, about 30 seconds. Transfer to small bowl.

3. Set wire rack in rimmed baking sheet. Remove chicken from brine and pat with paper towels. Combine flour, ½ teaspoon salt, and ½ teaspoon pepper in large bowl. Dredge chicken pieces two at a time in flour mixture. Shake excess flour from chicken and transfer to prepared baking sheet. (Do not discard seasoned flour.)

4. Adjust oven rack to middle position and heat oven to 200 degrees. Set second wire rack in second rimmed baking sheet. Add remaining oil to large Dutch oven until it measures about 2 inches deep

and heat over medium-high heat to 350 degrees. Return chicken pieces to flour mixture and turn to coat. Fry half of chicken, adjusting burner as necessary to maintain oil temperature between 300 and 325 degrees, until deep golden brown and breast meat registers 160 degrees and legs register 175 degrees, 20 to 25 minutes. Drain chicken on prepared baking sheet and place in oven. Return oil to 350 degrees and repeat with remaining chicken. Stir spicy oil mixture to recombine and brush over both sides of chicken. Serve.

NASHVILLE EXTRA-HOT FRIED CHICKEN
For spiced oil in step 2, increase oil to ¼ cup, cayenne to 3½ tablespoons, and sugar to ¾ teaspoon and add 1 teaspoon dry mustard. Continue with recipe as directed.

The American Table: The Prince of Shacks
Prince's Hot Chicken Shack, the granddaddy of all hot chicken shacks, sits in a nondescript strip mall in east Nashville. The business got its start in 1945, when, according to legend, Thornton Prince's "lady friend" doused his chicken dinner in hot sauce to teach him a lesson—she'd caught him fooling around. But, her plan backfired: He liked the chicken, and the seed of Prince's Hot Chicken Shack was born. Word spread. The turquoise walls of the "shack" are papered with tacked-up Styrofoam plates that bear autographs from the many Grand Ole Opry stars who have made Prince's famous. Country singers drop in after their shows for late-night snacks of the blazingly hot chicken, says the current proprietor—and Thornton's grandniece—André Prince Jeffries. These days, Prince's attracts club-goers in the wee hours as well as young couples, old couples, and families. Everybody in Nashville, it seems, has a taste for hot chicken.

Why This Recipe Works Mimicking the heat of the hot fried chicken we sweated through at Prince's Hot Chicken Shack in Nashville was harder than we anticipated. We created a spicy exterior to the chicken by blooming the spices (cooking them in oil for a short period) to create a complex yet still lip-burning spicy flavor. We also added a healthy amount of hot sauce to our brine to inject into the chicken, making the flavor more than skin deep.

Why This Recipe Works Really good honey fried chicken is juicy and tender on the inside with a crispy, sticky, honey-flavored coating. To keep the meat moist, we brined the chicken first. For the coating, we dusted the chicken in cornstarch and dipped it in a thin cornstarch-and-water batter. The hardest part was glazing the fried chicken in honey without making the crust soggy. We found that the key was to double-fry the chicken: We partially fried the chicken, let it rest to allow moisture from the skin to evaporate, then fried it again for an incredibly crunchy crust that stayed crispy when dunked in a glaze of warm honey and hot sauce.

HONEY FRIED CHICKEN

SERVES 4

If using kosher chicken, do not brine. Use a Dutch oven that holds 6 quarts or more for this recipe.

Brine and Chicken
½ cup salt
½ cup sugar
3 pounds bone-in chicken pieces (breasts halved crosswise and leg quarters separated into drumsticks and thighs), trimmed

Batter
1½ cups cornstarch
¾ cup cold water
2 teaspoons pepper
1 teaspoon salt
3 quarts peanut or vegetable oil

Honey Glaze
¾ cup honey
2 tablespoons hot sauce

1. For the Brine and Chicken Dissolve salt and sugar in 2 quarts cold water in large container. Submerge chicken in brine, cover, and refrigerate for 30 minutes to 1 hour.

2. For the Batter While chicken is brining, whisk 1 cup cornstarch, water, pepper, and salt together in large bowl until smooth. Refrigerate batter.

3. Set wire rack inside rimmed baking sheet. Sift remaining ½ cup cornstarch into shallow bowl. Remove chicken from brine and dry thoroughly with paper towels. Working with 1 piece at a time, coat chicken thoroughly with cornstarch, shaking to remove excess; transfer to platter.

4. Add oil to large Dutch oven until it measures about 2 inches deep and heat over medium-high heat to 350 degrees. Whisk batter to recombine. Using tongs, transfer half of chicken to batter and turn to coat. Remove chicken from batter, 1 piece at a time, allowing excess to drip back into bowl, and transfer to hot oil. Fry chicken, stirring to prevent pieces from sticking together, until slightly golden and just beginning to crisp, 5 to 7 minutes. Adjust burner, if necessary, to maintain oil temperature between 325 and 350 degrees. (Chicken will not be cooked through at this point.) Transfer parcooked chicken to platter. Return oil to 350 degrees and repeat with remaining raw chicken and batter. Let each batch of chicken rest for 5 to 7 minutes.

5. Return oil to 350 degrees. Return first batch of chicken to oil and fry until breasts register 160 degrees and thighs/drumsticks register 175 degrees, 5 to 7 minutes. Transfer to prepared baking sheet. Return oil to 350 degrees and repeat with remaining chicken.

6. For the Honey Glaze Combine honey and hot sauce in large bowl and microwave until hot, about 1½ minutes. Add chicken pieces to honey mixture, one at a time, and turn to coat. Return to baking sheet, skin side up, to drain. Serve.

Why This Recipe Works For fried chicken loaded with garlic flavor, we started by tossing a mix of chicken pieces in a marinade chock-full of both fresh and granulated garlic. We further reinforced our key flavor by dipping the parts in beaten egg whites and dredging them in flour boosted with more granulated garlic. After frying the chicken in peanut oil, we created a potent garlic-parsley butter that took the chicken's flavor right over the top.

GARLIC FRIED CHICKEN

SERVES 4

Use a Dutch oven that holds 6 quarts or more for this recipe. Mince the garlic with a knife rather than with a garlic press.

Chicken

- 3 tablespoons extra-virgin olive oil
- 2 tablespoons granulated garlic
- 5 garlic cloves, minced
  Kosher salt and pepper
- 3 pounds bone-in chicken pieces (split breasts cut in half crosswise, drumsticks, thighs, and/or wings), trimmed
- 2 cups all-purpose flour
- 4 large egg whites
- 3 quarts peanut or vegetable oil

Garlic Butter

- 8 tablespoons unsalted butter, softened
- 2 tablespoons minced fresh parsley
- ¼ teaspoon kosher salt
- ¼ teaspoon pepper
- 8 garlic cloves, minced
- 1 tablespoon water

1. For the Chicken Combine olive oil, 1 tablespoon granulated garlic, minced garlic, 2 teaspoons salt, and 2 teaspoons pepper in large bowl. Add chicken and toss to thoroughly coat with garlic mixture. Cover with plastic wrap and refrigerate for at least 1 hour or up to 24 hours.

2. Set wire rack in rimmed baking sheet. Whisk flour, remaining 1 tablespoon granulated garlic, 2 teaspoons salt, and 2 teaspoons pepper together in separate bowl. Lightly beat egg whites together in shallow dish.

3. Remove chicken from marinade and brush away any solidified clumps of oil with paper towels. Working with 1 piece at a time, dip chicken into egg whites to thoroughly coat, letting excess drip back into dish; then dredge in flour mixture, pressing firmly to adhere. Transfer chicken to prepared wire rack and refrigerate, uncovered, for at least 30 minutes or up to 2 hours.

4. Set second wire rack in second rimmed baking sheet and line with triple layer of paper towels. Add peanut oil to large Dutch oven until it measures about 2 inches deep and heat over medium-high heat to 325 degrees. Add half of chicken to hot oil and fry until breasts register 160 degrees and drumsticks/thighs register 175 degrees, 13 to 16 minutes. Adjust burner, if necessary, to maintain oil temperature between 300 and 325 degrees. Transfer to paper towel–lined rack, return oil to 325 degrees, and repeat with remaining chicken.

5. For the Garlic Butter While chicken rests, combine 7 tablespoons butter, parsley, salt, and pepper in bowl; set aside. Melt remaining 1 tablespoon butter in 8-inch nonstick skillet over medium heat. Add garlic and water and cook, stirring frequently, until garlic is softened and fragrant, 1 to 2 minutes. Add hot garlic mixture to butter-parsley mixture and whisk until well combined.

6. Transfer chicken to platter and spoon garlic butter over top. Serve.

On the Road: Basque Cooking in California

Though it might seem out of place, Basque food is as comfortable in California as any other cuisine. Immigrants from the Basque lands—primarily the Pyrenees Mountains separating Spain and France—flooded California during the Gold Rush in the mid-19th century; when gold proved elusive, they turned to agriculture and shepherding in and around Bakersfield, California, which boasts one of the largest Basque populations in the United States.

During our visit to this region, we were struck by how the vibrant fare at the Pyrenees Cafe stands firmly against the city's ever-present heat. There we feasted on plates of garlic fried chicken, Basque-style green beans, cabbage and bean soup dotted with spicy salsa, thin slices of pickled veal tongue, and a few glasses of chilled house wine, before enjoying the customary Basque dessert: vanilla ice cream doused with red wine.

Why This Recipe Works For this unusual sauced, or "dipped," fried chicken, we started by brining chicken pieces to keep the meat moist and tender. We then coated the pieces in a seasoned flour mixture containing flour, cornstarch, and baking powder, and let them sit briefly in the refrigerator to ensure that the coating adhered. We based our sauce on Texas Pete Original Hot Sauce, a North Carolina specialty. After the chicken cooled for a few minutes to let the steam escape, we spooned the sauce over it, which was less messy than dipping. The coating absorbed the lip-tingling sauce and still retained crisp texture.

NORTH CAROLINA DIPPED FRIED CHICKEN

SERVES 4

Plan ahead: The chicken needs to brine for at least 1 hour before being coated in step 3. Do not brine the chicken longer than 4 hours or it will be too salty. Use a Dutch oven that holds 6 quarts or more. You'll need one 12-ounce bottle of Texas Pete Original Hot Sauce for this recipe.

Chicken
Salt and pepper
¼ cup sugar
3 pounds bone-in chicken pieces (split breasts cut in half, drumsticks, thighs, and/or wings), trimmed
1¼ cups all-purpose flour
¾ cup cornstarch
1 teaspoon granulated garlic
1 teaspoon baking powder
3 quarts peanut or vegetable oil

Sauce
1¼ cups Texas Pete Original Hot Sauce
5 tablespoons Worcestershire sauce
5 tablespoons peanut or vegetable oil
2 tablespoons molasses
1 tablespoon cider vinegar

1. For the Chicken Dissolve ½ cup salt and sugar in 2 quarts cold water in large container. Submerge chicken in brine, cover, and refrigerate for at least 1 hour or up to 4 hours.

2. Whisk flour, cornstarch, granulated garlic, baking powder, 2 teaspoons pepper, and 1 teaspoon salt together in large bowl. Add 2 tablespoons water to flour mixture; using your fingers, rub flour mixture and water together until water is evenly incorporated and shaggy pieces of dough form.

3. Set wire rack in rimmed baking sheet. Working with 1 piece at a time, remove chicken from brine, letting excess drip off; dredge chicken in flour mixture, pressing to adhere. Transfer to prepared rack. Refrigerate chicken, uncovered, for at least 30 minutes or up to 2 hours.

4. Set second wire rack in second rimmed baking sheet and line half of rack with triple layer of paper towels. Add oil to large Dutch oven until it measures 2 inches deep and heat over medium-high heat to 350 degrees. Add half of chicken to pot and fry until breasts register 160 degrees and drumsticks/thighs/wings register 175 degrees, 13 to 16 minutes. Adjust burner, if necessary, to maintain oil temperature between 325 and 350 degrees.

5. Transfer chicken to paper towel–lined side of prepared rack. Let chicken drain on each side for 30 seconds, then move to unlined side of rack. Return oil to 350 degrees and repeat with remaining chicken. Let chicken cool for 10 minutes.

6. For the Sauce Meanwhile, whisk all ingredients together in bowl. Microwave, covered, until hot, about 2 minutes, stirring halfway through microwaving.

7. Transfer chicken to shallow platter. Spoon sauce over chicken. Serve.

The American Table: The Rise of Texas Pete

Thad W. Garner's initial plan was to take the money he'd put aside for college and, rather than pursue his studies, buy and run a barbecue restaurant near his family's home in North Carolina. And he did just that. But it was 1929, and within months the Great Depression killed the business. Garner was left with nothing—nothing, that is, except a recipe for a bracing, peppery hot sauce his customers loved.

Determined, Garner spent the next decade selling the sauce door to door. He called it "Texas Pete" to capitalize on the country's Hollywood-driven nostalgia for cowboy movies; even in a troubled economy, enough households could afford it for Garner to eke out a living.

By the mid-1940s, the economy was booming again, and the newly incorporated T. W. Garner Food Company was booming, too, selling hot sauce, jams, jellies, and more. But Texas Pete was—and remains—its most popular product.

HAWAIIAN-STYLE FRIED CHICKEN

SERVES 4 TO 6

Use a Dutch oven that holds 6 quarts or more for this recipe. Plan ahead: The chicken marinates for at least an hour before breading. Pressing the chicken after dredging it in the starch ensures a more uniform coating.

Chicken

- 1 (3-ounce) piece ginger, unpeeled, cut into ½-inch pieces
- 4 garlic cloves, peeled
- 1 cup water
- ½ cup soy sauce
- 3 tablespoons packed light brown sugar
- 1 tablespoon toasted sesame oil
- 2 pounds boneless, skinless chicken thighs, trimmed and halved crosswise
- 2¼ cups potato starch
- 2 tablespoons sesame seeds
- 1½ teaspoons baking powder
  Salt and pepper
- 3 quarts peanut or vegetable oil

Dipping Sauce

- ½ cup seasoned rice vinegar
- ¼ cup soy sauce
- ¼ cup lemon juice (2 lemons)
  Pepper

1. For the Chicken Process ginger and garlic in food processor until finely chopped, about 15 seconds; transfer to large bowl. Add water, soy sauce, sugar, and sesame oil and whisk to combine. Add chicken and press to submerge. Cover bowl with plastic wrap and refrigerate for at least 1 hour or up to 3 hours.

2. For the Dipping Sauce Whisk vinegar, soy sauce, and lemon juice together in bowl. Season with pepper to taste.

3. Line rimmed baking sheet with parchment paper. Set wire rack in second rimmed baking sheet. Whisk potato starch, sesame seeds, baking powder, 1 teaspoon salt, and 1 teaspoon pepper together in large bowl.

4. Working with 1 piece of chicken at a time, remove from marinade, allowing excess to drip back into bowl. Dredge chicken in potato starch mixture, pressing to adhere. Gently shake off excess and transfer chicken to parchment-lined sheet. Coating will look mottled; using your hand, press on chicken to smooth out coating. Cover sheet tightly with plastic wrap and refrigerate for at least 30 minutes or up to 1 hour.

5. Add peanut oil to large Dutch oven until it measures about 2 inches deep; heat oil over medium-high heat to 375 degrees. Carefully add one-third of chicken to pot and fry until deep golden brown and cooked through, about 5 minutes, stirring gently as needed to prevent pieces from sticking together. Adjust burner, if necessary, to maintain oil temperature between 350 and 375 degrees.

6. Transfer chicken to prepared rack. Return oil to 375 degrees and repeat in 2 more batches with remaining chicken. Serve chicken with sauce.

Ingredient Spotlight: Potato Starch

Potato starch is made by peeling potatoes, drying them, grinding them, and then putting them through a wash to remove the starch, which is then dried. We call for potato starch to coat our Hawaiian-Style Fried Chicken because it produced the crunchiest results, besting cornstarch, flour, and a combination of the two in side-by-side tests.

That's because potato starch fries up into a crispy, porous coating faster than either cornstarch or wheat starch (flour). This means potato starch can develop into a crunchy coating in the time required to fry the chicken, whereas a cornstarch or flour coating would need to fry longer, resulting in overcooked chicken.

Why This Recipe Works In Hawaii, fried chicken comes in many varieties. Our favorite is karaage, which is marinated in soy sauce, brown sugar, sake, ginger, and garlic, before being coated in potato flour, fried until shatteringly crisp, and then served with a tangy dipping sauce. Potato flour offered maximum crunch, but we couldn't get it to stick on its own, so we added baking powder and sesame seeds, firmly pressed the coating into the marinated chicken thighs, and then refrigerated them until the coating became fully saturated with the marinade. Rice vinegar, soy sauce, and lemon juice made a sweet and sour sauce that was ripe for dunking.

Why This Recipe Works Hot oil is the key to crunchy fried chicken, but it can be deadly to fresh herbs. To get the flavors to last throughout the frying process, the key was to fry for as little time as possible. Thin boneless chicken thighs took half as long to fry as bone-in chicken parts, which allowed the fresh herb flavors to flourish. Also, thighs are less expensive. After a few tests, we settled on a three-part technique for the chives, dill, and cilantro; we added them to the tangy buttermilk dip, the flour coating, and the dipping sauce. This triple punch provided the classic aroma and flavor we know and love as "ranch."

RANCH FRIED CHICKEN

SERVES 4 TO 6

Use a Dutch oven that holds 6 quarts or more for this recipe.

Chicken
8 (5- to 7-ounce) boneless, skinless chicken thighs, trimmed
   Salt and pepper
2 quarts peanut or vegetable oil

Buttermilk Mixture
1 cup buttermilk
2 tablespoons minced fresh chives
2 tablespoons minced fresh cilantro
2 teaspoons minced fresh dill
2 teaspoons distilled white vinegar
1 garlic clove, minced
½ teaspoon salt
   Pinch cayenne pepper

Coating
1¼ cups all-purpose flour
½ cup cornstarch
3 tablespoons minced fresh chives
3 tablespoons minced fresh cilantro
1 tablespoon minced fresh dill
1½ teaspoons garlic powder
1½ teaspoons salt
¾ teaspoon pepper

Ranch Sauce
½ cup mayonnaise
   Salt and pepper

1. For the Chicken Pat chicken dry with paper towels and season with salt and pepper.

2. For the Buttermilk Mixture Whisk all ingredients together in bowl. Set aside ¼ cup buttermilk mixture for ranch sauce.

3. For the Coating Whisk all ingredients together in large bowl.

4. Set wire rack in rimmed baking sheet. Set second wire rack in second rimmed baking sheet and line half of rack with triple layer of paper towels.

5. Working with 1 piece at a time, dip chicken in remaining buttermilk mixture to coat, letting excess drip back into bowl; then dredge in coating, pressing to adhere. Transfer chicken to first wire rack (without paper towels). (At this point, coated chicken may be refrigerated, uncovered, for up to 2 hours.)

6. Heat oil in large Dutch oven over medium-high heat until it reaches 350 degrees. Add half of chicken to hot oil and fry until golden brown and registers 175 degrees, 7 to 9 minutes. Adjust burner, if necessary, to maintain oil temperature between 325 and 350 degrees.

7. Transfer chicken to paper towel–lined side of second wire rack to drain on each side for 30 seconds, then move to unlined side of rack. Return oil to 350 degrees and repeat with remaining chicken.

8. For the Ranch Sauce Whisk mayonnaise into reserved buttermilk mixture. Season with salt and pepper to taste.

9. Transfer chicken to platter and serve with ranch sauce.

Key Ingredients: Three Herbs, Three Ways

We use the defining herbs of ranch flavor—dill, chives, and cilantro—in three ways for this chicken: in the buttermilk dip, in the flour coating, and in the dipping sauce.

Why This Recipe Works Some chicken nugget recipes take the least desirable parts of the chicken and put them through a grinder. We opted for boneless, skinless chicken breasts. Brining the chicken prevented it from drying out, and seasoning the breast meat combated its inherently bland flavor. Ground-up panko (Japanese-style bread crumbs) combined with flour and a pinch of baking soda provided a crispy brown exterior for our nuggets. Using whole eggs to adhere the coating made the nuggets too eggy. Egg whites alone didn't have enough binding power, but we found that resting the nuggets before frying solved the problem.

CHICKEN NUGGETS

SERVES 4 TO 6

Do not brine the chicken longer than 30 minutes or it will be too salty. To crush the bread crumbs, place them inside a zipper-lock bag and lightly beat it with a rolling pin. Use a Dutch oven that holds 6 quarts or more for this recipe. This recipe doubles easily and freezes well.

- 4 (6-ounce) boneless, skinless chicken breasts, trimmed
- 2 cups water
- 2 tablespoons Worcestershire sauce
  Salt and pepper
- 1 cup all-purpose flour
- 1 cup panko bread crumbs, crushed
- 2 teaspoons onion powder
- ½ teaspoon garlic powder
- ½ teaspoon baking soda
- 3 large egg whites
- 1 quart peanut or vegetable oil
- 1 recipe dipping sauce (recipes follow)

1. Cut each chicken breast diagonally into thirds, then cut each third diagonally into ½-inch-thick pieces. Whisk water, Worcestershire, and 1 tablespoon salt in large bowl until salt dissolves. Add chicken pieces, cover, and refrigerate for 30 minutes.

2. Remove chicken from brine and pat dry with paper towels. Combine flour, panko, onion powder, 1 teaspoon salt, ¾ teaspoon pepper, garlic powder, and baking soda in shallow dish. Whisk egg whites in second shallow dish until foamy. Coat half of chicken with egg whites and dredge in flour mixture, pressing gently to adhere. Transfer to plate and repeat with remaining chicken (don't discard flour mixture). Let sit for 10 minutes.

3. Adjust oven rack to middle position and heat oven to 200 degrees. Set wire rack in rimmed baking sheet. Add oil to large Dutch oven until it measures about ¾ inch deep and heat over medium-high heat to 350 degrees. Return chicken pieces to flour mixture and turn to coat, pressing flour mixture gently to adhere. Fry half of chicken until deep golden brown, about 3 minutes, turning halfway through cooking. Transfer chicken to prepared baking sheet and place in oven. Return oil to 350 degrees and repeat with remaining chicken. Serve with dipping sauce.

To Make Ahead Let fried nuggets cool, transfer to zipper-lock bag, and freeze for up to 1 month. To serve, adjust oven rack to middle position and heat oven to 350 degrees. Place nuggets on rimmed baking sheet and bake, flipping once, until heated through, about 15 minutes.

HONEY-MUSTARD SAUCE
MAKES ¾ CUP

- ½ cup yellow mustard
- ⅓ cup honey
  Salt and pepper

Whisk mustard and honey in medium bowl until smooth. Season with salt and pepper to taste.

SWEET AND SOUR SAUCE
MAKES ¾ CUP

- ¾ cup apple, apricot, or hot pepper jelly
- 1 tablespoon white vinegar
- ½ teaspoon soy sauce
- ⅛ teaspoon garlic powder
  Pinch ground ginger
  Pinch cayenne pepper
  Salt and pepper

Whisk jelly, vinegar, soy sauce, garlic powder, ginger, and cayenne in medium bowl until smooth. Season with salt and pepper to taste.

POPCORN CHICKEN

SERVES 6 TO 8

Use a Dutch oven that holds 6 quarts or more. We prefer Frank's RedHot Original Cayenne Pepper Sauce here, but you can substitute your favorite hot sauce, if desired. Freezing the chicken breasts makes them easier to cut.

1½ pounds boneless, skinless chicken breasts, trimmed
2¾ cups all-purpose flour
½ cup cornstarch
1½ tablespoons granulated garlic
1½ tablespoons sugar
1 tablespoon baking powder
Kosher salt and pepper
2 teaspoons onion powder
1 teaspoon cayenne pepper
½ cup water
2 large eggs, lightly beaten
1½ quarts peanut or vegetable oil
6 tablespoons honey
2 tablespoons Frank's RedHot Original Cayenne Pepper Sauce

1. Place chicken on large plate and freeze until firm but still malleable, about 40 minutes.

2. Whisk 2½ cups flour, cornstarch, granulated garlic, sugar, baking powder, 1 tablespoon salt, onion powder, cayenne, and 1 teaspoon pepper together in large bowl. Add water and rub flour mixture between your hands until tiny craggy bits form throughout and mixture holds together like damp sand when squeezed.

3. Cut chicken into ½-inch pieces. Toss chicken, eggs, and 2 teaspoons salt together in second bowl. Transfer half of chicken to flour mixture and toss with your hands, pressing on coating to adhere and breaking up clumps, until chicken is coated on all sides. Pick chicken out of flour mixture and spread in even layer on rimmed baking sheet. Whisk remaining ¼ cup flour into flour mixture until combined, then repeat coating process with remaining chicken.

4. Line second rimmed baking sheet with triple layer of paper towels. Add oil to large Dutch oven until it measures about 1 inch deep and heat over medium-high heat to 400 degrees.

5. Using spider skimmer or slotted spoon, carefully add half of chicken to hot oil in several spoonfuls. Immediately stir to break up clumps. Fry until chicken is evenly golden brown and cooked through, 2 to 3 minutes, stirring occasionally. Using clean spider skimmer or slotted spoon, transfer chicken to paper towel–lined sheet. Return oil to 400 degrees and repeat with remaining chicken. Let cool for 5 minutes.

6. Whisk honey, hot sauce, and pinch salt together in small bowl. Serve chicken with honey sauce.

The Slice Is Right

1. Slice the chilled breasts lengthwise into ½-inch-wide strips.

2. Turn the strips on their sides and cut them into ½-inch pieces.

The American Table: Patent the Process?

When Eugene Gagliardi Jr.'s family business that sold meat to restaurant chains in the Philadelphia area found its sales declining in the 1960s, he got creative. First came his most famous patent: Steak-Umms. He pressed unused meat scraps into a loaf before freezing, slicing, and packaging it. The beef slices took only 30 seconds to cook on both sides and flew off grocery store shelves. He sold the product to the Heinz Corporation for $20 million. He also patented other methods of meat preparation—including popcorn chicken, which he sold to Kentucky Fried Chicken for $33 million in 1992. KFC sold 15 million pounds of popcorn chicken in the first five weeks. Holding these patents secured Gagliardi's reputation as an inventor and gave him leverage when selling or licensing his ideas to big food companies.

Why This Recipe Works Popcorn chicken can require a lot of work for all those little pieces. Some versions are easier to make but have just a thin layer of fried flour that flakes off. Tossing our chicken pieces in beaten egg helped the dredge stick, and working water into a mixture of flour and cornstarch created craggy bits that fried up extra-crunchy. A small amount of sugar added to the dredge helped it brown more quickly while imparting a faint, pleasing sweetness. We brought the frying oil to a higher temperature so that the chicken could brown and cook through quickly without drying out. A simple honey–hot sauce dip completed this fun snack.

GREEK CHICKEN

SERVES 4

Use a vegetable peeler to remove six strips of zest from the lemon. If you have a rasp-style grater and prefer to use it to zest the lemon, you will need about 1 tablespoon of zest. Make sure to use kosher salt here; we developed this recipe using Diamond Crystal Kosher Salt.

¼ cup extra-virgin olive oil
2 tablespoons chopped fresh rosemary
2 tablespoons chopped fresh thyme
5 garlic cloves, chopped
6 (3-inch) strips lemon zest, chopped, plus 1 tablespoon juice
1 tablespoon kosher salt
1½ teaspoons dried oregano
1 teaspoon ground coriander
½ teaspoon red pepper flakes
½ teaspoon pepper
3 pounds bone-in chicken pieces (2 split breasts, 2 drumsticks, 2 thighs, and 2 wings, wingtips discarded)

1. Combine oil, rosemary, thyme, garlic, lemon zest, salt, oregano, coriander, pepper flakes, and pepper in large bowl. Cut three ½-inch-deep slits in skin side of each chicken breast, two ½-inch-deep slits in skin side of each thigh, and two ½-inch-deep slits in each drumstick; leave wings whole. Transfer chicken to bowl with marinade and turn to thoroughly coat, making sure marinade gets into slits. Cover and refrigerate for at least 30 minutes or up to 2 hours.

2. Adjust oven rack 6 inches from broiler element and heat oven to 425 degrees. Place chicken, skin side up, in 12-inch ovensafe skillet. Using rubber spatula, scrape any remaining marinade from bowl over chicken. Roast until breasts register 160 degrees and drumsticks/thighs register 175 degrees, 30 to 35 minutes.

3. Remove skillet from oven and spoon pan juices over top of chicken to wet skin. Heat broiler. Broil chicken until skin is lightly browned, about 3 minutes, rotating skillet as necessary for even browning. Let chicken rest in skillet for 10 minutes. Transfer chicken to shallow platter. Stir lemon juice into pan juices, then spoon over chicken. Serve.

Herbs and Slashing

In addition to lemon zest, we flavor this dish with a mix of herbs to create an incredibly aromatic Greek-inspired flavor profile. We use two fragrant fresh herbs—rosemary and thyme—plus potent dried oregano and ground coriander. To make sure those flavors find their way into the chicken, we slash the raw pieces (above) before combining them with the marinade.

Why This Recipe Works We found inspiration for this tasty Greek baked chicken at Johnny's Restaurant in Homewood, Alabama. Their chicken is juicy, marinated and roasted to perfection, and flavored with tons of herbs and lemon. To be sure the marinade penetrated the chicken, we cut ½-inch-deep slashes in each piece and tossed the chicken with the herb mixture. For cooking, a 12-inch skillet kept the pieces relatively tightly packed to minimize evaporation of the marinade and the chicken juices, transforming that liquid into a deeply flavorful pan sauce. In order to achieve a lovely brown color, we finished the chicken with a blast under the broiler.

CHICKEN SAUCE PIQUANT

SERVES 6 TO 8

Louisiana seasoning is typically a mix of paprika, garlic powder, thyme, cayenne, celery salt, oregano, salt, and black pepper. If you don't want to make your own, the test kitchen's taste test winner is Tony Chachere's Original Creole Seasoning.

- ½ cup all-purpose flour
- 2 pounds boneless, skinless chicken thighs, trimmed and quartered
- 3½ teaspoons Louisiana seasoning
- 5 tablespoons vegetable oil
- 1 onion, chopped
- 1 green bell pepper, stemmed, seeded, and chopped
- 1 celery rib, chopped
- 2 garlic cloves, minced
- 1 (28-ounce) can crushed tomatoes
- 3 cups chicken broth
- 2 slices bacon
- 2 tablespoons Worcestershire sauce
- 1 bay leaf
- 1 teaspoon Tabasco sauce, plus extra for serving
  Salt and pepper
- 4 cups cooked rice
- 4 scallions, sliced thin

1. Adjust oven rack to lower-middle position and heat oven to 350 degrees. Place flour in large bowl. Season chicken with 1 tablespoon Louisiana seasoning. Transfer chicken to bowl with flour and toss to coat.

2. Heat ¼ cup oil in Dutch oven over medium-high heat until shimmering. Shaking off excess flour, add half of chicken to pot and cook until golden brown, 3 to 5 minutes per side; transfer to plate. Repeat with remaining chicken. Reserve remaining flour.

3. Add onion, bell pepper, celery, garlic, remaining ½ teaspoon Louisiana seasoning, remaining 1 tablespoon oil, and reserved flour to now-empty pot. Cook, stirring often, until vegetables are just softened, about 5 minutes.

4. Stir in tomatoes, broth, bacon, Worcestershire, and bay leaf, scraping up any browned bits. Nestle chicken into pot and add any accumulated juices. Bring to simmer, cover, and transfer to oven. Cook until chicken is tender, about 45 minutes.

5. Remove pot from oven. Discard bacon and bay leaf, stir in Tabasco, and season with salt and pepper to taste. Serve over rice, sprinkled with scallions, passing extra Tabasco separately.

LOUISIANA SEASONING
MAKES ABOUT ¾ CUP

- 5 tablespoons paprika
- 2 tablespoons garlic powder
- 1 tablespoon dried thyme
- 1 tablespoon cayenne pepper
- 1 tablespoon celery salt
- 1 tablespoon salt
- 1 tablespoon pepper

Combine all ingredients in a bowl.

Why This Recipe Works A lively mix of Creole and Cajun flavors, spicy Sauce Piquant features chicken (though locals sometimes use wild game or alligator tail) braised in a cayenne-spiked, roux-thickened tomato sauce. We found we could skip the roux and mimic its consistency and flavor by dredging boneless chicken thighs in flour and shallow-frying them, and then cooking vegetables with the leftover flour before adding crushed tomatoes and chicken broth. We stirred in a few glugs of Worcestershire and Tabasco for salty depth and peppery heat, and some bacon for a meaty, smoky edge and popped it into the oven to thicken and finish cooking.

FISH AND CHIPS

SERVES 4

Try to find large Yukon Gold potatoes, 10 to 12 ounces each, that are similar in size. We prefer peanut or vegetable oil for frying and do not recommend using canola oil since it can impart off-flavors. Use a Dutch oven that holds 6 quarts or more. A light-bodied American lager, such as Budweiser, works best here. If you prefer to cook without alcohol, substitute seltzer for the beer. We prefer to use cod for this recipe, but haddock and halibut will also work well. Serve with Tartar Sauce (recipe follows), if desired.

- 1 cup (5 ounces) all-purpose flour
- 1 cup (4 ounces) cornstarch
  Salt and pepper
- 1 teaspoon baking powder
- 1½ cups beer
- 1 (2-pound) skinless cod fillet, about 1 inch thick
- 2½ pounds large Yukon Gold potatoes, unpeeled
- 8 cups peanut or vegetable oil
  Lemon wedges

1. Whisk flour, cornstarch, 1½ teaspoons salt, and baking powder together in large bowl. Add beer and whisk until smooth. Cover with plastic wrap and refrigerate for at least 20 minutes.

2. Cut cod crosswise into 8 equal fillets (about 4 ounces each). Pat cod dry with paper towels and season with salt and pepper; refrigerate until ready to use.

3. Square off each potato by cutting ¼-inch-thick slice from each of its 4 long sides. Cut potatoes lengthwise into ¼-inch-thick planks. Stack 3 to 4 planks and cut into ¼-inch fries. Repeat with remaining planks. (Do not place potatoes in water.)

4. Line rimmed baking sheet with triple layer of paper towels. Combine potatoes and oil in large Dutch oven. Cook over high heat until oil has reached rolling boil, about 7 minutes. Continue to cook, without stirring, until potatoes are limp but exteriors are beginning to firm, about 15 minutes longer. Using tongs, stir potatoes, gently scraping up any that stick, and continue to cook, stirring occasionally, until just lightly golden brown, about 4 minutes longer (fries will not be fully cooked

at this point). Using spider skimmer or slotted spoon, transfer fries to prepared sheet. Skim off any browned bits left in pot.

5. Set wire rack in second rimmed baking sheet. Transfer fish to batter and toss to evenly coat. Heat oil over medium-high heat to 375 degrees. Using fork, remove 4 pieces of fish from batter, allowing excess batter to drip back into bowl, and add to hot oil, briefly dragging fish along surface of oil to prevent sticking. Adjust burner, if necessary, to maintain oil temperature between 350 and 375 degrees.

6. Cook fish, stirring gently to prevent pieces from sticking together, until deep golden brown and crispy, about 4 minutes per side. Using spider skimmer or slotted spoon, transfer fish to prepared rack and skim off any browned bits left in pot. Return oil to 375 degrees and repeat with remaining 4 pieces of fish.

7. Return oil to 375 degrees. Add fries to oil and cook until deep golden brown and crispy, about 1 minute. Using spider skimmer or slotted spoon, transfer fries back to prepared sheet and season with salt. Transfer fish and chips to platter. Serve with lemon wedges.

TARTAR SAUCE
MAKES ABOUT 1 CUP
The test kitchen's favorite mayo is Blue Plate Real Mayonnaise, which is not available in all areas of the United States. Hellmann's Real Mayonnaise, which is available nationwide, was a close second and is a great option.

- ¾ cup mayonnaise
- ¼ cup dill pickle relish
- 1½ teaspoons distilled white vinegar
- ½ teaspoon Worcestershire sauce
- ½ teaspoon pepper
- ⅛ teaspoon salt

Combine all ingredients in small bowl. Cover with plastic wrap and refrigerate until flavors meld, about 15 minutes.

Why This Recipe Works The best fish and chips are usually found at a proper English pub, but we wanted to create a worthy version at home. To make the crispiest coating, we needed just four ingredients: beer, flour, cornstarch, and baking powder. The beer helped to create a coating that stuck well to the tender pieces of cod and also added a malty sweetness to each bite. For the chips, we fry the potatoes first, then the fish, then quickly finish the fries until deep golden brown. Yukon Gold potatoes worked best; they were less starchy and more crisp once fried than other potato varieties.

EASTERN NORTH CAROLINA FISH STEW

SERVES 8

Any mild, firm-fleshed whitefish, such as bass, rockfish, cod, hake, haddock, or halibut, will work well in this stew. Our favorite supermarket bacon is Oscar Mayer Naturally Hardwood Smoked Bacon. Serve this rustic stew with soft white sandwich bread or saltines.

6 slices thick-cut bacon, cut into ½-inch-wide strips
2 onions, halved and sliced thin
   Salt
½ teaspoon red pepper flakes
6 cups water
1 (6-ounce) can tomato paste
1 pound red potatoes, unpeeled, sliced ¼ inch thick
1 bay leaf
1 teaspoon Tabasco sauce, plus extra for serving
2 pounds skinless whitefish fillets, 1 to 1½ inches thick, cut into 2-inch chunks
8 large eggs

1. Cook bacon in Dutch oven over medium heat until crispy, 9 to 11 minutes, stirring occasionally. Add onions, 1½ teaspoons salt, and pepper flakes and cook until onions begin to soften, about 5 minutes.

2. Stir in water and tomato paste, scraping up any browned bits. Add potatoes and bay leaf. Increase heat to medium-high and bring to boil. Reduce heat to medium and cook at vigorous simmer for 10 minutes.

3. Reduce heat to medium-low and stir in Tabasco. Nestle fish into stew but do not stir. Crack eggs into stew, spacing them evenly. Cover and cook until eggs are just set, 17 to 22 minutes. Season with salt to taste. Serve, passing extra Tabasco separately.

Fishing for Stew in Deep Run

"Throwing a fish stew" is what they say in Deep Run, North Carolina, and it's as good an excuse as any for a low-key gathering. They usually happen in the fall, during vest season.

Walking behind the main house, Greg Smith and his father, Emmett, are gathering supplies outside their party shack (formerly a tobacco packhouse). To one side sits a large, black iron kettle. Emmett found this cauldron years ago in a "manure field," as he describes it, and this gets a rise out of the guests, all longtime friends who grew up together in the small town. He clarifies: It was technically a cow pasture, but you can see the connection. The pot was nearly completely buried when he unearthed it, but with determination, he scrubbed it back to life. Emmett estimates that his pot has held more than 500 stews.

Emmett and Greg fire up the propane burner under the pot and then drop in a pound and a half of chopped bacon to cook until its fat has rendered. Guests emerge from the kitchen in a procession, each bearing an offering for the stew: 10 pounds of sliced potatoes, 5 pounds of sliced onions, and 7 pounds of local rockfish. Emmett layers it all into the pot. One guest spoons in a couple of cans of tomato paste—his only job, but he performs it with authority.

Emmett throws in a heavy handful of red pepper flakes and stands guard as the stew simmers away. He eventually adds the final, and most surprising, ingredient: four dozen eggs, cracked and dropped one by one into the stew—just enough for 20 people.

Why This Recipe Works Locals in the Tar Heel State have loved this hearty tomatoey, bacon-infused Sunday stew for decades. After crisping bacon, we cooked onion and red pepper flakes in the rendered fat before adding a whole can of tomato paste for intense tomato flavor. With the spicy broth in place, we turned to the rest of the stew. We gave potato slices a head start before nestling chunks of whitefish into the pot. A surprising addition to this dish is poached eggs, which we layered atop the stew and cooked gently in the covered pot until just set.

Why This Recipe Works To create a home recipe inspired by the richer and more complex cioppino served at Phil's Fish Market & Eatery in Moss Landing, California, we simply added pesto's key ingredients (olive oil, basil, and garlic) to the mix, instead of making a traditional basil pesto to flavor the stew like Phil does. Phil's version includes a wide range of seafood, but we wanted to tighten the roster for our version, so we bypassed clams and calamari, opting instead for easy-to-find shrimp, scallops, sea bass, and mussels. Adding our seafood to the pot in stages and finishing the cooking off the heat ensured that each item was perfectly cooked.

MONTEREY BAY CIOPPINO

SERVES 6 TO 8

We recommend buying "dry" scallops, which don't have chemical additives and taste better than "wet" scallops. Dry scallops will look ivory or pinkish; wet scallops are bright white. If you can't find fresh dry scallops, you can substitute thawed frozen scallops. If you can't find sea bass, you can substitute cod, haddock, or halibut fillets.

Marinara

- 3 tablespoons extra-virgin olive oil
- 1 large onion, halved and sliced thin
- 3 garlic cloves, sliced thin
- ¾ teaspoon salt
- 1 (15-ounce) can tomato sauce
- 1 cup canned tomato puree
- ½ cup chopped fresh basil
- 1 tablespoon packed light brown sugar
- 1½ teaspoons Worcestershire sauce
- ¼ teaspoon ground cinnamon

Cioppino

- 1½ pounds skinless sea bass fillets, 1 to 1½ inches thick, cut into 1½-inch pieces
- 12 ounces extra-large shrimp (21 to 25 per pound), peeled, deveined, and tails removed
- 12 ounces large scallops, tendons removed, cut in half horizontally
  Salt and pepper
- 3 tablespoons extra-virgin olive oil
- 1 pound mussels, scrubbed and debearded
- ½ cup chopped fresh basil
- ¼ cup dry sherry
- 3 garlic cloves, minced
- 1 teaspoon Worcestershire sauce
- ½ teaspoon saffron threads, crumbled
- 2 (8-ounce) bottles clam juice
- 1 (12-inch) baguette, sliced and toasted
  Lemon wedges

1. For the Marinara Heat oil in large saucepan over medium heat until shimmering. Add onion, garlic, and salt and cook until onion is softened and just

beginning to brown, about 8 minutes. Add tomato sauce, tomato puree, basil, sugar, Worcestershire, and cinnamon and bring to boil. Reduce heat to medium-low and simmer until marinara is slightly thickened, 10 to 12 minutes. Remove from heat, cover, and set aside.

2. For the Cioppino Season sea bass, shrimp, and scallops with salt and pepper; set aside. Heat oil in Dutch oven over medium-high heat until shimmering. Add mussels, basil, sherry, garlic, Worcestershire, saffron, and ½ teaspoon salt. Cover and cook until mussels start to open, about 2 minutes.

3. Stir in clam juice and marinara until combined. Nestle sea bass and scallops into pot and bring to boil. Reduce heat to medium, cover, and simmer until seafood is just turning opaque, about 2 minutes. Nestle shrimp into pot and return to simmer. Cover and cook until all seafood is opaque, about 3 minutes. Remove from heat and let sit, covered, for 5 minutes. Serve with baguette slices and lemon wedges.

Seafood Substitutions

Our version of Phil's cioppino uses a carefully considered collection of seafood, but that doesn't mean you can't make it if you can't find everything on the ingredient list. For instance, sea bass is our first choice, but you can also use cod, haddock, or halibut fillets of a similar size. Here are a few more options:

- Double the amount of shrimp or scallops if you can't find one or the other.

- Use small clams in place of the mussels, or use half clams and half mussels.

- Garnish the stew with cooked crabmeat—or, for the full Phil's effect, cooked crab legs—before serving.

Why This Recipe Works This hearty Louisiana specialty combines culinary traditions from many different cultures (gombo means okra in many parts of West Africa). Our challenge was to find an easier way to prepare the dark-brown roux, the fat and flour paste that thickens the stew and adds flavor. We created a relatively hands-off roux by toasting the flour on the stovetop, adding the oil, and finishing the roux in the oven. For the soup base, instead of making our own shrimp stock, we switched to store-bought chicken broth fortified with fish sauce. Tasters preferred meaty chicken thighs to breasts because they had a lot more flavor.

GUMBO

SERVES 6 TO 8

A heavy cast-iron Dutch oven yields the fastest oven roux. If a lightweight pot is all you've got, increase the oven time by 10 minutes. The chicken broth must be at room temperature to prevent lumps from forming. Fish sauce lends an essential savory quality. Since the salt content of fish sauce varies among brands, taste the finished gumbo before seasoning with salt.

¾ cup plus 1 tablespoon all-purpose flour
½ cup vegetable oil
1 onion, chopped fine
1 green bell pepper, stemmed, seeded, and chopped
1 celery rib, chopped fine
5 garlic cloves, minced
1 teaspoon minced fresh thyme
¼ teaspoon cayenne pepper
1 (14.5-ounce) can diced tomatoes, drained
3¾ cups chicken broth, room temperature
¼ cup fish sauce
2 pounds bone-in chicken thighs, skin removed, trimmed
  Salt and pepper
8 ounces andouille sausage, halved lengthwise and sliced thin
2 cups frozen okra, thawed (optional)
2 pounds extra-large shrimp (21 to 25 per pound), peeled and deveined

1. Adjust oven rack to lowest position and heat oven to 350 degrees. Toast ¾ cup flour in Dutch oven over medium heat, stirring constantly, until just beginning to brown, about 5 minutes. Off heat, whisk in oil until smooth. Cover, transfer pot to oven, and cook until mixture is deep brown and fragrant, about 45 minutes. (Roux can be refrigerated for 1 week. To use, heat in Dutch oven over medium-high heat, whisking constantly, until just smoking, and continue with step 2.)

2. Transfer Dutch oven to stovetop and whisk cooked roux to combine. Add onion, bell pepper, and celery and cook over medium heat, stirring frequently, until vegetables are softened, about 10 minutes. Stir in remaining 1 tablespoon flour, garlic, thyme, and cayenne and cook until fragrant, about 1 minute. Add tomatoes and cook until dry, about 1 minute. Slowly whisk in broth and fish sauce until smooth. Season chicken with pepper. Add chicken to vegetable mixture and bring to boil.

3. Reduce heat to medium-low and simmer, covered, until chicken is tender, about 30 minutes. Skim fat and transfer chicken to plate. When chicken is cool enough to handle, cut into bite-size pieces and return to pot; discard bones.

4. Stir in sausage and okra, if using, and simmer until heated through, about 5 minutes. Add shrimp and simmer until cooked through, about 5 minutes. Season with salt and pepper to taste. Serve. (Gumbo can be refrigerated for 1 day.)

To Make Ahead Gumbo can be made through step 3 and refrigerated for 3 days. To serve, bring gumbo to simmer, covered, in Dutch oven. Remove lid and proceed with recipe as directed.

Newcomer to the Bayou

Asian fish sauce in a gumbo recipe? Admittedly, it's an unconventional idea. And here's the cool part: New Orleans has a well-established Vietnamese community that began after the Vietnam War. As far as we know, we're the first to put fish sauce in gumbo, but there's no question that these immigrants to New Orleans are having an impact on the city's storied food traditions: They've tossed lemongrass into crawfish boils, organized a farmers' market with such items as ngo gai (an herb), banana buds, and longan fruit, and put banh mi on the city's must-eat food list, right there next to the city's signature po' boys.

SHRIMP MOZAMBIQUE

SERVES 4

We prefer untreated shrimp—those without added sodium or preservatives such as sodium tripolyphosphate. Most frozen E-Z peel shrimp have been treated (the ingredient list should tell you). If you're using treated shrimp, do not sprinkle the shrimp with salt in step 2. We developed this recipe with Frank's RedHot Original Cayenne Pepper Sauce, which is similar to the piri-piri sauce called for in the traditional recipe. Serve with crusty bread or over white rice.

Sauce

- 2 tablespoons Frank's RedHot Original Cayenne Pepper Sauce
- 2 tablespoons extra-virgin olive oil
- 2 tablespoons water
- ¼ slice hearty white sandwich bread, torn into small pieces
- 1 tablespoon chopped fresh parsley
- 2 garlic cloves, chopped
- 2 teaspoons paprika
- ½ teaspoon pepper

Shrimp

- 2 pounds extra-large shrimp (21 to 25 per pound), peeled, deveined, and tails removed
  Salt and pepper
- 1 tablespoon extra-virgin olive oil
- ½ cup finely chopped onion
- 3 garlic cloves, sliced thin
- 1 cup dry white wine
- 2 tablespoons unsalted butter, cut into 2 pieces
- 2 tablespoons chopped fresh parsley

1. For the Sauce Process all ingredients in blender until smooth, about 2 minutes, scraping down sides of blender jar as needed.

2. For the Shrimp Sprinkle shrimp with ½ teaspoon salt and ¼ teaspoon pepper; set aside. Heat oil in 12-inch nonstick skillet over medium heat until shimmering. Add onion and ½ teaspoon salt and cook until softened, about 5 minutes. Add garlic and cook until fragrant, about 1 minute. Add wine and bring to boil. Cook until reduced by half, about 4 minutes.

3. Add shrimp and cook, stirring occasionally, until opaque and just cooked through, about 4 minutes. Stir in butter and sauce and cook until butter is melted and sauce is heated through, about 1 minute. Season with salt and pepper to taste. Sprinkle with parsley and serve.

Frank's RedHot

Traditional recipes for shrimp Mozambique call for using a spicy piri-piri sauce as a base. Since piri-piri sauce is unavailable in some parts of the United States, we searched far and wide for an alternative. The solution: our winning all-purpose hot sauce, **Frank's RedHot Original Cayenne Pepper Sauce.** Frank's is made with cayenne peppers, which have a similar kick to piri-piris; furthermore, the vinegar, salt, and oil in Frank's are common ingredients in piri-piri sauce. This supermarket staple was a perfect fit for our lively Shrimp Mozambique.

Why This Recipe Works This buttery, garlicky, peppery shrimp dish has roots in southeast Africa, where Portuguese colonists cultivated the piri-piri pepper that traditionally gives this dish its heat. While looking for a stand-in for the piri-piri pepper, we realized Frank's RedHot Original Cayenne Pepper Sauce was, like many piri-piri sauces, a puree of peppers, vinegar, and oil. To give it body and balance, we blended Frank's with olive oil, garlic, parsley, paprika, and torn bread. Cooking the shrimp until just opaque in the sauce with a splash of white wine and finishing it off with butter brought together this spicy and velvety seafood dish.

Why This Recipe Works Perloo (pronounced "PUHR-low"), a staple in South Carolina's Low Country, is a tomatoey rice dish simmered in broth. To start, we went the classic route and used reserved shrimp shells to create and flavor shrimp stock, which is surprisingly easy and practical to make from scratch. For the rice, we stuck to the traditional flavor base of onions, celery, and bell pepper. Sautéing the rice with the vegetables firmed up the grains' exterior and prevented mushiness. Just before removing the rice from the heat, we folded in the shrimp and let them rest, covered, for perfectly cooked shrimp and tender rice in a delicious one-pot meal.

CHARLESTON SHRIMP PERLOO

SERVES 4 TO 6

After adding the shrimp to the pot, fold it in gently; stirring the rice too vigorously will make it mushy. Any extra stock can be refrigerated for 3 days or frozen for up to 1 month. Serve with hot sauce.

5 tablespoons unsalted butter
1½ pounds extra-large shrimp (21 to 25 per pound), peeled and deveined, shells reserved
2 onions, chopped
4 celery ribs, chopped
  Salt
4 cups water
1 tablespoon peppercorns
5 sprigs fresh parsley
2 bay leaves
1 green bell pepper, stemmed, seeded, and chopped
2 cups long-grain white rice
2 garlic cloves, minced
1 teaspoon minced fresh thyme
¼ teaspoon cayenne pepper
1 (14.5-ounce) can diced tomatoes

1. Melt 1 tablespoon butter in large saucepan over medium heat. Add shrimp shells, 1 cup onion, ½ cup celery, and 1 teaspoon salt and cook, stirring occasionally, until shells are spotty brown, about 10 minutes. Add water, peppercorns, parsley, and bay leaves. Increase heat to high and bring to boil. Reduce heat to low, cover, and simmer for 30 minutes. Strain shrimp stock through fine-mesh strainer set over large bowl, pressing on solids to extract as much liquid as possible; discard solids.

2. Melt remaining 4 tablespoons butter in Dutch oven over medium heat. Add bell pepper, remaining onion and celery, and ½ teaspoon salt and cook until vegetables are beginning to soften, 5 to 7 minutes. Add rice, garlic, thyme, and cayenne and cook until fragrant and rice is translucent, about 2 minutes. Stir in tomatoes and their juice and 3 cups shrimp stock (reserve remainder for another use) and bring to boil. Reduce heat to low, cover, and cook for 20 minutes.

3. Gently fold shrimp into rice until evenly distributed, cover, and continue to cook 5 minutes longer. Remove pot from heat and let sit, covered, until shrimp are cooked through and all liquid is absorbed, about 10 minutes. Serve.

Peeling and Deveining Shrimp

1. Break shell under swimming legs, which will come off as shell is removed. Leave tail intact if desired, or tug tail to remove shell.

2. Use paring knife to make shallow cut along back of shrimp to expose vein. Use tip of knife to lift out vein. Discard vein by wiping blade against paper towel.

SHRIMP AND GRITS

SERVES 4

We prefer untreated shrimp—those without added sodium or preservatives like sodium tripolyphosphate. Most frozen E-Z peel shrimp have been treated (the ingredient list should tell you). If you're using treated shrimp, do not add the salt in step 4. If you use our winning grits (Anson Mills Pencil Cob Grits) or other fresh-milled grits, you will need to increase the simmering time by 25 minutes.

Grits
3 tablespoons unsalted butter
1 cup grits
2¼ cups whole milk
2 cups water
Salt and pepper

Shrimp
3 tablespoons unsalted butter
1½ pounds extra-large shrimp (21 to 25 per pound), peeled and deveined, shells reserved
1 tablespoon tomato paste
2¼ cups water
3 slices bacon, cut into ½-inch pieces
1 garlic clove, minced
Salt and pepper
2 tablespoons all-purpose flour
1 tablespoon lemon juice
½ teaspoon Tabasco sauce, plus extra for serving
4 scallions, sliced thin

1. For the Grits Melt 1 tablespoon butter in medium saucepan over medium heat. Add grits and cook, stirring often, until fragrant, about 3 minutes. Add milk, water, and ¾ teaspoon salt. Increase heat to medium-high and bring to boil. Reduce heat to low, cover, and simmer, whisking often, until thick and creamy, about 25 minutes. Remove from heat, stir in remaining 2 tablespoons butter, and season with salt and pepper to taste. Cover and keep warm.

2. For the Shrimp Meanwhile, melt 1 tablespoon butter in 12-inch nonstick skillet over medium heat. Add shrimp shells and cook, stirring occasionally, until shells are spotty brown, about 7 minutes. Stir in tomato paste and cook for 30 seconds. Add water and bring to boil. Reduce heat to low, cover, and simmer for 5 minutes.

3. Strain shrimp stock through fine-mesh strainer set over bowl, pressing on solids to extract as much liquid as possible; discard solids. You should have about 1½ cups stock (add more water if necessary to equal 1½ cups). Wipe out skillet with paper towels.

4. Cook bacon in now-empty skillet over medium-low heat until crisp, 7 to 9 minutes. Increase heat to medium-high and stir in shrimp, garlic, ½ teaspoon salt, and ½ teaspoon pepper. Cook until edges of shrimp are just beginning to turn pink, but shrimp are not cooked through, about 2 minutes. Transfer shrimp mixture to bowl.

5. Melt 1 tablespoon butter in now-empty skillet over medium-high heat. Whisk in flour and cook for 1 minute. Slowly whisk in shrimp stock until incorporated. Bring to boil, reduce heat to medium-low, and simmer until thickened slightly, about 5 minutes.

6. Stir in shrimp mixture, cover, and cook until shrimp are cooked through, about 3 minutes. Off heat, stir in lemon juice, Tabasco, and remaining 1 tablespoon butter. Season with salt and pepper to taste. Serve over grits, sprinkled with scallions, and passing extra Tabasco.

Shrimp Jumps the Shark
For decades, the savory Southern dish known as "shrimp and grits" was little known outside a small swath of the southeastern U.S. coast. There, the entrenched combination was an inevitable outcome of abundance—the Carolina shores teemed with shrimp, and grits were plentiful and cheap. Its profile grew through places like Crook's Corner restaurant in Chapel Hill, North Carolina, where Chef Bill Neal's Brunswick stew, hoppin' John, and shrimp and grits preserved the regional dishes of the area.

Why This Recipe Works Known locally in the Carolinas for generations as "breakfast shrimp", there are many modern versions of shrimp and grits. We set out to keep it simple: tender flavorful shrimp, silky sauce, and creamy grits. To avoid overcooking the shrimp, we lightly sautéed them in rendered bacon fat and set them aside while creating the sauce in the same skillet. We used the shrimp shells to make a stock for the base of the sauce. To finish cooking, we added the shrimp back into the sauce. Toasting the grits in butter coaxed the most corn flavor out of them before we added more-than-usual liquid. Sliced scallions added a fresh finish.

NEW ORLEANS BARBECUE SHRIMP

SERVES 4

Although traditional barbecue shrimp is always made with shell-on shrimp, peeled and deveined shrimp may be used. Light- or medium-bodied beers work best here. Serve with Tabasco sauce and French bread, if desired.

- 2 pounds extra-large (21 to 25 per pound) shrimp
- ½ teaspoon salt
- ½ teaspoon cayenne pepper
- 2 tablespoons vegetable oil
- 6 tablespoons unsalted butter, cut into 6 pieces
- 2 teaspoons all-purpose flour
- 1 teaspoon tomato paste
- 1 teaspoon minced fresh rosemary
- 1 teaspoon minced fresh thyme
- ½ teaspoon dried oregano
- 3 garlic cloves, minced
- ¾ cup bottled clam juice
- ½ cup beer
- 1 tablespoon Worcestershire sauce

1. Pat shrimp dry with paper towels and sprinkle with salt and cayenne. Heat 1 tablespoon oil in large skillet over medium-high heat until just smoking. Cook half of shrimp, without moving, until spotty brown on one side, about 1 minute; transfer to large plate. Repeat with remaining oil and shrimp.

2. Melt 1 tablespoon butter in empty skillet over medium heat. Add flour, tomato paste, rosemary, thyme, oregano, and garlic and cook until fragrant, about 30 seconds. Stir in clam juice, beer, and Worcestershire, scraping up any browned bits, and bring to boil. Return shrimp and any accumulated juices to skillet. Reduce heat to medium-low and simmer, covered, until shrimp are cooked through, about 2 minutes. Off heat, stir in remaining butter until incorporated. Serve.

Not Your Average Barbecue Sauce

Barbecue sauce conjures up an image of a thick, sticky tomato-based mop, but New Orleans Barbecue Shrimp is bathed in a spicy herbed butter sauce made with these ingredients.

CLAM JUICE

The briny bite makes a simple replacement for fish stock.

BEER

The mellow, slightly hoppy bitterness balances the rich butter.

WORCESTERSHIRE

Often used to add bold, ultrasavory flavor to dishes.

BUTTER

Adding butter twice makes a rich, satiny sauce.

Why This Recipe Works Named for the "barbecue" color rather than the cooking method, this New Orleans skillet shrimp dish relies on a velvety, butter-based sauce to flavor shell-on shrimp. To achieve perfectly cooked shrimp, we started by searing them first to partially cook them and then later returned the shrimp to the finished sauce to gently cook through. By using a roux to thicken the sauce and sautéing the aromatics with tomato paste, we were able to create a silky, flavorful sauce that clung perfectly to the shrimp. We replaced time-consuming seafood stock with bottled clam juice, a technique the test kitchen has used before.

Why This Recipe Works For our version of the New Orleans poor boy sandwich served on pillowy bread slathered with a pungent rémoulade and piled with fried shrimp, we packed flavor into every element. We started by tossing the shrimp in a flour, cornmeal, and Creole seasoning mixture. Next, to ensure that the batter stayed put when fried, we first dipped the shrimp in a paste-like batter of beaten eggs bolstered with a bit of the Creole-seasoned dry mixture, and dredged them again in the flour mixture before letting them rest in the refrigerator. Our superflavorful rémoulade dressing added another jazzed-up layer of flavor.

SHRIMP PO' BOYS

SERVES 4

Use refrigerated prepared horseradish, not the shelf-stable kind, which contains preservatives and additives. Frank's RedHot Original Cayenne Pepper Sauce is best here. Use a Dutch oven that holds 6 quarts or more. Do not refrigerate the breaded shrimp for longer than 30 minutes, or the coating will be too wet. It may seem like you're spreading a lot of rémoulade on the rolls, but it will be absorbed by the other ingredients.

Rémoulade
⅔ cup mayonnaise
2 tablespoons prepared horseradish
1 tablespoon Worcestershire sauce
1 tablespoon hot sauce
¼ teaspoon pepper

Shrimp
2 cups all-purpose flour
¼ cup cornmeal
2 tablespoons Creole seasoning
4 large eggs
1 pound medium-large shrimp (31 to 40 per pound), peeled, deveined, and tails removed
2 quarts peanut or vegetable oil
4 (8-inch) sub rolls, toasted
2 cups shredded iceberg lettuce
2 large tomatoes, cored and sliced thin
1 cup dill pickle chips

1. For the Rémoulade Whisk all ingredients together in bowl. Set aside.

2. For the Shrimp Set wire rack in rimmed baking sheet. Whisk flour, cornmeal, and Creole seasoning together in shallow dish. Whisk eggs and ½ cup flour mixture together in second shallow dish.

3. Place half of shrimp in flour mixture and toss to thoroughly coat. Shake off excess flour mixture, dip shrimp into egg mixture, then return to flour mixture, pressing gently to adhere. Transfer shrimp to prepared wire rack. Repeat with remaining half of shrimp. Refrigerate shrimp for at least 15 minutes or up to 30 minutes.

4. Line large plate with triple layer of paper towels. Add oil to large Dutch oven until it measures about 1½ inches deep and heat over medium-high heat

to 375 degrees. Carefully add half of shrimp to oil. Cook, stirring occasionally, until golden brown, about 4 minutes. Using slotted spoon or spider skimmer, transfer shrimp to prepared plate. Return oil to 375 degrees and repeat with remaining shrimp.

5. Spread rémoulade evenly on both cut sides of each roll. Divide lettuce, tomatoes, pickle chips, and shrimp evenly among rolls. Serve.

The American Table: The Birth of a Sandwich

Nineteen twenty-nine was a bumpy year for New Orleans—and not just because of the famous October stock market crash. Several months earlier, streetcar workers went on strike. They took to the streets on July 1, stomachs growling. Bennie Martin and his brother Clovis, former streetcar workers who'd since opened their Martin Brothers' Coffee Stand and Restaurant, came along to feed the picketers with their "poor boy" sandwiches, distributed free of charge. The sometimes-violent strike lasted in varying degrees for several years, and the sandwiches, originally filled with beef, became a signature New Orleans lunch. Eventually variations on po' boys—shrimp, for one—caught on and spread to other Gulf Coast towns.

Creole Seasoning

Recipes for Louisiana spice blends vary in name, but whether called Cajun or Creole (the terms are often used interchangeably), most contain paprika, garlic, thyme, salt, pepper, and cayenne. We prefer to make our own, but our favorite store-bought brand is **Tony Chachere's Original Creole Seasoning**. It's "vibrant" and "zesty," with strong notes of garlic and red pepper, a "punch of heat," and a "slightly sweet" aftertaste.

Why This Recipe Works South Carolina is the undisputed home of the shrimp burger. The best ones are almost pure shrimp, with no bready fillers. To achieve the perfect consistency, we finely chopped a third of our raw, peeled shrimp in a food processor, then coarsely chopped the remaining shrimp. This step made the shrimp slightly sticky for easy binding, aided further by some cayenne-seasoned mayo. Chopped scallions gave our burgers extra fresh flavor. Before pan-frying our patties, we dredged them in finely ground panko bread crumbs. We like to serve our shrimp burgers on a soft bun with a smear of homemade tartar sauce.

SOUTH CAROLINA SHRIMP BURGERS

SERVES 4

We prefer untreated shrimp—those without added sodium or preservatives like sodium tripolyphosphate (STPP). Most frozen shrimp have been treated (the ingredient list should tell you). If you're using untreated shrimp, increase the amount of salt to ½ teaspoon. If you're purchasing shell-on shrimp, you should buy about 1½ pounds.

Tartar Sauce
¾ cup mayonnaise
3 tablespoons finely chopped dill pickles plus 1 teaspoon brine
1 small shallot, minced
1 tablespoon capers, rinsed and chopped fine
¼ teaspoon pepper

Burgers
1 cup panko bread crumbs
1¼ pounds peeled and deveined large shrimp (26 to 30 per pound), tails removed
2 tablespoons mayonnaise
¼ teaspoon pepper
⅛ teaspoon salt
⅛ teaspoon cayenne pepper
3 scallions, chopped fine
3 tablespoons vegetable oil
4 hamburger buns
4 leaves Bibb lettuce

1. For the Tartar Sauce Combine all ingredients in bowl and refrigerate until needed.

2. For the Burgers Pulse panko in food processor until finely ground, about 15 pulses; transfer to shallow dish. Place one-third of shrimp (1 cup), mayonnaise, pepper, salt, and cayenne in now-empty processor and pulse until shrimp are finely chopped, about 8 pulses. Add remaining two-thirds of shrimp (2 cups) to shrimp mixture in processor and pulse until coarsely chopped, about 4 pulses, scraping down sides of bowl as needed. Transfer shrimp mixture to bowl and stir in scallions.

3. Divide shrimp mixture into four ¾-inch-thick patties (about ½ cup each). Working with 1 patty at a time, dredge both sides of patties in panko, pressing lightly to adhere, and transfer to plate.

4. Heat oil in 12-inch nonstick skillet over medium heat until shimmering. Place patties in skillet and cook until golden brown on first side, 3 to 5 minutes. Carefully flip and continue to cook until shrimp registers 140 to 145 degrees and second side is golden brown, 3 to 5 minutes longer. Transfer burgers to paper towel–lined plate and let drain, about 30 seconds per side. Spread tartar sauce on bun bottoms, then place burgers and lettuce on top. Cover with bun tops. Serve.

A Family Affair

Plenty of restaurants in Beaufort, South Carolina, offer shrimp burgers, but only the Shrimp Shack, an institution since 1978, uses "Captain Bob" Upton's special recipe, which relies on local shrimp—and not much else. Upton, a local fisherman, and his wife, Hilda Upton, opened the Shack in his front yard that year, after a particularly poor fishing season. Daughters Hilda "Sis" Godley and Julie Madlinger run the place now, using local shrimp and Captain Bob's recipe.

CHINESE CHICKEN SALAD

SERVES 6

You can substitute 1 minced clove of garlic and ¼ teaspoon of cayenne pepper for the Asian chili-garlic sauce.

- 2 oranges
- ¼ cup rice vinegar
- ¼ cup soy sauce
- 3 tablespoons grated fresh ginger
- 3 tablespoons sugar
- 1 tablespoon Asian chili-garlic sauce
- 3 tablespoons vegetable oil
- 2 tablespoons toasted sesame oil
- 4 (6- to 8-ounce) boneless, skinless chicken breasts, trimmed
- 2 romaine lettuce hearts (12 ounces), sliced thin
- ½ small head napa cabbage, cored and sliced thin (6 cups)
- 2 red bell peppers, stemmed, seeded, and cut into 2-inch-long matchsticks
- 1 cup fresh cilantro leaves
- 1 cup salted, dry-roasted peanuts, chopped
- 6 scallions, sliced thin

1. Cut thin slice from top and bottom of each orange, exposing fruit. Slice off rind and pith, cutting from top to bottom. Working over bowl, cut orange segments from thin membrane and transfer segments to second bowl; set aside. Squeeze juice from membrane into first bowl (juice should measure ¼ cup).

2. Combine orange juice, vinegar, soy sauce, ginger, sugar, and chili-garlic sauce in bowl. Transfer ½ cup of orange juice mixture to 12-inch skillet. Slowly whisk vegetable oil and sesame oil into remaining orange juice mixture to make vinaigrette; set aside.

3. Bring orange juice mixture in skillet to boil. Add chicken, reduce heat to medium-low, cover, and simmer until meat registers 160 degrees, 10 to 15 minutes, flipping halfway through cooking. Transfer chicken to plate and let rest for 5 to 10 minutes.

4. Meanwhile, boil pan juices until reduced to ¼ cup, 1 to 3 minutes, and set aside. Using 2 forks, shred chicken into bite-size pieces. Off heat, add chicken, any accumulated juices, and 2 tablespoons vinaigrette to skillet. Toss to coat and let sit for 10 minutes.

5. Toss lettuce, cabbage, bell peppers, cilantro, peanuts, and scallions with remaining vinaigrette in large bowl. Transfer to serving platter and top with chicken and oranges. Serve.

Shopping for Aromatic Asian Ingredients

Consider keeping these three versatile ingredients on hand to add layers of Asian flavor to a variety of dishes, including our Chinese Chicken Salad.

RICE VINEGAR
This Japanese vinegar is sweet and mild.

ASIAN CHILI-GARLIC SAUCE
If you like garlic and heat, you'll reach for this bottle often.

TOASTED SESAME OIL
This aromatic, boldly flavored oil is made from roasted sesame seeds. Its flavor doesn't hold up to cooking, so add it off heat.

Why This Recipe Works Despite its name, Chinese chicken salad is an American dish and although beloved, we wanted to give it a fresh makeover. The salad-bar pile ons, from chow mein noodles to water chestnuts, got the ax. Instead, we started with crisp romaine lettuce, napa cabbage, bell peppers, cilantro, and scallions. To keep the chicken from tasting like an afterthought, we poached boneless, skinless chicken breasts in a flavorful mixture of soy sauce, orange juice, rice vinegar, and ginger, setting aside some of the mixture to whisk with sesame and vegetable oils for a bold dressing. We finished the dish with fresh oranges and roasted peanuts.

CHICKEN CHOW MEIN

SERVES 4

Purchase thin, round fresh Chinese egg noodles, not flat and/or dried noodles, or substitute 6 ounces of dried chow mein, ramen, or wheat vermicelli.

- 1 (9-ounce) package fresh Chinese noodles
- 1 tablespoon toasted sesame oil
- 1 teaspoon baking soda
- 2 (6-ounce) boneless, skinless chicken breasts, trimmed and cut crosswise into 1/4-inch-thick slices
- 3 tablespoons Shaoxing or dry sherry
- 1 tablespoon cornstarch
- 1/2 cup chicken broth
- 3 tablespoons soy sauce
- 3 tablespoons oyster sauce
- 1/4 teaspoon white pepper
- 2 tablespoons vegetable oil
- 6 ounces shiitake mushrooms, stemmed and sliced thin
- 1 carrot, peeled and cut into 2-inch matchsticks
- 2 celery ribs, cut on bias into 1/4-inch-thick slices
- 4 scallions, white and green parts separated and sliced thin
- 3 garlic cloves, minced
- 1 tablespoon grated fresh ginger
- 4 ounces (2 cups) mung bean sprouts

1. Bring 4 quarts water to boil in large pot. Add noodles to boiling water and cook until tender, 2 to 4 minutes. Drain noodles, rinse thoroughly with cold water, then drain again. Toss noodles with sesame oil in bowl; set aside.

2. Meanwhile, dissolve baking soda in 1/2 cup cold water in bowl. Add chicken and let sit at room temperature for 15 minutes. Drain chicken, rinse under cold water, then drain again. Pat chicken dry with paper towels. Combine 1 tablespoon rice wine, 2 teaspoons cornstarch, and chicken in bowl; set aside.

3. Whisk broth, soy sauce, oyster sauce, pepper, remaining 2 tablespoons rice wine, and remaining 1 teaspoon cornstarch together in bowl; set aside.

4. Heat oil in 12-inch nonstick skillet over high heat until just smoking. Add chicken and cook, stirring frequently, until opaque, about 2 minutes. Add mushrooms and carrot and cook, stirring frequently, until tender, about 2 minutes. Add celery and cook until crisp-tender, about 1 minute. Add scallion whites, garlic, and ginger and cook until fragrant, about 30 seconds.

5. Whisk broth mixture to recombine, then add to skillet and cook until thickened and chicken is cooked through, about 2 minutes. Add bean sprouts and noodles and toss until sauce evenly coats noodles, about 1 minute. Transfer to platter and sprinkle with scallion greens. Serve.

Fresh Egg Noodles

You'll find chow mein in Chinese restaurants prepared with wheat noodles, Italian pastas, ramen noodles, or egg noodles. But our tasters preferred fresh Chinese egg noodles, available in the Asian section of most grocery stores.

Why This Recipe Works Like many dishes you'll find in America's Chinese restaurants, chow mein has deep roots in China, where chao mian ("fried noodles") has been around for centuries. To help the chicken in this takeout standard retain moisture, we soaked sliced chicken in water and baking soda followed by a quick soak in Shaoxing wine and cornstarch. For the chow mein's sauce, oyster sauce added meaty notes, and more rice wine added sweet brightness. To avoid a gloppy sauce, we used just a bit of cornstarch as thickener then added plenty of bean sprouts for fresh crunch.

Why This Recipe Works Also known as ABC, this Chinese American staple is on menus in the Detroit region. When we were testing batter recipes, one puffed up like a doughnut, while a thinner batter produced a coating that wasn't crisp enough. So we turned to an ingredient often used in coatings: beer. It added a welcome flavor, and its carbonation lightened the batter. Almond boneless chicken is traditionally sprinkled with chopped almonds, but we wanted to include the nuts more deeply. Adding toasted almonds to the batter made the almond flavor much more pronounced and our tasters, even the Michigan purists, called it an improvement.

ALMOND BONELESS CHICKEN

SERVES 4 TO 6

Use a Dutch oven that holds 6 quarts or more. Choose a mild lager or pilsner for this recipe. In addition to iceberg lettuce, this dish is usually served with rice.

Sauce
1 tablespoon cornstarch
1 tablespoon cold water
1 cup chicken broth
2 teaspoons dry sherry
2 teaspoons hoisin sauce
2 teaspoons soy sauce
⅛ teaspoon salt

Chicken
4 (6- to 8-ounce) boneless, skinless chicken breasts, trimmed
Salt and pepper
½ cup sliced almonds, toasted
2 cups all-purpose flour
1 cup cornstarch
1 teaspoon garlic powder
1 teaspoon baking powder
½ teaspoon baking soda
1¼ cups lager or pilsner beer
1 large egg, lightly beaten
2 quarts peanut or vegetable oil
½ head iceberg lettuce (4½ ounces), cored and sliced thin crosswise
3 scallions, sliced thin on bias

1. For the Sauce Dissolve cornstarch in water in small bowl and set aside. Combine broth, sherry, hoisin, soy sauce, and salt in small saucepan and bring to boil over medium-high heat. Whisk in reserved cornstarch mixture, return to boil, and cook until thickened, about 30 seconds. Remove from heat, cover, and keep warm, stirring occasionally.

2. For the Chicken Line rimmed baking sheet with parchment paper. Set wire rack in second rimmed baking sheet and line rack with triple layer of paper towels. Halve chicken breasts horizontally to form 8 cutlets. Pat cutlets dry with paper towels and season with salt and pepper.

3. Finely chop ¼ cup almonds. Whisk chopped almonds, 1 cup flour, cornstarch, garlic powder, baking powder, baking soda, 1 teaspoon salt, and ¾ teaspoon pepper together in large bowl. Whisk in beer and egg. Combine remaining 1 cup flour and 1 teaspoon salt in shallow dish.

4. Working with 1 at a time, dip cutlets into batter to thoroughly coat, letting excess drip back into bowl. Dredge battered cutlets in flour to coat, shaking off excess, and place on parchment-lined sheet. Let cutlets sit while oil heats.

5. Add oil to large Dutch oven until it measures about 1½ inches deep and heat over medium-high heat to 350 degrees. Working in batches, add half of cutlets to hot oil. Adjust burner as necessary to maintain oil temperature between 325 and 350 degrees. Fry, stirring gently to prevent pieces from sticking together, until cutlets are golden and register 160 degrees, about 4 minutes, flipping halfway through frying. Transfer to prepared wire rack to cool while frying remaining cutlets.

6. Place lettuce on platter. Cut each cutlet crosswise into ½-inch-thick slices. Arrange slices over lettuce and drizzle with sauce. Sprinkle with scallions and remaining ¼ cup almonds. Serve.

Cool Oil, Uncool Chicken
To achieve the perfect golden exterior, it's essential to have the cooking oil at the correct temperature—350 degrees. Adding too many pieces to the pot will drop the oil's temperature, producing pale, greasy chicken.

PALE FAIL
An overcrowded pot leads to underbrowned, unappetizing chicken.

Why This Recipe Works Unlike what we typically think of as barbecue, Chinese barbecued pork is made neither on a grill nor in a smoker: It's usually cooked (and then glazed) in an oven. But we made this dish even more convenient—by adapting it to the slow cooker. Boneless pork butt renders lots of flavorful fat and pork juices as it cooks. Because this fat diluted any sauce we tried, we instead used a dry rub and then cooked the pork with a glazy sauce under the broiler. The finished "barbecued" pork was tender with a shiny, slightly charred exterior that tasted even better than it looked, earning it the nickname "meat candy" in the test kitchen.

SLOW-COOKER CHINESE BARBECUED PORK

SERVES 8

Pork butt roast is often labeled Boston butt in the supermarket. Look for five-spice powder and hoisin sauce near the Asian ingredients at your supermarket.

1½ teaspoons salt
1½ teaspoons five-spice powder
½ teaspoon pepper
1 (5- to 6-pound) boneless pork butt roast, trimmed and sliced crosswise into 1-inch-thick steaks
⅓ cup hoisin sauce
⅓ cup honey
¼ cup sugar
¼ cup soy sauce
¼ cup ketchup
2 tablespoons dry sherry
1 tablespoon toasted sesame oil
1 tablespoon grated fresh ginger
2 garlic cloves, minced

1. Combine salt, ¾ teaspoon five-spice powder, and pepper in bowl. Rub spice mixture all over pork and transfer to slow cooker. Cover and cook on low until pork is just tender, 5 to 6 hours.

2. When pork is nearly done, combine hoisin, honey, sugar, soy sauce, ketchup, sherry, oil, ginger, garlic, and remaining ¾ teaspoon five-spice powder in bowl. Set wire rack inside aluminum foil–lined rimmed baking sheet. Pour 1 cup water into sheet. Adjust oven rack 4 inches from broiler element and heat broiler.

3. Using tongs, transfer pork from slow cooker to prepared wire rack in single layer. Brush pork with one-third of hoisin mixture and broil until lightly caramelized, 5 to 7 minutes. Flip pork, brush with half of remaining hoisin mixture, and broil until lightly caramelized on second side, 5 to 7 minutes. Brush pork with remaining hoisin mixture and broil until deep mahogany and crispy around edges, about 3 minutes. Transfer to carving board and let rest for 10 minutes. Slice crosswise into thin strips. Serve.

Pork Butt (Blade Shoulder)

This large, flavorful cut (often labeled Boston butt or pork shoulder at supermarkets) can weigh as much as 8 pounds when sold with the bone in. Many markets take out the bone and sell this cut in smaller chunks, often wrapped in netting to hold the roast together. This cut is ideal for slow roasting, barbecuing, stewing, or braising.

ST. PAUL SANDWICH

SERVES 4

Be sure to pat the ham steak dry with paper towels before adding it to the skillet in step 1; this will keep it from splattering as it cooks.

- 4 large eggs
- ½ teaspoon table salt
- ½ teaspoon white pepper
- ½ teaspoon granulated garlic
- 2 ounces (1 cup) mung bean sprouts, coarsely chopped
- 1 cup chopped onion
- 5 ounces ham steak, patted dry and cut into ½-inch pieces
- ½ cup vegetable oil for frying
- 4 tablespoons mayonnaise
- 8 slices hearty white sandwich bread
- 2 cups shredded iceberg lettuce
- 8 thin tomato slices
- 16 dill pickle chips

1. Beat eggs, salt, white pepper, and granulated garlic together in medium bowl. Stir in bean sprouts, onion, and ham until thoroughly combined.

2. Heat oil in 12-inch nonstick skillet over medium heat until just smoking. Using ½-cup dry measuring cup, portion 4 evenly spaced scoops of egg mixture in skillet. (Eggs may run together; this is OK.) Cover and cook, without stirring, until bottoms of egg foo yong patties are browned and tops are set, about 5 minutes.

3. Using spatula, cut and separate egg foo yong patties in skillet. Flip each patty and continue to cook, covered, until browned on second side, about 3 minutes longer. Transfer egg foo yong patties to paper towel–lined plate and let drain for 1 minute.

4. Spread mayonnaise on 1 side of each piece of bread. Top each of 4 slices of bread with ½ cup lettuce, 1 egg foo yong patty, 2 tomato slices, 4 pickles, and 1 slice of bread. Serve.

On the Road: A Misleading Name

Rudy Lieu first ate egg foo yong (a deep-fried omelet filled with bean sprouts, onions, and meat smothered in a savory brown gravy) at the age of 15 on a visit to his uncle's Chinese restaurant in St. Louis. On the same trip, Rudy tried St. Louis's famous St. Paul sandwich: an egg foo yong patty nestled between two slices of white bread with iceberg lettuce, tomatoes, pickles, and mayonnaise. "When you have it for the first time, it's like, Whoa! This is interesting." In the early 1980s, Rudy's uncle, Anthony Lieu, worked for a man named Stephen Yuen at his restaurant Park Chop Suey. Rudy refers to Yuen as a "pioneer" of the Chinese restaurant scene at that time. Yuen had moved to St. Louis from St. Paul, Minnesota, a city he loved, so he invented the St. Paul sandwich as an homage. "It started selling like hotcakes," says Rudy. He smiles and says, "In St. Louis, nobody doesn't know what a St. Paul sandwich is." Luckily for us, this crispy egg foo yong sandwich tastes great in any city.

Why This Recipe Works The traditional version of this regionally famous sandwich is made by deep-frying a large omelet filled with bean sprouts, onions, and meat; to make handling and cleanup easier, we chose to shallow-fry smaller patties in a skillet. Transferring the egg foo yong patties to a paper towel–lined plate after frying kept them from being greasy. Arranging them on white bread with a slather of mayonnaise and shredded iceberg lettuce we topped the patties with shredded iceberg lettuce, tomato slices, and dill pickle chips. The final sandwich features salty and tangy flavors with soft yet crispy textures in every bite.

Why This Recipe Works This Italian sandwich is a New Orleans classic, and we wanted to do it justice. We started by inspecting Central Grocery's famous olive salad. Then we got to work on our own version and found that combining olives, capers, giardiniera, garlic, herbs, and spices gave us the salty, tangy mixture we wanted. We baked store-bought pizza dough into perfect puffy rounds, which we sprinkled with sesame seeds. Alternating layers of meats and cheese gave our sandwich stability, making it easier to eat. Lastly, we pressed the assembled sandwiches for an hour to allow the olive salad to properly soak into the bread.

NEW ORLEANS MUFFULETTAS

SERVES 8

You will need one 16-ounce jar of giardiniera to yield 2 cups drained; our favorite brand is Pastene. If you like a spicier sandwich, increase the amount of pepper flakes to ½ teaspoon.

- 2 (1-pound) balls pizza dough
- 2 cups drained jarred giardiniera
- 1 cup pimento-stuffed green olives
- ½ cup pitted kalamata olives
- 2 tablespoons capers, rinsed
- 1 tablespoon red wine vinegar
- 1 garlic clove, minced
- ½ teaspoon dried oregano
- ¼ teaspoon red pepper flakes
- ¼ teaspoon dried thyme
- ½ cup extra-virgin olive oil
- ¼ cup chopped fresh parsley
- 1 large egg, lightly beaten
- 5 teaspoons sesame seeds
- 4 ounces thinly sliced Genoa salami
- 6 ounces thinly sliced aged provolone cheese
- 6 ounces thinly sliced mortadella
- 4 ounces thinly sliced hot capicola

1. Form dough balls into 2 tight round balls on oiled baking sheet, cover loosely with greased plastic wrap, and let sit at room temperature for 1 hour.

2. Meanwhile, pulse giardiniera, green olives, kalamata olives, capers, vinegar, garlic, oregano, pepper flakes, and thyme in food processor until coarsely chopped, about 6 pulses, scraping down sides of bowl as needed. Transfer to bowl and stir in oil and parsley. Let sit at room temperature for 30 minutes. (Olive salad can be refrigerated for up to 1 week.)

3. Adjust oven rack to middle position and heat oven to 425 degrees. Keeping dough balls on sheet, flatten each into 7-inch disk. Brush tops of disks with egg and sprinkle with sesame seeds. Bake until golden brown and loaves sound hollow when tapped, 18 to 20 minutes, rotating sheet halfway through baking. Transfer loaves to wire rack and let cool completely, about 1 hour. (Loaves can be wrapped in plastic and stored at room temperature for up to 24 hours.)

4. Slice loaves in half horizontally. Spread one-fourth of olive salad on cut side of each loaf top and bottom, pressing firmly with rubber spatula to compact. Layer 2 ounces salami, 1½ ounces provolone, 3 ounces mortadella, 1½ ounces provolone, and 2 ounces capicola in order on each loaf bottom. Cap with loaf tops and individually wrap sandwiches tightly in plastic.

5. Place baking sheet on top of sandwiches and weigh down with heavy Dutch oven or two 5-pound bags of flour or sugar for 1 hour, flipping sandwiches halfway through pressing. Unwrap and slice each sandwich into quarters and serve. (Pressed, wrapped sandwiches can be refrigerated for up to 24 hours. Bring to room temperature before serving.)

A Weighty Solution

If you don't have a heavy Dutch oven, use two 5-pound bags of flour or sugar to weigh down the wrapped muffulettas.

Pressing the assembled sandwiches for an hour helps the olive salad properly soak into the bread.

CROQUE MONSIEUR

SERVES 4

For the best results, be sure to use a good-quality Gruyère here.

Sandwiches

8 slices hearty white sandwich bread
4 tablespoons unsalted butter, melted
12 ounces thinly sliced Black Forest deli ham
¼ cup grated Parmesan cheese
4 ounces Gruyère cheese, shredded (1 cup)

Mornay Sauce

2 tablespoons unsalted butter
2 tablespoons all-purpose flour
1 cup whole milk
4 ounces Gruyère cheese, shredded (1 cup)
¼ cup grated Parmesan cheese
½ teaspoon salt
¼ teaspoon pepper
Pinch ground nutmeg

1. For the Sandwiches Adjust oven rack 6 inches from broiler element and heat oven to 375 degrees. Line rimmed baking sheet with aluminum foil and spray with vegetable oil spray.

2. Brush bread on both sides with melted butter and place on prepared sheet. Bake until light golden brown on top, about 10 minutes. Remove sheet from oven and flip slices. Return to oven and bake until golden brown on second side, about 3 minutes. Reserve 4 slices for sandwich tops; evenly space remaining 4 slices on sheet.

3. For the Mornay Sauce Melt butter in small saucepan over medium heat. Whisk in flour and cook for 1 minute. Slowly whisk in milk and bring to boil. Once boiling, remove from heat and quickly whisk in Gruyère, Parmesan, salt, pepper, and nutmeg until smooth.

4. Spread 1 tablespoon Mornay on each slice of toast on sheet. Then, folding ham slices over themselves multiple times so they bunch up, divide ham evenly among slices of toast. Spread 2 tablespoons Mornay on 1 side of each reserved slice of toast and place slices Mornay side down on top of ham.

5. Spread 2 tablespoons Mornay evenly over top of each sandwich, making sure to completely cover toast, including edges (exposed edges can burn under broiler). Sprinkle sandwiches with Parmesan, followed by Gruyère.

6. Bake until cheese on top of sandwiches is melted, about 5 minutes. Turn on broiler and broil until cheese bubbles across tops of sandwiches and edges are spotty brown, about 5 minutes. Serve.

CROQUE MADAME
Top each sandwich with a fried egg.

Why This Recipe Works Croque monsieur's are the perfect mix of crisp, buttery toast; salty-sweet ham; a creamy white sauce; and plenty of nutty Gruyère cheese. For a truly impressive version of this French bistro favorite we chose to amp up the béchamel sauce by adding both Gruyère and Parmesan cheeses. To ensure that the sandwiches were ready to eat at the same time, we assembled all four of them on a baking sheet, layering in the cheese sauce and slices of Black Forest ham before topping them with more sauce and cheese. A trip under the broiler was all that was needed to meld the sandwich together and create a bubbly-browned top.

Why This Recipe Works This sandwich bears a passing resemblance to the classic sloppy joe, but it's bigger and bolder, spicier and tangier. The Detroit staple was reinvented at Chef Greg's Soul "N" the Wall and features spicy, saucy ground beef that's topped with American cheese and sautéed onions and piled onto soft sub rolls. The original recipe for the sauce is top secret, so we puzzled out our own version, adding chili powder and dry mustard for heat and spice. Toasting the sandwiches in the oven created crunchy edges on the bread and melted the cheese. We reserved some sauce to spoon over the toasted sandwiches for a zesty finish.

BOOGALOO WONDERLAND SANDWICHES

SERVES 4

Heinz Organic Tomato Ketchup and Heinz Filtered Apple Cider Vinegar are our favorites. Both light and dark brown sugar will work in this recipe. Don't be tempted to substitute another kind of cheese for the American; nothing melts like it. Serve with your favorite hot sauce, if desired.

Sauce

- 1 cup ketchup
- 3 tablespoons cider vinegar
- 2 tablespoons packed brown sugar
- 2 tablespoons Worcestershire sauce
- ¾ teaspoon dried thyme
- ¾ teaspoon dry mustard
- ¾ teaspoon granulated garlic
- ¾ teaspoon chili powder
- ¼ teaspoon pepper

Sandwiches

- 1 tablespoon vegetable oil
- 1¼ pounds 85 percent lean ground beef
- 1 onion, sliced thin
- 1 teaspoon pepper
- ¾ teaspoon salt
- 4 (6-inch) Italian sub rolls, sliced lengthwise with 1 side intact
- 8 slices American cheese

1. For the Sauce Combine all ingredients in small saucepan and bring to boil over medium-high heat. Cook, whisking constantly, until slightly thickened, about 3 minutes.

2. For the Sandwiches Adjust oven rack to middle position and heat oven to 350 degrees. Heat oil in 12-inch nonstick skillet over medium-high heat until just smoking. Add beef, onion, pepper, and salt and cook, breaking meat into small pieces with spoon, until liquid has evaporated and meat begins to sizzle, about 10 minutes. Add 1 cup sauce and bring to boil. Reduce heat to medium and simmer until slightly thickened, about 1 minute.

3. Place rolls on rimmed baking sheet. Divide meat mixture evenly among roll bottoms. Top each sandwich with 2 slices American cheese. Bake until cheese is melted and rolls are warmed through, about 5 minutes. Divide remaining sauce equally among sandwiches. Fold roll tops over meat and serve.

On the Road: New Life for an Old Sandwich

Chef Gregory Emilis Beard opened Chef Greg's Soul "N" the Wall in Detroit in 2006 where he serves his own style of food that he calls "urban flavor with a twist." The spot was formerly occupied by Brother's Bar-B-Que, one of whose specialties was the so-called Boogaloo sandwich, a barbecue-flavored Sloppy Joe–style hero smothered with cheese and sauce and served on a sub roll. Beard had never heard of, much less tasted, a Boogaloo but customers kept asking for it. Through trial and error and with plenty of feedback from fans, he finessed a recipe and brought the sandwich back to life. He named this new version the Boogaloo Wonderland sandwich in honor of his friend, Grammy award-winning songwriter and Detroit native Allee Willis, who wrote the song "Boogie Wonderland" for Earth, Wind & Fire in 1979.

As Beard sees it, he "found something old, borrowed the concept, and turned it into something new."

PATTY MELTS

SERVES 4

To make sure that the melts hold together, use rye bread that's sliced about ½ inch thick.

10 slices hearty rye sandwich bread
2 tablespoons whole milk
¾ teaspoon onion powder
   Salt and pepper
1½ pounds 85 percent lean ground beef
3 tablespoons unsalted butter
2 onions, halved and sliced thin
8 ounces Swiss cheese, shredded (2 cups)

1. Adjust oven rack to middle position and heat oven to 200 degrees. Tear 2 pieces of bread into ½-inch pieces. Using potato masher, mash torn bread, milk, onion powder, ¾ teaspoon salt, and ½ teaspoon pepper in large bowl until smooth. Add beef and gently knead until well combined. Divide meat into 4 equal portions. Shape each portion into 6 by 4-inch oval.

2. Melt 1 tablespoon butter in 12-inch nonstick skillet over medium-high heat. Cook 2 patties until well browned on first side, about 5 minutes. Transfer to large plate, browned side up, and repeat with remaining 2 patties.

3. Pour off all but 1 teaspoon fat from pan. Add onions and ½ teaspoon salt and cook, stirring occasionally, until golden brown, 5 to 7 minutes. Arrange patties, browned side up, on top of onions, pouring any accumulated juices into pan. Reduce heat to medium and cook, shaking pan occasionally, until onions are tender and burgers are cooked through, about 5 minutes.

4. Divide 1 cup cheese among 4 slices bread. Top with patties, onions, remaining cheese, and remaining bread. Wipe out skillet with paper towels. Melt 1 tablespoon butter in now-empty skillet over medium heat. Cook 2 sandwiches until golden brown and cheese is melted, 3 to 4 minutes per side. Transfer to rimmed baking sheet and keep warm in oven. Repeat with remaining 1 tablespoon butter and remaining 2 sandwiches. Serve.

The American Table: Heyday of the Sandwich

When it comes to inventive sandwiches, you can't top 1920s America. Just a decade earlier, New Yorkers were said to eat only six types of sandwich: sardine, tongue, roast beef, Swiss cheese, liverwurst, and egg, according to William Grimes's book *Appetite City: A Culinary History of New York*. But three factors—Prohibition, the newfound popularity of automobiles, and women's increasing independence—had created a tearoom craze across the country, making sandwiches so popular that one New Yorker counted nearly 1,000 different types. In these newly minted salons of sandwiches, customers chose among dubious combinations like cheese-ketchup, lemon-prune, and baked bean–celery. Cookbooks reflected the trend, offering other odd partnerships, such as peanut butter and chili sauce, not to mention shredded coconut, cucumber, and mayonnaise. Makes Elvis's prized sandwich of fried peanut butter, banana, and bacon sound almost tame.

Why This Recipe Works Because the ground beef patty for patty melts is traditionally cooked twice—browned once in butter and a second time while the sandwich is griddled—many recipes produce something resembling dried-out hockey pucks. To solve the problem, we incorporated a panade (a paste of bread and milk) into the meat. To bump up the flavor of our burgers, we used rye bread and onion powder in the panade. Covering the cooking onions with the patties trapped some of the steam and helped the onions to soften quicker. This also allowed the flavors of the meat to seep into the onions and vice versa.

Why This Recipe Works Miniature burgers known as sliders (popularized by the White Castle chain) satisfy a lot of cravings: tender burger, soft roll, gooey cheese, and sweet onions. Since the burgers are small, it's extra-important they're all the same size to prevent overcooking. To portion the patties correctly, we weighed the beef and pressed it with a clear pie plate. The trick to achieving classic slider flavor is to sprinkle finely chopped onion on the patties when they first hit the skillet and then press the onion into the meat. Finally, adding water and covering the skillet softened the buns, finished cooking the onion, and fully melted the cheese.

SLIDERS

MAKES 12 SLIDERS

Plan ahead: This recipe moves quickly, so be sure to have everything ready before you begin cooking. We recommend using Martin's Dinner Potato Rolls in this recipe.

Sauce

¼ cup mayonnaise
2 tablespoons ketchup
1 teaspoon sweet pickle relish
1 teaspoon sugar
1 teaspoon distilled white vinegar
1 teaspoon pepper

Sliders

1½ pounds 85 percent lean ground beef
12 (2½-inch) slider buns or soft dinner rolls, halved horizontally
6 slices deli American cheese (6 ounces)
1½ teaspoons kosher salt
1 teaspoon pepper
2 teaspoons vegetable oil
½ cup finely chopped onion
¼ cup water

1. For the Sauce Whisk all ingredients together in bowl; refrigerate until ready to use.

2. For the Sliders Cut sides of 1-quart zipper-lock bag, leaving bottom seam intact. Divide beef into twelve 2-ounce portions, then roll into balls. Working with 1 ball at a time, enclose in split bag. Using clear pie plate (so you can see size of patty), press ball into even 4-inch-diameter patty. Remove patty from bag and place on baking sheet. Cover sheet with plastic wrap and refrigerate until ready to cook. (Patties can be shaped up to 24 hours in advance.)

3. Divide sauce evenly among bun bottoms. Arrange bun bottoms, sauce side up, on platter; set aside. Stack American cheese and cut into quarters (you will have 24 pieces). Combine salt and pepper in bowl.

4. Sprinkle both sides of patties with salt-pepper mixture. Heat 1 teaspoon oil in 12-inch nonstick skillet over medium heat until just smoking. Using spatula, transfer 6 patties to skillet. Sprinkle ¼ cup onion evenly over tops of patties and press firmly into patties with back of spatula.

5. Cook patties, uncovered and without moving them, for 2 minutes. Flip patties and top each with 2 pieces American cheese; add bun tops. Add 2 tablespoons water to skillet (do not wet buns), cover, and continue to cook until cheese is melted, about 90 seconds longer.

6. Transfer sliders to prepared bun bottoms and tent with aluminum foil. Wipe skillet clean with paper towels. Repeat with remaining 1 teaspoon oil, 6 patties, ¼ cup onion, American cheese, bun tops, and 2 tablespoons water. Serve immediately.

Slider Assembly Line

With burgers this small, consistent cooking is dependent on consistent sizing. To that end, we weigh each portion of beef before pressing it under a pie plate to form a patty.

Why This Recipe Works This Oklahoma specialty features a thin patty of ground beef topped with a crispy crust of caramelized onions cooked on a griddle. Served on a buttery grilled bun with yellow mustard, dill pickles, and a slice of American cheese, this exceptional burger is well worth a road trip. To make them at home, we sliced and salted the onions, then squeezed out their excess moisture so they'd brown quickly and stick to the burgers. We mashed the onions into the burgers, then put the burgers on a buttered skillet onion side down to brown the onions. Then we flipped the burgers and turned up the heat to finish cooking and get a nice sear.

OKLAHOMA FRIED ONION BURGERS

SERVES 4

A mandoline makes quick work of slicing the onion thinly. Squeeze the salted onion slices until they're as dry as possible, or they won't adhere to the patties. These burgers are traditionally served with yellow mustard and slices of dill pickle.

  1 large onion, halved and sliced ⅛ inch thick
      Salt and pepper
12 ounces 85 percent lean ground beef
  1 tablespoon unsalted butter
  1 teaspoon vegetable oil
  4 slices American cheese (4 ounces)
  4 hamburger buns, buttered and toasted

1. Combine onion and 1 teaspoon salt in bowl and toss to combine. Transfer to colander and let sit for 30 minutes, tossing occasionally. Using tongs, transfer onion to clean dish towel, gather edges, and squeeze onion dry. Sprinkle with ½ teaspoon pepper.

2. Divide onion mixture into 4 separate mounds on rimmed baking sheet. Form beef into 4 lightly packed balls and season with salt and pepper. Place beef balls on top of onion mounds and flatten beef firmly so onion adheres and patties measure 4 inches in diameter.

3. Melt butter with oil in 12-inch nonstick skillet over medium heat. Using spatula, transfer patties to skillet, onion side down, and cook until onion is deep golden brown and beginning to crisp around edges, 6 to 8 minutes. Flip burgers, increase heat to high, and cook until well browned on second side, about 2 minutes. Place 1 slice cheese on each bottom bun. Place burgers on buns, add desired toppings, and serve.

Keys to Fried Onion Burgers
A few tricks helped the onions adhere to the burgers and caramelize rather than burn.

1. After salting and squeezing onions dry, divide into four piles, place beef balls on top, and press.

2. Brown onion side over medium heat, then flip burgers and turn up heat to sear beef side.

Why This Recipe Works Atlanta brisket is a Southern braise featuring onion soup mix, ketchup, and Atlanta's own Coca-Cola. We wanted to keep the regional charm but update the convenience-product flavor. To season the brisket, we pierced it with a fork, salted it, and let it sit overnight. For a great crust, we seared the brisket weighed down with a heavy pot. Finally, for the characteristic braising liquid, we mixed cola and ketchup and replaced the artificial-tasting soup mix with our own blend of sautéed onions, onion and garlic powders, brown sugar, and dried thyme. The mixture both flavored the meat and became a sweet, tangy sauce for serving.

ATLANTA BRISKET

SERVES 6

Parchment paper provides a nonreactive barrier between the cola-based braising liquid and the aluminum foil. A whole brisket is comprised of two smaller roasts: the flat cut and the point cut. For this recipe, we prefer the flat cut, which is rectangular in shape and leaner than the knobby, well-marbled point cut. The flat cut is topped with a thick fat cap; make sure that the fat cap isn't overtrimmed.

1 (3½-pound) beef brisket, flat cut, fat trimmed to ¼ inch thick
   Salt and pepper
4 teaspoons vegetable oil
1 pound onions, halved and sliced ½ inch thick
2 cups cola
1½ cups ketchup
4 teaspoons onion powder
2 teaspoons packed dark brown sugar
1 teaspoon garlic powder
1 teaspoon dried thyme

1. Using fork, poke holes all over brisket. Rub entire surface of brisket with 1 tablespoon salt. Wrap brisket in plastic wrap and refrigerate for at least 6 or up to 24 hours.

2. Adjust oven rack to lower-middle position and heat oven to 325 degrees. Pat brisket dry with paper towels and season with pepper. Heat 2 teaspoons oil in 12-inch nonstick skillet over medium-high heat until just smoking. Place brisket fat side down in skillet; weigh down brisket with heavy Dutch oven or cast-iron skillet and cook until well browned on bottom, about 4 minutes. Remove pot, flip brisket, and replace pot on top of brisket. Cook on second side until well browned, about 4 minutes longer. Transfer brisket to plate.

3. Heat remaining 2 teaspoons oil in now-empty skillet over medium heat until shimmering. Add onions and cook, stirring occasionally, until soft and golden brown, 10 to 12 minutes. Transfer onions to 13 by 9-inch baking dish and spread out in even layer.

4. Combine cola, ketchup, onion powder, sugar, garlic powder, thyme, 1 teaspoon salt, and 1 teaspoon pepper in bowl. Place brisket fat side up on top of onions and pour cola mixture over brisket. Place parchment paper over brisket and cover dish tightly with aluminum foil. Bake until tender and fork slips easily in and out of meat, 3½ to 4 hours. Let brisket rest in liquid, uncovered, for 30 minutes.

5. Transfer brisket to carving board. Skim any fat from top of sauce with large spoon. Slice brisket against grain into ¼-inch-thick slices and return to baking dish. Serve brisket with sauce.

To Make Ahead Follow recipe through step 4. Allow brisket to cool in sauce, cover, and refrigerate overnight or up to 24 hours. To serve, slice brisket, return to sauce, and cover with parchment paper. Cover baking dish with aluminum foil and cook in 350-degree oven until heated through, about 1 hour.

Getting a Great Sear

Brisket is a flat cut of meat that curls up when you try to sear it. We fixed this problem by weighing down the brisket with a heavy Dutch oven (wrapped in foil to make cleanup easier) to ensure a more even sear.

SLOW-COOKER BBQ BEEF BRISKET

SERVES 8 TO 10

Scoring the fat on the brisket at ½-inch intervals will allow the rub to penetrate the meat. Two disposable aluminum loaf pans stacked inside one another can be substituted for the metal loaf pan.

Spice Rub and Brisket

½ cup packed dark brown sugar
2 tablespoons minced canned chipotle chile in adobo sauce
1 tablespoon ground cumin
1 tablespoon paprika
2 teaspoons pepper
1 teaspoon salt
1 (4- to 5-pound) brisket roast, fat trimmed to ¼ inch thick and scored lightly

Aromatics and Sauce

3 tablespoons vegetable oil
1 onion, chopped fine
2 tablespoons tomato paste
1 tablespoon chili powder
1 tablespoon minced canned chipotle chile in adobo sauce
2 garlic cloves, minced
½ cup water, plus extra as needed
¼ cup ketchup
1 tablespoon cider vinegar
¼ teaspoon liquid smoke
Salt and pepper

1. For the Spice Rub and Brisket Combine sugar, chipotle, cumin, paprika, pepper, and salt in bowl. Rub sugar mixture all over brisket. Cover with plastic wrap and let sit at room temperature for 1 hour or refrigerate for up to 24 hours.

2. For the Aromatics and Sauce Heat oil in 12-inch skillet over medium-high heat until shimmering. Cook onion until softened, about 5 minutes. Add tomato paste and cook until beginning to brown, about 1 minute. Stir in chili powder, chipotle, and garlic and cook until fragrant, about 30 seconds. Mound onion mixture in center of slow cooker, arrange inverted metal loaf pan over onion mixture, and place brisket fat side up on top of loaf pan. Add water

to slow cooker, cover, and cook on high until fork inserted in brisket can be removed with no resistance, 7 to 8 hours (or cook on low for 10 to 12 hours).

3. Transfer brisket to 13 by 9-inch baking dish, cover with aluminum foil, and let rest for 30 minutes. Carefully remove loaf pan from slow cooker. Pour onion mixture and accumulated juices into large bowl and skim fat. (You should have about 2 cups defatted juices; if you have less, supplement with water.)

4. Transfer brisket to carving board, slice thin against grain, and return to baking dish. Pour 1 cup reserved defatted juices over sliced brisket. Whisk ketchup, vinegar, and liquid smoke into remaining juices. Season with salt and pepper to taste. Serve, passing sauce at table.

To Make Ahead In step 3, wrap brisket tightly in foil and refrigerate for up to 3 days. (Refrigerate juices separately.) To serve, transfer foil-wrapped brisket to baking dish and heat in 350-degree oven until brisket is heated through, about 1 hour. Reheat juices in microwave or saucepan set over medium heat. Continue with recipe as directed.

Preventing Waterlogged Brisket

To minimize the moisture absorbed by the brisket, we place the meat on top of a loaf pan. The juices exuded by the meat are drawn under the pan by a vacuum effect, creating less moisture directly below the meat.

1. Pile onion mixture under inverted loaf pan and place brisket on top.

2. After cooking, release juices from loaf pan and reserve for use in barbecue sauce.

Why This Recipe Works Barbecued brisket in the slow cooker? You bet. To minimize the moisture absorbed by the brisket (which traditionally isn't cooked directly in liquid), we came up with an unorthodox solution: elevating the meat off the bottom of the slow cooker with an inverted loaf pan. The liquid exuded from the meat during cooking was drawn under the loaf pan by a vacuum effect, which meant that the slow cooker more closely mimicked the dry heat of real barbecue. To bump up the flavor of this liquid, we added sautéed onion, garlic, tomato paste, and chipotle chiles.

Why This Recipe Works We wanted a foolproof recipe for this Southern specialty. We started by making a whiskey-flavored marinade, then steeped the chops in it for at least 1 hour prior to cooking. We cooked the chops in a hot skillet and then used the same pan to prepare the glaze—browned bits left behind by the chops in the pan added deep, meaty flavor. Allowing the cooked chops to sit in the pan in the glaze for a few minutes before serving helped ensure that it clung to the meat.

TENNESSEE WHISKEY PORK CHOPS

SERVES 4

Bourbon tastes fine, but we think it's worth purchasing the real deal—Jack Daniel's Tennessee Whiskey—for this recipe. Watch the glaze closely during the last few minutes of cooking—the bubbles become very small as it approaches the right consistency.

½ cup Jack Daniel's Tennessee Whiskey or bourbon

½ cup apple cider

2 tablespoons packed light brown sugar

4 teaspoons cider vinegar

1 tablespoon Dijon mustard

½ teaspoon vanilla extract

⅛ teaspoon cayenne pepper

4 (8- to 10-ounce) bone-in, center-cut pork chops, about 1 inch thick, trimmed

2 teaspoons vegetable oil
Salt and pepper

1 tablespoon unsalted butter

1. Whisk whiskey, cider, sugar, 2 teaspoons vinegar, mustard, vanilla, and cayenne together in bowl. Transfer ¼ cup whiskey mixture to 1-gallon zipper-lock bag, add pork chops, press air out of bag, and seal. Turn bag to coat chops with marinade and refrigerate 1 to 2 hours. Reserve remaining whiskey mixture separately.

2. Remove chops from bag, pat dry with paper towels, and discard marinade. Heat oil in 12-inch skillet over medium-high heat until just beginning to smoke. Season chops with salt and pepper and cook until well browned on both sides and a peek into thickest part of a chop using paring knife yields still-pink meat ¼ inch from surface, 6 to 8 minutes, flipping chops halfway through cooking. Transfer chops to plate and cover tightly with aluminum foil.

3. Add reserved whiskey mixture to skillet and bring to boil, scraping up any browned bits with wooden spoon. Cook until reduced to thick glaze, 3 to 5 minutes. Reduce heat to medium-low and, holding on to chops, tip plate to add any accumulated juices back to skillet. Add remaining 2 teaspoons vinegar, whisk in butter, and simmer glaze until thick and sticky, 2 to 3 minutes. Remove pan from heat.

4. Return chops to skillet and let rest in pan, turning chops occasionally to coat both sides, until sauce clings to chops and meat registers 145 degrees, about 5 minutes. Transfer chops to platter and spoon sauce over. Serve.

Break Out the Good Stuff

Bourbon was fine, but we loved the deep, caramel-flavored glaze we got when using Jack Daniel's in this recipe. Nathan "Nearest" Green, the first known African American master distiller and Jack's right hand, gave birth to Tennessee whiskey. Tennessee whiskey differs from Kentucky bourbon because of Nearest's technique called the Lincoln County process, in which the distilled whiskey is filtered over hard maple charcoal. Then, like bourbon, it is aged in charred oak barrels, where it picks up its distinctive caramel color and smoky flavor.

MEMPHIS-STYLE WET RIBS FOR A CROWD

SERVES 8 TO 12

Spice Rub
¼ cup paprika
2 tablespoons packed brown sugar
2 tablespoons salt
2 teaspoons pepper
2 teaspoons onion powder
2 teaspoons granulated garlic

Barbecue Sauce and Mop
1½ cups ketchup
1¼ cups apple juice
¼ cup molasses
½ cup cider vinegar
¼ cup Worcestershire sauce
3 tablespoons yellow mustard
2 teaspoons pepper

Ribs
4 (2½- to 3-pound) racks St. Louis–style spareribs, trimmed, membrane removed
2 cups wood chips, soaked in water for 15 minutes and drained
1 (13 by 9-inch) disposable aluminum roasting pan (if using charcoal) or 1 (8½ by 6-inch) disposable aluminum pan (if using gas)

1. For the Spice Rub Combine all ingredients in bowl.

2. For the Barbecue Sauce and Mop Combine ketchup, ¾ cup apple juice, molasses, ¼ cup vinegar, Worcestershire, 2 tablespoons mustard, and 2 tablespoons spice rub in medium saucepan and bring to boil over medium heat. Reduce heat to medium-low and simmer until thickened and reduced to 2 cups, about 20 minutes. Off heat, stir in pepper; set barbecue sauce aside. For the mop, whisk ½ cup apple juice, ¼ cup vinegar, 1 tablespoon mustard, and ¼ cup barbecue sauce together in bowl.

3. For the Ribs Pat ribs dry with paper towels and season with remaining spice rub. Place 1 rack of ribs, meaty side down, on cutting board. Place second rack of ribs, meaty side up, directly on top of first rack, arranging thick end over tapered end. Tie racks together at 2-inch intervals with kitchen twine. Repeat with remaining 2 racks of ribs for two bundles. Using large piece of heavy-duty aluminum foil, wrap soaked chips in foil packet and cut several vent holes in top.

4A. For a Charcoal Grill Open bottom vent halfway and place disposable roasting pan on 1 side of grill. Fill pan with 2 quarts water. Arrange 3 quarts unlit charcoal briquettes on other side of grill. Light large chimney starter half filled with charcoal briquettes (3 quarts). When top coals are partially covered with ash, pour evenly over unlit coals. Place wood chip packet on coals. Set cooking grate in place, cover, and open lid vent halfway. Heat grill until hot and wood chips are smoking, about 5 minutes.

4B. For a Gas Grill Place wood chip packet and disposable pan over primary burner and fill pan with 2 cups water. Turn primary burner to high (leave other burners off), cover, and heat grill until hot and wood chips are smoking, about 15 minutes. (Adjust primary burner as needed to maintain grill temperature of 275 to 300 degrees.)

5. Clean and oil cooking grate. Place ribs on cooler side of grill and baste with one-third of mop. Cover (positioning lid vent over ribs for charcoal) and cook for 2 hours, flipping and switching positions of ribs and basting again with half of remaining mop halfway through cooking.

6. Adjust oven racks to upper-middle and lower-middle positions and heat oven to 300 degrees. Line 2 rimmed baking sheets with foil. Cut kitchen twine from racks. Transfer 2 racks, meaty side up, to each sheet. Baste with remaining mop and bake for 2 hours, switching and rotating sheets halfway through baking.

7. Remove ribs from oven and brush evenly with ½ cup barbecue sauce. Return to oven and continue to bake until tender, basting with ½ cup barbecue sauce and switching and rotating sheets twice during baking, about 45 minutes. (Ribs do not need to be flipped and should remain meaty side up during baking.) Transfer ribs to carving board. Brush evenly with remaining ½ cup barbecue sauce, tent loosely with foil, and let rest for 20 minutes. Cut ribs in between bones to separate. Serve.

Why This Recipe Works For these saucy Memphis wet ribs, a potent spice rub performs double duty, seasoning the meat and creating the backbone for our barbecue sauce. Tying two racks together allowed us to double our yield and cook four hefty racks of ribs at once. To keep the ribs moist, we grilled them over indirect heat and basted them with a traditional "mop" of juice and vinegar. After a few hours of smoking on the grill, we brushed the ribs with our flavorful barbecue sauce and transferred them to the steady, even heat of the oven to finish tenderizing.

SLOW-COOKER MEMPHIS-STYLE WET RIBS

SERVES 4 TO 6

Try to find ribs of equal shape to ensure even cooking. These ribs should be tender but not falling off the bone.

Ribs

2 tablespoons paprika
1 tablespoon packed brown sugar
1 tablespoon kosher salt
2 teaspoons pepper
2 teaspoons onion powder
2 teaspoons granulated garlic
2 (2½- to 3-pound) racks St. Louis–style spareribs, trimmed and each rack cut in half

Barbecue Sauce

¾ cup ketchup
6 tablespoons apple juice
2 tablespoons molasses
2 tablespoons cider vinegar
2 tablespoons Worcestershire sauce
1 tablespoon yellow mustard
1 teaspoon pepper
¼ teaspoon liquid smoke

1. For the Ribs Combine paprika, sugar, salt, pepper, onion powder, and granulated garlic in bowl. Reserve 1 tablespoon spice rub for sauce. Pat ribs dry with paper towels and coat all over with remaining 5 tablespoons rub.

2. Arrange ribs vertically with thick ends pointing down and meaty side against interior wall of slow cooker (ribs will overlap). Cover and cook until ribs are just tender, 5 to 6 hours on high or 6 to 7 hours on low.

3. For the Barbecue Sauce Meanwhile, whisk ketchup, apple juice, molasses, vinegar, Worcestershire, mustard, pepper, liquid smoke, and reserved 1 tablespoon spice rub together in medium saucepan. Bring to boil over medium heat, then reduce heat to medium-low and simmer, stirring occasionally, until thickened and reduced to 1 cup, about 10 minutes. (Sauce can be refrigerated for up to 3 days.)

4. Line rimmed baking sheet with aluminum foil and set wire rack in sheet. Using tongs, transfer ribs, meaty side up, to prepared rack. Let ribs sit for 10 minutes to allow surface to dry out.

5. Adjust oven rack 3 inches from broiler element and heat broiler. Liberally brush ribs with ½ cup sauce and broil until sauce is bubbling and beginning to char, about 4 minutes. Remove ribs from oven, brush with remaining ½ cup sauce, tent with foil, and let rest for 20 minutes. Cut ribs in between bones to separate. Serve.

How Hot Is Your Broiler?

It's good to know if your broiler runs relatively hot, average, or cold. This information allows you to adjust the cooking time for this recipe (and others) accordingly. To see how your broiler stacks up, heat it on high and place a slice of white sandwich bread directly under the heating element on the upper-middle rack. If the bread toasts to golden brown in 30 seconds or less, your broiler runs very hot, and you will need to reduce the cooking time by a minute or two. If the bread toasts perfectly in 1 minute, your broiler runs about average. If the bread takes 2 minutes or longer to toast, your broiler runs cool and you may need to increase the cooking time by a minute or two.

Why This Recipe Works To serve up saucy Memphis wet ribs without ever leaving the kitchen, we turned to our slow cooker. After applying a zesty spice rub, we arranged two racks of St. Louis–style ribs in the slow cooker. The ribs cooked low and slow in their own flavorful juices, no other liquid required. Hours later, the ribs were tender and perfectly cooked. We created a thick glazy sauce and brushed it over our deeply seasoned ribs before sliding them under the broiler to create truly "wet" barbecue ribs indoors.

Why This Recipe Works In the Midwest, pork is king. Also known as "the Hog Belt," it produces most of the pork we eat in this country. But Iowa stands out for its production and its preparation with the "skinny"—a crunchy fried pork tenderloin sandwich pounded comically thin and oversized, then breaded, fried, and served on a hamburger bun. A mixture of flour, egg, bread crumbs, and saltine crumbs created a crunchy, golden-brown coating: mayonnaise on the bun contributed richness and sweet tang that enhanced the pork flavor without weighing down the crust. Lettuce and sliced tomatoes added a fresh contrast to the hot, crispy cutlet.

IOWA SKINNY

SERVES 4

1 pork tenderloin (about 1 pound), prepared
   according to photos (below)
   Salt and pepper
½ cup all-purpose flour
2 large eggs
¼ cup mayonnaise, plus extra for serving
3 slices hearty white sandwich bread, torn
   into rough pieces
16 saltines
1 cup vegetable oil
4 soft hamburger buns
¼ head iceberg lettuce, shredded
1 medium tomato, sliced

1. Adjust oven rack to middle position and heat oven to 200 degrees. Pat pork cutlets dry with paper towels and season with salt and pepper.

2. Place flour in shallow dish. Beat eggs and ¼ cup mayonnaise in second shallow dish. Combine bread and saltines in food processor and pulse to fine crumbs; transfer to third shallow dish.

3. Coat cutlets in flour, shaking off excess. Dip both sides of cutlets in egg mixture, then dredge in crumbs, pressing on crumbs to adhere. Place cutlets on wire rack set over baking sheet and let dry 5 minutes (or refrigerate up to 1 hour).

4. Heat ½ cup oil in large nonstick skillet over medium heat until shimmering. Lay 2 cutlets in skillet and fry until crisp and deep golden, about 2 minutes per side. Transfer to large paper towel–lined plate and place in warm oven. Discard oil, wipe out skillet, and repeat with remaining oil and cutlets. Place 1 cutlet on each bun and top with lettuce, tomato, and mayonnaise. Serve.

How to Make Pork Cutlets

1. Use a paring knife to remove any silverskin or extraneous fat from the tenderloin.

2. Cut the tenderloin into 4 equal pieces.

3. Arrange pieces of tenderloin cut side up on cutting board. Cover with plastic wrap and pound into 1/4-inch-thick cutlets.

Why This Recipe Works Baltimore is known for its pit beef, replete with a well-seasoned, charred crust and a rosy pink interior. The meat is shaved paper thin, piled onto a kaiser roll, topped with a horseradish-y mayo known as tiger sauce, and finally covered with sliced onions. We started by cutting a beefy top sirloin roast in half and slow-cooked the meat on the cool side of the grill—a foil shield provided maximum protection so the meat didn't dry out. Then for maximum char, we generously seared both pieces all over.

BALTIMORE PIT BEEF

SERVES 10

When shopping for the prepared horseradish, buy the brined (not creamy) variety and, if necessary, drain it.

Tiger Sauce

- ½ cup mayonnaise
- ½ cup hot prepared horseradish
- 1 teaspoon lemon juice
- 1 garlic clove, minced
  - Salt and pepper

Pit Beef

- 4 teaspoons kosher salt
- 1 tablespoon paprika
- 1 tablespoon pepper
- 1 teaspoon garlic powder
- 1 teaspoon dried oregano
- ¼ teaspoon cayenne pepper
- 1 (4- to 5-pound) boneless top sirloin roast, trimmed and halved crosswise
- 10 kaiser rolls
- 1 onion, sliced thin

1. For the Tiger Sauce Whisk mayonnaise, horseradish, lemon juice, and garlic together in bowl. Season with salt and pepper to taste. (Sauce can be refrigerated for up to 2 days.)

2. For the Pit Beef Combine salt, paprika, pepper, garlic powder, oregano, and cayenne in bowl. Pat roasts dry with paper towels and rub with 2 tablespoons seasoning mixture. Wrap meat tightly with plastic wrap and refrigerate for 6 to 24 hours.

3A. For a Charcoal Grill Open bottom vent halfway. Light large chimney starter filled with charcoal briquettes (6 quarts). When top coals are partially covered with ash, pour evenly over half of grill. Set cooking grate in place, cover, and open lid vent halfway. Heat grill until hot, about 5 minutes.

3B. For a Gas Grill Turn all burners to high, cover, and heat grill until hot, about 15 minutes. Leave primary burner on high and turn other burner(s) off.

4. Clean and oil cooking grate. Unwrap roasts and place end to end on long side of 18 by 12-inch sheet of aluminum foil. Loosely fold opposite long side of foil around top of roasts. Place meat on cool part of grill with foil-covered side closest to heat source. Cover (positioning lid vent over meat if using charcoal) and cook until meat registers 100 degrees, 45 minutes to 1 hour.

5. Transfer roasts to plate and discard foil. Turn all burners to high if using gas. If using charcoal, carefully remove cooking grate and light large chimney starter three-quarters filled with charcoal briquettes (4½ quarts). When top coals are partially covered with ash, pour evenly over spent coals. Set cooking grate in place and cover. Heat grill until hot, about 5 minutes.

6. Pat roasts dry with paper towels and rub with remaining spice mixture. Place meat on hot part of grill. Cook (covered if using gas), turning occasionally, until charred on all sides and meat registers 120 to 125 degrees (for medium-rare), 10 to 20 minutes. Transfer meat to carving board, tent loosely with foil, and let rest for 15 minutes. Slice meat thin against grain. Transfer sliced beef to rolls, top with onion slices, and drizzle with sauce. Serve.

Preventing Pit Beef from Drying Out

Even with indirect heat, the sides of the roasts closest to the fire can overcook. A simple foil shield protects them.

Why This Recipe Works Warm spices and unexpected garnishes lend Cincinnati chili recipes their unique flavors—but can sometimes muddle the dish. To re-create this Midwestern recipe in our own kitchen, we narrowed our ingredient list to four spices. Tomato paste added richness to our chili, while dark brown sugar gave it a sweet tang. Boiling the beef in water kept it tender during cooking—we cooked ours directly in our spices and liquid to infuse the meat with their intense flavor. Serving our chili over spaghetti, plus cheese, onions, red beans, and oyster crackers, gave us the true Cincinnati chili experience.

CINCINNATI CHILI

SERVES 6 TO 8

Use canned tomato sauce for this recipe—do not use jarred spaghetti sauce.

- 1 tablespoon vegetable oil
- 2 onions, chopped fine
- 2 tablespoons tomato paste
- 2 tablespoons chili powder
- 1 tablespoon dried oregano
- 1½ teaspoons ground cinnamon
- 1 garlic clove, minced
   Salt and pepper
- ¼ teaspoon ground allspice
- 2 cups chicken broth
- 2 cups canned tomato sauce
- 2 tablespoons cider vinegar
- 2 teaspoons packed dark brown sugar
- 1½ pounds 85 percent lean ground beef

1. Heat oil in Dutch oven over medium-high heat until shimmering. Cook onions until soft and browned around edges, about 8 minutes. Add tomato paste, chili powder, oregano, cinnamon, garlic, 1 teaspoon salt, ¾ teaspoon pepper, and allspice and cook until fragrant, about 1 minute. Stir in chicken broth, tomato sauce, vinegar, and sugar.

2. Add beef and stir to break up meat. Bring to boil, reduce heat to medium-low, and simmer until chili is deep brown and slightly thickened, 15 to 20 minutes. Season with salt to taste and serve. (Chili can be refrigerated for up to 3 days or frozen for up to 2 months.)

Five Ways to Cincinnati

Those in the know can order their chili without a second thought, but for the uninitiated, here's a quick guide to the five ways of Cincinnati chili. The chili is almost never served on its own (one-way). Just don't forget the oyster crackers!

TWO-WAY CHILI
Served over spaghetti

THREE-WAY CHILI
Served over spaghetti
and topped with cheese

FOUR-WAY CHILI
Served over spaghetti and
topped with onions and cheese

FIVE-WAY CHILI
Served over spaghetti and topped
with onions, red beans, and cheese

COLORADO GREEN CHILI

SERVES 6

The chiles can be roasted and refrigerated up to 24 hours in advance.

3 pounds boneless pork butt roast, trimmed and cut into 1-inch pieces
  Salt
2 pounds (10 to 12) Anaheim chiles, stemmed, halved lengthwise, and seeded
3 jalapeño chiles
1 (14.5-ounce) can diced tomatoes
1 tablespoon vegetable oil
2 onions, chopped fine
8 garlic cloves, minced
1 tablespoon ground cumin
¼ cup all-purpose flour
4 cups chicken broth
  Cayenne pepper
  Lime wedges

1. Combine pork, ½ cup water, and ½ teaspoon salt in Dutch oven over medium heat. Cover and cook for 20 minutes, stirring occasionally. Uncover, increase heat to medium-high, and continue to cook, stirring frequently, until liquid evaporates and pork browns in its own fat, 15 to 20 minutes. Transfer pork to bowl and set aside.

2. Meanwhile, adjust 1 oven rack to lowest position and second rack 6 inches from broiler element. Heat broiler. Line rimmed baking sheet with aluminum foil and spray with vegetable oil spray. Arrange Anaheims, skin side up, and jalapeños in single layer on prepared sheet. Place sheet on upper rack and broil until chiles are mostly blackened and soft, 15 to 20 minutes, rotating sheet and flipping only jalapeños halfway through broiling. Place Anaheims in large bowl and cover with plastic wrap; let cool for 5 minutes. Set aside jalapeños. Heat oven to 325 degrees.

3. Remove skins from Anaheims. Chop half of Anaheims into ½-inch pieces and transfer to bowl. Process remaining Anaheims in food processor until smooth, about 10 seconds; transfer to bowl with chopped Anaheims. Pulse tomatoes and their juice in now-empty food processor until coarsely ground, about 4 pulses.

4. Heat oil in now-empty Dutch oven over medium heat until shimmering. Add onions and cook until lightly browned, 5 to 7 minutes. Stir in garlic and cumin and cook until fragrant, about 30 seconds. Stir in flour and cook for 1 minute. Stir in broth, Anaheims, tomatoes, and pork with any accumulated juices and bring to simmer, scraping up any browned bits. Cover pot, transfer to lower oven rack, and cook until pork is tender, 1 to 1¼ hours.

5. Without peeling, stem and seed jalapeños and reserve seeds. Finely chop jalapeños and stir into chili. Season chili with salt, cayenne, and reserved jalapeño seeds to taste. Serve with lime wedges.

Easier Roasted Chiles

Roasting chiles whole and then seeding them— the usual procedure—makes a mess: The wet seeds stick to everything. We halve and seed the raw Anaheims. It's neater and lets us skip the usual flipping step. We leave the jalapeños whole; they soften but don't deeply roast.

READY FOR ROASTING
Arrange the chiles head to foot for the best fit.

Why This Recipe Works This popular Southwestern dish boasts rich bites of pork in a sauce dominated by green chiles. For our version, we used a combination of Anaheim and jalapeño peppers. To achieve the cohesive flavor and mild vegetal taste that we liked, we used canned, diced tomatoes and more than 2 pounds of chiles, along with 3 pounds of boneless pork butt—our preferred cut for its rich meatiness. To reduce the hands-on time, we started the pork with water in a covered pan to render the fat, then let the even heat of the oven cook the chili. Adding the jalapeños just before serving gave a fresh hit of heat.

Why This Recipe Works Similar to Latin American empanadas, these deep-fried hand pies from Louisiana are filled with savory ground meat and spices. For the filling, we used equal parts ground beef and pork along with the classic Creole combination of onions, green bell peppers, and a pinch of cayenne for heat. Chicken broth and flour made the filling cohesive. Using chicken broth rather than milk in the dough gave the crust a subtle savory flavor. After a few minutes in hot oil, they emerged with a crisp, flaky crust and piping-hot filling.

NATCHITOCHES MEAT PIES

MAKES 16 PIES

You can make the dough and the filling up to 24 hours ahead and refrigerate them separately. You can also shape and fill the pies, refrigerating them for up to 24 hours before frying. Use a Dutch oven that holds 6 quarts or more for this recipe.

Filling

- 5 teaspoons vegetable oil
- ¾ pound 85 percent lean ground beef
- ¾ pound ground pork
  Salt and pepper
- 1 onion, chopped fine
- 1 green bell pepper, stemmed, seeded, and minced
- 6 scallions, white parts minced, green parts sliced thin
- 3 garlic cloves, minced
- ¼ teaspoon cayenne pepper
- 2 tablespoons all-purpose flour
- 1 cup chicken broth

Dough

- 4 cups (20 ounces) all-purpose flour
- 2 teaspoons salt
- 1 teaspoon baking powder
- 8 tablespoons vegetable shortening, cut into ½-inch pieces
- 1 cup chicken broth
- 2 large eggs, lightly beaten
- 1 quart vegetable oil for frying

1. For the Filling Heat 2 teaspoons oil in 12-inch skillet over medium-high heat until just smoking. Add beef, pork, 1 teaspoon salt, and ½ teaspoon pepper and cook, breaking up pieces with spoon, until no longer pink, 8 to 10 minutes. Transfer meat to bowl.

2. Add remaining 1 tablespoon oil to now-empty skillet and heat over medium-high heat until shimmering. Add onion, bell pepper, scallion whites, ½ teaspoon salt, and ½ teaspoon pepper and cook until vegetables are just starting to brown, 3 to 5 minutes. Stir in garlic and cayenne and cook until fragrant, about 30 seconds.

3. Return meat and any accumulated juices to skillet with vegetables. Sprinkle flour over meat and cook, stirring constantly, until evenly coated, about 1 minute. Add broth, bring to boil, and cook until slightly thickened, about 3 minutes. Transfer filling to bowl and stir in scallion greens. Refrigerate until completely cool, about 1 hour. (Filling can be refrigerated for up to 24 hours.)

4. For the Dough Process flour, salt, and baking powder in food processor until combined, about 3 seconds. Add shortening and pulse until mixture resembles coarse cornmeal, 6 to 8 pulses. Add broth and eggs and pulse until dough just comes together, about 5 pulses. Transfer dough to lightly floured counter and knead until dough forms smooth ball, about 20 seconds. Divide dough into 16 equal pieces. (Dough can be covered and refrigerated for up to 24 hours.)

5. Line rimmed baking sheet with parchment paper. Working with 1 piece of dough at a time, roll into 6-inch circle on lightly floured counter. Place ¼ cup filling in center of dough round. Brush edges of dough with water and fold dough over filling. Press to seal, trim any ragged edges, and crimp edges with tines of fork. Transfer to prepared sheet. (Filled pies can be covered and refrigerated for up to 24 hours.)

6. Adjust oven rack to middle position and heat oven to 200 degrees. Set wire rack in second rimmed baking sheet. Add oil to large Dutch oven until it measures about ¾ inch deep and heat over medium-high heat to 350 degrees. Place 4 pies in oil and fry until golden brown, 3 to 5 minutes per side, using slotted spatula or spider to flip. Adjust burner, if necessary, to maintain oil temperature between 325 and 350 degrees. Transfer pies to prepared wire rack and place in oven to keep warm. Return oil to 350 degrees and repeat with remaining pies. Serve.

DELTA HOT TAMALES

SERVES 6 TO 8

Use a saucepan that holds 4 quarts or more, with at least 5-inch sides. Corn husks can be found in the international aisle of grocery stores.

24 corn husks
1½ tablespoons chili powder
 1 tablespoon paprika
 1 tablespoon salt
 2 teaspoons ground cumin
 2 teaspoons sugar
 ¾ teaspoon pepper
 ¾ teaspoon cayenne pepper
2½ cups (12½ ounces) yellow cornmeal
 1 tablespoon baking powder
12 tablespoons unsalted butter, cut into 12 pieces
 ½ teaspoon baking soda
 1 pound 85 percent lean ground beef
 2 garlic cloves, minced
 2 tablespoons cornstarch combined with 2 tablespoons cold water

1. Place husks in large bowl and cover with hot water; soak until pliable, about 30 minutes. Combine chili powder, paprika, salt, cumin, sugar, pepper, and cayenne in bowl.

2. Pulse cornmeal and baking powder in food processor until combined, about 3 pulses. Add butter and 1½ tablespoons spice mixture and pulse to chop butter into small pieces, about 8 pulses. Add 1¼ cups water and process until dough forms, about 30 seconds. Reserve ½ cup cornmeal mixture. Divide remaining cornmeal mixture into 24 equal portions, about 1½ tablespoons each, and place on plate.

3. Dissolve baking soda in 2 tablespoons water in large bowl. Add beef, garlic, reserved ½ cup cornmeal mixture, and 1½ tablespoons spice mixture and knead with your hands until thoroughly combined. Divide meat mixture into 24 equal portions, about 1½ tablespoons each, and place on plate.

4. Remove husks from water and pat dry with dish towel. Working with 1 husk at a time, lay husk on counter, smooth side up, with long side parallel to counter edge and wide end oriented toward right. Using small offset spatula, spread 1 portion of cornmeal mixture in 3½-inch square over lower right corner of husk, flush to bottom edge but leaving ¼-inch border on right edge.

5. Place 1 portion of meat mixture in log across center of cornmeal (end to end), parallel to long side of husk. Roll husk away from you and over meat mixture so cornmeal mixture surrounds meat and forms cylinder; continue rolling to complete tamale. Fold tapered end (left side) of tamale up leaving top open. Using scissors, trim tapered end of tamale to align with filled end (if tapered end hangs over). Set tamales aside seam side down.

6. Stack tamales on their sides in groups of 6 and tie into bundles with kitchen twine. Add remaining 2 tablespoons spice mixture to large saucepan. Stand tamales, open ends up, in pot (walls of pot should clear tops of tamales). Add about 5½ cups water to pot to come within 1 inch of tops of tamales, being careful not to pour water into tamales.

7. Bring tamales to boil. Cover, reduce heat to low to maintain gentle simmer, and cook until tamales are firm and beginning to pull away from husks, about 30 minutes. Using tongs and slotted spoon, carefully transfer tamales to serving platter and remove twine.

8. Return liquid to simmer over medium heat. Whisk in cornstarch slurry and cook until slightly thickened, about 1 minute. Serve sauce with tamales.

Cooking with Corn Husks

Cooking the tamales in corn husks—which are available in most supermarkets near the dried chiles—adds a subtle depth of flavor. Working with the husks is actually quite easy, as they become pliable when soaked in hot water.

Why This Recipe Works Hot tamales—rich, spicy meat wrapped in flavorful corn dough—are a favorite in the Mississippi Delta. A bit of this cornmeal mixture stirred into the uncooked ground beef kept the filling moist, and baking soda was the trick for a more tender bite. We used butter instead of the traditional lard with coarsely ground cornmeal for a more balanced taste. We cooked the tamales in groups of six for more stability in the pot and made a spicy, glazy sauce with the seasoned stewing liquid and a cornstarch slurry. This was as close as we could come to being in the Delta without a plane ticket.

ST. LOUIS–STYLE PIZZA

MAKES TWO 12-INCH PIZZAS

If you can find Provel cheese, use 10 ounces in place of the American cheese, Monterey Jack cheese, and liquid smoke.

Sauce and Cheeses
1 (8-ounce) can tomato sauce
3 tablespoons tomato paste
2 tablespoons chopped fresh basil
1 tablespoon sugar
2 teaspoons dried oregano
8 ounces white American cheese, shredded (2 cups)
2 ounces Monterey Jack cheese, shredded (½ cup)
3 drops liquid smoke

Dough
2 cups (10 ounces) all-purpose flour
2 tablespoons cornstarch
2 teaspoons sugar
1 teaspoon baking powder
1 teaspoon salt
½ cup plus 2 tablespoons water
2 tablespoons olive oil

1. For the Sauce and Cheeses Whisk together tomato sauce, tomato paste, basil, sugar, and oregano in small bowl; set aside. Toss cheeses with liquid smoke in medium bowl; set aside.

2. For the Dough Combine flour, cornstarch, sugar, baking powder, and salt in large bowl. Combine water and olive oil in liquid measuring cup. Stir water mixture into flour mixture until dough starts to come together. Turn dough onto lightly floured surface and knead 3 or 4 times, until cohesive.

3. Adjust oven rack to lower-middle position, place baking stone (or inverted baking sheet) on rack, and heat oven to 475 degrees. Divide dough into 2 equal pieces. Working with 1 piece of dough at a time, press into small circle and transfer to parchment paper dusted lightly with flour. Using rolling pin, roll and stretch dough to form 12-inch circle, rotating parchment as needed. Lift parchment and pizza off work surface onto inverted baking sheet.

4. Top each piece of dough with half of sauce and half of cheese. Carefully pull parchment paper and pizza off baking sheet onto hot baking stone. Bake until underside is golden brown and cheese is completely melted, 9 to 12 minutes. Remove pizza and parchment from oven. Transfer pizza to wire rack and let cool briefly. Assemble and bake second pizza. Cut into 2-inch squares. Serve.

To Make Ahead The dough can be made in advance. At end of step 2, tightly wrap ball of dough in plastic wrap and refrigerate for up to 2 days.

Meet Me in St. Louis
You can make terrific pizza without yeast. It may sound crazy to most of us, but folks in St. Louis have been doing it for years. With its wafer-thin crust; thick, sweet tomato sauce; gooey Provel cheese (another local secret); and signature square slices, St. Louis–style pizza is unmistakable. Imo's, a popular local chain, is credited with creating it, and it's said that founder Ed Imo, a former tile-layer, subconsciously cut the circular pizza into tile-shaped squares (the "square beyond compare," as the jingle goes). The chain and its pizza have since crossed into Illinois and Kansas.

Why This Recipe Works St. Louis–style pizza is uniquely its own category with barely-there thin crust, sweet sauce, and melty Provel cheese. Adding cornstarch to the dough absorbed moisture and allowed the crust to crisp in a conventional oven. We doctored a simple pizza sauce by adding sugar, tomato paste, dried oregano, and fresh basil. The fresh herb wasn't typical, but it gave the pizza a flavorful lift. Smoky, melty Provel cheese was difficult to find outside the St. Louis area, so we crafted a respectable substitute with American cheese, Monterey Jack, and liquid smoke.

Why This Recipe Works Chicago thin-crust—sometimes called "tavern"—pizza is the slimmer, crunchier sibling of the city's famous deep-dish version, with a lightly sweet sauce and spotty-brown cheese reaching all the way to its charred edges. Since this pizza's success rests on its snappy crust (similar to St. Louis–style) we used a food processor to ensure the dough came together quickly, minimizing gluten development. After a 2- to 2½-hour rise, we rolled out the dough and slathered it with a no-cook tomato sauce, homemade Italian sausage, and shredded mozzarella, slid it onto a preheated baking stone, and baked it until the edges were crisp.

CHICAGO THIN-CRUST PIZZA

MAKES TWO 12-INCH PIZZAS

Using cold water keeps the dough from overheating in the food processor. A baking peel is the best tool for moving the pizza in and out of the oven, but you can also use a rimless baking sheet. You can swap the sweet Italian sausage for 12 ounces of homemade Easy Sweet Italian Sausage (page 163), crumbled.

Pizza

- 2½ cups (12½ ounces) all-purpose flour
- 2 teaspoons sugar
- 1½ teaspoons instant or rapid-rise yeast
- 1 teaspoon salt
- ¾ cup plus 2 tablespoons cold water
- 2 tablespoons extra-virgin olive oil
- Cornmeal
- 12 ounces sweet Italian sausage, casings removed
- 12 ounces whole-milk mozzarella cheese, shredded (3 cups)
- ½ teaspoon dried oregano

Sauce

- 1 (8-ounce) can tomato sauce
- 1 tablespoon tomato paste
- 2 teaspoons sugar
- ½ teaspoon Italian seasoning
- ½ teaspoon fennel seeds

1. For the Pizza Process flour, sugar, yeast, and salt in food processor until combined, about 3 seconds. With processor running, slowly add cold water and oil and process until dough forms sticky ball that clears sides of bowl, 30 to 60 seconds.

2. Transfer dough to lightly oiled counter and knead until smooth, about 1 minute. Shape dough into tight ball and place in greased bowl. Cover bowl with plastic wrap and let dough rise at room temperature until almost doubled in size, 2 to 2½ hours. One hour before baking, adjust oven rack to lowest position, set baking stone on rack, and heat oven to 500 degrees.

3. For the Sauce Whisk all ingredients together in bowl. (Sauce can be refrigerated for up to 2 days.)

4. Transfer dough to lightly floured counter, divide in half, and gently shape each half into ball. Return 1 dough ball to bowl and cover with plastic. Coat remaining dough ball lightly with flour and gently flatten into 8-inch disk using your fingertips. Using rolling pin, roll dough into 12-inch circle, dusting dough lightly with flour as needed. (If dough springs back during rolling, let rest for 10 minutes before rolling again.)

5. Sprinkle pizza peel with cornmeal. Transfer dough to prepared pizza peel and carefully stretch to return to 12-inch circle. Using back of spoon or ladle, spread scant ½ cup sauce in thin layer over surface of dough, leaving ⅛-inch border around edge. Pinch 6 ounces sausage into approximate dime-size pieces and evenly distribute over sauce. Sprinkle 1½ cups mozzarella evenly over sausage to edge of pie. Sprinkle ¼ teaspoon oregano over top.

6. Carefully slide pizza onto baking stone and bake until cheese is well browned and edges of pizza are crisp and dark, 10 to 14 minutes. Slide pizza peel underneath pizza and remove pizza from oven. Slide pizza onto cutting board and let cool for 5 minutes. Repeat with remaining dough, sauce, sausage, mozzarella, and oregano. Cut pizzas into 2- to 3-inch squares and serve.

Why This Recipe Works For an easy, all-purpose Italian sausage—the perfect topping for our Chicago Thin-Crust Pizza (page 161)—we started with coarsely ground pork. We toasted fennel seeds in a skillet to jump-start their flavor, crushed them with a rolling pin to break them down slightly, and added them to the pork with sugar for sweetness, black and red peppers for spice, and garlic for pungency. Using a stand mixer to combine the pork and seasonings helped extract more sticky proteins to bind the sausage, and letting it chill in the refrigerator for at least an hour (or up to 48 hours) aided in balancing and rounding out the flavors.

EASY SWEET ITALIAN SAUSAGE

MAKES ABOUT 1½ POUNDS

Let the toasted fennel seeds cool completely before cracking them in step 1. A rasp-style grater makes quick work of turning the garlic into a paste. If you can't find coarsely ground pork (you may have to ask your butcher), you can substitute finer, more commonly available regular-grind pork, but the texture of the sausage will be denser. If desired, you can grill the patties over a medium-hot fire until they're lightly charred and register 160 degrees, about 4 minutes per side.

- 1 tablespoon fennel seeds, toasted
- 1½ pounds coarsely ground pork
- 1½ teaspoons sugar
- 1½ teaspoons salt
- 1 large garlic clove, minced to paste
- ¾ teaspoon pepper
- ¼ teaspoon dried oregano
- ¼ teaspoon red pepper flakes
- 2 teaspoons vegetable oil

1. Place fennel seeds in small zipper-lock bag and seal bag. Using rolling pin, roll over seeds 2 or 3 times to coarsely crack.

2. Combine pork, sugar, salt, garlic, pepper, oregano, pepper flakes, and fennel seeds in bowl of stand mixer. Fit mixer with paddle and mix on low speed until mixture is thoroughly combined and looks sticky, 60 to 90 seconds, scraping down bowl as needed. Cover and refrigerate mixture for at least 1 hour to allow flavors to meld before using. (Sausage mixture can be refrigerated for up to 2 days.)

3. Using your wet hands and working with ½ cup sausage at a time, form six 4-inch-diameter patties, about ½ inch thick. Heat 1 teaspoon oil in 12-inch nonstick skillet over medium heat until shimmering. Add 3 patties to skillet and cook until browned on both sides and meat registers 160 degrees, about 4 minutes per side. Transfer patties to serving platter and tent with aluminum foil. Repeat with remaining 1 teaspoon oil and remaining 3 patties. Transfer to platter and serve.

Mix It Up

Using a stand mixer to incorporate the seasonings into the pork increases the contact between the salt and the meat and aids in extracting more of the sticky proteins in the meat that help bind the sausage.

COARSELY GROUND PORK
Makes the best textured sausage

REGULAR-GRIND PORK
Makes acceptable but slightly dense sausage

Why This Recipe Works Our challenge in creating a recipe for Detroit pizza—a crispy, buttery pizza from the Motor City—was figuring out how to mimic the tender crumb, melty brick cheese (which can be found only in Michigan), and vibrant sauce. The stand mixer did most of the kneading for us; the rich, hydrated dough required a 15-minute rest and a 2-hour rise to produce the tender, buttery crust we were after. We topped the dough with handfuls of shredded Monterey Jack cheese, the only acceptable substitute we found for the brick cheese typically used. Dried herbs, sugar, and canned tomatoes gave our sauce deep flavor and thick texture.

DETROIT-STYLE PIZZA

SERVES 4

When kneading the dough on medium speed, the mixer can wobble and move on the counter. Place a towel or shelf liner under the mixer to keep it in place, and watch it closely. To add more toppings, such as pepperoni or sausage, to your pizza, press them into the dough before adding the cheese.

Pizza

- 1 tablespoon extra-virgin olive oil
- 2¼ cups (11¼ ounces) all-purpose flour
- 1½ teaspoons instant or rapid-rise yeast
- 1½ teaspoons sugar
- 1 cup water, room temperature
- ¾ teaspoon salt
- 10 ounces Monterey Jack cheese, shredded (2½ cups)

Sauce

- 1 cup canned crushed tomatoes
- 1 tablespoon extra-virgin olive oil
- 1 tablespoon chopped fresh basil
- 1 garlic clove, minced
- 1 teaspoon dried oregano
- 1 teaspoon dried basil
- ½ teaspoon sugar
- ½ teaspoon pepper
- ¼ teaspoon salt

1. For the Pizza Spray 13 by 9-inch nonstick baking pan with vegetable oil spray, then brush bottom and sides of pan with oil. Using stand mixer fitted with dough hook, mix flour, yeast, and sugar on low speed until combined, about 10 seconds. With mixer running, slowly add room-temperature water and mix until dough forms and no dry flour remains, about 2 minutes, scraping down bowl as needed. Cover with plastic wrap and let stand for 10 minutes.

2. Add salt to bowl and knead on medium speed until dough forms satiny, sticky ball that clears sides of bowl, 6 to 8 minutes. Turn dough onto lightly floured counter and knead until smooth, about 1 minute.

3. Transfer dough to prepared pan, cover with plastic, and let rest for 15 minutes. Using your well-oiled hands, press dough into corners of pan. (If dough resists stretching, let it rest for another 10 minutes before trying again to stretch.) Cover with plastic and let dough rise at room temperature until nearly tripled in volume and large bubbles form, 2 to 3 hours. Adjust oven rack to lowest position and heat oven to 500 degrees.

4. For the Sauce Combine all ingredients in bowl. (Sauce can be refrigerated for up to 24 hours.)

5. Sprinkle Monterey Jack evenly over dough to edges of pan. Spoon three 1-inch-wide strips of sauce, using ⅓ cup sauce for each, over cheese evenly down length of pan.

6. Bake until cheese is bubbly and browned, about 15 minutes. Let pizza cool in pan on wire rack for 5 minutes. Run knife around edge of pan to loosen pizza. Using spatula, slide pizza onto cutting board. Cut into 8 pieces and serve.

On the Road: It Couldn't Have Happened Anywhere But in Detroit

As a child in Sicily, Connie Piccinato grew up eating squared-off wedges of focaccia studded with leftover meats. As an adult in 1946, while working as a waitress at Buddy's in Detroit, she found herself craving the pies of her youth. But she faced a dilemma. Food-grade rectangular pizza pans simply didn't exist at the time, so "square pizza" wasn't known in the States. But Piccinato found inspiration in a discarded rectangular "blue steel" pan used for collecting errant nuts and bolts in the string of automobile-related factories along Six Mile Road. She and Buddy's owner August "Gus" Guerra pressed a batch of dough into one of the pans, nudging it into the sharp corners; topped it with cheese and sauce; and baked it off. The square pizza was a hit, and it gave Buddy's, originally a "blind pig" speakeasy selling contraband booze during Prohibition, a new lease on life.

POTATO-CHEDDAR PIEROGI

MAKES ABOUT 30 PIEROGI

When rolling the dough in step 4, be sure not to dust the top surface with too much flour, as that will prevent the edges from forming a tight seal when pinched.

Filling

- 1 pound russet potatoes, peeled and sliced ½ inch thick
  Salt and pepper
- 4 ounces sharp cheddar cheese, shredded (1 cup)
- 2 tablespoons unsalted butter

Dough

- 2½ cups (13¾ ounces) bread flour
- 1 teaspoon baking powder
  Salt
- 1 cup sour cream
- 1 large egg plus 1 large yolk

Topping

- 4 tablespoons unsalted butter
- 1 large onion, chopped fine
- ½ teaspoon salt

1. For the Filling Combine potatoes and 1 tablespoon salt in large saucepan and cover with water by 1 inch. Bring to boil over medium-high heat; reduce heat to medium and cook at vigorous simmer until potatoes are very tender, about 15 minutes.

2. Drain potatoes in colander. While still hot, combine potatoes, cheddar, butter, ½ teaspoon salt, and ½ teaspoon pepper in bowl of stand mixer. Fit mixer with paddle and mix on medium speed until potatoes are smooth and all ingredients are fully combined, about 1 minute. Transfer filling to 8-inch square baking dish and refrigerate until fully chilled, about 30 minutes, or cover with plastic wrap and refrigerate for up to 24 hours.

3. For the Dough Whisk flour, baking powder, and ½ teaspoon salt together in clean bowl of stand mixer. Add sour cream and egg and yolk. Fit mixer

with dough hook and knead on medium-high speed for 8 minutes (dough will be smooth and elastic). Transfer dough to floured bowl, cover with plastic, and refrigerate until ready to assemble.

4. Line rimmed baking sheet with parchment paper and dust with flour. Roll dough on lightly floured counter into 18-inch circle, about ⅛ inch thick. Using 3-inch biscuit cutter, cut 20 to 24 circles from dough. Place 1 tablespoon chilled filling in center of each dough round. Fold dough over filling to create half-moon shape and pinch edges firmly to seal. Transfer to prepared sheet.

5. Gather dough scraps and reroll to ⅛-inch thickness. Cut 6 to 10 more circles from dough and repeat with remaining filling. (It may be necessary to reroll dough once more to yield 30 pierogi.) Cover pierogi with plastic and refrigerate until ready to cook, up to 3 hours.

6. For the Topping Melt butter in 12-inch skillet over medium-low heat. Add onion and salt and cook until onion is caramelized, 15 to 20 minutes. Remove skillet from heat and set aside.

7. Bring 4 quarts water to boil in Dutch oven. Add 1 tablespoon salt and half of pierogi to boiling water and cook until tender, about 5 minutes. Using spider or slotted spoon, remove pierogi from water and transfer to skillet with caramelized onion. Return water to boil, cook remaining pierogi, and transfer to skillet with first batch.

8. Add 2 tablespoons cooking water to pierogi in skillet. Cook over medium-low heat, stirring gently, until onion mixture is warmed through and adhered to pierogi. Transfer to platter and serve.

To Make Ahead Uncooked pierogi can be frozen for several weeks. After sealing pierogi in step 4, freeze them on baking sheet, about 3 hours. Transfer frozen pierogi to zipper-lock freezer bag. When ready to cook, extend boiling time in step 7 to about 7 minutes.

Why This Recipe Works Our take on the Polish dumplings known as pierogi combined potatoes and cheese tucked into a tender dough. We began by thoroughly combining boiled russet potatoes, shredded cheddar cheese, and butter in a stand mixer. The heat from the potatoes melted the butter and cheese for an even consistency. We created a pliable, rollable dough using higher-protein bread flour, sour cream, and egg. We stamped out rounds with a biscuit cutter and sealed in the filling by pinching the edges together before boiling the pierogi. A caramelized onion topping mixed with the dumplings made for a traditional sweet-savory finish.

Why This Recipe Works These buttermilk biscuits found around Rocky Mount, North Carolina, are big, golden, and stuffed with gooey cheese. Regional recipes call for hoop cheese, a yellow cheese common in North Carolina but hard to find elsewhere. We settled on yellow sharp cheddar cheese for its tangy flavor and melt-ability. We found, while trying to stuff a loose handful of shredded cheese into a wad of wet dough, that pressing the cheese into firmly packed balls made assembly easier and didn't sacrifice meltability. Baking the wet dough in a cake pan produced a higher rise and a more tender, fluffy texture due to the increase in trapped steam.

NORTH CAROLINA CHEESE BISCUITS

MAKES 6 BISCUITS

The biscuit dough will be wet and soft. Keep your hands well floured and don't be afraid to sprinkle extra flour on the biscuits to keep them from sticking. To prevent overbrowning, use a light-colored cake pan.

8 ounces yellow sharp cheddar cheese, shredded (2 cups)
3½ cups (17 ½ ounces) all-purpose flour
1 tablespoon sugar
1 tablespoon baking powder
½ teaspoon baking soda
1 teaspoon salt
4 tablespoons unsalted butter, cut into ¼-inch pieces and chilled, plus 2 tablespoons melted
1½ cups buttermilk

1. Adjust oven rack to middle position and heat oven to 500 degrees. Grease light-colored 9-inch round cake pan. Working with ⅓ cup cheese, use your hands to squeeze cheese tightly into firm ball. Repeat with remaining cheese to form 5 more balls; set cheese balls aside.

2. Pulse 2 ½ cups flour, sugar, baking powder, baking soda, and salt in food processor until combined, about 6 pulses. Add chilled butter and pulse until mixture resembles pebbly, coarse cornmeal, 8 to 10 pulses. Transfer mixture to large bowl. Stir in buttermilk until just combined. (Dough will be very wet and slightly lumpy.)

3. Spread remaining 1 cup flour in rimmed baking sheet. Using greased ½-cup dry measuring cup, transfer 6 portions of dough to prepared sheet. Dust top of each portion with flour from sheet.

4. Using your well-floured hands, gently flatten 1 portion of dough into 3 ½-inch circle and coat with flour. Pick up dough and place 1 cheese ball in center. Gently pull edges of dough over cheese to enclose and pinch together to seal. Shake off excess flour and transfer to prepared pan. Repeat with remaining dough and cheese, placing 5 biscuits around edge of pan and one in center. (Biscuits will be soft and will spread slightly as they sit.)

5. Brush biscuit tops with melted butter. Bake for 5 minutes, then reduce oven temperature to 450 degrees. Continue to bake until biscuits are deep golden brown, 15 to 20 minutes longer. Let biscuits cool in pan for 2 minutes, then invert onto plate. Break biscuits apart and turn right side up. Let cool for 5 minutes; serve warm.

Filling the Biscuits with Cheese

1. Using your hands, squeeze ⅓ cup shredded cheese into firm ball. Repeat to form 5 more balls.

2. Using greased ½-cup dry measuring cup, transfer 6 portions of dough to prepared sheet. Dust top of each with flour.

3. Flatten each dough ball into 3½-inch circle and coat with flour. Enclose cheese ball in center of dough and pinch to seal.

Why This Recipe Works We wanted a recipe for fast-food-style crunchy potato wedges that we could prepare at home. Microwaving the potatoes in a tightly covered bowl helped them obtain perfectly cooked interiors and nicely crisped exteriors. For the coating, adding baking soda to buttermilk and replacing some of the flour with cornstarch resulted in crunchy, deep-golden-brown wedges. Finally, seasoning our crunchy potato wedges with a spice blend as they precooked in the microwave, then tossing the wedges in the seasonings when they came out of the oil, produced potatoes that were flavored from the inside out.

CRUNCHY POTATO WEDGES

SERVES 6

If you don't have buttermilk, substitute 1 cup milk mixed with 1 tablespoon lemon juice. Let the mixture sit 15 minutes before using. Use a Dutch oven that holds 6 quarts or more for this recipe.

- 4 teaspoons kosher salt
- 2 teaspoons onion powder
- 1 teaspoon garlic powder
- 1 teaspoon dried oregano
- ¾ teaspoon cayenne pepper
- ½ teaspoon pepper
- 3 large russet potatoes (about 1¾ pounds), cut into ¼-inch wedges
- ¼ cup peanut or vegetable oil, plus 3 quarts for frying
- 1½ cups all-purpose flour
- ½ cup cornstarch
- 1 cup buttermilk
- ½ teaspoon baking soda

1. Combine salt, onion powder, garlic powder, oregano, cayenne, and pepper in small bowl.

2. Toss potato wedges with 4 teaspoons spice mixture and ¼ cup oil in large bowl; cover. Microwave until potatoes are tender but not falling apart, 7 to 9 minutes, shaking bowl to redistribute potatoes halfway through cooking. Uncover and drain potatoes. Arrange potatoes on rimmed baking sheet and let cool until potatoes firm up, about 10 minutes. (Potatoes can be held at room temperature for up to 2 hours.)

3. Set wire rack in rimmed baking sheet and line second baking sheet with triple layer of paper towels. Add remaining 3 quarts oil to large Dutch oven until it measures about 2 inches deep and heat over medium-high heat to 340 degrees. Meanwhile, combine flour and cornstarch in medium bowl and whisk buttermilk and baking soda together in large bowl. Working in 2 batches, dredge potato wedges in flour mixture, shaking off excess. Dip in buttermilk mixture, allowing excess to drip back into bowl, then coat again in flour mixture. Shake off excess and place on wire rack. (Potatoes can be coated up to 30 minutes in advance.)

4. When oil is ready, add half of coated wedges and fry until deep golden brown, 4 to 6 minutes. Transfer wedges to large bowl and toss with 1 teaspoon spice mixture. Drain wedges on paper towel–lined baking sheet. Return oil to 340 degrees and repeat with second batch of wedges. Serve with extra spice mixture.

To Make Ahead Our Crunchy Potato Wedges freeze very well. Follow steps 1 through 4, frying each batch of wedges until they are light golden brown, 2 to 3 minutes. Do not toss with seasoning, and drain and cool potatoes completely on baking sheet lined with paper towels. Freeze wedges on baking sheet until completely frozen, about 2 hours, then transfer potatoes to zipper-lock bag for up to 2 months. When ready to eat, heat 3 quarts oil to 340 degrees and cook in 2 batches until deep golden brown, about 3 minutes. Toss with seasonings, drain, and serve.

CREAMY BBQ SAUCE
MAKES 1¼ CUPS

Combine ¾ cup mayonnaise, ¼ cup barbecue sauce, 3 tablespoons cider vinegar, 1 minced garlic clove, ¼ teaspoon pepper, and ⅛ teaspoon salt in small bowl.

BUFFALO BLUE CHEESE SAUCE
MAKES 1½ CUPS

Combine ¾ cup mayonnaise, ¼ cup blue cheese salad dressing, 3 tablespoons hot sauce, 1 minced garlic clove, ¼ teaspoon pepper, and ⅛ teaspoon celery salt in small bowl.

CURRIED CHUTNEY SAUCE
MAKES 1¼ CUPS

Combine ¾ cup mayonnaise, ¼ cup yogurt, ¼ cup minced fresh cilantro, 3 tablespoons mango chutney, 2 teaspoons curry powder, ¼ teaspoon pepper, and ⅛ teaspoon salt in small bowl.

Why This Recipe Works Let's face it, frozen potato tots don't live up to our childhood memories. And many recipes simply mix coarsely ground potato with flour and egg, which fry up into raw, dense nuggets. We found that parcooking the chopped potato in the microwave was a step in the right direction, but the tots were still too heavy. Reducing the flour and omitting the egg helped, but they were still not light and fluffy. To minimize the gluey texture of potato starch, we tried processing the potatoes with water. Perfection. This step rinsed off the excess starch, and a small amount of salt in the mixture kept the interior downy white.

CRISPY POTATO TOTS

MAKES 48 POTATO TOTS

If any large pieces of potato remain after processing, chop them coarsely by hand. To make handling the uncooked tots easier, use a wet knife blade and wet hands. Once the tots are added to the hot oil, they may stick together; resist the temptation to stir and break them apart until after they have browned and set. You will need at least a 6-quart Dutch oven for this recipe.

2¼ teaspoons salt
2½ pounds russet potatoes, peeled and cut into 1½-inch pieces
1½ tablespoons all-purpose flour
½ teaspoon pepper
1 quart peanut or vegetable oil

1. Whisk 1 cup water and salt together in bowl until salt dissolves. Pulse potatoes and salt water in food processor until coarsely ground, 10 to 12 pulses, stirring occasionally. Drain mixture in fine-mesh strainer, pressing potatoes with rubber spatula until dry (liquid should measure about 1½ cups); discard liquid. Transfer potatoes to bowl and microwave, uncovered, until dry and sticky, 8 to 10 minutes, stirring halfway through cooking.

2. Stir flour and pepper into potatoes. Spread potato mixture into thin layer over large sheet of aluminum foil and let cool for 10 minutes. Push potatoes to center of foil and place foil and potatoes in 8-inch square baking pan. Push foil into corners and up sides of pan, smoothing it flush to pan. Press potato mixture tightly and evenly into pan. Freeze, uncovered, until firm, about 30 minutes.

3. Meanwhile, adjust oven rack to middle position and heat oven to 200 degrees. Set wire rack in rimmed baking sheet. Add oil to large Dutch oven until it measures about ¾ inch deep and heat over high heat until 375 degrees. Using foil overhang, lift potatoes from pan and cut into 48 pieces (5 cuts in 1 direction and 7 in other). Fry half of potato tots until golden brown and crisp, 5 to 7 minutes, stirring only after they are browned and set. Transfer to prepared baking sheet and place in oven. Return oil to 375 degrees and repeat with remaining potato tots. Serve.

To Make Ahead Let fried potato tots cool, transfer to zipper-lock bag, and freeze for up to 1 month. To serve, adjust oven rack to middle position and heat oven to 400 degrees. Place potato tots on rimmed baking sheet and bake until heated through, 12 to 15 minutes.

CRISPY POTATO TOTS FOR A CROWD

Double all ingredients for Crispy Potato Tots. Process and drain potato mixture in 2 batches. Microwave entire potato mixture for 12 to 14 minutes, stirring halfway through cooking. Spread potato mixture over large sheet of foil to cool and press into 13 by 9-inch baking pan. After freezing, cut potato rectangle in half crosswise before cutting into potato tots per recipe. Fry in 4 batches.

BACON-RANCH POTATO TOTS

Stir 1 tablespoon cider vinegar into potatoes after microwaving. Add 4 slices finely chopped cooked bacon, 1 teaspoon onion powder, ½ teaspoon garlic powder, and ½ teaspoon dried dill to potatoes with flour in step 2.

PARMESAN-ROSEMARY POTATO TOTS

Stir 2 minced garlic cloves into drained potatoes before microwaving. Add 1 cup grated Parmesan cheese and 2 tablespoons minced fresh rosemary to potatoes with flour in step 2.

SOUTHWESTERN POTATO TOTS

Add ½ cup shredded smoked gouda cheese, 3 tablespoons minced fresh cilantro, and 2 tablespoons minced jarred jalapeños to potatoes with flour in step 2.

GOBI MANCHURIAN

SERVES 4

A whole 2½-pound head of cauliflower should yield 1 pound of florets. You can also buy precut florets if available. Use a Dutch oven that holds 6 quarts or more.

Cauliflower
1   cup water
⅔   cup cornstarch
⅔   cup all-purpose flour
1   teaspoon table salt
1   teaspoon baking powder
1   pound (1½-inch) cauliflower florets (4 cups)
2   quarts peanut or vegetable oil for frying

Sauce
¼   cup ketchup
3   tablespoons water
2   tablespoons soy sauce
1   tablespoon Asian chili-garlic sauce
2   teaspoons lime juice, plus lime wedges for serving
¾   teaspoon pepper
½   teaspoon ground cumin
2   tablespoons vegetable oil
3   scallions, white and green parts separated and sliced thin
1   tablespoon grated fresh ginger
3   garlic cloves, minced

1. For the Cauliflower Whisk water, cornstarch, flour, salt, and baking powder in large bowl until smooth. Add cauliflower florets to batter and toss with rubber spatula to evenly coat; set aside.

2. Line baking sheet with triple layer of paper towels. Add oil to large Dutch oven until it measures about 1½ inches deep and heat over medium-high heat to 375 degrees.

3. Using tongs, add florets to hot oil 1 piece at a time. Cook, stirring occasionally to prevent florets from sticking, until coating is firm and very lightly golden, about 5 minutes. (Adjust burner, if necessary, to maintain oil temperature between 300 and 325 degrees.) Using spider skimmer, transfer florets to prepared sheet.

4. For the Sauce Combine ketchup, water, soy sauce, chili-garlic sauce, lime juice, pepper, and cumin in bowl. Heat oil in small saucepan over medium-high heat until shimmering. Add scallion whites, ginger, and garlic and cook, stirring frequently, until fragrant, about 1½ minutes. Stir in ketchup mixture and bring to simmer, scraping up any bits of ginger mixture from bottom of saucepan. Transfer sauce to clean large bowl.

5. Add cauliflower and scallion greens to bowl with sauce and toss to combine. Transfer to platter and serve with lime wedges.

From Head to Floret

1. Cut the stem flush with the base of the head, then snap off the leaves.

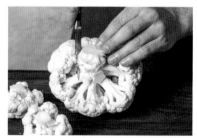

2. Place the head on the cutting board, rounded side down. Using a paring knife, cut down through the floret stems, rotating the head after each cut.

3. Pull off the loose florets, then continue cutting until all the florets are removed. Cut the florets into 1½-inch pieces.

Why This Recipe Works Gobi Manchurian, a multinational dish with roots in the Chinese immigrant communities of Kolkata, India, features cauliflower florets that are battered and fried until crisp and then served with or tossed in a spicy, umami-rich sauce. The dish has proven popular in Indian restaurants across the United States. for its powerful flavors and mix of crisp and soft textures. For our "wet-style" version, we coated cauliflower florets in a light batter (made of water, cornstarch, flour, baking powder, and salt) that was wonderfully crisp when fried and could hold up to being dressed in a thick and flavorful sauce.

Why This Recipe Works The Texas version of Kartoffelpuffer (German potato pancakes) boasts moist, fluffy interiors with supremely crunchy, lacy exteriors. When developing our recipe, we found that the potatoes' water content inhibited crispiness. Wringing out the shredded potatoes in a dish towel helped, but it wasn't enough. Using russet potatoes and some absorbent flour turned our pancakes from squishy to french-fry crisp. In Texas, the pancakes can be 10 inches across, but we found that smaller cakes were easier to flip and less likely to fall apart. Traditionally served with sour cream or applesauce, these crunchy cakes are just as good on their own.

TEXAS POTATO PANCAKES

SERVES 4 TO 6

Shred the potatoes and onion on the large holes of a box grater or with the shredding disk of a food processor. The potato shreds may take on a red hue if left to sit out for a few minutes before cooking. This does not affect their flavor.

2 pounds russet potatoes, peeled and shredded
½ cup all-purpose flour
2 large eggs, lightly beaten
⅓ cup shredded onion
   Salt and pepper
1¼ cups vegetable oil, plus extra as needed
   Sour cream
   Applesauce

1. Adjust oven rack to middle position and heat oven to 200 degrees. Set wire rack in rimmed baking sheet and place in oven. Line large plate with triple layer of paper towels.

2. Place half of potatoes in center of clean dish towel. Gather ends together and twist tightly to squeeze out as much liquid as possible. Transfer to large bowl and repeat with remaining potatoes.

3. Stir flour, eggs, onion, and 1¼ teaspoons salt into potatoes until combined. Heat oil in 12-inch skillet over medium heat to 325 degrees. Using ⅓-cup dry measuring cup, place 3 portions of potato mixture in skillet and press into 4-inch disks with back of spoon.

4. Cook until deep golden brown, 3 to 4 minutes per side, carefully flipping pancakes with 2 spatulas. Transfer pancakes to paper towel–lined plate to drain, about 15 seconds per side, then transfer to prepared wire rack in oven.

5. Repeat with remaining potato mixture in 3 batches, stirring mixture, if necessary, to recombine and adding extra oil to skillet as needed to maintain ¼-inch depth. Season pancakes with salt and pepper to taste. Serve immediately, passing sour cream and applesauce separately.

Shaping the Cakes

1. Use ⅓-cup dry measuring cup to evenly portion potato mixture.

2. Press mounds with back of spoon to flatten them.

3. Use 2 spatulas to flip pancakes to minimize splashing oil.

Why This Recipe Works Making crispy vegetable fritters can transform a fridgeful of imperfect produce into something that's crisp, delicious, and fun to eat. For a smooth batter that was light enough to not overpower the vegetables—they are the starring role in this dish, after all—we swapped tap water for seltzer, whisking it into equal parts cornstarch and flour (the perfect ratio for tender, not chewy, fritters), and added a dash of baking powder for leavening. Shallow-frying the fritters in just 1½ cups of oil yielded crispy morsels bursting with flavor, and a quick tangy horse-radish and bright lemon juice dipping sauce added a final finish.

CRISPY VEGETABLE FRITTERS

MAKES 12 FRITTERS; SERVES 4 TO 6

You can use tap water instead of seltzer, but the fritters won't be as light. Shred the zucchini and carrot on the large shredding disk of a food processor or the large holes of a box grater. Do not add corn; it pops in the hot oil. We season the batter just before frying because the salt causes the vegetables to shed water that thins the batter. Hold cooked fritters on a wire rack in a 200-degree oven.

Sauce
- ⅓ cup mayonnaise
- 1 tablespoon prepared horseradish, drained
- 1 tablespoon lemon juice
-   Salt and pepper

Fritters
- ½ cup (2½ ounces) plus 1 tablespoon all-purpose flour
- ½ cup (2 ounces) plus 1 tablespoon cornstarch
- ½ teaspoon baking powder
- ¾ cup seltzer
- 1 cup thinly sliced red bell pepper
- 1 cup shredded zucchini
- ½ cup shredded carrot
- ½ cup thinly sliced onion
- ½ cup fresh cilantro leaves
- 2 scallions, cut into ½-inch pieces
- 1 garlic clove, minced
- 1½ cups vegetable oil
-   Salt and pepper

1. For the Sauce Whisk mayonnaise, horseradish, and lemon juice together in bowl and season with salt and pepper to taste; set aside.

2. For the Fritters Set wire rack in rimmed baking sheet and line half of rack with triple layer of paper towels. Whisk flour, cornstarch, and baking powder together in large bowl. Add seltzer and whisk until smooth, thick batter forms. Add bell pepper, zucchini, carrot, onion, cilantro, scallions, and garlic to batter and stir until vegetables are evenly coated.

3. Add oil to 12-inch nonstick skillet until it measures about ¼ inch deep and heat over medium-high heat to 350 degrees. Stir ½ teaspoon salt and ½ teaspoon pepper into vegetable batter.

4. Using ¼-cup dry measuring cup, place 1 portion of vegetable batter in skillet; immediately spread to 4-inch diameter with spoon so top sits slightly below surface of oil. Repeat 3 times, so you have 4 fritters in skillet. Make sure vegetables do not mound in centers of fritters. Adjust burner, if necessary, to maintain oil temperature between 300 and 325 degrees.

5. Cook on first side until deep golden brown on bottom, 2 to 4 minutes. Using 2 spatulas, flip and continue to cook until golden brown on second side, 2 to 4 minutes longer, moving fritters around skillet as needed for even browning.

6. When second side of fritters is golden brown, turn off burner so oil doesn't overheat. Transfer fritters to paper towel–lined side of prepared rack to drain for about 15 seconds per side, then move to unlined side of rack and season with salt.

7. Return oil to 350 degrees and repeat with remaining vegetable batter in 2 batches, stirring to recombine batter as needed. Serve with sauce.

Press for Success

After portioning the batter into the hot oil, use the back of a spoon to press each fritter flat into a 4-inch circle; the tops of the fritters should sit below the surface of the oil.

BEER-BATTERED ONION RINGS

SERVES 4 TO 6

In step 1, do not soak the onion rounds longer than 2 hours or they will turn soft and become too saturated to crisp properly. Ordinary yellow onions will produce acceptable rings here. We like full-bodied beers like Sam Adams in this recipe. Cider vinegar can be used in place of malt vinegar. Use a Dutch oven that holds 6 quarts or more for this recipe.

- 2 sweet onions, peeled and sliced into ½-inch thick rounds
- 3 cups ale or lager
- 2 teaspoons malt vinegar
  Salt and pepper
- 2 quarts peanut or vegetable oil
- ¾ cup all-purpose flour
- ¾ cup cornstarch
- 1 teaspoon baking powder

1. Place onion rounds, 2 cups beer, vinegar, ½ teaspoon salt, and ½ teaspoon pepper in 1-gallon zipper-lock bag; refrigerate for 30 minutes or up to 2 hours.

2. Line rimmed baking sheet with triple layer of paper towels. Add oil to large Dutch oven until it measures about 1½ inches deep and heat over medium-high heat to 350 degrees. While oil is heating, combine flour, cornstarch, baking powder, ½ teaspoon salt, and ¼ teaspoon pepper in large bowl. Slowly whisk in ¾ cup beer until just combined (some lumps will remain). Whisk in remaining beer as needed, 1 tablespoon at a time, until batter falls from whisk in steady stream and leaves faint trail across surface of batter.

3. Adjust oven rack to middle position and heat oven to 200 degrees. Remove onions from refrigerator and pour off liquid. Pat onion rounds dry with paper towels and separate into rings. Transfer one-third of rings to batter. One at a time, carefully transfer battered rings to oil. Fry until rings are golden brown and crisp, about 5 minutes, flipping halfway through frying. Drain rings on prepared baking sheet, season with salt and pepper to taste, and transfer to oven. Return oil to 350 degrees and repeat 2 more times with remaining onion rings and batter. Serve.

Troubleshooting Onion Rings

1. To prevent raw, crunchy onions, soak rings in combination of beer, vinegar, and salt, which softens and flavors raw onion.

2. If batter is too thick, rings will be doughy; too thin and it will run off. Add beer gradually until batter falls from whisk to form ribbon trail.

3. To prevent fused rings, fry battered onion rings in small batches and transfer to hot oil one at a time so they don't stick together.

Why This Recipe Works We wanted sweet, tender onions for our beer-battered onion rings. We found that sweet onions worked best, and after testing many different batters, we settled on a beer, flour, salt, pepper, baking powder, and cornstarch batter. The beer gave the coating flavor, and the carbonation also provided lift to the batter. Baking powder yielded a coating that was thick and substantial, yet light, while cornstarch added crunch to the coating. Before frying our onion rings, we soaked the onions in a mixture of beer, malt vinegar, and salt to soften them and build flavor.

HAWAIIAN MACARONI SALAD

SERVES 8 TO 10

Low-fat milk or mayonnaise will make the dressing too thin.

2 cups whole milk
2 cups mayonnaise
1 tablespoon brown sugar
2 teaspoons pepper
½ teaspoon salt, plus extra for cooking pasta
1 pound elbow macaroni
½ cup cider vinegar
4 scallions, sliced thin
1 large carrot, peeled and grated
1 celery rib, chopped fine

1. Whisk milk, mayonnaise, sugar, pepper, and ½ teaspoon salt together in bowl. Reserve and refrigerate 1 cup dressing for finishing salad. Set both aside.

2. Bring 4 quarts water to boil in large pot. Add 1 tablespoon salt and pasta and cook until very soft, about 15 minutes. Drain pasta in colander and shake to remove excess water. Transfer pasta to large bowl, add vinegar, and toss until vinegar is absorbed. Let pasta cool for 10 minutes.

3. Stir remaining dressing (larger portion) into pasta mixture until combined. Stir in scallions, carrot, and celery until combined. Cover and refrigerate until fully chilled, about 1 hour. Stir in reserved 1 cup dressing. Season with salt and pepper to taste. Serve.

Why This Recipe Works No al dente noodles here—the Hawaiian tradition of overcooking the pasta for their creamy macaroni salad until it's "fat," enables the noodles to absorb more dressing. To achieve maximum flavor absorption, we added 2 cups each of mayonnaise and milk to make sure that the dressing was thin enough to soak into the macaroni. For an extra boost of flavor, we added cider vinegar only to discover that it curdled the milk, so we poured the vinegar directly over the hot macaroni and let it cool slightly before stirring in the dressing and vegetables.

BALLPARK PRETZELS

MAKES 12 PRETZELS

We use kosher salt on the exterior of our pretzels, but coarse pretzel salt may be substituted. However, be sure to still use kosher salt in the dough. Keep in mind that the dough needs to rise for 60 minutes, and then the shaped pretzels require a 20-minute rise before boiling and baking. These pretzels are best served warm, with mustard.

1½ cups warm water (110 degrees)
 3 tablespoons vegetable oil
 2 tablespoons packed dark brown sugar
 2 teaspoons instant or rapid-rise yeast
3¾ cups (20⅔ ounces) bread flour
    Kosher salt
 ¼ cup baking soda

1. Lightly grease large bowl. In bowl of stand mixer, combine warm water, 2 tablespoons oil, sugar, and yeast and let sit until foamy, about 3 minutes. Combine flour and 4 teaspoons salt in separate bowl. Add flour mixture to yeast mixture. Fit stand mixer with dough hook and knead on low speed until dough comes together and clears sides of bowl, 4 to 6 minutes.

2. Turn out dough onto lightly floured counter and knead by hand until smooth, about 1 minute. Transfer dough to greased bowl and cover with plastic wrap. Let dough rise at room temperature until almost doubled in size, about 60 minutes.

3. Gently press center of dough to deflate. Transfer dough to lightly greased counter, divide into 12 equal pieces, and cover with plastic.

4. Lightly flour 2 rimmed baking sheets. Working with 1 piece of dough at a time, roll into 22-inch-long rope. Shape rope into U with 2-inch-wide bottom curve and ends facing away from you. Crisscross ropes in middle of U, then fold ends toward bottom of U. Firmly press ends into bottom curve of U 1 inch apart to form pretzel shape. Transfer pretzels to prepared sheets, knot side up, 6 pretzels per sheet. Cover pretzels loosely with plastic and let rise at room temperature until slightly puffy, about 20 minutes.

5. Adjust oven racks to upper-middle and lower-middle positions and heat oven to 425 degrees. Dissolve baking soda in 4 cups water in Dutch oven and bring to boil over medium-high heat. Using slotted spatula, transfer 4 pretzels, knot side down, to boiling water and cook for 30 seconds, flipping halfway through cooking. Transfer pretzels to wire rack, knot side up, and repeat with remaining 8 pretzels in 2 additional batches. Let pretzels rest for 5 minutes.

6. Wipe flour from sheets and grease with remaining 1 tablespoon oil. Sprinkle each sheet with ½ teaspoon salt. Transfer pretzels to prepared sheets, knot side up, 6 pretzels per sheet. Sprinkle 1 teaspoon salt evenly over pretzels.

7. Bake pretzels until mahogany brown and any yellowish color around seams has faded, 15 to 20 minutes, switching and rotating sheets halfway through baking. Transfer pretzels to wire rack and let cool for 10 minutes. Serve.

Shape Shifter

Pretzel dough is fairly dry, so instead of working on a surface dusted with flour, we've found that rolling and shaping pretzels is easier and neater on a kitchen counter that's been lightly greased with vegetable oil. To achieve an even thickness when rolling the balls into ropes, use both hands. Start in the center and work your way toward the ends, using a gentle rocking motion.

1. After rolling each ball into 22-inch rope, bend into U shape with ends facing away.

2. Cross rope ends in middle of U, then cross again. Fold ends over top toward bottom of U and press ends firmly into bottom of curve, about 1 inch apart.

Why This Recipe Works Soft pretzels are an ultimate snack—and hard to come by, unless you are at a ballpark. We wanted to make them worth staying at home. To start, we created a soft, sweet interior by using bread flour—its higher gluten content produced great chew—and brown sugar, which added a subtle malty flavor. Pretzels get their dark crust from an alkali solution, so we made our own with water and baking soda. Boiling the pretzels in this solution ensured proper browning and set the crust to protect the dough inside. After letting the pretzels dry, we sprinkled them with kosher salt and baked them until they turned a beautiful mahogany-brown.

steakhouse specials

Why This Recipe Works The cornerstone of this bistro favorite is perfectly caramelized onions. First, we cooked sliced onions covered to steam and soften them, and then we removed the lid to allow the liquid to evaporate and cook the onions until they were soft and browned. Deglazing the pot with red wine ensured that all the tasty fond ended up in the soup, while stirring in beef broth and herbal arromatics completed the overall flavor. After ladling the soup into individual crocks, we sprinkled on a layer of Gruyère, followed by croutons and more cheese. The Gruyère under the croutons protected the bread from getting too soggy. C'est magnifique!

FRENCH ONION SOUP

SERVES 6

Be patient when caramelizing the onions; the entire process takes 55 to 70 minutes. If you don't have ovensafe soup crocks, form six individual piles of croutons on a baking sheet, cover them with the cheese, and broil them on the middle oven rack until the cheese is melted, 1 to 3 minutes. Then use a spatula to transfer the crouton portions to the individual filled soup bowls.

- 4 tablespoons unsalted butter
- 4 pounds onions, halved and sliced thin
- 1¾ teaspoons table salt, divided
- 1 teaspoon sugar
- 1 cup dry red wine
- 8 cups beef broth
- 4 sprigs fresh thyme
- 2 bay leaves
- ¾ teaspoon pepper, divided
- 6 ounces baguette, cut into 1-inch cubes
- 3 tablespoons extra-virgin olive oil
- 8 ounces Gruyère cheese, shredded (2 cups)
- 1½ ounces Parmesan cheese, shredded (½ cup)

1. Melt butter in Dutch oven over medium-high heat. Stir in onions, 1 teaspoon salt, and sugar. Cover and cook, stirring occasionally, until onions release their liquid and are uniformly translucent, about 20 minutes.

2. Uncover and cook until liquid has evaporated and browned bits start to form on bottom of pot, 5 to 10 minutes. Reduce heat to medium and continue to cook, uncovered, until onions are caramel-colored, 30 to 40 minutes longer, stirring and scraping with wooden spoon as browned bits form on bottom of pot and spreading onions into even layer after stirring. (If onions or browned bits begin to scorch, reduce heat to medium-low.)

3. Stir in wine, scraping up any browned bits, and cook until nearly evaporated, about 1 minute. Stir in broth, thyme sprigs, bay leaves, ½ teaspoon pepper, and ½ teaspoon salt. Increase heat to high and bring to boil. Reduce heat to medium-low and simmer, uncovered, for 30 minutes.

4. While onions simmer, adjust oven rack to middle position and heat oven to 350 degrees. Toss baguette, oil, remaining ¼ teaspoon salt, and remaining ¼ teaspoon pepper together in bowl. Transfer to rimmed baking sheet and bake until golden and crisp, 15 to 18 minutes. Remove sheet from oven and set aside. Increase oven temperature to 500 degrees.

5. Set six 12-ounce ovensafe crocks on second rimmed baking sheet. Discard thyme sprigs and bay leaves and season soup with salt and pepper to taste. Divide soup evenly among crocks (about 1½ cups each). Divide 1 cup Gruyère evenly among crocks, top with croutons, and sprinkle with remaining Gruyère, then Parmesan. Bake until cheeses are melted and soup is bubbly around edges, 5 to 7 minutes. Let cool for 5 minutes before serving.

Getting the Top Right

1. Toss cubed baguette with olive oil, salt, and pepper in bowl.

2. Toast croutons in 350-degree oven until crisp and golden brown.

3. Top soup with Gruyère, croutons, more Gruyère, and grated Parmesan.

4. Bake in 500-degree oven until cheese is fully melted.

Why This Recipe Works It can be a hassle to stand over a pot of caramelized onions when a craving for this French classic strikes. We looked to the slow cooker for simplification. Replicating the meaty flavor of the soup was more of a challenge, as the slow, long cooking can result in washed-out flavor. We found that soy sauce, sherry, and thyme added early on helped boost flavor and the addition of beef bones to store-bought chicken and beef broths reproduced the rich meatiness of the classic. Apple butter highlighted the flavor of the onions without drawing attention to itself and also helped make for a rich, silky broth.

SLOW-COOKER FRENCH ONION SOUP

SERVES 6 TO 8

After halving the onions, slice them through the root end for hearty slices that will hold up to long cooking. Beef bones are stocked in the frozen foods aisle of most supermarkets.

Soup

- 2 pounds beef bones
- 4 tablespoons unsalted butter
- 4 pounds yellow onions, halved and sliced through root end into ¼-inch-thick slices
  Salt and pepper
- 1 tablespoon packed brown sugar
- 1 teaspoon minced fresh thyme
- ¾ cup apple butter
- ¾ cup dry sherry
- 5 tablespoons all-purpose flour
- ¼ cup soy sauce
- 2 cups chicken broth
- 2 cups beef broth

Cheese Croutons

- 1 small baguette, cut into ½-inch slices
- 10 ounces Gruyère cheese, shredded (2½ cups)

1. For the Soup Arrange beef bones on paper towel–lined plate. Microwave until well browned, 8 to 10 minutes. Meanwhile, set slow cooker to high. Add butter, cover, and cook until melted. Add onions, 2 teaspoons salt, 1 teaspoon pepper, brown sugar, and thyme. Stir apple butter, sherry, flour, and soy sauce together in small bowl until smooth. Pour over onions and toss to coat. Tuck bones under onions around edge of slow cooker. Cover and cook on high heat until onions are softened and deep golden brown, 10 to 12 hours (start checking onions after 8 hours). (Cooked onions can be refrigerated for 1 day.)

2. Remove bones from slow cooker. Heat broths in microwave until beginning to boil. Stir into slow cooker. Season with salt and pepper to taste.

3. For the Cheese Croutons Adjust oven rack to upper-middle position (about 6 inches from broiler element) and heat oven to 400 degrees. Arrange bread slices in single layer on baking sheet and bake until bread is golden at edges, about 10 minutes. Heat broiler. Divide cheese evenly among croutons and broil until melted and bubbly, 3 to 5 minutes.

4. Ladle soup into bowls and top each with 2 croutons. Serve.

Slicing Onions for French Onion Soup

For this soup, we found that cutting onions with the grain (rather than across it) yielded slices that retained their shape through 10 to 12 hours in the slow cooker.

1. Using chef's knife, trim off both ends of onion.

2. Turn onion onto cut end to steady it and slice in half, through root end.

3. Peel each half, place flat side down, and cut onion, lengthwise, into slices.

Why This Recipe Works The sizzling arrival of cast-iron plates of marinated steakhouse steak tips is often the most exciting part about them, because in reality, the first bite reveals chewy meat in an overly sweet marinade. For tender tips with great beefy flavor, we relied on sirloin steak tips. As for the marinade, we replaced the usual culprits—ketchup, barbecue sauce, and cola—with a mixture of soy sauce, oil, dark brown sugar, and tomato paste for enhanced meaty flavor and maximum char.

GRILLED STEAKHOUSE STEAK TIPS

SERVES 4 TO 6

Sirloin steak tips are often labeled "flap meat" and are sold as whole steaks, strips, and pieces. For even pieces, buy a whole steak of uniform size and cut it up yourself.

⅓ cup soy sauce
⅓ cup vegetable oil
3 tablespoons packed dark brown sugar
5 garlic cloves, minced
1 tablespoon tomato paste
1 tablespoon paprika
½ teaspoon pepper
¼ teaspoon cayenne pepper
2½ pounds sirloin steak tips, trimmed

1. Whisk soy sauce, oil, sugar, garlic, tomato paste, paprika, pepper, and cayenne together in bowl until sugar dissolves; transfer to zipper-lock bag. Pat beef dry with paper towels. Prick beef all over with fork and cut into 2½-inch pieces. Add meat to bag with soy sauce mixture and refrigerate for at least 2 or up to 24 hours, turning occasionally.

2A. For a Charcoal Grill Open bottom vent completely. Light large chimney starter filled with charcoal briquettes (6 quarts). When top coals are partially covered with ash, pour evenly over grill. Set cooking grate in place, cover, and open lid vent completely. Heat grill until hot, about 5 minutes. Leave burners on high.

2B. For a Gas Grill Turn all burners to high, cover, and heat grill until hot, about 15 minutes.

3. Clean and oil cooking grate. Grill beef (covered if using gas) until charred and registers 130 to 135 degrees (for medium), 8 to 10 minutes. Transfer meat to platter, tent loosely with aluminum foil, and let rest for 5 to 10 minutes. Serve.

Common Ingredients, Uncommon Results

We engineered our marinade to give the steak tips maximum meaty flavor and satisfying texture. These familiar ingredients make a strong team, each with its own part to play.

DARK BROWN SUGAR
Delivers depth, complexity, and a caramelized, crusty char.

VEGETABLE OIL
Distributes flavors and activates oil-soluble flavor compounds, such as those found in garlic.

TOMATO PASTE
Adds background savor and enough body to help the marinade cling.

SOY SAUCE
Its salt penetrates to deeply season the meat. Its glutamates boost meaty flavor.

Why This Recipe Works Adding sugar to steak may at first seem strange, but trust us, the sugar provides a hint of sweetness and helps create the ultimate charred crust. To keep the sugar-salt mixture from sliding off the steaks or melting away on the grill, we sprinkled the mixture onto the steaks, let them rest for at least an hour, and then seasoned the moist steaks again just before hitting the heat. Though we typically discourage fussing with meat once it's on the grill, in this case, moving the steaks around as they cooked minimized the hot spots and evened out the heavy browning caused by the sugar.

GRILLED SUGAR STEAK

SERVES 4 TO 6

These steaks need to sit for at least 1 hour after seasoning. You will have about 1 teaspoon of sugar mixture left over after the final seasoning of the steaks in step 3. If your steaks are more than 1 inch thick, pound them to 1 inch.

¼ cup sugar
3 tablespoons kosher salt
4 (9- to 11-ounce) boneless strip steaks, 1 inch thick, trimmed
Pepper

1. Mix sugar and salt together in bowl. Pat steaks dry with paper towels and place in 13 by 9-inch baking dish. Evenly sprinkle 1½ teaspoons sugar mixture on top of each steak. Flip steaks and sprinkle second side of each steak with 1½ teaspoons sugar mixture. Cover with plastic wrap and let sit at room temperature for 1 hour or refrigerate for up to 24 hours.

2A. For a Charcoal Grill Open bottom vent completely. Light large chimney starter mounded with charcoal briquettes (7 quarts). When top coals are partially covered with ash, pour evenly over half of grill. Set cooking grate in place, cover, and open lid vent completely. Heat grill until hot, about 5 minutes.

2B. For a Gas Grill Turn all burners to high, cover, and heat grill until hot, about 15 minutes. Turn all burners to medium-high.

3. Clean and oil cooking grate. Transfer steaks to plate. (Steaks will be wet; do not pat dry.) Sprinkle steaks with 1 teaspoon sugar mixture on each side, then season with pepper.

4. Place steaks on hotter side of grill (if using charcoal) and cook (covered if using gas) until evenly charred on first side, 3 to 5 minutes, rotating and switching positions for even cooking. Flip steaks and continue to cook until meat registers 120 to 125 degrees (for medium-rare), 3 to 5 minutes, rotating and switching positions for even cooking.

5. Transfer steaks to wire rack set in rimmed baking sheet and let rest for 5 minutes. Slice and serve.

On the Road: A Denver Gem

Shaped like a circus tent, Bastien's Restaurant is a historic family-owned restaurant in Denver, Colorado, where grilled sugar steak has been the signature dish and a customer favorite for decades. The restaurant sits prominently on Colfax Avenue, a 50-odd-mile street that bisects Denver. It's a notorious street of contrasts (one stretch abuts the state capital while the next teems with unlawful trade, and gentrification mixes with grit along its entire stretch), but as Denver's defining throughway, it was granted Heritage Corridor status in the late 1990s to help protect and preserve Bastien's and many other mid-century architectural gems.

BROILED STEAKS

SERVES 4

To minimize smoking, be sure to trim as much exterior fat and gristle as possible from the steaks before cooking. Try to purchase steaks of a similar size and shape for this recipe. Note that you will need 2 cups of salt to line the roasting pan; the salt will absorb drippings from the steak and minimize smoking.

- 4 tablespoons unsalted butter, softened
- 1 teaspoon minced fresh thyme
- 1 teaspoon Dijon mustard
  Salt and pepper
- 1 (13 by 9-inch) disposable aluminum roasting pan, 3 inches deep
- 4 strip, rib-eye, or tenderloin steaks, 1 to 2 inches thick, trimmed

1. Adjust oven racks to upper-middle and lower-middle positions and heat oven to 375 degrees. Beat butter, thyme, mustard, ¼ teaspoon salt, and ¼ teaspoon pepper in bowl and refrigerate.

2. Spread 2 cups salt over bottom of aluminum pan. Pat steaks dry with paper towels, season with salt and pepper, and transfer to wire rack. Set rack over aluminum pan and transfer to lower oven rack. Cook 6 to 10 minutes, then remove pan from oven. Flip steaks, pat dry with paper towels, and let rest for 10 minutes.

3. Heat broiler. Transfer pan to upper oven rack and broil steaks, flipping every 2 to 4 minutes, until meat registers 120 to 125 degrees (for medium-rare), 6 to 16 minutes, depending on thickness of steaks (see chart). Transfer steaks to platter, top with reserved butter mixture, and tent with aluminum foil. Let rest for 5 minutes. Serve.

Perfectly Broiled Steaks

The first step to perfectly broiled steaks is knowing exactly how thick your steaks are. Using a ruler, measure each steak and then follow the guidelines below.

STEAK THICKNESS	PRECOOK	BROIL
1 inch	6 minutes	Turn steaks every 2 minutes
1½ inches	8 minutes	Turn steaks every 3 minutes
2 inches	10 minutes	Turn steaks every 4 minutes

Broiler Prep

Since oven-rack positioning varies greatly from model to model, we suggest you ensure correct positioning with a dry run before turning on your oven.

Before preheating your oven and with your oven racks adjusted to the upper-middle and lower-middle positions, place a wire rack on top of a 3-inch-deep disposable aluminum pan and place it on the upper-middle rack. Place the steaks on top of the rack and use a ruler to measure the distance between the top of the steaks and the heating element of the broiler. For optimal searing, there should be ½ inch to 1 inch of space.

If there is more than 1 inch of space, here's how to close the gap: Elevate the aluminum pan by placing it on an inverted rimmed baking sheet; use a deeper-sided disposable aluminum pan; or stack multiple aluminum pans inside one another. If there's less than ½ inch of space, adjust the oven rack or use a shallower pan.

Why This Recipe Works We usually rely on a red-hot skillet or the grill for our recipes that include putting a crusty sear on steaks, but we wondered if our oven's broiler could do the job just as well. Starting the steaks at a moderate temperature took the chill off, and letting them rest before putting them under the broiler produced evenly cooked meat. Covering the bottom of the pan with salt helped absorb the grease from the meat and greatly minimized smoking. To ensure a good sear on our steaks, we placed a wire rack over a 3-inch disposable pan, to bring the meat closer to the heating element.

Why This Recipe Works In order to achieve a respectable crust on our restaurant-style grilled steak, the exterior of the meat must be dry. After trying numerous drying-out methods, including salting and aging, we considered the freezer. The freezer's intensely dry environment sufficiently dehydrated the steaks' exteriors, and since we were only freezing them for a short time, the interiors remained tender and juicy. We rubbed the steaks with a mixture of salt and cornstarch before freezing. The salt ensured they were well seasoned, and cornstarch, a champ at absorbing moisture, allowed us to cut the freezing time in half.

CHAR-GRILLED STEAKS

SERVES 4

Serve with one of the sauces that follow, if desired.

- 1 teaspoon salt
- 1 teaspoon cornstarch
- 4 strip, rib-eye, or tenderloin steaks, about 1½ inches thick, trimmed
  Pepper
- 1 recipe steak sauce (recipes follow)

1. Combine salt and cornstarch. Pat steaks dry with paper towels and rub with salt mixture. Arrange on wire rack set in rimmed baking sheet and freeze until steaks are firm and dry to touch, at least 30 minutes or up to 1 hour.

2A. For a Charcoal Grill Open bottom vent completely. Light large chimney starter filled with charcoal briquettes (6 quarts). When top coals are partially covered with ash, pour evenly over grill. Set cooking grate in place, cover, and open lid vent completely. Heat grill until hot, about 5 minutes.

2B. For a Gas Grill Turn all burners to high, cover, and heat grill until hot, about 15 minutes. Leave burners on high.

3. Clean and oil cooking grate. Season steaks with pepper. Grill (covered if using gas) until meat registers 120 to 125 degrees (for medium-rare), 8 to 16 minutes, flipping steaks halfway through cooking. Transfer to plate, tent with aluminum foil, and let rest for 5 minutes. Serve.

CLASSIC STEAK SAUCE
MAKES 1¼ CUPS
Raisins add depth and sweetness to this sauce.

- ½ cup boiling water
- ⅓ cup raisins
- ¼ cup ketchup
- 3 tablespoons Worcestershire sauce
- 2 tablespoons Dijon mustard
- 2 tablespoons distilled white vinegar
  Salt and pepper

Combine water and raisins in bowl and let sit, covered, until raisins are plump, about 5 minutes. Puree raisin mixture, ketchup, Worcestershire,

mustard, and vinegar in blender until smooth, 30 seconds to 1 minute. Season with salt and pepper to taste. (Sauce can be refrigerated for 1 week.)

SPICY RED PEPPER STEAK SAUCE
MAKES 1¼ CUPS
This peppery sauce is a simplified version of the Spanish classic, romesco.

- 1 slice hearty white sandwich bread, toasted until golden and torn into pieces
- 2 tablespoons slivered almonds, toasted
- 1 cup jarred roasted red peppers, drained
- 1 plum tomato, seeded and chopped
- 2 teaspoons red wine vinegar
- 1 garlic clove, minced
- ⅛ teaspoon cayenne pepper
- 1 tablespoon extra-virgin olive oil
  Salt

Process bread and almonds in food processor until finely ground, about 10 seconds. Add red peppers, tomato, vinegar, garlic, and cayenne and process until smooth, about 1 minute. Season with salt to taste. (Sauce can be refrigerated for 1 week.)

GARLIC-PARSLEY STEAK SAUCE
MAKES 1¼ CUPS
A little of this aromatic vinaigrette goes a long way.

- ½ cup finely chopped fresh parsley
- ¼ cup minced red onion
- ¼ cup red wine vinegar
- 2 garlic cloves, minced
- ⅛ teaspoon red pepper flakes
- ¼ cup extra virgin olive oil
  Salt and pepper

Combine parsley, onion, vinegar, garlic, and pepper flakes in bowl. Slowly whisk in oil. Season with salt and pepper to taste. (Sauce can be refrigerated for 1 week.)

Why This Recipe Works Too often spice-crusted steaks are overpoweringly potent and leave scorched spices stuck to the pan, not the meat. We started with rib-eye steaks, our choice for their rich and beefy flavor, that could stand up to a bold spice crust and were thick enough to provide the perfect ratio of interior meat to exterior spice. We covered them in ground coriander and dry mustard with some coarsely crushed black peppercorns and carefully cooked the steaks in a nonstick skillet (our trusty cast iron left too much crust behind). Flipping them gently with a fork every two minutes kept the crusts intact with nary a burned peppercorn in sight.

SPICE-CRUSTED STEAKS

SERVES 4

A rasp-style grater is the best tool for zesting lemons. Turning the steaks every 2 minutes helps prevent the spices from burning.

- 1 tablespoon black peppercorns
- 2 tablespoons chopped fresh rosemary
- 1 tablespoon kosher salt
- 2 teaspoons ground coriander
- 2 teaspoons grated lemon zest
- 1½ teaspoons dry mustard
- 1 teaspoon red pepper flakes
- 2 (1-pound) boneless rib-eye steaks, 1½ inches thick, trimmed
- 1 tablespoon vegetable oil

1. Place peppercorns in zipper-lock bag and seal bag. Using rolling pin, crush peppercorns coarse. Combine peppercorns, rosemary, salt, coriander, lemon zest, mustard, and pepper flakes in bowl. Season steaks all over, including sides, with spice mixture, pressing to adhere. (Use all of spice mixture.)

2. Set wire rack in rimmed baking sheet. Heat oil in 12-inch nonstick skillet over medium heat until just smoking. Add steaks and cook, flipping steaks with fork every 2 minutes, until well browned and meat registers 125 degrees (for medium-rare), 10 to 13 minutes. Transfer steaks to prepared rack, tent with aluminum foil, and let rest for 5 minutes. Slice and serve.

Key Steps to Better Spice-Crusted Steaks

It's a simple recipe, so the details matter. Here are two tips that really work.

'Corn Crushing
Coarsely crushing the peppercorns results in big, bold pepper flavor. We like to put the peppercorns in a zipper-lock bag and have at 'em with a rolling pin.

Fork Flipping
Use a fork—not a pair of tongs—to turn the steaks in the skillet. Tongs could scrape off the spice coating.

EASY STEAK FRITES

SERVES 4

For the best french fries, we recommend using large Yukon Gold potatoes (10 to 12 ounces each) that are similar in size. We prefer peanut oil for frying for its high smoke point and the clean taste it imparts to fried foods, but you can use vegetable oil, if desired. Use a Dutch oven that holds 6 quarts or more for this recipe.

4 tablespoons unsalted butter, softened
1 shallot, minced
1 tablespoon minced fresh parsley
1 garlic clove, minced
  Kosher salt and pepper
2½ pounds large Yukon Gold potatoes, unpeeled
6 cups plus 1 tablespoon peanut or vegetable oil
2 (1-pound) boneless strip steaks, 1¼ to 1½ inches thick, trimmed and halved crosswise

1. Mash butter, shallot, parsley, garlic, ½ teaspoon salt, and ¼ teaspoon pepper together in bowl; set compound butter aside.

2. Square off potatoes by cutting ¼-inch-thick slice from each of their 4 long sides; discard slices. Cut potatoes lengthwise into ¼-inch-thick planks. Stack 3 or 4 planks and cut into ¼-inch-thick fries. Repeat with remaining planks. (Do not place sliced potatoes in water.)

3. Line rimmed baking sheet with triple layer of paper towels. Combine potatoes and 6 cups oil in large Dutch oven. Cook over high heat until oil is vigorously bubbling, about 5 minutes. Continue to cook, without stirring, until potatoes are limp but exteriors are beginning to firm, about 15 minutes. Using tongs, stir potatoes, gently scraping up any that stick, and continue to cook, stirring occasionally, until golden and crispy, 7 to 10 minutes longer.

4. Meanwhile, pat steaks dry with paper towels and season with salt and pepper. Heat remaining 1 tablespoon oil in 12-inch skillet over medium-high heat until just smoking. Add steaks and cook until well browned and meat registers 125 degrees (for medium-rare), 4 to 7 minutes per side. Transfer steaks to platter, top each with compound butter, tent with aluminum foil, and let rest for 10 minutes.

5. Using spider or slotted spoon, transfer fries to prepared sheet and season with salt. Serve fries with steaks.

The American Table:
Our First Restaurant? French.

Roadside taverns in New England served food to travelers throughout the colonial period, but it wasn't until 1793 that America got its first restaurant—complete with menus and separate prices for each item. The place, Julien's Restorator, was decidedly French. Proprietor Jean Baptiste Gilbert Payplat, called Julien by his friends and acquaintances, cooked for the archbishop of Bordeaux before emigrating to the United States. He settled in Massachusetts and set up shop, specializing in "excellent wines and cordials, good soups and broths, pastry in all its delicious variety, . . . beef, bacon, poultry, and generally, all other refreshing viands." After Payplat's death in 1805, his customers demanded that the business remain open, so his wife Hannah took over. She went on to manage Julien's Restorator for another decade.

Why This Recipe Works Steak frites is a favorite bistro dinner of juicy steak and crispy french fries that we wanted to make at home. For fries that did not require double frying, we added the potatoes and oil to a cold Dutch oven before cranking the heat to high. Lower-starch Yukon Golds yielded fries with crunchy exteriors and creamy interiors. For the steaks, we found that thick-cut boneless strip steaks gave us more time to get a crust on the outside without overcooking the center. To ensure that the fries and steaks were ready at the same time, we prepared all ingredients and equipment before cooking and started the fries 30 minutes before serving time.

GRILLED COWBOY-CUT RIB EYES

SERVES 4 TO 6

Don't start grilling until the steaks' internal temperatures have reached 55 degrees. Otherwise, the times and temperatures in this recipe will be inaccurate.

- 2 (1¼- to 1½-pound) double-cut bone-in rib-eye steaks, 1¾ to 2 inches thick, trimmed
- 4 teaspoons kosher salt
- 2 teaspoons vegetable oil
- 2 teaspoons pepper

1. Set wire rack inside rimmed baking sheet. Pat steaks dry with paper towels and sprinkle all over with salt. Place steaks on prepared rack and let stand at room temperature until meat registers 55 degrees, about 1 hour. Rub steaks with oil and sprinkle with pepper.

2A. For a Charcoal Grill Open bottom vent halfway. Arrange 4 quarts unlit charcoal briquettes in even layer over half of grill. Light large chimney starter one-third filled with charcoal briquettes (2 quarts). When top coals are partially covered with ash, pour evenly over unlit coals. Set cooking grate in place, cover, and open lid vent halfway. Heat grill until hot, about 5 minutes.

2B. For a Gas Grill Turn all burners to high, cover, and heat grill until hot, about 15 minutes. Turn primary burner to medium-low and turn off other burner(s). Adjust primary burner as needed to maintain grill temperature of 300 degrees.

3. Clean and oil cooking grate. Place steaks on cooler side of grill with bones facing fire. Cover and cook until steaks register 75 degrees, 10 to 20 minutes. Flip steaks, keeping bones facing fire. Cover and continue to cook until steaks register 95 degrees, 10 to 20 minutes.

4. If using charcoal, slide steaks to hotter part of grill. If using gas, remove steaks from grill, turn primary burner to high, and heat until hot, about 5 minutes; place steaks over primary burner. Cover and cook until well browned and steaks register 120 degrees (for medium-rare), about 4 minutes per side. Transfer steaks to clean wire rack set in rimmed baking sheet, tent loosely with foil, and let rest for 15 minutes. Transfer steaks to carving board, cut meat from bone, and slice into ½-inch-thick slices. Serve.

In Praise of Cowboy Steaks

Rib-eye steaks are deeply marbled, tender, and beefy—they're from the same part of the steer that's used for prime rib. Bone-in steaks (like these) have more flavor than boneless, and the bone protects against overcooking. Of special interest is the exterior band of fat and meat on a rib eye called the deckle; connoisseurs say it is the most flavorful part of the cow.

BIGGER IS BETTER
Cowboy-cut rib eyes are double-thick bone-in steaks. They take longer to cook than single-serving rib eyes, so they have more time to soak up smoky grill flavor.

Why This Recipe Works Oversized cowboy-cut rib eyes offer big, beefy flavor, but cooking the huge steaks all the way through while achieving a flavorful seared crust is challenging. We used a bare minimum of seasonings—salt, pepper, and oil—to highlight the flavor of the steaks. To cook them, we opted for a low and slow approach to start. To keep the fire burning long enough, we layered unlit coals under lit ones. We let the steaks come to room temperature before grilling to cut down on cooking time, and then we slow-roasted the steaks on the cooler side of the grill until they were almost done. A quick sear over hot coals gave them a flavorful dark crust.

GRILLED STEAK BURGERS

SERVES 4

Use kaiser rolls or other hearty buns for these substantial burgers.

Burgers
- 8 tablespoons unsalted butter
- 2 garlic cloves, minced
- 2 teaspoons onion powder
- 1 teaspoon pepper
- ½ teaspoon salt
- 2 teaspoons soy sauce
- 1½ pounds 90 percent lean ground sirloin
- 4 hamburger buns

Steak Sauce
- 2 tablespoons tomato paste
- ⅔ cup beef broth
- ⅓ cup raisins
- 2 tablespoons soy sauce
- 2 tablespoons Dijon mustard
- 2 tablespoons balsamic vinegar
- 1 tablespoon Worcestershire sauce

1. For the Burgers Melt butter in 8-inch skillet over medium-low heat. Add garlic, onion powder, pepper, and salt and cook until fragrant, about 1 minute. Pour all but 1 tablespoon butter mixture into bowl and let cool for about 5 minutes.

2. For the Steak Sauce Meanwhile, add tomato paste to skillet and cook over medium heat until paste begins to darken, 1 to 2 minutes. Stir in broth, raisins, soy sauce, mustard, vinegar, and Worcestershire and simmer until raisins plump, about 5 minutes. Process sauce in blender until smooth, about 30 seconds; transfer to bowl.

3. Add 5 tablespoons cooled butter mixture and soy sauce to ground beef and gently knead until well combined. Shape into four ¾-inch-thick patties and press shallow divot in center of each. Brush each patty all over with 1 tablespoon steak sauce. Combine remaining 2 tablespoons cooled butter mixture with 2 tablespoons steak sauce; set aside.

4A. For a Charcoal Grill Open bottom vent completely. Light large chimney starter filled with charcoal briquettes (6 quarts). When top coals are partially covered with ash, pour evenly over grill. Set cooking grate in place, cover, and open lid vent completely. Heat grill until hot, about 5 minutes.

4B. For a Gas Grill Turn all burners to high, cover, and heat grill until hot, about 15 minutes. Leave burners on high.

5. Clean and oil cooking grate. Grill burgers (covered if using gas) until meat registers 120 to 125 degrees (for medium-rare), 3 to 4 minutes per side, or 130 to 135 degrees (for medium), 4 to 5 minutes per side. Transfer burgers to plate, tent loosely with aluminum foil, and let rest for 5 to 10 minutes. Brush cut side of buns with butter–steak sauce mixture. Grill buns, cut side down, until golden, 2 to 3 minutes. Place burgers on buns. Serve with remaining steak sauce.

Butter Makes It Better

Why are our steakhouse burgers so good? Yep, butter. Ground sirloin has great flavor, but it's a little dry: Butter helps keep the burgers moist. Butter also gives richness and body to our homemade steak sauce. And we slather butter on the buns before toasting them on the grill.

FLAVORED BUTTER
For the meat, sauce, and buns.

Why This Recipe Works We wanted a burger with the big beefy flavor and crusty char of a grilled steak. Ground sirloin, the most flavorful ground beef, was a natural choice, but unfortunately it's also quite lean. A seasoned butter added richness to the sirloin, but something was missing. Steak sauce! In about five minutes, we simmered up our own intensely flavored sauce, perfect for serving with the burger, smearing on the bun, and even mixing into the beef before cooking.

Why This Recipe Works Despite their name, grillades are not grilled; rather, they are thinly sliced cuts of meat browned and stewed in a supersavory tomato-based gravy. For consistency and ease we opted for pork blade chops (with the bones cut off) which cooked evenly and held up to stewing. When it came time to make a roux for the base of our gravy, dry-toasting the flour in a skillet in advance helped cut down on the cooking time. Adding our own Cajun seasoning spice blend, a traditional mix of vegetables, and a dash of Tabasco provided heat and complexity to this iconic Louisiana dish.

PORK GRILLADES

SERVES 6 TO 8

We prefer pork blade chops because they hold up to stewing better than loin chops. Blade chops aren't typically available boneless; ask your butcher to bone them for you. Use our recipe for Louisiana Seasoning (page 92) or the test kitchen's taste test winner, Tony Chachere's Original Creole Seasoning.

- 1 cup all-purpose flour
- 8 (6- to 8-ounce) bone-in pork-blade-cut chops, ½ inch thick, bones discarded, and trimmed
- 2 tablespoons Louisiana Seasoning
  Salt and pepper
- ½ cup vegetable oil
- 1 onion, chopped
- 1 green bell pepper, stemmed, seeded, and chopped
- 1 celery rib, chopped
- 2 garlic cloves, minced
- 2 cups chicken broth
- 1 (14.5-ounce) can whole peeled tomatoes, crushed by hand
- 2 slices bacon
- 1 tablespoon Worcestershire sauce
- 1 bay leaf
- 1 teaspoon Tabasco sauce, plus extra for serving
- 4 cups cooked white rice
- 2 scallions, sliced thin

1. Adjust oven rack to lower-middle position and heat oven to 350 degrees. Toast ¼ cup flour in small skillet over medium heat, stirring constantly, until just beginning to brown, about 3 minutes; set aside.

2. Season chops with 1½ teaspoons Louisiana Seasoning, salt, and pepper. Whisk remaining ¾ cup flour and remaining 1½ tablespoons Louisiana Seasoning together in shallow dish. Working with 1 chop at a time, dredge in seasoned flour, shaking off excess; transfer chops to plate.

3. Heat oil in Dutch oven over medium heat until shimmering. Add 4 chops and cook until browned, 3 to 5 minutes per side; transfer to plate. Repeat with remaining 4 chops.

4. Remove all but ¼ cup oil from Dutch oven and return to medium heat. Add toasted flour to pot and cook, whisking constantly, until deep brown, about 2 minutes. Add onion, bell pepper, celery, and 1 teaspoon salt and cook, stirring often, until vegetables are just softened, about 3 minutes. Add garlic and cook until fragrant, about 30 seconds.

5. Stir in broth, tomatoes and their juice, bacon, Worcestershire, and bay leaf, scraping up any browned bits. Nestle chops into liquid and add any accumulated pork juices from plate. Bring to simmer, cover, and transfer to oven. Cook until fork slips easily in and out of pork, about 1 hour.

6. Remove grillades from oven. Discard bacon and bay leaf; stir in Tabasco. Season with salt and pepper to taste. Serve over rice, sprinkled with scallions and passing extra Tabasco.

The Right Chop

The problem with buying pork chops is that markets call chops by different names. Since grillades are braised, it's important that you don't buy a lean chop, which would be better quickly grilled or sautéed. Flavorful blade chops may not look pretty, but their fat and connective tissue softens and melts out during braising.

BAKED STUFFED SHRIMP

SERVES 4 TO 6

In a pinch, chicken broth can be substituted for the clam juice. A sturdy rimmed baking sheet can be used in place of the broiler pan bottom. Shrimp that are labeled U12 contain 12 or fewer shrimp per pound.

4   slices hearty white sandwich bread, torn into quarters
½   cup mayonnaise
¼   cup bottled clam juice
¼   cup finely chopped fresh parsley
4   scallions, chopped fine
1   tablespoon Dijon mustard
2   garlic cloves, minced
2   teaspoons grated lemon zest plus 1 tablespoon juice
⅛   teaspoon cayenne pepper
    Salt
1¼   pounds colossal shrimp (U12), peeled and deveined

1. Adjust oven rack to upper-middle position and heat oven to 375 degrees. Pulse bread in food processor to coarse crumbs, about 10 pulses. Transfer crumbs to broiler pan bottom and bake until golden and dry, 8 to 10 minutes, stirring halfway through cooking time. Remove crumbs from oven and reduce temperature to 275 degrees.

2. Combine toasted bread crumbs, mayonnaise, clam juice, parsley, scallions, mustard, garlic, lemon zest and juice, cayenne, and ¼ teaspoon salt in bowl.

3. Pat shrimp dry with paper towels and season with salt. Grease empty broiler pan bottom. To butterfly shrimp, use sharp paring knife to cut along (but not through) vein line, then open up shrimp like a book. Using tip of paring knife, cut 1-inch opening through center of shrimp. Arrange shrimp cut side down on prepared pan. Divide bread-crumb mixture among shrimp, pressing to adhere. Bake until shrimp are opaque, 20 to 25 minutes.

4. Remove shrimp from oven and heat broiler. Broil shrimp until crumbs are deep golden brown and crispy, 1 to 3 minutes. Serve.

CREOLE BAKED STUFFED SHRIMP WITH SAUSAGE
The smoky, meaty flavor of kielbasa is a nice foil to the sweet shrimp in this variation.
Omit cayenne and add 1 teaspoon Creole seasoning in step 2. Fold 4 ounces kielbasa sausage, chopped fine, into filling and proceed as directed.

Easy Steps to Baked Stuffed Shrimp
Cutting a hole through the center of each butterflied shrimp helps the shrimp hold on to the stuffing.

1. Use paring knife to cut along but not through vein line, then open up shrimp like a book. Cut 1-inch opening all the way through center of shrimp.

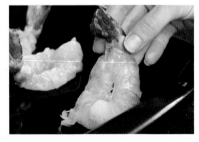

2. After shrimp have been butterflied and openings have been cut, flip shrimp over onto broiler pan so they will curl around stuffing.

3. Divide stuffing among shrimp, firmly pressing stuffing into opening and to edges of shrimp.

Why This Recipe Works There are often two problems with baked stuffed shrimp: mushy, bland stuffing and shrimp as chewy as rubber bands. We wanted a recipe that produced crisp, flavorful stuffing and perfectly cooked shrimp. For the stuffing, tasters preferred the sweet flavor of fresh bread crumbs, toasted to ensure crispness. Butterflying the shrimp allowed us to press the stuffing into the shrimp—as the shrimp contracted in the oven, the stuffing was sealed into place. To prevent over-cooked shrimp yet still achieve crisp stuffing, we cooked the shrimp for a longer time at a lower temperature.

FOOLPROOF CHICKEN CORDON BLEU

SERVES 4 TO 6

To help prevent the filling from leaking, thoroughly chill the stuffed breasts before breading. We like Black Forest ham here.

25 Ritz crackers (about ¾ sleeve)
 4 slices hearty white sandwich bread,
    torn into quarters
 6 tablespoons unsalted butter, melted
 8 thin slices deli ham (8 ounces)
 8 ounces Swiss cheese, shredded (2 cups)
 4 (8-ounce) boneless, skinless chicken breasts,
    trimmed
    Salt and pepper
 3 large eggs
 2 tablespoons Dijon mustard
 1 cup all-purpose flour

1. Adjust oven racks to lowest and middle positions and heat oven to 450 degrees. Pulse crackers and bread in food processor until coarsely ground, about 15 pulses. Drizzle in butter; pulse a few times to incorporate. Bake crumbs on rimmed baking sheet on middle rack, stirring occasionally, until light brown, 3 to 5 minutes. Transfer to shallow dish. Do not turn oven off.

2. Top each ham slice with ¼ cup cheese and roll tightly; set aside. Pat chicken dry with paper towels. Using paring knife, cut into thickest part of each chicken breast to create deep pocket with opening of 3 to 4 inches. Stuff each breast with 2 ham-and-cheese rolls and press closed. Season both sides of chicken with salt and pepper. Transfer chicken to plate, cover with plastic wrap, and refrigerate for at least 20 minutes.

3. Beat eggs and mustard in second shallow dish. Place flour in third shallow dish. One at a time, coat stuffed chicken lightly with flour, dip into egg mixture, and dredge in crumbs, pressing to adhere. (Breaded chicken can be refrigerated, covered, for 1 day.) Transfer chicken to clean rimmed baking sheet. Bake on lowest rack until bottom of chicken is golden brown, about 10 minutes, and then move baking sheet to middle rack and reduce oven temperature to 400 degrees. Bake until golden brown and chicken registers 160 degrees, 20 to 25 minutes. Transfer to platter, tent with aluminum foil, and let rest for 5 minutes. Serve.

Stuffing, Streamlined

1. Using paring knife, cut into thickest part of chicken breast to create deep pocket with opening of 3 to 4 inches.

2. Stuff each pocket with 2 ham-and-cheese rolls and seal. Refrigerate chicken for at least 20 minutes before breading.

Why This Recipe Works Making chicken cordon bleu can be fussy; we wanted an easier way. We found cutting a pocket into the breast to be much more efficient than the traditional method of pounding and rolling. To get the same swirl effect achieved by rolling the chicken around the ham and cheese, we simply rolled the ham slices into cylinders around shredded cheese and tucked the cylinders into each chicken breast. Adding a healthy dose of Dijon mustard to the egg wash boosted the flavor of our chicken, as did supplementing homemade bread crumbs with buttery Ritz cracker crumbs.

GARLIC MASHED POTATOES

SERVES 8 TO 10

Cutting the potatoes into ½-inch pieces ensures that the maximum surface area is exposed to soak up garlicky flavor.

 4 pounds russet potatoes, peeled, quartered, and cut into ½-inch pieces
 12 tablespoons unsalted butter, cut into pieces
 12 garlic cloves, minced
 1 teaspoon sugar
 1½ cups half-and-half
 ½ cup water
 Salt and pepper

1. Place cut potatoes in colander. Rinse under cold running water until water runs clear. Drain thoroughly.

2. Melt 4 tablespoons butter in Dutch oven over medium heat. Cook garlic and sugar, stirring often, until sticky and straw colored, 3 to 4 minutes. Add rinsed potatoes, 1¼ cups half-and-half, water, and 1 teaspoon salt to pot and stir to combine. Bring to boil, then reduce heat to low and simmer, covered and stirring occasionally, until potatoes are tender and most of liquid is absorbed, 25 to 30 minutes.

3. Off heat, add remaining 8 tablespoons butter to pot and mash with potato masher until smooth. Using rubber spatula, fold in remaining ¼ cup half-and-half until liquid is absorbed and potatoes are creamy. Season with salt and pepper to taste. Serve.

Folk Remedies for Removing Garlic Odor

Garlic odor is hard to remove from your hands, but folk remedies for doing so abound, from washing with baking soda, vinegar, lemon juice, salt, or toothpaste to rubbing your hands on stainless steel. To find out if any of these tricks worked, we rubbed minced garlic on our hands and tried each method.

Washing with all of these substances lessened the odor at least a little, with baking soda and lemon juice outperforming the others, and rubbing one's hands on stainless steel succeeding just as well. Why? Some of the aromatic compounds in garlic are weak acids that can be neutralized by alkaline baking soda. Because not all aroma compounds are acidic, baking soda can't neutralize the odor 100 percent. Stainless steel removes some of the odor when iron atoms in the stainless steel exchange some of their electrons with sulfur atoms from the volatile aroma compounds, rendering them nonvolatile (nonstinky). Lemon juice contains lemon oils that dissolve the oil-soluble aroma compounds in garlic, plus its own fragrance masks the remaining odor. The bottom line? Lemon juice, baking soda, and stainless steel all help a little, but there is no magic cure for removing garlic smell from your hands.

Secrets to Great Roasted Garlic Flavor

1. To bloom garlic flavor and temper harshness, cook minced garlic and sugar in butter until garlic is sticky and straw-colored.

2. For deeply integrated garlic flavor, toss raw potatoes with garlic-butter mixture, add half-and-half and water directly to pot, cover, and gently cook until tender.

Why This Recipe Works Making mashed potatoes isn't typically a quick endeavor—add roasted garlic to the mix and you've really got a project on your hands. We wanted a streamlined recipe. We cut the potatoes into small pieces to promote even, quicker cooking. The small pieces also meant the potatoes could better soak up garlicky flavor. To mimic the flavor of roasted garlic, we sprinkled in a little sugar while sautéing the garlic. Finally, we simmered the potatoes in half-and-half, butter, and the sautéed garlic to avoid the "washing away" of flavor that can come from boiling in just water.

MASHED POTATO CAKES

SERVES 4 TO 6

Using two spatulas to flip the cakes helps prevent splattering. We like to change the oil after frying the first batch of cakes because any dark panko remnants left behind will freckle the second batch. You can strain the oil through a fine-mesh strainer if you prefer to reuse it, but be careful because it is very hot. Plan ahead: The cooked mashed potatoes need to chill in the refrigerator for 1 hour, which makes it easier to form the cakes.

2½ pounds russet potatoes, peeled, halved
      lengthwise, and sliced ¼ inch thick
      Salt and pepper
  1 ounce Parmesan cheese, grated (½ cup)
  ¼ cup chopped fresh chives
  1 large egg yolk plus 2 large eggs
  2 cups panko bread crumbs
  1 cup vegetable oil
      Sour cream

1. Place potatoes in medium saucepan and add water to cover by 1 inch, then stir in 1 tablespoon salt. Bring to boil over high heat. Reduce heat to medium-low and simmer until tip of paring knife inserted into potatoes meets no resistance, 8 to 10 minutes. Drain potatoes and return to saucepan; let cool for 5 minutes.

2. Add Parmesan, chives, egg yolk, ¾ teaspoon salt, and ¼ teaspoon pepper to cooled potatoes. Using potato masher, mash until smooth and well combined. Transfer potato mixture to bowl and refrigerate until completely cool, about 1 hour.

3. Beat remaining 2 eggs together in shallow dish. Place panko in second shallow dish. Divide potato mixture into 8 equal portions (about ½ cup each) and shape into 3-inch-diameter cakes, about ¾ inch thick. Working with 1 cake at a time, carefully dip cakes in egg mixture, turning to coat both sides and allowing excess to drip off; then coat with panko, pressing gently to adhere. Transfer to plate and let sit for 5 minutes.

4. Line large plate with paper towels. Heat ½ cup oil in 12-inch nonstick skillet over medium-high heat until shimmering. Place 4 cakes in skillet and cook until deep golden brown on first side, about 3 minutes. Using 2 spatulas, carefully flip cakes and continue to cook until deep golden brown on second side, about 2 minutes longer, gently pressing on cakes with spatula for even browning.

5. Transfer cakes to prepared plate. Discard oil and wipe out skillet with paper towels. Repeat with remaining ½ cup oil and remaining 4 cakes. Serve with sour cream.

BLUE CHEESE AND BACON MASHED POTATO CAKES

Substitute ¾ cup crumbled blue cheese for Parmesan. Stir 6 slices cooked chopped bacon into potato mixture after mashing in step 2.

CHEDDAR AND SCALLION MASHED POTATO CAKES

Substitute 1 cup shredded sharp cheddar cheese for Parmesan and sliced scallions for chives.

Why This Recipe Works Mashed potato cakes—soft, fluffy mashed potatoes coated in bread crumbs and fried—are equally welcome at suppertime next to a piece of meat or at breakfast under a poached egg. Using leftover mashed potatoes yielded mushy cakes, so we started from scratch, mashing russet potatoes with Parmesan, chives, and an egg yolk for extra richness. Chilling the mashed potatoes before forming the cakes made shaping them easier. For a golden-brown and crisp crust, we dipped the disks in beaten egg to help the coating adhere. Serving the potato cakes with a dollop of sour cream offered a cool, tangy finish.

Why This Recipe Works Lyonnaise potatoes (hailing from Lyon, France) originated as a way to use up boiled potatoes from dinner the night before; they're peeled, sliced, and pan-fried with copious amounts of butter and thin slices of onion. To avoid waiting for leftovers, we started with raw Yukon Golds (chosen for their deep flavor and tender texture). Slicing them into ½-inch-thick rounds prevented over-crowding the pan, and giving the spuds a 15-minute head start before lowering the heat and adding the onions ensured that everything emerged tender and browned.

LYONNAISE POTATOES

SERVES 4

Use potatoes of similar size.

- 4 tablespoons unsalted butter
- 2 pounds Yukon Gold potatoes, peeled and sliced ½ inch thick
  Salt and pepper
- 1 onion, halved and sliced thin
- 1 tablespoon minced fresh parsley

1. Melt butter in 12-inch nonstick skillet over medium heat. Add potatoes and ¾ teaspoon salt and cook, covered, until just tender and golden brown, about 15 minutes, flipping potatoes occasionally to ensure even browning.

2. Reduce heat to medium-low. Add onion, ½ teaspoon salt, and ½ teaspoon pepper; cover and continue to cook until onion is tender and golden brown, about 10 minutes longer, stirring occasionally. Season with salt and pepper to taste. Transfer to serving platter and sprinkle with parsley. Serve.

Don't Make This Mistake: Raw Potatoes and Burnt Onion

Starting to cook the potatoes and onion at the same time will result in crunchy, undercooked spuds and scorched onion. Instead, we use a staggered approach, giving the potatoes a head start and a chance to soften before adding the onion to the pan.

Slice 'em Thick

Good news: There's no need for fussy thin potato slices. Cutting the potatoes a generous ½ inch thick (use the true-to-size photo below as a guide) helps the potatoes fit in the skillet so they brown evenly.

½ in

Why This Recipe Works To revive this classic potato dish, we first focused on how to prep the potatoes. Boiled cubed potatoes won out over shredded because they held their texture better in the casserole. Next, we sautéed onion and garlic, added cream and chicken broth (to cut the richness of the cream), and cooked the cubed potatoes in this mixture. Lemon juice and zest brought the casserole welcome brightness. For the crusty topping, we turned to an unexpected ingredient: frozen shredded hash browns. We sautéed the thawed hash browns in butter, cream, and chicken broth to enhance their flavor before topping the casserole.

DELMONICO POTATO CASSEROLE

SERVES 8 TO 10

We prefer the buttery flavor of Yukon Gold potatoes here, but all-purpose and red potatoes also work. Do not use russets—their high starch content will make the casserole gluey. For the topping, we had good results with Ore-Ida Country Style Hash Browns, available in the frozen foods aisle of most supermarkets.

3 tablespoons unsalted butter
1 onion, chopped fine
2 garlic cloves, minced
2½ cups heavy cream
1½ cups chicken broth
2½ pounds Yukon Gold potatoes, peeled and cut into ½-inch cubes
⅛ teaspoon ground nutmeg
Salt and pepper
1 teaspoon grated lemon zest plus 2 teaspoons juice
5 cups frozen shredded hash brown potatoes, thawed and patted dry with paper towels
1½ ounces Parmesan cheese, grated (¾ cup)
¼ cup finely chopped fresh chives

1. Adjust oven rack to upper-middle position and heat oven to 450 degrees. Melt 1 tablespoon butter in Dutch oven over medium-high heat. Cook onion until softened, about 3 minutes. Stir in garlic and cook until fragrant, about 30 seconds. Stir in 2 cups cream, 1 cup broth, Yukon Golds, nutmeg, 2 teaspoons salt, and 1 teaspoon pepper. Bring to boil, then reduce heat to medium and simmer until potatoes are translucent at edges and mixture is slightly thickened, about 10 minutes. Off heat, stir in lemon zest and juice.

2. Transfer potato mixture to 13 by 9-inch baking dish and bake until bubbling around edges and surface is just golden, about 20 minutes. Meanwhile, melt remaining 2 tablespoons butter in 12-inch nonstick skillet over medium-high heat. Cook shredded potatoes until beginning to brown, about 2 minutes. Add remaining ½ cup cream, remaining ½ cup broth, and ½ teaspoon pepper to skillet and cook, stirring occasionally, until liquid has evaporated, about 3 minutes. Off heat, stir in ½ cup Parmesan and 2 tablespoons chives.

3. Remove baking dish from oven and top with shredded potato mixture. Sprinkle with remaining ¼ cup Parmesan and continue to bake until top is golden brown, about 20 minutes. Let cool for 15 minutes. Sprinkle with remaining 2 tablespoons chives. Serve.

To Make Ahead Prepare through step 1, let cool completely, transfer to baking dish, and refrigerate, covered with plastic wrap, for 1 day. To serve, proceed as directed in step 2, increasing baking time to 25 to 30 minutes.

The American Table: Potatoes with Panache

In 1837, Delmonico's opened in lower Manhattan and a restaurant star was born. Owned by two Swiss men, the restaurant served French-style cuisine and became the model for many other fashionable restaurants of the era. Its lavish dining room served such luxurious fare as lobster Newburg, baked Alaska, and their signature potato side dish, Delmonico potatoes. The potatoes were boiled, finely shredded, and cooked with milk and heavy cream. When an order came in, a serving of potatoes was sprinkled with Parmesan cheese and "gratinéed" under the broiler. The result was a potato gratin with a creamy interior and a crusty, cheesy topping. But look up a modern recipe for this dish and you'll most likely find a casserole made of over-boiled chunks of potatoes baked in a creamy cheddar sauce and topped with more cheese. We wanted to bring back the simplicity and elegance of the original dish but make it more practical to feed a crowd.

Why This Recipe Works The Lighthouse Inn, an iconic Connecticut restaurant and hotel, was known for its rich potato side dish. But in re-creating the dish, we did not want to rely on leftover baked potatoes as the original recipe did. To ensure a creamy sauce, we cooked starchy russet potatoes in light cream and butter and then added it all into a baking dish, making sure the starch stayed in the sauce and left it rich and velvety. A little baking soda kept the sauce from curdling. Topping the potato mixture with cheesy bread crumbs and baking them until crunchy and golden brown took our recipe over the top.

LIGHTHOUSE INN POTATOES

SERVES 8 TO 10

We prefer the texture of light cream for this recipe, but heavy cream will also work. Do not use half-and-half; it has a tendency to break. Grate the Parmesan on a rasp-style grater. Our favorite panko bread crumbs are from Kikkoman.

2 ounces Parmesan cheese, grated (1 cup)
1 cup panko bread crumbs
4 tablespoons unsalted butter, melted, plus 6 tablespoons cut into 6 pieces
  Salt and pepper
2½ pounds russet potatoes, peeled and cut into 1-inch chunks
3 cups light cream
⅛ teaspoon baking soda

1. Adjust oven rack to middle position and heat oven to 375 degrees. Combine Parmesan, panko, melted butter, and ¼ teaspoon salt in bowl; set aside.

2. Bring potatoes, 2½ cups cream, baking soda, 2 teaspoons salt, and 1 teaspoon pepper to boil in large saucepan over medium-high heat. Reduce heat to low and cook at bare simmer, stirring often, until paring knife slides easily into potatoes without them crumbling, 20 to 25 minutes.

3. Off heat, stir remaining ½ cup cream and remaining 6 tablespoons butter into potato mixture until butter has melted, about 1 minute. Transfer potato mixture to 13 by 9-inch baking dish. Sprinkle Parmesan-panko mixture over top. Bake, uncovered, until bubbling around edges and surface is golden brown, 15 to 20 minutes. Let cool for at least 15 minutes. Serve.

To Make Ahead After potato mixture has been transferred to baking dish, let cool completely, cover with aluminum foil, and refrigerate for up to 24 hours. Before applying topping, bake, covered, until heated through, about 35 minutes. Apply topping and continue to bake, uncovered, 15 to 20 minutes longer.

The Lighthouse Inn

Locals claim that the Lighthouse Inn, originally a country house for wealthy businessmen before being turned into a resort, is haunted.

Lighthouse Inn, New London, Conn.

OLIVE OIL POTATO GRATIN

SERVES 6 TO 8

The test kitchen's favorite supermarket extra-virgin olive oils are Bertolli Extra Virgin Olive Oil, Rich Taste and California Olive Ranch Global Blend Medium Extra Virgin Olive Oil. We prefer to use a mandoline to create thin, even slices of potato.

  2 ounces Pecorino Romano cheese, grated (1 cup)
½ cup extra-virgin olive oil
¼ cup panko bread crumbs
     Salt and pepper
  2 onions, halved and sliced thin
  2 garlic cloves, minced
  1 teaspoon minced fresh thyme
  1 cup low-sodium chicken broth
  3 pounds Yukon Gold potatoes, peeled and sliced ⅛ inch thick

1. Adjust oven rack to upper-middle position and heat oven to 400 degrees. Grease 13 by 9-inch baking dish. Combine Pecorino, 3 tablespoons oil, panko, and ½ teaspoon pepper in bowl; set aside.

2. Heat 2 tablespoons oil in 12-inch skillet over medium heat until shimmering. Add onions, ½ teaspoon salt, and ¼ teaspoon pepper and cook, stirring frequently, until browned, about 15 minutes. Add garlic and ½ teaspoon thyme and cook until fragrant, about 30 seconds. Add ¼ cup broth and cook until nearly evaporated, scraping up any browned bits, about 2 minutes. Remove from heat; set aside.

3. Toss potatoes, remaining 3 tablespoons oil, 1 teaspoon salt, ½ teaspoon pepper, and remaining ½ teaspoon thyme together in bowl. Arrange half of potatoes in prepared dish, spread onion mixture in even layer over potatoes, and distribute remaining potatoes over onions. Pour remaining ¾ cup broth over potatoes. Cover dish tightly with aluminum foil and bake for 1 hour.

4. Remove foil, top gratin with reserved Pecorino mixture, and continue to bake until top is golden brown and potatoes are completely tender, 15 to 20 minutes. Let cool for 15 minutes. Serve.

Slicing Potatoes

A mandoline makes quick work of thinly slicing potatoes, but if you don't own one, cut a slice off of one side of each potato to create a flat, stable surface for thin slicing.

Why This Recipe Works Potato gratin is a notoriously heavy side dish, laden with cream and gooey cheese. We wanted to shift the focus of this classic side dish to the potatoes. We chose Yukon Gold potatoes for their rich flavor and moderate starch content, which helped them hold their shape when cooked. Tossing the potatoes with fruity, flavorful extra-virgin olive oil heightened the flavor of the potatoes but didn't overpower them. For a crisp, cheesy topping, we mixed more olive oil with panko bread crumbs and sprinkled the dish with sharp, salty Pecorino Romano. For added depth, we added sautéed onions, fresh thyme, and garlic.

Why This Recipe Works Boiled and buttered potatoes are a reliable side dish, but they can be a bit boring; all the flavor remains on the outsides of the potatoes, leaving the interiors bland. To fix that, we simmered 2 pounds of red potatoes until they were tender, drained them, and then melted butter in the empty pot before adding minced garlic, fresh chives, fresh parsley, salt, and pepper. We then added the hot potatoes, lightly pressed each with the back of a spoon until it broke apart, and gently stirred the potatoes with the buttery, herby goodness so that it worked its way into all the nooks and crannies. It's time to say goodbye to underseasoned spuds.

CRUSHED RED POTATOES WITH GARLIC AND HERBS

SERVES 4 TO 6

Be sure to use small red potatoes measuring 1 to 2 inches in diameter, and use a gentle hand when crushing them.

2 pounds small red potatoes, unpeeled
  Salt and pepper
6 tablespoons unsalted butter
1 garlic clove, minced
2 tablespoons minced fresh chives
2 tablespoons minced fresh parsley

1. Place potatoes and 2 tablespoons salt in Dutch oven and cover with water by 1 inch. Bring to boil over high heat. Reduce heat to medium-high and simmer until paring knife slips easily in and out of potatoes, about 20 minutes. (Potatoes should be very tender.) Drain potatoes in colander.

2. In now-empty pot, melt butter over medium heat. Add garlic and cook until fragrant, about 30 seconds. Off heat, stir in chives, parsley, ½ teaspoon salt, and ¼ teaspoon pepper.

3. Add potatoes to pot. Press each potato with back of spoon or spatula to lightly crush (do not mash; potatoes should still have texture). Stir to coat potatoes with butter mixture (potatoes will break up slightly; this is OK). Transfer to platter. Serve.

CRUSHED RED POTATOES WITH GARLIC AND SMOKED PAPRIKA

Substitute extra-virgin olive oil for butter and heat until shimmering. Sprinkle 1 teaspoon smoked paprika over crushed potatoes on platter before serving.

CRUSHED RED POTATOES WITH OREGANO AND CAPERS

Substitute 1 tablespoon chopped fresh oregano, 1 tablespoon rinsed capers, and 1 tablespoon lemon juice for chives and parsley. Decrease salt in step 2 to ¼ teaspoon.

Getting the Texture Just Right

1. Press on the cooked potatoes with a wooden spoon until they crack open and are lightly crushed.

2. Stir gently to further break down the crushed potatoes and distribute the seasoned butter mixture.

ROASTED SALT-AND-VINEGAR POTATOES

SERVES 4

Use small red potatoes, measuring 1 to 2 inches in diameter. If you prefer to use kosher salt, you will need 1½ cups of Morton's or 2½ cups of Diamond Crystal. Cider vinegar is a good substitute for the malt vinegar.

- 6 tablespoons olive oil
- 2 pounds small red potatoes, scrubbed
- 1¼ cups salt
- 3 tablespoons malt vinegar
  Pepper

1. Adjust oven rack to upper-middle position and heat oven to 500 degrees. Set wire rack inside rimmed baking sheet. Brush second rimmed baking sheet evenly with oil. Bring 2 quarts water to boil in Dutch oven over medium-high heat. Stir in potatoes and salt and cook until just tender and paring knife slips easily in and out of potatoes, 20 to 30 minutes. Drain potatoes and transfer to wire rack; let dry for 10 minutes.

2. Transfer potatoes to oiled baking sheet. Flatten each potato with underside of measuring cup until ½ inch thick. Brush potatoes with half of vinegar and season with pepper. Roast until potatoes are well browned, 25 to 30 minutes. Brush with remaining vinegar. Transfer potatoes to platter, smashed side up. Serve.

Scrub the Potatoes

Because the skins will be in the finished dish, it's important to scrub the potatoes well before cooking.

Salt of the Earth (and Sea)

A variety of salts are available in supermarkets today: table, iodized, kosher, and sea salt. What's the difference? Table and iodized salt (simply table salt with iodine added) have fine grains and contain anticaking agents that help them flow freely. Kosher salt, so named because it is used in the koshering process, has larger crystals and typically contains no additives. Both table and kosher salts are considered "refined salts" because they are mined from rock salt deposits and then purified. Sea salt is harvested by evaporating seawater and therefore has a full, slightly mineral flavor. Though we use table salt in the vast majority of our recipes, the choice is a matter of preference—except when it comes to our Roasted Salt-and-Vinegar Potatoes. While table, kosher, and sea salts all performed equally well in this recipe, we advise against using iodized salt as it gives the potatoes a noticeably chemical flavor.

Malt Vinegar Substitutes

For our salt-and-vinegar potatoes, we raided the English larder for a beloved condiment: malt vinegar. Brits commonly douse fish and chips with it, so we knew it would be a perfect match for roasted potatoes. The vinegar, which is made from sprouted barley grains, gives the potatoes a pleasantly malty, tangy taste. But if you don't have it, cider or white wine vinegars are good substitutes. Avoid balsamic and rice vinegars, which tasters found too sweet, and red wine and distilled white vinegars, which were too harsh.

Why This Recipe Works Cooking red potatoes in a super-saturated salt solution gave them incredibly creamy, well-seasoned interiors. After the potatoes were parcooked, we smashed them to expose some of the potato flesh, brushed them with malt vinegar, and roasted them on a well-oiled baking sheet until the exposed surface was golden and crispy. A final brush with more vinegar when the potatoes came out of the oven reinforced the addictive salty-sour flavor of these spuds.

Why This Recipe Works These crispy, cheesy Parmesan potatoes promised to be a habit-forming snack, but first we had to figure out how best to cook the potatoes and how to get the cheese to stick to them. Using thinly sliced, creamy Yukon Gold potatoes meant they wouldn't dry out during roasting. We tossed the potato slices with seasoned cornstarch to promote crisping. Parmesan, rosemary, and a little more cornstarch made for a savory coating that clung evenly to the slices. Baked in a very hot oven until golden brown and served with a cool chive sour cream, these were just the potatoes we craved.

CRISPY PARMESAN POTATOES

SERVES 6 TO 8

Try to find potatoes that are 2½ to 3 inches long. Spray the baking sheet with an aerosol (not pump) vegetable oil spray. Use a good-quality Parmesan cheese here. Serve with Chive Sour Cream (recipe follows), if desired.

- 2 pounds medium Yukon gold potatoes, unpeeled
- 4 teaspoons cornstarch
  Salt and pepper
- 1 tablespoon extra-virgin olive oil
- 6 ounces Parmesan cheese, cut into 1-inch chunks
- 2 teaspoons minced fresh rosemary

1. Adjust oven rack to lower-middle position and heat oven to 500 degrees. Spray rimmed baking sheet liberally with vegetable oil spray. Cut thin slice from 2 opposing long sides of each potato; discard slices. Cut potatoes crosswise into ½-inch-thick slices and transfer to large bowl.

2. Combine 2 teaspoons cornstarch, 1 teaspoon salt, and 1 teaspoon pepper in small bowl. Sprinkle cornstarch mixture over potatoes and toss until potatoes are thoroughly coated and cornstarch is no longer visible. Add oil and toss to coat.

3. Arrange potatoes in single layer on prepared sheet and bake until golden brown on top, about 20 minutes.

4. Meanwhile, process Parmesan, rosemary, ½ teaspoon pepper, and remaining 2 teaspoons cornstarch in food processor until cheese is finely ground, about 1 minute.

5. Remove potatoes from oven. Sprinkle Parmesan mixture evenly over and between potatoes (cheese should cover surface of baking sheet), pressing on potatoes with back of spoon to adhere. Using two forks, flip slices over into same spot on sheet.

6. Bake until cheese between potatoes turns light golden brown, 5 to 7 minutes. Transfer sheet to wire rack and let potatoes cool for 15 minutes. Using large metal spatula, transfer potatoes, cheese side up, and accompanying cheese to platter and serve.

CHIVE SOUR CREAM
MAKES ABOUT 1 CUP
This enhanced condiment makes an excellent topping for potatoes of all kinds.

- 1 cup sour cream
- ¼ cup minced fresh chives
- ½ teaspoon minced fresh rosemary
- ½ teaspoon salt
- ½ teaspoon pepper
- ½ teaspoon garlic powder
- ¼ teaspoon onion powder

Combine all ingredients in bowl. Cover and refrigerate at least 30 minutes to allow flavors to blend.

Flipping for Frico

Using 2 forks, turn each potato slice over and return it to the same spot on the sheet. As the Parmesan bakes, it will transform into crispy cheesy bits called frico.

Why This Recipe Works For this showstopper side dish, we found that using the right kind of potato is key. The russet potato was the best choice because of its starchy flesh and fluffy texture. Taking the time to rinse the potatoes of surface starch after they were sliced prevented them from sticking together, while trimming off the end of each potato gave the remaining slices room to fan out. To prevent overcooking our spuds in the punishing oven heat, we precooked them in the microwave before baking. A topping of fresh bread crumbs, melted butter, two kinds of cheese, garlic powder, and paprika was the crowning touch.

CRISPY BAKED POTATO FANS

SERVES 4

To ensure that the potatoes fan out evenly, look for uniformly shaped potatoes.

Bread Crumb Topping

- 1 slice hearty white sandwich bread, torn into quarters
- 4 tablespoons unsalted butter, melted
- 2 ounces Monterey Jack cheese, shredded (½ cup)
- ¼ cup grated Parmesan cheese
- 1 teaspoon paprika
- ½ teaspoon garlic powder
  Salt and pepper

Potato Fans

- 4 russet potatoes
- 2 tablespoons extra-virgin olive oil
  Salt and pepper

1. For the Bread Crumb Topping Adjust oven rack to middle position and heat oven to 200 degrees. Pulse bread in food processor until coarsely ground, about 5 pulses. Bake bread crumbs on rimmed baking sheet until dry, about 20 minutes. Let cool for 5 minutes, then combine crumbs, butter, Monterey Jack, Parmesan, paprika, garlic powder, ¼ teaspoon salt, and ¼ teaspoon pepper in large bowl. (Bread crumb mixture can be refrigerated in zipper-lock bag for 2 days.)

2. For the Potato Fans Heat oven to 450 degrees. Cut ¼ inch from bottom and ends of potatoes, then slice potatoes crosswise at ¼-inch intervals, leaving ¼ inch of potato intact. Gently rinse potatoes under running water, let drain, and transfer, sliced side down, to plate. Microwave until slightly soft to touch, 6 to 12 minutes, flipping potatoes halfway through cooking.

3. Line rimmed baking sheet with aluminum foil. Arrange potatoes, sliced side up, on prepared baking sheet. Brush potatoes all over with oil and season with salt and pepper. Bake until skin is crisp and potatoes are beginning to brown, 25 to 30 minutes. Remove potatoes from oven and heat broiler.

4. Top potatoes with bread crumb mixture, pressing gently to adhere. Broil until bread crumbs are deep golden brown, about 3 minutes. Serve.

BLUE CHEESE AND BACON BAKED POTATO FANS

In step 1, substitute ⅓ cup crumbled blue cheese for Monterey Jack. In step 4, sprinkle 4 slices bacon, cooked until crisp and then crumbled, over potatoes just prior to serving.

Prepping Baked Potato Fans

These potatoes may look difficult to make, but we found a few simple tricks to ensure perfect potato fans every time.

1. Trim ¼-inch slices from bottom and ends of each potato to allow them to sit flat and to give slices extra room to fan out during baking.

2. Chopsticks provide a foolproof guide for slicing potato petals without cutting all the way through.

3. Gently flex open fans while rinsing under cold running water; this rids potatoes of excess starch that can impede fanning.

Why This Recipe Works Our Super-Stuffed Baked Potatoes feature fluffy potato, garlic, herbs, and creamy cheese in crispy potato-skin shells. Precooking the potatoes in the microwave shaved an hour off the cooking time. And while most stuffed baked potato recipes call for cutting the potato in half, we preferred to lop off just the top quarter of the potato. Prepared this way, the potato shells held more filling. But after hollowing out the potatoes, there wasn't enough stuffing to fill each one and mound the filling on top. To make the filling go further, we cooked an extra potato and used its flesh to top off the other stuffed baked potatoes.

SUPER-STUFFED BAKED POTATOES

SERVES 6

This recipe calls for seven potatoes but makes six servings; the remaining potato is used for its flesh.

- 7 large russet potatoes
- 3 tablespoons unsalted butter, melted, plus 3 tablespoons unsalted butter
  Salt and pepper
- 1 (5.2-ounce) package Boursin cheese, crumbled
- ½ cup half-and-half
- 2 garlic cloves, minced
- ¼ cup chopped fresh chives

1. Adjust oven rack to middle position and heat oven to 475 degrees. Set wire rack in rimmed baking sheet. Prick potatoes all over with fork, place on paper towel, and microwave until tender, 20 to 25 minutes, turning potatoes over after 10 minutes.

2. Slice and remove top quarter of each potato, let cool for 5 minutes, then scoop out flesh, leaving ¼-inch layer of potato on inside. Discard 1 potato shell. Brush remaining shells inside and out with 3 tablespoons melted butter and sprinkle interiors with ¼ teaspoon salt. Transfer potatoes, scooped side up, to prepared baking sheet and bake until skins begin to crisp, about 15 minutes.

3. Meanwhile, mix half of Boursin with half-and-half in bowl until blended. Cook remaining 3 tablespoons butter and garlic in saucepan over medium-low heat until garlic is straw-colored, 3 to 5 minutes. Stir in Boursin mixture until combined.

4. Set ricer or food mill over medium bowl and press or mill potatoes into bowl. Gently fold in warm Boursin mixture, 3 tablespoons chives, 1 teaspoon pepper, and ½ teaspoon salt until well incorporated. Remove potato shells from oven and fill with potato-cheese mixture. Top with remaining crumbled Boursin and bake until tops of potatoes are golden brown, about 15 minutes. Sprinkle with remaining 1 tablespoon chives. Serve.

Bigger, Better Stuffed Potatoes

During testing for our Super-Stuffed Baked Potatoes, we found that most recipes called for the baked potatoes to be cut right in half before being filled. But these skimpy spuds were far from the super-stuffed garlic potatoes we were looking for. Instead, we found the best method was to cut off only the top quarter of the potato, leaving a much more substantial spud to stuff.

1. Slice off top quarter of microwaved potato.

2. Use spoon to scoop out interior of potato, being careful to leave ¼-inch layer of potato in shell.

Why This Recipe Works Roasting red peppers on the grill turns their juicy crunch smoky and tender. We tossed stemmed and cored peppers in garlic-infused olive oil, allowing the oil to soak into the interiors' exposed flesh. To prevent flare-ups, we grilled the peppers in a foil-covered disposable pan then drained them and placed them directly on the hot grates to char. After easily scraping the charred skins from the peppers, we tossed them in a vinaigrette made from the leftover oil and liquid released from the peppers. The finished peppers were tender, smoky, and infused with heady garlic flavor that complemented the intensified sweetness.

GRILL-ROASTED PEPPERS

SERVES 4

These peppers can be refrigerated for up to 5 days.

¼ cup extra-virgin olive oil
3 garlic cloves, peeled and smashed
   Salt and pepper
1 (13 by 9-inch) disposable aluminum pan
6 red bell peppers
1 tablespoon sherry vinegar

1. Combine oil, garlic, ½ teaspoon salt, and ¼ teaspoon pepper in disposable pan. Using paring knife, cut around stems of peppers and remove cores and seeds. Place peppers in pan and turn to coat with oil. Cover pan tightly with aluminum foil.

2A. For a Charcoal Grill Open bottom vent completely. Light large chimney starter filled with charcoal briquettes (6 quarts). When top coals are partially covered with ash, pour evenly over half of grill. Set cooking grate in place, cover, and open lid vent completely. Heat grill until hot, about 5 minutes.

2B. For a Gas Grill Turn all burners to high, cover, and heat grill until hot, about 15 minutes. Turn all burners to medium-high.

3. Clean and oil cooking grate. Place pan on grill (over hotter side for charcoal) and cook, covered, until peppers are just tender and skins begin to blister, 10 to 15 minutes, rotating and shaking pan halfway through cooking.

4. Remove pan from heat and carefully remove foil (reserve foil to use later). Using tongs, remove peppers from pan, allowing juices to drip back into pan, and place on grill (over hotter side for charcoal). Grill peppers, covered, turning every few minutes until skins are blackened, 10 to 15 minutes.

5. Transfer juices and garlic in pan to medium bowl and whisk in vinegar. Remove peppers from grill, return to now-empty pan, and cover tightly with foil. Let peppers steam for 5 minutes. Using spoon, scrape blackened skin off each pepper. Quarter peppers lengthwise, add to vinaigrette in bowl, and toss to combine. Season with salt and pepper to taste, and serve.

Steam Then Sear

We first steam the peppers in garlicky olive oil and their own juices. Then we sear the peppers and serve them with a vinaigrette made from the infused oil.

CAESAR GREEN BEAN SALAD

SERVES 4 TO 6

For maximum crunch, use a good-quality baguette for the croutons. The dressing can be made up to 1 day in advance.

Dressing and Green Beans

1½ tablespoons lemon juice
1 tablespoon Worcestershire sauce
1 tablespoon Dijon mustard
3 garlic cloves, minced
3 anchovy fillets, minced to paste
  Salt and pepper
3 tablespoons extra-virgin olive oil
1½ pounds green beans, trimmed
2 ounces Parmesan cheese, shaved with vegetable peeler

Croutons

3 ounces baguette, cut into ½-inch pieces
2 tablespoons extra-virgin olive oil
¼ teaspoon pepper

1. For the Dressing and Green Beans Whisk lemon juice, Worcestershire, mustard, garlic, anchovies, ½ teaspoon pepper, and ¼ teaspoon salt in bowl until combined. Slowly whisk in oil until emulsified; set aside.

2. Line baking sheet with clean dish towel. Bring 4 quarts water to boil in large Dutch oven. Add green beans and 1½ teaspoons salt, return to boil, and cook until tender, 5 to 7 minutes. Drain green beans in colander and spread in even layer on prepared sheet. Let green beans cool completely.

3. For the Croutons Meanwhile, toss baguette, oil, and pepper in large bowl until baguette pieces are coated with oil. Transfer to 12-inch nonstick skillet (reserve bowl). Cook over medium-high heat, stirring occasionally, until golden brown and crispy, 5 to 7 minutes. Return croutons to reserved bowl.

4. Transfer dressing, green beans, and half of Parmesan to bowl with croutons and toss to combine. Season with salt and pepper to taste. Transfer to serving dish. Sprinkle with remaining Parmesan. Serve.

Draining Green Beans

Instead of shocking the green beans in ice water to stop the cooking, we simply drain them and spread them onto a dish towel–lined baking sheet to cool.

Shaving Parmesan Cheese

Run a vegetable peeler over a block of Parmesan cheese to make paper-thin shavings.

Why This Recipe Works It's hard to beat a classic Caesar salad, so we wanted to translate the familiar flavor we love into a fuss-free green bean side dish. To keep the flavors bold and prevent the green beans from being waterlogged, we blanched the beans and then transferred them to a towel-lined baking sheet to cool. Dijon mustard provided great flavor and helped emulsify the dressing so it would cling well to the beans. We didn't want to skip the croutons, so we browned small baguette cubes in a skillet until they were perfectly crispy and would add just the right crunch to our beans.

STUFFED TOMATOES

SERVES 6

Look for large tomatoes, about 3 inches in diameter.

- 6 large vine-ripened tomatoes (8 to 10 ounces each)
- 1 tablespoon sugar
  Kosher salt and pepper
- 4½ tablespoons extra-virgin olive oil
- ¼ cup panko bread crumbs
- 3 ounces Gruyère cheese, shredded (¾ cup)
- 1 onion, halved and sliced thin
- 2 garlic cloves, minced
- ⅛ teaspoon red pepper flakes
- 8 ounces (8 cups) baby spinach, chopped coarse
- 1 cup couscous
- ½ teaspoon grated lemon zest
- 1 tablespoon red wine vinegar

1. Adjust oven rack to middle position and heat oven to 375 degrees. Cut top ½ inch off stem end of tomatoes and set aside. Using melon baller, scoop out tomato pulp and transfer to fine-mesh strainer set over bowl. Press on pulp with wooden spoon to extract juice; set aside juice and discard pulp. (You should have about ⅔ cup tomato juice; if not, add water as needed to equal ⅔ cup.)

2. Combine sugar and 1 tablespoon salt in bowl. Sprinkle each tomato cavity with 1 teaspoon sugar mixture, then turn tomatoes upside down on plate to drain for 30 minutes.

3. Combine 1½ teaspoons oil and panko in 10-inch skillet and toast over medium-high heat, stirring frequently, until golden brown, about 3 minutes. Transfer to bowl and let cool for 10 minutes. Stir in ¼ cup Gruyère.

4. Heat 2 tablespoons oil in now-empty skillet over medium heat until shimmering. Add onion and ½ teaspoon salt and cook until softened, 5 to 7 minutes. Stir in garlic and pepper flakes and cook until fragrant, about 30 seconds. Add spinach, 1 handful at a time, and cook until wilted, about 3 minutes. Stir in couscous, lemon zest, and reserved tomato juice. Cover, remove from heat, and let sit until couscous has absorbed liquid, about 7 minutes. Transfer couscous mixture to bowl and stir in remaining ½ cup Gruyère. Season with salt and pepper to taste.

5. Coat bottom of 13 by 9-inch baking dish with remaining 2 tablespoons oil. Blot tomato cavities dry with paper towels and season with salt and pepper. Pack each tomato with couscous mixture, about ½ cup per tomato, mounding excess. Top stuffed tomatoes with 1 heaping tablespoon panko mixture. Place tomatoes in prepared dish. Season reserved tops with salt and pepper and place in empty spaces in dish.

6. Bake, uncovered, until tomatoes have softened but still hold their shape, about 20 minutes. Using slotted spoon, transfer to serving platter. Whisk vinegar into oil remaining in dish, then drizzle over tomatoes. Place tops on tomatoes and serve.

STUFFED TOMATOES WITH BACON

Substitute shredded smoked cheddar for Gruyère. Stir 3 slices chopped, cooked bacon into cooked couscous mixture with cheddar in step 4.

STUFFED TOMATOES WITH CAPERS AND PINE NUTS

Substitute shredded mozzarella for Gruyère. Stir 2 tablespoons rinsed capers and 2 tablespoons toasted pine nuts into cooked couscous mixture with mozzarella in step 4.

STUFFED TOMATOES WITH CURRANTS AND PISTACHIOS

Substitute crumbled feta for Gruyère. Stir 2 tablespoons currants and 2 tablespoons chopped pistachios into cooked couscous mixture with feta in step 4.

STUFFED TOMATOES WITH OLIVES AND ORANGE

Substitute shredded Manchego for Gruyère. Substitute ¼ teaspoon grated orange zest for lemon zest. Stir ¼ cup pitted kalamata olives, chopped, into cooked couscous mixture with Manchego in step 4.

Why This Recipe Works Stuffed tomatoes always sound delicious, but too often you get tasteless tomatoes and a lackluster stuffing that falls out in a clump. To concentrate flavor and get rid of excess moisture, we seasoned hollowed-out tomato shells with salt and sugar and let them drain. Couscous proved the best base for the filling, and we rehydrated it with the reserved tomato juice, ensuring the savory tomato flavor we craved. A topping of panko bread crumbs—pretoasted for proper browning—mixed with more cheese added crunch and richness, and a drizzle of the cooking liquid mixed with red wine vinegar provided a piquant final touch.

our sunday best

OLD-FASHIONED ROAST TURKEY WITH GRAVY

SERVES 10 TO 12

You will need one 2-yard package of cheesecloth for this recipe. Because we layer the bird with salt pork, we prefer to use a natural turkey here; a self-basting turkey (such as a frozen Butterball) may become too salty. If using a self-basting turkey, omit the chicken broth in the gravy and increase the amount of water to 7 cups. Make sure to start the gravy as soon as the turkey goes into the oven.

Turkey
1 (2-yard) package cheesecloth
4 cups water
1 (12- to 14-pound) turkey, neck, giblets, and tailpiece removed and reserved for gravy
1 pound salt pork, cut into ¼-inch-thick slices

Gravy
1 tablespoon vegetable oil
1 onion, chopped
5 cups water
2 cups chicken broth
4 sprigs fresh thyme
1 bay leaf
6 tablespoons all-purpose flour
Salt and pepper

1. For the Turkey Adjust oven rack to lowest position and heat oven to 350 degrees. Fold cheesecloth into 18-inch square, place in large bowl, and cover with water. Tuck wings behind turkey and arrange, breast side up, on V-rack set in roasting pan. Prick skin of breast and legs of turkey all over with fork, cover breast and legs with salt pork, top with soaked cheesecloth (pouring any remaining water into roasting pan), and cover cheesecloth completely with heavy-duty aluminum foil.

2. Roast turkey until breast registers 140 degrees, 2½ to 3 hours. Remove foil, cheesecloth, and salt pork and discard. Increase oven temperature to 425 degrees. Continue to roast until breast registers 160 degrees and thighs register 175 degrees, 40 minutes to 1 hour longer. Transfer turkey to carving board and let rest 30 minutes.

3. For the Gravy Meanwhile, heat oil in large saucepan over medium-high heat until shimmering. Cook turkey neck and giblets until browned, about 5 minutes. Add onion and cook until softened, about 3 minutes. Stir in water, broth, thyme, and bay leaf and bring to boil. Reduce heat to low and simmer until reduced by half, about 3 hours. Strain mixture through fine-mesh strainer into 4-cup liquid measuring cup (you should have about 3½ cups), reserving giblets if desired.

4. Carefully strain contents of roasting pan into fat separator. Let liquid settle, then skim, reserving ¼ cup fat. Pour defatted pan juices into measuring cup with giblet broth to yield 4 cups liquid.

5. Heat reserved fat in empty saucepan over medium heat until shimmering. Stir in flour and cook until golden and fragrant, about 4 minutes. Slowly whisk in giblet broth and bring to boil. Reduce heat to medium-low and simmer until slightly thickened, about 5 minutes. Chop giblets and add to gravy, if desired, and season with salt and pepper to taste. Carve turkey and serve with gravy.

Salt Pork
Covering the breast and tops of the legs of the turkey with salt pork helps to season the meat and insulate it from overcooking. Don't confuse salt pork with bacon. Although both come from the belly of the pig and are salt-cured, bacon is heavily smoked and is typically leaner and meatier. Salt pork is unsmoked and used primarily as a flavoring agent (traditionally in dishes like baked beans) and is rarely actually consumed. We recommend buying blocks of salt pork (precut slices can dry out) and portioning it as needed. Look for salt pork that has at least a few streaks of meat throughout. Salt pork can be refrigerated for up to one month.

Why This Recipe Works For a roast turkey with moist, flavorful meat, we tried a number of options until we discovered a technique used for ages: barding. Similar to larding, it is a process of wrapping strips of lard (or other animal fat) around the meat so that it slowly releases flavor and moisture throughout roasting. After piercing the skin of the turkey breast and legs with a fork, we covered it with thin slices of salt pork before layering on cheesecloth that had been soaked in water and then aluminum foil. This insulated the meat and allowed the salt pork to slowly melt in the oven, basting the turkey with rich fat.

Why This Recipe Works For a lower-maintenance, holiday-worthy turkey and stuffing made in one pan, we started with bone-in turkey breast instead of a whole bird. This made for easier carving and eliminated the challenge of differing cook times for white and dark meat. For the stuffing, we used ciabatta, since it retained its chew, with a combo of herbs, onion, wine, and chicken broth (plus some hot Italian sausage for meaty savoriness and a bit of heat). We roasted the turkey breast on top of the stuffing and then removed it before returning the stuffing to the oven to crisp up. A vibrant sauce of pomegranate seeds and parsley added a final holiday flourish.

ONE-PAN TURKEY BREAST AND STUFFING WITH POMEGRANATE-PARSLEY SAUCE

SERVES 8 TO 10

The salted turkey needs to be refrigerated for at least 2 hours before cooking. If you can't find a loaf of ciabatta, you can substitute 2 pounds of another rustic, mild-tasting white bread. Do not use sourdough here; its flavor is too assertive.

Turkey

- 1½ tablespoons kosher salt
- 1 tablespoon pepper
- 1 tablespoon minced fresh thyme
- 1 (5- to 7-pound) bone-in turkey breast, trimmed

Stuffing

- ½ cup extra-virgin olive oil
- 3 cups chopped onion
- 1¾ teaspoons kosher salt, divided
- 6 garlic cloves, minced
- 3 cups chicken broth
- ⅓ cup dry white wine
- 2 tablespoons minced fresh sage
- 1 tablespoon minced fresh thyme
- ¼ teaspoon red pepper flakes
- 2 pounds ciabatta, cut into 1-inch cubes (about 20 cups)
- 1 pound hot Italian sausage, casings removed
- 1½ cups coarsely chopped fresh parsley

Sauce

- ¾ cup chopped fresh parsley
- ¾ cup pomegranate seeds
- ½ cup extra-virgin olive oil
- 1 shallot, minced
- 2 tablespoons lemon juice
- 2 garlic cloves, minced
- ¾ teaspoon kosher salt

1. For the Turkey Combine salt, pepper, and thyme in bowl. Place turkey on large plate and pat dry with paper towels. Sprinkle all over with salt mixture. Refrigerate, uncovered, for at least 2 hours or up to 24 hours.

2. For the Stuffing Adjust oven rack to lower-middle position and heat oven to 325 degrees. Spray large heavy-duty roasting pan with vegetable oil spray, then add oil to pan. Heat oil in roasting pan over medium heat until shimmering. Add onion and ¼ teaspoon salt and cook until onion is golden brown, about 10 minutes. Add garlic and cook until fragrant, about 30 seconds.

3. Off heat, stir in broth, wine, sage, thyme, pepper flakes, and remaining 1½ teaspoons salt, scraping up any browned bits. Add bread and, using tongs or your hands, toss until bread is evenly coated. Break sausage into ¾-inch chunks and toss with bread mixture to combine.

4. Nestle turkey, skin side up, into stuffing in center of roasting pan. Roast until thickest part of turkey registers 160 degrees, 2¼ to 2¾ hours.

5. For the Sauce Meanwhile, combine all ingredients in bowl; set aside.

6. Transfer turkey to carving board, skin side up, and let rest, uncovered, for at least 30 minutes or up to 1 hour.

7. Meanwhile, stir stuffing in roasting pan. Return pan to oven and cook until top of bread looks golden brown and is evenly dry, 10 to 15 minutes.

8. Remove breast meat from bone and slice thin crosswise. Toss parsley with stuffing in roasting pan. Arrange turkey over stuffing in pan. Drizzle with sauce. Serve, passing remaining sauce separately.

CORNBREAD AND SAUSAGE STUFFING

SERVES 10 TO 12

We prefer spicy andouille sausage in this recipe, but chorizo or kielbasa work well, too. For the cornbread, use your favorite recipe, store-bought cornbread, or Betty Crocker Golden Corn Muffin and Bread Mix or Jiffy Corn Muffin Mix, both of which will work fine in stuffing.

- 12 cups prepared cornbread cut into ¾-inch cubes
- 1½ pounds andouille sausage, halved lengthwise and sliced into ¼-inch-thick half-moons
- 2 tablespoons unsalted butter
- 2 small onions, chopped fine
- 3 celery ribs, chopped fine
- 2 tablespoons minced fresh sage
- 3 garlic cloves, minced
- 1 teaspoon salt
- 1 teaspoon pepper
- 4 cups chicken broth

1. Adjust oven racks to upper-middle and lower-middle positions and heat oven to 400 degrees. Spread cornbread evenly over 2 rimmed baking sheets. Bake until slightly crisp, 15 to 20 minutes; let cool. Carefully remove upper-middle rack from oven.

2. Cook sausage in Dutch oven over medium-high heat until lightly browned, 5 to 7 minutes. Transfer to paper towel–lined plate and pour off fat left behind in pot. Melt butter over medium-high heat, add onions and celery, and cook until softened, about 5 minutes. Stir in sage, garlic, salt, and pepper and cook until fragrant, about 1 minute. Add broth and sausage, scraping up browned bits with wooden spoon. Add cornbread and gently stir until liquid is absorbed. Cover and set aside for 10 minutes. (Stuffing can be refrigerated for 1 day; let sit at room temperature for 30 minutes before baking.)

3. Remove lid and bake until top of stuffing is golden brown and crisp, about 30 minutes. Serve.

CORNBREAD AND BACON STUFFING

Substitute 1 pound bacon, chopped, for sausage, 3 cups fresh or frozen corn kernels for celery, and 3 thinly sliced scallions for sage.

Drying Cornbread

Although cornbread gives stuffing great flavor, it also adds a lot of moisture, making a soggy baked mess. If you have the time, cube the cornbread, spread it out on baking sheets, and let it sit overnight on the counter. If you're in a hurry (and who isn't around the holidays?), pop the baking sheets holding the cornbread into a 400-degree oven and bake until slightly crisp, 15 to 20 minutes.

Why This Recipe Works We wanted a stuffing rich enough to stand on its own without gravy. We found our answer in cornbread and sausage. Cornbread gives the stuffing more flavor than plain white bread. We wanted plenty of stuffing, so we chose to cook it in a Dutch oven, which is large enough to accommodate 10 to 12 portions. To compensate for the loss in richness and poultry flavor we didn't just rely on any sausage—we chose spicy andouille sausage. Adding chicken broth to the stuffing further boosted the meaty flavor of our stuffing and helped keep it from drying out.

Why This Recipe Works Developing a recipe for a classic herb roast chicken proved surprisingly tricky. Stuffing the chicken with fresh herbs delivered zero flavor, herb butter melted off the chicken, and infused oil failed to really penetrate the meat. Our solution was to slather the chicken with a thick paste of fresh herbs and garlic, processed until smooth, then let it rest to develop a pronounced herbal flavor. So that there was plenty of meat to go around, we used two whole chickens instead of one. For a simple pan sauce, we whisked the drippings with chicken broth, white wine, cornstarch, butter, and additional herb paste while the chicken rested.

HERB ROAST CHICKEN

SERVES 6 TO 8

For even cooking, arrange the chickens side by side a few inches apart on the V-rack, with the legs pointing in opposite directions.

1 cup chopped fresh parsley
2 tablespoons chopped fresh thyme
1 tablespoon chopped fresh rosemary
2 garlic cloves, minced
   Salt and pepper
2 tablespoons olive oil
2 (3½- to 4-pound) whole chickens,
   giblets discarded
1 cup plus 2 tablespoons water
2 teaspoons cornstarch
1¼ cups chicken broth
¼ cup dry white wine
2 tablespoons unsalted butter, chilled

1. Process parsley, thyme, rosemary, garlic, 2 teaspoons salt, and 1 teaspoon pepper in food processor until paste forms, about 30 seconds. Reserve 1 teaspoon herb paste for sauce. Combine 2 tablespoons herb paste with oil in bowl. Set aside herb-oil paste and remaining herb paste.

2. Adjust oven rack to middle position and heat oven to 450 degrees. Pat chickens dry with paper towels. Using your fingers, gently loosen skin covering breast and thighs. Rub remaining herb paste under skin of each chicken, making sure to coat breast, thigh, and leg meat. Rub herb-oil paste over outside of each chicken. Tuck wings behind back and tie legs together with kitchen twine. Transfer chickens to platter. Cover and refrigerate 1 hour.

3. Arrange chickens 2 inches apart, breast side down, on V-rack set inside large roasting pan. Roast until thigh meat registers 135 to 140 degrees, 35 to 40 minutes. Remove chickens from oven and, using 2 bunches of paper towels, flip breast side up (meat that was facing in should now be facing out). Pour 1 cup water into roasting pan. Return chickens to oven and roast until breast registers 160 degrees and thighs register 175 degrees, 25 to 30 minutes. Transfer to carving board and let rest for 20 minutes.

4. Whisk cornstarch with remaining 2 tablespoons water in bowl until no lumps remain. Pour pan juices and any accumulated chicken juices into liquid measuring cup; skim fat. Transfer ½ cup defatted pan juices to medium saucepan. Add broth and wine and bring to boil. Reduce heat to medium-low and simmer until sauce is slightly thickened and reduced to 1¼ cups, 8 to 10 minutes. Whisk in cornstarch mixture and simmer until thickened, 3 to 5 minutes. Off heat, whisk in butter and reserved 1 teaspoon herb paste. Season with salt and pepper to taste. Carve chickens and serve, passing sauce at table.

Herb Flavor Times Three

To get deeply flavored roast chicken, we triple up on the herb paste.

1. Separate skin from meat and rub herb paste under skin.

2. Apply herb paste mixed with olive oil to exterior of each chicken.

3. Whisk teaspoon of herb paste into sauce for a fresh finish.

ROAST LEMON CHICKEN

SERVES 3 TO 4

Avoid using nonstick or aluminum roasting pans in this recipe. The former can cause the chicken to brown too quickly, while the latter may react with the lemon juice, producing off-flavors.

1 (3½- to 4-pound) whole chicken, giblets discarded
3 tablespoons grated lemon zest plus ⅓ cup juice (3 lemons)
1 teaspoon sugar
Salt and pepper
2 cups chicken broth
Water
1 teaspoon cornstarch
3 tablespoons unsalted butter
1 tablespoon finely chopped fresh parsley

1. Adjust oven rack to middle position and heat oven to 475 degrees. Pat chicken dry with paper towels. Using kitchen shears, cut along both sides of backbone to remove it. Flatten breastbone and tuck wings behind back. Using your fingers, gently loosen skin covering breast and thighs. Combine lemon zest, sugar, and 1 teaspoon salt in small bowl. Rub 2 tablespoons zest mixture under skin of chicken. Season chicken with salt and pepper and transfer to roasting pan. (Seasoned chicken can be refrigerated for 2 hours.)

2. Whisk broth, 1 cup water, lemon juice, and remaining zest mixture in 4-cup liquid measuring cup, then pour into roasting pan. (Liquid should just reach skin of thighs. If it does not, add enough water to reach skin of thighs.) Roast until skin is golden brown and breast registers 160 degrees and thighs register 175 degrees, 40 to 45 minutes. Transfer to carving board and let rest for 20 minutes.

3. Carefully pour liquid from pan, along with any accumulated chicken juices, into saucepan (you should have about 1½ cups). Skim fat, then cook over medium-high heat until reduced to 1 cup, about 5 minutes. Whisk cornstarch with 1 tablespoon water in small bowl until no lumps remain, then whisk into saucepan. Simmer until sauce is slightly thickened, about 2 minutes. Off heat, whisk in butter and parsley and season with salt and pepper. Carve chicken and serve, passing sauce at table.

More Lemon Flavor in Less Time

Butterflying the chicken may be unfamiliar, but this surprisingly simple process makes it easier to flavor the chicken with lemon—and it speeds roasting, too.

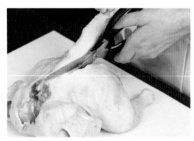

1. Use kitchen shears to cut out backbone. Flip bird and press to flatten breastbone.

2. Carefully loosen skin, then rub zest mixture into breast, thigh, and leg meat.

3. Roast flattened chicken in lemony sauce so flavor can permeate meat.

Why This Recipe Works The citrus flavor in roasted lemon chicken can be harsh or, on the flip side, totally absent. To infuse the meat with bright flavor, we combined lemon zest, sugar, and salt and rubbed it into the chicken under the skin. For even more lemon flavor, we roasted the chicken in a sauce of lemon juice mixed with water, more zest, and chicken broth. Roasting the bird at a high temperature ensured that the exposed skin became crisp. Before serving, we reduced the sauce to concentrate its flavor and thickened it with butter and cornstarch for sheen, body, and richness.

APPLE CIDER CHICKEN

SERVES 3 TO 4

Plain brandy, cognac, or Calvados (a French apple brandy) can be used in place of the apple brandy.

- 3 pounds bone-in chicken pieces, (split breasts halved crosswise, legs separated into thighs and drumsticks), trimmed
  Salt and pepper
- 2 teaspoons vegetable oil
- 1 onion, chopped fine
- 2 garlic cloves, minced
- 2 teaspoons minced fresh thyme
- 2 teaspoons all-purpose flour
- 1 large Golden Delicious, Cortland, or Jonagold apple (8 ounces), peeled, cored, and cut into ¾-inch pieces
- 1 cup apple cider
- ¼ cup apple brandy
- 1 teaspoon cider vinegar

1. Adjust oven rack to middle position and heat oven to 450 degrees. Pat chicken dry with paper towels and season with salt and pepper. Heat oil in 12-inch ovenproof skillet over medium-high heat until just smoking. Cook chicken skin side down until well browned, about 10 minutes. Flip and brown on second side, about 5 minutes. Transfer to plate.

2. Pour off all but 1 tablespoon fat from skillet. Add onion and cook until softened, about 5 minutes. Stir in garlic, thyme, and flour and cook, stirring frequently, until fragrant and flour is absorbed, about 1 minute. Add apple, apple cider, and 3 tablespoons apple brandy and bring to boil.

3. Nestle chicken skin side up into sauce and roast in oven until breasts register 160 degrees and thighs/drumsticks register 175 degrees, about 10 minutes. Transfer chicken to platter. Stir vinegar and remaining 1 tablespoon brandy into sauce and season with salt and pepper to taste. Serve, passing sauce at table.

Preventing Flabby Skin
We avoid flabby skin with a hybrid technique that combines braising and pan roasting.

1. Brown chicken skin side down in skillet for 10 minutes until deep brown. Brown second side for 5 more minutes.

2. Finish chicken, skin side up and uncovered, in hot oven. Be sure liquid does not submerge chicken pieces.

Apple Cider versus Apple Juice
To make cider, apples are simply cored, chopped, mashed, and then pressed to extract their liquid. Most cider is pasteurized before sale, though unpasteurized cider is also available. To make apple juice, manufacturers follow the same steps used to make cider, but they also filter the extracted liquid to remove pulp and sediment. Apple juice is then pasteurized, and potassium sorbate (a preservative) is often mixed in to prevent fermentation. Finally, apple juice is sometimes sweetened with sugar or corn syrup. We tried using unsweetened apple juice in recipes for pork chops and glazed ham that call for cider. Tasters were turned off by excessive sweetness in the dishes made with apple juice, unanimously preferring those made with cider. This made sense: The filtration process used in making juice removes some of the complex, tart, and bitter flavors that are still present in cider. (When we tested the pH level of both liquids, the cider had a lower pH than the apple juice, confirming its higher level of acidity.) The bottom line: When it comes to cooking, don't swap apple juice for cider.

Why This Recipe Works We had a tall order with our Apple Cider Chicken: It had to taste like apples, and it had to have supercrisp skin. Cooking the chicken skin side down in a skillet and then moving it to a hot oven kept the skin exceptionally crisp. When it came to flavor, apple cider alone didn't do the trick. We also needed fresh apples, apple brandy, and cider vinegar to flavor the chicken with apple goodness. For the sauce, Granny Smith apples were too sour, while other varieties turned to mush when cooked. In the end, we preferred Golden Delicious, Cortland, or Jonagold apples, which held their shape and offered sweet flavor.

Why This Recipe Works Cooking vegetables and chicken together in the same pan often leads to unevenly cooked chicken and greasy, soggy vegetables. To get the chicken and vegetables to cook at the same rate, we used chicken parts, which contain less overall fat than a whole chicken and don't smother the vegetables underneath, which would cause them to steam. To ensure that the delicate white meat stayed moist while the darker meat cooked through, we placed the chicken breasts in the center of the pan and the thighs and drumsticks around the perimeter.

ONE-PAN ROAST CHICKEN WITH ROOT VEGETABLES

SERVES 4

We halve the chicken breasts crosswise for even cooking. Use brussels sprouts no bigger than golf balls, as larger ones are often tough and woody.

12 ounces brussels sprouts, trimmed and halved
12 ounces red potatoes, cut into 1-inch pieces
 8 ounces shallots, peeled and halved
 4 carrots, peeled and cut into 2-inch pieces, thick ends halved lengthwise
 6 garlic cloves, peeled
 4 teaspoons minced fresh thyme
 1 tablespoon vegetable oil
 2 teaspoons minced fresh rosemary
 1 teaspoon sugar
    Salt and pepper
 2 tablespoons unsalted butter, melted
3½ pounds bone-in chicken pieces (2 split breasts halved crosswise, 2 drumsticks, and 2 thighs), trimmed

1. Adjust oven rack to upper-middle position and heat oven to 475 degrees. Toss brussels sprouts, potatoes, shallots, carrots, garlic, 2 teaspoons thyme, oil, 1 teaspoon rosemary, sugar, ¾ teaspoon salt, and ¼ teaspoon pepper together in bowl. Combine butter, remaining 2 teaspoons thyme, remaining 1 teaspoon rosemary, ¼ teaspoon salt, and ⅛ teaspoon pepper in second bowl; set aside.

2. Pat chicken dry with paper towels and season with salt and pepper. Place vegetables in single layer on rimmed baking sheet, arranging brussels sprouts in center. Place chicken, skin side up, on top of vegetables, arranging breast pieces in center and leg and thigh pieces around perimeter of sheet.

3. Brush chicken with herb butter and roast until breasts register 160 degrees and thighs/drumsticks register 175 degrees, 35 to 40 minutes, rotating pan halfway through cooking. Transfer chicken to serving platter, tent loosely with aluminum foil, and let rest for 5 to 10 minutes. Toss vegetables in pan juices and transfer to platter with chicken. Serve.

ONE-PAN ROAST CHICKEN WITH FENNEL AND PARSNIPS

Replace brussels sprouts and carrots with 1 fennel bulb, stalks discarded, bulb halved, cored, and sliced into ½-inch wedges, and 8 ounces (4 medium) parsnips, peeled and cut into 2-inch pieces.

Preparing Fennel

1. Cut off stalks and feathery fronds. Trim very thin slice from base and remove any tough or blemished outer layer.

2. Cut bulb in half through base. Use small sharp knife to remove pyramid-shaped cone.

3. Cut each half into ½-inch wedges.

SKILLET-ROASTED CHICKEN AND POTATOES

SERVES 4

Use uniform, medium potatoes.

- 3 tablespoons olive oil
- 2 teaspoons minced fresh thyme
- 1½ teaspoons smoked paprika
- 1½ teaspoons grated lemon zest,
  plus lemon wedges for serving
  Salt and pepper
- 1 (4-pound) whole chicken, giblets discarded
- 2 pounds Yukon Gold potatoes, peeled,
  ends squared off, and sliced into
  1-inch-thick rounds

1. Adjust oven rack to lower middle position and heat oven to 400 degrees. Combine 2 tablespoons oil, thyme, paprika, lemon zest, 1 teaspoon salt, and ½ teaspoon pepper in bowl. Pat chicken dry with paper towels and use your fingers or handle of wooden spoon to carefully separate skin from breast. Rub oil mixture all over chicken and underneath skin of breast. Tie legs together with kitchen twine and tuck wingtips behind back.

2. Toss potatoes with remaining 1 tablespoon oil, 1½ teaspoons salt, and ½ teaspoon pepper. Arrange potatoes, flat sides down, in single layer in 12-inch ovensafe nonstick skillet. Place skillet over medium heat and cook potatoes, without moving them, until brown on bottom, 7 to 9 minutes (do not flip).

3. Place chicken, breast side up, on top of potatoes and transfer skillet to oven. Roast until breast registers 160 degrees and thighs register 175 degrees, 1 to 1¼ hours. Transfer chicken to carving board, tent loosely with aluminum foil, and let rest for 20 minutes.

4. Meanwhile, cover skillet, return potatoes to oven, and roast until tender, about 20 minutes. Carve chicken and serve with potatoes and lemon wedges.

Keys to Potatoes That Are Tender and Brown

Potatoes don't cook at the same rate as a chicken. Here's how we got the dish to work.

1. On the Stove Brown one side of potatoes on stovetop, then top spuds with chicken and roast.

2. In the Oven Once chicken is done, set aside; cover pan and return to oven to finish cooking potatoes.

Prepping Fresh Thyme

For thin-stemmed thyme, chop stems along with leaves. If stems are thick, hold sprig upright and run your thumb and forefinger along stem to release leaves.

Why This Recipe Works For this convenient, one-pan meal, we were challenged to deliver tender potatoes and moist chicken at the same time. First, we quickly browned one side of the potatoes (an entire 2 pounds of potatoes fit into a 12-inch skillet when sliced into 1-inch-thick rounds). We placed the bird on top and moved everything to the oven, where flavorful juices basted the potatoes. An hour later, the chicken was golden and juicy and the potatoes had a caramelized crust on the bottom. While the chicken rested, we returned the potatoes to the oven. By the time the chicken was ready to be served, the potatoes were soft and flavorful.

Why This Recipe Works To simplify Sunday-style stuffed chicken into a one-pan meal, we sped things up by taking the stuffing out of the chicken and making the entire dish in just one skillet. First we sautéed the aromatics for the stuffing, then we placed the chicken—brushed with a flavorful herb butter—right on top. We scattered the bread cubes around the bird and moved the skillet to the oven to simultaneously roast the chicken and toast the bread. As the chicken cooked, the bread soaked up its flavorful juices. Finally, while the chicken rested, a quick stir and a splash of broth mixed up the aromatics and moistened the stuffing.

SKILLET-ROASTED CHICKEN WITH STUFFING

SERVES 4

You can find Italian bread in the bakery section of your grocery store. Take care when stirring the contents of the skillet in steps 4 and 5, as the skillet handle will be very hot.

- 1 (4-pound) whole chicken, giblets discarded
- 6 tablespoons unsalted butter
- 2 tablespoons minced fresh sage
- 2 tablespoons minced fresh thyme
  Salt and pepper
- 2 onions, chopped fine
- 2 celery ribs, minced
- 7 ounces Italian bread, cut into ½-inch cubes (6 cups)
- ⅓ cup chicken broth

1. Adjust oven rack to lower-middle position and heat oven to 375 degrees. Pat chicken dry with paper towels. Melt 4 tablespoons butter in small bowl in microwave, about 45 seconds. Stir in 1 tablespoon sage, 1 tablespoon thyme, 1 teaspoon salt, and ½ teaspoon pepper. Brush chicken with herb butter.

2. Melt remaining 2 tablespoons butter in 12-inch ovensafe skillet over medium heat. Add onions, celery, ½ teaspoon salt, and ½ teaspoon pepper and cook until softened, about 5 minutes. Add remaining 1 tablespoon sage and remaining 1 tablespoon thyme and cook until fragrant, about 1 minute. Off heat, place chicken, breast side up, on top of vegetables. Arrange bread cubes around chicken in bottom of skillet.

3. Transfer skillet to oven and roast until breasts register 160 degrees and thighs register 175 degrees, about 1 hour, rotating skillet halfway through roasting.

4. Carefully transfer chicken to plate and tent loosely with aluminum foil. Holding skillet handle with potholder (handle will be hot), stir bread and vegetables to combine, cover, and let stand for 10 minutes.

5. Add broth and any accumulated chicken juice from plate and cavity to skillet and stir to combine. Warm stuffing, uncovered, over low heat until heated through, about 3 minutes. Remove from heat, cover, and let sit while carving chicken. Transfer chicken to carving board, carve, and serve with stuffing.

Chopping Onions Finely

1. Halve onion through root end, then peel onion and trim top. Make several horizontal cuts from 1 end of onion to other but don't cut through root end.

2. Make several vertical cuts. Be sure to cut up to but not through root end.

3. Rotate onion so root end is in back; slice onion thinly across previous cuts. As you slice, onion will fall apart into chopped pieces.

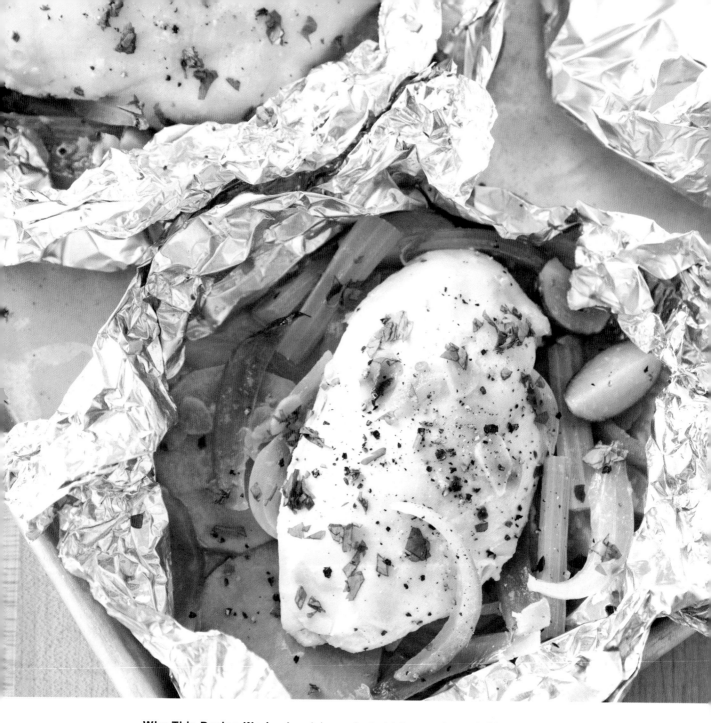

Why This Recipe Works A quick meal of chicken and vegetables baked in foil sounded great to us, but our first attempts were not much better than an old-style TV dinner. Seasoning the chicken with salt on both sides and refrigerating it for at least an hour proved ideal, as did using sturdy vegetables, which held up during cooking. Placing the potato slices under the chicken insulated the meat from the oven's direct heat, and we found that leaving plenty of headroom above the chicken within the pouch gave the steam room to circulate, ensuring even cooking. An added bonus? No pots or pans to clean.

CHICKEN BAKED IN FOIL WITH SWEET POTATO AND RADISH

SERVES 4

To ensure even cooking, cut the vegetables as directed and buy chicken breasts of the same size. Refrigerate the pouches for at least 1 hour before cooking.

- 5 tablespoons extra-virgin olive oil
- 6 garlic cloves, sliced thin
- 1 tablespoon grated fresh ginger
- ¼ teaspoon red pepper flakes
- 12 ounces sweet potatoes, peeled and sliced ¼ inch thick
- 4 radishes, trimmed and quartered
- 2 celery ribs, quartered lengthwise and cut into 2-inch lengths
- ½ large red onion, sliced ½ inch thick, layers separated
  Kosher salt and pepper
- 4 (6-ounce) boneless, skinless chicken breasts, trimmed
- 2 tablespoons rice vinegar
- 2 tablespoons minced fresh cilantro

1. Spray centers of four 20 by 12-inch sheets of heavy-duty aluminum foil with vegetable oil spray. Microwave oil, garlic, ginger, and pepper flakes in small bowl until garlic begins to brown, 1 to 1½ minutes. Combine potato slices, radishes, celery, onion, 1 teaspoon salt, and garlic oil in large bowl.

2. Pat chicken dry with paper towels. Sprinkle ⅛ teaspoon salt evenly over each side of each chicken breast, then season with pepper. Position 1 piece of prepared foil with long side parallel to counter edge. In center of foil, arrange one-quarter of potato slices in 2 rows perpendicular to counter edge. Lay 1 chicken breast on top of potato slices. Place one-quarter of vegetables around chicken. Repeat with remaining foil, potato slices, chicken, and vegetables. Drizzle any remaining oil mixture from bowl over chicken.

3. Bring short sides of foil together and crimp to seal tightly. Crimp remaining open ends of packets, leaving as much headroom as possible inside packets. Refrigerate for at least 1 hour or up to 24 hours.

4. Adjust oven rack to lowest position and heat oven to 475 degrees. Arrange packets on rimmed baking sheet. Bake until chicken registers 160 degrees, 18 to 23 minutes. (To check temperature, poke thermometer through foil and into chicken.) Let chicken rest in packets for 3 minutes.

5. Transfer chicken packets to individual dinner plates, carefully open (steam will escape), and slide contents onto plates. Drizzle vinegar over chicken and vegetables and sprinkle with cilantro. Serve.

CHICKEN BAKED IN FOIL WITH POTATOES AND CARROTS

Substitute 12 ounces Yukon Gold potatoes (unpeeled, sliced ¼ inch thick) and 2 carrots (peeled, quartered lengthwise and cut into 2-inch lengths), for sweet potatoes, radishes, and celery; lemon juice for rice vinegar. Substitute 1 teaspoon minced fresh thyme for ginger and 2 tablespoons minced fresh chives for cilantro.

CHICKEN BAKED IN FOIL WITH FENNEL AND SUN-DRIED TOMATOES

Substitute 1 fennel bulb, stalks discarded, bulb halved, cored, and cut into ½-inch-thick wedges, layers separated, for celery; balsamic vinegar for rice vinegar; and minced fresh basil for cilantro. Add ¼ cup oil-packed sun-dried tomatoes, rinsed, patted dry, and chopped fine and ¼ cup pitted kalamata olives, chopped fine, to vegetables in step 1.

CHICKEN AND SLICKS

SERVES 4 TO 6

If you're short on chicken fat at the end of step 1, supplement it with vegetable oil.

1½ pounds bone-in chicken thighs, trimmed
 2 (12-ounce) bone-in split chicken breasts, halved crosswise and trimmed
   Salt and pepper
 6 tablespoons plus 2 cups all-purpose flour
 3 tablespoons vegetable oil
 1 onion, chopped
 2 teaspoons minced fresh thyme
7½ cups chicken broth
 2 bay leaves
 ¼ cup chopped fresh parsley

1. Pat chicken dry with paper towels and season with salt and pepper. Toast 6 tablespoons flour in Dutch oven over medium heat, stirring constantly, until just beginning to brown, about 5 minutes. Transfer flour to medium bowl and wipe out pot. Heat 1 tablespoon oil in now-empty Dutch oven over medium-high heat until just smoking. Cook chicken until browned all over, about 10 minutes; transfer to plate. When chicken is cool enough to handle, remove and discard skin. Pour fat (you should have about 2 tablespoons) into small bowl; reserve.

2. Add onion and 1 tablespoon oil to now-empty pot and cook over medium heat until softened, about 5 minutes. Stir in thyme and cook until fragrant, about 30 seconds. Add 7 cups broth, chicken, and bay leaves and bring to boil. Reduce heat to low and simmer, covered, until breasts register 160 degrees and thighs register 175 degrees, 20 to 25 minutes. Remove from heat and transfer chicken to clean plate. When chicken is cool enough to handle, shred into bite-size pieces, discarding bones.

3. Meanwhile, combine remaining ½ cup chicken broth, reserved fat, and remaining 1 tablespoon oil in liquid measuring cup. Process remaining 2 cups flour and ½ teaspoon salt in food processor until combined. With processor running, slowly pour in broth mixture and process until mixture resembles coarse meal. Turn dough onto lightly floured surface and knead until smooth. Divide in half.

4. Roll each dough half into 10-inch square about ⅛ inch thick. Cut each square into twenty 5 by 1-inch rectangles. Place handful of noodles in single layer on parchment paper–lined plate, cover with another sheet of parchment, and repeat stacking with remaining noodles and additional parchment, ending with parchment. Freeze until firm, at least 10 minutes or up to 30 minutes.

5. Return broth to simmer and add noodles. Cook until noodles are nearly tender, 12 to 15 minutes, stirring occasionally to separate. Remove 1 cup broth from pot and whisk into reserved toasted flour. Stir broth-flour mixture into pot, being careful not to break up noodles, and simmer until slightly thickened, 3 to 5 minutes. Add shredded chicken and parsley and cook until heated through, about 1 minute. Season with salt and pepper to taste. Serve.

Making Slicks

1. Roll each dough half into 10-inch square of ⅛-inch thickness. Then, using sharp knife, cut dough into twenty 5 by 1-inch rectangles.

2. Stack slicks between layers of parchment and freeze briefly before simmering.

Why This Recipe Works A distant cousin to chicken and dumplings, chicken and slicks offers tender chicken in a rich, flavorful broth but swaps the traditional biscuit-style dumpling for a thick, chewy, noodlelike version. For a flavorful base, we browned the chicken before simmering it in the broth; bone-in pieces provided the best flavor. While traditional recipes call for lard in the slicks, we replaced it with more readily available vegetable oil, plus some of the rendered fat from our chicken. Cooking the slicks in an already thickened broth caused them to break apart, so we cooked them in the broth before adding toasted flour to thicken it.

MORAVIAN CHICKEN PIE

SERVES 8

Crust

½ cup sour cream, chilled
1 large egg, lightly beaten
2½ cups (12½ ounces) all-purpose flour
1½ teaspoons salt
12 tablespoons unsalted butter, cut into ½-inch pieces and chilled

Filling

2 (10- to 12-ounce) bone-in split chicken breasts, halved crosswise and trimmed
3 (5- to 7-ounce) bone-in chicken thighs, trimmed
   Salt and pepper
1 tablespoon vegetable oil
3 cups chicken broth
1 bay leaf
2 tablespoons unsalted butter
¼ cup all-purpose flour
¼ cup half-and-half
1 large egg, lightly beaten

1. For the Crust Combine sour cream and egg in bowl. Process flour and salt in food processor until combined, about 3 seconds. Add butter and pulse until only pea-size pieces remain, about 10 pulses. Add half of sour cream mixture and pulse until combined, 5 pulses. Add remaining sour cream mixture and pulse until dough begins to form, about 10 pulses.

2. Transfer mixture to lightly floured counter and knead briefly until dough comes together. Divide dough in half and form each half into 4-inch disk. Wrap each disk in plastic wrap and refrigerate for at least 1 hour or up to 2 days.

3. Line rimmed baking sheet with parchment paper. Remove 1 dough disk from refrigerator and let sit for 10 minutes. Working on lightly floured counter, roll into 12-inch round and transfer to 9-inch pie plate, leaving ½-inch overhang all around. Repeat with second dough disk and transfer to prepared baking sheet. Cover both dough rounds with plastic wrap and refrigerate for 30 minutes.

4. For the Filling Pat chicken dry with paper towels and season with salt and pepper. Heat oil in large Dutch oven over medium-high heat until just smoking. Cook chicken until browned, about 10 minutes; transfer to plate. Pour fat (you should have 2 tablespoons; supplement with butter if necessary) into bowl; reserve. When chicken is cool enough to handle, remove and discard skin. Add broth, chicken, and bay leaf to now-empty pot and bring to boil. Reduce heat to low and simmer, covered, until breasts register 160 degrees and thighs register 175 degrees, 14 to 18 minutes. Transfer chicken to bowl. When chicken is cool enough to handle, shred into bite-size pieces, discarding bones. Pour broth through fine-mesh strainer into second bowl and reserve (you should have about 2¾ cups); discard bay leaf.

5. Adjust oven rack to lowest position and heat oven to 450 degrees. Heat butter and reserved fat in now-empty pot over medium heat until shimmering. Add flour and cook, whisking constantly, until golden, 1 to 2 minutes. Slowly whisk in 2 cups reserved broth and half-and-half and bring to boil. Reduce heat to medium-low and simmer gravy until thickened and reduced to 1¾ cups, 6 to 8 minutes. Season with salt and pepper to taste. Combine 1 cup gravy with shredded chicken; reserve remaining gravy for serving.

6. Transfer chicken mixture to dough-lined pie plate and spread into even layer. Top with second dough round, leaving at least ½-inch overhang all around. Fold dough under so that edge of fold is flush with rim of pie plate. Flute edges using thumb and forefinger or press with tines of fork to seal. Cut four 1-inch slits in top. Brush pie with egg and bake until top is light golden brown, 18 to 20 minutes. Reduce oven temperature to 375 degrees and continue to bake until crust is deep golden brown, 10 to 15 minutes. Let pie cool on wire rack for at least 45 minutes.

7. When ready to serve, bring remaining ¾ cup reserved gravy and remaining ¾ cup reserved broth to boil in medium saucepan. Simmer over medium-low heat until slightly thickened, 5 to 7 minutes. Season with salt and pepper to taste. Serve pie with gravy.

Why This Recipe Works Protestant immigrants from the Czech province Moravia settled in Pennsylvania and later North Carolina and brought with them such homey dishes as Moravian cake, cookies, and chicken pie, a satisfying double-crusted pie filled with shredded chicken and served with a rich gravy. Searing the chicken (a mix of breasts and thighs) helped to render its fat, which we used in a roux to thicken the gravy. For moist chicken, we poached it in chicken broth and used that broth to give our gravy flavor. As for the pie crust, we found that sour cream helped make for a rich, flaky crust that was remarkably easy to roll out.

Why This Recipe Works Guinness beef stew often captures only the bitterness and none of the deep, caramelized flavors of the beer. We found the trick to rich, malty flavor was to add some of the beer at the end of cooking so that the heat didn't dull the complex flavors. We also added a little brown sugar to balance some of the bitterness. We loved the idea of just dumping the meat into the pot without searing, but the flavor was lacking. To compensate, we first browned the onions and tomato paste, then cooked the stew uncovered so that the meat could brown in the oven.

GUINNESS BEEF STEW

SERVES 6 TO 8

Use Guinness Draught, not Guinness Extra Stout, which is too bitter.

1   (3½- to 4-pound) boneless beef chuck-eye roast, pulled apart at seams, trimmed, and cut into 1½-inch pieces
    Salt and pepper
3   tablespoons vegetable oil
2   onions, chopped fine
1   tablespoon tomato paste
2   garlic cloves, minced
¼   cup all-purpose flour
3   cups chicken broth
1¼ cups Guinness Draught
1½ tablespoons packed dark brown sugar
1   teaspoon minced fresh thyme
1½ pounds Yukon Gold potatoes, unpeeled, cut into 1-inch pieces
1   pound carrots, peeled and cut into 1-inch pieces
2   tablespoons minced fresh parsley

1. Adjust oven rack to lower-middle position and heat oven to 325 degrees. Season beef with salt and pepper. Heat oil in Dutch oven over medium-high heat until shimmering. Add onions and ¼ teaspoon salt and cook, stirring occasionally, until well browned, 8 to 10 minutes.

2. Add tomato paste and garlic and cook until rust-colored and fragrant, about 2 minutes. Stir in flour and cook for 1 minute. Whisk in broth, ¾ cup Guinness, sugar, and thyme, scraping up any browned bits. Bring to simmer and cook until slightly thickened, about 3 minutes. Stir in beef and return to simmer. Transfer to oven and cook, uncovered, for 90 minutes, stirring halfway through cooking.

3. Stir in potatoes and carrots and continue cooking until beef and vegetables are tender, about 1 hour, stirring halfway through cooking. Stir in remaining ½ cup Guinness and parsley. Season with salt and pepper to taste and serve.

Cook It Uncovered

Most stew recipes start by searing meat in batches on the stovetop. For an easier beef stew, we skip that step but keep the flavor by cooking the stew uncovered in the oven; the open pot allows the meat on top to take on flavorful browning. In addition, the liquid reduces, concentrating in flavor and texture, while the meat cooks.

Preparing a Chuck Roast

1. Pull apart roast at major seams (marked by lines of fat and silverskin). Use knife as necessary.

2. With sharp chef's knife or boning knife, trim off thick layers of fat and silverskin. Cut meat into 1½-inch pieces.

BRUNSWICK STEW

SERVES 4 TO 6

Our favorite kielbasa is Wellshire Farms Smoked Polska Kielbasa.

- 1 tablespoon vegetable oil
- 1 onion, chopped fine
- ¾ cup ketchup
- 4 cups water
- 2 pounds boneless, skinless chicken thighs, trimmed
- 1 pound russet potatoes, peeled and cut into ½-inch chunks
- 8 ounces kielbasa sausage, sliced ¼ inch thick
- 6–8 tablespoons cider vinegar
- 2 tablespoons Worcestershire sauce
- 1 tablespoon yellow mustard
- 1 teaspoon garlic powder
  Salt and pepper
- ¼ teaspoon red pepper flakes
- 1 cup canned crushed tomatoes
- ½ cup frozen lima beans
- ½ cup frozen corn

1. Heat oil in Dutch oven over medium-high heat until shimmering. Add onion and cook until softened, 3 to 5 minutes. Add ketchup and ¼ cup water and cook, stirring frequently, until fond begins to form on bottom of pot and mixture has thickened, about 6 minutes.

2. Add chicken, potatoes, kielbasa, 6 tablespoons vinegar, 1½ tablespoons Worcestershire, mustard, garlic powder, 1 teaspoon salt, 1 teaspoon pepper, pepper flakes, and remaining 3¾ cups water and bring to boil. Reduce heat to low, cover, and simmer until potatoes are tender, 30 to 35 minutes, stirring frequently.

3. Transfer chicken to plate and let cool for 5 minutes, then shred into bite-size pieces with 2 forks. While chicken cools, stir tomatoes, lima beans, and corn into stew and continue to simmer, uncovered, for 15 minutes. Stir in shredded chicken and remaining 1½ teaspoons Worcestershire and cook until warmed through, about 2 minutes. Season with salt, pepper, and remaining vinegar (up to 2 tablespoons) to taste. Serve.

Browning Ketchup

Ketchup offers a lot of culinary bang for the buck, with sweet, tangy, and savory flavors in a single bottle. For this recipe, we cook the ketchup until it thickens and browns, making it even more complex.

Why This Recipe Works Brunswick stew is a fixture at many Southern barbecues, but because there is no definitive recipe for the stew, many cooks use it as a kitchen sink dump-all, resulting in variations that simply aren't appealing. After testing various versions, we settled on an eastern North Carolina style made with barbecue sauce for complex flavor and potatoes for thickness. We kept the meats simple, opting for tender chicken thighs and flavorful kielbasa. Because barbecue sauce flavors vary across brands, we created our own. Browning the ketchup before adding other ingredients helped to soften its raw edge and created a rich tomato base.

Why This Recipe Works Is there a more affordable roast beef alternative to pricey prime rib? One that is faster to cook and full of rich, beefy, tender flavor? In our testing, we found our answer with top sirloin. Skipping a stovetop sear, we browned the roast in the oven at a high temperature and then reduced the oven temperature to cook the roast through without losing too much moisture. And to give our roast an extra layer of savory flavor, we turned to garlic. A three-pronged attack yielded roast beef with great garlic flavor: We studded the roast beef with toasted garlic, rubbed it with garlic salt, and coated it while it cooked with a garlic paste.

SUNDAY-BEST GARLIC ROAST BEEF

SERVES 6 TO 8

Look for a top sirloin roast that has a thick, substantial fat cap still attached. The rendered fat will help to keep the roast moist. When making the jus, taste the reduced broth before adding any of the accumulated meat juices from the roast. The meat juices are well seasoned and may make the jus too salty. If you don't have a heavy-duty nonstick roasting pan, a broiler pan bottom works well, too.

Beef

8 large garlic cloves, unpeeled
1 (4-pound) top sirloin roast, fat trimmed to ¼ inch

Garlic-Salt Rub

3 large garlic cloves, minced
1 teaspoon dried thyme
½ teaspoon salt

Garlic Paste

½ cup olive oil
12 large garlic cloves, cut in half lengthwise
2 sprigs fresh thyme
2 bay leaves
½ teaspoon salt
Pepper

Jus

1½ cups beef broth
1½ cups chicken broth

1. For the Beef Toast garlic in 8-inch skillet over medium-high heat, tossing frequently, until spotty brown, about 8 minutes. Set aside. When cool enough to handle, peel and cut into ¼-inch slivers. Using paring knife, make 1-inch-deep slits all over roast and insert toasted garlic into slits.

2. For the Garlic-Salt Rub Combine garlic, thyme, and salt in small bowl and rub all over roast. Place roast on large plate and refrigerate, uncovered, for at least 4 hours or preferably overnight.

3. For the Garlic Paste Heat oil, garlic, thyme, bay leaves, and salt in small saucepan over medium-high heat until bubbles start to rise to surface. Reduce heat to low and cook until garlic is soft, about 30 minutes. Let cool completely, then strain, reserving oil. Discard herbs and transfer garlic to small bowl. Mash garlic with 1 tablespoon garlic oil until paste forms. Cover and refrigerate paste until ready to use. Cover and reserve garlic oil.

4. Adjust oven rack to middle position, place nonstick roasting pan on rack, and heat oven to 450 degrees. Using paper towels, wipe garlic-salt rub off beef. Rub beef with 2 tablespoons reserved garlic oil and season with pepper. Transfer meat, fat side down, to preheated pan and roast, turning as needed until browned on all sides, 10 to 15 minutes.

5. Reduce oven temperature to 300 degrees. Remove pan from oven, turn roast fat side up, and, using spatula, coat top with garlic paste. Return meat to oven and roast until it registers 120 to 125 degrees (for medium-rare), 50 minutes to 1 hour, 10 minutes. Transfer to carving board, cover loosely with aluminum foil, and let rest for 20 minutes.

6. For the Jus Pour off fat from roasting pan and place pan over high heat. Add beef broth and chicken broth and bring to boil, scraping up browned bits with wooden spoon. Simmer, stirring occasionally, until reduced to 2 cups, about 5 minutes. Add accumulated juices from roast and cook for 1 minute, then pour through fine-mesh strainer. Slice roast crosswise into ¼-inch-thick slices. Serve with jus.

Why This Recipe Works For tender, juicy roast beef, we chose top sirloin roast with a thick fat cap, which rendered as the beef roasted and kept it moist. Searing each side before roasting helped to develop a flavorful crust. Though the right roasting temperature produced juicy meat (our roast having expelled very little liquid), it left precious few drippings in the roasting pan from which to make gravy. A good amount of beef broth, plus the rendered fat and fond left behind from searing the meat, provided volume and richness, while mushrooms, red wine, and Worcestershire sauce amped up the flavor.

CLASSIC ROAST BEEF AND GRAVY

SERVES 6 TO 8

For the best flavor and texture, refrigerate the roast overnight after salting. If you don't have a V-rack, cook the roast on a wire rack set inside a rimmed baking sheet.

- 1 (4-pound) top sirloin roast, fat trimmed to ¼ inch
  Salt and pepper
- 1 tablespoon vegetable oil
- 8 ounces white mushrooms, trimmed and chopped
- 2 onions, chopped fine
- 1 carrot, peeled and chopped
- 1 celery rib, minced
- 1 tablespoon tomato paste
- 4 garlic cloves, minced
- ¼ cup all-purpose flour
- 1 cup red wine
- 4 cups beef broth
- 1 teaspoon Worcestershire sauce

1. Pat roast dry with paper towels. Rub 2 teaspoons salt evenly over meat. Cover with plastic wrap and refrigerate for at least 1 hour or up to 24 hours.

2. Adjust oven rack to lower-middle position and heat oven to 275 degrees. Pat roast dry with paper towels and rub with 1 teaspoon pepper. Heat oil in Dutch oven over medium-high heat until just smoking. Brown roast all over, 8 to 12 minutes, then transfer to V-rack set inside roasting pan (do not wipe out Dutch oven). Transfer to oven and cook until meat registers 120 to 125 degrees (for medium-rare), 1½ to 2 hours.

3. Meanwhile, add mushrooms to fat left in Dutch oven and cook until golden, about 5 minutes. Stir in onions, carrot, and celery and cook until browned, 5 to 7 minutes. Stir in tomato paste, garlic, and flour and cook until fragrant, about 2 minutes. Stir in wine and broth, scraping up any browned bits with wooden spoon. Bring to boil, then reduce heat to medium and simmer until thickened, about 10 minutes. Strain gravy, then stir in Worcestershire and season with salt and pepper; cover and keep warm.

4. Transfer roast to carving board, tent with aluminum foil, and let rest for 20 minutes. Slice roast crosswise into ½-inch-thick slices. Serve with gravy.

Flavor Builders

A combination of sautéed mushrooms, tomato paste, beef broth, and Worcestershire sauce mimicked the roasted, beefy flavor of traditional gravy made with pan drippings.

Top Sirloin—The Right Cut

Through extensive testing of every cut of beef, the test kitchen has settled on top sirloin as our favorite inexpensive roast. Look for a roast with at least a ¼-inch fat cap on top; the fat renders in the oven, basting the roast and helping to keep it moist.

HERBED ROAST BEEF

SERVES 6 TO 8

For even deeper seasoning, refrigerate the roast overnight after filling it with the herb mixture in step 2.

⅓ cup minced fresh parsley
1 shallot, minced
2 tablespoons minced fresh thyme
2 tablespoons olive oil
1 tablespoon Dijon mustard
4 tablespoons unsalted butter, softened
1 (4-pound) top sirloin roast, fat trimmed to ¼ inch
1 tablespoon salt
1 tablespoon pepper

1. Combine parsley, shallot, and thyme in bowl. Transfer 2 tablespoons herb mixture to second bowl and stir in 1 tablespoon oil and mustard until combined; set aside. Add butter to remaining herb mixture and mash with fork until combined.

2. Butterfly roast by slicing horizontally through middle of meat, leaving about ½ inch of meat intact, and rub roast inside and out with salt and pepper. Spread herb-mustard mixture over interior of meat, fold roast back together, and tie securely with kitchen twine at 1-inch intervals. Refrigerate for at least 1 hour or up to 24 hours.

3. Adjust oven rack to middle position and heat oven to 275 degrees. Pat roast dry with paper towels.

Heat remaining 1 tablespoon oil in 12-inch skillet over medium-high heat until just smoking. Brown roast all over, 8 to 12 minutes, then arrange on V-rack set inside roasting pan. Transfer to oven and roast until meat registers 120 to 125 degrees (for medium-rare), 1½ to 2 hours.

4. Transfer roast to carving board, spread with herb-butter mixture, tent with aluminum foil, and let rest for 20 minutes. Remove twine and slice roast crosswise into ¼-inch-thick slices. Serve.

Fast Sear, Slow Roast for Beef
We brown most beef roasts on the stovetop to build a flavorful crust, then roast them gently for a uniformly rosy, juicy interior.

1. Searing roast assures a flavorful, deep brown crust.

2. Roasting at a low temperature (275 degrees) keeps the meat moist and succulent.

Herbs Galore
Fresh parsley and thyme flavor both the interior and exterior of our roast.

1. Butterfly roast by slicing horizontally through middle of the meat. Leave about ½ inch of meat intact, then open it like a book.

2. After seasoning meat, spread herb-mustard mixture over interior of meat.

3. Fold meat back to its original position, then tie securely at 1-inch intervals with kitchen twine.

4. For second hit of herb flavor after roast is cooked, spread it with herb butter.

Why This Recipe Works For a roast beef dressed to impress without much effort, we turned to a swirl of herbs and mustard. To start, we combined fresh herbs with the mustard, butterflied the roast, and spread the herbs over the interior of the meat before folding it back together and securing it with twine. A simple herb butter, spread over the resting roast, melted and mingled with the natural juices of the meat, creating a flavorful sauce without the need to dirty another pan.

HERB-CRUSTED BEEF TENDERLOIN

SERVES 12 TO 16

Make sure to begin this recipe 2 hours before you plan to put the roast in the oven. The tenderloin can be trimmed, tied, rubbed with the salt mixture, and refrigerated up to 24 hours in advance; make sure to bring the roast back to room temperature before putting it into the oven.

1 (6-pound) whole beef tenderloin, trimmed, tail end tucked, and tied at 1½-inch intervals
  Kosher salt and cracked peppercorns
2 teaspoons sugar
2 slices hearty white sandwich bread, torn into pieces
2½ ounces Parmesan cheese, grated (1¼ cups)
½ cup chopped fresh parsley
6 tablespoons olive oil
2 teaspoons plus 2 tablespoons chopped fresh thyme
4 garlic cloves, minced
1 recipe Horseradish Cream Sauce

1. Set wire rack in rimmed baking sheet. Pat tenderloin dry with paper towels. Combine 1 tablespoon salt, 1 tablespoon pepper, and sugar in small bowl and rub all over tenderloin. Transfer to prepared baking sheet and let sit at room temperature for 2 hours.

2. Meanwhile, pulse bread in food processor to fine crumbs, about 15 pulses. Transfer bread crumbs to medium bowl and toss with ½ cup Parmesan, 2 tablespoons parsley, 2 tablespoons oil, and 2 teaspoons thyme until evenly combined. Wipe out food processor with paper towels and process remaining ¾ cup Parmesan, 6 tablespoons parsley, ¼ cup oil, 2 tablespoons thyme, and garlic until smooth paste forms. Transfer herb paste to small bowl.

3. Adjust oven rack to upper-middle position and heat oven to 400 degrees. Roast tenderloin for 20 minutes and remove from oven. Using scissors, carefully cut kitchen twine and remove it. Coat tenderloin with herb paste, then bread-crumb topping. Roast until meat registers 120 to 125 degrees (for medium-rare)

and topping is golden brown, 20 to 25 minutes. (If topping browns before meat reaches preferred internal temperature, lightly cover with aluminum foil for remainder of roasting time and remove while roast rests.) Let roast rest, uncovered, for 30 minutes on wire rack. Transfer to carving board and carve. Serve with Horseradish Cream Sauce.

HORSERADISH CREAM SAUCE
MAKES ABOUT 1 CUP

½ cup sour cream
½ cup heavy cream
¼ cup prepared horseradish, drained
2 teaspoons Dijon mustard
1 garlic clove, minced
¼ teaspoon sugar
  Salt and pepper

Mix all ingredients in bowl; add salt and pepper to taste. Cover and let stand at room temperature for 1 to 1½ hours to thicken. (Sauce can be refrigerated for up to 2 days.)

Preparing Herb-Crusted Beef Tenderloin

1. To ensure even cooking, fold thin, tapered end under roast, then tie entire roast with kitchen twine every 1½ inches. Roast for 20 minutes.

2. Remove roast from oven, snip twine with scissors, and remove before adding herb paste and bread-crumb mixture. Return to oven to finish cooking.

Why This Recipe Works Though beef tenderloin offers incomparable tenderness, its flavor could often use some embellishment. To give the meat a flavor boost, we turned to a thick herbed crust. But herbs can burn easily, lose their flavor in a hot oven, or just fall off the meat. Cooking the roast in the oven at a high temperature for part of the time gave us a perfectly caramelized exterior that made applying an herb paste easy. Adding grated Parmesan cheese to the paste gave it nutty flavor and helped the paste adhere to the meat. Fresh parsley and thyme provided a flavorful coating, and for a crisp texture, we relied on bread crumbs.

Why This Recipe Works A 5-pound trimmed whole beef tenderloin is a showstopping, crowd-pleaser of a dish, but it can be unwieldy and too large to fit in a skillet to sear (our favorite method for developing a nice crust). So we started by cutting it in half, yielding two smaller roasts that were easier to manage. We salted them overnight and then roasted both pieces gently in a low oven before searing them in a piping-hot skillet just before serving, ensuring a nicely browned, burnished exterior that added flavor and visual appeal without compromising the rosy interior. A rich, glossy red wine sauce took the roast over the top.

CLASSIC ROAST BEEF TENDERLOIN

SERVES 12 TO 16

Plan ahead: The roast must be salted and refrigerated for at least 12 hours before cooking. If you're buying an untrimmed tenderloin, be sure it weighs 6 to 7 pounds. Serve with Red Wine Sauce (recipe follows), if desired.

 1 (5-pound) trimmed whole beef tenderloin
    Kosher salt and pepper
 2 tablespoons vegetable oil

1. Cut tenderloin crosswise at base of head to make 2 roasts. Using kitchen twine, tie head at 1-inch intervals. Tuck tail end of second roast underneath by 3 to 5 inches to create more even shape. Tie tucked portion with kitchen twine at 1-inch intervals to secure.

2. Place 1 roast on large sheet of plastic wrap and sprinkle all over with 1 tablespoon salt. Wrap tightly in double layer of plastic. Repeat with remaining roast and 1 tablespoon salt. Refrigerate roasts for at least 12 hours or up to 24 hours.

3. Adjust oven rack to middle position and heat oven to 250 degrees. Set wire rack in rimmed baking sheet. Season roasts with pepper and place on prepared wire rack. Roast until meat registers 125 degrees (for medium-rare) or 130 degrees (for medium), 1 hour, 20 minutes to 1 hour, 40 minutes for tail-end roast and 1 hour, 40 minutes to 2 hours for head-end roast. Transfer roasts to carving board, tent with aluminum foil, and let rest for 20 minutes.

4. Pat roasts dry with paper towels. Heat oil in 12-inch nonstick skillet over medium-high heat until just smoking. Add both roasts and sear on all sides until well browned, 5 to 7 minutes. Transfer roasts to carving board, remove twine, and slice ½ inch thick. Serve.

RED WINE SAUCE
MAKES ABOUT 2 CUPS
Medium-bodied red wines, such as Côtes du Rhône or Pinot Noir, are best for this recipe. You can substitute chain meat trimmed from a beef tenderloin for the stew meat called for here.

 5 tablespoons unsalted butter,
    cut into 5 pieces and chilled
12 ounces beef stew meat,
    cut into 1-inch pieces
 2 tablespoons tomato paste
 2 cups red wine
 2 cups beef broth
 1 shallot, sliced thin
 2 tablespoons soy sauce
1½ tablespoons sugar
 6 sprigs fresh thyme
2½ teaspoons cornstarch
 1 tablespoon cold water
    Salt and pepper

1. Melt 1 tablespoon butter in large saucepan over medium-high heat. Add beef and cook, stirring occasionally, until well browned and fond forms on bottom of saucepan, 10 to 12 minutes.

2. Add tomato paste and cook until darkened in color and fragrant, about 1 minute. Stir in wine, broth, shallot, soy sauce, sugar, and thyme sprigs and bring to boil, scraping up any browned bits. Cook until reduced to 4 cups, 12 to 15 minutes.

3. Strain sauce through fine-mesh strainer set over bowl; discard solids. Return sauce to saucepan and bring to boil over medium-high heat. Dissolve cornstarch in cold water. Whisk cornstarch mixture into sauce and boil until slightly thickened, about 30 seconds. Reduce heat to low and whisk in remaining 4 tablespoons butter, 1 piece at a time. Season with salt and pepper to taste. Remove from heat and cover to keep warm.

Why This Recipe Works For an occasion-worthy, beefy top-loin roast, we wanted a seared crust and a perfect medium-rare throughout, but most recipes we found could only give us one or the other. Gently roasting in a low oven until the meat was almost done and then setting it under the broiler for a few minutes achieved both results without the hassle of pan-searing. Scoring the fat cap before cooking helped the fat to render and the surface to crisp. We let the meat sit overnight with a spice and herb rub (and plenty of salt) to ensure a perfectly seasoned, flavorful roast, and served it with a bright, fresh salsa verde to complement the rich meat.

HOLIDAY STRIP ROAST

SERVES 8 TO 10

Serve with Salsa Verde (recipe follows).

- 1 (5- to 6-pound) boneless top loin roast, fat trimmed to ¼ inch
- 2 tablespoons peppercorns
- 1 tablespoon coriander seeds
- 1 tablespoon yellow mustard seeds
- 3 tablespoons olive oil
- 2 tablespoons kosher salt
- 2 tablespoons chopped fresh rosemary
- 1 teaspoon red pepper flakes

1. Pat roast dry with paper towels. Using sharp knife, cut ½-inch crosshatch pattern through fat cap, ¼ inch deep. Tie kitchen twine around roast at 2-inch intervals. Grind peppercorns, coriander seeds, and mustard seeds to texture of coarse sand in spice grinder. Combine spice mixture, oil, salt, rosemary, and pepper flakes in bowl until thick paste forms. Rub paste all over roast and into crosshatch. Wrap roast with plastic wrap and refrigerate for 6 to 24 hours.

2. Set wire rack inside rimmed baking sheet. One hour before cooking, unwrap meat and place on prepared rack, fat side up. Adjust oven rack to middle position and heat oven to 275 degrees. Transfer roast to oven and cook until meat registers 115 degrees, about 90 minutes, rotating sheet halfway through cooking. Remove roast from oven and heat broiler.

3. Return roast to oven and broil on middle oven rack until fat cap is deep brown and interior of roast registers 125 degrees, 3 to 5 minutes. Transfer to carving board, tent loosely with aluminum foil, and let rest for 20 minutes. Remove twine and carve into thin slices. Serve.

SALSA VERDE
MAKES ABOUT 1½ CUPS
Mince the garlic before processing it, or it won't break down enough. This sauce can be prepared up to two days in advance and refrigerated. Before serving, bring it to room temperature and stir to recombine.

- 2 slices hearty white sandwich bread, torn into 1-inch pieces
- 1 cup extra-virgin olive oil
- ¼ cup lemon juice (2 lemons)
- 4 cups fresh parsley leaves
- ¼ cup capers, rinsed
- 4 anchovy fillets, rinsed
- 2 garlic cloves, minced
- ½ teaspoon kosher salt

Process bread, oil, and lemon juice in food processor until smooth, about 10 seconds. Add parsley, capers, anchovies, garlic, and salt and pulse until mixture is finely chopped, about 5 pulses, scraping down bowl as needed.

The Right Grind

As part of the rub for the roast, we grind peppercorns with mustard seeds and coriander seeds to the texture of coarse sand. Since these ingredients are irregularly sized and of varying densities, the texture won't be uniform, which is OK. The correct grind looks like this.

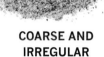

COARSE AND IRREGULAR

BOTTOM ROUND ROAST BEEF WITH ZIP-STYLE SAUCE

SERVES 8

We recommend cooking this roast to medium for ease of slicing. Open the oven door as little as possible, and remove the roast from the oven when taking its temperature to prevent dropping the oven temperature too drastically. Because the sauce contains butter, it will solidify as it cools, so it's best kept warm for serving.

Beef

1 (4-pound) boneless beef bottom round roast, trimmed
  Kosher salt and pepper
1 tablespoon minced fresh rosemary
1 tablespoon minced fresh thyme
2 tablespoons vegetable oil

Zip-Style Sauce

8 tablespoons unsalted butter
½ cup Worcestershire sauce
2 garlic cloves, minced
2 teaspoons minced fresh rosemary
1 teaspoon minced fresh thyme
½ teaspoon kosher salt
½ teaspoon pepper

1. For the Beef Pat roast dry with paper towels and sprinkle with 2 teaspoons salt. Wrap in plastic wrap and refrigerate for at least 1 hour or up to 24 hours.

2. Adjust oven rack to middle position and heat oven to 250 degrees. Set wire rack in rimmed baking sheet. Combine rosemary, thyme, 2 teaspoons pepper, and 1 teaspoon salt in bowl.

3. Pat roast dry with paper towels. Brush roast all over with oil and sprinkle with herb mixture; place on prepared wire rack. Transfer to oven and cook until meat registers 120 degrees, 1¾ hours to 2¼ hours. Turn off oven and leave roast in oven, without opening door, until meat registers 135 degrees (for medium), 20 to 30 minutes longer. Transfer roast to carving board, tent with aluminum foil, and let rest for 30 minutes.

4. For the Zip-Style Sauce Meanwhile, bring butter, Worcestershire, garlic, rosemary, thyme, salt, and pepper to bare simmer in small saucepan over medium heat, whisking constantly. Remove from heat, cover, and keep warm.

5. Slice roast thin against grain and serve with sauce.

The American Table: Zip Sauce

Zip Sauce—a lively, butter-based condiment for steak—was invented more than 75 years ago at Lelli's Inn, a northern Italian restaurant in Detroit. Customers couldn't get enough of the flavorful sauce, and it became so popular that neighboring restaurants concocted copycat versions. In 2006, Chef Michael Esshaki capitalized on a good thing when he started selling bottled Zip Sauce (just mix it with melted butter at home) online and in Detroit-area markets.

Why This Recipe Works Over the years, many cooks have decried the poor bottom round roast as unfit to serve as a centerpiece— too tough, too liver-y, nothing at all like a tender, melty rib roast or eye round. We wanted to find a way to serve this less-expensive cut as the main event—and not to have to apologize for it. By cooking the roast in a low oven for a few hours, then turning off the heat and letting the roast finish cooking, we were able to bring the roast to a perfect, tender medium. After letting it rest, we had a beautiful, herb-covered roast that was easy to slice paper-thin and looked much more elegant than any of us had expected.

DEVILED BEEF SHORT RIBS

SERVES 4 TO 6

English-style short ribs contain a single rib bone. For a milder sauce, use only one jalapeño and discard the seeds.

⅔ cup yellow mustard
⅓ cup orange juice
⅓ cup packed light brown sugar
1–2 jalapeño chiles, stemmed, seeds reserved, and roughly chopped
4 teaspoons dry mustard
1 tablespoon lemon juice plus 1 teaspoon grated lemon zest
Salt and pepper
½ teaspoon cayenne pepper
5 pounds bone-in English-style short ribs, bones 4 to 5 inches long, 1 to 1½ inches of meat on top of bone, trimmed
2 tablespoons unsalted butter
1½ cups panko bread crumbs
1 tablespoon chopped fresh parsley

1. Adjust oven rack to middle position and heat oven to 325 degrees. Combine yellow mustard, orange juice, sugar, jalapeños and reserved seeds, dry mustard, lemon juice, and 2 teaspoons pepper in food processor and process until smooth, about 30 seconds; set aside. (Mustard mixture can be refrigerated for up to 1 week.)

2. Combine 1 tablespoon salt, 1 tablespoon pepper, and cayenne in bowl. Sprinkle ribs all over with spice mixture. Arrange ribs, meat side down, in 13 by 9-inch baking dish. Cover dish tightly with aluminum foil and roast until meat is nearly tender, about 3 hours.

3. Meanwhile, melt butter in 12-inch skillet over medium-high heat. Add panko and cook, stirring often, until golden brown, about 3 minutes. Off heat, stir in parsley and lemon zest and transfer to shallow dish.

4. Remove baking dish from oven and increase oven temperature to 425 degrees; transfer ribs to plate. Discard rendered fat and juices from dish. Brush meat (not bone) all over with one-fourth of mustard sauce and return ribs to dish, meat side up. Roast, uncovered, until beginning to brown, about 10 minutes. Brush meat again with one-third of remaining mustard sauce and continue to roast until well browned and completely tender, 10 to 15 minutes longer. Transfer ribs to serving platter, tent loosely with foil, and let rest for 15 minutes.

5. Brush meat once more with half of remaining mustard sauce and roll in panko mixture, taking care to entirely coat meat. Serve, passing remaining mustard sauce separately.

A Roasting-Braising Hybrid Method

Most short rib recipes call for searing, then braising, and finally turning the braising liquid into a sauce. For our Deviled Beef Short Ribs, we took a different road: We put the ribs in a baking dish, meat side down, and roasted them (covered) until tender, about 3 hours. The meat cooked in its own rendered fat and juices, giving us fully rendered, supertender short ribs without much hands-on work. To finish, we uncovered the ribs, brushed them with a glaze, roasted them meat side up, repeated, and then rolled them in toasted crumbs.

Why This Recipe Works "Deviling" food usually involves flavoring it with mustard, black pepper, and other seasonings, but for our deviled short ribs we really wanted to feel the heat. We first roasted the seasoned ribs meat side down in a covered baking dish, allowing the meat to cook in its own rendered fat and juices. After cranking the heat and pouring off the juices, we brushed the ribs with a spicy glaze of dry and prepared mustards, citrus, brown sugar, and pureed jalapeños. A few rounds of brushing and roasting created a browned crust, and for a crunchy finish we coated the ribs with buttery, toasted panko bread crumbs.

Why This Recipe Works We focused on two parts of the classic British Sunday roast dinner—beef rib roast and Yorkshire pudding—to create a foolproof recipe that would have both ready simultaneously. The key was using one pan. We started with a nicely marbled, easy-to-carve boneless beef rib roast, our cut of choice, and used rendered fat from the roast and trimmings to make a Yorkshire pudding infused with meaty flavor. A quick, savory jus and horseradish sauce provided the perfect complements.

BONELESS RIB ROAST WITH YORKSHIRE PUDDING AND JUS

SERVES 8 TO 10

At the butcher counter, ask for a roast with an untrimmed fat cap, ideally ½ inch thick, in order to get enough trimmings to cook the pudding. Plan ahead: The roast must be salted and refrigerated for at least 24 hours before cooking. If you're using a dark, nonstick roasting pan, reduce the cooking time for the Yorkshire pudding by 5 minutes.

Horseradish Sauce
- ½ cup sour cream
- ½ cup prepared horseradish
- 1½ teaspoons kosher salt
- ⅛ teaspoon pepper

Roast and Pudding
- 1 (5- to 5½-pound) first-cut boneless beef rib roast with ½-inch fat cap
  Kosher salt and pepper
- 2½ cups (12½ ounces) all-purpose flour
- 4 cups milk
- 4 large eggs
- 1 tablespoon vegetable oil, plus extra as needed

Jus
- 1 onion, chopped fine
- 1 teaspoon cornstarch
- 2½ cups beef broth
- 1 sprig fresh thyme

1. For the Horseradish Sauce Combine all ingredients in bowl. Cover and refrigerate until ready to serve. (Sauce can be refrigerated for up to 2 days.)

2. For the Roast and Pudding Using sharp knife, trim roast's fat cap to even ¼-inch thickness and refrigerate trimmings for later use. Cut 1-inch cross-hatch pattern in fat cap, being careful not to cut into meat. Rub 2 tablespoons salt over entire roast and into crosshatch. Transfer to large plate and refrigerate, uncovered, for at least 24 hours or up to 4 days.

3. Adjust oven rack to lower-middle position and heat oven to 250 degrees. Spray roasting pan with vegetable oil spray. Cut reserved trimmings into ½-inch pieces. Place 3 ounces (about ¾ cup) trimmings in bottom of prepared pan. Set V-rack over trimmings in pan.

4. Season roast with pepper and place fat side up on V-rack. Roast until meat registers 115 degrees for rare, 120 degrees for medium-rare, or 125 degrees for medium, 2½ to 3 hours.

5. Meanwhile, combine flour and 1 tablespoon salt in large bowl. Whisk milk and eggs in second bowl until fully combined. Slowly whisk milk mixture into flour mixture until smooth. Cover with plastic wrap and let rest for 1 hour. (Batter can be covered and refrigerated for up to 24 hours. Let come to room temperature before proceeding.)

6. Transfer V-rack with roast to carving board, tent with aluminum foil, and let rest for 1 hour. Using fork, remove solids in pan, leaving liquid fat behind (there should be about 6 tablespoons; if not, supplement with extra vegetable oil). Increase oven temperature to 425 degrees.

7. When oven reaches 425 degrees, return pan to oven and heat until fat is just smoking, 3 to 5 minutes. Rewhisk batter and pour into center of pan. Bake until pudding is dark golden brown and edges are crisp, 40 to 45 minutes.

8. Meanwhile, pat roast dry with paper towels. Heat 1 tablespoon oil in 12-inch skillet over medium-high heat until just smoking. Sear roast on all sides until evenly browned, 5 to 7 minutes. Transfer roast to carving board.

9. For the Jus Return skillet to medium-high heat, add onion, and cook until softened, about 3 minutes, scraping up any browned bits. Whisk cornstarch into broth. Add broth mixture and thyme sprig to skillet and bring to boil. Reduce heat to medium-low and simmer until reduced by half and slightly thickened, about 7 minutes. Strain jus through fine-mesh strainer set over small saucepan; discard solids. Cover and keep warm.

10. Slice roast ¾ inch thick. Cut pudding into squares in roasting pan. Serve beef with Yorkshire pudding, jus, and horseradish sauce.

ONE-PAN PRIME RIB AND ROASTED VEGETABLES

SERVES 8 TO 10

The roast must be salted and then refrigerated for at least 24 hours before cooking; salting and refrigerating for the full 4 days results in the most tender, flavorful meat.

- 1 (7-pound) first-cut beef standing rib roast (3 bones), fat trimmed to ¼ inch Kosher salt and pepper Vegetable oil
- 2 pounds carrots, peeled, cut into 2-inch lengths, halved or quartered lengthwise to create ½-inch-diameter pieces
- 1 pound parsnips, peeled and sliced ½ inch thick on bias
- 1 pound Brussels sprouts, trimmed and halved
- 1 red onion, halved and sliced through root end into ½-inch wedges
- 2 teaspoons minced fresh thyme

1. Using sharp knife, cut through roast's fat cap in 1-inch crosshatch pattern, being careful not to cut into meat. Rub 2 tablespoons salt over entire roast and into crosshatch. Transfer to large plate and refrigerate, uncovered, for at least 24 hours or up to 4 days.

2. Adjust oven rack to lower-middle position and heat oven to 250 degrees. Season roast with pepper and arrange, fat side up, on V-rack set in large roasting pan. Roast until meat registers 115 degrees for rare, 120 degrees for medium-rare, or 125 degrees for medium, 3 to 3½ hours. Transfer V-rack with roast to carving board, tent loosely with aluminum foil, and let rest for about 1 hour.

3. Meanwhile, increase oven temperature to 425 degrees. Pour off all but 2 tablespoons fat from pan. (If there isn't enough fat in pan, add vegetable oil to equal 2 tablespoons.) Toss carrots, parsnips, brussels sprouts, onion, thyme, 1 teaspoon salt, and ½ teaspoon pepper with fat in pan. Roast vegetables, stirring halfway through roasting, until tender and browned, 45 to 50 minutes.

4. Remove pan from oven and heat broiler. Carefully nestle V-rack with roast among vegetables in pan. Broil roast until fat cap is evenly browned, about 5 minutes, rotating pan as necessary. Transfer roast to carving board, carve meat from bones, and cut into ¾-inch-thick slices. Season vegetables with salt and pepper to taste. Serve roast with vegetables.

Buy the Right Roast

This recipe calls for a first-cut, bone-in standing rib roast, which contains ribs 9, 10, and 11 (the ribs that are closest to the tail of the steer; butchers often label this cut "loin-end"). First-cut roasts contain the largest eye of meat. While second-cut roasts are pretty good, too, they are slightly fattier and more irregular, making them more difficult to cook evenly. Since these cuts are often priced the same, it's worth your while to ask for the superior first-cut roast.

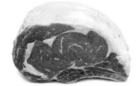 

FIRST CUT
More meat, larger eye

SECOND CUT
More fat, smaller eye (but still good)

Carving a Standing Rib Roast

To carve a bone-in rib roast, simply hold the roast in place with a carving fork and cut parallel to the rib bones to remove the meat in one big piece. Then slice and serve the meat.

Why This Recipe Works Our goal was to produce a recipe for holiday prime rib with roasted vegetables that was simple and foolproof. We scored and salted a first-cut standing rib roast and refrigerated it for 24 hours for tender beef. A low-and-slow cooking method yielded evenly red and juicy meat, and an additional stint under the broiler turned the outside crispy and golden. Instead of forcing the vegetables to work in concert with the beef, we roasted them solo in the flavorful beef fat while the prime rib was resting. It was definitely a feast fit for a holiday—with only one pan to wash.

Why This Recipe Works To ensure a juicy roast, we trimmed the excess fat, made shallow crosshatch cuts in the remaining fat cap, and rubbed the roast with salt 24 hours before cooking. We saved the trimmed fat and placed it under the roast as it cooked, creating intensely flavored drippings. To achieve a creamy interior, we pre-cooked the potatoes in the microwave before tossing them with the rendered fat and roasting them until crisp. Searing the cooked roast in a hot skillet added some last-minute browning to the roast's exterior without overcooking it. An easy red wine–orange sauce proved a bright contrast to the savory beef.

PRIME RIB WITH POTATOES AND RED WINE–ORANGE SAUCE

SERVES 8 TO 10

The roast must be salted and refrigerated for at least 24 hours before cooking. Wait until the roast is done cooking before peeling and cutting the potatoes so they don't discolor. It is crucial to use a sturdy rimmed baking sheet for this recipe. Serve with Red Wine–Orange Sauce (recipe follows).

1 (7-pound) first-cut beef standing rib roast (3 bones), with untrimmed fat cap
  Kosher salt and pepper
4 pounds Yukon gold potatoes, peeled and cut into 1½-inch pieces
1 tablespoon minced fresh rosemary
1 tablespoon vegetable oil

1. Using sharp knife, trim roast's fat cap to even ¼-inch-thickness; reserve and refrigerate trimmings. Cut 1-inch crosshatch pattern in fat cap, being careful not to cut into meat. Rub 2 tablespoons salt over roast and into crosshatch. Transfer to large plate and refrigerate, uncovered, for at least 24 hours or up to 4 days.

2. Adjust oven rack to lower-middle position and heat oven to 250 degrees. Cut reserved trimmings into ½-inch pieces. Place 1 cup of trimmings in rimmed baking sheet, then set wire rack in sheet. Season roast with pepper and place, fat side up, on wire rack.

3. Roast until meat registers 115 degrees for rare, 120 degrees for medium-rare, or 125 degrees for medium, 3 to 3½ hours. Transfer roast to carving board, tent with aluminum foil, and let rest for 1 hour. Carefully remove wire rack and reserve beef fat in baking sheet (there should be about ½ cup; if not, add vegetable oil).

4. Increase oven temperature to 450 degrees. Microwave potatoes, covered, in large bowl until they begin to release moisture and surfaces look wet, about 7 minutes. Pat potatoes dry with paper towels. Toss potatoes with rosemary, 2 teaspoons salt, and ½ teaspoon pepper. Transfer potatoes to baking sheet and carefully toss with reserved fat (fat may be hot).

Roast until tender and browned, 35 to 40 minutes, redistributing halfway through cooking. Season potatoes with salt and pepper to taste.

5. Pat roast dry with paper towels. Heat oil in 12-inch skillet over medium-high heat until just smoking. Sear all sides until browned, 6 to 8 minutes total. Transfer roast to carving board. Carve meat from bones and cut into ¾-inch-thick slices. Serve with potatoes.

RED WINE–ORANGE SAUCE
MAKES ABOUT 1½ CUPS
Medium-bodied red wines are best for this sauce.

6 tablespoons unsalted butter, cut into 6 pieces and chilled
3 shallots, minced
1½ tablespoons tomato paste
1 tablespoon sugar
4 garlic cloves, minced
1 tablespoon all-purpose flour
3 cups beef broth
1½ cups red wine
⅓ cup orange juice
1½ tablespoons Worcestershire sauce
1 sprig fresh thyme
  Salt and pepper

1. Melt 2 tablespoons butter in medium saucepan over medium-high heat. Add shallots, tomato paste, and sugar and cook, stirring frequently, until deep brown, 4 to 5 minutes. Stir in garlic and flour and cook until garlic is fragrant and vegetables are well coated with flour, about 30 seconds.

2. Stir in broth, wine, orange juice, Worcestershire, and thyme, scraping up any browned bits. Bring to boil, reduce heat to medium, and cook at low boil until reduced to 2 cups, about 40 minutes.

3. Strain sauce through fine-mesh strainer set over bowl; discard solids. Return sauce to pot and place over low heat. Whisk in remaining 4 tablespoons butter, 1 piece at a time. Season with salt and pepper to taste.

Why This Recipe Works Traditionally, this lazy cook's pot roast involves rubbing a chuck roast with onion soup mix, wrapping it in foil, and cooking it in the oven until tender. While we liked the ease of this dish, we weren't fans of its artificial, salty taste. To develop oniony flavor with ease, we started with onion powder and salt. Drizzling the vegetables with soy sauce before roasting enhanced the beefy flavor of the pan juices. Brown sugar added sweetness and depth, while a surprise ingredient, a little espresso powder, provided toasty complexity. Dividing the roast into two halves allowed us to apply more of the flavorful spice rub to its exterior.

CHUCK ROAST IN FOIL

SERVES 4 TO 6

You will need an 18-inch-wide roll of heavy-duty aluminum foil for wrapping the roast. We prefer to use small red potatoes, measuring 1 to 2 inches in diameter, in this recipe.

Rub

- 3 tablespoons cornstarch
- 4 teaspoons onion powder
- 2 teaspoons packed light brown sugar
- 2 teaspoons salt
- 1 teaspoon pepper
- 1 teaspoon garlic powder
- 1 teaspoon instant espresso powder
- 1 teaspoon dried thyme
- ½ teaspoon celery seeds

Chuck Roast

- 1 (4-pound) boneless beef chuck-eye roast, pulled apart at seams, fat trimmed to ¼ inch, and tied at 1-inch intervals
- 2 onions, peeled and quartered
- 1 pound small red potatoes, quartered
- 4 carrots, peeled and cut into 1½-inch pieces
- 2 bay leaves
- 2 tablespoons soy sauce

1. For the Rub Adjust oven rack to lower-middle position and heat oven to 300 degrees. Combine all ingredients in small bowl.

2. For the Chuck Roast Pat roast dry with paper towels. Place two 30 by 18-inch sheets of heavy-duty aluminum foil perpendicular to each other inside large roasting pan. Place onions, potatoes, carrots, and bay leaves in center of foil and drizzle with soy sauce. Set roasts on top of vegetables. Rub roasts all over with rub. Fold opposite corners of foil toward each other and crimp edges tightly to seal. Transfer pan to oven and cook until meat is completely tender, about 4½ hours.

3. Remove roasts from foil pouch and place on carving board. Tent meat with foil and let rest for 20 minutes. Remove onions and bay leaves. Using slotted spoon, place carrots and potatoes on serving platter. Strain contents of roasting pan through fine-mesh strainer into fat separator. Let liquid settle, then pour defatted pan juices into serving bowl.

4. Remove kitchen twine from roasts. Slice roasts thin against grain and transfer to platter with vegetables. Pour ½ cup pan juices over meat. Serve with remaining pan juices.

The American Table: Back in Fashion

Family Circle magazine once asked Peg Bracken, author of the mega-bestselling *I Hate to Cook Book*, to select her greatest-hits list for the hate-to-cook set. Her list included such gems as Stayabed Stew ("For those days when you're en negligee, en bed, with a murder story and a box of bonbons") and the Basic I-Hate-to-Cook Muffin (made by combining beer and muffin mix). But one classic super-easy dish of the day was notably absent: chuck roast with instant onion soup. "Done to death," Bracken explained, adding, "I remember years ago when every working wife in the land was sprinkling a package of dried onion soup mix onto a chunk of chuck steak...the thing was bigger than a Hula-Hoop, and it died, of course, of over-exposure." But guess what? The hula hoop is back, and in its new incarnation, chuck roast in foil is poised for a comeback, too.

CROWN ROAST OF PORK

SERVES 10 TO 12

A crown roast is two bone-in pork loin roasts tied into a crown shape, with the rib bones frenched and chine bones removed. This can be difficult to do, so ask your butcher to make this roast for you. We wrap extra kitchen twine around the widest part of the roast to provide more support when flipping. Use potatoes that measure 1 to 2 inches in diameter.

Kosher salt and pepper
3 tablespoons minced fresh thyme
2 tablespoons minced fresh rosemary
5 garlic cloves, minced
1 (8- to 10-pound) pork crown roast
2 pounds small red potatoes
10 ounces shallots, peeled and halved
2 Golden Delicious apples, peeled, cored, and halved
8 tablespoons unsalted butter, melted
½ cup apple cider
1 cup chicken broth

1. Combine 3 tablespoons salt, 1 tablespoon pepper, thyme, rosemary, and garlic in bowl; reserve 2 teaspoons for vegetables. Pat pork dry with paper towels and rub with remaining herb salt. Wrap kitchen twine twice around widest part of roast and tie tightly. Refrigerate roast, covered, for 6 to 24 hours.

2. Adjust oven rack to lower-middle position and heat oven to 475 degrees. Place V-rack inside large roasting pan. Toss potatoes, shallots, apples, 4 tablespoons butter, and reserved herb salt in large bowl and transfer to pan. Arrange roast bone side down in V-rack and brush with remaining 4 tablespoons butter. Roast until meat is well browned and registers 110 degrees, about 1 hour.

3. Remove roast from oven and reduce oven temperature to 300 degrees. Using 2 bunches of paper towels, flip roast bone side up. Add apple cider to pan and return to oven, rotating direction of pan. Roast until meat registers 140 degrees, 30 to 50 minutes. Place meat on carving board, tent loosely with aluminum foil, and let rest for 15 to 20 minutes.

4. Transfer apple halves to blender and potatoes and shallots to bowl. Pour pan juices into fat separator, let liquid settle for 5 minutes, then pour into blender. Add chicken broth to blender with apples and pan juices and process until smooth, about 1 minute. Transfer sauce to medium saucepan and bring to simmer over medium heat. Season with salt and pepper to taste. Cover and keep warm. Remove twine from roast and slice meat between bones. Serve with vegetables and sauce.

Cooking Crown Roast of Pork Evenly

1. Using kitchen twine, make 2 loops around widest part of roast and tie securely to help crown hold its shape when flipped.

2. Place pork bone side down on V-rack and adjust bones to steady roast. Roast about 1 hour, until meat registers 110 degrees.

3. Using paper towels to protect your hands, flip hot roast bone side up and set it back on V-rack to finish cooking in gentle oven.

Why This Recipe Works A crown roast—two bone-in pork loin roasts tied together in a round—can feed a holiday crowd and offers a dramatic presentation, but its shape presents serious challenges to even cooking. Simply roasting it yielded meat overcooked on the outside and undercooked around the inner circle. The solution? We turned the roast upside down to allow more air to circulate and to better expose the thickest part of the roast to the heat. For a side, we opted for potatoes, shallots, and apples roasted in the pan alongside the meat. Pureeing the apples into a rich pan sauce gave us both fruity flavor and a nice, thick consistency.

Why This Recipe Works Pork shoulder's fat content and marbling mean it requires low and slow cooking to become tender—making it a natural for the slow cooker. For a full-flavored sauce, we browned the pork, then sautéed onions and garlic with tomato paste in the browned bits left behind before adding them to the slow cooker. A little instant tapioca produced just the right texture in the braising liquid. White wine added brightness and a splash of white wine vinegar, stirred in at the end of cooking, refreshed the wine flavor. Hearty root vegetables and diced tomatoes, which cooked along with the roast, balanced the flavors.

SLOW-COOKER PORK POT ROAST

SERVES 8

This roast is sometimes sold in elastic netting that must be removed before cooking. If you cannot find 2½- to 3-pound pork picnic shoulder roasts, you can substitute one 6-pound pork picnic shoulder roast; cut it into two pieces and prepare as directed.

2 (2½- to 3-pound) boneless pork picnic shoulder roasts, trimmed
  Salt and pepper
2 tablespoons vegetable oil
2 onions, chopped
6 garlic cloves, minced
1 tablespoon tomato paste
½ cup white wine
1 (28-ounce) can diced tomatoes, drained
3 tablespoons instant tapioca
2 teaspoons minced fresh thyme
1 pound carrots, peeled, halved lengthwise, and cut into 2-inch pieces
1 pound parsnips, peeled, halved lengthwise, and cut into 2-inch pieces
2 teaspoons white wine vinegar

1. Open each roast and trim any excess fat, then tie each roast with kitchen twine at 1½-inch intervals and once around length of roasts. Pat roasts dry with paper towels and season with salt and pepper. Heat 2 teaspoons oil in 12-inch skillet over medium-high heat until just smoking. Brown roasts all over, about 10 minutes. Transfer to slow cooker.

2. Add onions and 2 teaspoons oil to now-empty skillet and cook until browned, about 5 minutes. Add garlic and tomato paste and cook until fragrant, about 1 minute. Stir in wine and simmer, scraping up browned bits with wooden spoon, until thickened, about 2 minutes. Stir in tomatoes, tapioca, and thyme; transfer to slow cooker.

3. Toss carrots, parsnips, ¼ teaspoon salt, ¼ teaspoon pepper, and remaining 2 teaspoons oil in bowl until vegetables are well coated. Scatter vegetable mixture over pork. Cover and cook on low until meat is tender, 9 to 10 hours (or cook on high 4 to 5 hours).

4. Transfer roasts to carving board, tent with aluminum foil, and let rest for 10 minutes. Remove twine from roasts and cut meat into ½-inch-thick slices; transfer to serving platter. Using slotted spoon, transfer carrots and parsnips to platter with pork. Stir vinegar into sauce and season with salt and pepper to taste. Serve, passing sauce separately.

Two Roasts Are Better than One

We like to use two smaller roasts for this recipe, because the meat cooks more quickly and the small roasts are easier to manage in the slow cooker—and to find in the supermarket. Most boneless pork shoulder roasts come bound in string netting, which is difficult to remove after cooking. We prefer to cut the netting off before cooking, trim the roasts, and then tie each one with kitchen twine.

1. Remove netting from pork roasts. Open each roast and trim any excess fat.

2. Tie roasts separately. To ensure even cooking, fold smaller lobes under, then tie each roast with kitchen twine every 1½ inches around circumference and once around length.

Why This Recipe Works For this Sunday dinner–worthy pork roast, we skipped lean loins and opted for a meaty and inexpensive pork butt roast, which we flavored with a spice rub of cracked peppercorns, rosemary, sage, fennel seeds, and garlic. Cooking the roast in a low oven for seven hours rendered its fat and softened its tough connective tissue. For easy slicing, we refrigerated the cooked roast overnight until firm, then reheated it in the oven while we made a simple sauce from apple cider, apple jelly, and cider vinegar.

OLD-FASHIONED ROAST PORK

SERVES 8

A heavy roasting pan with 3-inch sides is the best choice for this recipe, but a shallow broiler pan also works well. Boneless pork butt roast is often labeled Boston butt in the supermarket.

- 6 pounds boneless pork butt roast, fat trimmed to ⅛ inch, tied lengthwise and crosswise
- 3 garlic cloves, minced
- 2 teaspoons peppercorns, cracked
- 1½ teaspoons salt
- 1 tablespoon chopped fresh rosemary
- 1 tablespoon chopped fresh sage
- 1 tablespoon fennel seeds, chopped
- 2 large red onions, cut into 1-inch wedges
- 1 cup apple cider
- ¼ cup apple jelly
- 2 tablespoons cider vinegar

1. Adjust oven rack to lower-middle position and heat oven to 300 degrees. Pat pork dry with paper towels. Combine garlic, peppercorns, salt, rosemary, sage, and fennel seeds in small bowl. Rub roast with herb mixture.

2. Transfer to roasting pan and cook for 3 hours. Scatter onion wedges around roast, tossing onions in pan drippings to coat. (If roast has not produced any juices, toss onions with 1 tablespoon vegetable oil before adding to pan.) Continue roasting until meat is extremely tender and skewer inserted in center meets no resistance, 3½ to 4 hours. (Check pan juices every hour to make sure they have not evaporated. If necessary, add 2 cups water to pan and scrape up browned bits.)

3. Transfer roast to large baking dish, place onions in medium bowl, and pour pan drippings into 2-cup liquid measuring cup, adding enough water to measure 1½ cups. Let roast, onions, and drippings cool for 30 minutes, cover each with plastic wrap, and refrigerate overnight.

4. One hour before serving, adjust oven rack to middle position and heat oven to 300 degrees. Cut meat into ¼-inch slices and overlap in large baking dish. Skim off fat from pan drippings and transfer drippings and reserved onions to medium saucepan. Add cider, jelly, and vinegar and bring to boil over medium-high heat, then reduce to simmer. Spoon ½ cup sauce over pork slices and cover baking dish with aluminum foil. Place in oven and heat until very hot, 30 to 40 minutes.

5. Just before serving, reduce sauce until dark and thickened, 10 to 15 minutes. Serve pork, spooning onion mixture over meat or passing separately.

Secrets to Old-Fashioned Flavor

1. Trim any excess fat from pork, leaving behind ⅛-inch-thick layer. Tie trimmed roast tightly into uniform shape, lengthwise and then crosswise.

2. Rub mixture of rosemary, sage, fennel seeds, garlic, salt, and pepper over roast.

3. Roast pork for 3 hours, add onion wedges, and continue to roast until meat is extremely tender, 3½ to 4 hours more.

PORK PERNIL

SERVES 8 TO 10

Depending on their size, you may need two bunches of cilantro. Crimp the foil tightly over the edges of the roasting pan in step 2 to minimize evaporation. Make sure to spray the V-rack in step 3. Serve over white rice.

1½ cups chopped fresh cilantro leaves and stems
1 onion, chopped coarse
¼ cup kosher salt
¼ cup olive oil
10 garlic cloves, peeled
2 tablespoons pepper
1 tablespoon dried oregano
1 tablespoon ground cumin
1 (7-pound) bone-in pork picnic shoulder
1 tablespoon grated lime zest plus ⅓ cup juice (3 limes)

1. Pulse 1 cup cilantro, onion, salt, oil, garlic, pepper, oregano, and cumin in food processor until finely ground, about 15 pulses, scraping down sides of bowl as needed. Pat pork dry with paper towels and rub sofrito all over. Wrap pork in plastic wrap and refrigerate for at least 12 hours or up to 24 hours.

2. Adjust oven rack to lower-middle position and heat oven to 450 degrees. Pour 8 cups water in large roasting pan. Unwrap pork and place skin side down in pan. Cover pan tightly with aluminum foil and roast for 90 minutes. Remove foil, reduce oven temperature to 375 degrees, and continue to roast for 2½ hours.

3. Remove pan from oven. Spray V-rack with vegetable oil spray. Gently slide metal spatula under pork to release skin from pan. Using folded dish towels, grasp ends of pork and transfer to V-rack, skin side up. Wipe skin dry with paper towels. Place V-rack with pork in roasting pan. If pan looks dry, add 1 cup water. Return to oven and roast until pork registers 195 degrees, about 1 hour. (Add water as needed to keep bottom of pan from drying out.)

4. Line rimmed baking sheet with foil. Remove pan from oven. Transfer V-rack and pork to prepared sheet and return to oven. Immediately increase oven temperature to 500 degrees. Cook until pork skin is well browned and crispy (when tapped lightly with tongs, skin will sound hollow), 15 to 30 minutes, rotating sheet halfway through cooking. Transfer pork to carving board and let rest for 30 minutes.

5. Meanwhile, pour juices from pan into fat separator. Let liquid settle for 5 minutes, then pour off 1 cup defatted juices into large bowl. (If juices measure less than 1 cup, make up difference with water.) Whisk remaining ½ cup cilantro and lime zest and juice into bowl.

6. Remove crispy skin from pork in 1 large piece. Coarsely chop skin into bite-size pieces and set aside. Trim and discard excess fat from pork. Remove pork from bone and chop coarse. Transfer pork to bowl with cilantro-lime sauce and toss to combine. Serve pork, with crispy skin on side.

Creating Crispy Skin

Elevating the roast on a V-rack to finish cooking crisps up the flavorful skin.

Why This Recipe Works Famous for its crispy skin, this Puerto Rican dish of long-cooked, heavily seasoned pork roast should result in flavorful meat along with its trademark crispy exterior. We rubbed a picnic shoulder with a salty sofrito (a paste of aromatics and herbs) the day before roasting, which kept the meat moist and packed a flavor punch. We then roasted the pork skin side down, covered, which helped transform tough collagen into gelatin. Next, we removed the foil cover to ensure that our pork didn't taste steamed, and then we turned the roast skin side up on a V-rack to dry the skin to prepare it for the last step—a quick roast at very high heat.

CIDER-BRAISED PORK ROAST

SERVES 8

Pork butt roast is often labeled Boston butt in the supermarket. Plan ahead: This roast needs to cure for 18 to 24 hours before cooking. If you can't find Braeburn apples, substitute Jonagold. If you don't have a fat separator, strain the liquid through a fine-mesh strainer into a medium bowl in step 4 and wait for it to settle.

- 1 (5- to 6-pound) bone-in pork butt roast
- ¼ cup packed brown sugar
  Kosher salt and pepper
- 3 tablespoons vegetable oil
- 1 onion, halved and sliced thin
- 6 garlic cloves, smashed and peeled
- 2 cups apple cider
- 6 sprigs fresh thyme
- 2 bay leaves
- 1 cinnamon stick
- 2 Braeburn apples, cored and cut into 8 wedges each
- ¼ cup apple butter
- 1 tablespoon cornstarch
- 1 tablespoon cider vinegar

1. Using sharp knife, trim fat cap on roast to ¼ inch. Cut 1-inch crosshatch pattern, ¹⁄₁₆ inch deep, in fat cap. Place roast on large sheet of plastic wrap. Combine sugar and ¼ cup salt in bowl and rub mixture over entire roast and into slits. Wrap roast tightly in double layer of plastic, place on plate, and refrigerate for 18 to 24 hours.

2. Adjust oven rack to middle position and heat oven to 275 degrees. Unwrap roast and pat dry with paper towels, brushing away any excess salt mixture from surface. Season roast with pepper.

3. Heat oil in Dutch oven over medium-high heat until just smoking. Sear roast until well browned on all sides, about 3 minutes per side. Turn roast fat side up. Scatter onion and garlic around roast and cook until fragrant and beginning to brown, about 2 minutes. Add 1¾ cups cider, thyme sprigs, bay leaves, and cinnamon stick and bring to simmer. Cover,

transfer to oven, and braise until fork slips easily in and out of meat and meat registers 190 degrees, 2 hours 15 minutes to 2 hours 45 minutes.

4. Transfer roast to carving board, tent with aluminum foil, and let rest for 30 minutes. Strain braising liquid through fine-mesh strainer into fat separator; discard solids and let liquid settle for at least 5 minutes.

5. About 10 minutes before roast is done resting, wipe out pot with paper towels. Spoon 1½ tablespoons of clear, separated fat from top of fat separator into now-empty pot and heat over medium-high heat until shimmering. Season apples with salt and pepper. Space apples evenly in pot, cut side down, and cook until well browned on both cut sides, about 3 minutes per side. Transfer to platter and tent with foil.

6. Wipe out pot with paper towels. Return 2 cups defatted braising liquid to now-empty pot and bring to boil over high heat. Whisk in apple butter until incorporated. Whisk cornstarch and remaining ¼ cup cider together in bowl and add to pot. Return to boil and cook until thickened, about 1 minute. Off heat, add vinegar and season with salt and pepper to taste. Cover sauce and keep warm.

7. To carve roast, cut around inverted T-shaped bone until it can be pulled free from roast (use clean dish towel to grasp bone if necessary). Slice pork and transfer to serving platter with apples. Pour 1 cup sauce over pork and apples. Serve, passing remaining sauce at table.

Removing the Bone

Holding on to tip of T-shaped bone, use long knife to cut meat away from all sides of bone until bone is loose enough to pull out of roast.

Why This Recipe Works Pork and apples are a classic combination, so we paired flavorful bone-in pork butt roast with apple cider. Rubbing the meat with a brown sugar–salt mixture and refrigerating it overnight seasoned the pork and helped keep it juicy. Onions, garlic, bay leaf, cinnamon, and thyme were welcome additions that kept the clean, sweet-tart taste of cider in focus. Apple butter and cider vinegar added more apple-y punch, and a slurry of cornstarch and reserved cider thickened the braising liquid into a beautiful sauce. Apple wedges seared in flavorful pork fat united the elements of this hearty roast.

Why This Recipe Works Wrapping a pork loin roast in bacon not only adds big, smoky flavor to the mild meat but also encases the roast in a layer of protective fat that bastes the pork as it renders. Achieving a rosy, moist roast with a beautifully browned bacon crust required a two-pronged cooking approach: We roasted the pork in a low 250-degree oven until it reached 90 degrees, and then we cranked the oven to 475 degrees to brown the bacon and finish cooking the pork. Brushing the bacon with a sweet-savory, quick-cooking peach sauce gave it a rich, lacquered appearance and rounded out the dish.

BACON-WRAPPED PORK ROAST WITH PEACH SAUCE

SERVES 8

Buy a pork loin roast that measures about 9 inches long and is between 4 and 5 inches in diameter. Oscar Mayer Naturally Hardwood Smoked Bacon is our winning thin-sliced bacon. Do not use thick-cut bacon here. The peaches needn't be thawed before you make the sauce. The pork needs to cure for at least an hour before cooking.

Pork

Kosher salt and pepper
1 tablespoon sugar
1 (3 ½-pound) boneless center-cut pork loin roast
2 teaspoons herbes de Provence
10 slices bacon

Sauce

20 ounces frozen peaches, cut into ½-inch pieces (3 cups)
1 cup dry white wine
½ cup sugar
⅓ cup cider vinegar
4 sprigs fresh thyme
½ teaspoon kosher salt
2 tablespoons whole-grain mustard

1. For the Pork Combine 4 teaspoons salt and sugar in bowl. Remove fat cap and silverskin from roast. Rub roast with salt-sugar mixture, wrap in plastic wrap, and refrigerate for at least 1 hour or up to 24 hours.

2. For the Sauce Bring peaches, wine, sugar, vinegar, thyme sprigs, and salt to simmer in medium saucepan over medium-high heat. Reduce heat to medium and cook at strong simmer, stirring occasionally, until reduced to about 2 cups and spatula leaves trail when dragged through sauce, about 30 minutes. Remove from heat and discard thyme sprigs. Reserve 2 tablespoons of liquid portion of sauce (without peach segments) in small bowl for glazing. Cover and set aside remaining sauce.

3. Meanwhile, adjust oven rack to upper-middle position and heat oven to 250 degrees. Line rimmed baking sheet with aluminum foil and spray with vegetable oil spray. Unwrap roast and pat dry with paper towels. Sprinkle with herbes de Provence and 1 teaspoon pepper.

4. Arrange bacon slices on cutting board parallel to counter's edge, overlapping them slightly to match length of roast. Place roast in center of bacon, perpendicular to slices. Bring ends of bacon up and around sides of roast, overlapping ends of slices as needed.

5. Place bacon-wrapped roast, seam side down, in center of prepared sheet. Roast until center of pork registers 90 degrees, 30 to 40 minutes. Remove roast from oven and increase oven temperature to 475 degrees.

6. Brush top and sides of roast with reserved 2 tablespoons sauce. Once oven reaches temperature, return pork to oven and roast until bacon is well browned and meat registers 130 degrees, 15 to 20 minutes longer. Transfer roast to wire rack and let rest for 15 minutes.

7. Stir mustard into sauce and rewarm over low heat. Transfer roast to carving board and cut into ½-inch-thick slices. Serve with peach sauce.

Why This Recipe Works Unlike the hams that most people are familiar with, fresh ham isn't cured, smoked, or aged. This big cut is basically an oddly shaped bone-in, skin-on pork roast, and slow roasting turned it tender and flavorful. Roasting the ham in an oven bag created a moist environment that conducted heat more effectively than a dry oven does, so the ham stays moist and reaches the ideal cooking temperature faster and remains there longer. A simple tangy glaze brushed on toward the end of roasting made for a flavorful finish. This rich ham may be just the thing to serve as a simple yet elegant centerpiece for your next big gathering.

SLOW-ROASTED FRESH HAM

SERVES 12 TO 14

Use a turkey-size oven bag for this recipe.

1 (8- to 10-pound) bone-in, shank-end fresh ham
⅓ cup packed brown sugar
⅓ cup kosher salt
3 tablespoons minced fresh rosemary
1 tablespoon minced fresh thyme
1 large oven bag
2 tablespoons maple syrup
2 tablespoons molasses
1 tablespoon soy sauce
1 tablespoon Dijon mustard
1 teaspoon pepper

1. Place ham flat side down on cutting board. Using sharp knife, remove skin, leaving ½- to ¼-inch layer of fat intact. Cut 1-inch diagonal crosshatch pattern in fat, being careful not to cut into meat. Place ham on its side. Cut one 4-inch horizontal pocket about 2 inches deep in center of flat side of ham, being careful not to poke through opposite side.

2. Combine sugar, salt, rosemary, and thyme in bowl. Rub half of sugar mixture in ham pocket. Tie 1 piece of kitchen twine tightly around base of ham. Rub exterior of ham with remaining sugar mixture. Wrap ham tightly in plastic wrap and refrigerate for at least 12 hours or up to 24 hours.

3. Adjust oven rack to lowest position and heat oven to 325 degrees. Set V-rack in large roasting pan. Unwrap ham and place in oven bag flat side down. Tie top of oven bag closed with kitchen twine. Place ham, flat side down, on V-rack and cut ½-inch slit in top of oven bag. Roast until thermometer inserted in center of ham, close to but not touching bone, registers 160 degrees, 3½ to 5 hours. Remove ham from oven and let rest in oven bag on V-rack for 1 hour. Heat oven to 450 degrees.

4. Whisk maple syrup, molasses, soy sauce, mustard, and pepper together in bowl. Cut off top of oven bag and push down with tongs, allowing accumulated juices to spill into roasting pan; discard oven bag. Leave ham sitting flat side down on V-rack.

5. Brush ham with half of glaze and roast for 10 minutes. Brush ham with remaining glaze, rotate pan, and roast until deep amber color, about 10 minutes longer. Move ham to carving board, flat side down, and let rest for 20 minutes. Pour pan juices into fat separator. Carve ham into ¼-inch-thick slices, arrange on platter, and moisten lightly with defatted pan juices. Serve, passing remaining pan juices separately.

How to Season Deeply and Cook Evenly
We found two tricks for deep seasoning and even cooking of a fresh ham.

CUT a pocket in the meaty end and season the ham inside the pocket.

TIE twine around the base to create a more even shape, then season the exterior.

CIDER-BAKED HAM

SERVES 16 TO 20

We prefer a bone-in, uncut, cured ham for this recipe, because the exterior layer of fat can be scored and helps create a nice crust. A spiral-sliced ham can be used instead, but there won't be much exterior fat, so skip the trimming and scoring in step 2. This recipe requires nearly a gallon of cider and a large oven bag. In step 4, be sure to stir the reduced cider mixture frequently to prevent scorching.

- 1 cinnamon stick, broken into rough pieces
- ¼ teaspoon whole cloves
- 3¼ quarts apple cider
- 8 cups ice cubes
- 1 (7- to 10-pound) cured bone-in half ham, preferably shank end
- 2 tablespoons Dijon mustard
- 1 cup packed dark brown sugar
- 1 teaspoon pepper
  Large oven bag

1. Toast cinnamon and cloves in large saucepan over medium heat until fragrant, about 3 minutes. Add 4 cups cider and bring to boil. Pour spiced cider into large stockpot or clean bucket, add 4 cups cider and ice, and stir until melted.

2. Meanwhile, remove skin from exterior of ham and trim fat to ¼-inch thickness. Score remaining fat at 1-inch intervals in crosshatch pattern. Transfer ham to container with chilled cider mixture (liquid should nearly cover ham) and refrigerate for at least 4 hours or up to 12 hours.

3. Discard cider mixture and transfer ham to large oven bag. Add 1 cup fresh cider to bag, tie securely, and cut 4 slits in top of bag. Transfer to large roasting pan and let stand at room temperature for 1½ hours.

4. Adjust oven rack to lowest position and heat oven to 300 degrees. Bake until ham registers 100 degrees, 1½ to 2½ hours. Meanwhile, bring remaining 4 cups cider and mustard to boil in saucepan. Reduce heat to medium-low and simmer, stirring often, until mixture is very thick and reduced to ⅓ cup, about 1 hour.

5. Combine sugar and pepper in bowl. Remove ham from oven and let rest for 5 minutes. Increase oven temperature to 400 degrees. Roll back oven bag and brush ham with reduced cider mixture. Using your fingers, carefully press sugar mixture onto exterior of ham. Return to oven and bake until dark brown and caramelized, about 20 minutes. Transfer ham to carving board, tent loosely with aluminum foil, and let rest for 15 minutes. Carve and serve.

Secrets to Cider-Baked Ham

1. Soaking ham in spice-infused cider lends concentrated flavor.

2. Baking ham with cider in oven bag keeps meat moist and lends even more cider flavor.

3. Brushing ham with sticky cider reduction provides big apple flavor and base for crust.

4. Pressing mixture of brown sugar and pepper onto ham gives exterior spicy-sweet, crackly crust.

Why This Recipe Works Ham glazed with sweet apple cider certainly sounds great, but most recipes lack serious apple flavor, not to mention they call for frequent basting. For a relatively hands-off ham that was infused with lots of apple flavor, we marinated the ham in apple cider spiked with warm spices. Baking the ham in an oven bag guarded against dried-out meat. And to give our ham a crusty, spicy-sweet exterior, we rolled back the bag once the ham was heated through, slathered on reduced apple cider, pressed a mixture of brown sugar and black pepper all over, and slid it back into the oven until it caramelized.

Why This Recipe Works A rack of lamb with a nicely burnished exterior is the perfect festive centerpiece for a special-occasion meal, but trying to get a brown crust in the oven left us with overcooked meat. So instead we employed a two-step process, first searing the racks on the stovetop and then roasting them in a relatively low oven until they emerged tender, juicy, and rosy-pink throughout. Panko crumbs seasoned with thyme, garlic, lemon zest, and anchovies added crunch and assertive flavor, and sharp, tangy Dijon mustard acted as a flavorful glue to adhere the mixture to the lamb. A lemony mint sauce added a bright and zippy finish.

CRUMB-CRUSTED RACK OF LAMB

SERVES 6 TO 8

We prefer the milder taste and bigger size of domestic lamb, but you may substitute lamb imported from New Zealand or Australia. Since imported lamb is generally smaller, if you can find only racks that are 1½ to 1¾ pounds, decrease the salt for each rack to ¾ teaspoon in step 2 and reduce the cooking time by about 5 minutes in step 3. Serve with Fresh Mint Sauce (recipe follows), if desired.

- 1 cup panko bread crumbs
- 2 tablespoons plus 1 teaspoon extra-virgin olive oil
- 2 tablespoons minced fresh thyme
- 6 garlic cloves, minced
- 4 anchovy fillets, rinsed, patted dry, and minced (optional)
  Kosher salt and pepper
- 2 tablespoons minced fresh parsley
- 1 tablespoon grated lemon zest
- 2 (1¾- to 2-pound) racks of lamb, fat trimmed to ⅛ inch
- ¼ cup Dijon mustard

1. Adjust oven rack to middle position and heat oven to 300 degrees. Combine panko; 2 tablespoons oil; thyme; garlic; anchovies, if using; 2 teaspoons salt; and 1 teaspoon pepper in 12-inch nonstick skillet. Cook over medium heat, stirring frequently and breaking up any clumps, until golden brown, about 5 minutes. Transfer to shallow dish. Stir in parsley and lemon zest.

2. Wipe skillet clean with paper towels. Set wire rack in rimmed baking sheet. Pat lamb dry with paper towels, sprinkle each rack with 1 teaspoon salt, and season with pepper. Heat remaining 1 teaspoon oil in now-empty skillet over medium-high heat until just smoking. Place 1 rack in skillet and cook until well browned, 2 to 4 minutes per side, using tongs as necessary to stand up rack to brown loin portion. Transfer to prepared wire rack. Pour off all but 1 teaspoon fat from skillet and repeat cooking with remaining rack of lamb. Let lamb cool for 5 minutes.

3. Brush lamb all over with mustard. Working with 1 rack at a time, transfer lamb to panko mixture, turning to coat all sides and pressing gently to adhere. Return lamb to wire rack, fat side up. Roast until lamb registers 135 degrees for medium, 40 to 50 minutes. Transfer to carving board and let rest for 15 minutes. Cut between bones to separate chops. Serve.

FRESH MINT SAUCE
MAKES ABOUT ½ CUP
Use a good-quality extra-virgin olive oil here for the best results.

- ½ cup chopped fresh mint
- 6 tablespoons extra-virgin olive oil
- ¼ cup chopped fresh parsley
- 2 tablespoons lemon juice
- 1 garlic clove, minced
- ½ teaspoon kosher salt
- ¼ teaspoon pepper

Combine all ingredients in bowl.

The Details Matter

1. Trim Fat Much of lamb's stronger flavor resides in its fat; we trim the fat on the racks' exteriors to ⅛ inch to control it.

2. Stand Up to Brown To ensure even cooking, brown the racks on all sides, including the "bottom" of the loin.

SLOW-ROASTED SALMON WITH CHIVES AND LEMON

SERVES 6

You can substitute granulated sugar for the brown sugar, if desired. If a 2½-pound salmon fillet is unavailable, you can use six 6- to 8-ounce skinless salmon fillets instead. In step 1, sprinkle both sides of the fillets evenly with the sugar mixture and arrange them side by side in the baking dish so that they are touching. The cooking time remains the same. We prefer farm-raised salmon here; if using wild salmon, reduce the cooking time to 45 to 50 minutes, or until the salmon registers 120 degrees. If you're using table salt, use ¾ teaspoon (½ teaspoon in step 1 and ¼ teaspoon in step 3).

1 tablespoon packed brown sugar
1½ teaspoons kosher salt, divided
½ teaspoon pepper
1 (2½-pound) skinless center-cut salmon fillet, about 1½ inches thick
¼ cup extra-virgin olive oil
2 tablespoons sliced fresh chives
2 teaspoons grated lemon zest plus 1½ tablespoons juice

1. Adjust oven rack to middle position and heat oven to 250 degrees. Combine sugar, 1 teaspoon salt, and pepper in small bowl. Sprinkle salmon all over with sugar mixture.

2. Place salmon, flesh side up, in 13 by 9-inch baking dish. Roast until center is still translucent when checked with tip of paring knife and registers 125 degrees (for medium-rare), 55 to 60 minutes.

3. Meanwhile, combine oil, chives, lemon zest and juice, and remaining ½ teaspoon salt in bowl.

4. Remove dish from oven and immediately pour oil mixture evenly over salmon. Let rest for 5 minutes. Using spatula and spoon, portion salmon and sauce onto serving platter. Stir together any juices left in dish and spoon over salmon. Serve.

SLOW-ROASTED SALMON WITH DILL AND GARLIC

Substitute 1 teaspoon dry mustard for pepper. Add 1 teaspoon granulated garlic to sugar mixture. Substitute chopped fresh dill for chives.

SLOW-ROASTED SALMON WITH PARSLEY AND CAYENNE

Substitute cayenne pepper for pepper and chopped fresh parsley for chives.

Pull Out the Pin Bones

To remove the pin bones from a salmon fillet, drape the fillet skin side down on an overturned bowl and remove the protruding bones with tweezers or needle-nose pliers.

Why This Recipe Works Though slow roasting is an uncommon method for cooking fish, here it results in ultratender, buttery salmon. To feed six people, we opted to work with a single 2½-pound fillet, which would be less likely to overcook than separate, smaller pieces. We sprinkled the fish with a mixture of brown sugar and salt to evoke the flavors of cured salmon and slid it into the oven. A very low, 250-degree oven kept the fish from overcooking and minimized any residual cooking once it was out of the oven. A light, bright vinaigrette of extra-virgin olive oil, lemon zest and juice, and fresh chives perfectly complemented our succulent fish.

Why This Recipe Works We embraced the challenge of a one-pan dinner with salmon, broccoli, and red potatoes even though all require different cooking times. We started the potatoes and broccoli together, roasting them at 500 degrees—enough time for the broccoli to brown and the spuds to soften. Then we removed the broccoli, keeping it warm under foil, and arranged the salmon fillets in its place. Reducing the oven temperature let the salmon roast gently while the potatoes finished cooking. A sharp stir-together sauce of chives, mustard, and lemon gave this simple meal some pizzazz and added a fresh note.

ONE-PAN ROASTED SALMON WITH BROCCOLI AND RED POTATOES

SERVES 4

Use small red potatoes measuring 1 to 2 inches in diameter for this recipe.

4   (6- to 8-ounce) center-cut skinless salmon fillets, 1 to 1½ inches thick
2   teaspoons plus 5 tablespoons extra-virgin olive oil
    Salt and pepper
1   pound small red potatoes, unpeeled, halved
1   pound broccoli florets, cut into 2-inch pieces
¼   cup minced fresh chives
2   tablespoons whole-grain mustard
2   teaspoons lemon juice
1   teaspoon honey
    Lemon wedges

1. Adjust oven rack to lowest position and heat oven to 500 degrees. Pat salmon dry with paper towels, then rub all over with 2 teaspoons oil and season with salt and pepper. Refrigerate until needed.

2. Brush rimmed baking sheet with 1 tablespoon oil. Toss potatoes, 1 tablespoon oil, ½ teaspoon salt, and ½ teaspoon pepper together in bowl. Arrange potatoes cut side down on half of sheet. Toss broccoli, 1 tablespoon oil, ¼ teaspoon salt, and ¼ teaspoon pepper together in now-empty bowl. Arrange broccoli on other half of sheet.

3. Roast until potatoes are light golden brown and broccoli is dark brown on bottom, 22 to 24 minutes, rotating sheet halfway through baking.

4. Meanwhile, combine chives, mustard, lemon juice, honey, remaining 2 tablespoons oil, pinch salt, and pinch pepper in bowl; set chive sauce aside.

5. Remove sheet from oven and transfer broccoli to platter, browned side up; cover with foil to keep warm. Using spatula, remove any bits of broccoli remaining on sheet. (Leave potatoes on sheet.)

6. Place salmon skinned side down on now-empty side of sheet, spaced evenly. Place sheet in oven and immediately reduce oven temperature to 275 degrees. Bake until centers of fillets register 125 degrees (for medium-rare), 11 to 15 minutes, rotating sheet halfway through baking. Transfer potatoes and salmon to platter with broccoli. Serve with lemon wedges and chive sauce.

Broccoli-Salmon Switcheroo

To ensure that all three components emerge from the oven well browned and cooked just right, we roast the potatoes the entire time on the baking sheet (they take the longest) but remove the broccoli before placing the salmon fillets on the sheet.

BAKED SHRIMP WITH FENNEL, POTATOES, AND OLIVES

SERVES 4 TO 6

We prefer all-natural shrimp that aren't treated with sodium or preservatives. If buying frozen shrimp, the ingredient label should list only "shrimp."

1½ pounds Yukon Gold potatoes, peeled and
    sliced ½ inch thick

2 fennel bulbs, stalks discarded, bulbs halved
    lengthwise and cut into 1-inch-thick wedges
    through stem end

3 tablespoons extra-virgin olive oil, plus
    extra for drizzling
    Salt and pepper

2 pounds jumbo shrimp (16 to 20 per pound),
    peeled, deveined, and tails removed

2 teaspoons dried oregano

1 teaspoon grated lemon zest, plus lemon
    wedges for serving

4 ounces feta cheese, crumbled (1 cup)

½ cup pitted kalamata olives, halved

2 tablespoons chopped fresh parsley

1. Adjust oven rack to lower-middle position and heat oven to 450 degrees. Toss potatoes, fennel, 2 tablespoons oil, 1 teaspoon salt, and ¼ teaspoon pepper together in bowl. Spread vegetables in single layer on rimmed baking sheet and roast until just tender, about 25 minutes.

2. Pat shrimp dry with paper towels. Toss shrimp, oregano, lemon zest, remaining 1 tablespoon oil, ½ teaspoon salt, and ¼ teaspoon pepper together in bowl.

3. Using spatula, flip potatoes and fennel so browned sides are facing up. Scatter shrimp and feta over top. Return to oven and roast until shrimp are cooked through, 6 to 8 minutes. Sprinkle olives and parsley over top and drizzle with extra oil. Serve with lemon wedges.

Roast Veggies First

Roast the longer-cooking potatoes and fennel until they are just tender. Then, flip the vegetables so that their browned sides are facing up and scatter the oregano-and-lemon-scented shrimp and the feta on top to cook the shrimp. Sprinkle with parsley and kalamata olives before serving.

Why This Recipe Works Unlike other proteins that look anemic if not seared over direct heat, naturally vibrant pink shrimp are a great candidate for the oven. But since shrimp cook so quickly, we needed to give the rest of our one-pan meal a head start. Potatoes browned nicely in the oven, and licorice-y fennel stayed intact when sliced into wedges though the stem end. To achieve a bright flavor profile, we tossed the shrimp with oregano and lemon zest before adding them to the baking sheet with the vegetables. Salty feta cheese and kalamata olives gave our simple dish a savory finish, and a squeeze of lemon brought it all to life.

PARMESAN-CRUSTED ASPARAGUS

SERVES 4 TO 6

Avoid pencil-thin asparagus for this recipe. Work quickly when tossing the asparagus with the egg whites, as the salt on the asparagus will rapidly begin to deflate the whites.

2 pounds (½-inch-thick) asparagus, trimmed
  Salt and pepper
3 ounces Parmesan cheese, grated (1½ cups)
¾ cup panko bread crumbs
1 tablespoon unsalted butter, melted and cooled
  Pinch cayenne
2 large egg whites
1 teaspoon honey

1. Adjust oven rack to middle position and heat oven to 450 degrees. Line rimmed baking sheet with aluminum foil and spray with vegetable oil spray. Using fork, poke holes up and down stalks of asparagus. Toss asparagus with ½ teaspoon salt and let stand for 30 minutes on a paper towel–lined baking sheet.

2. Meanwhile, combine 1 cup Parmesan, panko, butter, ¼ teaspoon salt, ⅛ teaspoon pepper, and cayenne in bowl. Transfer half of panko mixture to shallow dish and reserve remaining mixture. Using stand mixer fitted with whisk, whip egg whites and honey on medium-low speed until foamy, about 1 minute. Increase speed to medium-high and whip until soft peaks form, 2 to 3 minutes. Scrape into 13 by 9-inch baking dish and toss asparagus in mixture. Working with 1 spear at a time, dredge half of asparagus in panko and transfer to aluminum foil–lined baking sheet. Refill shallow dish with reserved panko mixture and repeat with remaining half of asparagus.

3. Bake asparagus until just beginning to brown, 6 to 8 minutes. Sprinkle with remaining ½ cup Parmesan and continue to bake until cheese is melted and panko is golden brown, 6 to 8 minutes. Transfer to platter. Serve.

Making the Coating Stick

1. Perforate and salt asparagus to draw out excess moisture that could saturate crumbs.

2. Whip egg whites to help crumbs adhere. Add honey for flavor and extra sticking power.

3. Work with 1 spear at a time to keep bread crumbs from clumping.

Why This Recipe Works Simply roasting asparagus and topping it with shaved Parmesan gives you limp spears and rubbery cheese. To get perfectly crisp-tender asparagus, we first salted it to rid it of excess moisture. For a cheesy coating that would stay put on the slender spears, we whipped a combination of honey and egg whites to soft peaks, dipped the asparagus in the mixture, then coated them with a mixture of bread crumbs and Parmesan. Finally, to reinforce the Parmesan flavor, we sprinkled the spears with more cheese at the end of roasting.

Why This Recipe Works It's easy to mask the taste of an unpopular vegetable with cheese, but we think the flavors of properly cooked brussels sprouts are worth showing off. We roasted them to bring out their nutty and slightly sweet notes, and meanwhile whipped up a Mornay sauce—a creamy cheese sauce (using Gruyère and Parmesan) spiked with nutmeg, cayenne, and sweet-sharp aromatics. We poured the sauce over the roasted sprouts, and then for the crunchiest possible topping for our gratin, we jump-started some panko by sautéing it in butter, sprinkled it over the top with cheese, and popped the whole dish back in the oven to crisp up.

BRUSSELS SPROUT GRATIN

SERVES 6 TO 8

Look for smaller brussels sprouts, no bigger than a golf ball, as they're likely to be sweeter and more tender than large sprouts. If you can find only large sprouts, quarter them. A broiler-safe dish is important because the sprouts cook at such a high temperature.

2½ pounds brussels sprouts, trimmed and halved through stem
 1 tablespoon vegetable oil
    Salt and pepper
 3 tablespoons unsalted butter
 ¼ cup panko bread crumbs
 1 shallot, minced
 1 garlic clove, minced
 1 tablespoon all-purpose flour
1¼ cups heavy cream
 ¾ cup chicken broth
 2 ounces Gruyère cheese, shredded (½ cup)
 1 ounce Parmesan cheese, grated (½ cup)
    Pinch ground nutmeg
    Pinch cayenne pepper

1. Adjust oven rack to middle position and heat oven to 450 degrees. Grease 13 by 9-inch broiler-safe baking dish. Toss brussels sprouts, oil, ½ teaspoon salt, and ¼ teaspoon pepper together in prepared baking dish. Bake until sprouts are well browned and tender, 30 to 35 minutes. Transfer to wire rack and set aside to cool for at least 5 minutes or up to 30 minutes.

2. Meanwhile, melt 1 tablespoon butter in medium saucepan over medium heat. Add panko and cook, stirring frequently, until golden brown, about 3 minutes. Transfer to bowl and stir in ¼ teaspoon salt and ¼ teaspoon pepper; set aside. Wipe saucepan clean with paper towels.

3. Melt remaining 2 tablespoons butter in now-empty saucepan over medium heat. Add shallot and garlic and cook until just softened, about 1 minute. Stir in flour and cook for 1 minute. Whisk in cream and broth and bring to boil over medium-high heat. Once boiling, remove from heat and whisk in ¼ cup Gruyère, Parmesan, nutmeg, cayenne, ¼ teaspoon pepper, and ⅛ teaspoon salt until smooth.

4. Pour cream mixture over brussels sprouts in baking dish and stir to combine. Sprinkle evenly with panko mixture and remaining ¼ cup Gruyère. Bake until bubbling around edges and golden brown on top, 5 to 7 minutes. Transfer dish to wire rack and let cool for 10 minutes. Serve.

Choose the Right Size Sprouts

For this recipe, the brussels sprouts should be relatively small, no larger than a golf ball. Larger sprouts can be tougher and more bitter.

BRUSSELS SPROUT SALAD

SERVES 8

Slice the sprouts as thin as possible. Shred the Pecorino Romano on the large holes of a box grater.

- 3 tablespoons lemon juice
- 2 tablespoons Dijon mustard
- 1 small shallot, minced
- 1 garlic clove, minced
  Salt and pepper
- 6 tablespoons extra-virgin olive oil
- 2 pounds brussels sprouts, trimmed, halved, and sliced very thin
- 3 ounces Pecorino Romano cheese, shredded (1 cup)
- ½ cup pine nuts, toasted

1. Whisk lemon juice, mustard, shallot, garlic, and ½ teaspoon salt together in large bowl. Slowly whisk in oil until incorporated. Toss brussels sprouts with vinaigrette and let sit for at least 30 minutes or up to 2 hours.

2. Fold in Pecorino and pine nuts. Season with salt and pepper to taste. Serve.

BRUSSELS SPROUT SALAD WITH CHEDDAR, HAZELNUTS, AND APPLE

Substitute 1 cup shredded sharp cheddar for Pecorino and ½ cup hazelnuts, toasted, skinned, and chopped, for pine nuts. Add 1 Granny Smith apple, cored and cut into ½-inch pieces.

BRUSSELS SPROUT SALAD WITH SMOKED GOUDA, PECANS, AND DRIED CHERRIES

Substitute 1 cup shredded smoked gouda for Pecorino and ½ cup pecans, toasted and chopped, for pine nuts. Add ½ cup chopped dried cherries.

How to Slice Brussels Sprouts

You can use the slicing disk of your food processor or slice the sprouts with a chef's knife. Follow these steps to do the latter safely and quickly.

1. Trim stem end of each sprout and then cut each sprout in half through cut end.

2. With flat surface on cutting board, thinly slice each half.

Why This Recipe Works Raw brussels sprout salad isn't as weird as it sounds: brussels sprouts are very much like miniature cabbages in both texture and taste. To make this slaw-like salad, we thinly sliced the sprouts and tossed them with a bright, lemony vinaigrette with a touch of Dijon. We briefly marinated the salad in the vinaigrette to soften and season the sprouts. We topped the sprouts with toasted pine nuts and salty Pecorino Romano for a salad that's so delicious it can turn brussels sprout loathers into brussels sprout lovers.

Why This Recipe Works Conventional wisdom holds that anything but the gentlest treatment turns mashed potatoes into wallpaper paste, but we think our mixer-whipped spuds prove otherwise. For the lightest, fluffiest potatoes, we found high-starch russets worked best. Boiling the potatoes added extra water, resulting in a flat, not fluffy, finished dish. The best technique was to rinse excess starch from the raw potatoes, steam them, and then dry them in a pot on the stovetop over low heat. This process made them fluffier and better able to absorb the warm butter-and-milk mixture during whipping.

WHIPPED POTATOES

SERVES 8 TO 10

If your steamer basket has short legs (under 1¾ inches), the potatoes will sit in water as they cook and get wet. To prevent this, use balls of aluminum foil as steamer basket stilts. A stand mixer fitted with a whisk yields the smoothest potatoes, but a handheld mixer may be used as well.

  4 pounds russet potatoes, peeled and cut into
     1-inch pieces
1½ cups whole milk
  8 tablespoons unsalted butter, cut into 8 pieces
  2 teaspoons salt
  ½ teaspoon pepper

1. Place cut potatoes in colander. Rinse under cold water until water runs clear, about 1 minute. Drain potatoes. Fill Dutch oven with 1 inch water and bring to boil. Place steamer basket in Dutch oven and fill with potatoes. Reduce heat to medium and cook, covered, until potatoes are tender, 20 to 25 minutes.

2. Heat milk, butter, salt, and pepper in small saucepan over medium-low heat, whisking until smooth, about 3 minutes; cover and keep warm.

3. Pour contents of Dutch oven into colander and return potatoes to dry pot. Stir over low heat until potatoes are thoroughly dried, about 1 minute. Using stand mixer fitted with whisk, break potatoes into small pieces on low speed, about 30 seconds. Add milk mixture in steady stream until incorporated. Increase speed to high and whip until potatoes are light and fluffy and no lumps remain, about 2 minutes. Serve.

Choosing Your Mixing Method

Don't try this recipe in your food processor—its sharp blades cut open the starch granules and turn the potatoes to glue. The beating motion of the mixer makes smooth, fluffy potatoes every time.

DON'T DO IT
A food processor's blade makes gluey mashed potatoes.

WHIP SMART
Use the mixer for light, fluffy whipped potatoes.

The American Table: Whip It Good

In all likelihood, whipped potatoes owe their mid 20th-century fame to the Sunbeam Mixmaster. The appliance, first manufactured in 1930 and quickly enshrined as the must-have kitchen tool for American housewives, actually had a Mix-Finder Dial setting for whipped potatoes— speed 4 or 5, depending on the model. Whipping potatoes in the Mixmaster, the manufacturer claimed, saved "one-third the time usually taken by hand." But then, this machine promised time savings on just about every kitchen task. The 17 available attachments on early models included not only a slicer/shredder and an ice cream maker but also a butter churn, a string bean slicer, and (our personal favorite) a pea sheller. It's no wonder this kitchen tool became perhaps the most famous appliance of the 20th century.

Why This Recipe Works Duchess potatoes take mashed potatoes to the next level, enriching them with egg and piping them into decorative rosettes before baking. To cook our spuds, we tried boiling, but this made them waterlogged; baking dried them out. Parcooking them in the microwave and finishing the rosettes in a hot oven proved best. For a potato mixture that was the right texture for piping, we stirred in butter, eggs, and cream while the potatoes were still hot, then added more butter once the potatoes had cooled. Baking powder ensured our picture-perfect Duchess Potatoes had the perfect airy, light texture to match.

DUCHESS POTATOES

SERVES 8

For the smoothest, most uniform texture, use a food mill or ricer to mash the potatoes. Choose potatoes of the same size so that they cook evenly.

3 pounds russet potatoes
1 cup heavy cream
6 tablespoons unsalted butter, cut into ¼-inch pieces and softened
1 large egg plus 1 large yolk, lightly beaten
1¼ teaspoons salt
½ teaspoon pepper
½ teaspoon baking powder
Pinch nutmeg
Vegetable oil spray

1. Adjust oven rack to upper-middle position and heat oven to 475 degrees. Meanwhile, prick potatoes all over with fork, place on plate, and microwave until tender, 18 to 25 minutes, turning potatoes over after 10 minutes.

2. Cut potatoes in half. When cool enough to handle, scoop flesh into large bowl and mash until no lumps remain. Add cream, 3 tablespoons butter, egg and yolk, salt, pepper, baking powder, and nutmeg and continue to mash until potatoes are smooth. Let cool to room temperature, about 10 minutes. Gently fold in remaining butter until pieces are evenly distributed.

3. Transfer potato mixture to piping bag fitted with ½-inch star tip. Pipe eight 4-inch-wide mounds of potato onto rimmed baking sheet. Spray lightly with vegetable oil spray and bake until golden brown, 15 to 20 minutes. Serve.

To Make Ahead Once piped onto baking sheet, potatoes can be covered loosely with plastic wrap and refrigerated for 24 hours. Remove plastic and spray lightly with vegetable oil spray before baking.

Two Paths to Perfect Piping

With a pastry bag fitted with a star tip, making beautiful duchess potatoes is child's play. If you don't have a pastry bag, don't worry: There's another easy way.

With Pastry Bag
Pipe 4-inch circle of potato mixture onto baking sheet. Continue to pipe upward in circles to form 3-inch-high peak.

Without Pastry Bag
Scoop potato mixture into zipper-lock bag, snip off 1 corner, and pipe as directed. Use tines of fork to create rippled surface.

Freezer Friendly

Our Duchess Potatoes freeze beautifully, which is handy, as they're ideal for a party. Pipe the mounds onto a rimmed baking sheet and then cover them lightly with plastic wrap. Freeze the potatoes for 2 hours until they're solid and then transfer them to an airtight container (or leave them on the baking sheet if you've got the space). When you are ready to bake, arrange them on a rimmed baking sheet (or simply remove the plastic), spray the mounds lightly with vegetable oil spray, and bake according to our recipe. They can go straight from the freezer to the oven, and they won't even need any extra time.

Why This Recipe Works Most recipes for mashed potato casserole simply dump mashed potatoes in a baking dish and pop it in the oven, but these dishes always end up bland, gluey, and dense. We wanted a casserole that delivered fluffy, buttery, creamy potatoes nestled under a savory golden crust. Using half-and-half instead of the traditional heavy cream lightened the recipe, and cutting it with chicken broth kept the potatoes moist. Beating eggs into the potato mixture helped it achieve a fluffy, airy texture. For bold flavor, we added Dijon mustard and fresh chives.

MASHED POTATO CASSEROLE

SERVES 8

The casserole may also be baked in a 13 by 9-inch pan.

4 pounds russet potatoes, peeled and cut into 1-inch chunks
12 tablespoons unsalted butter, cut into 12 pieces
½ cup half-and-half
½ cup chicken broth
2 teaspoons Dijon mustard
1 garlic clove, minced
2 teaspoons salt
4 large eggs
¼ cup finely chopped fresh chives

1. Adjust oven rack to upper-middle position and heat oven to 375 degrees. Bring potatoes and water to cover by 1 inch to boil in large pot over high heat. Reduce heat to medium and simmer until potatoes are tender, about 20 minutes.

2. Heat butter, half-and-half, broth, mustard, garlic, and salt in saucepan over medium-low heat until smooth, about 5 minutes. Keep warm.

3. Drain potatoes and transfer to large bowl. Using stand mixer fitted with paddle, beat potatoes on medium-low speed, slowly adding half-and-half mixture, until smooth and creamy, about 1 minute. Scrape down bowl; beat in eggs, 1 at a time, until incorporated, about 1 minute. Fold in chives.

4. Transfer potato mixture to greased 3-quart baking dish. Smooth surface of potatoes, then use fork to make peaked design on top of casserole. Bake until potatoes rise and begin to brown, about 35 minutes. Let cool for 10 minutes. Serve.

To Make Ahead The baking dish with the potatoes can be covered with plastic and refrigerated for up to 24 hours. When ready to bake, let the casserole sit at room temperature for 1 hour. Increase baking time by 10 minutes.

Secrets to Perfect Mashed Potato Casserole

1. When poured into casserole dish, mashed potatoes will look very soupy. They will firm up and rise in oven.

2. For better browning and an impressive presentation, use fork to make peaked design on top of casserole.

Can Evaporated Milk Be Substituted for Half-and-Half?

Sorry, the answer is no. We substituted evaporated milk in a handful of recipes that call for half-and-half. The savory dishes made with evaporated milk in place of half-and-half tasted tinny, and the desserts were too sweet.

Not willing to give up, we diluted the evaporated milk with water and then used it in place of the half-and-half in our test recipes. Tasters didn't like that either, detecting a mildly cooked taste. We tried heavy cream, but its high milk-fat content muted the other flavors. Whole milk made the food less rich, but the flavors remained lively.

With heavy cream and either skim or whole milk, you can mix up a good substitute for half-and-half. If you don't mind a slightly thinner consistency and lighter flavor, whole milk will work in most recipes.

⅓ cup heavy cream + ⅔ cup skim milk =
1 cup half-and-half

¼ cup heavy cream + ¾ cup whole milk =
1 cup half-and-half

SYRACUSE SALT POTATOES

SERVES 6 TO 8

You will need 1¼ cups of noniodized table salt, 1½ cups of Morton kosher salt, or 2½ cups of Diamond Crystal kosher salt to equal 14 ounces. We prefer to use small potatoes, measuring 1 to 2 inches in diameter, in this recipe.

  8 cups water
14 ounces salt
  3 pounds small white or red potatoes
  8 tablespoons unsalted butter, cut into 8 pieces
  2 tablespoons minced fresh chives
  1 teaspoon pepper

1. Set wire rack in rimmed baking sheet. Bring water to boil in Dutch oven over medium-high heat. Stir in salt and potatoes and cook until potatoes are just tender, 20 to 30 minutes. Drain potatoes and transfer to prepared baking sheet. Let dry until salty crust forms, about 1 minute.

2. Meanwhile, microwave butter, chives, and pepper in medium bowl until butter is melted, about 1 minute. Transfer potatoes to serving bowl and serve, passing butter separately.

Salt Magic

Just out of the salty water, the potatoes will look like any other boiled potato.

One minute after they've been drained, the characteristic salt crust will appear on the potato skins.

The high salinity means the cooking water gets hotter than normal, resulting in extra-creamy potato flesh.

Selling Salt Potatoes

Salt potatoes have their origin in the mid-1800s when Irish salt workers in the Syracuse area would cook unpeeled new potatoes in huge evaporation vats filled with boiling salt water. In 1914, John Hinerwadel, owner of an eponymous central New York clambake company, began offering salt potatoes on his menu. They became so popular that Mr. Hinerwadel started selling salt potato kits—complete with a sack of small white potatoes and a packet of salt—so people could make the potatoes at home. The red and white bags of potatoes with the signature red and yellow sun are still sold in the Syracuse area.

Why This Recipe Works For Syracuse salt potatoes with a well-seasoned crust and ultra-creamy interior, we cut back on the usual 3 cups of salt, which resulted in overly salty potatoes. We found that white or red potatoes proved best, but they needed to be boiled in the salted water whole—if they were cut or peeled, they absorbed too much salt. Though these potatoes are usually served with plain melted butter for dipping, we found that adding chives and black pepper to the butter brought this dish to new heights.

CREAMY MASHED SWEET POTATOES

SERVES 4 TO 6

This recipe can be doubled and prepared in a Dutch oven, but the cooking time will need to be doubled as well.

  2 pounds sweet potatoes, peeled, quartered, and sliced ¼ inch thick
  4 tablespoons unsalted butter, cut into 4 pieces
  3 tablespoons heavy cream
  1 teaspoon sugar
     Salt and pepper

1. Combine sweet potatoes, butter, 2 tablespoons cream, sugar, ½ teaspoon salt, and ¼ teaspoon pepper in large saucepan. Cook, covered, over low heat until potatoes are fall-apart tender, 35 to 40 minutes.

2. Off heat, add remaining 1 tablespoon cream and mash sweet potatoes with potato masher. Serve.

HERBED MASHED SWEET POTATOES WITH CARAMELIZED ONION

If you prefer, substitute ¼ teaspoon of dried thyme for the thyme sprig.

Add 1 sprig fresh thyme to saucepan in step 1. While sweet potatoes are cooking, melt 1 tablespoon butter in 8-inch nonstick skillet and add 1 small onion, chopped, ¼ teaspoon sugar, and ¼ teaspoon salt. Cook over low heat until onion is caramelized, about 15 minutes. Remove thyme and mash potatoes as directed. Stir in onion and 1 tablespoon sour cream.

SMOKEHOUSE MASHED SWEET POTATOES

Add ⅛ teaspoon cayenne pepper to saucepan in step 1. Mash sweet potatoes with ½ cup shredded smoked Gouda cheese and cover with lid until cheese melts, about 1 minute. Sprinkle with 6 slices chopped cooked bacon and 1 thinly sliced scallion.

No-Boil Sweet Potatoes

Boiling sweet potatoes in lots of liquid—as you would regular potatoes—is not a good idea. Sweet potatoes will soak up too much water, and the resulting mash will be a soggy mess. Better to cook them in a small amount of liquid. Just 2 tablespoons of heavy cream (plus a little butter), along with the water released from the sweet potatoes as they cook, is enough to steam them to tenderness.

The Slice Is Right

It is imperative to cut the sweet potato into thin, even slices to ensure perfect cooking.

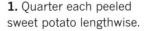

1. Quarter each peeled sweet potato lengthwise.

2. Cut each quarter into ¼-inch slices crosswise.

Why This Recipe Works Deeply flavored, earthy, and subtly sweet, mashed sweet potatoes hardly need a layer of marshmallows to make them into a tempting side. For a silky and full-flavored mash, we found the secret was to thinly slice the potatoes and cook them covered, on the stovetop, over low heat in a small amount of butter and cream. Once the sweet potatoes were fall-apart tender, they could be mashed right in the pot—no draining, no straining, no fuss. Adding another spoonful of cream when we mashed the potatoes enriched them even more.

Why This Recipe Works Butternut squash is one of our favorite fall vegetables, but it can be a chore to prepare. To streamline the process, we began by peeling the tough exterior of the squash. Instead of meticulously dicing the squash into cubes, we cut the squash in half lengthwise and then crosswise into 1-inch-thick pieces. The larger pieces of squash caramelized beautifully while their interiors remained ultracreamy. For a mix of sweet and tart flavors, we added an apple partway through cooking. After removing the squash and apple from the oven, we drizzled them with a zippy vinaigrette of minced shallot, red wine vinegar, and parsley.

ROASTED BUTTERNUT SQUASH WITH APPLE

SERVES 4 TO 6

When peeling the squash, be sure to also remove the fibrous yellow flesh just beneath the skin.

Vinaigrette
3 tablespoons red wine vinegar
1 tablespoon sugar
⅛ teaspoon table salt
3 tablespoons minced shallot
2 tablespoons chopped fresh parsley
2 tablespoons extra-virgin olive oil
¼ teaspoon red pepper flakes

Squash and Apple
1 (2¼- to 2¾-pound) butternut squash
3 tablespoons extra-virgin olive oil, divided
1 teaspoon table salt
1 Gala, Fuji, or Braeburn apple, unpeeled, cored, halved, and cut into ½-inch-thick wedges

1. For the Vinaigrette Stir vinegar, sugar, and salt in small bowl until sugar is dissolved. Stir in shallot, parsley, oil, and pepper flakes; set aside.

2. For the Squash And Apple Adjust oven rack to lowest position and heat oven to 450 degrees. Trim ends from squash and peel squash. Halve squash lengthwise and scrape out seeds. Place squash cut side down on cutting board and slice crosswise 1-inch thick.

3. Toss squash, 2 tablespoons oil, and salt together in bowl. Spread squash in even layer on rimmed baking sheet, cut side down. Roast until squash is tender and bottoms are beginning to brown, 14 to 16 minutes.

4. Toss apple and remaining 1 tablespoon oil together in now-empty bowl. Remove sheet from oven. Place apple between squash on sheet, cut side down. (Do not flip squash.) Return sheet to oven and continue to roast until apple is tender and squash is fully browned on bottoms (tops of squash will not be browned), about 8 minutes longer.

5. Using spatula, transfer squash and apple to shallow platter and spread into even layer. Drizzle vinaigrette over top. Serve warm or at room temperature.

ROASTED BUTTERNUT SQUASH WITH PEAR AND PANCETTA
Reduce salt for squash to ½ teaspoon. Substitute 1 teaspoon minced fresh thyme for parsley and 1 Bosc pear for apple. Add 3 ounces pancetta, cut into ½-inch pieces, to sheet with pears in step 4.

Why This Recipe Works "Galette" is the French term for a freeform, round crusty cake, generally with a savory filling. The idea of a rustic tomato galette is simple: slice tomatoes, season them, pile them onto flaky dough, fold the edges up, and bake until the crust is golden and crisp. The hard part about baking with fresh tomatoes is their unpredictable juice. To draw out the tomatoes' excess juice, we salted the slices and let them sit in a colander for just 30 minutes. We spread mustard and sprinkled Gruyère right onto the dough to water proof it before layering the tomato slices on top and finished with a sprinkle of Parmesan.

FRESH TOMATO GALETTE

SERVES 4 TO 6

Sharp cheddar can be used in place of the Gruyère.

1½ cups (7½ ounces) all-purpose flour
2 teaspoons table salt, divided
10 tablespoons unsalted butter, cut into ½-inch pieces and chilled
6–7 tablespoons ice water
1½ pounds mixed tomatoes, cored and sliced ¼ inch thick
1 shallot, sliced thin
2 tablespoons extra-virgin olive oil
1 teaspoon minced fresh thyme
1 garlic clove, minced
¼ teaspoon pepper
2 teaspoons Dijon mustard
3 ounces Gruyère cheese, shredded (¾ cup)
2 tablespoons grated Parmesan cheese
1 large egg, lightly beaten
1 tablespoon chopped fresh basil

1. Process flour and ½ teaspoon salt in food processor until combined, about 3 seconds. Scatter butter over top and pulse until mixture resembles coarse crumbs, about 10 pulses. Transfer to large bowl. Sprinkle 6 tablespoons ice water over flour mixture. Using rubber spatula, stir and press dough until it sticks together, adding up to 1 tablespoon more ice water if dough doesn't come together.

2. Turn out dough onto lightly floured counter, form into 4-inch disk, wrap tightly in plastic wrap, and refrigerate for 1 hour. (Wrapped dough can be refrigerated for up to 2 days or frozen for up to 1 month.)

3. Toss tomatoes and 1 teaspoon salt together in second large bowl. Transfer tomatoes to colander and set in sink. Let tomatoes drain for 30 minutes.

4. Adjust oven rack to lower-middle position and heat oven to 375 degrees. Line rimmed baking sheet with parchment paper. Let chilled dough sit on counter to soften slightly, about 10 minutes, before rolling. Roll dough into 12-inch circle on lightly floured counter, then transfer to prepared sheet (dough may run up lip of sheet slightly; this is OK).

5. Shake colander well to rid tomatoes of excess juice. Combine tomatoes, shallot, oil, thyme, garlic, pepper, and remaining ½ teaspoon salt in now-empty bowl. Spread mustard over dough, leaving 1½-inch border. Sprinkle Gruyère in even layer over mustard. Shingle tomatoes and shallot on top of Gruyère in concentric circles, keeping within 1½-inch border. Sprinkle Parmesan over tomato mixture.

6. Carefully grasp 1 edge of dough and fold up about 1 inch over filling. Repeat around circumference of tart, overlapping dough every 2 inches, gently pinching pleated dough to secure. Brush folded dough with egg (you won't need it all).

7. Bake until crust is golden brown and tomatoes are bubbling, 45 to 50 minutes. Transfer sheet to wire rack and let galette cool for 10 minutes. Using metal spatula, loosen galette from parchment and carefully slide onto wire rack; let cool until just warm, about 20 minutes. Sprinkle with basil. Cut into wedges and serve.

Three Keys to a Savory, Not Soggy, Tart

Drain tomatoes Slice, salt, and transfer to colander to drain.

"Waterproof" crust Cover dough with mustard and Gruyère.

Shape tart Fold up dough edges and crimp to seal.

SWEET CORN SPOONBREAD

SERVES 6

You will need three ears of corn to yield 2 cups. Frozen corn, thawed and drained well, can be substituted for the fresh corn.

- 1 cup cornmeal
- 2¾ cups whole milk
- 4 tablespoons unsalted butter
- 2 cups fresh corn
- 1 teaspoon sugar
- 1 teaspoon salt
- ⅛ teaspoon cayenne pepper
- 3 large eggs, separated
- ¼ teaspoon cream of tartar

1. Adjust oven rack to middle position and heat oven to 400 degrees. Grease 1½-quart soufflé dish or 8-inch baking dish. Whisk cornmeal and ¾ cup milk in bowl until combined; set aside.

2. Melt butter in Dutch oven over medium-high heat. Cook corn until beginning to brown, about 3 minutes. Stir in remaining 2 cups milk, sugar, salt, and cayenne and bring to boil. Off heat, cover mixture and let steep for 15 minutes.

3. Transfer warm corn mixture to blender or food processor and puree until smooth. Return to pot and bring to boil. Reduce heat to low and add cornmeal mixture, whisking constantly, until thickened, 2 to 3 minutes; transfer to large bowl and let cool to room temperature, about 20 minutes. Once mixture is cool, whisk in egg yolks until combined.

4. Using stand mixer fitted with whisk, beat egg whites and cream of tartar on medium-low speed until foamy, about 1 minute. Increase speed to medium-high and whip until stiff peaks form, 3 to 4 minutes. Whisk one-third of whites into corn mixture, then gently fold in remaining whites until combined. Scrape mixture into prepared dish and transfer to oven. Reduce oven temperature to 350 degrees and bake until spoonbread is golden brown and has risen above rim of dish, about 45 minutes. Serve immediately.

INDIVIDUAL SPOONBREADS

To make individual spoonbreads, divide batter among 6 greased 7-ounce ramekins. Arrange ramekins on rimmed baking sheet and bake as directed, reducing cooking time to 30 to 35 minutes.

Egg Whites 101

Egg whites are most easily whipped in a very clean metal bowl with a pinch of cream of tartar, which promotes stabilization.

Soft Peaks
Soft peaks will droop slightly downward from tip of whisk or beater.

Stiff Peaks
Stiff peaks will stand up tall on their own.

Overwhipped
Overwhipped egg whites will look curdled and separated; if you reach this point, start over with new whites and clean bowl.

Why This Recipe Works For a fluffy, soufflé-style sweet corn spoonbread with deep corn flavor, we focused on flavor, then texture. Sautéing the corn in butter, before steeping it in milk and pureeing it, ensured that the sweet corn flavor permeated our spoonbread. To make sure the cornmeal didn't impart a gritty texture, we soaked it in the milk beforehand. And to guarantee a stable foam and an impressive rise, we beat the egg whites with a bit of cream of tartar.

tex-mex and more

Why This Recipe Works Some nacho recipes produce soggy chips loaded down with bland, greasy beef, dry beans, and cold strings of cheese. Instead, we wanted hearty nachos that are crisp, flavorful, and fresh. Boldly seasoning our beef with a mixture of spices and other flavorings caused the flavor to pop. While many nacho recipes call for cheddar cheese, we found it didn't melt nearly as well as pepper Jack, which melted smoothly and added a kick, too.

ULTIMATE SPICY BEEF NACHOS

SERVES 8

Garnish the nachos with sour cream, chopped cilantro, and diced avocado.

Refried Beans
½ cup canned refried beans
3 tablespoons shredded pepper Jack cheese
1 tablespoon chopped canned jalapeños

Spicy Beef
2 teaspoons vegetable oil
1 small onion, chopped fine
3 garlic cloves, minced
1 tablespoon chili powder
1 teaspoon ground cumin
½ teaspoon dried oregano
1 teaspoon salt
1 pound 90 percent lean ground beef
2 tablespoons tomato paste
1 teaspoon packed brown sugar
1½ teaspoons minced canned chipotle chile in adobo sauce, plus 1 teaspoon adobo sauce
½ cup water
2 teaspoons lime juice

1 (9.5-ounce) bag tortilla chips
1 pound pepper Jack cheese, shredded (4 cups)
2 jalapeño chiles, sliced into thin rings
1 recipe One-Minute Salsa (recipe follows)

1. Adjust oven rack to middle position and heat oven to 400 degrees.

2. For the Refried Beans Pulse ingredients in food processor until smooth, about 10 pulses. Transfer to bowl and cover with plastic wrap.

3. For the Spicy Beef Heat oil in large skillet over medium heat until shimmering. Cook onion until softened, about 4 minutes. Add garlic, chili powder, cumin, oregano, and salt and cook until fragrant, about 1 minute. Add beef and cook, breaking meat

into small bits with wooden spoon and scraping pan bottom to prevent scorching, until no longer pink, about 5 minutes. Add tomato paste, sugar, chipotle, and adobo sauce and cook until paste begins to darken, about 1 minute. Add water, bring to simmer, and cook over medium-low until mixture is nearly dry, 5 to 7 minutes. Stir in lime juice and transfer mixture to plate lined with several layers of paper towels. Use more paper towels to blot up excess grease.

4. Spread half of chips on large ovensafe serving platter or in 13 by 9-inch baking dish. Dollop half of bean mixture over chips, then spread evenly. Scatter half of beef mixture over beans, top with 2 cups cheese and half of jalapeños. Repeat with remaining chips, beans, beef, cheese, and jalapeños. Bake until cheese is melted and just beginning to brown, 12 to 14 minutes. Serve with salsa.

ONE-MINUTE SALSA
MAKES ABOUT 1 CUP
Make sure to drain both the tomatoes and the jalapeños before processing. The salsa will keep for two days in the refrigerator. Season to taste before serving.

½ small red onion
¼ cup fresh cilantro leaves
2 tablespoons jarred jalapeños, drained
1 tablespoon lime juice
1 garlic clove, peeled
¼ teaspoon salt
1 (14.5-ounce) can diced tomatoes, drained

Pulse onion, cilantro, jalapeños, lime juice, garlic, and salt in food processor until roughly chopped, about 5 pulses. Add tomatoes and pulse until chopped, about 2 pulses. Transfer mixture to fine-mesh strainer and drain briefly. Serve.

Why This Recipe Works With bold Southwestern flavors and an appealing ingredient list, seven-layer dip recipes sound like a hit. But most versions of this party classic assume that guests won't notice the messy layers and muted flavors. In our version, canned black beans stood in for refried beans, while garlic, chili powder, and lime juice added flavor. We found that sour cream on its own quickly watered down our dip, but combining it with cheese gave this layer more structure.

ULTIMATE SEVEN-LAYER DIP

SERVES 8 TO 10

This recipe is usually served in a clear dish so you can see the layers. For a crowd, double the recipe and serve in a 13 by 9-inch glass baking dish. If you don't have time to make fresh guacamole as called for, simply mash three avocados with 3 tablespoons lime juice and ½ teaspoon salt.

- 4 large tomatoes, cored, seeded, and chopped fine
- 2 jalapeño chiles, stemmed, seeded, and minced
- 3 tablespoons chopped fresh cilantro
- 6 scallions (2 minced, 4 with green parts sliced thin and white parts discarded)
- 2 tablespoons plus 2 teaspoons lime juice (2 limes)
  Salt
- 1 (15-ounce) can black beans, drained but not rinsed
- 2 garlic cloves, minced
- ¾ teaspoon chili powder
- 1½ cups sour cream
- 1 pound pepper Jack cheese, shredded (4 cups)
- 1 recipe Chunky Guacamole (page 348)
  Tortilla chips

1. Combine tomatoes, jalapeños, cilantro, minced scallions, and 2 tablespoons lime juice in medium bowl. Stir in ⅛ teaspoon salt and let stand until tomatoes begin to soften, about 30 minutes. Strain mixture into bowl and discard liquid.

2. Pulse black beans, garlic, remaining 2 teaspoons lime juice, chili powder, and ⅛ teaspoon salt in food processor until mixture resembles chunky paste, about 15 pulses. Transfer to bowl and wipe out food processor. Pulse sour cream and 2½ cups pepper Jack until smooth, about 15 pulses. Transfer to separate bowl.

3. Spread bean mixture evenly over bottom of 8-inch square baking dish or 1-quart glass bowl. Spread sour cream mixture evenly over bean layer and sprinkle evenly with remaining 1½ cups cheese. Spread guacamole over cheese and top with tomato mixture. Sprinkle with sliced scallion greens and serve with tortilla chips. (Dip can be refrigerated for up to 24 hours. Let dip stand at room temperature for 1 hour before serving.)

ULTIMATE SMOKY SEVEN-LAYER DIP

Cook 4 slices bacon in 10-inch skillet over medium-high heat until crisp, about 8 minutes. Drain on paper towel–lined plate and crumble. Pulse 1 to 3 teaspoons minced canned chipotle chile in adobo sauce with black beans in step 2. Garnish dip with crumbled bacon along with scallions.

Processing Your Pico

Although the pico de gallo topping in our Ultimate Seven-Layer Dip adds lots of fresh flavor, chopping all the ingredients by hand takes some work. We found that a food processor gets the job done, but the texture won't be as perfectly uniform as pico de gallo made by hand. To make pico de gallo in the food processor, start by pulsing jalapeños with cilantro until finely chopped. Then add quartered, cored, and seeded tomatoes and pulse in 1-second bursts until the tomatoes are evenly chopped. Add minced scallions and lime juice. Strain as instructed.

Seeding Jalapeños

Halve pepper lengthwise. Starting at end opposite stem, use melon baller to scoop down inside of each half.

CHUNKY GUACAMOLE

MAKES ABOUT 3 CUPS

Preparing the guacamole ahead of time helps the flavors marry, but it should not be prepared more than 24 hours in advance. To prevent the dip from turning brown, press a sheet of plastic wrap directly onto the surface and refrigerate until ready to use. We prefer pebbly Hass avocados to the smoother Fuerte variety.

- 2 scallions, green and white parts separated and sliced thin
- 1 jalapeño chile, stemmed, seeded, and minced
- 1 small garlic clove, minced
- ¼ teaspoon finely grated lime zest plus 2 tablespoons juice
- 3 avocados, halved, pitted, and cubed
- 3 tablespoons chopped fresh cilantro
  Salt

1. Combine scallion whites, jalapeño, garlic, and lime juice in large bowl. Let sit for 30 minutes.

2. Add two-thirds of avocado pieces to bowl with jalapeño mixture and mash with potato masher until smooth. Gently fold remaining avocado pieces into mashed avocado mixture. Gently stir in lime zest, scallion greens, and cilantro. Season with salt to taste. Serve.

Ripening Avocados

Avocados have a small window of perfect ripeness. To see if we could broaden this time frame, we ripened avocados four ways: on the counter or refrigerator shelf, enclosed in a paper bag, and enclosed in a paper bag with pieces of green apple (fruit gives off ethylene gas, which helps many fruits and vegetables ripen more quickly). We also tried burying the avocados at room temperature in flour and in rice. In the end, the only thing that mattered was the temperature at which the avocados were stored.

At room temperature, rock-hard avocados ripened within two days, but many of them ripened unevenly, developing soft spots and air pockets on one side just as the other side was ripening. Once ripe, they lasted two days on average if kept at room temperature (stored in the fridge after ripening, they lasted five days). Avocados ripened in the refrigerator, whether in a bag or out in the open, took around four days to soften, but did so evenly. Stored in the fridge, they lasted a full five days before starting to show signs of overripening.

The bottom line: If you need avocados to ripen sooner rather than later, keep them on the counter. Otherwise, you're better off putting them in the fridge and allowing them to ripen slowly. In either case, store the ripened fruit in the fridge to extend its shelf life.

Preparing Avocado for Guacamole

1. Halve avocado. Strike pit sharply with chef's knife. Twist blade to remove pit, then use dish towel to pull pit off blade.

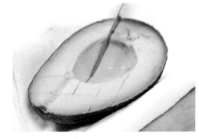

2. Place avocado half on dish towel to secure it and make ½-inch crosshatch slices into flesh without cutting through skin.

3. Insert spoon between skin and flesh to separate the two. Gently scoop out avocado cubes.

Why This Recipe Works The best guacamole starts with ripe avocados, but other ingredients often overwhelm their delicate flavor. Tasters liked the flavor of minced garlic in guacamole but thought raw onions were just too harsh. Instead, scallions contributed a mellower onion flavor. Steeping them in lime juice for a few minutes before combining them with the avocados mellowed their flavor even more. To provide some textural contrast to our guacamole, we chopped the avocados and then mashed just two-thirds of the chunks.

Why This Recipe Works Huevos rancheros has made its way northward from Mexico, becoming common on breakfast menus around the United States. To make this crowd-pleasing but involved dish of fried eggs, cheese, and tomato-chile sauce manageable for a group, we roasted the sauce components to brown the vegetables and replicate the char from a cast-iron skillet. We then transferred everything to a casserole dish and nestled the eggs into the sauce so that we could cook eight eggs at once. Moving this spicy dish of eggs and charred chiles to the oven gave us a perfectly timed meal that's not just for breakfast.

HUEVOS RANCHEROS

SERVES 4

Use a heavyweight rimmed baking sheet; flimsy sheets will warp. Our winning sheet is the Nordic Ware Baker's Half Sheet. Serve with refried beans and hot sauce.

2   (28-ounce) cans diced tomatoes
1   tablespoon packed brown sugar
1   tablespoon lime juice
1   onion, chopped
½   cup chopped canned green chiles
¼   cup extra-virgin olive oil
3   tablespoons chili powder
4   garlic cloves, sliced thin
    Salt and pepper
4   ounces pepper Jack cheese, shredded (1 cup)
8   large eggs
1   avocado, halved, pitted, and diced
3   scallions, sliced thin
⅓   cup minced fresh cilantro
8   (6-inch) corn tortillas, warmed

1. Adjust oven rack to middle position and heat oven to 500 degrees. Line rimmed baking sheet with parchment paper. Drain tomatoes in fine-mesh strainer set over bowl, pressing with rubber spatula to extract as much juice as possible. Reserve 1¾ cups tomato juice and discard remainder. Whisk sugar and lime juice into reserved tomato juice and set aside.

2. In separate bowl, combine onion, chiles, oil, chili powder, garlic, ½ teaspoon salt, and drained tomatoes. Transfer tomato mixture to prepared baking sheet and spread in even layer to edges of sheet. Roast until charred in spots, 35 to 40 minutes, stirring and redistributing into even layer halfway through baking. Reduce oven temperature to 400 degrees.

3. Transfer roasted tomato mixture to 13 by 9-inch baking dish and stir in tomato juice mixture. Season with salt and pepper to taste, then spread into even layer. Sprinkle pepper Jack over tomato mixture. Using spoon, hollow out 8 holes in tomato mixture in 2 rows. Crack 1 egg into each hole. Season eggs with salt and pepper.

4. Bake until whites are just beginning to set but still have some movement when dish is shaken, 13 to 16 minutes. Transfer dish to wire rack, tent loosely with aluminum foil, and let sit for 5 minutes. Spoon avocado over top, then sprinkle with scallions and cilantro. Serve with warm tortillas.

To Make Ahead The sauce can be made 24 hours in advance. Microwave until hot, about 2 minutes (stirring halfway), before transferring to baking dish and proceeding with recipe.

Roast the Vegetables, Bake the Eggs

To evoke the charred flavors in traditional huevos rancheros, we roast vegetables in a hot oven before layering them into a dish and sprinkling cheese on top. Using a 13 by 9-inch baking dish allows us to bake eight eggs at once—no more standing at the stove frying egg after egg for an impatient crowd.

ARROZ CON POLLO

SERVES 6

Sazón is a spice blend common in Latin American cooking. We developed this recipe with Goya Sazón with Coriander and Annatto (or con Culantro y Achiote). It can be found in the Latin American aisle of most supermarkets; however, other brands will work. (One tablespoon of Goya Sazón equals about two packets.) If you can't find sazón, use our homemade version (recipe follows). You can substitute ¾ cup of chopped green bell pepper for the Cubanelle pepper. Allow the rice to rest for the full 15 minutes before lifting the lid to check it. Long-grain rice may be substituted for medium-grain, but the rice will be slightly less creamy.

- 1 cup fresh cilantro leaves and stems, chopped
- 1 onion, chopped (1 cup)
- 1 Cubanelle pepper, stemmed, seeded, and chopped (¾ cup)
- 5 garlic cloves, chopped coarse
- 1 teaspoon ground cumin
- ½ cup mayonnaise
- 3½ tablespoons lemon juice (2 lemons), plus lemon wedges for serving
  Salt and pepper
- 6 (5- to 7-ounce) bone-in chicken thighs, trimmed
- 1 tablespoon vegetable oil
- 2 cups medium-grain rice, rinsed
- 1 tablespoon Goya Sazón with Coriander and Annatto
- 2½ cups chicken broth
- ¼ cup pimento-stuffed green olives, halved
- 2 tablespoons capers, rinsed
- 2 bay leaves
- ½ cup frozen peas, thawed (optional)

1. Adjust oven rack to middle position and heat oven to 350 degrees. Process cilantro, ½ cup onion, Cubanelle, garlic, and cumin in food processor until finely chopped, about 20 seconds, scraping down bowl as needed. Transfer sofrito to bowl.

2. Process mayonnaise, 1½ tablespoons lemon juice, ⅛ teaspoon salt, and 2 tablespoons sofrito in now-empty processor until almost smooth, about

30 seconds. Transfer mayonnaise-herb sauce to small bowl, cover, and refrigerate until ready to serve.

3. Pat chicken dry with paper towels and sprinkle with 1 teaspoon salt and ¼ teaspoon pepper. Heat oil in Dutch oven over medium heat until shimmering. Add chicken to pot skin side down and cook without moving it until skin is crispy and golden, 7 to 9 minutes. Flip chicken and continue to cook until golden on second side, 7 to 9 minutes longer. Transfer chicken to plate; discard skin.

4. Pour off all but 2 tablespoons fat from pot and heat over medium heat until shimmering. Add remaining ½ cup onion and cook until softened, 3 to 5 minutes. Stir in rice and Sazón and cook until edges of rice begin to turn translucent, about 2 minutes.

5. Stir in broth, olives, capers, bay leaves, remaining sofrito, remaining 2 tablespoons lemon juice, 1 teaspoon salt, and ½ teaspoon pepper, scraping up any browned bits. Nestle chicken into pot along with any accumulated juices and bring to vigorous simmer. Cover, transfer to oven, and bake for 20 minutes.

6. Transfer pot to wire rack and let stand, covered, for 15 minutes. Fluff rice with fork and stir in peas, if using. Discard bay leaves. Serve with mayonnaise-herb sauce and lemon wedges.

HOMEMADE SAZÓN
MAKES 1 TABLESPOON
We add paprika in place of annatto for color. In addition to flavoring our Arroz con Pollo, this blend makes a great seasoning for eggs, beans, and fish.

- 1 teaspoon garlic powder
- ¾ teaspoon salt
- ½ teaspoon paprika
- ½ teaspoon ground coriander
- ¼ teaspoon ground cumin

Combine all ingredients in bowl.

Why This Recipe Works Arroz con pollo is a classic Latin take on chicken and rice. For our version, we first created the dish's flavor backbone: a sofrito of onions, peppers, garlic, and spices. Next, after browning meaty skin-on chicken thighs, we used the rendered fat to soften chopped onion, toast the rice, and bloom the starring spice blend, sazón. We removed the skin from the thighs and finished cooking them nestled into the rice, studded with halved green olives, capers, and our zesty sofrito. We served our arroz con pollo with a drizzle of herby lemon sauce for a final punch of freshness.

GARLIC-LIME FRIED CHICKEN

SERVES 4

Don't let the chicken marinate any longer than 2 hours or it will toughen from the lime juice. Use a Dutch oven that holds 6 quarts or more for this recipe.

Marinade and Chicken

- 2 tablespoons kosher salt
- 6 garlic cloves, chopped coarse
- 1 tablespoon pepper
- 1 tablespoon ground cumin
- 2 teaspoons smoked paprika
- 2 teaspoons dried oregano
- 2 teaspoons grated lime zest plus ¼ cup juice (2 limes)
- 3 pounds bone-in chicken pieces (split breasts cut in half crosswise, drumsticks, thighs, and/or wings), trimmed

Coating

- 1¼ cups all-purpose flour
- ¾ cup cornstarch
- 1 tablespoon pepper
- 1 tablespoon granulated garlic
- 1 teaspoon baking powder
- 1 teaspoon white pepper
- 1 teaspoon kosher salt
- 1 teaspoon ground cumin
- ¼ teaspoon cayenne pepper
- 3 large egg whites, lightly beaten

- 3 quarts peanut or vegetable oil

1. For the Marinade and Chicken Combine salt, garlic, pepper, cumin, paprika, oregano, and lime zest and juice in bowl. Add chicken and turn to coat thoroughly. Cover with plastic wrap and refrigerate for at least 1 hour or up to 2 hours.

2. For the Coating Whisk flour, cornstarch, pepper, granulated garlic, baking powder, white pepper, salt, cumin, and cayenne together in bowl. Place egg whites in shallow dish.

3. Set wire rack in rimmed baking sheet. Remove chicken from marinade and scrape off solids. Pat chicken dry with paper towels. Working with 1 piece at a time, dip chicken into egg whites to thoroughly coat, letting excess drip back into dish. Dredge chicken in flour mixture, pressing to adhere. Transfer chicken to prepared wire rack and refrigerate for at least 30 minutes or up to 2 hours.

4. Add oil to large Dutch oven until it measures about 2 inches deep and heat over medium-high heat to 325 degrees. Add half of chicken to hot oil and fry until breasts register 160 degrees and drumsticks/thighs register 175 degrees, 13 to 16 minutes. Adjust burner, if necessary, to maintain oil temperature between 300 and 325 degrees. Transfer chicken to second wire rack set in second rimmed baking sheet. Return oil to 325 degrees and repeat with remaining chicken. Serve.

White Pepper

White peppercorns are fully ripe black peppercorns—the black outer husk is removed and the berries are dried. They lose much of their heat in this process but have a sharpness and a pronounced citrus flavor. Their taste is especially welcome in our spicy Garlic-Lime Fried Chicken coating. Many chefs like the way that these peppercorns blend into white sauces, while Asian cooks use them in stir-fries and hot-and-sour soup.

Why This Recipe Works Fried chicken is a classic comfort food across Latin America. Each country has its own variation, but most feature a citrus and garlic marinade and a crunchy spiced coating. For our version, we used a combination of flour cut with cornstarch for a nice, light coating, and a little baking powder made it extra-crisp. Refrigerating the marinated dredged chicken before frying ensured that the coating set up nicely and thus stayed put on the chicken. Dipping the chicken in egg whites before coating it enhanced the lightness, and after frying, it was crunchy, juicy, and golden brown.

Why This Recipe Works We wanted our California-style fish tacos to be light, fresh, and simple, with a perfect balance of flavors and textures. An ultrathin beer batter using a combination of flour, cornstarch, and baking powder proved to be ideal for getting a light, crispy coating on the delicate white fish. Quick-pickled onions and jalapeños added tart spiciness, and tossing shredded cabbage with the pickling liquid just before serving added flavor without overcomplicating the dish. Lime juice and sour cream added tang to the traditional creamy white sauce.

CALIFORNIA-STYLE FISH TACOS

SERVES 6

Light-bodied American lagers, such as Budweiser, work best here. Cod, haddock, or halibut are good choices for the fish. Cut the fish on a slight bias if your fillets aren't quite 4 inches wide. You should end up with about 24 pieces of fish. Serve with green salsa, if desired.

Pickled Onions

- 1 small red onion, halved and sliced thin
- 2 jalapeño chiles, stemmed and sliced into thin rings
- 1 cup white wine vinegar
- 2 tablespoons lime juice
- 1 tablespoon sugar
- 1 teaspoon salt

Cabbage

- 3 cups shredded green cabbage
- ¼ cup pickling liquid from pickled onions
- ½ teaspoon salt
- ½ teaspoon pepper

White Sauce

- ½ cup mayonnaise
- ½ cup sour cream
- 2 tablespoons lime juice
- 2 tablespoons milk

Fish

- 2 pounds skinless white-flesh fish fillets, cut crosswise into 4 by 1-inch strips
  Salt and pepper
- ¾ cup all-purpose flour
- ¼ cup cornstarch
- 1 teaspoon baking powder
- 1 cup beer
- 1 quart peanut or vegetable oil

- 24 (6-inch) corn tortillas, warmed
- 1 cup fresh cilantro leaves

1. For the Pickled Onions Combine onion and jalapeños in medium bowl. Bring vinegar, lime juice, sugar, and salt to boil in small saucepan. Pour vinegar mixture over onion mixture and let sit for at least 30 minutes. (Pickled onions can be made and refrigerated up to 2 days in advance.)

2. For the Cabbage Toss all ingredients together in bowl.

3. For the White Sauce Whisk all ingredients together in bowl. (Sauce can be made and refrigerated up to 2 days in advance.)

4. For the Fish Adjust oven rack to middle position and heat oven to 200 degrees. Set wire rack inside rimmed baking sheet. Pat fish dry with paper towels and season with salt and pepper. Whisk flour, cornstarch, baking powder, and 1 teaspoon salt together in large bowl. Add beer and whisk until smooth. Transfer fish to batter and toss until evenly coated.

5. Add oil to large Dutch oven until it measures about ¾ inch deep and heat over medium-high heat to 350 degrees. Working with 5 to 6 pieces at a time, remove fish from batter, allowing excess to drip back into bowl, and add to hot oil, briefly dragging fish along surface of oil to prevent sticking. Adjust burner, if necessary, to maintain oil temperature between 325 and 350 degrees. Fry fish, stirring gently to prevent pieces from sticking together, until golden brown and crispy, about 2 minutes per side. Transfer fish to prepared wire rack and place in oven to keep warm. Return oil to 350 degrees and repeat with remaining fish.

6. Divide fish evenly among tortillas. Top with pickled onions, cabbage, white sauce, and cilantro. Serve.

SHRIMP TACOS

SERVES 4 TO 6

We developed this recipe using Mission White Corn Tortillas, Restaurant Style, but any 100 percent corn tortillas will work here. Mexican hot sauces, such as Valentina Salsa Picante and Tapatío Salsa Picante, pair best with these tacos. For a spicier taco filling, reserve the jalapeño seeds and add them to the tomato mixture in step 1.

- 2 tomatoes, cored and chopped
- 1 small onion, chopped fine
- 1 jalapeño chile, stemmed, seeded, and minced
- 2 tablespoons ketchup
- 1 tablespoon lime juice, plus lime wedges for serving
- 2 garlic cloves, minced
  Salt and pepper
- 1 pound large shrimp (26 to 30 per pound), peeled, deveined, and tails removed
- 5 tablespoons vegetable oil
- 12 (6-inch) corn tortillas
- 8 ounces Monterey Jack cheese, shredded (2 cups)
  Shredded iceberg lettuce
  Diced avocado
  Chopped fresh cilantro
  Hot sauce

1. Adjust oven rack to lowest position and heat oven to 450 degrees. Combine tomatoes, onion, jalapeño, ketchup, lime juice, garlic, 1 teaspoon salt, and ¼ teaspoon pepper in large bowl; set aside. Cut shrimp into ½-inch pieces.

2. Heat 1 tablespoon oil in 12-inch skillet over medium-high heat until shimmering. Add tomato mixture and cook until liquid is slightly thickened and tomatoes begin to break down, 5 to 7 minutes. Reduce heat to medium, stir in shrimp, and cook until shrimp are just opaque, about 2 minutes.

3. Brush 2 rimmed baking sheets with 2 tablespoons oil (1 tablespoon per sheet). Arrange tortillas in single layer on prepared sheets (6 tortillas per sheet). Brush tops of tortillas with remaining 2 tablespoons oil. Divide Monterey Jack evenly among tortillas, then top with shrimp mixture. Bake, 1 sheet at a time, until cheese melts and edges of tortillas just begin to brown and crisp, 7 to 9 minutes.

4. Garnish with lettuce, avocado, cilantro, and hot sauce, then fold tacos in half. Transfer tacos to platter. Serve, passing lime wedges separately.

Crisp and Melt

First, we top oiled corn tortillas with shredded Monterey Jack cheese and the shrimp filling and bake them in a 450-degree oven until the cheese melts and becomes gooey. Then we add the garnishes, fold the tortillas in half, and serve them as tacos. You get the best of both worlds.

Why This Recipe Works Our goal was to combine the best parts of a taco and a quesadilla—crisped corn tortillas, gooey cheese, and a fiesta of shrimp. To do this without time-consuming stovetop batch cooking, we placed corn tortillas on baking sheets and topped them with cheese and a quick-cooked shrimp filling, baking them until the tortillas crisped and the cheese melted. To give our shrimp filling a secret boost, we stirred in some ketchup. This gave the sauce extra body, subtle sweetness, and a vinegary punch. Topping with fresh ingredients just before serving gave us the vibrancy of a taco with the warmth and comfort of a quesadilla.

EASY CHICKEN TACOS

SERVES 6

To warm the tortillas, wrap them in foil and heat them in a 350-degree oven for 15 minutes. Top the tacos with shredded lettuce, grated cheese, diced avocado, chopped tomato, and sour cream.

  3 tablespoons unsalted butter
  4 garlic cloves, minced
  2 teaspoons minced canned chipotle chile
     in adobo sauce
  ¾ cup chopped fresh cilantro
  ½ cup orange juice
  1 tablespoon Worcestershire sauce
  4 (6-ounce) boneless, skinless chicken breasts,
     trimmed
  1 teaspoon yellow mustard
     Salt and pepper
12 (6-inch) flour tortillas

1. Melt butter in large skillet over medium-high heat. Add garlic and chipotle and cook until fragrant, about 30 seconds. Stir in ½ cup cilantro, orange juice, and Worcestershire and bring to boil. Add chicken and simmer, covered, over medium-low heat until meat registers 160 degrees, 10 to 15 minutes, flipping chicken halfway through cooking. Transfer to plate and tent with aluminum foil.

2. Increase heat to medium-high and cook until liquid is reduced to ¼ cup, about 5 minutes. Off heat, whisk in mustard. Using 2 forks, shred chicken into bite-size pieces and return to skillet. Add remaining ¼ cup cilantro to skillet and toss until well combined. Season with salt and pepper to taste. Serve with tortillas.

Storing Canned Chipotle Chiles

When a recipe uses just a teaspoon or two of chipotle chiles, here's how to store the rest of the can.

Canned chipotle chiles are jalapeños that have been ripened until red, smoked, and packed in a tangy tomato-based adobo sauce. Since the size of chipotles varies, in the test kitchen we measure them by minced teaspoons. Could we store leftovers in the freezer, or would they lose their potency? To see, we pureed several cans and froze measured teaspoons on a plastic wrap–covered plate. Once our "chipotle chips" were hard, we peeled them off the plastic and transferred them to a zipper-lock freezer bag.

Weeks later we made a salsa and a casserole with the frozen chipotles and compared them with the same dishes made with chiles from a newly opened can. Most tasters couldn't tell the two apart. The chipotles will keep for up to two months in the freezer and should be thawed before you use them. The chiles will also last for two weeks in the refrigerator.

Shredding Chicken

Hold 1 fork in each hand, with tines facing down. Insert tines into chicken and gently pull forks away from each other, breaking meat apart and into long thin shreds.

Why This Recipe Works We like the convenience of boneless, skinless chicken breasts in tacos, but they can be dry. After trying a variety of cooking methods, we found that poaching produced meat that was tender and moist. Chipotle chiles gave our poaching liquid a smoky, full-bodied flavor and orange juice offered a touch of sweetness that tempered its vivid acidity. For more robust flavor, we called on two kitchen staples: Worcestershire mimicked the complex flavor of dark meat, and mustard added sharpness that balanced the sweet orange juice and smoky chipotle.

CARNE GUISADA

SERVES 8 TO 10

*Note that you are browning only half the beef in
step 1. If your Dutch oven holds less than 6 quarts,
you may need to brown the beef in batches to avoid
overcrowding the pot. This recipe yields enough filling
for about 24 tacos.*

    3   pounds boneless beef chuck-eye roast,
        trimmed and cut into 1-inch pieces
        Salt and pepper
    2   tablespoons vegetable oil
    2   onions, chopped
    2   tablespoons tomato paste
    4   garlic cloves, minced
    1   tablespoon chili powder
    1   tablespoon dried oregano
    2   teaspoons ground coriander
 1½   teaspoons ground cumin
    1   tablespoon all-purpose flour
    1   (14.5-ounce) can diced tomatoes, drained
    1   cup chicken broth
    1   pound Yukon Gold potatoes, peeled and
        cut into ½-inch pieces
    2   green bell peppers, stemmed, seeded, and
        cut into ¼-inch strips
  24   flour tortillas, warmed
        Fresh cilantro leaves
        Lime wedges

1. Adjust oven rack to lower-middle position and
heat oven to 325 degrees. Pat beef dry with paper
towels and season with salt and pepper. Heat oil
in Dutch oven over medium-high heat until just
smoking. Add half of beef and cook until browned
on all sides, 7 to 10 minutes; transfer to plate.

2. Reduce heat to medium-low, add onions and
1 teaspoon salt to pot, and cook until softened, about
5 minutes. Stir in tomato paste, garlic, chili powder,
oregano, coriander, and cumin and cook until fragrant, about 30 seconds. Stir in flour and cook for
1 minute. Stir in tomatoes and broth and bring to
simmer, scraping up any browned bits. Stir in all of
beef and any accumulated juices. Cover, transfer pot
to oven, and cook for 1½ hours.

3. Remove pot from oven and stir in potatoes and
bell peppers. Cover, return pot to oven, and continue
to cook until beef and potatoes are tender, about
45 minutes longer.

4. Season with salt and pepper to taste. Spoon
small amount of stew into center of each tortilla,
top with cilantro, and serve with lime wedges.

Why This Recipe Works Carne guisada is a bold and satisfying beef, tomato, and potato stew eaten in many Latin American countries. To re-create the Mexican-style version of this comfort food enjoyed in Texas, in place of fresh and dried chiles we used a delicious mix of chili powder, oregano, cumin, and coriander. Using chicken broth for the braising liquid really let the tender beef chuck shine, and adding the potatoes and bell peppers partway through cooking guaranteed tender and intact vegetables. Using less liquid and adding some flour gave us the perfect texture, making it equally delicious as a taco filling or served with beans and rice.

Why This Recipe Works Puffy taco fans in San Antonio, Texas, cite Diana Barrios-Treviño's restaurant, Los Barrios, as having the best in the city. Determined to recreate a similar version, instead of using the traditional masa de maíz (finely ground hominy) we used the more widely available masa harina (dried masa flour) for our tortilla dough. Pressing the dough with a clear pie plate allowed us to gauge the diameter and to get a consistent thickness. Using a large saucepan containing just 2 quarts of oil made our taco shell prep much easier. For a flavorful filling, picadillo made with ground beef, green bell pepper, onion, garlic, and cumin fit the bill.

PUFFY TACOS

SERVES 6 TO 8

We used Maseca Instant Masa Corn Flour for our taco shells. The dough should not be sticky and should have the texture of Play-Doh. If the dough cracks or falls apart when pressing the tortillas, just reroll and press again.

Picadillo

12 ounces 85 percent lean ground beef
½ russet potato (4 ounces), peeled and cut into ¼-inch pieces
  Salt and pepper
1 onion, chopped fine
1 small green bell pepper, stemmed, seeded, and chopped fine
3 garlic cloves, minced
1½ teaspoons ground cumin
2 teaspoons all-purpose flour
¾ cup water

Taco Shells

2½ cups (10 ounces) masa harina
1 teaspoon salt
1⅔ cups warm water
2 quarts vegetable oil

  Shredded iceberg lettuce
  Chopped tomato
  Shredded sharp cheddar cheese
  Hot sauce

1. For the Picadillo Combine beef, potato, 1 teaspoon pepper, and ¾ teaspoon salt in 12-inch nonstick skillet. Cook over medium-high heat until meat and potatoes begin to brown, 6 to 8 minutes, breaking up meat with spoon. Add onion and bell pepper and cook until softened, 4 to 6 minutes. Add garlic and cumin and cook until fragrant, about 30 seconds.

2. Stir in flour and cook for 1 minute. Stir in water and bring to boil. Reduce heat to medium-low and simmer until thickened slightly, about 1 minute. Season with salt and pepper to taste. Remove from heat, cover, and keep warm.

3. For the Taco Shells Mix masa harina and salt together in medium bowl. Stir in warm water with rubber spatula. Using your hands, knead mixture in bowl until it comes together fully (dough should be soft and tacky, not sticky), about 30 seconds. Cover dough with damp dish towel and let rest for 5 minutes.

4. Divide dough into 12 equal portions, about ¼ cup each, then roll each into smooth ball between your hands. Transfer to plate and keep covered with damp dish towel. Cut sides of 1-gallon zipper-lock bag, leaving bottom seam intact.

5. Set wire rack in rimmed baking sheet and line rack with triple layer of paper towels. Add oil to large saucepan until it measures 2½ inches deep and heat over medium-high heat to 375 degrees.

6. When oil comes to temperature, enclose 1 dough ball at a time in split bag. Using clear pie plate (so you can see size of tortilla), press dough flat into 6-inch circle (about ⅛ inch thick).

7. Carefully remove tortilla from plastic and drop into hot oil. Fry tortilla until it puffs up, 15 to 20 seconds. Using 2 metal spatulas, carefully flip tortilla. Immediately press down in center of tortilla with 1 spatula to form taco shape, submerging tortilla into oil while doing so. Using second spatula, spread top of tortilla open about 1½ inches. Fry until golden brown, about 60 seconds. Adjust burner, if necessary, to maintain oil temperature between 350 and 375 degrees.

8. Transfer taco shell to prepared rack and place upside down to drain. Return oil to 375 degrees and repeat with remaining dough balls.

9. Divide picadillo evenly among taco shells, about ¼ cup each. Serve immediately, passing lettuce, tomato, cheddar, and hot sauce separately.

Why This Recipe Works Traditional cochinita pibil requires a suckling pig and banana leaves. To make these richly flavored tacos on a smaller scale, we replaced annatto seeds with bay leaves and tomato paste and swapped in well-marbled, collagen-rich pork butt for the pig. Our savory braising liquid delivered layers of flavor. Cooking the pork butt low and slow produced luscious meat that shredded easily with a potato masher. Served on warm tortillas with punchy quick-pickled red onions and a fiery homemade habanero sauce, our finished filling bursted with flavor.

CITRUS-BRAISED PORK TACOS

SERVES 6

Pork butt roast is often labeled Boston butt in the supermarket. For a spicier sauce, add an extra habanero or two; if you are spice-averse, substitute jalapeños for the habaneros. Pickled onions and habanero sauce can each be refrigerated for up to 1 week.

Pork

- 2 tablespoons vegetable oil
- 1 onion, chopped fine
- 3 garlic cloves, minced
- 1 teaspoon ground cumin
- 1 teaspoon dried oregano
- ½ teaspoon ground allspice
- ½ teaspoon ground cinnamon
- ⅓ cup tomato paste
- 1½ cups water
- ¼ cup frozen orange juice concentrate, thawed
- 3 tablespoons distilled white vinegar
- 1½ tablespoons Worcestershire sauce
- 5 bay leaves
  Salt and pepper
- 1 (2½- to 3-pound) boneless pork butt roast, trimmed and cut into 1-inch chunks

Pickled Red Onions

- 1 red onion, halved and sliced thin
- 1 cup distilled white vinegar
- ⅓ cup sugar
- ¼ teaspoon salt

Habanero Sauce

- 1 cup water
- 1 carrot, peeled and chopped
- 1 vine-ripened tomato, cored and chopped
- ¼ cup chopped onion
- ½ habanero chile, stemmed
- 1 garlic clove, smashed and peeled
  Salt and pepper
- 1 tablespoon distilled white vinegar
- 1½ teaspoons lime juice, plus lime wedges for serving

18 (6-inch) corn tortillas, warmed

1. For the Pork Adjust oven rack to lower-middle position and heat oven to 300 degrees. Heat oil in Dutch oven over medium heat until shimmering. Add onion and cook until lightly browned, 4 to 6 minutes.

2. Add garlic, cumin, oregano, allspice, and cinnamon and cook until fragrant, about 30 seconds. Stir in tomato paste and cook, stirring constantly, until paste begins to darken, about 45 seconds. Stir in water, orange juice concentrate, 2 tablespoons vinegar, Worcestershire, bay leaves, 2 teaspoons salt, and 1 teaspoon pepper, scraping up any browned bits.

3. Add pork and bring to boil. Transfer to oven, uncovered, and cook until pork is tender, about 2 hours, stirring once halfway through cooking.

4. For the Pickled Red Onions Meanwhile, place onion in medium bowl. Bring vinegar, sugar, and salt to simmer in small saucepan over medium-high heat, stirring occasionally, until sugar dissolves. Pour over onions and cover loosely. Let onions cool completely, about 30 minutes.

5. For the Habanero Sauce Combine water, carrot, tomato, onion, habanero, garlic, and ½ teaspoon salt in now-empty saucepan. Bring to boil over medium heat and cook until carrot is tender, about 10 minutes. Remove from heat and let carrot mixture cool slightly, about 5 minutes. Transfer carrot mixture to blender, add vinegar and lime juice, and process until sauce is smooth, 1 to 2 minutes. Season with salt and pepper to taste; set aside.

6. Transfer pot to stovetop; discard bay leaves. Using potato masher, mash pork until finely shredded. Bring to simmer over medium-high heat, then reduce heat to medium-low and cook until most of liquid has evaporated, 3 to 5 minutes.

7. Off heat, stir in remaining 1 tablespoon vinegar and season with salt and pepper to taste. Serve on tortillas with pickled red onions, habanero sauce, and lime wedges.

PORK CARNITAS

SERVES 8 TO 10

We developed this recipe using Morrell Snow Cap Lard, but you can substitute 4 cups of peanut or vegetable oil. Pork butt roast is often labeled Boston butt in the supermarket. The pork doesn't need to be cut into perfect 2-inch pieces; a little variation in size is fine. Serve with Quick Tomatillo Salsa (recipe follows), if desired.

- 4 pounds boneless pork butt roast, cut into 2-inch pieces
  Kosher salt
- 2 pounds lard, cut into 8 pieces
- 24 (6-inch) corn tortillas, toasted
  Finely chopped onion
  Coarsely chopped fresh cilantro
  Lime wedges

1. Adjust oven rack to lower-middle position and heat oven to 300 degrees. Sprinkle pork with 1½ tablespoons salt. Melt lard in large Dutch oven over medium-low heat. Add pork, increase heat to medium-high, and cook until bubbling vigorously all over, about 5 minutes. Transfer to oven and cook, uncovered, until pork is tender, about 2½ hours.

2. Remove pot from oven and let stand for 30 minutes. Using spider skimmer or tongs, transfer pork to carving board; chop into bite-size pieces. Transfer pork to bowl and season with salt to taste. Divide pork among warm tortillas and garnish with onion and cilantro. Serve with lime wedges.

QUICK TOMATILLO SALSA
MAKES ABOUT 2 CUPS

We developed this recipe using a 28-ounce can of tomatillos, but they are also available in 26-ounce cans. If you can find only a 26-ounce can, there's no need to buy a second can to make up the extra 2 ounces. For more heat, reserve and add the jalapeño seeds.

- 1 (28-ounce) can whole tomatillos, drained
- 1 tablespoon extra-virgin olive oil
- 1 small onion, chopped
- ½ cup fresh cilantro leaves
- 1 jalapeño chile, stemmed, seeded, and chopped
- 3 tablespoons lime juice (2 limes)
- 1 garlic clove, minced
  Salt
- ½ teaspoon sugar

1. Adjust oven rack 6 inches from broiler element and heat broiler. Line rimmed baking sheet with aluminum foil. Toss half of tomatillos with 1 teaspoon oil and transfer to prepared sheet. Broil until tomatillos are spotty brown and skins begin to burst, 7 to 10 minutes. Transfer tomatillos to food processor and let cool completely.

2. Add onion, cilantro, jalapeño, lime juice, garlic, ¾ teaspoon salt, sugar, remaining tomatillos, and remaining 2 teaspoons oil to processor. Pulse until slightly chunky, 16 to 18 pulses. Season with salt to taste. Serve. (Salsa can be refrigerated for up to 2 days.)

The American Table: Advocating for Lard

Many home cooks think that lard—which is simply rendered and clarified pork fat—is an antiquated, unhealthy cooking medium. We'll leave the health debate up to the professionals (many of whom claim that lard has more health benefits than butter, by the way), but we can confidently declare that lard produces great results in the kitchen. While you can cook our Pork Carnitas in vegetable oil and they'll taste great, the meat is more deeply savory when cooked in lard. Like frying oil, lard can be strained, refrigerated, and reused once or twice before being discarded.

Why This Recipe Works We used 86 pounds of meat and 26 pounds of lard to develop our recipe for carnitas. While testing we noticed that a tiny difference in our stovetop heat dial could produce surprisingly varied results, so we decided to move the carnitas operation to the more controlled heat of the oven. At 300 degrees, the pork cooked evenly and was tender, except for the corners that poked above the surface of the lard, which browned into crisp edges. Since we didn't add any seasonings or spices, the result was soft pork with unparalleled flavor. These carnitas are best chopped into bite-size pieces served in a warm tortilla with a tangy tomatillo salsa.

EASIER CHICKEN CHIMICHANGAS

SERVES 4

If using a cast-iron Dutch oven, increase the broth to 1¾ cups, adding 1¼ cups in step 2. Serve with Smoky Salsa Verde (page 372).

1¼ cups chicken broth
1 tablespoon minced canned chipotle chile in adobo sauce
½ cup long-grain white rice
  Salt and pepper
2 (6-ounce) boneless, skinless chicken breasts, trimmed
1 tablespoon peanut or vegetable oil, plus 3 cups for frying
1 onion, chopped fine
2 garlic cloves, minced
1 teaspoon chili powder
½ teaspoon ground cumin
1 (15-ounce) can pinto beans, rinsed
4 ounces sharp cheddar cheese, shredded (1 cup)
⅓ cup chopped fresh cilantro
1 tablespoon all-purpose flour
1 tablespoon water
4 (10-inch) flour tortillas

1. Whisk broth and chipotle together in 2-cup liquid measuring cup. Combine ½ cup chipotle broth, rice, and ¼ teaspoon salt in bowl. Cover bowl and microwave until liquid is completely absorbed, about 5 minutes. Meanwhile, pat chicken dry with paper towels and season with salt and pepper.

2. Heat 1 tablespoon oil in Dutch oven over medium-high heat until just smoking. Add onion and cook until softened, about 5 minutes. Stir in garlic, chili powder, and cumin and cook until fragrant, about 30 seconds. Add remaining ¾ cup chipotle broth, parcooked rice, and beans and bring to boil.

3. Reduce heat to medium-low, add chicken, and cook, covered, until chicken registers 160 degrees and rice is tender, about 15 minutes, flipping chicken halfway through cooking. Transfer chicken to cutting board and let rest for 5 to 10 minutes. Cut chicken into ½-inch pieces and combine with rice and bean mixture, cheddar, and cilantro in large bowl. Wash now-empty pot.

4. Whisk flour and water together in small bowl. Stack tortillas on plate and microwave, covered, until pliable, about 1 minute. Working with one at a time, place one-quarter of chicken mixture in center of warm tortilla. Brush edges of tortilla with flour paste. Wrap top and bottom of tortilla tightly over filling. Brush ends of tortilla with paste and fold into center, pressing firmly to seal.

5. Set wire rack in rimmed baking sheet. Heat remaining 3 cups oil in clean pot over medium-high heat until 325 degrees. Place 2 chimichangas, seam side down, in oil. Fry, adjusting burner as necessary to maintain oil temperature between 300 and 325 degrees, until chimichangas are deep golden brown, about 4 minutes, turning them halfway through frying. Drain on prepared wire rack. Bring oil back to 325 degrees and repeat with remaining chimichangas. Serve.

Glue and Fold

The usual burrito-style wrapping method left us between the devil and the deep blue sea: Either the filling leaked out in the pot of oil or the ends of the tortilla never crisped. Our new chimichanga folding technique solves both problems.

1. Place filling in middle of tortilla. Brush tortilla's circumference with flour-and-water paste.

2. After folding opposing sides toward center and pressing to seal, brush open flaps with more paste. Fold flaps in and press firmly to seal chimichanga shut.

Why This Recipe Works Forget about tasteless fillings. We simmer the chicken and rice for our chimichangas in a chipotle broth, infusing them with a smoky bite through and through. As for construction, we noticed that the standard burrito-style wrapping method left us with doughy tortilla ends and filling that fell out. We created an easy new folding technique that kept the filling put without any floury bites.

SMOKY SALSA VERDE

MAKES 1¼ CUPS

This salsa is especially good served with our Easier Chicken Chimichangas (page 370), or try it with just about anything you'd serve salsa with, such as tortilla chips, grilled steak, or scrambled eggs.

- 1 pound tomatillos, husks and stems removed, rinsed well, and dried
- 1 small onion, quartered
- 1 jalapeño chile, stemmed, halved, and seeded
- 1 garlic clove, peeled
- 1 teaspoon olive oil
- ½ cup fresh cilantro leaves
- 1 tablespoon lime juice
  Salt

1. Adjust oven rack 5 inches from broiler element and heat broiler. Toss tomatillos, onion, jalapeño, and garlic with oil and place on aluminum foil–lined rimmed baking sheet. Broil, shaking pan occasionally, until vegetables are lightly charred, 10 to 12 minutes. Cool slightly, about 5 minutes.

2. Add vegetables, cilantro, lime juice, and ¼ teaspoon salt to food processor and pulse until coarsely ground, 5 to 7 pulses. Season with salt to taste. Serve. (Salsa can be refrigerated for up to 3 days.)

Tomatillos

Called tomates verdes (green tomatoes) in much of Mexico, small green tomatillos have a tangier, more citrusy flavor than true green tomatoes. When choosing tomatillos, look for pale-green orbs with firm flesh that fills and splits open the fruit's outer papery husk, which must be removed before cooking. Avoid tomatillos that are too yellow and soft, as these specimens are past their prime and will taste sour and muted.

Reviving Tired Herbs

We rarely use an entire bunch of herbs at once, and inevitably a few days later they are looking less-than-fresh and we have to throw them out and start all over. Is there a way to revive tired herbs? With a little research, we found that soaking herbs in water restores the pressure of the cell contents against the cell wall, causing them to become firmer as the dehydrated cells plump up. So, after purposely letting several bunches of parsley, cilantro, and mint sit in the refrigerator until they became limp, sorry-looking versions of their former selves, we tried bringing the herbs back to life by soaking them in tepid and cold water. We found that soaking herbs (stems trimmed) for 10 minutes in cold water perks them up better than tepid water. These herbs had a fresher look and an improved texture.

Why This Recipe Works Our recipe for salsa verde includes the typical ingredients: tomatillos, onions, garlic, jalapeño, and lots of cilantro. To temper their sharply acidic flavor, we broiled the tomatillos just until tender. We also broiled the other vegetables to provide subtle smokiness. Our recipe calls for a large amount of cilantro to ensure that its flavor stands out from the other ingredients.

Why This Recipe Works Tex-Mex cheese enchiladas are a wildly popular dish in the Lone Star State, beloved for their relative simplicity and their chile gravy, a red sauce that's a cross between beef gravy and Mexican enchilada sauce. We found that two toasted ancho chiles ground with a combination of spices gave the sauce smoky flavors that we brightened with a little white vinegar. We skipped frying the corn tortillas, instead brushing them with oil and microwaving, resulting in soft, easy-to-roll tortillas without excess grease. For the cheesy filling, we combined sharp cheddar and Monterey Jack and used the oven to ensure melty, gooey cheese.

TEX-MEX CHEESE ENCHILADAS

SERVES 6

Dried chiles vary in size and weight. You'll get a more accurate measure if you seed and tear them first; you need about ½ cup of prepped chiles. You'll lose some flavor, but you can substitute 2 tablespoons ancho chile powder and 1 tablespoon ground cumin for the whole ancho chiles and cumin seeds, decreasing the toasting time to 1 minute.

Gravy

2 dried ancho chiles, stemmed, seeded, and torn into ½-inch pieces (½ cup)
1 tablespoon cumin seeds
1 tablespoon garlic powder
2 teaspoons dried oregano
3 tablespoons vegetable oil
3 tablespoons all-purpose flour
   Salt and pepper
2 cups chicken broth
2 teaspoons distilled white vinegar

Enchiladas

12 (6-inch) corn tortillas
1½ tablespoons vegetable oil
8 ounces Monterey Jack cheese, shredded (2 cups)
6 ounces sharp cheddar cheese, shredded (1½ cups)
1 onion, chopped fine

1. For the Gravy Toast chiles and cumin in 12-inch skillet over medium-low heat, stirring frequently, until fragrant, about 2 minutes. Transfer to spice grinder and let cool for 5 minutes. Add garlic powder and oregano and grind to fine powder.

2. Heat oil in now-empty skillet over medium-high heat until shimmering. Whisk in flour, ½ teaspoon salt, ½ teaspoon pepper, and spice mixture and cook until fragrant and slightly deepened in color, about 1 minute. Slowly whisk in broth and bring to

simmer. Reduce heat to medium-low and cook, whisking frequently, until gravy has thickened and reduced to 1½ cups, about 5 minutes. Whisk in vinegar and season with salt and pepper to taste. Remove from heat, cover, and keep warm.

3. For the Enchiladas Adjust oven rack to middle position and heat oven to 450 degrees. Brush both sides of tortillas with oil. Stack tortillas, then wrap in damp dish towel. Place tortillas on plate and microwave until warm and pliable, about 1 minute.

4. Spread ½ cup gravy in bottom of 13 by 9-inch baking dish. Combine cheeses in bowl; set aside ½ cup cheese mixture for topping enchiladas. Sprinkle ¼ cup cheese mixture and 1 tablespoon onion across center of each tortilla. Tightly roll tortillas around filling and lay them seam side down in dish (2 columns of 6 tortillas will fit neatly across width of dish). Pour remaining 1 cup gravy over enchiladas, then sprinkle with reserved cheese mixture.

5. Cover dish with aluminum foil and bake until sauce is bubbling and cheese is melted, about 15 minutes. Let enchiladas cool for 10 minutes, then sprinkle with remaining onion. Serve.

To Make Ahead The sauce can be made up to 24 hours in advance. To reheat, add 2 tablespoons water and microwave until loose, 1 to 2 minutes, stirring halfway through microwaving.

Enchilada Orientation

After spreading ½ cup chile gravy in 13 by 9-inch baking dish, fit 12 enchiladas by creating 2 snug columns of 6.

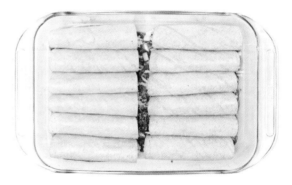

EASY GREEN CHILE CHICKEN ENCHILADAS

SERVES 4 TO 6

For more heat, reserve the jalapeño seeds and add them to the blender in step 3. Don't spend a lot of time chopping the cilantro stems and leaves for the sauce; chop them just enough to measure them, and then let the blender do the bulk of the work. Serve with hot sauce, if desired.

Sauce

- 1 (28-ounce) can whole tomatillos, drained
- 3 poblano chiles, stemmed, halved, and seeded
- 1 onion, cut into 8 wedges through root end
- 1 jalapeño chile, stemmed, halved, and seeded
- 5 garlic cloves, peeled
- 1 tablespoon vegetable oil
- ¼ cup water
- ¼ cup coarsely chopped fresh cilantro leaves and stems
- 1 teaspoon ground cumin
- 1 teaspoon dried oregano
- 1 teaspoon sugar
- 1 teaspoon table salt
- 1 teaspoon pepper

Enchiladas

- 1 (2½-pound) rotisserie chicken, skin and bones discarded, meat shredded into bite-size pieces (3 cups)
- 12 ounces sharp cheddar cheese, shredded (3 cups), divided
- 12 (6-inch) corn tortillas
- 1 tablespoon chopped fresh cilantro
   Sour cream
   Lime wedges
   Avocado
   Finely chopped onion

1. For the Sauce Adjust oven rack 6 inches from broiler element and heat broiler. Line rimmed baking sheet with aluminum foil.

2. Place tomatillos, poblanos, onion, jalapeño, and garlic on prepared sheet. Drizzle with oil and toss gently to coat. Arrange poblanos and jalapeño skin side up. Broil until poblanos, jalapeño, and tomatillos are blistered and blackened and onion wedges are dark at edges, about 15 minutes, rotating sheet halfway through broiling. (Vegetables may appear to be burning, but they are not.) Let vegetables cool on sheet for 15 minutes.

3. Turn off broiler and heat oven to 400 degrees. Transfer broiled vegetables and any accumulated juices to blender. Add water, cilantro, cumin, oregano, sugar, salt, and pepper and process until smooth, about 30 seconds, scraping down sides of blender jar as needed (you should have about 3½ cups sauce).

4. For the Enchiladas Spread ½ cup sauce in bottom of 13 by 9-inch baking dish. Combine chicken, 1½ cups cheddar, and 1 cup sauce in bowl. Stack tortillas and wrap in damp dish towel. Microwave until hot and pliable, about 1½ minutes.

5. Arrange tortillas on counter and place ¼ cup filling in center of each. Distribute any remaining filling evenly among tortillas. Roll tortillas tightly around filling and place seam side down in prepared dish.

6. Pour remaining 2 cups sauce over enchiladas and spread evenly with back of spoon. Sprinkle with remaining 1½ cups cheddar and cover dish with foil. Bake until enchiladas are heated through and cheese is melted, about 30 minutes.

7. Uncover and let cool for 15 minutes. Sprinkle with cilantro and serve with sour cream, lime wedges, avocado, and onion.

Why This Recipe Works Enchiladas can be a tall order, so to cut down on preparation we started with shredded rotisserie chicken. Store-bought enchilada sauces tasted too acidic, but homemade ones required sometimes out-of-season fresh tomatillos, so we turned to canned tomatillos and bolstered them with fresh poblanos and jalapeño. Broiling before blending with cilantro and spices added complexity, while a little water kept the sauce fluid so that the filled and rolled enchiladas did not dry out in the oven. To ensure that the enchiladas rolled neatly, we microwaved the tortillas in a damp towel before filling to make them nice and pliable.

BEEF ENCHILADAS

SERVES 4 TO 6

Cut back on the jalapeños if you like your enchiladas on the mild side.

3 tablespoons chili powder
3 garlic cloves, minced
2 teaspoons ground coriander
2 teaspoons ground cumin
1 teaspoon sugar
   Salt
1¼ pounds top blade steaks, trimmed
1 tablespoon vegetable oil
2 onions, chopped
1 (15-ounce) can tomato sauce
½ cup water
8 ounces Monterey Jack or mild cheddar cheese, shredded (2 cups)
⅓ cup chopped fresh cilantro
¼ cup chopped canned jalapeños
12 (6-inch) corn tortillas

1. Combine chili powder, garlic, coriander, cumin, sugar, and 1 teaspoon salt in small bowl. Pat meat dry with paper towels and sprinkle with salt. Heat oil in Dutch oven over medium-high heat until shimmering. Cook meat until browned on both sides, about 6 minutes. Transfer meat to plate. Add onions to pot and cook over medium heat until golden, about 5 minutes. Stir in garlic mixture and cook until fragrant, about 1 minute. Add tomato sauce and water and bring to boil. Return meat and juices to pot, cover, reduce heat to low, and gently simmer until meat is tender and can be broken apart with wooden spoon, about 1½ hours.

2. Adjust oven rack to middle position and heat oven to 350 degrees. Strain beef mixture over medium bowl, breaking meat into small pieces; reserve sauce. Transfer meat to bowl and mix with 1 cup cheese, cilantro, and jalapeños.

3. Spread ¾ cup sauce in bottom of 13 by 9-inch baking dish. Place 6 tortillas on plate and microwave until soft, about 1 minute. Spread ⅓ cup beef mixture down center of each tortilla, roll tortillas tightly, and set in baking dish seam side down. Repeat with remaining tortillas and beef mixture (you may have to fit 2 or more enchiladas down the sides of the baking dish). Pour remaining sauce over enchiladas and spread to coat evenly. Sprinkle remaining 1 cup cheese evenly over enchiladas, wrap with aluminum foil, and bake until heated through, 20 to 25 minutes. Remove foil and continue baking until cheese browns slightly, 5 to 10 minutes. Serve.

Trimming Blade Steaks

Halve each steak lengthwise and slice away center strip of gristle.

Why This Recipe Works Traditional beef enchilada recipes require simmering steak for hours. Convenience recipes call for hamburger and canned sauce. We wanted to find a middle ground. For a deeply flavored sauce, we relied on chili powder and tomato sauce, along with onions, garlic, and spices. Slicing beefy, inexpensive blade steaks into small pieces cut our cooking time considerably. Traditional recipes fry the corn tortillas and then dip them in sauce to soften and season them. Instead, we softened the tortillas in the microwave. Once filled, topped with sauce and cheese, and baked, our enchiladas tasted like the real deal.

Why This Recipe Works Arrachera en adobo, a chili-like dish of steak slowly stewed in a pungent adobo sauce, is a gem of Mexican American cuisine and popular in Texas. We wanted to re-create its flavors in the test kitchen. For a simple but rich adobo sauce, we used two kinds of dried chiles—anchos for their fruitiness and pasillas for their bitter earthiness. Seeding them tamed their heat, while toasting them gave them more complex flavor. Flank steak proved to be the ideal cut of meat, since it is leaner and it did not add greasiness to the sauce. Browning the meat before braising added another layer of meaty depth.

FLANK STEAK IN ADOBO

SERVES 4 TO 6

Salsa verde is a green salsa made from tomatillos and green chiles. Our favorite store-bought brand is Frontera Tomatillo Salsa. You can substitute skirt steak for flank steak here, if desired. If queso fresco is unavailable, you can substitute farmer's cheese or a mild feta. This dish is also great served over rice.

Adobo

- 1½ ounces dried ancho chiles, stemmed and seeded
- 1 ounce dried pasilla chiles, stemmed and seeded
- ¾ cup salsa verde
- ¾ cup chicken broth
- ½ cup orange juice
- ⅓ cup packed brown sugar
- ¼ cup lime juice (2 limes)
- 1½ teaspoons dried oregano
- 1 teaspoon salt
- ½ teaspoon pepper

Flank Steak

- 2½–3 pounds flank steak, trimmed and cut into 1½-inch cubes
  Salt and pepper
- 2 tablespoons vegetable oil
- 1 onion, chopped fine
- 8 garlic cloves, minced
- 1 tablespoon ground cumin
- 12 (8-inch) flour tortillas, warmed
- 4 ounces queso fresco, crumbled (1 cup)
- ½ cup coarsely chopped fresh cilantro

1. For the Adobo Adjust oven rack to lower-middle position and heat oven to 350 degrees. Arrange anchos and pasillas on rimmed baking sheet and bake until fragrant, about 5 minutes. Immediately transfer chiles to bowl and cover with hot tap water. Let stand until chiles are softened and pliable, about 5 minutes. Drain.

2. Process salsa verde, broth, orange juice, sugar, lime juice, oregano, salt, pepper, and drained chiles in blender until smooth, 1 to 2 minutes. Set aside.

3. For the Flank Steak Reduce oven temperature to 300 degrees. Pat beef dry with paper towels and sprinkle with ½ teaspoon salt and ½ teaspoon pepper. Heat 1 tablespoon oil in Dutch oven over medium-high heat until just smoking. Add half of beef and cook, stirring occasionally, until well browned on all sides, 6 to 9 minutes. (Adjust heat, if necessary, to keep bottom of pot from scorching.) Using slotted spoon, transfer beef to large bowl. Repeat with remaining 1 tablespoon oil and remaining beef.

4. Add onion and ½ teaspoon salt to now-empty pot. Reduce heat to medium and cook, stirring occasionally, until golden brown, 3 to 5 minutes, scraping up any browned bits. Add garlic and cumin and cook until fragrant, about 30 seconds. Stir in adobo, beef, and any accumulated juices until well incorporated and bring mixture to simmer.

5. Cover pot and transfer to oven. Cook until beef is tender and sauce has thickened, about 1½ hours. Season with salt and pepper to taste. Serve with flour tortillas, sprinkled with queso fresco and cilantro.

CHICKEN CHILAQUILES

SERVES 6

New Mexican or Anaheim chiles can be substituted for the guajillo chiles. If queso fresco is unavailable, you can substitute farmer's cheese or a mild feta. When baking the tortillas, stir them well to promote even browning.

16 (6-inch) corn tortillas, each cut into 8 wedges
¼ cup olive oil
   Salt
5 dried guajillo chiles, stemmed and seeded
1 (28-ounce) can whole peeled tomatoes
1 cup finely chopped onion
1 poblano chile, stemmed, seeded, and chopped
1 jalapeño chile, stemmed, seeded, and chopped
8 sprigs fresh cilantro, plus 2 tablespoons chopped
3 garlic cloves, chopped
1½ cups chicken broth
1½ pounds boneless, skinless chicken breasts, trimmed
4 ounces queso fresco, crumbled (1 cup)
1 avocado, halved, pitted, and cut into ½-inch chunks
2 radishes, trimmed and sliced thin
   Sour cream
   Lime wedges

1. Adjust oven racks to upper-middle and lower-middle positions and heat oven to 425 degrees. Divide tortillas evenly between 2 rimmed baking sheets and drizzle with oil and ½ teaspoon salt. Toss until tortillas are evenly coated with oil. Bake until golden brown and crisp, 15 to 20 minutes, stirring chips and switching and rotating sheets halfway through baking.

2. Toast guajillos in Dutch oven over medium heat until fragrant and slightly darkened, about 5 minutes. Transfer to blender and process until finely ground, 60 to 90 seconds, scraping down sides of blender jar as needed.

3. Add tomatoes and their juice, ¾ cup onion, poblano, jalapeño, cilantro sprigs, garlic, and ¾ teaspoon salt to guajillos and process until very smooth, 60 to 90 seconds. Transfer sauce to now-empty Dutch oven and stir in broth. Bring sauce to boil over medium-high heat. Add chicken breasts; reduce heat to low and simmer, uncovered, until chicken registers 160 degrees, 15 to 20 minutes, flipping halfway through cooking.

4. Using tongs, transfer chicken to large plate. Increase heat to medium and continue to simmer sauce until thickened and reduced to about 4½ cups, about 5 minutes longer. While sauce simmers, shred chicken into bite-size pieces using 2 forks. Return chicken to sauce and cook until warmed through, about 2 minutes.

5. Add chips to pot and toss to coat. Remove from heat and season with salt to taste. Cover and let stand for 2 to 5 minutes, depending on how soft you like your chips.

6. Transfer chilaquiles to serving dish and top with queso fresco, avocado, radishes, remaining ¼ cup onion, and chopped cilantro. Serve with sour cream and lime wedges.

Entrée-Worthy Chilaquiles

1. Use 3 types of chiles.

2. Make easy homemade chips.

3. Cook chicken in sauce.

4. Finish with fresh garnishes.

Why This Recipe Works Chilaquiles are often made from leftover meats and are considered a side dish, but we started from scratch for the best flavor and turned the dish into a meal. We began by baking our own tortilla chips. For the tomato-based red sauce, we toasted dried guajillo chiles to intensify their flavor before pureeing them with fresh poblanos, jalapeños, and other aromatic ingredients. To make the chilaquiles a complete meal, we poached boneless, skinless chicken breasts in the red sauce before shredding and mixing the tender meat back in with the chips. Finishing the dish with sour cream and queso fresco balanced the heat.

Why This Recipe Works Many chili con carne recipes call for toasting and grinding whole chiles. We wanted to create a simpler, but still satisfying version. For the meat, we settled on beef chuck, our favorite cut for stews because its substantial marbling provides rich flavor and tender texture after prolonged cooking. To add a smoky meatiness to our chili, we browned the beef in bacon fat instead of oil. We added a jalapeño for brightness and heat and minced chipotle for smoky, spicy depth. A few tablespoons of corn muffin mix, in place of masa harina (corn flour), helped thicken our chili and gave it a silky texture.

EASY CHILI CON CARNE

SERVES 6 TO 8

If the bacon does not render a full 3 tablespoons of fat in step 1, supplement it with vegetable oil. If desired, serve chili with chopped onion, avocado, shredded cheese, lime wedges, and/or hot sauce.

1 (14.5-ounce) can diced tomatoes
2 teaspoons minced canned chipotle chile in adobo sauce
4 slices bacon, chopped fine
1 (3½- to 4-pound) boneless beef chuck-eye roast, pulled apart at seams, trimmed, and cut into 1-inch pieces
   Salt and pepper
1 onion, chopped fine
1 jalapeño chile, stemmed, seeded, and chopped fine
3 tablespoons chili powder
4 garlic cloves, minced
1½ teaspoons ground cumin
½ teaspoon dried oregano
4 cups water
1 tablespoon packed brown sugar
2 tablespoons yellow corn muffin mix

1. Process tomatoes and chipotle in food processor until smooth. Cook bacon in Dutch oven over medium heat until crisp, about 8 minutes. Transfer bacon to paper towel–lined plate and reserve 3 tablespoons bacon fat.

2. Pat beef dry with paper towels and season with salt and pepper. Heat 1 tablespoon reserved bacon fat in now-empty Dutch oven over medium-high heat until just smoking. Brown half of beef, about 8 minutes. Transfer to bowl and repeat with 1 tablespoon bacon fat and remaining beef.

3. Add remaining 1 tablespoon bacon fat, onion, and jalapeño to again-empty Dutch oven and cook until softened, about 5 minutes. Stir in chili powder, garlic, cumin, and oregano and cook until fragrant, about 30 seconds. Stir in water, pureed tomato mixture, bacon, browned beef, and sugar and bring to boil. Reduce heat to low and simmer, covered, for 1 hour. Skim fat and continue to simmer uncovered until meat is tender, 30 to 45 minutes.

4. Ladle 1 cup chili liquid into medium bowl and stir in muffin mix; cover with plastic wrap. Microwave until mixture is thickened, about 1 minute. Slowly whisk mixture into chili and simmer until chili is slightly thickened, 5 to 10 minutes. Season with salt and pepper to taste. Serve. (Chili can be refrigerated for up to 3 days.)

Silky Sauce

Our chili gets silky texture and a hint of corn flavor from the addition of corn muffin mix.

Why This Recipe Works As the name implies, five-alarm chili should be spicy enough to make you break a sweat—but it has to have rich, complex chile flavor as well. We used a combination of dried anchos, smoky chipotle chiles in adobo sauce, fresh jalapeños, and chili powder to create layers of spicy flavor. Ground beef added meaty bulk, and pureeing the chiles along with canned tomatoes and corn chips added extra body and another layer of flavor. Mellowed with a bit of sugar and enriched with creamy pinto beans, our chili was well balanced and spicy without being harsh.

FIVE-ALARM CHILI

SERVES 8 TO 10

Look for ancho chiles in the Latin American aisle at the supermarket. Light-bodied American lagers, such as Budweiser, work best here. Serve chili with lime, sour cream, diced tomato, diced avocado, scallions, and cornbread.

2 ounces (4 to 6) dried ancho chiles, stemmed, seeded, and cut into 1-inch pieces

3½ cups water

1 (28-ounce) can whole peeled tomatoes

¾ cup crushed corn tortilla chips

¼ cup canned chipotle chile in adobo sauce plus 2 teaspoons adobo sauce

2 tablespoons vegetable oil

2 pounds 85 percent lean ground beef

Salt and pepper

2 pounds onions, chopped fine

2 jalapeño chiles, stemmed, seeds reserved, and minced

6 garlic cloves, minced

2 tablespoons ground cumin

2 tablespoons chili powder

1 tablespoon dried oregano

2 teaspoons ground coriander

2 teaspoons sugar

1 teaspoon cayenne pepper

1½ cups beer

3 (15-ounce) cans pinto beans, rinsed

1. Combine anchos and 1½ cups water in bowl and microwave until softened, about 3 minutes. Drain and discard liquid. Process anchos, tomatoes and their juice, remaining 2 cups water, tortilla chips, chipotle, and adobo sauce in blender until smooth, about 1 minute; set aside.

2. Heat 2 teaspoons oil in Dutch oven over medium-high heat until just smoking. Add beef, 1 teaspoon salt, and ½ teaspoon pepper and cook, breaking up pieces with spoon, until all liquid has evaporated and meat begins to sizzle, 10 to 15 minutes. Drain in colander and set aside.

3. Heat remaining 4 teaspoons oil in now-empty Dutch oven over medium-high heat until simmering. Add onions and jalapeños and seeds and cook until onions are lightly browned, about 5 minutes. Stir in garlic, cumin, chili powder, oregano, coriander, sugar, and cayenne and cook until fragrant, about 30 seconds. Pour in beer and bring to simmer. Stir in beans, reserved chile-tomato mixture, and reserved cooked beef and return to simmer. Cover, reduce heat to low, and cook, stirring occasionally, until thickened, 50 to 60 minutes. Season with salt to taste. Serve.

Five Hits for Five-Alarm Chili

JALAPEÑO
Brings fresh vegetable flavor

CHIPOTLE IN ADOBO
Instant shortcut to smokiness

CHILI POWDER
Wouldn't be chili without it

CAYENNE
Adds raw heat

ANCHO
Adds depth, complexity, and mild heat

SO-CAL CHURROS

MAKES ABOUT 18 CHURROS

We used a closed star #8 pastry tip, ⅝ inch in diameter, to create deeply grooved ridges in the churros. However, you can use any large, closed star tip of similar diameter, though your yield may vary slightly. It's important to mix the dough for 1 minute in step 2 before adding the eggs to keep them from scrambling.

Dough
- 2 cups water
- 2 tablespoons unsalted butter
- 2 tablespoons sugar
- 1 teaspoon vanilla extract
- ½ teaspoon salt
- 2 cups (10 ounces) all-purpose flour
- 2 large eggs
- 2 quarts vegetable oil

Chocolate Sauce
- ¾ cup heavy cream
- 4 ounces semisweet chocolate chips
  Pinch salt
- ¼ teaspoon vanilla extract

Coating
- ½ cup (3½ ounces) sugar
- ¾ teaspoon ground cinnamon

1. For the Dough Line 1 rimmed baking sheet with parchment paper and spray with vegetable oil spray. Combine water, butter, sugar, vanilla, and salt in large saucepan and bring to boil over medium-high heat. Remove from heat; add flour all at once and stir with rubber spatula until well combined, with no streaks of flour remaining.

2. Transfer dough to bowl of stand mixer. Fit mixer with paddle and mix on low speed until cooled slightly, about 1 minute. Add eggs, increase speed to medium, and beat until fully incorporated, about 1 minute.

3. Transfer warm dough to piping bag fitted with ⅝-inch closed star pastry tip. Pipe 18 (6-inch) lengths of dough onto prepared sheet, using scissors to snip dough at tip. Refrigerate, uncovered, for 15 minutes to 1 hour.

4. Adjust oven rack to middle position and heat oven to 200 degrees. Set wire rack in second rimmed baking sheet and place in oven. Line large plate with triple layer of paper towels. Add oil to Dutch oven until it measures about 1½ inches deep and heat over medium-high heat to 375 degrees.

5. Gently drop 6 churros into hot oil and fry until dark golden brown on all sides, about 6 minutes, turning frequently for even cooking. Adjust burner, if necessary, to maintain oil temperature between 350 and 375 degrees. Transfer churros to paper towel–lined plate for 30 seconds to drain off excess oil, then transfer to wire rack in oven. Return oil to 375 degrees and repeat with remaining dough in 2 more batches.

6. For the Chocolate Sauce Microwave cream, chocolate chips, and salt in bowl at 50 percent power, stirring occasionally, until melted, about 2 minutes. Stir in vanilla until smooth.

7. For the Coating Combine sugar and cinnamon in shallow dish. Roll churros in cinnamon sugar, tapping gently to remove excess. Transfer churros to platter and serve warm with chocolate sauce.

Churning Out Churros

Pipe eighteen 6-inch lengths of warm dough, snipping at tip. Refrigerate 15 minutes to 1 hour to firm up before frying.

Why This Recipe Works The fried pastries known as churros should be crisp on the outside and soft on the inside, but piping thick pâte à choux dough into hot oil is no easy feat. We began by preparing a simple dough, precooking a mixture of water, butter, sugar, vanilla, and salt before stirring in flour and beating in eggs. The dough proved easier to work with when still warm, so we transferred it to a pastry bag right away. Piping the dough onto a baking sheet and frying the churros in batches made it easier to monitor when they were done. A roll in cinnamon sugar and a dip in a simple chocolate sauce made for a sweet finish.

everybody loves italian

Why This Recipe Works Every cook has a different take on "pasta fazool"—the hearty Italian American soup studded with creamy beans and little pieces of pasta. For our slightly sweet, full-bodied version, we started with chicken broth and added pancetta for meaty richness, tomato paste for savory punch, and plenty of garlic. To build body, we pureed half of the cannellini beans and added them to the broth with the remaining whole beans. Finally, for simplicity, we cooked ditalini pasta directly in the simmering soup before serving—their small size prevents them from bloating and sucking up too much of the brothy goodness.

PASTA E FAGIOLI

SERVES 4 TO 6

You can use any small pasta shape, such as tubettini, elbow macaroni, or small shells, in place of the ditalini. To make this soup vegetarian, omit the pancetta and substitute vegetable broth for the chicken broth. If you do not have a food processor, you can use a blender to process the beans and water in step 1.

2 (15-ounce) cans cannellini beans, rinsed
1 cup water
2 tablespoons extra-virgin olive oil, plus extra for drizzling
2 onions, chopped fine
2 carrots, peeled and chopped fine
1 celery rib, chopped fine
2 ounces pancetta, chopped fine
¾ teaspoon salt
½ teaspoon pepper
2 tablespoons tomato paste
4 garlic cloves, minced
¼ teaspoon red pepper flakes (optional)
4 cups chicken broth
4 ounces (1 cup) ditalini
2 ounces Parmesan cheese, grated (1 cup), plus extra for serving
½ cup finely chopped fresh basil

1. Process 1 can of beans and water in food processor until smooth, about 30 seconds. Set aside.

2. Heat oil in large saucepan over medium heat until shimmering. Add onions, carrots, celery, pancetta, salt, and pepper and cook until vegetables are softened, about 10 minutes.

3. Add tomato paste, garlic, and pepper flakes, if using, and cook until fragrant, about 2 minutes. Stir in broth, remaining can of beans, and pureed bean mixture. Bring to boil, reduce heat to medium-low, and simmer, stirring occasionally, until flavors have melded, about 10 minutes.

4. Increase heat to medium and bring to boil. Add pasta and cook, stirring occasionally, until pasta is al dente, about 12 minutes. Off heat, stir in Parmesan and basil. Serve, drizzled with extra oil and passing extra Parmesan separately.

To Make Ahead At end of step 3, let soup cool completely. Refrigerate soup for up to 2 days or freeze for up to 1 month. Let frozen soup thaw completely in refrigerator before reheating. To serve, bring soup to boil and continue with step 4.

Texture Trick

This soup features creamy cannellini beans floating in the thick broth but also where you can't see them: pureed with water into a mixture that helps thicken and flavor the soup base. In both cases, we drain and rinse the canned beans before using them.

Tiny Tubes

Ditalini is just the right size to add heft while still being easy to eat.

Why This Recipe Works To translate a classic minestrone to the slow cooker, we needed to find a combination of vegetables that would cook through in the same amount of time. Green beans took too long to become tender. We scrapped cauliflower because its flavor overwhelmed the soup. Zucchini squash and Swiss chard won out for texture and their similar cooking times. Canned beans disintegrated in the soup, so we used dried white beans. We started cooking the beans in the soup along with some softened carrots and onions, then added the squash, chard, and pasta toward the end of cooking so they would be perfectly tender.

SLOW-COOKER MINESTRONE

SERVES 6 TO 8

We recommend using great Northern or cannellini beans here. Serve the minestrone with grated Parmesan cheese.

- 1 cup dried medium-size white beans, rinsed and picked over
- 6 tablespoons extra-virgin olive oil
- 2 onions, chopped fine
- 4 carrots, peeled and cut into ½-inch pieces
- 8 garlic cloves, minced
- 1 (28-ounce) can whole peeled tomatoes, coarsely crushed by hand
- 8 cups chicken broth
- 3 cups water
- 2 cups fresh basil leaves, chopped
- 1 teaspoon dried oregano
- ¼ teaspoon red pepper flakes
- 2 medium zucchini, quartered lengthwise, seeded, and sliced ¼ inch thick
- 8 ounces Swiss chard, stemmed and chopped
- ½ cup small dried pasta, such as ditalini, orzo, or small elbows
  Salt and pepper

1. Bring beans and enough water to cover by 1 inch to boil in medium saucepan over high heat. Reduce heat to low and simmer, covered, until beans are just beginning to soften, about 20 minutes. Drain beans and transfer to slow cooker.

2. Heat 3 tablespoons oil in Dutch oven over medium heat until shimmering. Add onions and carrots and cook until softened, about 5 minutes. Stir in garlic and cook until fragrant, about 30 seconds. Add tomatoes and their juice and cook until pan is nearly dry, 8 to 12 minutes. Stir in broth, water, ½ cup basil, oregano, and pepper flakes and bring to boil; transfer to slow cooker. Cover and cook until beans are tender, 6 to 7 hours on low or 5 to 6 hours on high.

3. Stir zucchini, Swiss chard, and pasta into slow cooker and cook on high, covered, until pasta is tender, 20 to 30 minutes. Stir in remaining 1½ cups basil and remaining 3 tablespoons oil. Season with salt and pepper to taste and serve.

To Make Ahead Recipe can be made through step 2 and refrigerated for up to 2 days. To finish, bring to boil in Dutch oven. Stir in zucchini, chard, and pasta; reduce heat to low; and simmer until pasta is tender, about 10 minutes.

Timing Is Everything

First the onions, carrots, and tomatoes go into the slow cooker with the broth to create a rich, long-simmered backbone of flavor. Then we add the quick-cooking zucchini, Swiss chard, and pasta toward the end so they don't overcook.

HEAD START
Sautéed vegetables and canned whole tomatoes season the broth.

LAST MINUTE
The more delicate vegetables are added with the pasta near the end of cooking.

Why This Recipe Works We love the flavor and heartiness of Sunday gravy, but traditional recipes feature a long ingredient list and involve hours of monitoring the stovetop. For a streamlined recipe, we turned to our slow cooker and narrowed the meat selection down to three: flank steak, for meaty flavor; country-style spareribs, for tender, fall-off-the-bone meat; and sausage, for its spicy, sweet kick. Using the flavorful drippings left behind from browning the sausage to sauté our aromatics infused the whole dish with flavor. And a combination of drained diced tomatoes, canned tomato sauce, and tomato paste ensured a rich, thick sauce.

SLOW-COOKER ITALIAN SUNDAY GRAVY

SERVES 8 TO 10

Most sausage has enough seasoning to make extra salt unnecessary. This recipe makes enough to sauce 2 pounds of pasta. We like rigatoni, ziti, or penne with this sauce.

1 tablespoon vegetable oil
1 pound sweet Italian sausage
1 pound hot Italian sausage
2 onions, chopped
12 garlic cloves, minced
2 teaspoons dried oregano
1 (6-ounce) can tomato paste
½ cup dry red wine
1 (28-ounce) can diced tomatoes, drained
1 (28-ounce) can tomato sauce
2 pounds bone-in country-style pork spareribs, trimmed
1 (1½-pound) flank steak, trimmed
3 tablespoons chopped fresh basil
Pepper

1. Heat oil in Dutch oven over medium-high heat until just smoking. Add sweet sausage and cook until well browned and fat begins to render, about 8 minutes. Using slotted spoon, transfer sausage to paper towel–lined plate to drain, then place in slow cooker. Repeat with hot sausage; transfer to slow cooker.

2. Cook onions in rendered fat over medium heat until well browned, about 6 minutes. Stir in garlic and oregano and cook until fragrant, about 1 minute. Add tomato paste and cook until it begins to brown, about 5 minutes. Stir in wine and simmer, scraping up browned bits, until wine is slightly reduced, about 3 minutes. Transfer to slow cooker. Stir in diced tomatoes and tomato sauce.

3. Submerge spareribs and steak in sauce in slow cooker. Cover and cook until meat is tender, 8 to 10 hours on low or 4 to 5 hours on high.

4. About 30 minutes before serving, remove ribs, steak, and sausages and set aside until cool enough to handle. Shred ribs and steak into small pieces, discarding excess fat and bones; slice sausages in half crosswise. Skim fat from surface of sauce, then stir sausages and shredded meat back into sauce. Stir in basil and season with pepper to taste. Serve. (Gravy can be refrigerated for up to 3 days.)

To Make Ahead Recipe can be made in advance through step 2. After stirring in diced tomatoes and tomato sauce, add browned sausages and simmer over medium-low heat until cooked through, about 12 minutes. Refrigerate sausage and sauce for up to 2 days. To cook gravy, warm sauce and sausages together over medium heat until heated through; transfer to slow cooker. Proceed with step 3.

The Meat Matters

For our easy Slow-Cooker Italian Sunday Gravy, we narrowed down the meat to the following combination, which offers the best taste and texture.

ITALIAN SAUSAGES
Browning the sausages in advance helps build deep flavor.

FLANK STEAK
This lean cut adds beefy flavor without too much grease.

COUNTRY-STYLE SPARERIBS
These meaty ribs become fall-apart tender in a slow cooker.

PORK RAGU

MAKES ABOUT 8 CUPS

This recipe makes enough sauce to coat 2 pounds of pasta. Leftover sauce may be refrigerated for up to 3 days or frozen for up to 1 month.

- 2 (2¼- to 2½-pound) racks baby back ribs, trimmed and each rack cut into fourths
- 2 teaspoons ground fennel
  Kosher salt and pepper
- 3 tablespoons olive oil
- 1 large onion, chopped fine
- 1 large fennel bulb, stalks discarded, bulb halved, cored, and chopped fine
- 2 large carrots, peeled and chopped fine
- ¼ cup minced fresh sage
- 1½ teaspoons minced fresh rosemary
- 1 cup plus 2 tablespoons dry red wine
- 1 (28-ounce) can whole peeled tomatoes, drained and chopped coarse
- 3 cups chicken broth
- 1 garlic head, outer papery skins removed and top fourth of head cut off and discarded
- 1 pound pappardelle or tagliatelle
  Grated Parmesan cheese

1. Adjust oven rack to middle position and heat oven to 300 degrees. Sprinkle ribs with ground fennel and generously season with salt and pepper, pressing spices to adhere. Heat oil in Dutch oven over medium-high heat until just smoking. Add half of ribs, meat side down, and cook, without moving them, until meat is well browned, 6 to 8 minutes; transfer to plate. Repeat with remaining ribs; set aside.

2. Reduce heat to medium and add onion, fennel, carrots, 2 tablespoons sage, rosemary, and ½ teaspoon salt to now-empty pot. Cook, stirring occasionally and scraping up any browned bits, until vegetables are well browned and beginning to stick to pot bottom, 12 to 15 minutes.

3. Add 1 cup wine and cook until evaporated, about 5 minutes. Stir in tomatoes and broth and bring to simmer. Submerge garlic and ribs, meat side down, in liquid; add any accumulated juices from plate. Cover and transfer to oven. Cook until ribs are fork-tender, about 2 hours.

4. Remove pot from oven and transfer ribs and garlic to rimmed baking sheet. Using large spoon, skim any fat from surface of sauce. Once cool enough to handle, shred meat from bones; discard bones and gristle. Return meat to pot. Squeeze garlic from its skin into pot. Stir in remaining 2 tablespoons sage and remaining 2 tablespoons wine. Season with salt and pepper to taste.

5. Meanwhile, bring 4 quarts water to boil in large pot. Add pasta and 2 tablespoons salt and cook, stirring often, until al dente. Reserve ½ cup cooking water, then drain pasta and return it to pot. Add half of sauce and toss to combine, adjusting consistency with reserved cooking water as needed. Serve, passing Parmesan separately.

Cutting Baby Back Ribs for Ragu

Before browning ribs, divide each rack into three-rib segments using a chef's knife.

Why This Recipe Works Earthy and intense, pork ragu takes pasta to a new level. Most recipes call for pork shoulder and a hard-to-find, bony cut like neck, shank, or feet. We tried using all baby back ribs and found the resulting ragu rich and meaty. For a classic Italian flavor profile, fennel took the place of celery in the ragu's base and ground fennel rubbed into the ribs echoed the anise flavor. Simmering the garlic head whole right in the sauce yielded sweeter softened cloves that we squeezed back into the sauce when tender. With fresh herbs and red wine, our ragu tasted balanced and far more complex than its simple preparation would suggest.

Why This Recipe Works For the long-cooked flavor of pork ragu in under 90 minutes, we looked to our food processor. Whirring fennel, onion, and fennel seeds together created a savory flavor base. Pulsing canned whole tomatoes created a silky tomato sauce, and processing sweet Italian sausage delivered bites of well-seasoned meat in every forkful. We cooked the components in stages, browning the sausage before softening the soffritto in the rendered fat. Minced garlic and dried oregano, bloomed in tomato paste, further defined the Italian flavors, and red wine offered brightness. A 45-minute simmer produced a rich ragu with the perfect consistency.

PASTA WITH SAUSAGE RAGU

SERVES 4 TO 6

For a spicier sauce, substitute hot Italian sausage for sweet. You will have 3 cups of extra sauce, which can be used to sauce 1 pound of pasta.

½ fennel bulb, stalks discarded, bulb cored and chopped coarse
½ onion, chopped coarse
1 tablespoon fennel seeds
1 (28-ounce) can whole peeled tomatoes
2 pounds sweet Italian sausage, casings removed
1 tablespoon extra-virgin olive oil, plus extra for drizzling
   Salt and pepper
2 tablespoons tomato paste
4 garlic cloves, minced
1½ teaspoons dried oregano
¾ cup red wine
1 pound pappardelle or tagliatelle
   Grated Parmesan cheese

1. Pulse fennel, onion, and fennel seeds in food processor until finely chopped, about 10 pulses, scraping down sides of bowl as needed; transfer to separate bowl. Process tomatoes in now-empty processor until smooth, about 10 seconds; transfer to second bowl. Pulse sausage in now-empty processor until finely chopped, about 10 pulses, scraping down sides of bowl as needed.

2. Heat oil in Dutch oven over medium-high heat until shimmering. Add sausage and cook, breaking up meat with spoon, until all liquid has evaporated and meat begins to sizzle, 10 to 15 minutes.

3. Add fennel mixture and ½ teaspoon salt and cook, stirring occasionally, until softened, about 5 minutes. (Fond on bottom of pot will be deeply browned.) Add tomato paste, garlic, and oregano and cook, stirring constantly, until fragrant, about 30 seconds.

4. Stir in wine, scraping up any browned bits, and cook until nearly evaporated, about 1 minute. Add 1 cup water and pureed tomatoes and bring to simmer. Reduce heat to low and simmer gently, uncovered, until thickened, about 45 minutes. (Wooden spoon should leave trail when dragged through sauce.) Season with salt and pepper to taste; cover and keep warm.

5. Bring 4 quarts water to boil in large pot. Add pasta and 1 tablespoon salt and cook, stirring often, until al dente. Reserve 1 cup cooking water, then drain pasta and return it to pot. Add 3 cups sauce and ½ cup reserved cooking water to pasta and toss to combine. Adjust consistency with remaining reserved cooking water as needed. Transfer to serving dish. Drizzle with extra oil, sprinkle with Parmesan, and serve. (Remaining 3 cups sauce can be refrigerated for up to 3 days or frozen for up to 1 month.)

Spotlight on Fennel

The vegetable that we slice and eat raw or cooked is Florence fennel, or finocchio; its bulb, stems, and feathery fronds boast a mildly sweet, faint anise flavor. Fennel seeds, which are a key part of the flavor profile of Italian sausage, come from a perennial herb called common fennel (also referred to as herb, sweet, or wild fennel) that has no bulb.

FLORENCE FENNEL
A vegetable grown for its edible bulb, stems, and fronds.

COMMON FENNEL
A perennial herb grown for its ornamental fronds and aromatic seeds.

Why This Recipe Works Fettuccine with butter and cheese, aka fettuccine Alfredo, has simple roots and a rich sauce of only a few ingredients: Parmigiano-Reggiano, butter, and salt. The secret to getting a silky sauce that coats each strand? Using the pasta's cooking water. After cooking a pound of fettuccine in exactly 3 quarts of water, we reserved 1 cup of the starchy liquid and added it back to the drained pasta along with the sauce's ingredients. After a rest and some vigorous stirring, the butter, cheese, and pasta water formed a creamy, emulsified sauce. Serving the pasta in warm bowls kept the pasta hot and the sauce velvety right to the last bite.

FETTUCCINE WITH BUTTER AND CHEESE

SERVES 4 TO 6

Be sure to use imported Parmigiano-Reggiano cheese here and not the bland domestic cheese labeled "Parmesan." For the best results, grate the cheese on a rasp-style grater. Do not adjust the amount of water for cooking the pasta. Stir the pasta frequently while cooking so that it doesn't stick together. It's important to move quickly after draining the pasta, as the residual heat from the reserved cooking water and pasta will help the cheese and butter melt. For best results, heat ovensafe dinner bowls in a 200-degree oven for 10 minutes prior to serving and serve the pasta hot. If you are using fresh pasta, increase the amount to 1¼ pounds.

1 pound fettuccine
  Salt
4 ounces Parmigiano-Reggiano, grated (2 cups), plus extra for serving
5 tablespoons unsalted butter, cut into 5 pieces

1. Bring 3 quarts water to boil in large Dutch oven. Add pasta and 1 tablespoon salt and cook, stirring frequently, until al dente. Reserve 1 cup cooking water, then drain pasta and return it to pot.

2. Add Parmigiano-Reggiano, butter, reserved cooking water, and ½ teaspoon salt to pot. Set pot over low heat and, using tongs, toss and stir vigorously to thoroughly combine, about 1 minute. Remove pot from heat, cover, and let pasta sit for 1 minute.

3. Toss pasta vigorously once more so sauce thoroughly coats pasta and any cheese clumps are emulsified into sauce, about 30 seconds. (Mixture may look wet at this point, but pasta will absorb excess moisture as it cools slightly.) Season with salt to taste.

4. Transfer pasta to individual bowls. (Use rubber spatula as needed to remove any clumps of cheese stuck to tongs and bottom of pot.) Serve immediately, passing extra Parmigiano-Reggiano separately.

Keep On Stirring

When the grated Parmigiano-Reggiano cheese, butter pieces, and reserved pasta cooking water are stirred into the still-hot fettuccine, the dish 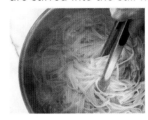 will appear very watery. But don't fret: After a covered 1-minute rest and a vigorous stir, the sauce will come together, forming a creamy emulsion.

PASTA WITH ROASTED GARLIC SAUCE, ARUGULA, AND WALNUTS

SERVES 4

It takes about four heads of garlic to yield 50 cloves, but you can use prepeeled.

50 garlic cloves, peeled (1 cup)
 3 tablespoons extra-virgin olive oil,
   plus extra for drizzling
 1 cup chicken broth
 2 teaspoons balsamic vinegar
   Salt and pepper
 1 pound spaghetti, linguine, or fettuccine
 8 ounces (8 cups) baby arugula
 1 cup walnuts, toasted and chopped
   Grated Pecorino Romano cheese

1. Combine garlic and oil in medium saucepan over medium-low heat. Cover and cook, stirring occasionally, until garlic is browned all over, 6 to 8 minutes. Add broth, vinegar, ¾ teaspoon salt, and ½ teaspoon pepper and bring to boil. Reduce heat to low and simmer, uncovered, until garlic is fork-tender, 5 to 7 minutes. Pour garlic mixture into food processor and process until smooth, about 1 minute.

2. Meanwhile, bring 4 quarts water to boil in large pot. Add pasta and 1 tablespoon salt and cook, stirring often, until al dente. Reserve ½ cup cooking water, then drain pasta and return it to pot. Add garlic sauce, arugula, and walnuts to pasta and toss to combine. Adjust consistency with reserved cooking water as needed. Season with salt and pepper to taste. Serve, drizzling individual servings with extra oil and passing Pecorino separately.

Speedy Stovetop "Roasting"

We love the mellow sweetness of roasted garlic, but we don't always have an hour to make it. Our stovetop method takes just 15 minutes. We sauté 50 cloves of garlic in olive oil in a covered pan for just 6 minutes or so. Later, we add balsamic vinegar, which helps mimic the complex, sweet flavor of oven-roasted garlic.

Why This Recipe Works Toasting mellows, softens, and sweetens a head of garlic. But rather than waiting the hour or more it can take to roast garlic in the oven, we set out to develop a quick pasta dish that could harness the same great flavor in short order. We browned a whopping 50 whole cloves on the stovetop and then poached the garlic in chicken broth seasoned with sweet, tangy balsamic vinegar. After a spin in the food processor, the final result was a complex and silky sauce that we combined with walnuts and spicy arugula. The best part? The whole thing took just 15 minutes—more than enough time to cook the pasta.

PASTA WITH MUSHROOM SAUCE

SERVES 4

If you can't find shiitake mushrooms, cremini mushrooms can be substituted or white mushrooms can be used exclusively, but don't omit the dried porcini. Parmesan cheese can be substituted for the Pecorino Romano.

- 12 ounces shiitake mushrooms, stemmed
- 12 ounces white mushrooms, trimmed
- 4 tablespoons unsalted butter
  Salt and pepper
- 2 shallots, minced
- 2 tablespoons minced fresh sage
- 4 garlic cloves, minced
- ¼ ounce dried porcini mushrooms, rinsed and chopped fine
- ½ cup dry white wine
- 4 cups water plus ¼ cup hot water
- 12 ounces (3¾ cups) campanelle, penne, or fusilli
- 2 ounces Pecorino Romano cheese, grated (1 cup), plus extra for serving
- 1 tablespoon lemon juice
- 2 tablespoons minced fresh chives

1. Coarsely chop half of shiitake mushrooms and white mushrooms; then quarter remaining shiitake mushrooms and white mushrooms. Melt 2 tablespoons butter in Dutch oven over medium-high heat. Add all shiitake mushrooms and white mushrooms (both chopped and quartered) and ¾ teaspoon salt. Cover and cook until mushrooms release their liquid, about 5 minutes. Uncover and continue to cook, stirring occasionally, until all liquid has evaporated and mushrooms begin to brown, about 10 minutes.

2. Add shallots, sage, garlic, and porcini mushrooms and cook until fragrant, about 1 minute. Add wine and cook until evaporated, about 2 minutes. Stir in 4 cups water, pasta, and 1¼ teaspoons salt and bring to boil. Reduce heat to medium, cover, and cook, stirring occasionally, until pasta is tender, 12 to 15 minutes.

3. Off heat, stir in Pecorino, ¼ cup hot water, lemon juice, remaining 2 tablespoons butter, and ½ teaspoon pepper. Stir vigorously for 1 minute, until sauce is thickened. Season with salt and pepper to taste. Transfer to serving dish and sprinkle with chives. Serve, passing extra Pecorino separately.

Doubling Down for Big Impact

Chopping half the mushrooms creates more fond for a flavorful sauce; quartering the rest gives big, meaty mushroom texture.

COARSELY CHOPPED   **QUARTERED**

Why This Recipe Works In order to coax as much earthy, meaty flavor as possible from supermarket mushrooms, we used fresh shiitake and white mushrooms, plus dried porcini. We coarsely chopped half of them, providing better browning due to the increased surface area, and we quartered the rest for visual appeal and meaty texture. After deglazing the pan with wine, we added the pasta directly to the pot so it could absorb the flavorful liquid. One minute of vigorous stirring drew out the pasta's starch, adding structure to the sauce and helping it cling to the pasta. The end result? An elegant one-pot dish with deep mushroom flavor.

Why This Recipe Works We visited Mike's Kitchen in Cranston, Rhode Island, and were inspired by Mike Lepizzera's famous creamy, light polenta. Cooking the cornmeal in water instead of dairy gave us clean, sweet corn flavor and an airy texture. Garlic oil boosted the dish's savory quality, and adding half-and-half and nutty Pecorino contributed some welcome richness. While the polenta chilled, we processed canned whole tomatoes into a smooth, thick puree and created a sweet-and-savory red sauce. We then sliced blocks of polenta and baked them long enough to brown and heat through before serving.

FLUFFY BAKED POLENTA WITH RED SAUCE

SERVES 6

We developed this recipe using Quaker Yellow Corn Meal for its desirable texture and relatively short cooking time. We recommend you use the same product for this recipe. The timing may be different for other types of cornmeal, so be sure to cook the polenta until it is thickened and tender. Whole milk can be substituted for the half-and-half. Plan ahead: The polenta needs to be cooled for at least 3 hours before being cut, baked, and served.

Polenta

4 tablespoons unsalted butter
2 tablespoons extra-virgin olive oil
2 garlic cloves, smashed and peeled
7 cups water
1½ teaspoons salt
½ teaspoon pepper
1½ cups cornmeal
3 ounces Pecorino Romano cheese, grated (1½ cups)
¼ cup half-and-half

Red Sauce

1 (14.5-ounce) can whole peeled tomatoes
¼ cup extra-virgin olive oil
1 onion, peeled and halved through root end
1 (15-ounce) can tomato sauce
1 ounce Pecorino Romano cheese, grated (½ cup)
1½ tablespoons sugar
¾ teaspoon salt
½ teaspoon garlic powder

1. For the Polenta Lightly grease 8-inch square baking pan. Heat butter and oil in Dutch oven over medium heat until butter is melted. Add garlic and cook until lightly golden, about 4 minutes. Discard garlic.

2. Add water, salt, and pepper to butter mixture. Increase heat to medium-high and bring to boil. Add cornmeal in slow, steady stream, whisking constantly. Reduce heat to medium-low and continue to cook, whisking frequently and scraping sides and bottom of pot, until mixture is thick and cornmeal is tender, about 20 minutes.

3. Off heat, whisk in Pecorino and half-and-half. Transfer to prepared pan and let cool completely on wire rack. Once cooled, cover with plastic wrap and refrigerate until completely chilled, at least 3 hours.

4. For the Red Sauce Process tomatoes and their juice in blender until smooth, about 30 seconds. Heat 1 tablespoon oil in large saucepan over medium heat until shimmering. Add onion, cut side down, and cook without moving until lightly browned, about 4 minutes. Add pureed tomatoes, tomato sauce, Pecorino, sugar, salt, garlic powder, and remaining 3 tablespoons oil. Bring mixture to boil, reduce heat to medium-low, and simmer until sauce is slightly thickened, about 15 minutes. Remove from heat, discard onion, cover, and keep warm.

5. Adjust oven rack to middle position and heat oven to 375 degrees. Line rimmed baking sheet with parchment paper, then grease parchment. Cut chilled polenta into 6 equal pieces (about 4 by 2⅔ inches each). Place on prepared sheet and bake until heated through and beginning to brown on bottom, about 30 minutes. Serve each portion covered with about ½ cup red sauce.

DROP MEATBALLS

SERVES 6 TO 8

You can use a #16 portion scoop to form the meatballs. To make shaping easier, wet your hands slightly. The recipe yields enough sauce for 2 pounds of pasta. To serve, toss the pasta with some sauce and top it with the meatballs.

Meatballs
- 22 square saltines
- 1 cup milk
- 2 pounds 85 percent lean ground beef
- 2 ounces Parmesan cheese, grated (1 cup)
- 1 teaspoon garlic powder
- 1 teaspoon dried oregano
- 1 teaspoon salt
- ½ teaspoon pepper

Sauce
- ¼ cup extra-virgin olive oil
- 10 garlic cloves, peeled and smashed
- ½ teaspoon red pepper flakes
- 2 (28-ounce) cans crushed tomatoes
  Salt and pepper
- 3 tablespoons chopped fresh basil

1. For the Meatballs Adjust oven rack to lower-middle position and heat oven to 400 degrees. Place saltines in large zipper-lock bag, seal bag, and crush saltines fine with rolling pin (you should have 1 cup). Combine saltines and milk in large bowl and let sit for 5 minutes for saltines to soften. Mash with fork until smooth paste forms.

2. Add beef, Parmesan, garlic powder, oregano, salt, and pepper to saltine mixture and mix with your hands until thoroughly combined. Divide meat mixture into 24 scant ¼-cup portions. Roll portions between your wet hands to form balls. Transfer to plate, cover with plastic wrap, and refrigerate until ready to use. (Meatballs can be refrigerated for up to 24 hours.)

3. For the Sauce Combine oil and garlic in large Dutch oven. Cook over low heat until garlic is soft and golden on all sides, 10 to 12 minutes, stirring occasionally. Add pepper flakes and cook until fragrant,

about 30 seconds. Stir in tomatoes and 1 teaspoon salt. Nestle meatballs into sauce. Bring to simmer over medium-high heat.

4. Cover and bake until meatballs are cooked through and tender, about 40 minutes. Let cool, uncovered, for 20 minutes. Gently stir in basil and season with salt and pepper to taste. Serve.

What's a Panade?

A panade is a paste typically made by combining milk and bread. We often use panades to help foods such as meatloaf and meatballs hold their shape and stay moist.

But how does it work? Starches from bread, or in this case saltines, absorb liquid from milk. The starches form a gel that, like fat, coats the proteins in the meat. This gel holds meat juices in. It also prevents the proteins from linking together and toughening. The result is a moister, more tender meatball.

All in the Family

Basil DeLuca, pictured below with his daughter Carmella Garofoli, hand-rolls nearly 150 meatballs every day at Philadelphia's Villa di Roma restaurant. To keep the meatballs tender, they're careful not to pack them too tightly. The restaurant is a touchstone in Philadelphia's Italian American community, one of the oldest and most dynamic in the United States.

Why This Recipe Works For a simpler meatball recipe, we skipped our usual browning step (good for developing a nice crust, but a lot of work) and went straight to simmering them in a sauce. But we discovered that the crust adds more than just flavor; it also keeps the meatballs intact. A crushed saltine panade (higher-moisture bread crumbs caused crumbling) saved the day, as did finishing everything in the oven so the meatballs could cook evenly without stirring. We liked the brighter, less meaty sauce, and added a hefty dose of smashed garlic and red pepper flakes for a savory edge and a slight kick.

MEATBALLS AND MARINARA

SERVES 8

To keep the recipe easy and streamlined, the meatballs and sauce start with the same onion mixture. This recipe makes enough to sauce 2 pounds of pasta.

Onion Mixture
¼ cup olive oil
3 onions, chopped fine
8 garlic cloves, minced
1 tablespoon dried oregano
¾ teaspoon red pepper flakes

Marinara
1 (6-ounce) can tomato paste
1 cup dry red wine
1 cup water
4 (28-ounce) cans crushed tomatoes
1 ounce Parmesan cheese, grated (½ cup)
¼ cup chopped fresh basil
Salt
1–2 teaspoons sugar

Meatballs
4 slices hearty white sandwich bread, torn into pieces
¾ cup milk
8 ounces sweet Italian sausage, casings removed
2 ounces Parmesan cheese, grated (1 cup)
½ cup chopped fresh parsley
2 large eggs
2 garlic cloves, minced
1½ teaspoons salt
2½ pounds 80 percent lean ground chuck

1. For the Onion Mixture Heat oil in Dutch oven over medium-high heat until shimmering. Cook onions until golden, 10 to 15 minutes. Add garlic, oregano, and pepper flakes and cook until fragrant, about 30 seconds. Transfer half of onion mixture to large bowl and set aside.

2. For the Marinara Add tomato paste to remaining onion mixture in pot and cook until fragrant, about 1 minute. Add wine and cook until slightly thickened, about 2 minutes. Stir in water and tomatoes and simmer over low heat until sauce is no longer watery, 45 minutes to 1 hour. Stir in Parmesan and basil and season with salt and sugar to taste.

3. For the Meatballs Meanwhile, adjust oven rack to upper-middle position and heat oven to 475 degrees. Add bread and milk to bowl with reserved onion mixture and mash together until smooth. Add sausage, Parmesan, parsley, eggs, garlic, and salt to bowl and mash to combine. Add beef and knead with hands until well combined. Lightly shape mixture into 2½-inch round meatballs (about 16 meatballs total), place on rimmed baking sheet, and bake until well browned, about 20 minutes.

4. Transfer meatballs to pot with sauce and simmer for 15 minutes. Serve. (Meatballs and marinara can be frozen for up to 1 month.)

Well-Seasoned Meatballs Without the Mess
We bypassed the messy frying step and baked our meatballs in a superhot oven instead to ensure a nicely browned crust. Simmering the meatballs in the sauce briefly allows the sauce to season the meat, and vice versa.

1. Bake meatballs in very hot oven to ensure browned crust.

2. Simmer meatballs in sauce for 15 minutes before serving for flavorful sauce and meatballs

Why This Recipe Works Meatballs and marinara sauce are the epitome of comfort food, except when you're the cook. Frying the meatballs can be messy and take a good chunk of time when working in batches. For an easier method, we turned to the oven and roasted our meatballs at a high temperature, which ensured they developed a nice, browned crust. To keep our meatballs moist and tender, we added a panade (a paste of milk and bread). In addition to ground beef, using Italian sausage for the pork gave the meatballs a flavor boost, as did simmering them in the sauce after baking.

Why This Recipe Works To infuse our Slow-Cooker Meatballs and Marinara with depth of flavor, we used lots of onion, garlic, and tomato paste and sautéed them before adding them to the slow cooker. Microwaving the meatballs before adding them to the slow cooker rendered just enough fat (which we discarded) to ensure the sauce wouldn't be greasy. To bind and moisten the meatballs, we traded in the usual panade (a paste of milk and bread), which caused them to break apart in the slow cooker, for cream and shredded mozzarella cheese.

SLOW-COOKER MEATBALLS AND MARINARA

SERVES 6

Microwave the meatballs on a large plate or in a casserole dish to contain the rendering fat. This recipe makes enough to sauce 1½ pounds of pasta.

Onion Mixture
- 2 tablespoons olive oil
- 2 onions, chopped fine
- 1 (6-ounce) can tomato paste
- 6 garlic cloves, minced
- 1 tablespoon dried oregano
- ½ teaspoon red pepper flakes
- ¼ teaspoon salt

Marinara
- ½ cup red wine
- 2 (28-ounce) cans crushed tomatoes

Meatballs
- 4 ounces Italian sausage, casings removed
- 2 ounces mozzarella cheese, shredded (½ cup)
- 1 ounce Parmesan cheese, grated (½ cup)
- 2 large eggs
- 2 garlic cloves, minced
- ¾ teaspoon salt
- 1¼ pounds 85 percent lean ground beef
- 3 tablespoons heavy cream

- 1 ounce Parmesan cheese, grated (½ cup)
- 2 tablespoons finely chopped fresh basil
  Salt

1. For the Onion Mixture Heat oil in Dutch oven over medium-high heat until shimmering. Add onions, tomato paste, garlic, oregano, pepper flakes, and salt and cook until softened and lightly browned, about 8 to 10 minutes. Transfer half of onion mixture to large bowl and set aside.

2. For the Marinara Add wine to remaining onion mixture in pot and cook until slightly thickened, about 2 minutes. Stir in tomatoes, then transfer to slow cooker.

3. For the Meatballs Add sausage, mozzarella, Parmesan, eggs, garlic, and salt to bowl with reserved onion mixture. Mash with potato masher until smooth. Add beef and cream to bowl and knead with hands until well combined. Lightly shape mixture into 2-inch round meatballs (about 12 total). Microwave meatballs on large plate until fat renders and meatballs are firm, 4 to 7 minutes. Nestle meatballs into slow cooker, discarding rendered fat. Cover and cook until meatballs are tender and sauce is slightly thickened, 4 to 5 hours on low.

4. Let meatballs and sauce settle for 5 minutes, then skim fat from surface and stir in Parmesan and basil. Season with salt to taste. Serve.

To Make Ahead Recipe can be made in advance through shaping meatballs in step 3. Uncooked meatballs and sauce can be refrigerated in separate containers for up to 24 hours. When ready to cook, add sauce to slow cooker and proceed with microwaving meatballs in step 3.

Microwaving Meatballs

Microwave meatballs uncovered until fat renders and meat is firm.

Why This Recipe Works Pasta in a slow cooker? You bet. But achieving well-cooked pasta and melty cheese in the slow cooker takes some strategy. Borrowing a technique from risotto was the key to perfect pasta—we stirred the raw pasta into the browned sausage and onion mixture, coating the starch in fat and preventing the pasta from bloating in the slow cooker. To get cheese that was evenly melted, we added it after cooking and let it sit in the residual warmth of the turned-off slow-cooker.

SLOW-COOKER BAKED ZITI

SERVES 6

Our favorite crushed tomatoes are SMT Crushed Tomatoes.

- 2 tablespoons olive oil
- 1 pound hot or sweet Italian sausage, casings removed
- 1 onion, chopped
- 3 garlic cloves, minced
- ½ teaspoon dried oregano
- ½ teaspoon salt
- ½ teaspoon pepper
- 8 ounces (2½ cups) ziti
- 1 (28-ounce) can crushed tomatoes
- 1 (15-ounce) can tomato sauce
- 8 ounces (1 cup) whole-milk ricotta cheese
- 4 ounces mozzarella cheese, shredded (1 cup)
- 2 tablespoons thinly sliced fresh basil

1. Make aluminum foil collar for slow cooker by folding 2 (18-inch-long) pieces of foil to make 2 (18 by 4-inch) strips. Line perimeter of slow cooker with foil strips and spray with vegetable oil spray.

2. Heat oil in Dutch oven over medium-high heat until just smoking. Cook sausage, breaking up pieces with spoon, until well browned, 6 to 8 minutes. Add onion and cook until lightly browned, about 5 minutes. Stir in garlic, oregano, salt, and pepper and cook until fragrant, about 1 minute.

3. Reduce heat to medium-low. Add ziti and cook, stirring constantly, until edges of pasta become translucent, about 4 minutes. Off heat, stir in crushed tomatoes and tomato sauce, scraping up any browned bits. Transfer mixture to prepared slow cooker. Cover and cook on low until pasta is tender, about 3 hours.

4. Using tongs, remove foil collar from slow cooker. Dollop ricotta over ziti and sprinkle with mozzarella. Cover and let sit for 20 minutes to let cheeses melt. Garnish with basil and serve.

Key Steps to Great Slow-Cooker "Baked" Ziti

1. To prevent burning, fold aluminum foil into 2 strips and use them to line perimeter of slow cooker.

2. To avoid slimy, bloated pasta, sauté it with sausage and onion.

Why This Recipe Works This Italian meatloaf is essentially an excellent, no-fuss meatballs and marinara recipe. We started with a flavorful meat mixture of ground beef, Italian sausage, Parmesan cheese, garlic, and oregano. Instead of rolling dozens of meatballs, we made one big loaf-shaped one. Mixing in a paste of crushed saltines, eggs, and milk helped the meatloaf hold its shape and stay moist. We whipped up a garlicky 5-minute tomato sauce, poured it on top, and baked the two together, elevating both meatloaf and sauce in the process. For a finishing touch, we topped the meatloaf with melty fontina and a sprinkling of fresh basil.

ITALIAN MEATLOAF

SERVES 6 TO 8

Grate the Parmesan using a rasp-style grater; shred the fontina on the large holes of a box grater.

Sauce
- 1 tablespoon extra-virgin olive oil
- 5 garlic cloves, sliced thin
- 1 (28-ounce) can crushed tomatoes
- 1 (15-ounce) can tomato sauce
- ¼ teaspoon red pepper flakes
- ¼ teaspoon table salt

Meatloaf
- 35 square saltines
- ¾ cup whole milk
- 2 large eggs
- 1 pound 85 percent lean ground beef
- 1 pound sweet Italian sausage, casings removed
- 2 ounces Parmesan cheese, grated (1 cup)
- 1 teaspoon granulated garlic
- 1 teaspoon dried oregano
- ½ teaspoon table salt
- ½ teaspoon pepper
- ¼ teaspoon red pepper flakes
- 4 ounces fontina cheese, shredded (1 cup)
- 3 tablespoons chopped fresh basil

1. For the Sauce Adjust oven rack to middle position and heat oven to 400 degrees. Heat oil in large saucepan over medium heat until shimmering. Add garlic and cook until lightly browned, about 1 minute. Stir in tomatoes, tomato sauce, pepper flakes, and salt. Bring to simmer and cook until flavors have melded, about 5 minutes. Remove from heat; cover to keep warm.

2. For the Meatloaf Spray broiler-safe 13 by 9-inch baking dish with vegetable oil spray. Place saltines in large zipper-lock bag, seal bag, and crush saltines to fine crumbs with rolling pin. Whisk saltines, milk, and eggs together in large bowl. Let sit until saltines are softened, about 5 minutes. Whisk saltine mixture until smooth paste forms. Add beef, sausage, Parmesan, granulated garlic, oregano, salt, pepper, and pepper flakes and mix with your hands until thoroughly combined.

3. Transfer beef mixture to prepared dish. Using your wet hands, shape into 9 by 5-inch rectangle; top should be flat and meatloaf should be 1½ inches thick. Pour sauce over meatloaf. Cover dish with aluminum foil and place on rimmed baking sheet. Bake until meatloaf registers 160 degrees, 1 hour 5 minutes to 1¼ hours.

4. Remove sheet from oven, uncover dish, and sprinkle meatloaf evenly with fontina. Heat broiler. Broil meatloaf until cheese is melted, about 2 minutes. Let rest for 15 minutes.

5. Using 2 spatulas, transfer meatloaf to cutting board. Spoon off any excess grease from tomato sauce. Slice meatloaf 1 inch thick. Transfer slices back to sauce in dish, sprinkle with basil, and serve.

Teaching Meatloaf to Speak Italian

1. Make 5-minute tomato sauce.

2. Shape beef mixture into loaf in dish.

3. Pour sauce over beef, cover, and bake.

4. Uncover, top with fontina, and broil.

SKILLET LASAGNA

SERVES 4 TO 6

A 12-inch nonstick skillet with a tight-fitting lid works best for this recipe.

- 1 (28-ounce) can diced tomatoes
  Water
- 1 tablespoon olive oil
- 1 onion, chopped fine
  Salt and pepper
- 3 garlic cloves, minced
- ⅛ teaspoon red pepper flakes
- 1 pound meatloaf mix
- 10 curly-edged lasagna noodles, broken into 2-inch lengths
- 1 (8-ounce) can tomato sauce
- 1 ounce Parmesan cheese, grated (½ cup), plus 2 tablespoons, grated
- 8 ounces (1 cup) whole-milk or part-skim ricotta cheese
- 3 tablespoons chopped fresh basil

1. Place tomatoes in 4-cup liquid measuring cup. Add water until mixture measures 4 cups.

2. Heat oil in 12-inch nonstick skillet over medium heat until shimmering. Add onion and ½ teaspoon salt and cook until onion begins to brown, about 5 minutes. Stir in garlic and pepper flakes and cook until fragrant, about 30 seconds. Add meat and cook, breaking up meat into small pieces with wooden spoon, until it is no longer pink, about 4 minutes.

3. Scatter pasta over meat but do not stir. Pour tomato mixture and tomato sauce over pasta, cover, and bring to simmer. Reduce heat to medium-low and simmer, stirring occasionally, until pasta is tender, about 20 minutes.

4. Off heat, stir in ½ cup Parmesan and season with salt and pepper to taste. Dollop heaping tablespoons of ricotta over top, cover, and let sit for 5 minutes. Sprinkle with basil and remaining 2 tablespoons Parmesan. Serve.

SKILLET LASAGNA WITH SAUSAGE AND RED PEPPER

Substitute 1 pound Italian sausage, casings removed, for meatloaf mix. Add 1 chopped red bell pepper to skillet with onion.

Secrets to Skillet Lasagna

1. Sauté onion, garlic, and meat in skillet, then scatter broken lasagna noodles over meat.

2. Pour diced tomatoes and tomato sauce over noodles, cover, and cook until pasta is tender, about 20 minutes.

3. Stir in Parmesan and dollop with ricotta, then cover skillet and let cheese soften off heat.

Why This Recipe Works To get our lasagna fix without spending hours in the kitchen, we made the entire dish, from start to finish, in a 12-inch skillet. After sautéing aromatics, we browned our meat in the pan, then added the noodles and sauce. Meatloaf mix (a blend of ground beef, pork, and veal) contributed deep, meaty flavor. Canned diced tomatoes and tomato sauce, thinned with water, provided ample liquid to cook our noodles and thickened to just the right consistency after a brief simmer. For a rich, creamy topping, we dropped big dollops of ricotta cheese over the noodles and covered the pan so they'd melt.

HEARTY BEEF LASAGNA

SERVES 10 TO 12

We developed this recipe using dried curly-edged lasagna noodles; do not use no-boil noodles. There are about 20 individual noodles in a 1-pound box of lasagna noodles, enough for this recipe.

Lasagna
Vegetable oil spray
17 curly-edged lasagna noodles
1 tablespoon salt
12 ounces mozzarella cheese, shredded (3 cups)
¼ cup grated Pecorino Romano cheese

Meat Sauce
2 slices hearty white sandwich bread, torn into small pieces
¼ cup milk
1½ pounds 90 percent lean ground beef
¾ teaspoon salt
½ teaspoon pepper
1 tablespoon extra-virgin olive oil
1 onion, chopped fine
6 garlic cloves, minced
1 teaspoon dried oregano
¼ teaspoon red pepper flakes
1 (28-ounce) can crushed tomatoes

Cream Sauce
8 ounces (1 cup) cottage cheese
4 ounces Pecorino Romano cheese, grated (2 cups)
1 cup heavy cream
2 garlic cloves, minced
1 teaspoon cornstarch
¼ teaspoon salt
¼ teaspoon pepper

1. For the Lasagna Adjust oven rack to middle position and heat oven to 375 degrees. Spray rimmed baking sheet and 13 by 9-inch baking dish with oil spray. Bring 4 quarts water to boil in large Dutch oven. Add noodles and salt and cook, stirring often, until al dente. Drain noodles and transfer them to prepared sheet. Using tongs, gently turn noodles to coat lightly with oil spray. Cut 2 noodles in half crosswise.

2. For the Meat Sauce Mash bread and milk in bowl until smooth. Add beef, salt, and pepper and knead with your hands until well combined; set aside. Heat oil in now-empty Dutch oven over medium heat until shimmering. Add onion and cook until softened, about 5 minutes. Stir in garlic, oregano, and pepper flakes and cook until fragrant, about 1 minute.

3. Add beef mixture, breaking meat into small pieces with wooden spoon, and cook until no longer pink, about 4 minutes. Stir in tomatoes and bring to simmer, scraping up any browned bits. Reduce heat to medium-low and simmer until flavors have melded, about 5 minutes.

4. For the Cream Sauce Whisk all ingredients in bowl until combined.

5. Lay 3 noodles lengthwise in prepared dish with ends touching 1 short side of dish, leaving gap at far end. Lay 1 half noodle crosswise to fill gap (if needed).

6. Spread 1½ cups meat sauce over noodles, followed by ½ cup cream sauce and finally ½ cup mozzarella. Repeat layering of noodles, meat sauce, cream sauce, and mozzarella 3 more times, switching position of half noodle to opposite end of dish each time.

7. Lay remaining 3 noodles over top (there is no half noodle for top layer). Spread remaining cream sauce over noodles, followed by remaining 1 cup mozzarella. Sprinkle Pecorino over top.

8. Spray sheet of aluminum foil with oil spray and cover lasagna. Set lasagna on rimmed baking sheet. Bake for 30 minutes. Discard foil and continue to bake until top layer of lasagna is spotty brown, 25 to 30 minutes longer. Let lasagna cool for 30 minutes. Slice and serve.

To Make Ahead At end of step 7, cover dish with greased aluminum foil and refrigerate for up to 24 hours. When ready to eat, bake lasagna as directed in step 8, increasing covered baking time to 55 minutes.

Why This Recipe Works Meat lasagna can take all day to make, so we tried to streamline the process and also amp up the meatiness. We chose 90 percent lean ground beef for its rich flavor and added a panade—a mixture of bread and milk—to it, which produced a soft-textured, easy-to-layer meat sauce. Instead of a traditional béchamel sauce or layer of grainy ricotta, we created a no-cook cream sauce made with cottage cheese and heavy cream, Pecorino Romano for a bold and salty hit, and cornstarch to bind and thicken it. Since the meat sauce continued to cook in the oven as the lasagna baked, we could skip the long simmer on the stovetop.

Why This Recipe Works To make a spinach lasagna worthy of its name, we increased the amount of spinach. Frozen spinach tasted just as good as fresh and cut down on kitchen time. For the most even texture, we used the food processor to chop the spinach. For extra spinach flavor we included some of the drained spinach liquid (we combined it with the ricotta in the food processor) but not enough to make the lasagna watery. To keep the spinach flavor front and center, we nixed the traditional creamy béchamel in favor of a fresh, herb-flecked tomato sauce but still layered in plenty of mozzarella and Parmesan for richness.

SPINACH AND TOMATO LASAGNA

SERVES 8 TO 10

Our favorite brand of no-boil lasagna noodles is Barilla. You can thaw the spinach overnight in the refrigerator instead of microwaving it, but be sure to warm the spinach liquid to help smooth the ricotta.

30 ounces frozen chopped spinach
2 tablespoons olive oil
1 onion, chopped fine
5 garlic cloves, minced
⅛ teaspoon red pepper flakes
2 (28-ounce) cans crushed tomatoes
Salt and pepper
6 tablespoons chopped fresh basil
1½ pounds (3 cups) whole-milk or part-skim ricotta cheese
3 ounces Parmesan cheese, grated (1½ cups)
2 large eggs
12 no-boil lasagna noodles
12 ounces whole-milk mozzarella cheese, shredded (3 cups)

1. Adjust oven rack to middle position and heat oven to 375 degrees. Microwave spinach in covered large bowl until completely thawed, about 15 minutes, stirring halfway through cooking. Squeeze spinach dry, reserving ⅓ cup liquid. Pulse spinach in food processor until ground, 8 to 10 pulses, scraping down bowl every few pulses. Wipe out large bowl with paper towels. Transfer spinach to now-empty bowl; set aside.

2. Heat oil in large saucepan over medium heat until shimmering. Add onion and cook until softened, about 5 minutes. Stir in garlic and pepper flakes and cook until fragrant, about 30 seconds. Add tomatoes, ½ cup processed spinach, 1 teaspoon salt, and ½ teaspoon pepper and cook until slightly thickened, about 10 minutes. Off heat, stir in 3 tablespoons basil; set aside.

3. Process ricotta and reserved spinach liquid in food processor until smooth, about 30 seconds. Add Parmesan, remaining 3 tablespoons basil, eggs, 1½ teaspoons salt, and ½ teaspoon pepper and process until combined. Stir ricotta mixture into remaining processed spinach.

4. Cover bottom of 13 by 9-inch baking dish with 1¼ cups sauce. Top with 3 noodles and spread one-third of ricotta mixture evenly over noodles. Sprinkle with ⅔ cup mozzarella and cover with 1¼ cups sauce. Repeat twice, beginning with noodles and ending with sauce. Top with remaining 3 noodles, remaining sauce, and remaining 1 cup mozzarella.

5. Cover pan tightly with aluminum foil sprayed with vegetable oil spray and bake until bubbling around edges, about 40 minutes. Discard foil and continue to bake until cheese is melted, about 10 minutes. Let cool on wire rack for 30 minutes. Serve.

Keys to Spinach Flavor

For lasagna that actually tastes like spinach, we took a three-pronged approach.

1. Increasing the amount of spinach to triple the amount called for in most recipes guaranteed it had a distinct presence.
2. Adding some of the spinach water, from squeezing the spinach dry to prevent a soggy lasagna, to the ricotta cheese ensured a creamy, spinach-flavored filling.
3. Chopping the spinach in the food processor produced a fine, even texture that distributed nicely in both the cheese filling and the sauce.

EGGPLANT PECORINO

SERVES 6

Do not use eggplants weighing more than 1 pound each or the slices won't fit in the baking dish. Use a rasp-style grater to grate the Pecorino Romano; shred the fontina on the large holes of a box grater. Depending on the size of your eggplants, you may not need to use all three to get the 20 slices needed to assemble the casserole.

Sauce
- 2 tablespoons unsalted butter
- ¼ cup finely chopped onion
- 3 garlic cloves, minced
- 2 anchovy fillets, rinsed and minced
- ¾ teaspoon table salt
- ¼ teaspoon red pepper flakes
- ¼ teaspoon dried oregano
- 1 (28-ounce) can crushed tomatoes
- 1 (14.5-ounce) can diced tomatoes
- ½ teaspoon sugar
- ¼ cup chopped fresh basil
- 1 tablespoon extra-virgin olive oil

Eggplant
- 3 (10- to 16-ounce) eggplants
- ½ cup all-purpose flour
- 4 large eggs
- 1 cup extra-virgin olive oil, for frying
- 4 ounces Pecorino Romano cheese, grated (2 cups)
- 4 ounces fontina cheese, shredded (1 cup)

1. For the Sauce Melt butter in medium saucepan over medium-low heat. Add onion, garlic, anchovies, salt, pepper flakes, and oregano and cook until onion is softened, about 3 minutes. Stir in crushed tomatoes, diced tomatoes and their juice, and sugar; increase heat to medium-high; and bring to simmer.

Reduce heat to medium-low and simmer until slightly thickened, about 10 minutes. Off heat, stir in basil and oil. Season with salt and pepper to taste. Set aside. (Sauce can be refrigerated for up to 48 hours.)

2. For the Eggplant Cut stem end off eggplants and discard. Cut ¼-inch-thick slice from 1 long side of each eggplant and discard. Using mandoline or slicing knife and starting on cut side, slice eggplants lengthwise ¼ inch thick until you have 20 slices total (you may not need all 3 eggplants).

3. Place flour in shallow dish. Beat eggs in second shallow dish. Line baking sheet with triple layer of paper towels. Heat oil in 12-inch skillet over medium heat to 350 degrees (to take temperature, tilt skillet so oil pools on 1 side). Working with 3 or 4 slices at a time (depending on size of eggplant), dredge eggplant in flour, shaking off excess; dip in egg, allowing excess to drip off; then place in hot oil. Fry until lightly browned on both sides, about 1½ minutes per side. Transfer to prepared sheet. (As eggplant slices cool, you can stack them to make room on sheet.)

4. Adjust oven rack 6 inches from broiler element and heat oven to 375 degrees. Spread 1 cup sauce in bottom of broiler-safe 13 by 9-inch baking dish. Starting with largest slices of eggplant, place 4 eggplant slices side by side over sauce in dish. Spread ½ cup sauce over eggplant, then sprinkle ½ cup Pecorino over top. Repeat layering 3 times to make 4 stacks of 4 slices. Place remaining eggplant slices on top. Spread remaining sauce over top layer of eggplant, then sprinkle with fontina.

5. Bake until bubbling around edges and center of casserole is hot, about 30 minutes. Broil until fontina is lightly browned, 1 to 3 minutes. Let cool for 20 minutes. Serve.

Why This Recipe Works For a more refined take on eggplant Parmesan that showcases the eggplant paired with a rich, bright sauce, we took inspiration from La Campagna, in Westlake, Ohio. For our version, we skipped bread crumbs and instead fried the eggplant in a thin flour and egg coating which created a light, fluffy shell around each thin eggplant slice rather than a thick bready coating. We replaced the traditional Parmesan with Pecorino Romano, which added a nutty, tangy flavor, elevating the mild eggplant. Topping our eggplant stacks with creamy shredded fontina and finishing them under the broiler gave them an irresistible melted browned top.

Why This Recipe Works For fuss-free but flavorful manicotti, we started by substituting no-boil lasagna noodles for the manicotti tubes. Briefly soaking them in hot water made them pliable and easy to roll up. Using the food processor to break down the ground beef allowed its flavor to permeate the sauce quickly so it needed just a short simmer. For even more meaty flavor, we added a popular pizza topping—pepperoni—which gave the sauce a spicy backbone. To liven up the filling, we included assertive provolone, plus a portion of the processed ground beef and pepperoni; a single egg helped to bind it all together.

BAKED MANICOTTI WITH MEAT SAUCE

SERVES 6 TO 8

You will need 16 no-boil lasagna noodles for this recipe. The test kitchen's preferred brand, Barilla, comes 16 noodles to a box, but other brands contain only 12. It is important to let the dish cool for 15 minutes after baking.

Meat Sauce

- 1 onion, chopped
- 6 ounces thinly sliced deli pepperoni
- 1 pound 85 percent lean ground beef
- 5 garlic cloves, minced
- 1 tablespoon tomato paste
- ¼ teaspoon red pepper flakes
- 2 (28-ounce) cans crushed tomatoes
  Salt and pepper

Manicotti

- 1½ pounds (3 cups) ricotta cheese
- 10 ounces mozzarella cheese, shredded (2½ cups)
- 6 ounces provolone cheese, shredded (1½ cups)
- 1 large egg, lightly beaten
- ¼ cup finely chopped fresh basil
- ½ teaspoon salt
- ½ teaspoon pepper
- 16 no-boil lasagna noodles

1. For the Meat Sauce Adjust oven rack to upper-middle position and heat oven to 375 degrees. Pulse onion and pepperoni in food processor until coarsely ground, about 10 pulses. Add beef and pulse until thoroughly combined, 5 to 8 pulses.

2. Transfer mixture to large saucepan and cook over medium heat, breaking up mixture with wooden spoon, until no longer pink, about 5 minutes. Using slotted spoon, transfer 1 cup meat mixture to paper towel–lined plate and reserve. Add garlic, tomato paste, and pepper flakes to pot and cook until fragrant, about 1 minute. Stir in tomatoes and simmer until sauce is slightly thickened, about 20 minutes. Season with salt and pepper to taste. (Meat sauce can be refrigerated for up to 3 days.)

3. For the Manicotti Combine ricotta, 2 cups mozzarella, 1 cup provolone, egg, basil, salt, pepper, and reserved meat mixture in large bowl. Pour 1 inch boiling water into 13 by 9-inch baking dish and slip noodles into water, one at a time. Let noodles soak until pliable, about 5 minutes, separating noodles with tip of knife to prevent sticking. Remove noodles from water and place in single layer on clean dish towels; discard water and dry off baking dish.

4. Spread half of meat sauce over bottom of baking dish. Spread ¼ cup ricotta mixture evenly over bottom of each noodle. Roll noodles up around filling and lay them seam side down in baking dish. Spread remaining sauce over top to cover pasta completely. Cover dish tightly with aluminum foil and bake until bubbling around edges, about 40 minutes. Remove foil and sprinkle with remaining ½ cup mozzarella and ½ cup provolone. Bake until cheese is melted, about 5 minutes. Let cool for 15 minutes. Serve.

Manicotti Made Easy

Manicotti shells are hard to fill without tearing. For easy-to-fill manicotti, we found a better solution in no-boil lasagna noodles.

1. After soaking no-boil lasagna noodles briefly in hot water, spread filling across bottom of each and roll into tube.

2. Arrange rolled manicotti seam side down over sauce in baking dish.

Why This Recipe Works Stuffed shell recipes can be frustrating. For a quicker version of stuffed shells with better results, we got right down to stuffing them. We chose raw jumbo shells with wide openings and piped in the filling. For a supercheesy filling, we mixed creamy ricotta, shredded fontina, and grated Pecorino Romano cheeses with savory minced garlic, fragrant chopped fresh basil, and dried oregano. Adding cornstarch to the ricotta kept it from becoming grainy when baked. Smothering the shells in a thin tomato sauce meant the raw pasta cooked during covered baking, absorbing the liquid while still leaving behind a full-bodied sauce.

CHEESY STUFFED SHELLS

SERVES 6 TO 8

Shred the fontina on the large holes of a box grater. Be sure to use only open, unbroken shells. We developed this recipe using Barilla Jumbo Shells and were able to find at least 25 open shells in each 1-pound box we used. Pipe each shell only about three-quarters full on your first pass, and then divide the remaining filling evenly among the shells.

Sauce

2 tablespoons extra-virgin olive oil
1 onion, chopped
½ teaspoon salt
½ teaspoon pepper
6 garlic cloves, minced
¼ teaspoon red pepper flakes
1 (28-ounce) can tomato puree
2 cups water
1 teaspoon sugar

Filling

10 ounces (1¼ cups) whole-milk ricotta cheese
4 ounces fontina cheese, shredded (1 cup)
2 ounces Pecorino Romano cheese, grated
   (1 cup)
2 large eggs
3 tablespoons chopped fresh basil
1½ tablespoons cornstarch
2 garlic cloves, minced
1 teaspoon dried oregano
½ teaspoon salt

Shells

25 jumbo pasta shells
8 ounces fontina cheese, shredded (2 cups)
1 tablespoon chopped fresh basil

1. For the Sauce Heat oil in large saucepan over medium heat until shimmering. Add onion, salt, and pepper and cook, stirring occasionally, until softened and lightly browned, about 10 minutes.

2. Stir in garlic and pepper flakes and cook until fragrant, about 30 seconds. Stir in tomato puree, water, and sugar and bring to simmer. Reduce heat

to medium-low and cook until flavors have melded, about 5 minutes. (Cooled sauce can be refrigerated for up to 3 days.)

3. For the Filling Stir all ingredients in bowl until thoroughly combined. Transfer filling to pastry bag or large zipper-lock bag (if using zipper-lock bag, cut 1 inch off 1 corner of bag).

4. For the Shells Adjust oven rack to middle position and heat oven to 400 degrees. Place shells open side up on counter. Pipe filling into shells until each is about three-quarters full. Divide remaining filling evenly among shells.

5. Spread 1 cup sauce over bottom of 13 by 9-inch baking dish. Transfer shells, open side up, to prepared dish. Pour remaining sauce evenly over shells to completely cover.

6. Cover dish tightly with aluminum foil and set on rimmed baking sheet. Bake until shells are tender and sauce is boiling rapidly, about 45 minutes. Remove dish from oven and discard foil; sprinkle fontina over top. Bake, uncovered, until fontina is lightly browned, about 15 minutes. Let shells cool for 25 minutes. Sprinkle with basil. Serve.

To Make Ahead At end of step 2, let sauce cool completely. At end of step 5, cover dish tightly with aluminum foil and refrigerate for up to 24 hours. When ready to eat, bake shells as directed in step 6.

Filling Station

We found that it was much easier to fill rigid uncooked pasta shells than it was to work with floppy boiled ones, so we designed a recipe that involved filling raw shells with the cheese mixture, assembling the casserole, and baking it—no precooking of the pasta required.

Sort through a box and select 25 shells that feature wide openings. Use a pastry bag (or a zipper-lock bag with one corner snipped off) to pipe in the cheese mixture until each shell is about three-quarters full (as shown above), and then divide the remaining filling among the shells.

GRANDMA PIZZA

SERVES 4

If the dough snaps back when you press it to the corners of the baking sheet, cover it, let it rest for 10 minutes, and try again.

Dough

- 3 tablespoons olive oil
- ¾ cup water
- 1½ cups (8¼ ounces) bread flour
- 2¼ teaspoons instant or rapid-rise yeast
- 1 teaspoon sugar
- ¾ teaspoon salt

Topping

- 1 (28-ounce) can diced tomatoes
- 1 tablespoon olive oil
- 2 garlic cloves, minced
- 1 teaspoon dried oregano
- ¼ teaspoon salt
- 8 ounces mozzarella cheese, shredded (2 cups)
- ¼ cup grated Parmesan cheese
- 2 tablespoons chopped fresh basil

1. For the Dough Coat rimmed baking sheet with 2 tablespoons oil. Combine water and remaining 1 tablespoon oil in 1-cup liquid measuring cup. Using stand mixer fitted with dough hook, mix flour, yeast, sugar, and salt on low speed until combined. With mixer running, slowly add water mixture and mix until dough comes together, about 1 minute. Increase speed to medium-low and mix until dough is smooth and comes away from sides of bowl, about 10 minutes.

2. Transfer dough to greased baking sheet and turn to coat. Stretch dough to 10 by 6-inch rectangle. Cover loosely with plastic wrap and let rise in warm place until doubled in size, 1 to 1½ hours. Stretch dough to corners of pan, cover loosely with plastic, and let rise in warm place until slightly puffed, about 45 minutes. Meanwhile, adjust oven rack to lowest position and heat oven to 500 degrees.

3. For the Topping Place tomatoes in colander and drain well. Combine drained tomatoes, oil, garlic, oregano, and salt in bowl. Combine mozzarella and Parmesan in second bowl. Sprinkle cheese mixture over dough, leaving ½-inch border around edges. Top with tomato mixture and bake until well browned and bubbling, about 15 minutes. Slide pizza onto wire rack, sprinkle with basil, and let cool for 5 minutes. Serve.

Easy Rise

Our method lets the dough proof right on the sheet. Spread dough on oiled baking sheet, then cover with plastic wrap, set aside, and let rise.

The American Table: Where Was Grandma Pizza Born?

In a 2003 piece in the Long Island newspaper *Newsday*, writer Erica Marcus traced grandma pizza's origins to Umberto's Pizzeria in New Hyde Park. According to Marcus, in the early 1970s proprietor Umberto Corteo would ask his pizza man to create a simple pizza like the one his mother used to make in Italy. The Corteos opened a second pizzeria, King Umberto's, in nearby Elmont. It was later bought by two former Umberto's pizza makers, who built a best-selling item out of their former boss's favorite lunch, naming it grandma pizza sometime in the late 1980s. Within 10 years, other Long Island pizzerias were offering the pie, and a phenomenon was born.

Why This Recipe Works Grandma pizza is a thin-crust pan pizza topped with a modest amount of cheese and chunks of tomatoes. To re-create this Long Island specialty, bread flour and lengthy kneading gave us the chewy crust we wanted, but the dough was difficult to stretch thin. Proofing the dough on the same sheet pan that we used to bake the pizza let it stretch on its own as it proofed. For a fresh, easy tomato topping that wouldn't make our crust soggy, we tossed drained diced tomatoes with salt, olive oil, garlic, and oregano. Baking the pizza on the lowest rack then cooling it on a wire rack perfectly crisped the bottom crust.

Why This Recipe Works Getting crisp pizza crust from your oven can be a challenge, but with just a few tweaks and the right tools, you'll have homemade pizza that's miles better than offerings from the freezer case or the delivery guy. We started by rolling out pizza dough thinly and then gently pressing it into our cast-iron skillet. Heating the pizza dough in the skillet on the stove gave our crust a jump start before going into the oven. Once in the oven, the skillet functioned like a pizza stone and crisped up our crust in just minutes. Our simple, classic pizza toppings—pizza sauce, mozzarella cheese, and basil—allowed our crust to really shine.

CAST-IRON SKILLET PIZZA

SERVES 4

We like to use our Classic Pizza Dough and No-Cook Pizza Sauce (recipes follow); however, you can use ready-made pizza dough and sauce from the local pizzeria or supermarket.

- ¼ cup extra-virgin olive oil
- 1 pound pizza dough, room temperature
- 1 cup pizza sauce
- 12 ounces fresh mozzarella cheese, sliced ¼ inch thick
- 2 tablespoons chopped fresh basil

1. Adjust oven rack to upper-middle position and heat oven to 500 degrees. Grease 12-inch cast-iron skillet with 2 tablespoons oil.

2. Place dough on lightly floured counter, divide in half, and cover with greased plastic wrap. Press and roll 1 piece of dough (keeping remaining dough covered) into 11-inch round. Transfer dough to prepared skillet and gently push it to corners of pan. Spread ½ cup sauce over surface of dough, leaving ½-inch border around edge. Top with half of mozzarella.

3. Set skillet over medium-high heat and cook until outside edge of dough is set, pizza is lightly puffed, and bottom crust is spotty brown when gently lifted with spatula, 2 to 4 minutes. Transfer skillet to oven and bake until edge of pizza is golden brown and cheese is melted, 7 to 10 minutes.

4. Using potholders, remove skillet from oven and slide pizza onto wire rack using spatula; let cool slightly. Sprinkle with 1 tablespoon basil, cut into wedges, and serve. Being careful of hot skillet, repeat with remaining 2 tablespoons oil, dough, sauce, mozzarella, and 1 tablespoon basil. Cut into wedges and serve.

CLASSIC PIZZA DOUGH
MAKES 1 POUND

- 2 cups (11 ounces) plus 2 tablespoons bread flour
- 1⅛ teaspoons instant or rapid-rise yeast
- ¾ teaspoon salt
- 1 tablespoon olive oil
- ¾ cup warm water (110 degrees)

1. Pulse flour, yeast, and salt together in food processor to combine, about 5 pulses. With processor running, add oil, then water, and process until rough ball forms, 30 to 40 seconds. Let dough rest for 2 minutes, then process for 30 seconds longer. (If after 30 seconds dough is very sticky and clings to blade, add extra flour as needed.)

2. Transfer dough to lightly floured counter and knead by hand to form smooth, round ball, about 1 minute. Place dough in large, lightly greased bowl, cover tightly with greased plastic wrap, and let rise until doubled in size, 1 to 1½ hours. (Alternatively, dough can be refrigerated for at least 8 hours or up to 16 hours.)

NO-COOK PIZZA SAUCE
MAKES 2 CUPS
While it is convenient to use ready-made pizza sauce, we think making your own yields tastier results.

- 1 (28-ounce) can whole peeled tomatoes, drained with juice reserved
- 1 tablespoon extra-virgin olive oil
- 1 teaspoon red wine vinegar
- 2 garlic cloves, minced
- 1 teaspoon dried oregano
  Salt and pepper

Process tomatoes with oil, vinegar, garlic, and oregano in food processor until smooth, about 30 seconds. Transfer mixture to 2-cup liquid measuring cup and add tomato juice until sauce measures 2 cups. Season with salt and pepper to taste. (Sauce can be refrigerated for up to 1 week or frozen for up to 1 month.)

SKILLET CHICKEN PARMESAN

SERVES 4

We like the assertive flavor of sharp provolone here, but mild provolone works well, too.

- 2 slices hearty white sandwich bread, torn into large pieces
- 3 tablespoons olive oil
- 2½ ounces Parmesan cheese, grated (1¼ cups)
- ¼ cup chopped fresh basil
- 1 (28-ounce) can crushed tomatoes
- 2 garlic cloves, minced
  Salt and pepper
- 4 (6-ounce) boneless, skinless chicken breasts, trimmed
- ½ cup all-purpose flour
- 3 tablespoons vegetable oil
- 3 ounces mozzarella cheese, shredded (¾ cup)
- 3 ounces provolone cheese, shredded (¾ cup)

1. Pulse bread in food processor to coarse crumbs, about 10 pulses. Toast bread crumbs in 12-inch non-stick skillet over medium-high heat until browned, about 5 minutes, and transfer to bowl. Toss with 1 tablespoon olive oil, ¼ cup Parmesan, and half of basil. In separate bowl, combine remaining 2 tablespoons olive oil, ¼ cup Parmesan, remaining basil, tomatoes, garlic, and salt and pepper to taste.

2. Using sharp knife, and holding chicken securely, slice each breast horizontally into 2 cutlets of even thickness. Place flour in shallow dish. Season chicken with salt and pepper and dredge in flour. Heat 2 tablespoons vegetable oil in now-empty skillet over medium-high heat until shimmering. Add 4 cutlets and cook until golden brown on both sides, about 5 minutes. Transfer to plate and repeat with remaining cutlets and remaining 1 tablespoon vegetable oil.

3. Reduce heat to medium-low and add tomato mixture to now-empty skillet. Return cutlets to pan in even layer, pressing down to cover with sauce. Sprinkle mozzarella, provolone, and remaining ¾ cup Parmesan over chicken. Cover and cook until cheese is melted, about 5 minutes. Sprinkle with bread crumb mixture and serve.

Making Cutlets from Breasts

Use your hand to hold breast in place, keeping your fingers straight and parallel to breast. Starting at thickest end of breast, slice in half horizontally, producing 2 even cutlets.

Shredding Semisoft Cheese

To keep grater holes from clogging, lightly coat side of box grater with vegetable oil spray before shredding cheese.

Why This Recipe Works To streamline chicken Parmesan and still keep its flavors and textures intact, we browned boneless, skinless chicken breasts, which we had sliced into cutlets, in a nonstick pan, then made a simple tomato sauce and simmered the chicken right in the sauce so it could absorb the flavors. For the cheesy layer, we supplemented the traditional mozzarella with provolone (preferably the sharp variety) for a much richer flavor. And rather than breading the chicken, we sprinkled the bread crumbs, which we toasted and seasoned with Parmesan and basil, over the finished dish so they stayed ultra-crisp.

Why This Recipe Works Chicken scampi is a popular restaurant dish, and we wanted to find out why. The dish consists of fried chicken tenders served in the style of shrimp scampi, with a classic lemony, garlicky sauce. To achieve a golden, crisp coating, we dredged chicken tenderloins in egg and flour, shallow-fried them in just 2 tablespoons of oil, and paired them with a garlicky sauce studded with strips of tender red bell pepper. We finished the sauce with lemon for brightness and butter for richness and the proper consistency—perfect for swiping up with crusty bread or pouring over pasta.

CHICKEN SCAMPI

SERVES 4 TO 6

If you can't find chicken tenderloins, slice boneless, skinless chicken breasts lengthwise into ¾-inch-thick strips. You can use torn basil in place of the parsley, if desired. Serve with crusty bread and lemon wedges.

- 2 large eggs
  Salt and pepper
- ¾ cup plus 1 tablespoon all-purpose flour
- 2 pounds chicken tenderloins, trimmed
- 6 tablespoons extra-virgin olive oil
- 1 red bell pepper, stemmed, seeded, and sliced thin
- 8 garlic cloves, sliced thin
- 1¼ cups chicken broth
- ¾ cup dry white wine
- 4 tablespoons unsalted butter, cut into 4 pieces
- 2 tablespoons chopped fresh parsley

1. Lightly beat eggs and ½ teaspoon salt together in shallow dish. Place ¾ cup flour in second shallow dish. Pat chicken dry with paper towels and season with salt and pepper. Working with 1 piece of chicken at a time, dip in eggs, allowing excess to drip off, then dredge in flour, shaking off any excess. Transfer to large plate.

2. Heat 2 tablespoons oil in 12-inch nonstick skillet over medium-high heat until just smoking. Add half of chicken and cook until golden brown and registering 160 degrees, about 3 minutes per side. Transfer chicken to clean plate and tent with aluminum foil. Wipe skillet clean with paper towels and repeat with 2 tablespoons oil and remaining chicken.

3. Wipe skillet clean with paper towels. Heat remaining 2 tablespoons oil in now-empty skillet over medium-high heat until just smoking. Add bell pepper and ½ teaspoon salt and cook until softened and well browned, 5 to 7 minutes. Add garlic and cook until fragrant and golden brown, about 1 minute. Stir in remaining 1 tablespoon flour and cook for 1 minute.

4. Stir in broth and wine and bring to boil, scraping up any browned bits. Cook until mixture is reduced to about 1½ cups, 5 to 7 minutes. Reduce heat to low and stir in butter until melted. Return chicken to skillet and cook, turning to coat with sauce, until heated through, about 2 minutes. Season with salt and pepper to taste. Transfer to shallow serving platter and sprinkle with parsley. Serve.

Why This Recipe Works Chicken scarpariello is an Italian American dish of chicken and sausage in a spicy sauce full of bell peppers, onion, and pickled cherry peppers. We wanted our version to be bright and flavorful, but not too briny or too spicy. Removing the cherry peppers' seeds tempered their heat, and using some of the vinegary cherry pepper brine added extra flavor. After browning the meats, we sautéed the vegetables and then nestled the chicken and sausage in the vegetables to finish cooking in the oven, which kept the chicken skin crispy. A bit of flour and chicken broth created a sauce that coated the chicken and sausage perfectly.

CHICKEN SCARPARIELLO

SERVES 4 TO 6

We used sweet Italian sausage to balance the spiciness of the cherry peppers. Feel free to substitute hot Italian sausage if you prefer a spicier dish.

- 3 pounds bone-in chicken pieces (2 split breasts cut in half crosswise, 2 drumsticks, and 2 thighs), trimmed Salt and pepper
- 1 tablespoon vegetable oil
- 8 ounces sweet Italian sausage, casings removed
- 1 onion, halved and sliced thin
- 1 red bell pepper, stemmed, seeded, and sliced thin
- 5 jarred hot cherry peppers, seeded, rinsed, and sliced thin (½ cup), plus 2 tablespoons brine
- 5 garlic cloves, minced
- 1 teaspoon dried oregano
- 1 tablespoon all-purpose flour
- ¾ cup chicken broth
- 2 tablespoons chopped fresh parsley

1. Adjust oven rack to middle position and heat oven to 350 degrees. Pat chicken dry with paper towels and season with salt and pepper. Heat oil in 12-inch skillet over medium-high heat until just smoking. Add chicken to skillet, skin side down, and cook without moving until well browned, about 5 minutes. Flip chicken and continue to cook until browned on second side, about 3 minutes. Transfer chicken to plate.

2. Add sausage to fat left in skillet and cook, breaking up with spoon, until browned, about 3 minutes. Transfer sausage to paper towel–lined plate.

3. Pour off all but 1 tablespoon fat from skillet and return to medium-high heat. Add onion and bell pepper and cook until vegetables are softened and lightly browned, about 5 minutes. Add cherry peppers, garlic, and oregano and cook until fragrant, about 1 minute. Stir in flour and cook for 30 seconds. Add broth and cherry pepper brine and bring to simmer, scraping up any browned bits.

4. Remove skillet from heat and stir in sausage. Arrange chicken pieces, skin side up, in single layer in skillet and add any accumulated juices. Transfer skillet to oven and cook until breasts register 160 degrees and drumsticks/thighs register 175 degrees, 20 to 25 minutes.

5. Carefully remove skillet from oven (handle will be very hot). Transfer chicken to serving platter. Season onion mixture with salt and pepper to taste, then spoon over chicken. Sprinkle with parsley. Serve.

ITALIAN POT ROAST

SERVES 4 TO 6

Start checking the roast for doneness after 2 hours; if there is a little resistance when prodded with a fork, it's done. Light, sweeter red wines, such as a Merlot or Beaujolais, work especially well with this recipe.

- 1 (3½- to 4-pound) boneless beef chuck-eye roast, trimmed, tied at 1-inch intervals
  Salt and pepper
- 2 tablespoons vegetable oil
- 1 onion, chopped
- 1 celery rib, minced
- 1 pound cremini or white mushrooms, trimmed and quartered
- 2 tablespoons tomato paste
- 1 (14.5-ounce) can diced tomatoes
- ½ cup canned tomato sauce
- ½ cup water
- 1 cup red wine
- 2 teaspoons sugar
- 1 large garlic head, outer papery skins removed, halved
- 1 sprig fresh thyme
- 1 sprig fresh rosemary

1. Adjust oven rack to middle position and heat oven to 300 degrees. Pat roast dry with paper towels and season with salt and pepper.

2. Heat oil in Dutch oven over medium-high heat until just smoking. Brown roast on all sides, 8 to 12 minutes. Transfer roast to large plate. Reduce heat to medium, add onion, celery, mushrooms, and tomato paste and cook until vegetables begin to soften, about 8 minutes. Add diced tomatoes, tomato sauce, water, ½ cup wine, sugar, garlic, and thyme. Add roast, with accumulated juices, to pot and bring to simmer over medium-high heat. Place piece of aluminum foil over pot, cover with lid, and transfer pot to oven.

3. Cook until roast is just fork-tender, 2½ to 3½ hours, turning roast after 1 hour. Remove lid and foil and let roast rest for 30 minutes, skimming fat from surface of liquid after 20 minutes. Transfer roast to carving board and tent with foil.

4. Remove and reserve garlic head and skim remaining fat. Add remaining ½ cup wine to pot, bring to boil over medium-high heat, and cook until sauce begins to thicken, about 12 minutes. Meanwhile, carefully squeeze garlic cloves from their skins and mash into paste. Add rosemary to pot and simmer until fragrant, about 2 minutes. Remove rosemary and thyme sprigs, stir in mashed garlic, and season with salt and pepper to taste.

5. Remove twine from roast and slice meat against grain into ½-inch-thick slices or pull apart into large pieces. Transfer meat to serving platter and pour ¾ cup sauce over meat. Serve, passing remaining sauce separately.

Fit to Be Tied

A tied roast will cook evenly and won't fall apart during the long cooking time. If your roast doesn't come tied, simply tie pieces of kitchen twine around it at 1-inch intervals.

Getting the Garlic Right

Here's how we tone down the garlic in our Italian Pot Roast so it offers mellow, not overpowering, flavor.

1. After slicing whole head of garlic in half, add it to pot to simmer with roast.

2. Once roast is done, squeeze garlic cloves from skins and mash garlic with fork to form paste. Stir garlic paste back into sauce.

Why This Recipe Works The bolder cousin of American-style pot roast, Italian Pot Roast trades the potatoes, carrots, and gravy for mushrooms, onion, and a thick sauce based on tomatoes, red wine, garlic, and herbs. For our version, we started with a chuck-eye roast for its beefy flavor and ample fat. Canned diced tomatoes, tomato sauce, and tomato paste gave us a thick, rich sauce; a double dose of red wine added depth and brightness. Simmering a whole head of garlic with our roast ensured the meat and sauce were infused with mellow garlic flavor.

PORK CHOPS WITH VINEGAR PEPPERS

SERVES 4

Our favorite chicken broth is Swanson Chicken Stock.

3 tablespoons sugar
  Salt and pepper
4 (8- to 10-ounce) bone-in pork rib chops,
  1 inch thick, trimmed
⅓ cup all-purpose flour
2 tablespoons olive oil
1 onion, halved and sliced thin
8 garlic cloves, lightly crushed and peeled
2 anchovy fillets, rinsed, patted dry, and minced
2 cups thinly sliced sweet green vinegar peppers
1 sprig fresh rosemary
1 cup chicken broth
½ cup red wine vinegar
1 tablespoon unsalted butter

1. Dissolve sugar and 3 tablespoons salt in 1½ quarts cold water in large container. Add chops, cover, and refrigerate for 30 minutes or up to 1 hour.

2. Place flour in shallow dish. Remove chops from brine. Pat chops dry with paper towels and season with pepper. Working with 1 chop at a time, dredge both sides in flour, shaking off excess. Heat 1 tablespoon oil in 12-inch skillet over medium-high heat until just smoking. Add chops and cook until well browned on first side, 5 to 7 minutes. Flip chops and cook on second side for 1 minute; transfer to plate, browned side up.

3. Reduce heat to medium and add remaining 1 tablespoon oil, onion, garlic, and anchovies to now-empty skillet. Cook, stirring frequently, until onion is softened and golden brown, 6 to 8 minutes. Add peppers and rosemary and cook until peppers begin to caramelize, about 5 minutes. Add broth and vinegar and bring to boil.

4. Arrange chops, browned side up, in skillet and add any accumulated juices from plate. Reduce heat to low, cover, and simmer until chops register 145 degrees, 6 to 10 minutes. Transfer chops to serving platter and tent loosely with aluminum foil.

5. Increase heat to high and boil sauce until slightly thickened, about 3 minutes. Off heat, stir in butter and season with salt and pepper to taste. Stir any accumulated juices from platter into sauce. Discard rosemary and spoon sauce over chops. Serve.

Finishing a Pan Sauce with Butter

Add butter to pan sauce off heat to prevent butter from separating and leaving an oil slick on top.

Why This Recipe Works Choosing the right pork chop and the right kind of peppers was essential to getting this dish right. We decided on thick-cut, bone-in rib chops, which we brined briefly to ensure seasoned and moist meat. Jarred sweet vinegar peppers held up to braising and had a mild tang that we liked. To give long-cooked flavor to our quick-cooked braising sauce, we added a secret ingredient—anchovy fillets—which contributed savory depth but did not impart any fishy flavor. We thickened the sauce in two ways: by flouring the chops (which also aided browning) and by reducing the sauce slightly after the pork was done.

PROSCIUTTO BREAD

MAKES 2 LOAVES

We love the combination of prosciutto, pepperoni, and capicola in this bread, but you can use 9 ounces of any combination of your favorite cured meats; just be sure to have each sliced ¼ inch thick at the deli counter. Do not use thinly sliced deli meats, as they will adversely affect the bread's texture. Use a mild lager, such as Budweiser; strongly flavored beers will make this bread taste bitter.

3 cups (16½ ounces) bread flour
1½ teaspoons instant or rapid-rise yeast
1 teaspoon salt
1 cup mild lager, room temperature
6 tablespoons water, room temperature
3 tablespoons extra-virgin olive oil
5 ounces (¼-inch-thick) sliced provolone cheese, cut into ½-inch pieces (optional)
3 ounces (¼-inch-thick) sliced prosciutto, cut into ½-inch pieces
3 ounces (¼-inch-thick) sliced pepperoni, cut into ½-inch pieces
3 ounces (¼-inch-thick) sliced capicola, cut into ½-inch pieces
1½ teaspoons coarsely ground pepper
Cornmeal

1. Whisk flour, yeast, and salt together in bowl of stand mixer. Whisk beer, room-temperature water, and oil together in 2-cup liquid measuring cup.

2. Fit mixer with dough hook. Mix flour mixture on low speed while slowly adding beer mixture until cohesive dough starts to form and no dry flour remains, about 2 minutes, scraping down bowl as needed. Increase speed to medium and knead until dough is smooth and elastic and clears sides of bowl, about 8 minutes.

3. Reduce speed to low and add provolone, if using, prosciutto, pepperoni, capicola, and pepper. Continue to knead until combined, about 2 minutes longer (some meats may not be fully incorporated into dough at this point; this is OK). Transfer dough and any errant pieces of meats to lightly floured counter and knead by hand to evenly incorporate meats into dough, about 1 minute.

4. Form dough into smooth, round ball and place seam side down in lightly greased large bowl. Cover tightly with plastic wrap and let dough rise at room temperature until doubled in size, about 1½ hours.

5. Line baking sheet with parchment paper and lightly dust with cornmeal. Turn out dough onto counter and gently press down to deflate any large air pockets. Cut dough into 2 even pieces. Press each piece of dough into 8 by 5-inch rectangle with long side parallel to counter's edge.

6. Working with 1 piece of dough at a time, fold top edge of rectangle down to midline, pressing to seal. Fold bottom edge of rectangle up to midline and pinch to seal. Flip dough seam side down and gently roll into 12-inch loaf with tapered ends. Transfer loaf to 1 side of prepared sheet. Repeat shaping with second piece of dough and place loaf about 3 inches from first loaf on sheet. Cover with greased plastic and let rise at room temperature until puffy and dough springs back slowly when pressed lightly with your finger, about 45 minutes.

7. Adjust oven rack to middle position and heat oven to 450 degrees. Using sharp paring knife in swift, fluid motion, make ½-inch-deep lengthwise slash along top of each loaf, starting and stopping about 1½ inches from ends. Bake until loaves register 205 to 210 degrees, 22 to 25 minutes. Transfer loaves to wire rack and let cool completely, about 3 hours. Serve.

To Make Ahead Make dough through step 3, form into ball, and place seam side down in lightly greased large bowl. Cover tightly with plastic wrap and refrigerate for at least 16 hours or up to 24 hours. Let dough come to room temperature, about 3 hours, before proceeding with step 5.

Shaping the Loaf

After patting half the dough into a rectangle, fold the top down and the bottom up, pressing to seal as you go. Flip it seam down and roll it into a 12-inch loaf.

Why This Recipe Works Prosciutto bread is a specialty at G. Esposito and Sons Jersey Pork Store in Brooklyn: a rustic loaf studded with tiny chunks of cured meats and flavored with black pepper. For a dough with a strong gluten structure that wouldn't collapse under the weight of the meat, we opted for high-protein bread flour. Adding beer boosted the bread's yeasty flavor while cutting down on rising time. Standard thin slices of deli meat got wadded up, but thick slabs cut into ½-inch pieces incorporated nicely. Prosciutto, capicola, and pepperoni gave the bread a balance of peppery sweetness, and provolone underscored the savoriness.

Why This Recipe Works To make zeppoles, a cross between doughnuts and fried dough, we discovered that two leaveners were better than one. Although typically used independently, in the case of these Italian fritters, a combination of baking powder and yeast created the perfect fluffy confection. We fried the wet, sticky dough at 350 degrees, which yielded a crispy exterior that didn't overcook by the time the interior had finished cooking. These light, tender zeppoles are best served warm with a dusting of powdery confectioners' sugar.

ZEPPOLES

MAKES 15 TO 18 ZEPPOLES

This dough is very wet and sticky. If you own a 4-cup liquid measuring cup, you can combine the batter in it to make it easier to tell when it has doubled in volume in step 1. Zeppoles are best served warm.

1⅓ cups (6⅔ ounces) all-purpose flour
1 tablespoon granulated sugar
2 teaspoons instant or rapid-rise yeast
1 teaspoon baking powder
½ teaspoon salt
1 cup warm water (110 degrees)
½ teaspoon vanilla extract
2 quarts peanut or vegetable oil
  Confectioners' sugar

1. Combine flour, granulated sugar, yeast, baking powder, and salt in large bowl. Whisk water and vanilla into flour mixture until fully combined. Cover tightly with plastic wrap and let rise at room temperature until doubled in size, 15 to 25 minutes.

2. Set wire rack in rimmed baking sheet and line rack with triple layer of paper towels. Adjust oven rack to middle position and heat oven to 200 degrees. Add oil to large Dutch oven until it measures about 1½ inches deep and heat over medium-high heat to 350 degrees.

3. Using greased tablespoon measure, add 6 heaping tablespoonfuls of batter to oil. (Use dinner spoon to help scrape batter from tablespoon if necessary.)

Fry until golden brown and toothpick inserted in center of zeppole comes out clean, 2 to 3 minutes, flipping once halfway through frying. Adjust burner, if necessary, to maintain oil temperature between 325 and 350 degrees.

4. Using slotted spoon, transfer zeppoles to prepared wire rack; roll briefly so paper towels absorb grease. Transfer sheet to oven to keep warm. Return oil to 350 degrees and repeat twice more with remaining batter. Dust zeppoles with confectioners' sugar and serve.

Instant Yeast

Instant, or rapid-rise, yeast is much like active dry yeast, but it has undergone a gentler drying process that has not destroyed the outer cells. Instant yeast does not require proofing and can be added directly to the dry ingredients when making bread—hence the name "instant." Our recipes call for instant yeast because it's easier to use. In breads that contain butter, sugar, and other flavorings, we find virtually no difference in flavor between instant and active dry yeasts. If you have a recipe that calls for active dry yeast, you can use instant as long as you reduce the amount of yeast by 25 percent. For example if the recipe calls for 1 packet, or 2¼ teaspoons, of active dry yeast, use 1¾ teaspoons of instant yeast.

the state of grilling

Why This Recipe Works Traditional Hawaiian huli huli chicken is typically something home cooks buy instead of make. The birds are continually basted with a sticky-sweet glaze and "huli"-ed, which means "turned" in Hawaiian. For the teriyaki-like glaze, we developed a version with soy sauce, rice vinegar, ginger, garlic, chili sauce, ketchup, brown sugar, and lots and lots of pineapple juice. We boiled the sauce down until it was thick, glossy, and sweet. To mimic a Hawaiian rotisserie, we spread the coals in a single layer. The direct heat rendered the fat and crisped the skin, but the chicken was far enough from the coals to avoid burning.

HULI HULI CHICKEN

SERVES 4 TO 6

Mesquite wood chips give this recipe the best flavor, but you can substitute another variety.

Chicken

2 (3½- to 4-pound) whole chickens
2 quarts water
2 cups soy sauce
1 tablespoon vegetable oil
6 garlic cloves, minced
1 tablespoon grated fresh ginger

Glaze

3 (6-ounce) cans pineapple juice
¼ cup packed light brown sugar
¼ cup soy sauce
¼ cup ketchup
¼ cup rice vinegar
4 garlic cloves, minced
2 tablespoons grated fresh ginger
2 teaspoons chili-garlic sauce
2 cups wood chips, soaked in water
   for 15 minutes and drained

1. For the Chicken Using kitchen shears, cut along both sides of backbone to remove it. Trim any excess fat or skin at neck. Flip chicken over and, using chef's knife, cut through breastbone to separate chicken into halves. Repeat with other chicken. Combine water and soy sauce in large bowl. Heat oil in large saucepan over medium-high heat until shimmering. Add garlic and ginger and cook until fragrant, about 30 seconds. Stir into soy sauce mixture. Add chicken and refrigerate, covered, for at least 1 hour or up to 8 hours.

2. For the Glaze Combine pineapple juice, sugar, soy sauce, ketchup, vinegar, garlic, ginger, and chili-garlic sauce in empty saucepan and bring to boil. Reduce heat to medium and simmer until thick and syrupy (you should have about 1 cup), 20 to 25 minutes. Using large piece of heavy-duty aluminum foil, wrap soaked chips in foil packet and cut several vent holes in top.

3A. For a Charcoal Grill Open bottom vent halfway. Light large chimney starter three-quarters filled with charcoal briquettes (4½ quarts). When top coals are partially covered with ash, pour evenly over grill. Place foil packet on coals. Set cooking grate in place, cover, and open lid vent halfway. Heat grill until hot and wood chips are smoking, about 5 minutes.

3B. For a Gas Grill Place wood chip packet directly on primary burner. Turn all burners to high, cover, and heat grill until hot and wood chips are smoking, about 15 minutes. Turn all burners to medium-low. (Adjust burners as needed to maintain grill temperature of 350 degrees.)

4. Clean and oil cooking grate. Remove chicken from brine and pat dry with paper towels. Place chicken skin side up on grill (do not place chicken directly above foil packet). Cover and cook chicken until well browned on bottom and thighs register 120 degrees, 25 to 30 minutes. Flip chicken skin side down and continue to cook, covered, until skin is well browned and crisp and thighs register 175 degrees, 20 to 25 minutes longer. Transfer chicken to platter, brush with half of glaze, and let rest for 5 minutes. Serve, passing remaining glaze at table.

To Make Ahead Both brine and glaze can be made ahead and refrigerated for up to 3 days. Do not brine chicken for longer than 8 hours or it will become too salty.

Huli History Lesson

In 1955, Hawaiian chicken farmer Ernie Morgado served local farmers barbecued chickens he'd made with his mom's homemade teriyaki-style sauce. They liked it so much that he launched a catering business using specially designed barbecue troughs that held chicken halves between two grates. When the chickens were ready to turn, the workers would yell "Huli!" ("turn," in Hawaiian), and all the chickens would be rotated in one go. Morgado named his sauce Huli Huli.

CORNELL BARBECUED CHICKEN

SERVES 4 TO 6

Do not brine the chicken longer than 2 hours or the vinegar will turn the meat mushy. Poultry seasoning is a mix of herbs and spices that can be found in the spice aisle of most supermarkets.

Chicken

2 (3½- to 4-pound) whole chickens
¼ cup salt
3½ cups cider vinegar

Seasoning and Sauce

1 tablespoon ground poultry seasoning
  Salt and pepper
½ cup cider vinegar
3 tablespoons Dijon mustard
1 tablespoon chopped fresh sage leaves
1 tablespoon chopped fresh rosemary
½ cup olive oil

1. For the Chicken Using kitchen shears, cut along both sides of backbone to remove it. Trim any excess fat or skin at neck. Flip chicken over and, using chef's knife, cut through breastbone to separate chicken into halves. Repeat with other chicken. In large container, dissolve salt in vinegar and 2 quarts water. Submerge chickens in brine, cover, and refrigerate for 1 to 2 hours.

2. For the Seasoning and Sauce Combine poultry seasoning, 2 teaspoons salt, and 2 teaspoons pepper in small bowl; set aside. Process vinegar, mustard, sage, rosemary, ½ teaspoon salt, and ½ teaspoon pepper in blender until smooth, about 1 minute. With blender running, slowly add oil until incorporated. Transfer vinegar sauce to small bowl and reserve for basting chicken in steps 5 and 6.

3. Remove chickens from brine, pat dry with paper towels, and rub evenly with poultry seasoning mixture. Measure out ¾ cup vinegar sauce and set aside for cooking; reserve remaining sauce for serving.

4A. For a Charcoal Grill Open bottom vent completely. Light large chimney starter three-quarters filled with charcoal briquettes (4½ quarts). When top coals are partially covered with ash, pour evenly over grill. Set cooking grate in place, cover, and open lid vent halfway. Heat grill until hot, about 5 minutes.

4B. For a Gas Grill Turn all burners to high, cover, and heat grill until hot, about 15 minutes. Turn all burners to medium-low. (Adjust burners as needed to maintain grill temperature around 350 degrees.)

5. Clean and oil cooking grate. Place chicken skin side up on grill and brush with 6 tablespoons vinegar sauce for cooking. Cover and cook chicken until well browned on bottom and thighs register 120 degrees, 25 to 30 minutes, brushing with more sauce for cooking halfway through grilling.

6. Flip chicken skin side down and brush with remaining sauce for cooking. Cover and continue to cook chicken until skin is golden brown and crisp and breasts register 160 degrees and thighs register 175 degrees, 20 to 25 minutes longer.

7. Transfer chicken to carving board and let rest for 10 minutes. Carve chicken and serve with reserved sauce.

The Chicken Man of Cornell University

Robert Baker (1921–2006) developed the recipe for Cornell chicken while employed at Pennsylvania State University, but his recipe didn't take off until he had moved on to the Animal Sciences Department at Cornell University (his alma mater) and published it in a school journal. This vinegary chicken wasn't Dr. Baker's only contribution to the culinary world: He also had a hand in developing the vacuum packaging still used by much of the poultry industry and was the inventor of chicken nuggets, turkey ham, and chicken hot dogs.

Why This Recipe Works Invented in the 1940s by Robert Baker, a Cornell University professor, this tangy, crisp-skinned grilled chicken recipe has been a star attraction at the New York State Fair ever since. Grilling two split chickens over gentle direct heat worked best here. To crisp the skin without burning it, we started the chicken skin side up to render the fat slowly, then flipped the chicken skin side down to brown until crisp. The traditional poultry seasoning worked great as a rub but tasted dusty in the sauce, so we replaced it with fresh rosemary and sage. Dijon mustard contributed even more flavor to the sauce and thickened it perfectly.

ALABAMA BARBECUED CHICKEN

SERVES 4 TO 6

Hickory wood chips are traditional here; however, any type of wood chips will work fine. Two medium wood chunks, soaked in water for 1 hour, can be substituted for the wood chips on a charcoal grill.

Sauce

¾ cup mayonnaise
2 tablespoons cider vinegar
2 teaspoons sugar
½ teaspoon prepared horseradish
½ teaspoon salt
½ teaspoon black pepper
¼ teaspoon cayenne pepper

Chicken

1 teaspoon salt
1 teaspoon black pepper
½ teaspoon cayenne pepper
2 (3½- to 4-pound) whole chickens
2 cups wood chips, soaked in water for 15 minutes and drained
1 (13 by 9-inch) disposable aluminum roasting pan (if using charcoal)

1. For the Sauce Process ingredients in blender until smooth, about 1 minute. Refrigerate for at least 1 hour or up to 2 days.

2. For the Chicken Combine salt, pepper, and cayenne in small bowl. Using kitchen shears, cut along both sides of backbone to remove it. Trim any excess fat or skin at neck. Flip chicken over and, using chef's knife, cut through breastbone to separate chicken into halves. Repeat with other chicken. Pat chickens dry with paper towels and rub them evenly with spice mixture. Using large piece of heavy-duty aluminum foil, wrap soaked chips in foil packet and cut several vent holes in top.

3A. For a Charcoal Grill Open bottom vent halfway and place disposable pan in center of grill. Light large chimney starter filled with charcoal briquettes (6 quarts). When top coals are partially covered with ash, pour into 2 even piles on either side of pan. Place wood chip packet on 1 pile of coals. Set cooking grate in place, cover, and open lid vent halfway. Heat grill until hot and wood chips are smoking, about 5 minutes.

3B. For a Gas Grill Place wood chip packet directly on primary burner. Turn all burners to high, cover, and heat grill until hot and wood chips are smoking, about 15 minutes. Turn all burners to medium-low. (Adjust burners as needed to maintain grill temperature around 350 degrees.)

4. Clean and oil cooking grate. Place chicken skin side down on grill (in center of grill if using charcoal). Cover (positioning lid vent over chicken if using charcoal) and cook chicken until well browned on bottom and thighs register 120 degrees, 35 to 45 minutes.

5. Flip chicken skin side up. Cover and continue to cook chicken until skin is golden brown and crisp and breasts register 160 degrees and thighs register 175 degrees, 15 to 20 minutes longer.

6. Transfer chicken to carving board and brush with 2 tablespoons sauce. Tent chicken with foil and let rest for 10 minutes. Brush chicken with remaining sauce, carve, and serve.

Keeping BBQ in the Family

Big Bob Gibson's, famous for its white mayonnaise-based sauce, has been serving hickory-smoked barbecue in Decatur, Alabama, since 1925. Now run by Big Bob's grandchildren and great-grandchildren, the restaurant has expanded several times. The current pit smoker can cook 175 chickens, 110 slabs of ribs, and 60 whole turkeys at the same time. Although Big Bob used the sauce mostly on chicken, his grandson Don McLemore says nowadays people put it on everything from pork to potato chips.

Why This Recipe Works For Alabama-inspired barbecued chicken, we ditched the tomato and slathered a mayonnaise-based sauce on hickory-smoked chicken. Smoking generally takes hours, but our recipe expedites the process by cutting the chickens in half and cooking them in the middle of the grill, sandwiched between piles of smoking coals topped with hickory chips. We coated our chickens with the traditional Alabama mixture of seasoned mayonnaise and vinegar two times during cooking so the hot chicken absorbed the sauce and was flavored through and through.

Why This Recipe Works Despite its popularity, barbecued chicken recipes cause grillers plenty of headaches. Most recipes call for searing chicken quickly over high heat, but we found that starting the chicken over low heat slowly rendered the fat without the danger of flare-ups. Using a method called "grill roasting" ensured that we had almost completely cooked chicken before we were ready to add our sauce. We created a thick, complex layer of barbecue flavor for our grilled chicken by applying the sauce in coats and turning the chicken frequently as it cooked over moderate heat and then finishing it over higher heat.

CLASSIC BARBECUED CHICKEN

SERVES 4 TO 6

Don't try to grill more than 10 pieces of chicken at a time; you won't be able to line them up on the grill as directed in step 5.

Quick Barbecue Sauce

- 3 cups store-bought barbecue sauce
- ½ cup molasses
- ½ cup ketchup
- ¼ cup cider vinegar
- 3 tablespoons brown mustard
- 2 teaspoons onion powder
- 1 teaspoon garlic powder

Chicken

- 1 teaspoon salt
- 1 teaspoon pepper
- ¼ teaspoon cayenne pepper
- 3 pounds bone-in chicken pieces, breasts halved crosswise and leg quarters separated into thighs and drumsticks, trimmed
- 1 (13 by 9-inch) disposable aluminum roasting pan (if using charcoal)

1. For the Quick Barbecue Sauce Whisk all ingredients in medium saucepan and bring to boil over medium-high heat. Reduce heat to medium and cook until sauce is thick and reduced to 3 cups, about 20 minutes. (Sauce can be refrigerated for up to 1 week.)

2. For the Chicken Combine salt, pepper, and cayenne in small bowl. Pat chicken dry with paper towels and rub evenly with spice mixture.

3A. For a Charcoal Grill Open bottom vent completely. Place disposable pan on 1 side of grill. Light large chimney starter filled with charcoal briquettes (6 quarts). When top coals are partially covered with ash, pour evenly over half of grill, opposite pan. Set cooking grate in place, cover, and open lid vent completely. Heat grill until hot, about 5 minutes.

3B. For a Gas Grill Turn all burners to high, cover, and heat grill until hot, about 15 minutes. Leave primary burner on high and turn other burner(s) off. (Adjust primary burner as needed to maintain grill temperature around 350 degrees.)

4. Clean and oil cooking grate. Place chicken, skin side down, on cool side of grill. Cover (positioning lid vent over chicken if using charcoal) and cook until chicken begins to brown, 30 to 35 minutes. Reserve 2 cups barbecue sauce for cooking; set aside remaining 1 cup sauce for serving.

5. Slide chicken into single line between hot and cool sides of grill and continue to cook, uncovered, flipping chicken and brushing with half of sauce for cooking every 5 minutes, until sticky, about 20 minutes.

6. Slide chicken to hot side of grill and continue to cook, flipping and brushing chicken with remaining sauce for cooking, until well glazed and breasts register 160 degrees and thighs/drumsticks register 175 degrees, about 5 minutes.

7. Transfer chicken to platter, tent loosely with aluminum foil, and let rest for 10 minutes. Serve with reserved sauce.

Barbecued Chicken, Slow and Low

First grill roasting, then basting over moderate heat, and finally finishing with more basting over higher heat ensures rendered, saucy, perfectly cooked chicken.

1. Cook chicken skin side down and covered on cool side of grill for about 30 minutes.

2. Move chicken into a single line near coals; baste and turn chicken. Then move pieces directly over coals to caramelize sauce.

GRILLED JERK CHICKEN

SERVES 4

Plan ahead: The chicken needs to marinate for at least 1 hour before cooking. Use more or fewer habaneros depending on your desired level of spiciness. You can also remove the seeds and ribs from the habaneros or substitute jalapeños for less heat. We recommend wearing rubber gloves or plastic bags on your hands when handling the chiles. Use thyme sprigs with a generous amount of leaves; there's no need to separate the leaves from the stems. Keep a close eye on the chicken in step 5 since it can char quickly.

  4 scallions
  ¼ cup vegetable oil
  ¼ cup soy sauce
  2 tablespoons cider vinegar
  2 tablespoons packed brown sugar
1–2 habanero chiles, stemmed
 10 sprigs fresh thyme
  5 garlic cloves, peeled
2½ teaspoons ground allspice
1½ teaspoons table salt
  ½ teaspoon ground cinnamon
  ½ teaspoon ground ginger
  3 pounds bone-in chicken pieces (split breasts cut in half crosswise, drumsticks, and/or thighs), trimmed
     Lime wedges

1. Process scallions, oil, soy sauce, vinegar, sugar, habanero(s), thyme sprigs, garlic, allspice, salt, cinnamon, and ginger in blender until smooth, about 30 seconds, scraping down sides of blender jar as needed. Measure out ¼ cup marinade and refrigerate until ready to use.

2. Place chicken and remaining marinade in 1-gallon zipper-lock bag. Press out air, seal bag, and turn to coat chicken in marinade. Refrigerate for at least 1 hour or up to 24 hours, turning occasionally.

3A. For a Charcoal Grill Open bottom vent completely. Light large chimney starter mounded with charcoal briquettes (7 quarts). When top coals are partially covered with ash, pour evenly over half of grill. Set cooking grate in place, cover, and open lid vent completely. Heat grill until hot, about 5 minutes.

3B. For a Gas Grill Turn all burners to high, cover, and heat grill until hot, about 15 minutes. Leave primary burner on high and turn off other burner(s). (Adjust primary burner [or, if using 3-burner grill, primary burner and second burner] as needed to maintain grill temperature between 450 and 500 degrees.)

4. Clean and oil cooking grate. Place chicken skin side up on cooler side of grill, with breast pieces farthest away from heat. Cover and cook until breasts register 160 degrees and drumsticks/thighs register 175 degrees, 22 to 30 minutes, transferring pieces to plate, skin side up, as they come to temperature. (Re-cover grill after checking pieces for doneness.)

5. Brush skin side of chicken with half of reserved marinade. Place chicken skin side down on hotter side of grill. (Turn all burners to high if using gas.) Brush with remaining reserved marinade and cook until lightly charred, 1 to 3 minutes per side. Check browning often and move pieces as needed to avoid flare-ups.

6. Transfer chicken to platter, tent with aluminum foil, and let rest for 5 to 10 minutes. Serve with lime wedges.

Why This Recipe Works Our bold but nuanced grilled jerk chicken starts with the paste. A blend of habaneros, scallions, garlic, and thyme sprigs made a big herby punch. Soy sauce added savory depth, cider vinegar brightness, and warm spices characteristic jerk flavor. After marinating the chicken, we cooked it on the cooler side of the grill, covered, which helped the marinade stick. Once the chicken was cooked through, we brushed it with a little marinade for a fresh burst of jerk flavor and seared it on the hotter side of the grill. Tasters preferred the chicken charred, not smoked per tradition, because the jerk flavor came through more clearly.

Why This Recipe Works The combination of bourbon and smoke flavors sounded perfect, but first we had get the savory taste we wanted while keeping the chicken from drying out. The key was a mopping sauce: a sauce that is applied during long-grilling recipes to help keep the meat moist. And since smoke is attracted to moisture, keeping the chicken skin damp enhanced the smoky flavor. For even tastier chicken, we split them in half and cut slashes into the meat to create more surface area to soak up the flavor. By basting the chicken every 15 minutes, we ended up with moist, browned chicken with smokin' good bourbon taste.

SMOKED BOURBON CHICKEN

SERVES 4

Use a bourbon you'd be happy drinking. Use all the basting liquid in step 5.

1¼ cups bourbon
1¼ cups soy sauce
½ cup packed brown sugar
1 shallot, minced
4 garlic cloves, minced
2 teaspoons pepper
2 (3½- to 4-pound) whole chickens, giblets discarded
1 cup wood chips
4 (12-inch) wooden skewers

1. Bring bourbon, soy sauce, sugar, shallot, garlic, and pepper to boil in medium saucepan over medium-high heat and cook for 1 minute. Remove from heat and let cool completely. Set aside ¾ cup bourbon mixture for basting chicken. (Bourbon mixture can be refrigerated for up to 3 days.)

2. With chickens breast side down, using kitchen shears, cut through bones on both sides of backbones; discard backbones. Flip chickens and, using chef's knife, split chickens in half lengthwise through centers of breastbones. Cut ½-inch-deep slits across breasts, thighs, and legs, about ½ inch apart. Tuck wingtips behind backs. Divide chicken halves between two 1-gallon zipper-lock bags and divide remaining bourbon mixture between bags. Seal bags, turn to distribute marinade, and refrigerate for at least 1 hour or up to 24 hours, flipping occasionally.

3. Just before grilling, soak wood chips in water for 15 minutes, then drain. Using large piece of heavy-duty aluminum foil, wrap soaked chips in foil packet and cut several vent holes in top. Remove chicken halves from marinade and pat dry with paper towels; discard marinade. Insert 1 skewer lengthwise through thickest part of breast down through thigh of each chicken half.

4A. For a Charcoal Grill Open bottom vent halfway. Light large chimney starter filled with charcoal briquettes (6 quarts). When top coals are partially covered with ash, pour into steeply banked pile against side of grill. Place wood chip packet on coals. Set cooking grate in place, cover, and open lid vent halfway. Heat grill until hot and wood chips are smoking, about 5 minutes.

4B. For a Gas Grill Remove cooking grate and place wood chip packet directly on primary burner. Set grate in place, turn all burners to high, cover, and heat grill until hot and wood chips are smoking, about 15 minutes. Leave primary burner on high and turn off other burners. (Adjust primary burner as needed to maintain grill temperature between 350 to 375 degrees.)

5. Clean and oil cooking grate. Place chicken halves skin side up on cooler side of grill with legs pointing toward fire. Cover and cook, basting every 15 minutes with reserved bourbon mixture, until breasts register 160 degrees and thighs register 175 degrees, 75 to 90 minutes, switching placement of chicken halves after 45 minutes. (All of bourbon mixture should be used.) Transfer chicken to carving board, tent loosely with foil, and let rest for 20 minutes. Carve and serve.

How to Cut a Chicken in Half

1. Remove backbone
Using poultry shears, cut through bones on both sides of backbone; discard backbone.

2. Cut through breast
Flip chicken and use chef's knife to halve chicken through center of breastbone.

GRILLED BUTTERFLIED LEMON CHICKEN

SERVES 8

Chicken and Rub

2 (3½- to 4-pound) whole chickens
2 teaspoons grated lemon zest (reserve lemon for vinaigrette)
2 teaspoons salt
1 teaspoon pepper
1 (13 by 9-inch) disposable aluminum roasting pan (if using charcoal)

Vinaigrette

4 lemons, halved; plus zested, halved lemon from rub
2 tablespoons minced fresh parsley
2 teaspoons Dijon mustard
1 garlic clove, minced
1 teaspoon sugar
½ teaspoon salt
½ teaspoon pepper
⅔ cup extra-virgin olive oil

1. For the Chicken and Rub Set wire rack in rimmed baking sheet. With 1 chicken breast side down, using kitchen shears, cut along both sides of backbone to remove it. Flip chicken and flatten breastbone. Use your hands to loosen skin over breast and thighs and remove any excess fat. Repeat with other chicken. Combine lemon zest, salt, and pepper in bowl. Rub zest mixture under chicken skin and tuck wings behind back. Transfer chickens to prepared baking sheet and refrigerate, uncovered, for 30 minutes. (Chickens may be prepared up to this point 24 hours in advance; allow chickens to sit at room temperature for 30 minutes before grilling.)

2A. For a Charcoal Grill Open bottom vent completely and place disposable pan on 1 side of grill. Light large chimney starter filled with charcoal briquettes (6 quarts). When top coals are partially covered in ash, pour into steeply banked pile against side of grill (opposite disposable pan). Evenly scatter 20 unlit coals on top of hot coals. Set cooking grate in place, cover, and open lid vent completely. Heat grill until hot, about 5 minutes.

2B. For a Gas Grill Turn all burners to high, cover, and heat grill until hot, about 15 minutes. Leave primary burner on high and turn off other burner(s). (Adjust primary burner as needed to maintain grill temperature around 350 degrees.)

3. Clean and oil cooking grate. Place lemon halves, cut side down, on hot side of grill and cook until deep brown and caramelized, 5 to 8 minutes. Transfer to bowl.

4. Place chicken skin side down on cool side of grill, with legs closer to hot side. Cover (positioning lid vent over chicken if using charcoal) and cook until skin is well browned, 45 to 55 minutes.

5. Slide chicken to hot side of grill and continue to cook (covered if using gas) until deeply browned and breasts register 160 degrees and thighs register 175 degrees, about 5 minutes longer. Transfer chicken to carving board, tent loosely with aluminum foil, and let rest for 10 minutes.

6. For the Vinaigrette While chicken cooks, squeeze ⅓ cup juice from grilled lemons into bowl. Stir in parsley, mustard, garlic, sugar, salt, and pepper, then slowly whisk in oil until emulsified.

7. Carve chicken and transfer to serving platter. Pour ⅓ cup vinaigrette over chicken and serve, passing remaining vinaigrette separately.

Butterflying a Whole Chicken

1. Cut through bones on either side of backbone and trim any excess fat or skin at neck.

2. Flip chicken and use heel of your hand to flatten breastbone.

Why This Recipe Works For perfectly grilled butterflied lemon chicken, we banked all the coals on one side of the grill, placing the chicken opposite the coals and setting the lid on the grill. This allowed the fat under the chicken's skin to render slowly and the relatively gentle heat resulted in a moister bird. Placing the chicken on the grill skin side down reduced cooking time and allowed the most fat to render—a final sear directly over the dying coals at the end of cooking crisped and browned the skin nicely. To finish the chicken with intense lemon flavor, we caramelized lemon halves over the grill and made a sauce from their juice.

Why This Recipe Works To get crisp, well-rendered chicken wings, we tossed the wings in cornstarch and pepper and grilled them over a gentle medium-low heat. We began grilling with the thicker skin side facing up so that the fat could slowly render, and then we flipped the wings at the end of cooking to crisp the skin. Also, though we normally cook white chicken meat to 160 degrees, wings are chock-full of collagen, which begins to break down upwards of 170 degrees. Cooking the wings to 180 degrees produced meltingly tender wings.

GRILLED CHICKEN WINGS

MAKES 24 WINGS

If you buy whole wings, cut them into two pieces before brining. Don't brine the wings for more than 30 minutes or they'll be too salty.

½ cup salt
2 pounds chicken wings, wingtips discarded, trimmed
1½ teaspoons cornstarch
1 teaspoon pepper

1. Dissolve salt in 2 quarts cold water in large container. Prick chicken wings all over with fork. Submerge chicken in brine, cover, and refrigerate for 30 minutes.

2. Combine cornstarch and pepper in bowl. Remove chicken from brine and pat dry with paper towels. Transfer wings to large bowl and sprinkle with cornstarch mixture, tossing until evenly coated.

3A. For a Charcoal Grill Open bottom vent completely. Light large chimney starter half filled with charcoal briquettes (3 quarts). When top coals are partially covered with ash, pour evenly over grill. Set cooking grate in place, cover, and open lid vent completely. Heat grill until hot, about 5 minutes.

3B. For a Gas Grill Turn all burners to high, cover, and heat grill until hot, about 15 minutes. Turn all burners to medium-low.

4. Clean and oil cooking grate. Grill wings (covered if using gas), thicker skin side up, until browned on bottom, 12 to 15 minutes. Flip chicken and grill until skin is crisp and lightly charred and meat registers 180 degrees, about 10 minutes. Transfer chicken to platter, tent loosely with aluminum foil, and let rest for 5 to 10 minutes. Serve.

BBQ GRILLED CHICKEN WINGS

Reduce pepper to ½ teaspoon. Add 1 teaspoon chili powder, 1 teaspoon paprika, ½ teaspoon garlic powder, ½ teaspoon dried oregano, and ½ teaspoon sugar to cornstarch mixture in step 2.

CREOLE GRILLED CHICKEN WINGS

Add ¾ teaspoon dried oregano, ½ teaspoon garlic powder, ½ teaspoon onion powder, ½ teaspoon white pepper, and ¼ teaspoon cayenne pepper to cornstarch mixture in step 2.

TANDOORI GRILLED CHICKEN WINGS

Reduce pepper to ½ teaspoon. Add 1 teaspoon garam masala, ½ teaspoon ground cumin, ¼ teaspoon garlic powder, ¼ teaspoon ground ginger, and ⅛ teaspoon cayenne pepper to cornstarch mixture in step 2.

Prepping Grilled Chicken Wings

1. Puncturing each wing with fork lets brine easily penetrate meat and helps fat render away.

2. Quick saltwater brine seasons wings and keeps them juicy.

3. Dusting wings with cornstarch and black pepper prevents sticking and encourages crisping.

Why This Recipe Works It's possible to make great fried chicken without deep frying. We found a way to get deeply seasoned meat and a crunchy coating on the grill. We separated whole chicken wings into drumettes and flats and brined them to ensure they stayed moist. Then we coated the chicken with heavily seasoned flour and built a hot fire with the coals banked on one side of the grill. We put the chicken on the cooler side of the grill, to cook until the coating was dry and set. Then, to get the fried texture we were looking for, we brushed the wings with vegetable oil halfway through cooking, which helped the coating turn golden brown.

GRILL-FRIED CHICKEN WINGS

SERVES 4 TO 6

We prefer to buy whole chicken wings and butcher them ourselves because they tend to be larger than wings that come presplit. If you can find only pre-split wings, opt for larger ones, if possible. Ideally, 12 whole wings should equal 3 pounds, which will yield 24 pieces of chicken (12 drumettes and 12 flats, tips discarded) once broken down. Do not brine the chicken for longer than 3 hours in step 1 or it will become too salty. Charcoal grills tend to produce more-intense heat than gas grills do, hence the difference in cooking times.

  Salt and pepper
¼ cup sugar
3 pounds chicken wings, cut at joints, wingtips discarded
2 cups all-purpose flour
1 tablespoon granulated garlic
2 teaspoons paprika
½ teaspoon cayenne pepper
3 tablespoons vegetable oil

1. Dissolve ¼ cup salt and sugar in 2 quarts cold water in large container. Add chicken and refrigerate, covered, for at least 1 hour or up to 3 hours.

2. Set wire rack in rimmed baking sheet. Whisk flour, granulated garlic, paprika, cayenne, 1 tablespoon pepper, and 1 teaspoon salt together in large bowl. Remove chicken from brine. Working in batches of four, dredge chicken pieces in flour mixture, pressing to adhere. Place chicken on prepared rack. Refrigerate chicken, uncovered, for at least 30 minutes or up to 2 hours.

3A. For a Charcoal Grill Open bottom vent completely. Light large chimney starter mounded with charcoal briquettes (7 quarts). When top coals are partially covered with ash, pour into steeply banked pile against side of grill. Set cooking grate in place, cover, and open lid vent completely. Heat grill until hot, about 5 minutes.

3B. For a Gas Grill Turn all burners to high, cover, and heat grill until hot, about 15 minutes. Turn primary burner to high and turn off other burner(s). (Adjust primary burner [or, if using three-burner grill, primary burner and second burner] as needed to maintain grill temperature of 425 degrees.)

4. Clean and oil cooking grate. Place chicken, fatty side up, on cooler side of grill, arranging drumettes closest to coals. Cook chicken, covered, until lightly browned and coating is set, about 30 minutes for charcoal or about 45 minutes for gas.

5. Brush chicken with oil until no traces of flour remain (use all oil). Cover and continue to cook until coating is golden brown and chicken registers between 180 and 200 degrees, about 30 minutes longer for charcoal or about 45 minutes longer for gas. Transfer chicken to clean wire rack and let cool for 10 minutes. Serve.

BUFFALO-STYLE GRILL-FRIED CHICKEN WINGS

Add ½ cup Frank's RedHot Original Cayenne Pepper Sauce to brine in step 1. While chicken is cooling, microwave ½ cup Frank's RedHot Original Cayenne Pepper Sauce and 4 tablespoons unsalted butter in covered large bowl until butter is melted, about 1 minute. Whisk to fully combine. Add chicken and toss to coat before serving.

SMOKED CHICKEN WINGS

SERVES 4 TO 6

We prefer to buy whole wings and butcher them ourselves because they tend to be larger than wings that come split. If you can find only split wings, look for larger ones. Twelve whole wings should ideally equal 3 pounds and will yield 24 pieces (12 drumettes and 12 flats, tips discarded). Do not brine the chicken for longer than 3 hours in step 1 or it will become too salty.

Wings

¼ cup table salt, for brining
¼ cup sugar, for brining
3 pounds chicken wings, cut at joints, wingtips discarded
2 teaspoons paprika
2 teaspoons chili powder
1¼ teaspoons dried oregano
1¼ teaspoons pepper
1¼ teaspoons garlic powder
1 teaspoon sugar
¼ teaspoon cayenne pepper
2 cups wood chips

Sauce

4 tablespoons unsalted butter
2 tablespoons cider vinegar
2 tablespoons ketchup
¼ teaspoon table salt

1. For the Wings Dissolve salt and ¼ cup sugar in 2 quarts cold water in large container. Submerge wings in brine, cover, and refrigerate for at least 1 hour or up to 3 hours. Combine paprika, chili powder, oregano, pepper, garlic powder, 1 teaspoon sugar, and cayenne in bowl. Measure out 1 tablespoon spice mixture and set aside.

2. For the Sauce Melt butter in small saucepan over medium-low heat. Add reserved 1 tablespoon spice mixture and cook until fragrant, about 30 seconds. Carefully add vinegar (mixture will bubble up). Bring to quick simmer, then remove from heat. Whisk in ketchup and salt. Cover and set aside.

3. Remove wings from brine and pat dry with paper towels. Sprinkle wings all over with remaining spice mixture.

4. Just before grilling, soak wood chips in water for 15 minutes, then drain. Using large piece of heavy-duty aluminum foil, wrap soaked chips in 8 by 4½-inch foil packet. (Make sure chips do not poke holes in sides or bottom of packet.) Cut 2 evenly spaced 2-inch slits in top of packet.

5A. For a Charcoal Grill Open bottom vent completely. Light large chimney starter mounded with charcoal briquettes (7 quarts). When top coals are partially covered with ash, place wood chip packet on 1 side of grill and pour coals evenly over half of grill, covering wood chip packet. Set cooking grate in place, cover, and open lid vent completely. Heat grill until hot and wood chips are smoking, about 5 minutes.

5B. For a Gas Grill Remove cooking grate and place wood chip packet directly on primary burner. Turn all burners to high, cover, and heat grill until hot and wood chips are smoking, about 15 minutes. Leave primary burner on high and turn off other burner(s). (Adjust primary burner [or, if using 3-burner grill, primary burner and second burner] as needed to maintain grill temperature of 400 degrees.)

6. Clean and oil cooking grate. Place wings, fatty side up, on cooler side of grill, arranging drumettes closest to coals. Cover and cook until wings are darkened in color and meat registers at least 180 degrees, about 40 minutes, flipping wings halfway through cooking.

7A. For a Charcoal Grill Slide half of wings to hotter side of grill and cook, uncovered, until charred in spots, 1 to 3 minutes per side. Transfer wings to platter and tent with foil. Repeat with remaining wings.

7B. For a Gas Grill Turn all burners to high and cook, uncovered, until wings are charred in spots, 5 to 7 minutes per side. Transfer wings to platter and tent with foil.

8. Reheat sauce over medium heat, about 2 minutes. Toss wings and sauce together in bowl. Serve.

Why This Recipe Works We wanted smoked wings with tender, juicy meat; a balanced, pronounced smokiness; and crisp, fully rendered skin. Our wings got a quick brine before they hit the grill to keep the meat from drying out. A spice rub including paprika, chili powder, oregano, garlic powder, and cayenne gave the wings heat and aromatic complexity. To let the wings cook through with plenty of smoke, we built a two-level fire in the grill, starting them over indirect heat and then moving them over the coals to sear and crisp the skin. To make the wings shine, we mixed melted butter with cider vinegar and ketchup to create a savory sauce.

GRILLED CHICKEN LEG QUARTERS

SERVES 4

A garlic press makes quick work of mincing the 6 cloves called for here. You can use 1 teaspoon of dried oregano in place of the fresh called for in the dressing. Do not use dried cilantro.

- 6 garlic cloves, minced
- 4 teaspoons kosher salt
- 1 tablespoon sugar
- 2 teaspoons grated lime zest plus 2 tablespoons juice
- 2 teaspoons plus ¼ cup extra-virgin olive oil
- 1½ teaspoons ground cumin
- 1 teaspoon pepper
- ½ teaspoon cayenne pepper
- 4 (10-ounce) chicken leg quarters, trimmed
- 2 tablespoons chopped fresh cilantro
- 2 teaspoons chopped fresh oregano

1. Combine garlic, salt, sugar, lime zest, 2 teaspoons oil, cumin, pepper, and cayenne in bowl and mix to form paste. Reserve 2 teaspoons garlic paste for dressing.

2. Position chicken skin side up on cutting board and pat dry with paper towels. Leaving drumsticks and thighs attached, make 4 parallel diagonal slashes in chicken: 1 across drumsticks, 1 across leg joints; and 2 across thighs (each slash should reach bone). Flip chicken over and make 1 more diagonal slash across back of drumsticks. Rub remaining garlic paste all over chicken and into slashes. Refrigerate chicken for at least 1 hour or up to 24 hours.

3A. For a Charcoal Grill Open bottom vent completely. Light large chimney starter filled with charcoal briquettes (6 quarts). When top coals are partially covered with ash, pour two-thirds evenly over half of grill, then pour remaining coals over other half of grill. Set cooking grate in place, cover, and open lid vent completely. Heat grill until hot, about 5 minutes.

3B. For a Gas Grill Turn all burners to high, cover, and heat grill until hot, about 15 minutes. Turn primary burner to medium and turn other burner(s) to low. (Adjust primary burner as needed to maintain grill temperature of 400 to 425 degrees.)

4. Clean and oil cooking grate. Place chicken on cooler side of grill, skin side up. Cover and cook until underside of chicken is lightly browned, 9 to 12 minutes. Flip chicken, cover, and cook until leg joint registers 165 degrees, 7 to 10 minutes.

5. Transfer chicken to hotter side of grill, skin side down, and cook (covered if using gas) until skin is well browned, 3 to 5 minutes. Flip chicken and continue to cook until leg joint registers 175 degrees, about 3 minutes longer. Transfer to platter, tent loosely with aluminum foil, and let rest for 5 to 10 minutes.

6. Meanwhile, whisk lime juice, remaining ¼ cup oil, cilantro, oregano, and reserved garlic paste together in bowl. Spoon half of dressing over chicken and serve, passing remaining dressing separately.

Making Flavorful, Well-Cooked Chicken Leg Quarters

1. Slash Make bone-deep slashes in each quarter so the seasonings can penetrate and the meat cooks more readily.

2. Rub Massage the garlicky seasoning paste into the slashes and all over the chicken and refrigerate for up to 24 hours.

Why This Recipe Works Chicken leg quarters seem like a perfect candidate for the grill—the rich leg and thigh meat has plenty of skin to crisp up. But the thick joint takes longer to cook than the rest of the leg, so grilling often results in overcooking. To remedy this, we took a two-pronged approach. To prepare the chicken, we made slashes down to the bone, a technique often used for large cuts of meat. This helped the chicken cook evenly, and also ensured deep seasoning. We then used our two-level grilling technique, starting the chicken over a low flame, then searing it over a hot fire. A citrus-y dressing provided a welcome hit of brightness.

BBQ CHICKEN THIGHS

SERVES 4 TO 6

The seasoned chicken thighs need to sit for 1 hour before grilling. We prefer Frank's RedHot Original Cayenne Pepper Sauce for this recipe. If you use Tabasco, reduce the amount to 2 teaspoons in the broth mixture and 1 teaspoon in the glaze.

- 2 tablespoons packed brown sugar
- 1 tablespoon kosher salt
- 1 tablespoon paprika
- 1 teaspoon pepper
- 1 teaspoon white pepper
- ¾ teaspoon granulated garlic
- 4 pounds bone-in chicken thighs, trimmed
- 1 (13 by 9-inch) disposable aluminum roasting pan
- ½ cup plus 2 tablespoons bottled barbecue sauce
- ½ cup chicken broth
- 7 garlic cloves (6 sliced thin, 1 minced)
- 3 tablespoons Worcestershire sauce
- 3 tablespoons hot sauce
- 2 tablespoons apple jelly
- 1½ cups wood chips

1. Combine 1 tablespoon sugar, salt, paprika, pepper, white pepper, and granulated garlic in bowl. Set aside 4 teaspoons spice mixture. Place chicken in disposable pan and season all over with remaining spice mixture. Flip chicken skin side down and let sit at room temperature for 1 hour.

2. Meanwhile, whisk ½ cup barbecue sauce, broth, sliced garlic, Worcestershire sauce, and 2 tablespoons hot sauce together in bowl; set aside. In separate bowl, microwave jelly until melted, about 30 seconds. Stir minced garlic, remaining 2 tablespoons barbecue sauce, remaining 1 tablespoon sugar, and remaining 1 tablespoon hot sauce into jelly; set glaze aside.

3. Just before grilling, soak wood chips in water for 15 minutes, then drain. Using large piece of heavy-duty aluminum foil, wrap soaked chips in foil packet and cut several vent holes in top.

4A. For a Charcoal Grill Open bottom vent completely. Light large chimney starter mounded with charcoal briquettes (7 quarts). When top coals are partially covered with ash, pour into steeply banked pile against side of grill. Place wood chip packet on coals. Set cooking grate in place, cover, and open lid vent completely. Heat grill until hot and wood chips are smoking, about 5 minutes.

4B. For a Gas Grill Remove cooking grate and place wood chip packet directly on primary burner. Set grate in place, turn all burners to high, cover, and heat grill until hot and wood chips are smoking, about 15 minutes. Leave primary burner on high and turn off other burners. (Adjust primary burner as needed to maintain grill temperature of 350 to 375 degrees.)

5. Pour broth mixture over chicken in pan. Place pan on cooler side of grill, cover (positioning lid vent over chicken for charcoal), and cook for 30 minutes (chicken will be about 140 degrees).

6. Remove pan from grill. Using tongs, transfer chicken skin side up to cooler side of grill. (Discard cooking liquid.) Brush chicken skin with half of glaze, then sprinkle with reserved spice rub. Cover and cook for 15 minutes.

7. Brush chicken skin with remaining glaze. Cover and cook until glaze has set and chicken registers 175 degrees, 25 to 30 minutes longer. Transfer chicken to platter, tent loosely with foil, and let rest for 15 minutes. Serve.

Why This Recipe Works For juicy grilled chicken thighs slick with a shiny barbecue glaze, we started by applying a sweet-meets-spicy rub. We braised spice-rubbed chicken thighs in a pan of flavorful bottled barbecue sauce and chicken broth. After 30 minutes, we poured off the cooking liquid, applied a sticky glaze and more spice rub, and arranged the thighs directly on the grill to render the skin. With a final layer of glaze and a brief rest, we had the ultimate finger-licking chicken.

Why This Recipe Works To make a chicken diavolo that was fiery and smoky, we took it to the grill. A mixture of herbs, spices, lemon, oil, sugar, and both black and red pepper performed double duty as a marinade and as a sauce. We built a two-level fire, starting the chicken on the cooler side of the grill to cook through and then searing it over the hotter side to char the outside and crisp the skin. For extra smoky flavor, we added a foil-wrapped packet of soaked wood chips. We cooked the reserved marinade mixture to mellow the garlic bite, added a shot of lemon juice, and spooned our supercharged vinaigrette over the grilled chicken.

GRILLED CHICKEN DIAVOLO

SERVES 4

If you are buying a whole chicken and cutting it into pieces yourself, reserve the backbone and wings to make stock. To use wood chunks on a charcoal grill, substitute one medium wood chunk, soaked in water for 1 hour, for the wood chip packet.

    3   pounds bone-in chicken pieces (split breasts
        cut in half, drumsticks, and/or thighs),
        trimmed
    ½   cup extra-virgin olive oil
    4   garlic cloves, minced
    1   tablespoon chopped fresh rosemary
    2   teaspoons grated lemon zest plus
        4 teaspoons juice
    2   teaspoons red pepper flakes
    1   teaspoon sugar
        Salt and pepper
    ½   teaspoon paprika
    1   cup wood chips

1. Pat chicken dry with paper towels. Whisk oil, garlic, rosemary, lemon zest, pepper flakes, sugar, 1 teaspoon pepper, and paprika together in bowl until combined. Reserve ¼ cup oil mixture for sauce. (Oil mixture can be covered and refrigerated for up to 24 hours.) Whisk 2¼ teaspoons salt into oil mixture remaining in bowl and transfer to 1-gallon zipper-lock bag. Add chicken, turn to coat, and refrigerate for at least 1 hour or up to 24 hours. Just before grilling, soak wood chips in water for 15 minutes, then drain. Using large piece of heavy-duty aluminum foil, wrap soaked chips in foil packet and cut several vent holes in top.

2A. For a Charcoal Grill Open bottom vent halfway. Light large chimney starter filled with charcoal briquettes (6 quarts). When top coals are partially covered with ash, pour two-thirds evenly over half of grill, then pour remaining coals over other half of grill. Place wood chip packet on larger pile of coals. Set cooking grate in place, cover, and open lid vent halfway. Heat grill until hot and wood chips are smoking, about 5 minutes.

2B. For a Gas Grill Place wood chip packet over primary burner. Turn all burners to high, cover, and heat grill until hot and wood chips are smoking, about 15 minutes. Turn primary burner to medium and turn other burner(s) to low. (Adjust primary burner as needed to maintain grill temperature of 400 to 425 degrees.)

3. Remove chicken from marinade and pat dry with paper towels. Discard used marinade. Clean and oil cooking grate. Place chicken on cooler side of grill, skin side up. Cover and cook until underside of chicken is lightly browned, 8 to 12 minutes. Flip chicken, cover, and cook until white meat registers 155 degrees and dark meat registers 170 degrees, 7 to 10 minutes.

4. Transfer chicken to hotter side of grill, skin side down, and cook (covered if using gas) until skin is well browned, about 3 minutes. Flip and continue to cook (covered if using gas) until white meat registers 160 degrees and dark meat registers 175 degrees, 1 to 3 minutes. Transfer chicken to platter, tent loosely with foil, and let rest for 5 to 10 minutes.

5. Meanwhile, heat reserved oil mixture in small saucepan over low heat until fragrant and garlic begins to brown, 3 to 5 minutes. Off heat, whisk in lemon juice and ¼ teaspoon salt. Spoon sauce over chicken. Serve.

The Right Fire

A two-level fire lets us gently cook the chicken on the cooler side and then sear it on the hotter side for flavorful char. To get good smoky flavor, we place an aluminum foil–wrapped packet of soaked wood chips on the larger pile of charcoal.

Why This Recipe Works Barbecuing is the perfect method for cooking fatty cuts of pork or beef, but relatively lean chicken is another story. For barbecued pulled chicken with a smoky flavor and moist, tender meat, we'd have to come up with some tricks. Brining the birds kept the white meat moist and juicy, and arranging the chickens on the grill with the breast meat farther from the heat source than the dark meat evened out the cooking times. We tweaked our favorite barbecue sauce to better complement the chicken, increasing the vinegar to balance the sweetness and swapping the root beer for coffee to boost the smoky flavor.

BARBECUED PULLED CHICKEN

MAKES ENOUGH FOR 8 SANDWICHES

We prefer to halve the chickens ourselves, but you may be able to buy halved chickens from your butcher.

Chicken

1 cup salt
2 (4-pound) whole chickens, giblets discarded
Pepper
2 cups wood chips, soaked in water
for 15 minutes and drained

Sauce

2 teaspoons vegetable oil
1 onion, chopped fine
4 cups chicken broth
1¼ cups cider vinegar
1 cup brewed coffee
¾ cup molasses
½ cup tomato paste
½ cup ketchup
2 tablespoons brown mustard
1 tablespoon hot sauce
½ teaspoon garlic powder
¼ teaspoon liquid smoke

1. For the Chicken Dissolve salt in 4 quarts cold water in large container. Remove backbones from chickens and split chickens in half lengthwise through center of breastbone. Using metal skewer, poke 20 holes all over each chicken half. Submerge chicken halves in brine, cover, and refrigerate for 1 hour. Remove chicken halves from brine, pat dry with paper towels, and season with pepper. Using large piece of heavy-duty aluminum foil, wrap soaked wood chips in foil packet and cut several vent holes in top.

2. For the Sauce Meanwhile, heat oil in Dutch oven over medium-high heat until shimmering. Add onion and cook until softened, about 5 minutes. Whisk in broth, vinegar, coffee, molasses, tomato paste, ketchup, mustard, hot sauce, and garlic powder and bring to boil. Reduce heat to medium-low and simmer until mixture is thick and reduced to 4 cups, about 65 to 75 minutes. Stir in liquid smoke; reserve 1 cup sauce for serving. (Sauce can be refrigerated for up to 2 days.)

3A. For a Charcoal Grill Open bottom vent halfway. Light large chimney starter filled with charcoal briquettes (6 quarts). When top coals are partially covered with ash, pour into steeply banked pile against side of grill. Place wood chip packet on coals. Set cooking grate in place, cover, and open lid vent halfway. Heat grill until hot and wood chips are smoking, about 5 minutes.

3B. For a Gas Grill Place wood chip packet over primary burner. Turn all burners to high, cover, and heat grill until hot and wood chips are smoking, about 15 minutes. Leave primary burner on high and turn off other burner(s).

4. Clean and oil cooking grate. Place chicken halves skin side up on cool side of grill with legs closest to heat source. Cover and cook until breasts register 160 degrees and thighs register 175 degrees, 75 to 85 minutes. Transfer chicken to carving board, tent loosely with foil, and let rest until cool enough to handle, about 15 minutes. Remove and discard skin. Pull meat off bones, separating dark and light meat. Roughly chop dark meat into ½-inch pieces. Shred white meat into thin strands.

5. Add chicken to pot with sauce and cook over medium-low heat until chicken is warmed through, about 5 minutes. Serve on hamburger rolls, passing reserved sauce separately.

Why This Recipe Works We love a good pulled pork sandwich, so we were interested in an equally moist, smoky version using turkey. Salting the turkey a day ahead helped keep the lean meat juicy. Positioning the boneless breasts on the grill so that the thicker ends were closer to the heat source evened out the cooking time. We then transferred the breasts to a disposable pan partway through cooking and topped them with butter to add richness and help keep the meat moist. And for even more moisture, we mixed the shredded meat with the juices and butter leftover in the pan. The crowning touch was a tangy white barbecue sauce.

TENNESSEE PULLED TURKEY SANDWICHES

SERVES 8 TO 10

We prefer a natural (unbrined) turkey breast here, but both self-basting and kosher work well. Plan ahead: The salted meat needs to be refrigerated for at least 8 hours. Skip the salting step if you buy a kosher or self-basting breast. Some stores sell only boneless turkey breasts with the skin still attached; the skin can be removed easily with a paring knife. If you don't have ½ cup of juices from the rested turkey, supplement with chicken broth.

Turkey

- 2 (1¾- to 2-pound) boneless, skinless split turkey breasts, trimmed
  Kosher salt and pepper
- 2 cups wood chips
- ½ teaspoon cayenne pepper
- 1 (13 by 9-inch) disposable aluminum roasting pan
- 4 tablespoons unsalted butter, cut into 4 pieces

White Barbecue Sauce

- 1 cup mayonnaise
- ⅓ cup cider vinegar
- 1 tablespoon prepared horseradish, drained
- 1½ teaspoons kosher salt
- 1 teaspoon Worcestershire sauce
- 1 garlic clove, minced
- 1 teaspoon pepper
- ¼ teaspoon cayenne pepper

- 8 hamburger buns
  Shredded iceberg lettuce

1. For the Turkey Pat turkey dry with paper towels, place on large sheet of plastic wrap, and sprinkle with 1 tablespoon salt. Wrap in plastic and refrigerate for at least 8 hours or overnight.

2. Just before grilling, soak wood chips in water for 15 minutes, then drain. Using large piece of heavy-duty aluminum foil, wrap soaked chips in 8 by 4½-inch foil packet. (Make sure chips do not poke holes in sides or bottom of packet.) Cut 2 evenly spaced 2-inch slits in top of packet.

3A. For a Charcoal Grill Open bottom vent completely. Light large chimney starter three-quarters filled with charcoal briquettes (4½ quarts). When top coals are partially covered with ash, pour evenly over half of grill. Place wood chip packet on coals. Set cooking grate in place, cover, and open lid vent completely. Heat grill until hot and wood chips are smoking, about 5 minutes.

3B. For a Gas Grill Remove cooking grate and place wood chip packet directly on primary burner. Set grate in place, turn all burners to high, cover, and heat grill until hot and wood chips are smoking, about 15 minutes. Leave primary burner on medium-high and turn off other burner(s). (Adjust primary burner as needed to maintain grill temperature between 300 and 350 degrees.)

4. Clean and oil cooking grate. Unwrap turkey and sprinkle with 2 teaspoons pepper and cayenne. Place turkey on cooler side of grill, with thicker parts of breasts closest to fire. Cover grill (positioning lid vent directly over turkey if using charcoal) and cook until breasts register 120 degrees, 30 to 40 minutes.

5. Transfer turkey to disposable pan and top with butter. Cover pan tightly with foil and return to cooler side of grill. Cover grill and continue to cook until breasts register 160 degrees, 25 to 35 minutes longer. Remove pan from grill and let turkey rest in covered pan for 20 minutes.

6. For the White Barbecue Sauce Whisk all ingredients in bowl until smooth.

7. Transfer turkey to cutting board. Using two forks or your hands, shred turkey into bite-size pieces. Transfer to large bowl. Add ½ cup juices from pan to shredded turkey and toss to combine. Season with salt and pepper to taste.

8. Serve turkey on buns with white barbecue sauce and lettuce.

BARBECUED BURNT ENDS

SERVES 8 TO 10

Look for a brisket with a significant fat cap. This recipe takes about 8 hours to prepare. The meat can be brined ahead of time, transferred to a zipper-lock bag, and refrigerated for up to a day. If you don't have ½ cup of juices from the rested brisket, supplement with beef broth.

Brisket and Rub

- 2 cups plus 1 tablespoon kosher salt
- ½ cup granulated sugar
- 1 (5- to 6-pound) beef brisket, flat cut, untrimmed
- ¼ cup packed brown sugar
- 2 tablespoons pepper
- 4 cups wood chips
- 1 (13 by 9-inch) disposable aluminum roasting pan (if using charcoal) or 2 (8½ by 6-inch) disposable aluminum pans (if using gas)

Barbecue Sauce

- ¾ cup ketchup
- ¼ cup packed brown sugar
- 2 tablespoons cider vinegar
- 2 tablespoons Worcestershire sauce
- 2 teaspoons granulated garlic
- ¼ teaspoon cayenne pepper

1. For the Brisket and Rub Dissolve 2 cups salt and granulated sugar in 4 quarts cold water in large container. Slice brisket with grain into 1½-inch-thick strips. Add brisket strips to brine, cover, and refrigerate for 2 hours. Remove brisket from brine and pat dry with paper towels.

2. Combine brown sugar, pepper, and remaining 1 tablespoon salt in bowl. Season brisket all over with rub. Just before grilling, soak wood chips in water for 15 minutes, then drain. Using 2 large pieces of heavy-duty aluminum foil, wrap soaked chips in 2 foil packets and cut several vent holes in tops.

3A. For a Charcoal Grill Open bottom vent halfway and place disposable pan filled with 2 quarts water on one side of grill, with long side of pan facing

center of grill. Arrange 3 quarts unlit charcoal briquettes on opposite side of grill and place 1 wood chip packet on coals. Light large chimney starter filled halfway with charcoal briquettes (3 quarts). When top coals are partially covered with ash, pour evenly over unlit coals and wood chip packet. Place remaining wood chip packet on lit coals. Set cooking grate in place, cover, and open lid vent halfway. Heat grill until hot and wood chips are smoking, about 5 minutes.

3B. For a Gas Grill Add ½ cup ice cubes to 1 wood chip packet. Remove cooking grate and place both wood chip packets directly on primary burner; place disposable pans each filled with 2 cups water directly on secondary burner(s). Set grate in place, turn all burners to high, cover, and heat grill until hot and wood chips are smoking, about 15 minutes. Leave primary burner on high and turn off other burner(s). (Adjust primary burner as needed to maintain grill temperature of 275 to 300 degrees.)

4. Clean and oil cooking grate. Arrange brisket on cooler side of grill as far from heat source as possible. Cover (positioning lid vent over brisket for charcoal) and cook without opening for 3 hours.

5. Adjust oven rack to middle position and heat oven to 275 degrees. Remove brisket from grill and transfer to rimmed baking sheet. Cover sheet tightly with foil. Roast until fork slips easily in and out of meat and meat registers 210 degrees, about 2 hours. Remove from oven, leave covered, and let rest for 1 hour. Remove foil, transfer brisket to carving board, and pour accumulated juices into fat separator.

6. For the Barbecue Sauce Combine ketchup, sugar, vinegar, Worcestershire, granulated garlic, cayenne, and ½ cup defatted brisket juices in medium saucepan. Bring to simmer over medium heat and cook until slightly thickened, about 5 minutes.

7. Cut brisket strips crosswise into 1- to 2-inch chunks. Combine brisket chunks and barbecue sauce in large bowl and toss to combine. Serve.

Why This Recipe Works Burnt ends are the extra crispy and slightly meaty pieces left after cutting brisket. They are the brainchild of Arthur Bryant, a legendary African American barbecuer in Kansas City who gave them to his customers as they waited for their food instead of throwing them away. Real burnt ends are all about moist meat and flavorful, charred bark, but most pit masters use fatty point-cut brisket. To make leaner, more widely available flat-cut brisket work, we cut it into strips and brined it for maximum moisture and flavor. Three hours of smoke on the grill plus a few hours in a low oven ensured tender brisket with plenty of char.

Why This Recipe Works Shashlik—a favorite street food in the Caucasus—is a grilled kebab with juicy, well-charred meat with a vibrant marinade. We chose sirloin steak tips because their loose grain enables them to soak up more marinade and they have big, beefy flavor. For our marinade we blended red wine vinegar, vegetable oil, chopped onion, and garlic with a blend of warm cumin, citrusy coriander, savory bay leaf, and aromatic cinnamon. Adding a little sugar and grilling the kebabs over a hot fire gave us excellent charring in spite of the wet marinade. A tangy sauce of caramelized onion and tart yogurt provided the perfect complement to the flame-kissed beef.

SHASHLIK-STYLE BEEF KEBABS

SERVES 4 TO 6

Sirloin steak tips are often sold as flap meat; we prefer to buy one large piece and cut it into pieces ourselves. We cook this beef past medium-rare in order to get more charring and to keep it from being too chewy. If you prefer it less cooked, remove it from the grill sooner (125 degrees for medium-rare).

Marinade

- ½ cup coarsely chopped onion
- ¼ cup vegetable oil
- 2 tablespoons red wine vinegar
- 4 garlic cloves
- 1 tablespoon soy sauce
- 1 tablespoon kosher salt
- 1 tablespoon sugar
- 1 teaspoon ground cumin
- ½ teaspoon pepper
- ½ teaspoon ground coriander
- ¼ teaspoon ground cinnamon
- ¼ teaspoon cayenne pepper
- 1 bay leaf, crumbled

Beef and Sauce

- 2 pounds sirloin steak tips, trimmed and cut into 1-inch pieces
- 1 onion, chopped fine
- ⅓ cup water
- 1 tablespoon vegetable oil
- ½ cup plain whole-milk yogurt
- ⅓ cup chopped fresh cilantro
- 2 teaspoons lemon juice
- 6 (10-inch) wooden skewers, soaked in water for at least 30 minutes

1. For the Marinade Process all ingredients in blender until smooth, about 30 seconds. Measure out 2 tablespoons marinade and set aside.

2. For the Beef and Sauce Combine beef and remaining marinade in 1-gallon zipper-lock bag. Press out air, seal bag, and turn to coat beef in marinade. Refrigerate for 1 to 2 hours.

3. While beef marinates, combine onion, water, oil, and reserved marinade in 10-inch skillet. Cover and cook over medium-high heat until liquid has evaporated and onion is beginning to brown, 5 to 7 minutes, stirring occasionally. Uncover, reduce heat to medium, and continue to cook until onion is well browned, 8 to 10 minutes longer. Transfer onion to bowl and stir in yogurt, cilantro, and lemon juice. Season with salt and pepper to taste.

4. Thread beef tightly onto skewers, leaving ends of skewers slightly exposed.

5A. For a Charcoal Grill Open bottom vent completely. Light large chimney starter mounded with charcoal briquettes (7 quarts). When top coals are partially covered with ash, pour evenly over half of grill. Set cooking grate in place, cover, and open lid vent completely. Heat grill until hot, about 5 minutes.

5B. For a Gas Grill Turn all burners to high, cover, and heat grill until hot, about 15 minutes. Leave all burners on high.

6. Clean and oil cooking grate. Arrange kebabs on grill (over hotter side if using charcoal) and cook (covered if using gas), turning every 2 to 3 minutes, until beef is well browned, charred around edges, and registering between 135 and 145 degrees, 8 to 12 minutes. Transfer kebabs to platter, tent with aluminum foil, and let rest for 5 minutes. Serve with sauce.

GRILLED BOURBON STEAKS

SERVES 6 TO 8

Use a bourbon you'd be happy drinking. Plan ahead: These steaks need to marinate for at least 4 hours before grilling.

- 1 cup bourbon
- 1 cup Worcestershire sauce
- 1 shallot, minced
- 2 garlic cloves, minced
  Kosher salt and pepper
- 4 (1-pound) boneless rib-eye steaks, 1 to 1½ inches thick, trimmed
- 2 tablespoons vegetable oil

1. Whisk bourbon, Worcestershire, shallot, garlic, 2 teaspoons salt, and 2 teaspoons pepper together in bowl. Place 2 steaks in each of two 1-gallon zipper-lock bags and divide bourbon mixture between bags, about 1 cup each. Seal bags, turn to distribute marinade, and refrigerate for at least 4 hours or up to 24 hours, flipping occasionally.

2. Remove steaks from marinade and pat dry with paper towels; discard marinade. Brush steaks all over with oil and season liberally with salt and pepper.

3A. For a Charcoal Grill Open bottom vent completely. Light large chimney starter filled with charcoal briquettes (6 quarts). When top coals are partially covered with ash, pour evenly over grill. Set cooking grate in place, cover, and open lid vent completely. Heat grill until hot, about 5 minutes.

3B. For a Gas Grill Turn all burners to high, cover, and heat grill until hot, about 15 minutes. Turn all burners to medium-high. (Adjust burners as needed to maintain grill temperature between 350 and 400 degrees.)

4. Clean and oil cooking grate. Place steaks on grill and cook (covered if using gas) until well charred and meat registers 125 degrees (for medium-rare), 6 to 8 minutes per side.

5. Transfer steaks to wire rack set in rimmed baking sheet, tent with aluminum foil, and let rest for 10 minutes. Serve.

The World of Whiskey

The word "whiskey" comes from the Celtic word "uisqebaugh" (whis-kee-BAW), meaning "water of life." It is traditionally made from barley, corn, rye, wheat, or oats, but artisanal makers now incorporate everything from buckwheat to farro to spelt.

A whiskey's distinct flavor is determined by a number of factors including the type of grain used, the aging time, the type of wood in which it is stored, and the distillation method. There are many types of whiskey, but American, Irish, Canadian, and Scotch are the most widely consumed. (Scotch and Canadian whiskys drop the e.)

AMERICAN
- Bourbon is the most popular form of American whiskey.
- It must contain at least 51 percent corn.
- It must be aged in charred new oak barrels for two years.
- Bourbon can't go into the barrel for aging at higher than a 62.5-percent alcohol level.

IRISH
- Irish whiskey is made from a blend of malted barley (grain that's been germinated or sprouted, which converts its starch to sugar) and unmalted barley.
- It's aged in wood for a minimum of three years.
- Often, it is triple-distilled, so it's extra-smooth.

CANADIAN
- Canadian whisky is typically made from a base whisky (usually a mix of grains but predominantly corn) and a flavoring whisky (often rye).
- Fifty-one percent of each batch must be aged in wood for three years.

SCOTCH
- Single-malt scotches are made from malted barley.
- Blends are made from a mix of single malt(s) and grain whisky made from various unmalted grains.
- Scotch whisky is usually distilled twice and is aged in oak for three years.

Why This Recipe Works We tried the Whiskey Steak at Jesse's Restaurant in Magnolia Springs, Alabama, and it was something special. Why marinate rib eyes in bourbon? The bourbon not only enhances the beef's meatiness, it also increases the char. To maximize the steaks' flavor, we soaked four hefty rib eyes in a mixture of bourbon, Worcestershire, shallot, and garlic. After marinating the meat for four hours, we fired up the grill, brushed the steaks with oil and a liberal dose of salt and pepper, and cooked them to a juicy medium-rare. The boozy marinade really delivered, giving us sweet-savory flavors and perfect char.

GRILLED THICK-CUT PORTERHOUSE STEAKS

SERVES 6

Flare-ups may occur when grilling over charcoal. If the flames become constant, slide the steaks to the cooler side of the grill until the flames die down.

2 (2½- to 3-pound) porterhouse steaks, 2 inches thick, fat trimmed to ¼ inch
   Kosher salt and pepper
4 teaspoons olive oil (if using gas)
3 tablespoons unsalted butter, melted

1. Pat steaks dry with paper towels and sprinkle each side of each steak with 1 teaspoon salt. Transfer steaks to large plate and refrigerate, uncovered, for at least 1 hour or up to 24 hours.

2A. For a Charcoal Grill Open bottom vent completely. Light large chimney starter filled with charcoal briquettes (6 quarts). When top coals are partially covered with ash, pour evenly over half of grill. Set cooking grate in place, cover, and open lid vent completely. Heat grill until hot, about 5 minutes.

2B. For a Gas Grill Turn all burners to high, cover, and heat grill until hot, about 15 minutes. Leave primary burner on high and turn off other burner(s). (Adjust primary burner [or, if using three-burner grill, primary burner and second burner] as needed to maintain grill temperature of 450 degrees.)

3. Pat steaks dry with paper towels. If using gas, brush each side of each steak with 1 teaspoon oil. Sprinkle each side of each steak with ½ teaspoon pepper.

4. Clean and oil cooking grate. Place steaks on hotter side of grill, with tenderloins facing cooler side. Cook (covered if using gas) until evenly charred on first side, 6 to 8 minutes. Flip steaks and position so tenderloins are still facing cooler side of grill. Continue to cook (covered if using gas) until evenly charred on second side, 6 to 8 minutes longer.

5. Flip steaks and transfer to cooler side of grill, with bone side facing fire. Cover and cook until thermometer inserted 3 inches from tip of strip side of steak registers 115 to 120 degrees (for medium-rare), 8 to 12 minutes, flipping halfway through cooking. Transfer steaks to wire rack set in rimmed baking sheet, tent with aluminum foil, and let rest for 10 minutes.

6. Stir ¼ teaspoon salt into melted butter. Transfer steaks to carving board. Carve strips and tenderloins from bones. Place bones on platter. Slice steaks thin against grain, then reassemble sliced steaks around bones. Drizzle with melted butter and season with salt and pepper to taste. Serve.

Orienting the Steaks on the Grill

1. Tenderloins Face the Cooler Side Char steaks on hotter side of grill for 6 to 8 minutes on each side with tenderloins facing cooler side of grill, then flip and turn steaks so tenderloins are still facing cooler side.

2. Bones Face the Fire Flip steaks and cook for 8 to 12 minutes on cooler side of grill, with bone sides positioned so that they are facing fire. To check temperatures, insert thermometer 3 inches from tips of strip sides of each steak.

Why This Recipe Works A giant, special-occasion steak can vex even experienced grillers. We wanted a simple route to perfect medium-rare. Setting up a half-grill fire with a cooler side and a hotter side allowed us to control the amount of crusty exterior and achieve a rosy interior for these steaks. To protect the leaner, quicker-cooking tenderloin portion of the porterhouse, we positioned the steaks with the tenderloins facing the cooler side of the grill. The T-shaped bone acted as a heat shield, further protecting the tenderloins from the heat. A final drizzle of melted butter added an even richer flavor before serving.

Why This Recipe Works With sizzling meat and an array of charred vegetables, fajitas are always an exciting option at a Tex-Mex restaurant. For an at-home version, we marinated beefy and rich skirt steak in soy sauce to enhance its meaty flavor and pineapple juice for balanced sweetness and acidity. Leaving bell peppers whole and onions in thick rounds secured by toothpicks prevented any from slipping through the grates. We seared them over a hot fire before moving them to the cooler side of the grill to gently steam in a disposable pan while we cooked our steak on the hotter side, yielding tender meat with a caramelized exterior.

GRILLED STEAK FAJITAS

SERVES 6

Serve the fajitas with Pico de Gallo (recipe follows), avocado pieces or guacamole, sour cream, and lime wedges. One (6-ounce) can of pineapple juice will yield ¾ cup. We cook the skirt steak to between medium and medium-well so that its texture is less chewy and the steak is therefore easier to eat.

¾ cup pineapple juice
½ cup plus 1 tablespoon vegetable oil
¼ cup soy sauce
3 garlic cloves, minced
2 pounds skirt steak, trimmed and cut crosswise into 6 equal pieces
3 yellow, red, orange, or green bell peppers
1 large red onion, sliced into ½-inch-thick rounds
  Salt and pepper
12 (6-inch) flour tortillas
1 (13 by 9-inch) disposable aluminum pan
1 tablespoon chopped fresh cilantro

1. Whisk pineapple juice, ½ cup oil, soy sauce, and garlic together in bowl. Reserve ¼ cup marinade. Transfer remaining 1¼ cups marinade to 1-gallon zipper-lock bag. Add steak, press out air, seal bag, and turn to distribute marinade. Refrigerate for at least 2 hours or up to 24 hours.

2. Using paring knife, cut around stems of bell peppers and remove cores and seeds. Push toothpick horizontally through each onion round to keep rings intact while grilling. Brush bell peppers and onion evenly with remaining 1 tablespoon oil and season with salt and pepper. Remove steak from marinade and pat dry with paper towels; discard marinade. Sprinkle steak with ¾ teaspoon salt and ½ teaspoon pepper. Wrap tortillas in aluminum foil; set aside.

3A. For a Charcoal Grill Open bottom vent completely. Light large chimney starter filled with charcoal briquettes (6 quarts). When top coals are partially covered with ash, pour evenly over half of grill. Set cooking grate in place, cover, and open lid vent completely. Heat grill until hot, about 5 minutes.

3B. For a Gas Grill Turn all burners to high, cover, and heat grill until hot, about 15 minutes.

Leave primary burner on high and turn other burner(s) to low.

4. Clean and oil cooking grate. Place bell peppers and onion on hotter side of grill and place tortilla packet on cooler side of grill. Cook (covered if using gas) until vegetables are char-streaked and tender, 8 to 13 minutes, flipping and moving as needed for even cooking, and until tortillas are warmed through, about 10 minutes, flipping halfway through cooking.

5. Remove tortillas from grill; keep wrapped and set aside. Transfer vegetables to disposable pan, cover pan tightly with foil, and place on cooler side of grill. (If using gas, cover grill and allow hotter side to reheat for 5 minutes.) Place steak on hotter side of grill and cook (covered if using gas) until charred and meat registers 135 to 140 degrees, 2 to 4 minutes per side. Transfer steak to cutting board and tent with foil. Remove disposable pan from grill.

6. Carefully remove foil from disposable pan (steam may escape). Slice bell peppers into thin strips. Remove toothpicks from onion rounds and separate rings. Return vegetables to disposable pan and toss with cilantro and reserved marinade. Season with salt and pepper to taste. Slice steak thin against grain. Transfer steak and vegetables to serving platter. Serve with tortillas.

PICO DE GALLO
SERVES 4
To make it spicier, include the jalapeño seeds.

3 tomatoes, cored and chopped
  Salt and pepper
¼ cup finely chopped red onion
¼ cup chopped fresh cilantro
1 jalapeño chile, stemmed, seeded, and minced
1 tablespoon lime juice
1 garlic clove, minced

Toss tomatoes with ¼ teaspoon salt in bowl. Transfer to colander and let drain for 30 minutes. Combine drained tomatoes, onion, cilantro, jalapeño, lime juice, and garlic in bowl. Season with salt and pepper to taste. Serve.

GRILLED FLANK STEAK WITH BASIL DRESSING

SERVES 6

We season this steak with sugar in addition to salt and pepper to help promote browning during the relatively short cooking time.

Steak

- 1 (2-pound) flank steak, trimmed
- 2 teaspoons sugar
- ½ teaspoon salt
- ½ teaspoon pepper

Basil Dressing

- ¼ cup extra-virgin olive oil
- ¼ cup chopped fresh basil
- 1 shallot, minced
- 2 tablespoons red wine vinegar
- 2 teaspoons lemon juice
- 1 teaspoon honey
- 1 garlic clove, minced
- ½ teaspoon red pepper flakes
- ½ teaspoon salt
- ¼ teaspoon pepper

1. For the Steak Pat steak dry with paper towels and sprinkle with sugar, salt, and pepper. Transfer steak to plate, cover with plastic wrap, and refrigerate for at least 1 hour or up to 24 hours.

2. For the Basil Dressing Whisk all ingredients in bowl until sugar has dissolved; set aside.

3A. For a Charcoal Grill Open bottom vent completely. Light large chimney starter mounded with charcoal briquettes (7 quarts). When top coals are partially covered with ash, pour evenly over half of grill. Set cooking grate in place, cover, and open lid vent completely. Heat grill until hot, about 5 minutes.

3B. For a Gas Grill Turn all burners to high, cover, and heat grill until hot, about 15 minutes. Leave primary burner on high and turn off other burner(s).

4. Set wire rack in rimmed baking sheet. Clean and oil cooking grate. Place steak on hotter side of grill and cook (covered if using gas) until browned on both sides, about 2 minutes per side. Flip steak again and rotate so that thin end is over cooler side of grill and thick end remains over hotter side. Continue to cook (covered if using gas), flipping steak every 2 minutes, until thick end of steak registers 125 degrees (for medium-rare) or 130 degrees (for medium), 2 to 6 minutes longer.

5. Transfer steak to prepared rack, tent with aluminum foil, and let rest for 10 minutes. Transfer steak to carving board and cut in half lengthwise with grain to create 2 narrow steaks. Slice each steak thin on bias against grain. Transfer steak to shallow platter and pour dressing over top. Serve.

Sear, Flip, and Rotate

Flank steaks are considerably thicker on one end, so cooking them evenly requires some technique. We build a half-grill fire with a hotter and a cooler zone and start by searing both sides of the steak directly over the hotter side of the grill until browned. Then we position the steak with its thin end over the cooler side and its thick end over the hotter side to finish cooking.

Why This Recipe Works For a grilled flank steak with a char-kissed exterior and a perfectly cooked interior, we had to revisit the idea of marinade. Since salt and sugar do dissolve and penetrate deep into the meat, we skipped the marinade and seasoned our steak with sugar, salt, and pepper. To cook this wedge-shaped cut to a consistent internal temperature, we set up our grill with a cooler side and a hotter side. After briefly grilling the steak on the hotter side, we positioned the steak so the thinner end was over the cooler side of the grill to prevent overcooking. Finally, we converted our marinade into a sauce that we drizzled over our perfectly grilled steak.

Why This Recipe Works Unlike other barbecue recipes, California barbecued tri-tip recipes call for cooking the meat (bottom sirloin roast) over high heat and seasoning it only with salt, pepper, garlic, and the sweet smoke of the grill. This consistently produces a charred exterior and very rare center—but we wanted the outside cooked less and the inside cooked more. To achieve this, we pushed all the coals in our grill to one side, which created a hot zone for cooking and a cooler one for finishing the meat slowly. To prevent the meat from tasting too smoky, we held off on the wood chips until after we'd seared the meat.

CALIFORNIA BARBECUED TRI-TIP

SERVES 4 TO 6

If you can't find tri-tip, bottom round steak will also work. Two medium wood chunks, soaked in water for 1 hour, can be substituted for the wood chips on a charcoal grill. Serve with Santa Maria Salsa (recipe follows) and California Barbecued Beans (page 560). We prefer this roast cooked medium-rare.

- 6 garlic cloves, minced
- 2 tablespoons olive oil
- ¾ teaspoon salt
- 1 (2-pound) tri-tip roast, trimmed
- 1 teaspoon pepper
- ¾ teaspoon garlic salt
- 2 cups wood chips, soaked in water for 15 minutes and drained

1. Combine garlic, oil, and salt in bowl. Pat meat dry with paper towels, poke it about 20 times on each side with fork, and rub it evenly with garlic mixture. Wrap meat in plastic wrap and let sit at room temperature for at least 1 hour or refrigerate for up to 24 hours. (If refrigerated, let sit at room temperature for 1 hour before grilling.) Before cooking, unwrap meat, wipe off garlic paste using paper towels, and rub it evenly with pepper and garlic salt. Using large piece of heavy-duty aluminum foil, wrap soaked chips in foil packet and cut several vent holes in top.

2A. For a Charcoal Grill Open bottom vent completely. Light large chimney starter filled with charcoal briquettes (6 quarts). When top coals are partially covered with ash, pour evenly over half of grill. Set cooking grate in place, cover, and open lid vent completely. Heat grill until hot, about 5 minutes.

2B. For a Gas Grill Turn all burners to high, cover, and heat grill until hot, about 15 minutes.

3. Clean and oil cooking grate. Grill meat on hot side of grill until well browned on both sides, about 10 minutes. Transfer meat to plate.

4. Place wood chip packet directly on coals or primary burner. If using gas, leave primary burner on high and turn other burner(s) off.

5. Place meat on cool side of grill. Cover (positioning lid vent over meat if using charcoal) and cook until meat registers 120 to 125 degrees (for medium-rare), about 20 minutes.

6. Transfer meat to carving board, tent loosely with aluminum foil, and let rest for 20 minutes. Slice meat thin against grain and serve.

SANTA MARIA SALSA
MAKES ABOUT 4 CUPS
The distinct texture of each ingredient is part of this salsa's identity and appeal, so we don't recommend using a food processor.

- 2 pounds tomatoes, cored and chopped
- 2 teaspoons salt
- 2 jalapeño chiles, stemmed, seeded, and chopped fine
- 1 small red onion, chopped fine
- 1 celery rib, chopped fine
- ¼ cup lime juice (2 limes)
- ¼ cup chopped fresh cilantro
- 1 garlic clove, minced
- ⅛ teaspoon dried oregano
- ⅛ teaspoon Worcestershire sauce

1. Place tomatoes in strainer set over bowl and sprinkle with salt; drain for 30 minutes. Discard liquid. Meanwhile, combine jalapeños, onion, celery, lime juice, cilantro, garlic, oregano, and Worcestershire in large bowl.

2. Add drained tomatoes to jalapeño mixture and toss to combine. Cover with plastic wrap and let stand at room temperature for 1 hour before serving. (Salsa can be refrigerated for up to 2 days.)

Why This Recipe Works For our Shredded Barbecued Beef, we cut a chuck roast into quarters. The smaller pieces of beef absorbed more smoke flavor and cooked much faster. After cooking the meat in a disposable roasting pan on the cooler side of the grill for a few hours, we flipped all four pieces, wrapped the pan in foil, and placed the roast in the oven to finish cooking. For a barbecue sauce with richer flavor, we sautéed the onions in beef fat from the pan. Chili powder and pepper added bite, while ketchup, vinegar, coffee, Worcestershire sauce, brown sugar, and the beef juices rounded out the flavors.

SHREDDED BARBECUED BEEF

SERVES 8 TO 10

If you prefer a smooth barbecue sauce, strain the sauce before tossing it with the beef in step 5. We like to serve this beef on white bread with plenty of pickle chips. Three medium wood chunks, soaked in water for 1 hour, can be substituted for the wood chips on a charcoal grill.

1 tablespoon salt
1 tablespoon pepper
1 teaspoon cayenne pepper
1 (5- to 6-pound) boneless beef chuck-eye roast, trimmed and quartered
1 (13 by 9-inch) disposable aluminum roasting pan
3 cups wood chips, soaked in water for 15 minutes and drained
1 onion, chopped fine
4 garlic cloves, minced
½ teaspoon chili powder
1¼ cups ketchup
¾ cup brewed coffee
½ cup cider vinegar
½ cup packed brown sugar
3 tablespoons Worcestershire sauce
½ teaspoon pepper

1. Combine salt, pepper, and cayenne in small bowl. Pat meat dry with paper towels and rub evenly with spice mixture. Wrap meat in plastic wrap and let sit at room temperature for at least 1 hour or refrigerate up to 24 hours. (If refrigerated, let sit at room temperature for 1 hour before grilling.) Before cooking, unwrap meat and transfer to disposable pan. Using 2 large pieces of heavy-duty aluminum foil, wrap soaked chips in 2 foil packets and cut several vent holes in tops.

2A. For a Charcoal Grill Open bottom vent completely. Light large chimney starter half filled with charcoal briquettes (3 quarts). When top coals are partially covered with ash, pour into steeply banked pile against 1 side of grill. Place wood chip packets on coals. Set cooking grate in place, cover, and open lid vent halfway. Heat grill until hot and wood chips are smoking, about 5 minutes.

2B. For a Gas Grill Place wood chip packets directly on primary burner. Turn all burners to high, cover, and heat grill until hot and wood chips are smoking, about 15 minutes. Leave primary burner on high and turn other burner(s) off. (Adjust primary burner as needed to maintain grill temperature between 250 and 300 degrees.)

3. Place pan of meat on cool side of the grill. Cover (positioning lid vent over meat if using charcoal) and cook until meat is deep red, about 2 hours. During final 20 minutes of grilling, adjust oven rack to lower-middle position and heat oven to 300 degrees.

4. Flip meat over in pan, cover pan tightly with foil, and roast beef in oven until fork slips easily in and out of beef, 2 to 3 hours.

5. Transfer meat to large bowl, tent loosely with foil, and let rest for 30 minutes. While meat rests, skim fat from accumulated juices in pan; reserve 2 tablespoons fat. Strain defatted juices; reserve ½ cup juice. Combine onion and reserved fat in medium saucepan and cook over medium heat until onion has softened, about 10 minutes. Add garlic and chili powder and cook until fragrant, about 30 seconds. Stir in ketchup, coffee, vinegar, sugar, Worcestershire, pepper, and any accumulated meat juices and simmer until thickened, about 15 minutes. Using 2 forks, pull meat into shreds, discarding any excess fat or gristle. Toss meat with ½ cup barbecue sauce. Serve, passing remaining sauce separately.

Why This Recipe Works A proper Texas-style smoked brisket is sublime eating; tender juicy meat encased in a dark, peppery crust or "bark." But smoking a 10-pound brisket on a charcoal grill took some creative thinking. We used a charcoal snake, a C-shaped array of briquettes that slowly burns from one end to the other. Topped with wood chips, it provided hours of low, smoky heat, needing to be refueled only once. Cooking the brisket fat side down offered protection against the coals, and wrapping it in aluminum foil toward the end of its cooking time and letting it rest in an insulated cooler for 2 hours kept the meat ultramoist.

TEXAS BARBECUE BRISKET

SERVES 12 TO 15

We developed this recipe using a 22-inch Weber Kettle charcoal grill. Plan ahead: The brisket must be seasoned at least 12 hours before cooking. We call for a whole beef brisket here, with both the flat and point cuts intact; you may need to special-order this cut. We recommend reading the entire recipe before starting.

- 1 (10- to 12-pound) whole beef brisket, untrimmed
- ¼ cup kosher salt
- ¼ cup pepper
- 5 (3-inch) wood chunks
- 1 (13 by 9-inch) disposable aluminum pan

1. With brisket positioned point side up, use sharp knife to trim fat cap to ½- to ¼-inch thickness. Remove excess fat from deep pocket where flat and point are attached. Trim and discard short edge of flat if less than 1 inch thick. Flip brisket and remove any large deposits of fat from underside.

2. Combine salt and pepper in bowl. Place brisket on rimmed baking sheet and sprinkle all over with salt mixture. Cover loosely with plastic wrap and refrigerate for 12 to 24 hours.

3. Open bottom vent of grill completely. Set up charcoal snake: Arrange 58 briquettes, 2 briquettes wide, around perimeter of grill, overlapping slightly so briquettes are touching, leaving 8-inch gap between ends of snake. Place second layer of 58 briquettes, also 2 briquettes wide, on top of first. (Completed snake should be 2 briquettes wide by 2 briquettes high.)

4. Starting 4 inches from 1 end of snake, evenly space wood chunks on top of snake. Place disposable pan in center of grill. Fill disposable pan with 6 cups water. Light chimney starter filled with 10 briquettes (pile briquettes on 1 side of chimney). When coals are partially covered with ash, pour over 1 end of snake. (Make sure lit coals touch only 1 end of snake.)

5. Set cooking grate in place. Clean and oil cooking grate. Place brisket, fat side down, directly over water pan, with point end facing gap in snake. Insert temperature probe into side of upper third of point. Cover grill, open lid vent completely, and position lid vent over gap in snake. Cook, undisturbed and without lifting lid, until meat registers 170 degrees, 4 to 5 hours.

6. Place 2 large sheets of aluminum foil on rimmed baking sheet. Remove temperature probe from brisket. Using oven mitts, lift brisket and transfer to center of foil, fat side down. Wrap brisket tightly with first layer of foil, minimizing air pockets between foil and brisket. Rotate brisket 90 degrees and wrap with second layer of foil. (Use additional foil, if necessary, to completely wrap brisket.) Make small mark on foil with marker to keep track of fat/point side. Foil wrap should be airtight.

7. Remove cooking grate. Starting at still-unlit end of snake, pour 3 quarts unlit briquettes about halfway around perimeter of grill over gap and spent coals. Replace cooking grate. Return foil-wrapped brisket to grill over water pan, fat side down, with point end facing where gap in snake used to be. Reinsert temperature probe into point. Cover grill and continue to cook until meat registers 205 degrees, 1 to 2 hours longer.

8. Remove temperature probe. Transfer foil-wrapped brisket to cooler, point side up. Close cooler and let rest for at least 2 hours or up to 3 hours. Transfer brisket to carving board, unwrap, and position fat side up. Slice flat against grain ¼ inch thick, stopping once you reach base of point. Rotate point 90 degrees and slice point against grain (perpendicular to first cut) ⅜ inch thick. Serve.

Buy the Right Brisket

A full brisket is from the lower chest of the cow and ranges from 8 to 20 pounds in size. It's made up of both the "point" and "flat" cuts. The ideal brisket will have an even, ½-inch-thick fat cap. If you can't get a whole brisket in the 10- to 12-pound range, it's better to buy a slightly larger brisket and trim it down to size (smaller briskets are more prone to drying out on the grill).

POINT
Thicker, fattier

FLAT
Thinner, leaner

JUCY LUCY BURGERS

SERVES 4

Buy the American cheese from the deli counter, and ask them to slice it into a ½-inch slab from which you can cut four big cubes to fill the center of the burgers. One or two percent low-fat milk can be substituted for the whole milk. The cheesy center of these burgers is molten hot when first removed from the grill, so be sure to let the burgers rest for at least 5 minutes before serving.

- 2 slices hearty white sandwich bread, torn into 1-inch pieces
- ¼ cup whole milk
- 1 teaspoon garlic powder
- ¾ teaspoon salt
- ½ teaspoon pepper
- 1½ pounds 85 percent lean ground beef
- 1 slice deli American cheese (½-inch-thick), quartered

1. In large bowl using potato masher, mash bread, milk, garlic powder, salt, and pepper into smooth paste. Add beef and lightly knead mixture until well combined.

2. Divide meat into 4 equal portions. Using half of each portion of meat, encase cheese to form mini burger patty. Mold remaining half-portion of meat around mini patty and seal edges to form ball. Flatten ball with palm of your hand, forming ¾-inch-thick patty. Cover and refrigerate patties for at least 30 minutes or up to 24 hours.

3A. For a Charcoal Grill Open bottom vent completely. Light large chimney starter half filled with charcoal briquettes (3 quarts). When top coals are partially covered with ash, pour evenly over grill. Set cooking grate in place, cover, and heat grill until hot, about 5 minutes.

3B. For a Gas Grill Turn all burners to high, cover, and heat grill until hot, about 15 minutes. Turn all burners to medium.

4. Clean and oil cooking grate. Lay burgers on grill and cook, without pressing on them, until well browned on both sides and cooked through, 12 to 16 minutes, flipping burgers halfway through grilling. Transfer burgers to platter, tent loosely with aluminum foil, and let rest for 5 minutes before serving.

How to Form a Jucy Lucy
To avoid a burger blowout, it's essential to completely seal in the cheese.

1. Using half of each portion of meat, encase cheese to form mini burger patty.

2. Mold remaining half-portion of meat around mini patty and seal edges to form a ball and flatten to form ¾-inch patty.

The Great Lucy Debate
A debate still rages as to where the Jucy Lucy was created. Two Minnesota taverns, Matt's Bar and the 5–8 Club, claim to have created the burger in the 1950s. As the story goes, a customer requested a burger with the cheese sealed in the middle. When he bit in, the hot cheese spurted out and he exclaimed, "That's one juicy Lucy!" As for the unusual spelling, that's still a mystery.

Why This Recipe Works Minneapolis taverns are famous for the Jucy Lucy, a moist beef burger stuffed with American cheese. Replicating the Jucy Lucy seemed easy enough—but our burgers, cooked to well-done to melt the cheese inside, were dry and tough or the cheese melted through the meat, leaving an empty cavern where the cheese had been. To keep the cheese in place, we created a double-sealed pocket by wrapping the cheese inside a small beef patty and then molding a second patty around it. Adding a mixture of bread and milk, mashed into a paste, to the ground beef kept the burgers moist and juicy.

GRILLED BACON BURGERS WITH CARAMELIZED ONION

SERVES 4

Martin's Sandwich Potato Rolls are our favorite hamburger buns, and Oscar Mayer Naturally Hardwood Smoked Bacon is our favorite thin-sliced bacon. Be gentle when shaping the patties, taking care not to overwork the meat, or the burgers will become dense. Serve the burgers with lettuce and tomato, if desired.

- 8 slices bacon
- 1 large onion, halved and sliced thin
  Salt and pepper
- 1½ pounds 85 percent lean ground beef
- 4 ounces blue cheese, crumbled and chilled (1 cup) (optional)
- 4 hamburger buns, toasted

1. Process bacon in food processor to smooth paste, about 1 minute, scraping down sides of bowl as needed. Cook bacon in 12-inch nonstick skillet over medium heat until lightly browned in spots but still pink (do not cook until crispy), about 5 minutes, breaking up pieces with spoon. Drain bacon in fine-mesh strainer set over bowl. Transfer bacon to paper towel–lined plate and let cool completely. Reserve bacon fat.

2. Add 2 tablespoons reserved fat to now-empty skillet and heat over medium heat until shimmering. Add onion and ¼ teaspoon salt and cook until well browned, about 20 minutes. Transfer to bowl and set aside.

3. Spread beef in even layer in rimmed baking sheet. Sprinkle bacon, 1 teaspoon pepper, and ⅛ teaspoon salt over beef. Gently toss with 2 forks to combine. Divide beef mixture into 4 equal mounds. Gently shape each mound into ¾-inch-thick patty about 4½ inches in diameter. Using your fingertips, press center of each patty down until about ½ inch thick, creating slight indentation. (Patties can be covered and refrigerated for up to 24 hours.)

4A. For a Charcoal Grill Open bottom vent completely. Light large chimney starter filled with charcoal briquettes (6 quarts). When top coals are partially covered with ash, pour evenly over grill. Set cooking grate in place, cover, and open lid vent completely. Heat grill until hot, about 5 minutes.

4B. For a Gas Grill Turn all burners to high, cover, and heat grill until hot, about 15 minutes. Leave all burners on high.

5. Clean and oil cooking grate. Season patties with pepper. Cook patties indentation side down, uncovered, until browned, about 3 minutes. Flip patties and top each with ¼ cup blue cheese, if using. Cover and continue to cook until burgers register 125 degrees (for medium-rare) or 130 degrees (for medium), about 2 minutes longer. Transfer burgers to buns, top with onion, and serve.

Making a Good Impression

When we make burgers, we always form a shallow indentation in the center of each patty before cooking it. That's because the collagen, or connective tissue, in ground meat shrinks when heated. This causes the bottom and sides of the meat to tighten like a belt, which forces the surface of the burger to expand. To prevent a bulging burger, press a ¼-inch-deep indentation into the center of each patty. When the collagen tightens, it will cause the indentation to fill out so that it is level with the rest of the patty.

Why This Recipe Works Bacon is a no-brainer burger topping, but we wanted bacony bliss in every bite, not just on top. Combining raw bacon with ground beef, however, led to overworked, dry patties, while adding crumbled cooked bacon left us with crunchy burgers. But we found that blitzing raw bacon in the food processor and then cooking it just until some of the fat was rendered before mixing it into our ground beef helped it incorporate easily, ensuring optimal flavor distribution. To take these burgers to even higher heights, we topped them with crumbled blue cheese (a classic pairing) and onion that we sautéed in some of the leftover bacon fat.

Why This Recipe Works For our version of New Mexico's green chile cheeseburgers—ground beef patties grilled to a crusty brown and topped with chopped fire-roasted chiles and a slice of cheese—we preferred the flavor and fat of 85 percent lean ground beef. For the topping, we used mild Anaheim chiles and spicy jalapeños for a complex chile flavor. We grilled the chiles with onions, then quickly chopped them with fresh garlic in the food processor. For even more chile flavor, we pureed some of the chile topping into a smooth paste and mixed it into the raw ground beef. This gave us burgers with satisfying heat through and through.

GREEN CHILE CHEESEBURGERS

SERVES 4

In step 3, you may need to add a teaspoon or two of water to the food processor to help process the chile mixture. Pressing a shallow indentation in the center of each patty keeps the burgers flat during grilling.

- 3 Anaheim chiles, stemmed, halved, and seeded
- 3 jalapeño chiles, stemmed, halved, and seeded
- 1 onion, sliced into ½-inch-thick rounds
- 1 garlic clove, minced
   Salt and pepper
- 1½ pounds 85 percent lean ground beef
- 4 slices deli American cheese

1A. For a Charcoal Grill Open bottom vent completely. Light large chimney starter filled with charcoal briquettes (6 quarts). When top coals are partially covered with ash, pour evenly over grill. Set cooking grate in place, cover, and open lid vent completely. Heat grill until hot, about 5 minutes.

1B. For a Gas Grill Turn all burners to high, cover, and heat grill until hot, about 15 minutes.

2. Clean and oil cooking grate. Place Anaheims, jalapeños, and onion on grill, cover, and cook until vegetables are lightly charred and tender, 4 to 6 minutes, flipping halfway through cooking. Transfer vegetables to bowl, cover, and let cool 5 minutes. Remove skins from chiles and discard; separate onion rounds into rings.

3. Transfer chiles and onion to food processor, add garlic, and pulse until coarsely chopped, about 5 pulses. Transfer all but ¼ cup chopped chile mixture to empty bowl and season with salt and pepper; set aside. Process remaining mixture until finely chopped, about 45 seconds, scraping down bowl as needed.

4. Combine beef, finely chopped chile mixture, ½ teaspoon salt, and ¼ teaspoon pepper in large bowl and lightly knead until well combined. Shape into four ¾-inch-thick patties and press shallow depression in center of each.

5. Place burgers on grill, cover, and cook until well browned on first side, 3 to 5 minutes. Flip burgers, top with reserved coarsely chopped chile mixture and cheese, and continue to cook, covered, until cheese is melted and burgers are cooked to desired doneness, 3 to 5 minutes. Serve.

Chile Pinch Hitter

For complex green chile flavor outside of New Mexico, we found that a combination of mild Anaheims and spicy jalapeños has a nice peppery balance.

MILD HEAT
Anaheim chiles add a mildly sweet, grassy flavor.

SPICE IS NICE
Jalapeño chiles have just enough heat to stand up to the beefiness of the burger.

CHICAGO-STYLE BARBECUED RIBS

SERVES 4 TO 6

The dry spices are used to flavor both the rub and the barbecue sauce. One medium wood chunk, soaked in water for 1 hour, can be substituted for the wood chips on a charcoal grill. When removing the ribs from the oven, be careful to not spill the hot water in the bottom of the baking sheet.

Spice Rub and Ribs
- 1 tablespoon dry mustard
- 1 tablespoon paprika
- 1 tablespoon packed dark brown sugar
- 1½ teaspoons garlic powder
- 1½ teaspoons onion powder
- 1½ teaspoons celery salt
- 1 teaspoon cayenne pepper
- ½ teaspoon ground allspice
- 2 racks baby back ribs (about 1½ pounds each), trimmed
- 1 cup wood chips, soaked in water for 15 minutes and drained
- 1 (13 by 9-inch) disposable aluminum roasting pan

Sauce
- 1¼ cups ketchup
- ¼ cup molasses
- ¼ cup cider vinegar
- ¼ cup water
- ⅛ teaspoon liquid smoke

1. For the Spice Rub and Ribs Combine dry mustard, paprika, sugar, garlic powder, onion powder, celery salt, cayenne, and allspice in bowl. Measure out and reserve 2 tablespoons spice mixture for sauce. To remove chewy membrane from ribs, loosen it with tip of paring knife and, with aid of paper towel, pull it off slowly in 1 big piece. Pat ribs dry with paper towels and rub evenly with spice mixture. Wrap meat in plastic wrap and let sit at room temperature for at least 1 hour or refrigerate for up to 24 hours. (If refrigerated, let sit at room temperature for 1 hour before grilling.)

2. For the Sauce Whisk all ingredients with reserved 2 tablespoons spice rub in bowl. Using large piece of heavy-duty aluminum foil, wrap soaked chips in foil packet and cut several vent holes in top.

3A. For a Charcoal Grill Open bottom vent completely. Light large chimney starter filled with charcoal briquettes (6 quarts). Add 2 cups water to disposable pan and place it on 1 side of grill. When top coals are partially covered with ash, pour into steeply banked pile against other side of grill, opposite pan of water. Place wood chip packet on coals. Set cooking grate in place, cover, and open lid vent completely. Heat grill until hot and wood chips are smoking, about 5 minutes.

3B. For a Gas Grill Place wood chip packet directly on primary burner. Add 2 cups water to disposable pan and place it on secondary burner. Turn all burners to high, cover, and heat grill until hot and wood chips are smoking, about 15 minutes. Turn primary burner to medium and turn other burner(s) off. (Adjust primary burner as needed to maintain grill temperature around 325 degrees.)

4. Clean and oil cooking grate. Place ribs meat side down on grill over water-filled pan; ribs may overlap slightly. Cover (positioning lid vent over meat if using charcoal) and cook until ribs are deep red and smoky, about 1½ hours, flipping and rotating racks halfway through grilling. During final 20 minutes of grilling, adjust oven rack to middle position and heat oven to 250 degrees.

5. Set wire rack in rimmed baking sheet and add just enough water to cover pan bottom. Transfer ribs to rack and cover tightly with foil. Continue to cook ribs in oven until fork slips easily in and out of meat, 1½ to 2 hours.

6. Remove ribs from oven, tent with foil, and let rest for 30 minutes. Brush ribs evenly with half of sauce. Slice ribs between bones and serve with remaining sauce.

Why This Recipe Works Chicago-style barbecued ribs recipes typically call for smoking the ribs at about 200 degrees for at least 8 hours. This slow-and-low cooking method delivers the moist, tender meat that defines Chicago ribs. We wanted to replicate the same method at home. To shorten cooking time, we started our recipe on the grill—where the ribs picked up good color and smoke flavor—and finished them in the oven. Placing pans of water on the grill and in the oven steamed the ribs, making them extra moist and tender. For Chicago-style barbecue sauce, we used celery salt, allspice, and plenty of cayenne pepper.

TEXAS BARBECUED BEEF RIBS

SERVES 4

Beef ribs are sold in slabs with up to seven bones, but slabs with three to four bones are easier to manage on the grill. If you cannot find ribs with a substantial amount of meat on the bones, don't bother making this recipe. One medium wood chunk, soaked in water for 1 hour, can be substituted for the wood chips on a charcoal grill.

Texas Barbecue Sauce

2 tablespoons unsalted butter
½ small onion, chopped fine
2 garlic cloves, minced
1½ teaspoons chili powder
1½ teaspoons pepper
½ teaspoon dry mustard
2 cups tomato juice
6 tablespoons distilled white vinegar
2 tablespoons Worcestershire sauce
2 tablespoons packed brown sugar
2 tablespoons molasses
Salt

Ribs

3 tablespoons packed brown sugar
4 teaspoons chili powder
1 tablespoon salt
2 teaspoons pepper
½ teaspoon cayenne pepper
3–4 beef rib slabs (3 to 4 ribs per slab, about 5 pounds total), trimmed
1 cup wood chips, soaked in water for 15 minutes and drained

1. For the Texas Barbecue Sauce Melt butter in medium saucepan over medium heat. Add onion and cook until softened, about 5 minutes. Stir in garlic, chili powder, pepper, and dry mustard and cook until fragrant, about 30 seconds. Stir in tomato juice, vinegar, Worcestershire, sugar, and molasses and simmer until sauce is reduced to 2 cups, about 20 minutes. Season with salt to taste. (Sauce can be refrigerated for 1 week.)

2. For the Ribs Combine sugar, chili powder, salt, pepper, and cayenne in bowl. Pat ribs dry with paper towels and rub them evenly with spice mixture. Cover ribs with plastic wrap and let sit at room temperature for 1 hour.

3. Adjust oven rack to middle position and heat oven to 300 degrees. Set wire rack in rimmed baking sheet and add just enough water to cover pan bottom. Arrange ribs on rack and cover tightly with aluminum foil. Bake until fat has rendered and meat begins to pull away from bones, about 2 hours. Using large piece of heavy-duty foil, wrap soaked chips in foil packet and cut several vent holes in top.

4A. For a Charcoal Grill Open bottom vent halfway. Light large chimney starter filled with charcoal briquettes (6 quarts). When top coals are partially covered with ash, pour into steeply banked pile against 1 side of grill. Place wood chip packet on coals. Set cooking grate in place, cover, and open lid vent halfway. Heat grill until hot and wood chips are smoking, about 5 minutes.

4B. For a Gas Grill Place wood chip packet directly on primary burner. Turn all burners to high, cover, and heat grill until hot and wood chips are smoking, about 15 minutes. Leave primary burner on high and turn other burner(s) off. (Adjust primary burner as needed to maintain grill temperature between 250 and 300 degrees.)

5. Clean and oil cooking grate. Place ribs meat side down on cool side of grill; ribs may overlap slightly. Cover (positioning lid vent over meat if using charcoal) and cook until ribs are lightly charred and smoky, about 1½ hours, flipping and rotating racks halfway through grilling. Transfer to cutting board, tent with foil, and let rest for 10 minutes. Serve with barbecue sauce.

Why This Recipe Works Traditional Texas barbecued beef ribs are placed in pits for up to 10 hours. The smoke slowly permeates the meat, melting away fat, building flavor, and creating an unforgettable crust. We wanted a streamlined recipe. To speed things up, we first turned to steaming the ribs in the oven on a tray of water covered with aluminum foil, which tenderized the ribs. We then moved the ribs to the grill, where we smoked them over indirect heat (banking all the coals to one side of the grill and placing the ribs on the empty side) using wood chips. The surface of the meat dried and formed a spicy, crusty bark.

Why This Recipe Works For a new take on pulled pork, we started with a shank-end fresh ham. We rubbed it with only salt to keep the flavor pure and let it rest overnight for deeply seasoned, juicy meat. To speed up the usually long cooking time, we smoked the ham on the grill to infuse it with flavor before covering it with foil and transferring it to the oven. For crisp and crackling skin, we removed the skin when the meat hit 200 degrees and roasted it separately. From there, we chopped the ham, stirring in the crisp bits of skin and the flavorful rendered juices, and served it on soft buns with a smear of tangy mustard sauce.

SOUTH CAROLINA SMOKED FRESH HAM

SERVES 8 TO 10

Plan ahead: The ham must be salted at least 18 hours before cooking. You'll have about 2½ cups of mustard sauce.

Ham

1   (6- to 8-pound) bone-in, skin-on shank-end fresh ham
    Kosher salt
2   cups wood chips

Mustard Sauce

1½ cups yellow mustard
½   cup cider vinegar
6   tablespoons packed brown sugar
2   tablespoons ketchup
2   teaspoons hot sauce
2   teaspoons Worcestershire sauce
1   teaspoon pepper

Hamburger buns

1. For the Ham Pat ham dry with paper towels. Place ham on large sheet of plastic wrap and rub all over with 2 tablespoons salt. Wrap tightly in plastic and refrigerate for 18 to 24 hours.

2. Just before grilling, soak wood chips in water for 15 minutes, then drain. Using large piece of heavy-duty aluminum foil, wrap soaked chips in 8 by 4½-inch foil packet. (Make sure chips do not poke holes in sides or bottom of packet.) Cut 2 evenly spaced 2-inch slits in top of packet.

3A. For a Charcoal Grill Open bottom vent completely. Light large chimney starter three-quarters filled with charcoal briquettes (4½ quarts). When top coals are partially covered with ash, pour evenly over half of grill. Place wood chip packet on coals. Set cooking grate in place, cover, and open lid vent completely. Heat grill until hot and wood chips are smoking, about 5 minutes.

3B. For a Gas Grill Remove cooking grate and place wood chip packet directly on primary burner. Set cooking grate in place, turn all burners to high, cover, and heat grill until hot and wood chips are smoking, about 15 minutes. Turn primary burner to medium-high and turn off other burner(s). (Adjust primary burner as needed to maintain grill temperature of 300 degrees.)

4. Clean and oil cooking grate. Unwrap ham and place flat side down on cooler side of grill. Cover grill (position lid vent directly over ham if using charcoal) and cook for 2 hours. Thirty minutes before ham comes off grill, adjust oven rack to middle position and heat oven to 300 degrees.

5. For the Mustard Sauce Meanwhile, whisk all ingredients together in bowl. (Sauce can be refrigerated for up to 1 week.)

6. Transfer ham to 13 by 9-inch baking pan, flat side down. Cover pan tightly with foil. Transfer to oven and roast until fork inserted in ham meets little resistance and meat registers 200 degrees, about 2½ hours.

7. Remove ham from oven and increase oven temperature to 400 degrees. Line rimmed baking sheet with foil. Using tongs, remove ham skin in 1 large piece. Place skin fatty side down on prepared sheet. Transfer to oven and roast until skin is dark and crispy and sounds hollow when tapped with fork, about 25 minutes, rotating sheet halfway through roasting. Tent ham with foil and let rest while skin roasts.

8. Transfer ham to carving board. Strain accumulated juices from pan through fine-mesh strainer set over bowl; discard solids. Trim and discard excess fat from ham. Remove bone and chop meat into bite-size pieces; transfer to large bowl.

9. When cool enough to handle, chop skin fine. Rewarm reserved ham juices in microwave for 1 minute. Add juices and chopped skin to ham and toss to combine. Season with salt to taste. Serve on buns, topped with mustard sauce.

Why This Recipe Works Traditional vinegar-based Lexington-style pulled pork recipes take hours to prepare. We wanted to simplify this recipe without sacrificing flavor. To do so, we used a combination of grilling and oven roasting to reduce the cooking time from all day to just a few hours. To infuse our Lexington-Style Pulled Pork with ample smoke flavor despite the abbreviated cooking time, we doubled the amount of wood chips we used.

LEXINGTON-STYLE PULLED PORK

SERVES 8

Boneless pork butt (also labeled Boston butt) is often wrapped in elastic netting; be sure to remove the netting before rubbing the meat with the spices in step 1. Four medium wood chunks, soaked in water for 1 hour, can be substituted for the wood chips on a charcoal grill.

Spice Rub and Pork

- 2 tablespoons paprika
- 2 tablespoons pepper
- 2 tablespoons packed brown sugar
- 1 tablespoon salt
- 1 (4- to 5-pound) boneless pork butt roast, trimmed
- 4 cups wood chips, soaked in water for 15 minutes and drained

Lexington Barbecue Sauce

- 1 cup water
- 1 cup cider vinegar
- ½ cup ketchup
- 1 tablespoon granulated sugar
- ¾ teaspoon salt
- ½ teaspoon pepper
- ½ teaspoon red pepper flakes

1. For the Spice Rub and Pork Combine paprika, pepper, sugar, and salt in bowl. Pat meat dry with paper towels and rub it evenly with spice mixture. Wrap meat in plastic wrap and let sit at room temperature for at least 1 hour or refrigerate for up to 24 hours. (If refrigerated, let sit at room temperature for 1 hour before grilling.) Using 2 large pieces of heavy-duty aluminum foil, wrap soaked chips in 2 foil packets and cut several vent holes in tops.

2A. For a Charcoal Grill Open bottom vent halfway. Light large chimney starter half filled with charcoal briquettes (3 quarts). When top coals are partially covered with ash, pour into steeply banked pile against 1 side of grill. Place wood chip packets on coals. Set cooking grate in place, cover, and open lid vent halfway. Heat grill until hot and wood chips are smoking, about 5 minutes.

2B. For a Gas Grill Place wood chip packets directly on primary burner. Turn all burners to high, cover, and heat grill until hot and wood chips are smoking, about 15 minutes. Turn primary burner to medium and turn other burner(s) off. (Adjust primary burner as needed to maintain grill temperature around 275 degrees.)

3. Clean and oil cooking grate. Place meat on cool side of grill. Cover (positioning lid vent over meat if using charcoal) and cook until pork has dark, rosy crust, about 2 hours. During final 20 minutes of grilling, adjust oven rack to lower-middle position and heat oven to 325 degrees.

4. Transfer pork to large roasting pan, cover pan tightly with foil, and roast pork in oven until fork slips easily into and out of meat, 2 to 3 hours. Remove pork from the oven and let rest, still covered with foil, for 30 minutes.

5. For the Lexington Barbecue Sauce Whisk together all ingredients until sugar and salt are dissolved. When cool enough to handle, unwrap pork and pull meat into thin shreds, discarding excess fat and gristle. Toss pork with ½ cup barbecue sauce, serving remaining sauce at table.

North Carolina Barbecue Battle

In the eastern part of North Carolina, it's just not barbecue unless it's a whole hog. Known as a pig pickin', this type of barbecue starts with a split hog and ends with succulent meat and crackling-crisp skin. The meat is then literally picked from the bones and lightly seasoned with a thin vinegar and pepper sauce. Western Carolinians eschew the whole hog and go straight for the pork shoulder—the most marbled and meatiest chunk of the animal. The pork shoulder is cooked just like the whole hog, but the sauce is enriched with just enough ketchup and sugar to take the edge off the acidity.

SOUTH CAROLINA PULLED PORK

SERVES 8

Boneless pork butt (also labeled Boston butt) is often wrapped in elastic netting; be sure to remove the netting before rubbing the meat with the spices in step 1. The cooked meat can be shredded or chopped. Four medium wood chunks, soaked in water for 1 hour, can be substituted for the wood chip packet on a charcoal grill.

Spice Rub and Pork

- 3 tablespoons dry mustard
- 2 tablespoons salt
- 1½ tablespoons packed light brown sugar
- 2 teaspoons pepper
- 2 teaspoons paprika
- ¼ teaspoon cayenne pepper
- 1 (4- to 5-pound) boneless pork butt roast, trimmed
- 4 cups wood chips, soaked in water for 15 minutes and drained

Mustard Barbecue Sauce

- ½ cup yellow mustard
- ½ cup packed light brown sugar
- ¼ cup distilled white vinegar
- 2 tablespoons Worcestershire sauce
- 1 tablespoon hot sauce
- 1 teaspoon salt
- 1 teaspoon pepper

1. For the Spice Rub and Pork Combine dry mustard, salt, sugar, pepper, paprika, and cayenne in bowl. Pat meat dry with paper towels and rub it evenly with spice mixture. Wrap meat in plastic wrap and let sit at room temperature for at least 1 hour or refrigerate up to 24 hours. (If refrigerated, let sit at room temperature for 1 hour before grilling.) Using 2 large pieces of heavy-duty aluminum foil, wrap soaked chips in 2 foil packets and cut several vent holes in tops.

2A. For a Charcoal Grill Open bottom vent completely. Light large chimney starter half filled with charcoal briquettes (3 quarts). When top coals are partially covered with ash, pour into steeply banked pile against 1 side of grill. Place wood chip packets on coals. Set cooking grate in place, cover, and open lid vent halfway. Heat grill until hot and wood chips are smoking, about 5 minutes.

2B. For a Gas Grill Place wood chip packets directly on primary burner. Turn all burners to high, cover, and heat grill until hot and wood chips are smoking, about 15 minutes. Turn primary burner to medium-high and turn other burner(s) off. (Adjust primary burner as needed to maintain grill temperature around 325 degrees.)

3. Clean and oil cooking grate. Place meat on cool side of grill. Cover (positioning lid vent over meat if using charcoal) and cook until pork has dark, rosy crust, about 2 hours. During final 20 minutes of grilling, adjust oven rack to lower-middle position and heat oven to 325 degrees.

4. For the Mustard Barbecue Sauce Whisk yellow mustard, sugar, vinegar, Worcestershire, hot sauce, salt, and pepper in bowl until smooth. Measure out ½ cup sauce and set aside for cooking, reserving remaining sauce for serving.

5. Transfer pork to roasting pan and brush evenly with sauce for cooking. Cover pan tightly with foil and roast pork in oven until fork slips easily in and out of meat, 2 to 3 hours.

6. Remove pork from oven and let rest, still covered with foil, for 30 minutes. When cool enough to handle, unwrap pork and pull meat into thin shreds, discarding excess fat and gristle. Toss pork with reserved sauce and serve.

Why This Recipe Works This regional recipe, nicknamed Carolina Gold, demands more than just a last-minute dose of bold flavors. A combination of grilling and oven roasting reduces the cooking time from all day to just four or five hours. We used a spice rub, which included dry mustard to jump-start the mustard flavor of the sauce. Most South Carolina barbecue sauce recipes use yellow mustard, which our tasters praised for its bright tang. Brushing the pork with the sauce before it went into the oven produced a second hit of mustard flavor; tossing the shredded pork with the remaining sauce gave the meat a final layer of mustard flavor.

TENNESSEE PULLED PORK SANDWICHES

SERVES 8 WITH LEFTOVERS

In step 8, shred the pork while it's still hot. Leftover pork can be refrigerated for up to three days.

Pork

1 (5- to 6-pound) bone-in pork butt roast, trimmed
  Kosher salt
2 cups wood chips
1 (13 by 9-inch) disposable aluminum roasting pan

Barbecue Sauce

1 cup ketchup
¼ cup cider vinegar
¼ cup water
2 tablespoons yellow mustard
1 tablespoon Worcestershire sauce
1 teaspoon granulated garlic
1 teaspoon pepper

1 recipe Hoecakes (page 519)
  Dill pickle chips
  Coleslaw

1. For the Pork Using sharp knife, cut 1-inch crosshatch pattern about ¼ inch deep in fat cap of roast, being careful not to cut into meat. Pat roast dry with paper towels. Place roast on large sheet of plastic wrap and rub 2 tablespoons salt over entire roast and into slits. Wrap tightly with plastic and refrigerate for 18 to 24 hours.

2. Just before grilling, soak wood chips in water for 15 minutes, then drain. Using large piece of heavy-duty aluminum foil, wrap soaked chips in foil packet and cut several vent holes in top.

3A. For a Charcoal Grill Open bottom vent completely. Light large chimney starter three-quarters filled with charcoal briquettes (4½ quarts). When top coals are partially covered with ash, pour evenly over half of grill. Place wood chip packet on coals. Set cooking grate in place, cover, and open lid vent completely. Heat grill until hot and wood chips are smoking, about 5 minutes.

3B. For a Gas Grill Remove cooking grate and place wood chip packet directly on primary burner. Set cooking grate in place, turn all burners to high, cover, and heat grill until hot and wood chips are smoking, about 15 minutes. Turn primary burner to medium-high and turn off other burner(s). (Adjust primary burner as needed to maintain grill temperature of 300 degrees.)

4. Unwrap pork and place fat side down in disposable pan. Place disposable pan on cooler side of grill. Cover grill (with lid vent directly over pork for charcoal) and cook until pork registers 120 degrees, about 2 hours. Thirty minutes before pork comes off grill, adjust oven rack to middle position and heat oven to 300 degrees.

5. Transfer disposable pan from grill to rimmed baking sheet. Cover pan tightly with foil and transfer to oven (still on sheet). Cook until fork inserted in pork meets little resistance and meat registers 210 degrees, about 3 hours.

6. For the Barbecue Sauce Meanwhile, combine all ingredients in medium saucepan and bring to boil over medium-high heat. Reduce heat to medium-low and simmer, whisking constantly, until slightly thickened, about 3 minutes. Transfer sauce to bowl and let cool completely.

7. Carefully remove foil from disposable pan (steam will escape). Remove blade bone from roast using tongs. Immediately transfer hot pork to bowl of stand mixer fitted with paddle attachment. Strain accumulated juices from pan through fine-mesh strainer set over separate bowl; discard solids.

8. Mix pork on low speed until meat is finely shredded, about 1½ minutes. Whisk pork juices to recombine, if separated, and add 1½ cups juices to shredded pork. Continue to mix pork on low speed until juices are incorporated, about 15 seconds longer. Season with salt to taste, adding more pork juices if desired. Serve pork on hoecakes with barbecue sauce, pickles, and coleslaw.

Why This Recipe Works Inspired by a central Tennessee sandwich of pulled pork on cornmeal griddle cakes called hoecakes, we wanted pork shredded so finely that it resembled pâté. A combination of grill smoking and oven roasting brought our meat to a higher temperature for a softer pork butt roast. Instead of hand-shredding the meat, we used a stand mixer fitted with a paddle attachment to handily get a superfine shred. To keep the meat moist, we returned some of the pork juices to the shredded meat and served our sandwich with barbecue sauce just like they do at Papa KayJoe's (see "A 30-Year Journey to Pulled Pork Perfection," page 519).

Why This Recipe Works To fully re-create our Papa KayJoe's experience in Centerville, Tennessee, we felt obligated to serve our Tennessee pulled pork on hoecakes. These cornmeal griddle cakes can be served on their own (with butter and syrup) or, in this case, as the perfect vehicle for a delicious barbecue sandwich. A loose batter with plenty of tangy buttermilk flavor gives the hoecakes a light texture, and the cornmeal makes them sturdy enough to hold up to a sandwich filling. Frying them in bacon fat adds a nice hit of smoky pork richness. Although our pulled pork is great on hamburger buns, we prefer to serve it on hoecakes.

HOECAKES

MAKES 16 HOECAKES

Papa KayJoe's makes their hoecakes with bacon fat.

    3   cups (15 ounces) white cornmeal
    2   tablespoons sugar
    2   teaspoons baking powder
 1½   teaspoons salt
    2   cups buttermilk
    2   large eggs
    2   tablespoons bacon fat or vegetable oil

1. Adjust oven rack to middle position and heat oven to 200 degrees. Set wire rack in rimmed baking sheet and place in oven. Whisk cornmeal, sugar, baking powder, and salt together in large bowl. Beat buttermilk and eggs together in separate bowl. Whisk buttermilk mixture into cornmeal mixture until combined.

2A. For a Skillet Heat 1 teaspoon fat in 12-inch nonstick skillet over medium heat until shimmering. Using level ¼-cup dry measuring cup, drop 3 evenly spaced scoops of batter into skillet, smoothing tops slightly if necessary.

2B. For a Griddle Heat 1 tablespoon fat on 400-degree nonstick griddle until shimmering. Using level ¼-cup dry measuring cup, drop 8 evenly spaced scoops of batter onto griddle, smoothing tops slightly if necessary.

3. Cook until small bubbles begin to appear on surface of cakes and edges are set, about 2 minutes. Flip and cook until second side is golden brown, about 2 minutes longer. Transfer hoecakes to prepared sheet in oven. Repeat with remaining fat and batter: 5 additional batches for skillet or 1 additional batch for griddle. Serve.

On The Road: A 30-Year Journey to Pulled Pork Perfection

Papa KayJoe's in Centerville, Tennessee, is a gray wooden building with a red tin roof at the end of a steep driveway. In the dining room, patrons tuck into Papa KayJoe's for their signature sandwiches—pulled pork on cornmeal griddle cakes—and share local news. Each morning owner Devin Pickard feeds armloads of hickory sticks into an outdoor furnace, where they slowly burn down to coals. Pickard then carries the hot embers to a nearby dirt-floored barbecue shack where a pair of cinder block pits sit waiting. At 11 a.m., Pickard lines up 24 heavily salted pork butts on the thick, black metal grate that sits over the pit and covers them with sheets of corrugated steel to trap the heat. The pork spends 6 to 8 hours on the grill, picking up the woodsy aroma of the smoldering hickory. After a day on the grill, the pork butts are packed into large aluminum roasting pans and transferred to a low oven where they'll spend the night. The next morning, Pickard slips on a pair of thick fireproof rubber gloves, picks out a pork butt, removes the blade bone and attacks the meat. In a clapping motion, he brings his fingertips together, pinching the pork; in less than a minute, the pork is in tiny shreds. He works in cupfuls of the juices that have accumulated in the roasting pan, moistening the pork with its own essence. Inside, Pickard's mother (Debbie) and daughter (Ruby) help pile the pork onto hot cornmeal griddle cakes (hoecakes) made to order with buttermilk and bacon fat. They'll produce dozens of these sandwiches today, and every day—including one for Pickard. "I would eat a barbecue sandwich every day of my life, that's how much I love it."

Why This Recipe Works Pork burgers can be notoriously dry and crumbly. To fix that problem we looked toward meatballs for inspiration. They use a bread and milk mixture (called a panade) to stay moist, so we adopted that technique to keep our burgers juicy. Bumping up the seasoning with Worcestershire and soy sauces provided big flavor. After adding the pork to this flavorful mix, we formed patties and pressed divots into each to prevent the burgers from bulging on the grill. Cooking the patties over moderate heat kept them moist. We like these burgers topped with an easy horseradish sauce.

GRILLED PORK BURGERS

SERVES 4

We developed this recipe with whole milk, but low-fat will work, too.

 1 slice hearty white sandwich bread, torn into pieces
 1 shallot, minced
 2 tablespoons milk
 4 teaspoons soy sauce
 1 tablespoon Worcestershire sauce
1¼ teaspoons minced fresh thyme
 1 teaspoon pepper
 ½ teaspoon salt
1½ pounds 80 to 85 percent lean ground pork
 4 hamburger buns, toasted and buttered
 1 recipe Horseradish Burger Sauce (optional; recipe follows)

1. Combine bread, shallot, milk, soy sauce, Worcestershire, thyme, pepper, and salt in large bowl. Mash to paste with fork. Using your hands, add pork and mix until well combined.

2. Divide pork mixture into 4 equal balls. Flatten balls into even ¾-inch-thick patties, about 4 inches in diameter. Using your fingertips, press centers of patties down until about ½ inch thick, creating slight divot.

3A. For a Charcoal Grill Open bottom vent completely. Light large chimney starter filled with charcoal briquettes (6 quarts). When top coals are partially covered with ash, pour evenly over grill. Set cooking grate in place, cover, and open lid vent completely. Heat grill until hot, about 5 minutes.

3B. For a Gas Grill Turn all burners to high, cover, and heat grill until hot, about 15 minutes. Turn all burners to medium.

4. Clean and oil cooking grate. Grill patties (covered if using gas) until browned on first side, 5 to 7 minutes. Flip and continue to grill until burgers register 150 degrees, 5 to 7 minutes longer. Serve burgers on buns with sauce, if using.

GRILLED PARMESAN PORK BURGERS
Add ½ cup grated Parmesan, 1 tablespoon minced fresh sage, 1 teaspoon ground fennel, and ½ teaspoon red pepper flakes to pork mixture in step 1.

GRILLED SOUTHWEST PORK BURGERS
Add 2 tablespoons minced jarred hot pepper rings, 1½ teaspoons chili powder, and ½ teaspoon minced fresh rosemary to pork mixture in step 1.

GRILLED THAI-STYLE PORK BURGERS
Substitute fish sauce for soy sauce. Add 3 tablespoons minced fresh cilantro, 2 teaspoons sriracha sauce, and 1 teaspoon grated lime zest to pork mixture in step 1.

HORSERADISH BURGER SAUCE
MAKES ½ CUP
Buy refrigerated prepared horseradish, not the shelf-stable kind, which contains preservatives and additives. Horseradish strength varies, so add it according to your taste.

 ¼ cup mayonnaise
 2 tablespoons sour cream
1–2 tablespoons prepared horseradish
 1 tablespoon whole-grain mustard
 1 garlic clove, minced
    Pinch sugar
    Salt and pepper
    Hot sauce

Whisk mayonnaise, sour cream, horseradish, mustard, garlic, and sugar together in bowl. Season with salt, pepper, and hot sauce to taste.

GRILLED SAUSAGES WITH BELL PEPPERS AND ONIONS

SERVES 6

You can substitute hot Italian sausages for sweet, if desired. Minimal flare-ups are to be expected when grilling the sausages on the hotter side of the grill; they give the sausages color and flavor. Our favorite instant-read thermometer is the ThermoWorks Thermapen Mk4.

3 red bell peppers, stemmed, seeded, and cut into ¼-inch-wide strips
2 onions, halved and sliced ¼ inch thick
3 tablespoons distilled white vinegar
2 tablespoons sugar
1 tablespoon vegetable oil
½ teaspoon salt
½ teaspoon pepper
1 (13 by 9-inch) disposable aluminum pan
2 pounds sweet Italian sausages
12 (6-inch) sub rolls (optional)

1. Toss bell peppers, onions, vinegar, sugar, oil, salt, and pepper together in bowl. Microwave, covered, until vegetables are just tender, about 6 minutes. Pour vegetable mixture and any accumulated juices into disposable pan.

2A. For a Charcoal Grill Open bottom vent completely. Light large chimney starter filled with charcoal briquettes (6 quarts). When top coals are partially covered with ash, pour evenly over half of grill. Set cooking grate in place, cover, and open lid vent completely. Heat grill until hot, about 5 minutes.

2B. For a Gas Grill Turn all burners to high, cover, and heat grill until hot, about 15 minutes. Leave primary burner on high and turn off other burner(s). (Adjust primary burner [or, if using three-burner grill, primary burner and second burner] as needed to maintain grill temperature between 375 and 400 degrees.)

3. Clean and oil cooking grate. Place disposable pan on hotter side of grill (over primary burner if using gas). Cover and cook for 20 minutes.

4. Place sausages on cooler side of grill and stir vegetable mixture; cover and cook for 8 minutes. Flip sausages and stir vegetable mixture again; cover and cook until sausages register 150 degrees and vegetables are softened and beginning to brown, about 8 minutes.

5. Transfer sausages to disposable pan with vegetables; slide disposable pan to cooler side of grill, then transfer sausages from disposable pan to hotter side of grill. Cook sausages, uncovered, turning often, until well browned and registering 160 degrees, 2 to 3 minutes (there may be flare-ups).

6. Return sausages to disposable pan with vegetables. Remove disposable pan from grill, tent with aluminum foil, and let rest for 5 minutes. Divide sausages and vegetables among rolls, if using. Serve.

Why This Recipe Works To get ballpark-worthy sausages with bell peppers and onions at home, we discovered that it's all about timing. We cooked the sausages gently on the cooler side of the grill until they were nearly done and then moved them to the hotter side to develop nice grill marks and a slight char. We used the microwave to parcook the vegetables and then transferred them to a disposable pan set on the hotter side of the grill, which mimicked a flat-top grill. The vegetables softened and browned just as the sausages finished cooking.

Why This Recipe Works Big chops demand big flavor. Soaking thick pork chops in a salt and sugar brine promised juicy, seasoned meat that would brown beautifully on the grill. For true Hill Country flavor, we applied a rub of kosher salt, pepper, onion powder, and granulated garlic and smoked the chops over mesquite chips. Before firing up the grill, we readied a kicked-up barbecue sauce, rendering strips of bacon and stirring in grated onion and cider vinegar for a pop of acidity; liquid smoke added extra flavor and hot sauce introduced some heat. Brushing the chops with some sauce before serving doubled down on the pork's smoky goodness.

TEXAS THICK-CUT SMOKED PORK CHOPS

SERVES 8

Each chop can easily serve two people. Grate the onion for the sauce on the large holes of a box grater. Our preferred hot sauce is Frank's RedHot Original Cayenne Pepper Sauce. If you'd like to use wood chunks instead of wood chips when using a charcoal grill, substitute two medium chunks, soaked in water for 1 hour, for the wood chip packet.

Pork

Kosher salt and pepper
3 tablespoons sugar
4 (18- to 20-ounce) bone-in pork rib chops, 2 inches thick
2 teaspoons onion powder
2 teaspoons granulated garlic
2 cups mesquite wood chips

Barbecue Sauce

2 slices bacon
¼ cup grated onion
Kosher salt and pepper
¾ cup cider vinegar
1¼ cups chicken broth
1 cup ketchup
2 tablespoons hot sauce
½ teaspoon liquid smoke

1. For the Pork Dissolve 6 tablespoons salt and sugar in 1½ quarts cold water in large container. Submerge chops in brine, cover, and refrigerate for 1 hour. Combine onion powder, granulated garlic, 1½ tablespoons salt, and 2 tablespoons pepper in bowl; set aside.

2. For the Barbecue Sauce Cook bacon in medium saucepan over medium heat until fat begins to render and bacon begins to brown, 4 to 6 minutes. Add onion and ¼ teaspoon salt and cook until softened, 2 to 4 minutes. Stir in vinegar, scraping up any browned bits, and cook until slightly thickened, about 2 minutes.

3. Stir in broth, ketchup, hot sauce, liquid smoke, and ¼ teaspoon pepper. Bring to simmer and cook until slightly thickened, about 15 minutes, stirring occasionally. Discard bacon and season with salt and pepper to taste. Remove from heat, cover, and keep warm.

4. Just before grilling, soak wood chips in water for 15 minutes, then drain. Using large piece of heavy-duty aluminum foil, wrap soaked chips in 8 by 4½-inch foil packet. (Make sure chips do not poke holes in sides or bottom of packet.) Cut 2 evenly spaced 2-inch slits in top of packet. Remove chops from brine and pat dry with paper towels. Season chops all over with reserved spice mixture.

5A. For a Charcoal Grill Open bottom vent completely. Light large chimney starter three-quarters filled with charcoal briquettes (4½ quarts). When top coals are partially covered with ash, pour evenly over half of grill. Place wood chip packet on coals. Set cooking grate in place, cover, and open lid vent completely. Heat grill until hot and wood chips are smoking, about 5 minutes.

5B. For a Gas Grill Remove cooking grate and place wood chip packet directly on primary burner. Set grate in place, turn all burners to high, cover, and heat grill until hot and wood chips are smoking, about 15 minutes. Leave primary burner on medium-high and turn off other burner(s). (Adjust primary burner as needed to maintain grill temperature around 325 degrees.)

6. Clean and oil cooking grate. Arrange chops on cooler side of grill with bone ends toward fire. Cook, covered (positioning lid vent over chops if using charcoal), until chops register 140 degrees, 45 to 50 minutes, flipping halfway through cooking.

7. Transfer chops to platter, tent with foil, and let rest for 10 minutes. Brush chops generously with warm sauce and serve, passing remaining sauce separately.

SMOKED DOUBLE-THICK PORK CHOPS

SERVES 6 TO 8

We prefer blade chops, which have more fat to prevent drying out on the grill, but leaner loin chops will also work. Two medium wood chunks, soaked in water for 1 hour, can be substituted for the wood chips on a charcoal grill. These chops are huge. You may want to slice the meat off the bone before serving.

- ¼ cup packed dark brown sugar
- 1 tablespoon ground fennel
- 1 tablespoon ground cumin
- 1 tablespoon ground coriander
- 1 tablespoon paprika
- 1 teaspoon salt
- 1 teaspoon pepper
- 4 (1¼- to 1½-pound) bone-in blade-cut pork chops, about 2 inches thick, trimmed
- 2 cups wood chips, soaked in water for 15 minutes and drained

1. Combine sugar, fennel, cumin, coriander, paprika, salt, and pepper in bowl. Pat pork chops dry with paper towels and rub them evenly with spice mixture. Wrap chops in plastic wrap and refrigerate for at least 1 hour or up to 24 hours. Using large piece of heavy-duty aluminum foil, wrap soaked chips in foil packet and cut several vent holes in top.

2A. For a Charcoal Grill Open bottom vent halfway. Light large chimney starter filled with charcoal briquettes (6 quarts). When top coals are partially covered with ash, pour into pile on 1 side of grill. Place wood chip packet on coals. Set cooking grate in place, cover, and open lid vent halfway. Heat grill until hot and wood chips are smoking, about 5 minutes.

2B. For a Gas Grill Place wood chip packet directly on primary burner. Turn all burners to high, cover, and heat grill until hot and wood chips are smoking, about 15 minutes. Turn primary burner to medium and turn other burner(s) off. (Adjust primary burner as needed to maintain grill temperature around 275 degrees.)

3. Clean and oil cooking grate. Place pork chops on cool side of grill with bone sides facing hot side of grill. Cover (positioning lid vent over pork if using charcoal) and cook until meat registers 145 degrees, 50 minutes to 1 hour. Slide chops directly over fire (hot side on gas grill) and cook, uncovered, until well browned, about 4 minutes, flipping chops halfway through grilling. Transfer to platter and let rest for 20 minutes. Serve.

Cutting Your Own Double-Thick Pork Chops

We like juicy blade-end chops that are at least 2 inches thick for our Smoked Double-Thick Pork Chops recipe. If you can't find them prepackaged at your grocery store, just buy a 4½- to 5-pound bone-in blade roast and cut it into 2-inch portions yourself. If cutting your own chops, ask your butcher or meat department manager if the chine bone (a part of the backbone) has been removed from the base of the roast—this thick bone can make carving difficult. If the chine bone has not been removed, ask the butcher to cut the chops for you.

Why This Recipe Works Most grilled double-thick pork chop recipes result in a charred exterior and raw meat, or gray meat that tastes steamed. We wanted our pork chops to have great taste and tenderness. Cooking our pork chops over indirect heat made for juicy and tender meat. We used wood chips on the grill to infuse the pork with a nice level of smoke flavor. Coating the double-thick pork chops with a rub of brown sugar and potent herbs and spices helped produce a flavorful crust, and quick grilling over hot coals at the end of cooking gave the crust a crisp texture and rich mahogany color.

Why This Recipe Works Usually, by the time thin-cut pork chops pick up char on the grill, the insides have dried out. To ensure that our pork chops would brown quickly, we partially froze them to eliminate excess moisture from the exterior. Salting them first prevented them from drying out and allowed us to skip brining. A combination of softened butter and brown sugar spread over the chops resulted in a flavorful golden-brown crust when they came off the grill. A chive-mustard butter added even more flavor to the finished chops.

GRILLED THIN-CUT PORK CHOPS

SERVES 4 TO 6

To prevent the chops from curling, cut two slits about 2 inches apart through the fat around the outside of each raw chop.

- 6 bone-in rib or center-cut pork chops, about ½ inch thick, trimmed
- ¾ teaspoon salt
- 4 tablespoons unsalted butter, softened
- 1 teaspoon packed brown sugar
- ½ teaspoon pepper
- 1 teaspoon minced fresh chives
- ½ teaspoon Dijon mustard
- ½ teaspoon grated lemon zest

1. Set wire rack in rimmed baking sheet. Pat chops dry with paper towels. Cut 2 slits, about 2 inches apart, through outer layer of fat and silverskin on each chop. Rub chops with salt. Arrange on prepared rack and freeze until chops are firm, at least 30 minutes but no more than 1 hour. Combine 2 tablespoons butter, sugar, and pepper in small bowl; set aside. Mix remaining 2 tablespoons butter, chives, mustard, and zest in second small bowl and refrigerate until firm, about 15 minutes. (Butter-chive mixture can be refrigerated, covered, for 1 day.)

2A. For a Charcoal Grill Open bottom vent completely. Light large chimney starter filled with charcoal briquettes (6 quarts). When top coals are partially covered with ash, pour evenly over grill. Set cooking grate in place, cover, and open lid vent completely. Heat grill until hot, about 5 minutes.

2B. For a Gas Grill Turn all burners to high, cover, and heat grill until hot, about 15 minutes.

3. Pat chops dry with paper towels. Spread softened butter-sugar mixture evenly over both sides of each chop. Grill, covered, over hot fire until well browned and meat registers 145 degrees, 6 to 8 minutes, flipping chops halfway through grilling. Transfer chops to platter and top with chilled butter-chive mixture. Tent with aluminum foil and let rest for 5 minutes. Serve.

SPICY GRILLED THIN-CUT PORK CHOPS WITH CILANTRO AND LIME

Substitute 1½ teaspoons Asian chili-garlic sauce, 1 teaspoon minced fresh cilantro, and ½ teaspoon grated lime zest for chives, mustard, and lemon zest.

GRILLED THIN-CUT PORK CHOPS WITH THYME AND GINGER

Substitute 1 teaspoon grated fresh ginger, ½ teaspoon minced fresh thyme, and ½ teaspoon grated orange zest for chives, mustard, and lemon zest.

GRILLED THIN-CUT PORK CHOPS WITH OLIVE TAPENADE

Substitute 1½ teaspoons black olive tapenade and ½ teaspoon minced fresh oregano for chives and mustard.

Thin Is the New Thick

For juicy, nicely charred chops, try our method: salting, freezing, and brushing with softened butter before grilling. Salting ensures juicy chops; freezing promotes crust formation by drying the exterior and adding valuable minutes to the cooking time; and butter accelerates browning and adds richness to the lean meat.

WOULD YOU EAT THIS?
Grilled straight from the package, this chop is dry, pale, and bland.

NOW WE'RE TALKING
Salted, frozen, buttered, then grilled, this chop is juicy, browned, and flavorful.

MONROE COUNTY–STYLE PORK CHOPS

SERVES 4

Thin pork chops buckle during cooking. To prevent this, we snip the fat surrounding the loin portion of each chop. In Monroe County, these chops are considered finger food.

- 2 tablespoons kosher salt
- 2 tablespoons pepper
- 1 tablespoon paprika
- ¾ teaspoon cayenne pepper
- 1 tablespoon cornstarch
- 8 (6-ounce) bone-in blade-cut pork chops, ½ inch thick, trimmed
- 8 tablespoons unsalted butter
- ½ cup distilled white vinegar

1. Combine salt, pepper, paprika, and cayenne in bowl. Transfer 2 tablespoons spice mixture to separate bowl and stir in cornstarch. Using kitchen shears, snip interior portion of fat surrounding loin muscle of each chop in 2 places, about 2 inches apart. Season chops all over with cornstarch mixture. Reserve remaining spice mixture for sauce.

2. Heat butter in small saucepan over medium-low heat. Cook, swirling pan constantly, until butter turns dark golden brown and has nutty aroma, 4 to 5 minutes. Add reserved spice mixture and cook until fragrant, about 30 seconds. Carefully add vinegar (mixture will bubble up), bring to quick simmer, then remove from heat. Let cool completely, but do not let butter solidify.

3A. For a Charcoal Grill Open bottom vent completely. Light large chimney starter mounded with charcoal briquettes (7 quarts). When top coals are partially covered with ash, pour evenly over grill. Set cooking grate in place, cover, and open lid vent completely. Heat grill until hot, about 5 minutes.

3B. For a Gas Grill Turn all burners to high, cover, and heat grill until hot, about 15 minutes. Leave all burners on high.

4. Clean and oil cooking grate. Place chops on grill and cook without moving them (covered if using gas) until well charred on first side, 3 to 5 minutes. Flip chops and continue to cook on second side until well charred and meat registers 140 degrees, 3 to 5 minutes longer.

5. Transfer chops to rimmed baking sheet. Pour sauce over chops, flipping to evenly coat. Tent with aluminum foil and let rest for 5 minutes, flipping chops halfway through resting. Serve.

On the Road: All About That Dip

Barbecue in Monroe County, Kentucky, is known (or rather not known) for being a little different. Take the 'cue found at Collins Bar-B-Q in Gamaliel. There, you won't find the slow-smoked fall-apart-tender hunk of pork prevalent at most Southern barbecue joints. Instead, you'll find slices of bone-in pork shoulder, cut thin on the butcher's band saw and quickly grilled over hickory coals.

The sauce, which doubles as the basting liquid, is atypical, too. Known locally as "dip"—basting or saucing is thus "dipping"—it's more spicy than traditional barbecue sauce. Made with lard, butter, vinegar, and black and cayenne peppers, it's thin, oily, and potent. It comes together in a tall pot that's left to sit on the back of the stove where the oily portion naturally rises to the top and the vinegary spice-laden part sinks to the bottom. Since much of the capsaicin in the peppers is oil-soluble, that's where most of the heat resides. If you like your shoulder spicy, the pit master will dip from the top of the pot; less spicy and they'll dive the ladle to the bottom, where it collects more of the spent pepper and sharp vinegar. It's as much about the dip as it is the pork. The shoulder is mopped with dip on the grill, smothered with dip on your plate, and then served with more dip on the side for dunking. And while this is essentially a bone-in pork chop, this is 100 percent finger food. Tear off a piece, dip, eat, repeat.

Why This Recipe Works The paper-thin pork "steaks" flash-grilled over hickory coals in Monroe County, Kentucky, stay moist and flavorful thanks in part to a healthy dose of a fiery crimson-colored sauce (ordering it "dipped" means the meat is dunked in the lip-numbing sauce). For our version of this spicy, smoky, and intoxicating delicacy, we used bone-in blade pork chops (thin enough to not require at-home slicing) with just enough fat to keep the pork tender while grilling over a screaming-hot fire. For our "dip," we browned butter to bring out its nuttiness and dialed back the cayenne pepper, delivering a flavor-packed yet balanced heat.

ST. LOUIS BBQ PORK STEAKS

SERVES 4

Boneless pork butt is also labeled Boston butt. If pork steaks are available, use them and increase the cooking time in the sauce to 1 to 1½ hours. We use Budweiser in this recipe, since it's made in St. Louis, but any mild-tasting beer will do.

Spice Rub and Pork Steaks

- 1 tablespoon packed brown sugar
- 1 tablespoon paprika
- 2 teaspoons dry mustard
- 2 teaspoons pepper
- 1 teaspoon onion powder
- 1 teaspoon garlic powder
- 1 teaspoon ground cumin
- 1 teaspoon salt
- ¼ teaspoon cayenne pepper
- 1 (5- to 6-pound) boneless pork butt roast, sliced crosswise, trimmed, and each half cut into three or four 1-inch-thick steaks

Barbecue Sauce

- 2 cups beer
- 1½ cups ketchup
- ¼ cup Heinz 57 Steak Sauce
- ¼ cup packed dark brown sugar
- 2 tablespoons cider vinegar
- 2 tablespoons Worcestershire sauce
- 1 teaspoon garlic powder
- 1 teaspoon hot sauce
- 1 teaspoon liquid smoke
- 1 (13 by 9-inch) disposable aluminum roasting pan

1. For the Spice Rub and Pork Steaks Combine sugar, paprika, dry mustard, pepper, onion powder, garlic powder, cumin, salt, and cayenne in bowl. Pat pork steaks dry with paper towels and rub them evenly with spice mixture. Wrap pork in plastic wrap and refrigerate for at least 1 hour or up to 24 hours.

2. For the Barbecue Sauce Whisk all ingredients together in bowl and transfer to disposable pan.

3A. For a Charcoal Grill Open bottom vent halfway. Light large chimney starter filled with charcoal briquettes (6 quarts). When top coals are partially covered with ash, pour evenly over grill. Set cooking grate in place, cover, and open lid vent halfway. Heat grill until hot, about 5 minutes.

3B. For a Gas Grill Turn all burners to high, cover, and heat grill until hot, about 15 minutes. Leave primary burner on high and turn other burner(s) off. (Adjust primary burner as needed to maintain grill temperature around 350 degrees.)

4. Clean and oil cooking grate. Place pork steaks on hot side of grill. Cook (covered if using gas) until well browned on both sides, about 10 minutes, flipping steaks halfway through grilling.

5. Transfer pork steaks to sauce in pan and coat thoroughly. Cover pan with aluminum foil and place on grill. Cover (positioning lid vent over pan if using charcoal) and cook steaks until fork-tender and they register 190 degrees, 45 minutes to 1 hour. Remove steaks from pan and grill until lightly charred around edges, 4 to 8 minutes, flipping steaks halfway through grilling.

6. Transfer steaks to serving platter, tent loosely with foil, and let rest for 10 minutes. Skim excess fat from sauce and serve with steaks.

Making Pork Steaks

1. Slice pork crosswise in half and remove any large pieces of fat.

2. Rotate and stand each half of pork butt on its cut end and cut each half into three or four 1-inch-thick steaks.

Why This Recipe Works St. Louis BBQ pork steaks are little-known in other parts of America, but in St. Louis, they are so popular that pork steaks are on permanent sale in family packs at the supermarket. We found there was no substitute for pork steak, so the only option was to cut our own. We ordered a boneless Boston butt and cut it in half crosswise, then turned each piece on end to slice 1-inch-thick steaks. Inspired by a test kitchen recipe for brats and beer, we used a method of sear, simmer, sear again. This untraditional process gives the steaks a nice char, candy-like edges, and succulent, slightly chewy interiors.

CHINESE-STYLE GLAZED PORK TENDERLOIN

SERVES 4 TO 6

Leftover pork makes an excellent addition to fried rice or noodle soup.

2 (12- to 16-ounce) pork tenderloins, trimmed
½ cup soy sauce
½ cup apricot preserves
¼ cup hoisin sauce
¼ cup dry sherry
2 tablespoons grated fresh ginger
1 tablespoon toasted sesame oil
2 garlic cloves, minced
1 teaspoon five-spice powder
1 teaspoon pepper
¼ cup ketchup
1 tablespoon molasses
2 teaspoons vegetable oil

1. Lay tenderloins on cutting board with long side running parallel to counter edge. Cut horizontally down length of each tenderloin, stopping ½ inch from edge so tenderloin remains intact. Working with one at a time, open up tenderloins, place between 2 sheets of plastic wrap, and pound to ¾-inch thickness.

2. Combine soy sauce, preserves, hoisin, sherry, ginger, sesame oil, garlic, five-spice powder, and pepper in bowl. Reserve ¾ cup marinade. Place pork in large zipper-lock bag and pour remaining marinade into bag with pork. Seal bag, turn to coat, and refrigerate for at least 30 minutes or up to 4 hours.

3. Combine reserved marinade, ketchup, and molasses in small saucepan. Cook over medium heat until syrupy and reduced to ¾ cup, 3 to 5 minutes. Reserve ¼ cup glaze for glazing cooked pork.

4A. For a Charcoal Grill Open bottom vent completely. Light large chimney starter filled with charcoal briquettes (6 quarts). When top coals are partially covered with ash, pour evenly over grill. Set cooking grate in place, cover, and open lid vent completely. Heat grill until hot, about 5 minutes.

4B. For a Gas Grill Turn all burners to high, cover, and heat grill until hot, about 15 minutes. Turn all burners to medium-high.

5. Clean and oil cooking grate. Pat pork dry with paper towels, then rub with vegetable oil. Grill pork (covered if using gas) until lightly charred on first side, about 2 minutes. Flip and brush grilled side of pork evenly with 2 tablespoons glaze. Continue grilling until lightly charred on second side, about 2 minutes. Flip and brush evenly with 2 more tablespoons glaze. Repeat flipping and glazing twice more, until pork registers 140 degrees and is thickly glazed, about 4 minutes longer. Transfer pork to cutting board and brush with reserved glaze. Tent loosely with aluminum foil and let rest for 5 minutes. Slice and serve.

Preparing the Tenderloins

1. Place tenderloins on cutting board and slice each down side, leaving ½ inch of meat uncut. Open each tenderloin like a book.

2. Place each butterflied tenderloin between two sheets of plastic wrap. Using meat pounder, pound each to ¾-inch thickness.

Why This Recipe Works For an easy take on Chinese-style glazed and charred pork, we turned to the grill and opted for pork tenderloin, which cooks quickly over a hot fire. Butterflying and pounding the meat gave us maximum surface area for our glaze. A combination of thick, sweet apricot preserves and ketchup flavored with hoisin, fresh ginger, sesame oil, sherry, garlic, and five-spice powder gave us a salty-sweet sauce that acted as both marinade and glaze. Continuously flipping and glazing the pork creates a charred, caramelized—but not burnt—exterior.

Why This Recipe Works We began our Chinese-Style Barbecued Spareribs by removing the tough membrane on the underside of the ribs. Instead of cooking the ribs on the grill the entire time, we found that cooking them in the sauce in the oven and then finishing them on the grill allowed for deeply seasoned Chinese-style ribs and eliminated the need to marinate them. Since the smoke from wood chips was overpowering, we replaced the wood chips with orange spice or Earl Grey tea bags soaked in water, wrapped in foil, and placed on the hot coals for a mellow, smoky flavor that complemented the seasonings in the sauce.

CHINESE-STYLE BARBECUED SPARERIBS

SERVES 6

Full-size spareribs are fatty, plus they're too large to fit on the grill. If you can't find St. Louis–style spareribs (which have been trimmed of the brisket bone and surrounding meat), substitute baby back ribs and begin to check for doneness after 1 hour on the grill. Cover the edges of the ribs loosely with foil if they begin to burn while grilling.

2 (2½- to 3-pound) racks St. Louis–style spareribs, trimmed
8 black tea bags, preferably orange spice or Earl Grey
1½ cups ketchup
1 cup soy sauce
1 cup hoisin sauce
1 cup sugar
½ cup dry sherry
6 garlic cloves, minced
2 tablespoons grated fresh ginger
2 teaspoons toasted sesame oil
1½ teaspoons cayenne pepper
1 (13 by 9-inch) disposable aluminum roasting pan
1 cup red currant jelly

1. To remove chewy membrane from ribs, loosen it with tip of paring knife and, with aid of paper towel, pull it off slowly in 1 big piece. Cut rib racks in half. Cover tea bags with water in small bowl and soak for 5 minutes. Squeeze water from tea bags. Using large piece of heavy-duty aluminum foil, wrap tea bags in foil packet and cut several vent holes in top.

2. Adjust oven rack to middle position and heat oven to 300 degrees. Whisk 1 cup ketchup, soy sauce, hoisin sauce, sugar, sherry, garlic, ginger, sesame oil, and cayenne in large bowl; reserve ½ cup for glaze. Arrange ribs, meaty side down, in disposable pan and pour remaining ketchup mixture over ribs. Cover pan tightly with foil and cook until fat has rendered and meat begins to pull away from bones, 2 to 2½ hours. Transfer ribs to large plate. Pour pan juices into fat separator. Let liquid settle and reserve 1 cup defatted pan juices.

3. Simmer reserved pan juices in medium saucepan over medium-high heat until reduced to ½ cup, about 5 minutes. Stir in jelly, reserved ketchup mixture, and remaining ½ cup ketchup and simmer until reduced to 2 cups, 10 to 12 minutes. Reserve one-third of glaze for serving.

4A. For a Charcoal Grill Open bottom vent completely. Light large chimney starter filled with charcoal briquettes (6 quarts). When top coals are partially covered with ash, pour evenly over half of grill. Place tea packet on coals. Set cooking grate in place, cover, and open lid vent completely. Heat grill until hot and tea is smoking, about 5 minutes.

4B. For a Gas Grill Place tea packet directly on primary burner. Turn all burners to high, cover, and heat grill until hot and tea is smoking, about 15 minutes. Leave primary burner on high and turn other burner(s) off.

5. Clean and oil cooking grate. Arrange ribs, meaty side down, on cool side of grill and cook, covered, until ribs are smoky and edges begin to char, about 30 minutes.

6. Brush ribs with glaze, flip, rotate, and brush again. Cover and cook, brushing with glaze every 30 minutes, until ribs are fully tender and glaze is browned and sticky, 1 to 1½ hours. Transfer ribs to cutting board, tent with foil, and let rest for 10 minutes. Serve with reserved glaze.

To Make Ahead Ribs and glaze can be prepared through step 3 up to 2 days in advance. Once ribs are cool, wrap tightly in foil and refrigerate. Transfer glaze to microwave-safe bowl, cover with plastic wrap, and refrigerate. Before proceeding with step 4, allow ribs to stand at room temperature for 1 hour. Before proceeding with step 6, microwave glaze until warm, about 1 minute.

Why This Recipe Works Boneless country-style ribs present several cooking challenges. Each piece not only varies wildly from the next, but is also a mishmash of lean white meat and rich dark meat. Unfortunately, if the ribs are cooked to optimize the white meat, then the dark meat stays tough, and if they are cooked to optimize the dark meat, the white meat turns dry. To even out the cooking, we brined the ribs so that the white meat would stay juicy and pounded the ribs to an even ¾-inch thickness to "break down" the fattier dark meat. As for flavor, a double layer of barbecue spice and sauce and a quick smoke on the grill worked wonders.

BARBECUED COUNTRY-STYLE RIBS

SERVES 4 TO 6

For easier pounding, cut any ribs that are longer than 5 inches in half crosswise.

- 1 tablespoon salt
- 2 pounds boneless country-style pork ribs, trimmed
- ¾ cup packed dark brown sugar
- 2 tablespoons chili powder
- 2 tablespoons paprika
- 1 tablespoon dry mustard
- 1 tablespoon onion powder
- ¾ teaspoon pepper
- ¼ teaspoon cayenne pepper
- 6 tablespoons ketchup
- 1 tablespoon cider vinegar
- ¼ cup wood chips, soaked in water for 15 minutes and drained

1. Dissolve salt in 2 cups cold water in large container. Place ribs, cut side down, between 2 sheets of plastic wrap and pound to ¾ inch thickness. Submerge pork in brine, cover, and refrigerate for 30 minutes to 1 hour.

2. Combine sugar, chili powder, paprika, dry mustard, onion powder, pepper, and cayenne in shallow dish. Transfer half of mixture to bowl and stir in ketchup and vinegar; set aside.

3. Remove pork from brine and pat dry with paper towels. Dredge pork in remaining spice mixture and transfer to plate. Using large piece of heavy-duty aluminum foil, wrap soaked chips in foil packet and cut several vent holes in top.

4A. For a Charcoal Grill Open bottom vent halfway. Light large chimney starter filled with charcoal briquettes (6 quarts). When top coals are partially covered with ash, pour evenly over half of grill. Place wood chip packet on coals. Set cooking grate in place, cover, and open lid vent halfway. Heat grill until hot and wood chips are smoking, about 5 minutes.

4B. For a Gas Grill Place wood chip packet directly on primary burner. Turn all burners to high, cover, and heat grill until hot and wood chips are smoking, about 15 minutes. Leave primary burner on high and turn other burner(s) off.

5. Clean and oil cooking grate. Place pork on cool side of grill, cover (positioning lid vent over meat if using charcoal), and cook until meat registers 125 degrees, 3 to 5 minutes. Brush pork with ketchup mixture and grill, brushed side down, over hot side of grill until lightly charred, 2 to 3 minutes. Brush second side of pork, flip, and grill until lightly charred and meat registers 145 degrees, 2 to 3 minutes. Transfer pork to platter, tent loosely with foil, and let rest for 5 to 10 minutes. Serve.

Country-Style Ribs

Country-style ribs aren't ribs at all. They're well-marbled pork chops cut from the blade end of the loin. We bought dozens of these chops while testing this recipe and found that they were inconsistently shaped and sized. What's more, these "ribs" had widely varying proportions of light and dark meat. To help level the culinary playing field and ensure even cooking, we pounded each piece into an even ¾ inch thickness.

MISMATCHED MEAT
Each "rib" contains both light and dark meat.

Ensuring Even Cooking

The white and dark meat in country-style ribs cook at different rates—the white meat cooks quickly, while the dark meat is slower to tenderize. To equalize them, we brined and pounded. Brining kept the white meat from drying out, while pounding the ribs thin let them cook faster, helpful since long cooking times accentuate differences in cooking. Think of a fast car and a slow car starting from a stoplight at the same time: 30 seconds after the light turns green, the two cars won't be far apart, but after 10 minutes, they will be.

SOUTH DAKOTA CORNCOB-SMOKED RIBS

SERVES 4 TO 6

A gas grill can't do these corncob ribs justice, so please use charcoal. The test kitchen's favorite ketchup is Heinz Organic. To use up some of the leftover corn, try our recipe for Sweet Corn Spoonbread (page 340).

Sauce
1 cup ketchup
¼ cup water
1 tablespoon pepper
1 tablespoon onion powder
1 tablespoon Worcestershire sauce
1 tablespoon light corn syrup
1 tablespoon granulated garlic
2 teaspoons celery seeds
½ teaspoon liquid smoke

Ribs
5 tablespoons packed light brown sugar
1 teaspoon salt
½ teaspoon pepper
2 (2½- to 3-pound) racks baby back pork ribs, trimmed and membrane removed
1 cup cornmeal
6 corncobs, kernels removed and reserved for another use
1 (13 by 9-inch) disposable aluminum roasting pan

1. For the Sauce Whisk all ingredients together in medium bowl; set aside.

2. For the Ribs Combine sugar, salt, and pepper in bowl. Pat ribs dry with paper towels and rub with sugar mixture; set aside. Using large piece of heavy-duty aluminum foil, wrap cornmeal in foil packet and cut several vent holes in top.

3. Open bottom vents of charcoal grill halfway. Place disposable pan on 1 side of grill and fill pan with 2 quarts water. Arrange 3 quarts unlit charcoal briquettes on opposite side of grill. Place cobs on top of unlit briquettes. Light large chimney starter filled halfway with charcoal briquettes (3 quarts). When top coals are partially covered with ash, pour over cobs and unlit briquettes. Place cornmeal packet on coals. Set cooking grate in place, cover, and open lid vent halfway. Heat grill until hot and cornmeal is smoking, about 5 minutes.

4. Clean and oil cooking grate. Place ribs, meat side up, on cool part of grill opposite coals. Cover, positioning lid vent over ribs, and cook until ribs are deep red and tender, 3½ to 4 hours, rotating and switching ribs every hour. (Do not flip ribs.) During last 30 minutes of cooking, baste ribs every 10 minutes, rotating and switching ribs each time. Transfer ribs to carving board, tent loosely with foil, and let rest for 15 to 20 minutes. Cut ribs in between bones. Serve, passing remaining sauce separately.

Failed Corncob Tests

In South Dakota, bushels of dried, stripped corncobs impart a special flavor to ribs. To replicate it, we left no kernel unturned. It was A for effort, but these attempts were a bust.

SOOTY
Unhusked ears of corn

SOOTY
Husked ears with the corn intact

TOO MUCH WORK
Husked, stripped, and oven-dried

BURNT TASTE
Popped popcorn

Why This Recipe Works Corncob smoking is a South Dakota specialty and pit master Larry Mart is its undisputed king. It gives meat a subtle smokiness hardwoods can't match. For barbecued ribs with mild, nutty sweetness but without a barbecuing rig, we layered charcoal on our grill with fresh corncobs (with the kernels removed) and a foil packet of cornmeal. The cornmeal gave the ribs an initial blast of smoky flavor, and the fresh cobs offered long-lasting smoke and a nutty aroma. We basted the ribs with a simple ketchup-based barbecue sauce with plenty of garlic and some celery seeds for sticky, sweet ribs that we couldn't get enough of.

Why This Recipe Works Two surefire ways to dress up a pork roast are to give it a flavorful, deeply caramelized crust on the grill and serve it with a savory-sweet mustard glaze. Our mustard-glazed pork loin has the best of both worlds. Leaving our roast untrimmed added moisture and flavor—and scoring the fat kept it from tasting too fatty. For the mustard glaze, apple jelly was a perfect complement to the spicy crunch of grainy mustard, and both married well with the other glaze ingredients—brown sugar, garlic, and fresh thyme. To fully infuse our pork loin with mustard flavor, we applied the glaze before, during, and after grilling.

GRILLED MUSTARD-GLAZED PORK LOIN

SERVES 6 TO 8

Dijon and yellow mustards also work well in the glaze, but make certain to use apple jelly, not apple butter. Look for a pork roast with about ¼ inch of fat on top and tie the roast at 1-inch intervals to ensure an even shape.

½ cup whole-grain mustard
6 tablespoons apple jelly
2 tablespoons packed dark brown sugar
2 tablespoons extra-virgin olive oil
1 large garlic clove, minced
2 teaspoons minced fresh thyme
¾ teaspoon pepper
½ teaspoon salt
1 boneless pork loin roast (2½ to 3 pounds), fat scored lightly, tied at 1-inch intervals

1. Whisk mustard, jelly, sugar, oil, garlic, thyme, pepper, and salt together in bowl. Measure out ⅔ cup sauce and set aside for cooking; reserve remaining sauce for serving. Before grilling, pat pork loin dry with paper towels and coat it evenly with ⅓ cup sauce for cooking.

2A. For a Charcoal Grill Open bottom vent halfway. Light large chimney starter filled with charcoal briquettes (6 quarts). When top coals are partially covered with ash, pour evenly over half of grill. Set cooking grate in place, cover, and open lid vent halfway. Heat grill until hot, about 5 minutes.

2B. For a Gas Grill Turn all the burners to high, cover, and heat grill until hot, about 15 minutes. Leave primary burner on high and turn other burner(s) off. (Adjust primary burner as needed to maintain grill temperature around 350 degrees.)

3. Clean and oil cooking grate. Place pork loin on hot side of grill. Cook (covered if using gas) until well browned on all sides, 12 to 15 minutes, turning as needed.

4. Flip pork loin fat side up and slide to cool side of grill. Brush pork with 2 tablespoons sauce for cooking. Cover (positioning lid vent over pork if using charcoal) and continue to cook until meat registers 140 degrees, 25 to 40 minutes longer, brushing every 10 minutes with remaining sauce for cooking.

5. Transfer pork loin to carving board, tent loosely with aluminum foil, and let rest for 15 minutes. Remove twine, cut meat into ¼-inch-thick slices, and transfer to serving platter. Whisk any accumulated juices into reserved sauce, spoon over meat, and serve.

The Benefits of Scoring

Gently scoring the fat helps it render (basting the meat and keeping it moist as it cooks) and creates an uneven surface that holds the glaze.

WOOD-GRILLED SALMON

SERVES 4

Any variety of wood chips will work here, but aromatic woods such as cedar and alder give the most traditional flavor.

1½ teaspoons sugar
½ teaspoon salt
¼ teaspoon pepper
4 (6- to 8-ounce) skin-on salmon fillets, about 1¼ inches thick
1 tablespoon olive oil
2 cups wood chips, soaked in water for 15 minutes and drained

1. Combine sugar, salt, and pepper in bowl. Pat salmon fillets dry with paper towels, then brush flesh sides with oil and rub evenly with sugar mixture. Using 4 large sheets of heavy-duty aluminum foil, crimp edges of each sheet to make 4 trays, each measuring 7 by 5 inches. Perforate bottom of each tray with tip of paring knife. Divide wood chips among trays and lay 1 fillet skin side down on top of wood chips in each tray.

2A. For a Charcoal Grill Open bottom vent completely. Light large chimney starter filled with charcoal briquettes (6 quarts). When top coals are partially covered with ash, pour evenly over grill. Set cooking grate in place, cover, and open lid vent completely. Heat grill until hot, about 5 minutes.

2B. For a Gas Grill Turn all burners to high, cover, and heat grill until hot, about 15 minutes.

3. Clean and oil cooking grate. Place trays on grill. Cook (covered if using gas) until center is still translucent when checked with tip of paring knife and registers 125 degrees (for medium-rare), about 10 minutes.

4. Transfer trays to wire rack, tent loosely with foil, and let rest for 5 minutes. Slide metal spatula between skin and flesh of fish, transfer fish to platter, and serve.

BARBECUED WOOD-GRILLED SALMON
Add ¾ teaspoon chili powder and ¼ teaspoon cayenne pepper to sugar mixture and substitute 1 tablespoon Dijon mustard mixed with 1 tablespoon maple syrup for oil in step 1.

LEMON-THYME WOOD-GRILLED SALMON
Add 2 teaspoons minced fresh thyme and 1½ teaspoons grated fresh lemon zest to sugar mixture and substitute 2 tablespoons Dijon mustard for oil in step 1.

Another Way to Planked Salmon
Cooking salmon on a cedar plank infuses it with gentle wood flavor rather than overwhelming smokiness. But sometimes they can be difficult to find. Here's how to get the same great taste, minus the plank.

1. Crimp 4 sheets of foil to make trays. Using paring knife, poke small slits in bottom of trays.

2. Place soaked wood chips in foil trays and arrange salmon skin side down directly on top of wood chips.

3. Once salmon is cooked, slide metal spatula between flesh and skin; fish should release easily.

Why This Recipe Works To create the flavor of cedar planks in our wood-grilled salmon (without having to mail-order them), we settled on wood chips and made individual aluminum foil trays to hold the chips and salmon. To prevent the salmon from sticking to the wood chips, we left the skin on, which easily separated from the cooked fish. Poking a few slits in the bottom of the foil allowed more heat to reach the wood chips, which caused them to release more of their woodsy—but not overly smoky—flavor. Coating each fillet with a thin layer of olive oil and a light sprinkling of granulated sugar produced a golden, mildly sweet exterior.

CEDAR-PLANKED SALMON
WITH CUCUMBER-YOGURT SAUCE

SERVES 4

Be sure to buy an untreated cedar plank specifically intended for cooking. To ensure uniform pieces of fish, we prefer to purchase a whole center-cut salmon fillet and cut it into four equal pieces. Note that the seasoned fillets must be refrigerated for at least 1 hour before grilling. When preheating the cedar plank, you will know it's ready when it is just giving off wisps of smoke. It should not ignite. Serve with lemon wedges and our Cucumber-Yogurt Sauce (recipe follows).

- 1 (2-pound) center-cut, skinless salmon fillet, about 1½ inches thick
- 2 tablespoons packed brown sugar
- 1½ tablespoons kosher salt
- 1 tablespoon chopped fresh dill
- 1 teaspoon pepper
- 1 (16 by 7-inch) cedar plank
- 1 teaspoon vegetable oil
  Lemon wedges

1. Cut salmon crosswise into 4 equal fillets and pat dry with paper towels. Combine sugar, salt, dill, and pepper in bowl. Sprinkle salmon all over with sugar mixture, place on plate, and refrigerate, uncovered, for at least 1 hour or up to 24 hours. One hour before grilling, soak cedar plank in water for 1 hour (or according to manufacturer's directions).

2A. For a Charcoal Grill Open bottom vent completely. Light large chimney starter filled with charcoal briquettes (6 quarts). When top coals are partially covered with ash, pour evenly over grill. Set cooking grate in place. Place cedar plank in center of grill. Cover and open lid vent completely. Heat grill until plank is lightly smoking and crackling (it should not ignite), about 5 minutes.

2B. For a Gas Grill Place cedar plank in center of grill. Turn all burners to medium-low, cover, and heat grill until plank is smoking and crackling (it should not ignite), about 15 minutes. Leave all burners on medium-low. Adjust burners as needed to maintain grill temperature between 300 and 325 degrees.

3. Brush 1 side of salmon fillets with oil, then place oiled side down on plank. Cover grill and cook until center of salmon is translucent when checked with tip of paring knife and registers 125 degrees (for medium-rare), 12 to 15 minutes. Using tongs, transfer plank with salmon to baking sheet, tent with aluminum foil, and let rest for 5 minutes. Serve with lemon wedges.

CUCUMBER-YOGURT SAUCE
MAKES ABOUT ¾ CUP

A spoon makes easy work of removing the cucumber seeds. Using Greek yogurt here is key; don't substitute regular plain yogurt, or the sauce will be very watery.

- ½ cucumber, peeled, halved lengthwise, and seeded
- ½ cup plain whole-milk Greek yogurt
- 1 tablespoon extra-virgin olive oil
- 1 tablespoon chopped fresh mint
- 1 tablespoon chopped fresh dill
- 1 small garlic clove, minced
- ¼ teaspoon pepper
- ⅛ teaspoon salt

Shred cucumber on large holes of box grater. Combine yogurt, oil, mint, dill, garlic, pepper, salt, and shredded cucumber in bowl. Cover and refrigerate until chilled, about 20 minutes. Serve.

Why This Recipe Works Our smoky, succulent salmon is surprisingly easy to make. Grilling the delicate fish on a cedar plank prevented it from sticking to the grill and provided subtle smoky flavor while keeping the grill grates pristine. While the plank soaked in water, we seasoned the salmon with a simple "cure" of brown sugar, kosher salt, fresh dill, and pepper. We preheated the plank on the grill before adding the salmon to get just the right woodsy flavor that wouldn't overwhelm the fish. Opting for skinless fillets allowed just enough cedar flavor to permeate the salmon. A Greek yogurt–cucumber tzatziki sauce balanced the salmon's smoky richness.

Why This Recipe Works Salmon steaks are a common choice for grilling: Their bone and thickness make them a far sturdier cut than a fillet. But the steak's thickness can also work against it, making it difficult for the interior and exterior to finish cooking at the same time. We began by tucking the belly flaps in toward the center of the steak and tying them to create medallions that would cook evenly and be easily maneuvered. To make sure our steaks were packed with flavor, we finished cooking them in a pan of zesty sauce on the cooler part of the grill. When they were done, our salmon steaks were flavorful, juicy, and moist.

GRILLED SALMON STEAKS WITH LEMON-CAPER SAUCE

SERVES 4

Before eating, lift out the small circular bone from the center of each steak.

4 (10-ounce) salmon steaks, 1 to 1½ inches thick
  Salt and pepper
2 tablespoons olive oil
1 teaspoon grated lemon zest and 6 tablespoons juice (2 lemons)
1 shallot, minced
3 tablespoons unsalted butter, cut into 3 pieces
1 tablespoon capers, rinsed
2 tablespoons minced fresh parsley
1 (13 by 9-inch) disposable aluminum pan

1. Pat salmon steaks dry with paper towels. Working with 1 steak at a time, carefully trim 1½ inches of skin from 1 tail. Tightly wrap other tail around skinned portion and tie steaks with kitchen twine. Repeat with remaining salmon steaks. Season salmon steaks with salt and pepper and brush both sides with oil. Combine lemon zest, lemon juice, shallot, butter, capers, and ⅛ teaspoon salt in disposable pan.

2A. For a Charcoal Grill Open bottom vent completely. Light large chimney starter filled with charcoal briquettes (6 quarts). When top coals are partially covered with ash, pour evenly over half of grill. Set cooking grate in place, cover, and open lid vent completely. Heat grill until hot, about 5 minutes.

2B. For a Gas Grill Turn all burners to high, cover, and heat grill until hot, about 15 minutes. Leave primary burner on high and turn off other burner(s).

3. Clean and oil cooking grate. Place salmon medallions on hot part of grill. Cook until browned, 2 to 3 minutes per side. Meanwhile, set pan on cool part of grill and cook until butter has melted, about 2 minutes. Transfer medallions to pan and gently turn to coat. Cook (covered if using gas) until center is still translucent when checked with tip of paring knife and registers 125 degrees (for medium-rare), 6 to 14 minutes, flipping salmon and rotating pan halfway through grilling. Remove twine and transfer salmon to platter. Off heat, whisk parsley into sauce and drizzle sauce over salmon. Serve.

Prepping Salmon Medallions

 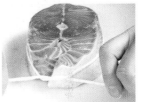

1. For salmon steaks sturdy enough to grill easily, remove 1½ inches of skin from 1 tail of each steak.

2. Tuck skinned portion into center of steak, wrap other tail around it, and tie with kitchen twine.

Why This Recipe Works The smoked salmon taco served at Ruddell's Smokehouse in Cayucos, California, won us over with its unbeatable (and unique) combination of smoky fish, creamy mustard sauce, and a crunchy-sweet apple slaw. For our version, we seasoned the salmon in a salt-sugar cure to firm up the flesh and brushed on an apricot glaze. Then we built a two-level fire and added some wood chips. Cooked gently on the grill's cooler side, the salmon took on smoky flavor and a silky texture without drying out, even when brought to medium-well, which made the fillets easier to flake over a tortilla.

SMOKED FISH TACOS

SERVES 4 TO 6

Hickory wood chips are widely available and work fine in this recipe. However, we prefer the flavor that applewood chips (if you can find them) impart to the fish. To ensure even cooking, we prefer to purchase a whole center-cut salmon fillet and cut it into four equal pieces. Note that the seasoned fillets must be refrigerated for at least 4 hours before grilling. If desired, you can serve the salmon as whole fillets rather than as a flaked taco filling. Smucker's makes our favorite apricot preserves, and our favorite brown mustard is Gulden's Spicy Brown Mustard.

Salmon

- 1 cup packed brown sugar
  Kosher salt
- 1 tablespoon granulated garlic
- 1 (2-pound) center-cut, skin-on salmon fillet, about 1½ inches thick
- 1 cup wood chips
- 2 tablespoons apricot preserves
- 1 tablespoon water

Tacos

- ½ cup mayonnaise
- ¼ cup spicy brown mustard
- 2 teaspoons lemon juice
- ¼ teaspoon ground cumin
- 1 small Granny Smith apple, peeled and chopped fine
- 1 small celery rib, chopped fine
- 1 small carrot, peeled and shredded
- 12 (6-inch) flour tortillas, warmed
- 3 ounces (3 cups) mesclun

1. For the Salmon Combine sugar, ¼ cup salt, and granulated garlic in bowl. Cut salmon crosswise into 4 equal fillets. Transfer salmon and sugar mixture to 1-gallon zipper-lock bag. Press out air, seal bag, and turn to evenly coat salmon with sugar mixture. Refrigerate for at least 4 hours or up to 24 hours.

2. Just before grilling, soak wood chips in water for 15 minutes, then drain. Using large piece of heavy-duty aluminum foil, wrap soaked chips in 8 by 4½-inch foil packet. (Make sure chips do not poke holes in sides or bottom of packet.) Cut 2 evenly spaced 2-inch slits in top of packet.

3. Remove salmon from sugar mixture; discard sugar mixture. Rinse excess sugar mixture from salmon and pat salmon dry with paper towels. Whisk preserves and water together in small bowl; microwave until mixture is fluid, about 30 seconds.

4A. For a Charcoal Grill Open bottom vent completely. Light large chimney starter one-third filled with charcoal briquettes (2 quarts). When top coals are partially covered with ash, pour evenly over half of grill. Place wood chip packet on coals. Set cooking grate in place, cover, and open lid vent completely. Heat grill until hot and wood chips are smoking, about 5 minutes.

4B. For a Gas Grill Remove cooking grate and place wood chip packet directly on primary burner. Set cooking grate in place, turn all burners to high, cover, and heat grill until hot and wood chips are smoking, about 15 minutes. Turn primary burner to medium and turn off other burner(s). (Adjust primary burner as needed to maintain grill temperature between 250 and 275 degrees.)

5. Clean and oil cooking grate. Brush tops and sides of salmon fillets evenly with apricot mixture. Place fillets, skin side down, on cooler side of grill, with thicker ends facing fire. Cover grill (position lid vent over salmon if using charcoal) and cook until centers of fillets register 135 degrees (for medium-well), 28 to 35 minutes. Transfer salmon to plate, tent with foil, and let rest for 5 minutes. (If skin sticks to cooking grate, insert fish spatula between skin and fillet to separate and lift fillet from skin.)

6. For the Tacos Meanwhile, whisk mayonnaise, mustard, lemon juice, and cumin together in bowl. Combine apple, celery, and carrot in second bowl.

7. Remove and discard salmon skin. Flake salmon into bite-size pieces and season with salt to taste. Divide salmon evenly among tortillas, about ⅓ cup per tortilla. Serve, topping each taco with desired amounts of mesclun, mayonnaise mixture, and apple mixture.

Why This Recipe Works We wanted tender, juicy, shrimp with a smoky, charred crust and chile flavor that was more than just superficial. To achieve this, we sprinkled one side of the shrimp with sugar to promote browning and cooked the shrimp sugar side down over the hot side of the grill for a few minutes. We then flipped the skewers to gently finish cooking on the cool side of the grill. Creating a flavorful marinade that doubled as a sauce gave our shrimp skewers a spicy, assertive kick. And butterflying the shrimp before marinating and grilling them opened up more shrimp flesh for the marinade and finishing sauce to flavor.

GRILLED JALAPEÑO AND LIME SHRIMP SKEWERS

SERVES 4

We prefer flat metal skewers that are at least 14 inches long for this recipe.

Marinade

1–2 jalapeño chiles, stemmed, seeded, and chopped
3 tablespoons olive oil
6 garlic cloves, minced
1 teaspoon grated lime zest plus 5 tablespoons juice (3 limes)
½ teaspoon ground cumin
¼ teaspoon cayenne pepper
½ teaspoon salt

Shrimp

1½ pounds extra-large shrimp (21 to 25 per pound), peeled and deveined
½ teaspoon sugar
1 tablespoon minced fresh cilantro

1. For the Marinade Process all ingredients in food processor until smooth, about 15 seconds. Reserve 2 tablespoons marinade; transfer remaining marinade to medium bowl.

2. For the Shrimp Pat shrimp dry with paper towels. To butterfly shrimp, use paring knife to make shallow cut down outside curve of shrimp. Add shrimp to bowl with marinade and toss to coat. Cover and refrigerate for 30 minutes to 1 hour.

3A. For a Charcoal Grill Open bottom vent completely. Light large chimney starter filled with charcoal briquettes (6 quarts). When top coals are partially covered with ash, pour evenly over half of grill. Set cooking grate in place, cover, and open lid vent completely. Heat grill until hot, about 5 minutes.

3B. For a Gas Grill Turn all burners to high, cover, and heat grill until hot, about 15 minutes.

4. Clean and oil cooking grate. Thread marinated shrimp on skewers. (Alternate direction of each shrimp as you pack them tightly on skewer to allow about a dozen shrimp to fit snugly on each skewer.) Sprinkle 1 side of skewered shrimp with sugar. Grill shrimp, sugared side down, over hot side of grill (covered if

using gas), until lightly charred, 3 to 4 minutes. Flip skewers and move to cool side of grill (if using charcoal) or turn all burners off (if using gas), and cook, covered, until other side of shrimp is no longer translucent, 1 to 2 minutes. Using tongs, slide shrimp into clean medium bowl and toss with reserved marinade. Sprinkle with cilantro and serve.

GRILLED RED CHILE AND GINGER SHRIMP SKEWERS

Replace marinade with 1 to 3 seeded and chopped small red chiles (or jalapeños), 1 minced scallion, 3 tablespoons rice vinegar, 2 tablespoons soy sauce, 1 tablespoon toasted sesame oil, 1 tablespoon grated fresh ginger, 2 teaspoons sugar, and 1 minced garlic clove. Prepare and grill shrimp as directed. Replace cilantro with 1 thinly sliced scallion and serve with lime wedges.

GRILLED HABANERO AND PINEAPPLE SHRIMP SKEWERS

Replace marinade with 1 to 2 seeded and chopped habanero or serrano chiles, ¼ cup pineapple juice, 2 tablespoons olive oil, 1 tablespoon white wine vinegar, 3 minced garlic cloves, 1 teaspoon grated fresh ginger, 1 teaspoon packed brown sugar, 1 teaspoon dried thyme, ½ teaspoon salt, and ¼ teaspoon ground allspice. Prepare and grill shrimp as directed. Replace cilantro with 1 tablespoon minced fresh parsley.

How to Skewer Shrimp

1. Make shallow cut down outside curve of shrimp to open up flesh.

2. Alternate direction of each shrimp as you pack them tightly on skewer.

HUSK-GRILLED CORN

SERVES 6

The flavored butter can be made ahead and refrigerated for up to three days; bring it to room temperature before using. Set up a cutting board and knife next to your grill to avoid traveling back and forth between the kitchen and grill.

- 6 ears corn (unshucked)
- 6 tablespoons unsalted butter, softened
- ½ teaspoon salt
- ½ teaspoon pepper

1. Cut and remove silk protruding from top of each ear of corn. Combine butter, salt, and pepper in bowl. Fold one 14 by 12-inch piece heavy-duty aluminum foil in half to create 7 by 12-inch rectangle; then crimp into boat shape long and wide enough to accommodate 1 ear of corn. Transfer butter mixture to prepared foil boat.

2A. For a Charcoal Grill Open bottom vent completely. Light large chimney starter mounded with charcoal briquettes (7 quarts). When top coals are partially covered with ash, pour evenly over half of grill. Set cooking grate in place, cover, and open lid vent completely. Heat grill until hot, about 5 minutes.

2B. For a Gas Grill Turn all burners to high, cover, and heat grill until hot, about 15 minutes.

3. Clean and oil grate. Place corn on grill (over coals, with stem ends facing cooler side of grill, for charcoal). Cover and cook, turning corn every 3 minutes, until husks have blackened all over, 12 to 15 minutes. (To check for doneness, carefully peel down small portion of husk. If corn is steaming and bright yellow, it is ready.) Transfer corn to cutting board. Using chef's knife, cut base from corn. Using dish towel to hold corn, peel away and discard husk and silk with tongs.

4. Roll each ear of corn in butter mixture to coat lightly and return to grill (over coals for charcoal). Cook, turning as needed to char corn lightly on each side, about 5 minutes total. Remove corn from grill and roll each ear again in butter mixture. Transfer corn to platter. Serve, passing any remaining butter mixture.

HUSK-GRILLED CORN WITH MUSTARD-PAPRIKA BUTTER

Stir 2 tablespoons spicy brown mustard and 1 teaspoon smoked paprika into butter mixture in step 1.

HUSK-GRILLED CORN WITH CILANTRO-LIME BUTTER

Stir ¼ cup minced fresh cilantro, 2 teaspoons grated lime zest plus 1 tablespoon juice, and 1 minced small garlic clove into butter mixture in step 1.

HUSK-GRILLED CORN WITH ROSEMARY-PEPPER BUTTER

Increase pepper to 1 teaspoon. Stir 1 tablespoon minced fresh rosemary and 1 minced small garlic clove into butter mixture in step 1.

HUSK-GRILLED CORN WITH BROWN SUGAR–CAYENNE BUTTER

Stir 2 tablespoons packed brown sugar and ¼ teaspoon cayenne pepper into butter mixture in step 1.

Why This Recipe Works Corn is the perfect vegetable to grill because its sweet flavor loves a smoky accent and it's large enough not to fall through the grate. But grilled corn seldom tastes as good as it sounds. Our goal was to prevent the corn from drying out while achieving a classic char. To keep the kernels moist, we found that initially cooking the ears of corn within their husks worked best. We then shucked the hot corn, rolled the ears in seasoned butter, and returned them to the grill to caramelize. This way, the kernels achieved a good char but weren't on the grill long enough to dry out. One last roll in the butter and our corn was ready.

Why This Recipe Works Grilling corn sounds like a simple proposition—but our research found dozens of variations on the cooking method for this classic summer vegetable. For a recipe that produced corn with a distinctly grilled taste and lightly charred kernels, we grilled the corn unhusked. The grill imparted great flavor to our grilled corn, but also made the kernels tough and dry. To avoid this, we soaked the husked corn in salted water before grilling, which kept the kernels moist and seasoned them as well.

GRILLED CORN ON THE COB

SERVES 4 TO 6

If your corn isn't as sweet as you'd like, stir ½ cup of sugar into the water along with the salt. Avoid soaking the corn for more than 8 hours, or it will become overly salty.

  Salt and pepper
8 ears corn, husks and silks removed
8 tablespoons unsalted butter, softened, or
  1 recipe flavored butter (recipes follow)

1. In large pot, stir ½ cup salt into 4 quarts cold water until dissolved. Add corn and let soak for at least 30 minutes or up to 8 hours.

2A. For a Charcoal Grill Open bottom vent completely. Light large chimney starter filled with charcoal briquettes (6 quarts). When top coals are partially covered with ash, pour evenly over grill. Set cooking grate in place, cover, and open lid vent completely. Heat grill until hot, about 5 minutes.

2B. For a Gas Grill Turn all burners to high, cover, and heat grill until hot, about 15 minutes.

3. Clean and oil cooking grate. Grill corn, turning every 2 to 3 minutes, until kernels are lightly charred all over, 10 to 14 minutes. Remove corn from grill, brush with softened butter, and season with salt and pepper. Serve.

CHESAPEAKE BAY BUTTER
MAKES ABOUT ½ CUP

Using fork, beat 8 tablespoons softened, unsalted butter with 1 tablespoon hot sauce, 1 teaspoon Old Bay seasoning, and 1 minced garlic clove.

CILANTRO-CHIPOTLE BUTTER
MAKES ABOUT ½ CUP

Using fork, beat 8 tablespoons softened, unsalted butter with 1 teaspoon chili powder, ½ teaspoon ground cumin, ½ teaspoon grated lime zest, and 1 minced garlic clove. (Sprinkle cobs with ½ cup grated Parmesan, if desired.)

BASIL PESTO BUTTER
MAKES ABOUT ½ CUP

Using fork, beat 8 tablespoons softened, unsalted butter with 1 tablespoon basil pesto and 1 teaspoon lemon juice.

BARBECUE-SCALLION BUTTER
MAKES ABOUT ½ CUP

Using fork, beat 8 tablespoons softened, unsalted butter with 2 tablespoons barbecue sauce and 1 minced scallion.

A Good Soak
The grill imparts great flavor but can make corn tough and dry. Soaking the husked corn in salted water keeps the kernels moist and seasons them, too.

Why This Recipe Works For a standout backyard barbecue side, we turned canned beans into a savory showstopper. Baked beans gave us an easy starting point, and mixing in pinto and cannellini beans built a multifaceted bean base. We boosted the beans' flavor with an easy pantry sauce made with cider vinegar, granulated garlic, cayenne, and liquid smoke for that off-the-grill flavor. Browned bratwurst gave the sauce some meaty heft. We stirred the beans into this rich mixture, arranged bite-size pieces of bacon over the surface, and baked, allowing the bacon to render, crisp, and infuse the dish with its smoky flavor.

BACKYARD BARBECUE BEANS

SERVES 12 TO 16

Be sure to use a 13 by 9-inch metal baking pan; the volume of the beans is too great for a 13 by 9-inch ceramic baking dish, and it will overflow. We found that Bush's Original Recipe Baked Beans are the most consistent product for this recipe. Our favorite supermarket barbecue sauce is Bull's-Eye Original BBQ Sauce.

½ cup barbecue sauce
½ cup ketchup
½ cup water
2 tablespoons spicy brown mustard
2 tablespoons cider vinegar
1 teaspoon liquid smoke
1 teaspoon granulated garlic
¼ teaspoon cayenne pepper
1¼ pounds bratwurst, casings removed
2 onions, chopped
2 (28-ounce) cans baked beans
2 (15-ounce) cans pinto beans, drained
2 (15-ounce) cans cannellini beans, drained
1 (10-ounce) can Ro-Tel Original Diced Tomatoes and Green Chilies, drained
6 slices thick-cut bacon, cut into 1-inch pieces

1. Adjust oven rack to middle position and heat oven to 350 degrees. Whisk barbecue sauce, ketchup, water, mustard, vinegar, liquid smoke, granulated garlic, and cayenne together in large bowl; set aside.

2. Cook bratwurst in 12-inch nonstick skillet over medium-high heat, breaking up into small pieces with spoon, until fat begins to render, about 5 minutes. Stir in onions and cook until sausage and onions are well browned, about 15 minutes.

3. Transfer bratwurst mixture to bowl with sauce. Stir in baked beans, pinto beans, cannellini beans, and tomatoes. Transfer bean mixture to 13 by 9-inch baking pan and place pan on rimmed baking sheet. Arrange bacon pieces in single layer over top of beans.

4. Bake until beans are bubbling and bacon is rendered, about 1½ hours. Let cool for 15 minutes. Serve.

To Make Ahead At end of step 3, beans can be wrapped in plastic and refrigerated for up to 24 hours. Proceed with recipe from step 4, increasing baking time to 1¾ hours.

Best for Baking

We tried several varieties of baked beans and found that firm, creamy **Bush's Original Recipe Baked Beans** held their shape best in this recipe. Plus, their meaty flavor is ideal for doctoring.

CALIFORNIA BARBECUED BEANS

SERVES 4 TO 6

If you can find them, pinquito beans (a variety grown in the Santa Maria Valley) are traditional in this dish. Bottled taco sauce is available in the Mexican aisle of most grocery stores. Don't add the tomato puree, taco sauce, brown sugar, and salt before the beans have simmered for an hour; they will hinder the proper softening of the beans.

  4 slices bacon, chopped fine
  ½ pound deli ham, chopped fine
  1 onion, chopped fine
  4 garlic cloves, minced
  1 pound pink kidney beans, soaked in 6 cups
     water overnight and drained
  6 cups water
  1 cup canned tomato puree
  ½ cup bottled taco sauce
  5 tablespoons packed light brown sugar
  1 tablespoon dry mustard
     Salt
  ¼ cup chopped fresh cilantro
  2 tablespoons cider vinegar

1. Cook bacon and ham in Dutch oven over medium heat until fat renders and bacon and ham are lightly browned, 5 to 7 minutes. Add onion and cook until softened, about 5 minutes. Stir in garlic and cook until fragrant, about 30 seconds. Add beans and water and bring to simmer. Reduce heat to medium-low, cover, and cook until beans are just soft, about 1 hour.

2. Stir in tomato puree, taco sauce, sugar, dry mustard, and 2 teaspoons salt. Continue to simmer, uncovered, until beans are completely tender and sauce is thickened, about 1 hour. (If mixture becomes too thick, add water.) Stir in cilantro and vinegar and season with salt. Serve. (Beans can be refrigerated for up to 4 days.)

Sorting Dried Beans

It is important to rinse and pick over dried beans to remove any stones or debris before cooking. To make the task easier, sort dried beans on a large white plate or on a white, rimmed cutting board. The neutral background makes any unwanted matter a cinch to spot and discard.

Quick-Soaking Beans

If you don't want to soak the beans overnight, there is a faster way. Simply cover the beans with water in a Dutch oven, bring them to a boil over high heat, and let them boil for 5 minutes. Remove the beans from the heat and allow them to sit, covered, in the hot water for 1 hour. Drain the beans and proceed with the recipe as directed. The quick-soaked beans taste just as good as beans that are soaked overnight.

Why This Recipe Works California barbecued beans recipes use a bean variety and chili sauce rarely found outside of California. We wanted to re-create this recipe with nationally available supermarket ingredients. Pink kidney beans proved to be a good stand-in for the traditional pinquito beans. Some recipes suggest using jarred taco sauce alone if the original recipe's requisite red chili sauce can't be found, but we found its taste and texture too thin. Instead, augmenting the sauce with a combination of fried bacon, ham, onion, and garlic with tomato puree, brown sugar, and dry mustard perfectly captured the chili sauce's bite.

GRILLED POTATO HOBO PACKS

SERVES 4

To keep the packs from tearing, use heavy-duty aluminum foil or two layers of regular foil. Also, scrape the cooking grate clean before grilling.

- 2 pounds Yukon Gold potatoes (about 3 large), scrubbed
- 1 tablespoon olive oil
- 2 garlic cloves, peeled and chopped
- 1 teaspoon minced fresh thyme
- 1 teaspoon salt
- ½ teaspoon pepper

1. Cut each potato in half crosswise, then cut each half into 8 wedges. Place potatoes in large bowl and wrap tightly with plastic wrap. Microwave until edges of potatoes are translucent, 4 to 7 minutes, shaking bowl (without removing plastic) to redistribute potatoes halfway through cooking. Carefully remove plastic and drain well. Gently toss potatoes with oil, garlic, thyme, salt, and pepper.

2. Cut four 14 by 10-inch sheets of heavy-duty aluminum foil. Working with 1 at a time, spread one-quarter of potato mixture over half of foil, fold foil over potatoes, and crimp edges tightly to seal.

3A. For a Charcoal Grill Open bottom vent completely. Light large chimney starter filled with charcoal briquettes (6 quarts). When top coals are partially covered with ash, pour evenly over grill. Set cooking grate in place, cover, and open lid vent completely. Heat grill until hot, about 5 minutes.

3B. For a Gas Grill Turn all burners to medium-high, cover, and heat grill until hot, about 15 minutes.

4. Grill hobo packs over hot fire, covered, until potatoes are completely tender, about 10 minutes, flipping packs halfway through cooking. Cut open foil and serve.

SPANISH-STYLE GRILLED POTATO HOBO PACKS

Add 6 ounces thinly sliced cured chorizo sausage, 1 seeded and chopped red bell pepper, and 1 teaspoon paprika to cooked potatoes as they are tossed in step 1.

VINEGAR AND ONION GRILLED POTATO HOBO PACKS

Microwave 1 halved and thinly sliced small onion with potatoes in step 1. Add 2 tablespoons white wine or red wine vinegar to cooked potatoes as they are tossed in step 1.

SPICY HOME FRY GRILLED POTATO HOBO PACKS

Omit chopped garlic. Add 1 teaspoon paprika, ½ teaspoon garlic powder, ½ teaspoon onion powder, and ¼ teaspoon cayenne pepper to cooked potatoes as they are tossed in step 1.

Making Potato Hobo Packs

1. Microwave potatoes first to help them cook quickly on grill.

2. Arrange microwaved potatoes on foil, fold over, and crimp.

3. Flip packs halfway through grilling for evenly charred potatoes.

Why This Recipe Works We wanted to rescue this campfire classic, which too often results in unevenly cooked spuds. After multiple tests, we found that Yukon Golds were preferred to starchy, mealy russets and "slippery" red potatoes. To ensure evenly grilled potatoes, we cut them into evenly sized wedges and microwaved them for a few minutes before grilling them. Tossing the potatoes with a little oil prevented them from sticking to the foil.

Why This Recipe Works Steaming or sautéing broccoli is fine, but if you want vivid green florets with flavorful char, there's no beating the grill. To avoid toughness, we peeled the stalks with a vegetable peeler and cut the head into spears small enough to cook quickly but large enough to grill easily. Since grilling alone would yield dry broccoli, we tossed the spears in olive oil and water and steamed them in sealed foil packets on the grill. As soon as the stems and florets were evenly cooked, we placed them directly on the grill to give them plenty of char. A squeeze of grilled lemon and a sprinkling of Parmesan sealed the deal.

GRILLED BROCCOLI WITH LEMON AND PARMESAN

SERVES 4

To keep the packs from tearing, use heavy-duty aluminum foil. Use the large holes of a box grater to shred the Parmesan.

¼ cup extra-virgin olive oil, plus extra for drizzling
1 tablespoon water
   Salt and pepper
2 pounds broccoli
1 lemon, halved
¼ cup shredded Parmesan cheese

1. Cut two 26 by 12-inch sheets of heavy-duty aluminum foil. Whisk oil, water, ¾ teaspoon salt, and ½ teaspoon pepper together in large bowl.

2. Trim stalk ends so each entire head of broccoli measures 6 to 7 inches long. Using vegetable peeler, peel away tough outer layer of broccoli stalks (about ⅛ inch). Cut stalks in half lengthwise into spears (stems should be ½ to ¾ inch thick and florets 3 to 4 inches wide). Add broccoli spears to oil mixture and toss well to coat.

3. Divide broccoli between sheets of foil, cut side down and alternating direction of florets and stems. Bring short sides of foil together and crimp tightly. Crimp long ends to seal packs tightly.

4A. For a Charcoal Grill Open bottom vent completely. Light large chimney starter filled with charcoal briquettes (6 quarts). When top coals are partially covered with ash, pour evenly over half of grill. Set cooking grate in place, cover, and open lid vent completely. Heat grill until hot, about 5 minutes.

4B. For a Gas Grill Turn all burners to high, cover, and heat grill until hot, about 15 minutes. Turn all burners to medium-high. (Adjust burners as needed to maintain grill temperature around 400 degrees.)

5. Clean and oil cooking grate. Arrange packs evenly on grill (over coals if using charcoal), cover, and cook for 8 minutes, flipping packs halfway through cooking.

6. Transfer packs to rimmed baking sheet and, using scissors, carefully cut open, allowing steam to escape away from you. (Broccoli should be bright green and fork inserted into stems should meet some resistance.)

7. Discard foil and place broccoli and lemon halves cut side down on grill (over coals if using charcoal). Grill (covered if using gas), turning broccoli about every 2 minutes, until stems are fork-tender and well charred on all sides, 6 to 8 minutes total. Transfer broccoli to now-empty sheet as it finishes cooking. Grill lemon halves until well charred on cut side, 6 to 8 minutes.

8. Transfer broccoli to cutting board and cut into 2-inch pieces; transfer to platter. Season with salt and pepper to taste. Squeeze lemon over broccoli to taste, sprinkle with Parmesan, and drizzle with extra oil. Serve.

GRILLED BROCCOLI WITH ANCHOVY-GARLIC BUTTER

Omit lemon and Parmesan cheese. In step 1, whisk together 4 tablespoons melted unsalted butter, 3 rinsed and minced anchovy fillets, 1 minced garlic clove, 1 teaspoon lemon juice, ¼ teaspoon red pepper flakes, ½ teaspoon salt, and ⅛ teaspoon pepper. Set aside, then rewarm in step 8 and drizzle over broccoli before serving.

GRILLED BROCCOLI WITH SWEET CHILI SAUCE

Omit lemon and Parmesan cheese. In step 1, whisk together 4 teaspoons toasted sesame oil, 1 teaspoon distilled white vinegar, 2½ teaspoons sugar, 2 teaspoons Asian chili-garlic sauce, and ¼ teaspoon salt. Set aside, then drizzle over broccoli before serving.

GRILLED CAESAR SALAD

SERVES 6

Our favorite Parmesan cheese is Boar's Head Parmigiano-Reggiano.

Dressing

1 tablespoon lemon juice
1 garlic clove, minced
½ cup mayonnaise
½ ounce Parmesan cheese, grated (¼ cup)
1 tablespoon white wine vinegar
1 tablespoon Worcestershire sauce
1 tablespoon Dijon mustard
2 anchovy fillets, rinsed
½ teaspoon salt
½ teaspoon pepper
¼ cup extra-virgin olive oil

Salad

1 (12-inch) baguette, cut on bias into 5-inch-long, ½-inch-thick slices
3 tablespoons extra-virgin olive oil
1 garlic clove, peeled
3 romaine lettuce hearts (18 ounces), halved lengthwise through cores
½ ounce Parmesan cheese, grated (¼ cup)

1. For the Dressing Combine lemon juice and garlic in bowl and let stand for 10 minutes. Process mayonnaise, Parmesan, lemon-garlic mixture, vinegar, Worcestershire, mustard, anchovies, salt, and pepper in blender for about 30 seconds. With blender running, slowly add oil. Reserve 6 tablespoons dressing for brushing romaine.

2A. For a Charcoal Grill Open bottom vent completely. Light large chimney starter filled with charcoal briquettes (6 quarts). When top coals are partially covered with ash, pour evenly over half of grill. Set cooking grate in place, cover, and open lid vent completely. Heat grill until hot, about 5 minutes.

2B. For a Gas Grill Turn all burners to high, cover, and heat grill until hot, about 15 minutes. Leave all burners on high.

3. For the Salad Clean and oil cooking grate. Brush bread with oil and grill (over coals if using charcoal), uncovered, until browned, about 1 minute per side. Transfer to platter and rub with garlic clove. Brush cut sides of romaine with reserved dressing; place half of romaine, cut side down, on grill (over coals if using charcoal). Grill, uncovered, until lightly charred, 1 to 2 minutes. Move to platter with bread. Repeat. Drizzle romaine with remaining dressing. Sprinkle with Parmesan. Serve.

Salad Prep for Grilled Caesar

We get twice the flavor by using the dressing before and after grilling.

1. Brush homemade Caesar dressing onto halved romaine hearts before grilling.

2. Grill dressed romaine halves on just 1 side to keep lettuce from wilting.

3. Once charred lettuce comes off grill, finish with more Caesar dressing.

Why This Recipe Works Grilled salad may seem like an oxymoron, but we were intrigued by the idea of the flavors of a classic Caesar salad enriched with the smoky char of the grill. We found that compact romaine hearts held their shape better than whole heads. We halved them lengthwise to increase their surface area, making sure to keep the core intact so the leaves didn't fall apart on the grill. To prevent sticking, we brushed the leaves with dressing. Just 1 to 2 minutes over a hot grill gave us a smoky and charred (not wilted) exterior. To keep things simple, we replaced the croutons with slices of crusty bread grilled alongside the lettuce.

Why This Recipe Works We wanted to discover the secrets to tender cabbage, crunchy apples, and the sweet and spicy dressing that brings them together in this Southern barbecue side dish. Because cabbage is relatively watery, we salted the cut cabbage to draw out excess moisture before dressing it, which prevented moisture from diluting the dressing later and leaving us with a watery slaw. Granny Smith apples work best in this slaw recipe—tasters loved their sturdy crunch and tart bite. Cider vinegar gave the dressing a fruity flavor, while red pepper flakes, chopped scallions, and mustard added some punch.

TANGY APPLE CABBAGE SLAW

SERVES 6 TO 8

In step 1, the salted, rinsed, and dried cabbage can be refrigerated in a zipper-lock bag for up to 24 hours. To prep the apples, cut the cored apples into ¼-inch-thick planks, then stack the planks and cut them into thin matchsticks.

- 1   medium head green cabbage (2 pounds), cored and chopped fine (12 cups)
- 2   teaspoons salt
- 2   Granny Smith apples, cored and cut into thin matchsticks
- 2   scallions, sliced thin
- 6   tablespoons vegetable oil
- ½   cup cider vinegar
- ½   cup sugar
- 1   tablespoon Dijon mustard
- ¼   teaspoon red pepper flakes

1. Toss cabbage and salt in colander set over medium bowl. Let stand until wilted, about 1 hour. Rinse cabbage under cold water, drain, dry well with paper towels, and transfer to large bowl. Add apples and scallions and toss to combine.

2. Bring oil, vinegar, sugar, mustard, and pepper flakes to boil in saucepan over medium heat. Pour over cabbage mixture and toss to coat. Cover with plastic wrap and refrigerate at least 1 hour or up to 24 hours. Serve.

Cutting Apples for Slaw

1. Cut each side of apple squarely away from core and cut each piece into ¼-inch-thick slices.

2. Stack planks and cut them into thin matchsticks.

Vinegar Primer

Although cider vinegar and white vinegar are made by the same process, the similarities end there. Vinegar is made by turning fermented liquid into acetic acid by adding certain bacteria to the liquid. Cider and distilled vinegars are made by the same process but start with different liquids: Cider vinegar begins with apple cider and distilled vinegar with ethyl alcohol (also known as grain alcohol). Although both vinegars are commonly used in pickle recipes (and are often substituted for each other), they do have distinctly different flavors. We like to use sweeter cider vinegar in sweet pickles, reserving white vinegar for applications such as sour pickles, where we want acidity without added flavor. While cider vinegar is fine in a sweet salad dressing, we don't think distilled vinegar adds much to any dressing. In general, we find that vinegars that start with wine are the best choice for salad dressings.

CIDER VINEGAR
Sweet cider vinegar begins with apple cider.

DISTILLED VINEGAR
Acidic distilled vinegar begins with ethyl alcohol.

Why This Recipe Works The high water content of cabbage is typically to blame for watery slaws. We salted our cabbage to draw out the excess moisture. Memphis Chopped Coleslaw is usually studded with celery seeds and crunchy green peppers and tossed with an unapologetically sugary mustard dressing that's balanced by a bracing hit of vinegar. To ensure our slaw boasted brash, balanced flavor, we quickly cooked the spicy dressing to meld the flavors and tossed the hot dressing with the cabbage. The salted cabbage absorbed the dressing and became seasoned inside and out.

MEMPHIS CHOPPED COLESLAW

SERVES 8 TO 10

In step 1, the salted, rinsed, and dried cabbage mixture can be refrigerated in a zipper-lock bag for up to 24 hours.

- 1 head green cabbage (2 pounds), cored and chopped fine (12 cups)
- 1 jalapeño chile, stemmed, seeded, and minced
- 1 carrot, peeled and shredded on box grater
- 1 small onion, peeled and shredded on box grater
- 2 teaspoons salt
- ¼ cup yellow mustard
- ¼ cup chili sauce
- ¼ cup mayonnaise
- ¼ cup sour cream
- ¼ cup cider vinegar
- 1 teaspoon celery seeds
- ⅔ cup packed light brown sugar

1. Toss cabbage, jalapeño, carrot, onion, and salt in colander set over medium bowl. Let stand until wilted, about 1 hour. Rinse cabbage mixture under cold water, drain, dry well with paper towels, and transfer to large bowl.

2. Bring mustard, chili sauce, mayonnaise, sour cream, vinegar, celery seeds, and sugar to boil in saucepan over medium heat. Pour over cabbage and toss to coat. Cover with plastic wrap and refrigerate 1 hour or up to 24 hours. Serve.

How to Chop Cabbage

1. Cut cabbage into quarters, then trim and discard hard core.

2. Separate cabbage into small stacks of leaves that flatten when pressed.

3. Cut each stack of cabbage leaves into ¼-inch strips.

4. Cut strips into ¼-inch pieces.

ALL-AMERICAN POTATO SALAD

SERVES 4 TO 6

Make sure not to overcook the potatoes or the salad will be quite sloppy. Keep the water at a gentle simmer and use the tip of a paring knife to judge the doneness of the potatoes. If the knife inserts easily into the potato pieces, they are done.

- 2 large eggs
  Salt
- 2 pounds Yukon Gold potatoes, peeled and cut into ¾-inch cubes
- 3 tablespoons dill pickle juice, plus ¼ cup finely chopped dill pickles
- 1 tablespoon yellow mustard
- ¼ teaspoon pepper
- ½ teaspoon celery seeds
- ½ cup mayonnaise
- ¼ cup sour cream
- ½ small red onion, chopped fine
- 1 celery rib, chopped fine

1. Bring eggs, 1½ teaspoons salt, and 1 quart water to boil in small saucepan. Remove pan from heat, cover, and let sit for 10 minutes. Transfer eggs to bowl filled with ice water and let cool for 5 minutes, then peel and chop coarse.

2. Place potatoes in large saucepan with cold water to cover by 1 inch. Bring to boil over high heat, add 1 teaspoon salt, reduce heat to medium-low, and simmer until potatoes are tender, 10 to 15 minutes.

3. Drain potatoes thoroughly, then spread out on rimmed baking sheet. Mix 2 tablespoons pickle juice and mustard together in small bowl, drizzle pickle juice mixture over hot potatoes, and toss until evenly coated. Refrigerate until cooled, about 30 minutes.

4. Mix remaining tablespoon pickle juice, chopped pickles, ½ teaspoon salt, pepper, celery seeds, mayonnaise, sour cream, red onion, and celery in large bowl. Toss in cooled potatoes, cover, and refrigerate until well chilled, about 30 minutes. (Salad can be refrigerated for up to 2 days.) Gently stir in eggs, just before serving.

Don't Throw Out the Juice

Pickle juice tossed with just-cooked potatoes gives them a tangy flavor that's not as harsh as straight vinegar and has a gentle sweetness, too.

Why This Recipe Works For flavorful all-American potato salad, we decided to use firm-textured Yukon Gold potatoes because they hold their shape after cooking and won't turn mushy in the salad. Our recipe benefited from the sweetness of an unexpected ingredient: pickle juice. We drizzled the still-warm potatoes with a mixture of pickle juice and mustard. The hot potatoes easily absorbed the acidic liquid and tasted seasoned through to the middle. A combination of mayonnaise and sour cream formed the base of our creamy dressing, seasoned with classic additions like celery seeds, celery, and chopped hard-cooked eggs.

SMOKY POTATO SALAD

SERVES 8

Use small red potatoes 1½ to 2 inches in diameter. If you don't have 2 tablespoons of fat in the skillet after frying the bacon, add olive oil to make up the difference.

- 6 slices bacon
- 3 tablespoons red wine vinegar
- 2 tablespoons mayonnaise
- 2 teaspoons minced canned chipotle chile in adobo sauce
   Salt and pepper
- 3 tablespoons olive oil, plus extra for brushing
- 3 pounds small red potatoes, unpeeled, halved
- 1 large onion, sliced into ½-inch-thick rounds
- 4 scallions, sliced thin

1. Cook bacon in 12-inch skillet over medium heat until crisp, 7 to 9 minutes; transfer to paper towel–lined plate. Set aside 2 tablespoons bacon fat. When cool enough to handle, crumble bacon and set aside. Whisk vinegar, mayonnaise, chile, ½ teaspoon salt, and ½ teaspoon pepper together in large bowl. Slowly whisk in 3 tablespoons oil until combined; set aside.

2A. For a Charcoal Grill Open bottom vent completely. Light large chimney starter three-quarters filled with charcoal briquettes (4½ quarts). When top coals are partially covered with ash, pour evenly over grill. Set cooking grate in place, cover, and open lid vent completely. Heat grill until hot, about 5 minutes.

2B. For a Gas Grill Turn all burners to high, cover, and heat grill until hot, about 15 minutes. Turn all burners to medium.

3. Clean and oil cooking grate. Toss potatoes with reserved bacon fat and ½ teaspoon salt. Push a toothpick horizontally through each onion round to keep rings intact while grilling. Brush onion rounds lightly with extra oil and season with salt and pepper. Place potatoes, cut side down, and onion rounds on grill and cook, covered, until charred on first side, 10 to 14 minutes.

4. Flip potatoes and onion rounds and continue to cook, covered, until well browned all over and potatoes are easily pierced with tip of paring knife, 10 to 16 minutes longer. Transfer potatoes and onion rounds to rimmed baking sheet and let cool slightly.

5. When cool enough to handle, halve potatoes; remove toothpicks and coarsely chop onion rounds. Add potatoes, onion, scallions, and bacon to dressing and toss to combine. Season with salt and pepper to taste. Serve warm or at room temperature.

Why This Recipe Works For a summery potato salad cooked on the grill from start to finish featuring smoky, tender potatoes with crispy outsides, we began with halved, unpeeled red potatoes: The skin helped them to stay intact, and their firm, waxy texture stood up to the heat of the grill. Prior to grilling, we coated the potatoes with flavorful bacon fat. For even more smokiness, we grilled rounds of onions along with the potatoes. A spicy, smoky vinaigrette with a touch of mayo, chipotle, and crumbled bacon was the perfect match for this backyard-ready potato salad.

Why This Recipe Works Amish potato salad is distinct for its creamy cooked dressing and sweet-and-sour flavor. We modernized this recipe by ditching the labor-intensive dressing, which is traditionally enriched with eggs and gently cooked over a double-boiler. To keep the rich taste with less work, we processed a hard-cooked egg yolk into the dressing base of vinegar and sugar. Sprinkling a few tablespoons of the tangy dressing over the hot potatoes infused them with flavor. Then we tossed the cooled potatoes with the rest of the dressing, enriched with sour cream, for a cool, creamy potato salad with great old-fashioned flavor.

AMISH POTATO SALAD

SERVES 8

You can substitute an equal amount of celery salt for the celery seed, but if you do, eliminate the table salt from the dressing. Make sure to use sturdy Yukon Golds here; fluffy russets will fall apart in the salad.

- 3 pounds Yukon Gold potatoes, peeled and cut into ¾-inch chunks
  Salt and pepper
- ⅓ cup cider vinegar
- ¼ cup sugar
- 2 tablespoons yellow mustard
- 1 recipe Foolproof Hard-Cooked Eggs (recipe follows)
- ½ teaspoon celery seeds
- ¾ cup sour cream
- 1 celery rib, chopped fine

1. Bring potatoes, 1 tablespoon salt, and enough water to cover by 1 inch to boil in large pot over high heat. Reduce heat to medium and simmer until potatoes are just tender, about 10 minutes.

2. Meanwhile, microwave vinegar and sugar in small bowl until sugar dissolves, about 30 seconds. Process vinegar mixture, mustard, 1 hard-cooked egg yolk (reserve white), celery seeds, and ½ teaspoon salt in food processor until smooth, about 30 seconds. Transfer to medium bowl.

3. Drain potatoes thoroughly and transfer to large bowl. Drizzle 2 tablespoons dressing over hot potatoes and, using rubber spatula, gently toss until evenly coated. Refrigerate until cooled, at least 30 minutes, stirring gently once to redistribute dressing.

4. Whisk sour cream into remaining dressing. Add reserved egg white and 3 hard-cooked eggs to dressing and, using potato masher, mash until only small pieces remain. Add dressing and celery to cooled potatoes, tossing gently to combine. Cover and refrigerate until chilled, about 30 minutes. Season with salt and pepper to taste. Serve. (Salad can be refrigerated for up to 2 days.)

FOOLPROOF HARD-COOKED EGGS
MAKES 4 EGGS
You can double or triple this recipe as long as you use a pot large enough to hold the eggs in a single later, covered by an inch of water.

- 4 large eggs

Bring eggs and enough water to cover by 1 inch to boil in medium saucepan over high heat. Remove pan from heat, cover, and let sit 10 minutes. Meanwhile, fill medium bowl with 4 cups water and 1 tray of ice cubes. Transfer eggs to ice water bath with slotted spoon; let sit for 5 minutes. Peel eggs.

The American Table: Sweet on Sweet-and-Sour

Like most other resourceful Colonial Americans, the Amish turned to pickling as a way to preserve fruits and vegetables for long (prerefrigeration) winters. It wasn't just practicality that drove them to pickling, however. The Amish people's penchant for these sweet-and-sour flavors is also rooted in the group's native Germany, where rich dishes are often finished with a splash of vinegar or served with vinegar-spiked sides, such as sauerkraut. The Amish table, it's said, is incomplete without "seven sweets and seven sours." A cornucopia of delicious foods reflects this Amish predilection, from watermelon rind and cantaloupe pickles to chow chow, pickled beets and eggs, and Amish potato salad, which is seasoned with plenty of vinegar and sugar.

RANCH POTATO SALAD

SERVES 6 TO 8

We prefer white wine vinegar here, but white and cider vinegars are acceptable substitutes.

- 3 pounds red potatoes, peeled and cut into ¾-inch chunks
  Salt
- ¾ cup mayonnaise
- ½ cup buttermilk
- ¼ cup white wine vinegar
- ¼ cup drained jarred roasted red peppers, chopped fine
- 3 tablespoons finely chopped fresh cilantro
- 3 scallions, chopped fine
- 1 garlic clove, minced
- ⅛ teaspoon dried dill
- 2 teaspoons pepper
- 2 tablespoons Dijon mustard

1. Bring potatoes, 1 tablespoon salt, and enough water to cover potatoes by 1 inch to boil in large pot over high heat. Reduce heat to medium and simmer until potatoes are just tender, about 10 minutes. While potatoes simmer, whisk mayonnaise, buttermilk, 2 tablespoons vinegar, red peppers, cilantro, scallions, garlic, dill, 1 teaspoon salt, and pepper in large bowl.

2. Drain potatoes thoroughly, then spread out on rimmed baking sheet. Whisk mustard and remaining vinegar in small bowl. Drizzle mustard mixture over hot potatoes and toss until evenly coated. Refrigerate until cooled, about 30 minutes.

3. Transfer cooled potatoes to bowl with mayonnaise mixture and toss to combine. Cover and refrigerate until well chilled, about 30 minutes. Serve. (Salad can be refrigerated for up to 2 days.)

Better Potato Texture, and Faster, Too

We discovered some interesting information about boiling potatoes while developing our recipe for Ranch Potato Salad. Most recipes for boiled potatoes call for starting the spuds in cold water so that they will come up to temperature slowly and cook evenly throughout. In an attempt to shorten the cooking time, we tried letting the water boil before adding the potatoes. In a side-by-side test, we weren't surprised that tasters preferred the potatoes started in cold water for their uniformly creamy texture. We were surprised, however, to find that the total cooking time for potatoes started in cold water was less than for those started in boiling water.

Hidden Valley Ranch Dressing

The original ranch dressing first became popular at the Hidden Valley Guest Ranch near Santa Barbara, California in the late 1950s. It began as a dried herb mixture that Steve Henson, the ranch's owner, combined with mayonnaise and buttermilk to make a creamy, tangy dressing for the ranch's house salad. It was so well received that guests clamored for bottles of the dressing to take home with them. Recognizing the potential of his concoction, Henson began marketing the mix in small packets, and the rest is culinary history. The little packets are still around, but the dressing really took off in 1983, when manufacturers figured out how to bottle this creamy dressing in a shelf-stable format.

Why This Recipe Works Bottled ranch dressing sounds like a quick way to dress up potato salad, but many recipes are surprisingly dull and bland. We found that peeling the potatoes (we liked red spuds) allowed them to absorb more dressing. For the dressing, we doubled the amount of cilantro used in most recipes and added fresh garlic and scallions for a welcome bite. Dijon mustard and vinegar provided acidity and bite, while chopped roasted red peppers made a sweet counterpoint. To better season the potatoes, we tossed the hot spuds first with just the Dijon mustard and vinegar. And just a dash of dried dill lent more herb flavor.

Why This Recipe Works We wanted potato salad with vibrant dill flavor through and through. To do so, we seasoned our potato salad with three rounds of dill: first as an herb sachet while the potatoes simmered, next as a piquant dill vinegar, and finally as a fresh sprinkle. A dressing based on a combination of creamy mayonnaise and tangy sour cream, accented with Dijon mustard, provided the perfect backdrop for our dill flavor to shine.

DILL POTATO SALAD

SERVES 8

Use both dill stems and chopped leaves (sometimes called fronds) in the herb sachet. Trois Petits Cochons is our favorite brand of Dijon mustard.

¼ cup white wine vinegar
3 tablespoons minced fresh dill, plus ½ cup leaves and stems, chopped coarse
3 pounds Yukon Gold potatoes, peeled and cut into ¾-inch pieces
   Salt and pepper
½ cup mayonnaise
¼ cup sour cream
1 tablespoon Dijon mustard
3 scallions, green parts only, sliced thin

1. Combine vinegar and 1 tablespoon minced dill in bowl and microwave until steaming, 30 to 60 seconds. Set at room temperature until cool, 15 to 20 minutes.

2. Meanwhile, place chopped dill inside disposable coffee filter and tie closed with kitchen twine. Bring potatoes, dill sachet, 1 tablespoon salt, and enough water to cover potatoes by 1 inch to boil in large pot over high heat. Reduce heat to medium and simmer until potatoes are just tender, about 10 minutes.

3. Drain potatoes thoroughly, then transfer to large bowl; discard sachet. Drizzle 2 tablespoons dill vinegar over hot potatoes and gently toss until evenly coated. Refrigerate until cooled, about 30 minutes, stirring once.

4. Whisk mayonnaise, sour cream, remaining dill vinegar, mustard, ½ teaspoon salt, and ¼ teaspoon pepper together until smooth. Add dressing to cooled potatoes. Stir in scallions and remaining 2 tablespoons minced dill. Cover and refrigerate to let flavors meld, about 30 minutes. Season with salt and pepper to taste. Serve. (Salad can be refrigerated for up to 2 days.)

Dill Three Ways

Three rounds of fresh dill season our Dill Potato Salad.

Infuse
We add a packet of chopped dill to the water in which the potatoes simmer.

Marinate
We steep vinegar with minced dill and use it to dress the hot potatoes.

Mince
We sprinkle extra minced dill over the dressed potato salad.

Why This Recipe Works Texans take their potato salad up a notch with plenty of mustard and spicy chopped jalapeños. For our version, we started with classic potato salad, using firm Yukon Gold potatoes, which have a rich earthy flavor and hold their shape after cooking, and a mayonnaise-based dressing seasoned with onion, celery seeds, and dill pickles. To this we added plenty of bold yellow mustard and spicy jalapeños. We tempered the jalapeños' raw bite by quick-pickling them in a mixture of vinegar, sugar, and mustard seeds. We used the leftover pickling solution to flavor the hot potatoes. A pinch of cayenne added extra kick.

TEXAS POTATO SALAD

SERVES 8

Heinz is our favorite brand of yellow mustard.

½ cup red wine vinegar
1½ tablespoons sugar
    Salt and pepper
 1 teaspoon yellow mustard seeds
½ small red onion, sliced thin
 2 jalapeño chiles (1 sliced into thin rings;
    1 stemmed, seeded, and minced)
 3 pounds Yukon Gold potatoes, peeled and
    cut into ¾-inch pieces
 6 tablespoons mayonnaise
 6 tablespoons yellow mustard
¼ teaspoon cayenne pepper
 2 large hard-cooked eggs, cut into ¼-inch pieces
 1 celery rib, minced

1. Combine vinegar, sugar, 1½ teaspoons salt, and mustard seeds in bowl and microwave until steaming, about 2 minutes. Whisk until sugar and salt are dissolved. Add onion and jalapeños and set aside until cool, 15 to 20 minutes. Strain onion and jalapeños through fine-mesh strainer set over bowl. Reserve pickled vegetables and vinegar mixture separately.

2. Meanwhile, combine potatoes, 8 cups water, and 1 tablespoon salt in Dutch oven and bring to boil over high heat. Reduce heat to medium and simmer until potatoes are just tender, 10 to 15 minutes.

3. Drain potatoes thoroughly, then transfer to large bowl. Drizzle 2 tablespoons reserved vinegar mixture over hot potatoes and toss gently until evenly coated. (Reserve remaining vinegar mixture for another use.) Refrigerate until cool, about 30 minutes, stirring once halfway through chilling.

4. Whisk mayonnaise, mustard, ½ teaspoon pepper, and cayenne together in bowl until combined. Add mayonnaise mixture, reserved pickled vegetables, eggs, and celery to potatoes and stir gently to combine. Season with salt and pepper to taste. Cover and refrigerate to let flavors blend, about 30 minutes. Serve. (Salad can be refrigerated for up to 2 days.)

Keeping Potato Salad Safe

Though mayonnaise is often blamed for spoiled potato salads, it is rarely the problem. In fact, it's the potatoes that are more likely to go bad. The bacteria usually responsible for spoiled potato salad is found in soil and dust, and it thrives on starchy foods like potatoes. No matter what kind of dressing you use, don't leave any potato salad out for more than 2 hours (1 hour if the temperature is above 90 degrees), and promptly refrigerate any leftovers in a covered container.

SMASHED POTATO SALAD

SERVES 8 TO 10

Use the tip of a paring knife to judge the doneness of the potatoes. If the tip inserts easily into the potato pieces, they are done. Hellmann's Real Mayonnaise is our favorite nationally available mayonnaise. Note that the salad needs to be refrigerated for about 2 hours before serving.

- 3 pounds Yukon Gold potatoes, unpeeled, cut into 1-inch chunks
  Salt and pepper
- 2 tablespoons distilled white vinegar
- 1 cup mayonnaise
- 3 tablespoons yellow mustard
- ¼ teaspoon cayenne pepper
- 3 hard-cooked large eggs, chopped
- 3 scallions, sliced thin
- ½ cup chopped sweet pickles
- ½ cup finely chopped celery
- ¼ cup finely chopped onion

1. Combine potatoes, 8 cups water, and 1 tablespoon salt in Dutch oven and bring to boil over high heat. Reduce heat to medium and cook at vigorous simmer until potatoes are tender, 14 to 17 minutes.

2. Drain potatoes in colander. Transfer 3 cups potatoes to large bowl, add 1 tablespoon vinegar, and coarsely mash with potato masher. Transfer remaining potatoes to rimmed baking sheet, drizzle with remaining 1 tablespoon vinegar, and toss gently to combine. Let cool completely, about 15 minutes.

3. Whisk mayonnaise, ½ cup water, mustard, cayenne, 1 teaspoon salt, and 1 teaspoon pepper together in bowl. Stir mayonnaise mixture into mashed potatoes. Fold in eggs, scallions, pickles, celery, onion, and remaining potatoes until combined. (Mixture will be lumpy.)

4. Cover and refrigerate until fully chilled, about 2 hours. Season with salt and pepper to taste. Serve.

Mayo Showdown

Commercial mayonnaise is one of the most hotly debated ingredients out there, with impassioned salad- and sandwich-makers insisting that only their favorite will do. Here are three of the most well-loved mayos.

HELLMANN'S
(Sold as Best Foods west of the Rockies) The most popular brand in the U.S., Hellmann's accounts for about half of all mayonnaise sales.

DUKE'S
This spread is made with cider vinegar, which gives it a sharp flavor. It has ardent fans in many Southern states.

BLUE PLATE
The test kitchen's favorite mayo is made with egg yolks, not whole eggs. It must be mail-ordered in most of the country.

Why This Recipe Works For our take on this Southern picnic staple, wanted both the creamy texture of mashed potatoes and the tender chunks of traditional potato salad. Yukon Gold potatoes worked best—their soft skins cooked up tender and saved us from peeling. For a mix of textures, we smashed a third of the boiled spuds with some vinegar before tossing the mashed portion with the cubes. Yellow mustard contributed some extra bite, which we balanced with chopped sweet pickles, and a touch of cayenne. Hard-cooked eggs, scallions, celery, and onion added even more textural variety to finish off our smooth-yet-chunky potato salad.

LEMON AND HERB RED POTATO SALAD

SERVES 8

To rinse the onion, place it in a fine-mesh strainer and run it under cold water. This removes some of the onion's harshness. Drain, but do not rinse, the capers here.

- 3 pounds red potatoes, unpeeled, cut into 1-inch chunks
- 2 tablespoons distilled white vinegar
  Salt and pepper
- 2 teaspoons grated lemon zest plus 3 tablespoons juice
- ⅓ cup extra-virgin olive oil
- ½ cup finely chopped onion, rinsed
- 3 tablespoons minced fresh tarragon
- 3 tablespoons minced fresh parsley
- 3 tablespoons minced fresh chives
- 2 tablespoons capers, minced

1. Combine potatoes, 8 cups water, vinegar, and 2 tablespoons salt in Dutch oven and bring to boil over high heat. Reduce heat to medium and cook at strong simmer until potatoes are just tender, 10 to 15 minutes.

2. Meanwhile, whisk lemon zest and juice, 1 teaspoon salt, and ½ teaspoon pepper together in large bowl. Slowly whisk in oil until emulsified; set aside.

3. Drain potatoes thoroughly, then transfer to rimmed baking sheet. Drizzle 2 tablespoons dressing over hot potatoes and toss gently until evenly coated. Let potatoes cool, about 30 minutes, stirring once halfway through cooling.

4. Whisk dressing to recombine and stir in onion, tarragon, parsley, chives, and capers. Add cooled potatoes to dressing and stir gently to combine. Season with salt and pepper to taste. Serve warm or at room temperature.

Capers 101

Capers are actually pickles made from the unopened flower buds of the *Capparis spinosa* shrub, which grows in the Mediterranean. In France, Italy, and Spain, the shrubs are cultivated for capers, and Roquevaire, in Provence, is known as the "caper capital." Capers are never used fresh, and are preserved one of two ways: in a salt and water brine, sometimes with added vinegar, or in salt. More often, the flower buds are soaked in saltwater, then packed in brine or a mixture of brine and vinegar. This is how capers are sold in most supermarkets. The other option is to cure them with salt. This kind of caper costs more and is available only in specialty markets. Capers also vary in size, from the tiny non-pareilles to surfines, capucines, fines, and capotes—increasing in size and decreasing in value.

Why This Recipe Works Too often potato salad is weighed down by a heavy mayonnaise-based dressing; we sought a lighter alternative. We used waxy red potatoes, as they are lower in starch than russets and more colorful than Yukon Golds. To prevent them from breaking down too much, we added vinegar to the cooking water, giving us tender but firm potatoes that held their shape. A mixture of capers, olive oil, and lemon juice and zest complemented the potatoes' earthiness, while tarragon, parsley, and chives provided freshness. Adding some of the herbed vinaigrette while the potatoes were still hot ensured they best absorbed all of its flavor.

Why This Recipe Works For a substantial salad that is simple to make and heavy on the vegetables, potatoes, green beans, and tomatoes do the trick. The secret to getting tender potatoes and vibrant green beans was to stagger the cooking. We cooked the potatoes in boiling water until just tender and then added the beans so that both vegetables finished cooking at the same time, which simplified the cooking process. Marinating the tomatoes in the dressing while the vegetables cooked infused them with flavor; we then tossed everything together before serving. An easy vinaigrette plus lots of fresh parsley leaves and dill tied our hearty salad together.

POTATO, GREEN BEAN, AND TOMATO SALAD

SERVES 4

Make sure to scrub the potatoes well. High-quality extra-virgin olive oil makes a big difference here. You can substitute cherry tomatoes for the grape tomatoes, if desired. For the best results, use a rubber spatula to combine the ingredients in steps 3 and 4.

1½ pounds Yukon Gold potatoes, unpeeled, cut into ¾-inch chunks
¾ teaspoon table salt, plus salt for cooking vegetables
1 pound green beans, trimmed and cut into 1-inch pieces
½ cup extra-virgin olive oil
¼ cup white wine vinegar
¾ teaspoon pepper
6 ounces grape tomatoes, halved
¼ cup capers
1 shallot, sliced thin
2 anchovy fillets, rinsed and minced (optional)
½ cup fresh parsley leaves
¼ cup chopped fresh dill

1. Place potatoes and 2 teaspoons salt in large saucepan and cover with water by 1 inch. Bring to boil over high heat. Reduce heat to medium-low and simmer until potatoes are almost tender, about 7 minutes. Add green beans and continue to cook until both vegetables are tender, about 7 minutes longer.

2. Meanwhile, whisk oil, vinegar, pepper, and salt together in large bowl; measure out ¼ cup dressing and set aside. Add tomatoes; capers; shallot; and anchovies, if using, to bowl with remaining dressing and toss to coat; set aside.

3. Drain potatoes and green beans thoroughly in colander, then spread out on rimmed baking sheet. Drizzle reserved dressing over potatoes and green beans and, using rubber spatula, gently toss to combine. Let cool slightly, about 15 minutes.

4. Add parsley, dill, and potato mixture to bowl with tomato mixture and toss to combine. Season with salt and pepper to taste. Serve.

rise-and-shine breakfast and breads

Why This Recipe Works For a tall, fluffy diner-worthy omelet, we ditched the whisk for an electric mixer, which helped us incorporate air into the eggs. Cream added richness, but when we added it to the whipped eggs, the omelet lost its fluffiness. Combining the cream and eggs before whipping didn't work either—the fat in the cream made it impossible to whip air into the eggs. Instead, we whipped the dairy first, then folded it into the whipped eggs. After letting the bottom of the omelet set on the stovetop, we popped the skillet into a preheated oven, and just six minutes later had a puffy, fluffy omelet, cooked to perfection.

FLUFFY DINER-STYLE CHEESE OMELET

SERVES 2

Although this recipe will work with a stand mixer, a handheld mixer makes quick work of whipping such a small amount of cream. To make two omelets, double this recipe and cook the omelets simultaneously in two skillets. If you have only one skillet, prepare a double batch of ingredients and set half aside for the second omelet. Be sure to wipe out the skillet in between omelets.

- 3 tablespoons heavy cream, chilled
- 5 large eggs, room temperature
- ¼ teaspoon salt
- 2 tablespoons unsalted butter
- 2 ounces sharp cheddar cheese, shredded (½ cup)
- 1 recipe omelet filling (optional) (recipes follow)

1. Adjust oven rack to middle position and heat oven to 400 degrees. Using stand mixer fitted with whisk, whip cream on medium-low speed until foamy, about 1 minute. Increase speed to high and whip until soft peaks form, 1 to 3 minutes. Set whipped cream aside. Using dry, clean bowl and whisk attachment, whip eggs and salt on high speed until frothy and eggs have tripled in size, about 2 minutes. Gently fold whipped cream into eggs.

2. Melt butter in ovensafe 10-inch nonstick skillet over medium-low heat, swirling pan to coat bottom and sides. Add egg mixture and cook until edges are nearly set, 2 to 3 minutes. Sprinkle with ¼ cup cheddar and half of omelet filling, if using, and transfer to oven. Bake until eggs are set and edges are beginning to brown, 6 to 8 minutes.

3. Carefully remove pan from oven (handle will be very hot), sprinkle eggs with remaining ¼ cup cheddar and remaining omelet filling, if using, and let sit, covered, until cheese begins to melt, about 1 minute. Tilt pan and, using rubber spatula, push half of omelet onto cutting board, then fold omelet over itself to form half-moon shape. Cut omelet in half and serve.

SAUSAGE AND PEPPER FILLING
MAKES ABOUT 1 CUP

- 4 ounces hot or sweet Italian sausage, casings removed
- 1 tablespoon unsalted butter
- 1 small onion, chopped
- ½ red bell pepper, chopped
  Salt and pepper

Cook sausage in 10-inch nonstick skillet over medium heat, breaking up clumps with wooden spoon, until browned, about 6 minutes. Transfer to paper towel–lined plate. Add butter, onion, and bell pepper to now-empty skillet and cook until softened, about 10 minutes. Stir in sausage and season with salt and pepper to taste.

LOADED BAKED POTATO FILLING
MAKES ABOUT 1 CUP

- 1 large Yukon Gold potato, peeled and cut into ½-inch pieces
- 4 slices bacon, chopped
- 2 scallions, sliced thin
  Salt and pepper

Microwave potato, covered, in large bowl until just tender, 2 to 5 minutes. Cook bacon in 10-inch nonstick skillet over medium heat until crisp, about 8 minutes. Transfer bacon to paper towel–lined plate; pour off all but 1 tablespoon bacon fat. Add potato to skillet and cook until golden brown, about 6 minutes. Transfer potato to bowl, add cooked bacon, and stir in scallions. Season with salt and pepper to taste.

Why This Recipe Works "Impossible" pie is a 1970s phenomenon that promises a pie "crust" without rolling out finicky dough. Traditionally, a simple Bisquick batter was whisked with eggs and poured over vegetables, meat, and cheese and baked. To give our "crust" a crispy, browned exterior, we buttered the pie dish and coated it with Parmesan cheese. We replaced the Bisquick with a simple batter of flour, baking powder, eggs, and creamy half-and-half. Doubling the number of eggs made for a richer, custardy pie. For the filling, we chose ingredients that required a minimum of prep work: scallions, diced deli ham, and Gruyère cheese.

"IMPOSSIBLE" HAM-AND-CHEESE PIE

SERVES 8

Use a rasp-style grater or the smallest holes on a box grater for the Parmesan.

1 tablespoon unsalted butter, softened, plus 2 tablespoons melted
3 tablespoons finely grated Parmesan cheese
8 ounces Gruyère cheese, shredded (2 cups)
4 ounces thickly sliced deli ham, chopped
4 scallions, minced
½ cup (2½ ounces) all-purpose flour
¾ teaspoon baking powder
½ teaspoon pepper
¼ teaspoon salt
1 cup half-and-half
4 large eggs, lightly beaten
2 teaspoons Dijon mustard
⅛ teaspoon ground nutmeg

1. Adjust oven rack to lowest position and heat oven to 350 degrees. Grease 9-inch pie plate with softened butter, then coat plate evenly with Parmesan.

2. Combine Gruyère, ham, and scallions in bowl. Sprinkle cheese-and-ham mixture evenly in bottom of prepared pie dish. Combine flour, baking powder, pepper, and salt in now-empty bowl. Whisk in half-and-half, eggs, melted butter, mustard, and nutmeg until smooth. Slowly pour batter over cheese-and-ham mixture in pie dish.

3. Bake until pie is light golden brown and filling is set, 30 to 35 minutes. Let cool on wire rack for 15 minutes. Slice into wedges. Serve warm.

Finger Food

To serve our "Impossible" Ham-and-Cheese Pie as an hors d'oeuvre at your next party, forgo the pie plate and instead bake it in an 8-inch square baking dish. Slice it into 1-inch squares and serve warm or at room temperature.

Grating Hard Cheese

Using a rasp-style grater to grate hard cheeses like Parmesan produces lighter, fluffier shreds that melt seamlessly into all kinds of dishes.

BREAKFAST PIZZA

SERVES 6

Small-curd cottage cheese is sometimes labeled "country-style." Room-temperature dough is much easier to shape than cold, so pull the dough from the fridge about 1 hour before you start cooking.

- 3 tablespoons extra-virgin olive oil, plus extra for drizzling
- 6 slices bacon
- 8 ounces mozzarella cheese, shredded (2 cups)
- 1 ounce Parmesan cheese, grated (½ cup)
- 4 ounces (½ cup) small-curd cottage cheese
- ¼ teaspoon dried oregano
  Salt and pepper
  Pinch cayenne pepper
- 1 pound store-bought pizza dough, room temperature
- 6 large eggs
- 2 scallions, sliced thin
- 2 tablespoons minced fresh chives

1. Adjust oven rack to lowest position and heat oven to 500 degrees. Grease rimmed baking sheet with 1 tablespoon oil.

2. Cook bacon in 12-inch skillet over medium heat until crisp, 7 to 9 minutes. Transfer to paper towel–lined plate; when cool enough to handle, crumble bacon. Combine mozzarella and Parmesan in bowl; set aside. Combine cottage cheese, oregano, ¼ teaspoon pepper, cayenne, and 1 tablespoon oil in separate bowl; set aside.

3. Press and roll dough into 15 by 11-inch rectangle on lightly floured counter, pulling on corners to help make distinct rectangle. Transfer dough to prepared sheet and press to edges of sheet. Brush edges of dough with remaining 1 tablespoon oil. Bake dough until top appears dry and bottom is just beginning to brown, about 5 minutes.

4. Remove crust from oven and, using spatula, press down on any air bubbles. Spread cottage cheese mixture evenly over top, leaving 1-inch border around edges. Sprinkle bacon evenly over cottage cheese mixture.

5. Sprinkle mozzarella mixture evenly over pizza, leaving ½-inch border. Create 2 rows of 3 evenly spaced small wells in cheese, each about 3 inches in diameter (6 wells total). Crack 1 egg into each well, then season each with salt and pepper.

6. Return pizza to oven and bake until crust is light golden around edges and eggs are just set, 9 to 10 minutes for slightly runny yolks or 11 to 12 minutes for soft-cooked yolks, rotating sheet halfway through baking.

7. Transfer pizza to wire rack and let cool for 5 minutes. Transfer pizza to cutting board. Sprinkle with scallions and chives and drizzle with extra oil. Slice and serve.

SMOKED SALMON BREAKFAST PIZZA

In step 7, after cooling, omit scallions and top pizza with ¼ cup sliced red onion, 3 ounces sliced smoked salmon (cut into thin strips), and ¼ cup sour cream. Sprinkle with chives and 1 tablespoon chopped fresh dill and drizzle with extra oil.

SAUSAGE AND RED BELL PEPPER BREAKFAST PIZZA

Substitute 6 ounces bulk breakfast sausage for bacon and extra-sharp cheddar for mozzarella. Combine sausage; 1 stemmed, seeded, and chopped red bell pepper; 1 chopped onion; and ¼ teaspoon salt in 12-inch skillet. Cook over medium heat, breaking up sausage with spoon, until sausage begins to brown and bell pepper and onion are translucent, about 6 minutes. Transfer to paper towel–lined plate. Let mixture cool completely before proceeding.

CHORIZO AND MANCHEGO BREAKFAST PIZZA

Substitute 6 ounces chorizo sausage, halved lengthwise and cut into ½-inch slices, for bacon and 1 cup shredded Manchego cheese for Parmesan. Cook chorizo in 12-inch skillet over medium heat until lightly browned, 7 to 9 minutes. Let cool completely before proceeding.

Why This Recipe Works Eggs and bacon on a cheese pizza? Sounded like an excellent breakfast to us. Our challenge was to achieve a crisp, golden-brown crust without overcooking the eggs. We gave the crust a head start by parbaking it for 5 minutes. The remaining oven time cooked the eggs and other toppings to perfection. To keep the eggs in place while they cooked, we created wells in the cheese. Though we initially used ricotta, it became dry and grainy in the oven. Then we tried cottage cheese and were pleasantly surprised to find the curds melted in the oven, leaving a creamy, silky cheese layer that tied everything together.

Why This Recipe Works Adjaruli khachapuri is a bread stuffed with melty cheese hailing from the country of Georgia. When the bread is hot from the oven, the molten cheese is topped with an egg and butter and stirred together. We used a simple pizza dough since it was easy to shape, provided structure to contain the cheese, and had a chewy texture. We found that a mix of mozzarella and feta approximated the tang and stringy texture found in Georgian cheeses. Stirring in an egg yolk and a pat of butter right before serving kept the cheese filling smooth and stretchy. While khachapuri is perfect party food, it can also be enjoyed as a savory breakfast.

ADJARULI KHACHAPURI

SERVES 6

Using cold water to make the dough keeps it from overheating in the food processor. Use block mozzarella, not fresh here.

1¾ cups (8¾ ounces) all-purpose flour
1½ teaspoons sugar
1 teaspoon instant or rapid-rise yeast
¾ teaspoon table salt
½ cup plus 2 tablespoons cold water
1 tablespoon extra-virgin olive oil
6 ounces whole-milk mozzarella cheese, shredded (1½ cups)
6 ounces feta cheese, crumbled (1½ cups)
1 large egg yolk
1 tablespoon unsalted butter

1. Process flour, sugar, yeast, and salt in food processor until combined, about 3 seconds. With processor running, slowly add cold water and oil and process until dough forms sticky ball that clears sides of bowl, 30 to 60 seconds.

2. Transfer dough to counter and knead until smooth, about 1 minute. Shape dough into tight ball and place in greased bowl. Cover bowl with plastic wrap and let dough rise at room temperature until almost doubled in size, 2 to 2½ hours. (Alternatively, dough can rise in refrigerator until doubled in size, about 24 hours. Let come to room temperature, about 2 hours, before proceeding.)

3. Turn out dough onto lightly floured 16 by 12-inch sheet of parchment paper and coat lightly with flour. Flatten into 8-inch disk using your hands. Using rolling pin, roll dough into 12-inch circle, dusting dough lightly with flour as needed.

4. Roll bottom edge of dough 2½ inches in toward center. Rotate parchment 180 degrees and roll bottom edge of dough (directly opposite first rolled side) 2½ inches toward center. (Opposing edges of rolled sides should be 7 inches apart.)

5. Roll ends of rolled sides toward centerline and pinch firmly together to form football shape about 12 inches long and about 7 inches across at its widest point. Transfer parchment with dough to rimmed baking sheet. Cover loosely with plastic and let rise until puffy, 30 minutes to 1 hour. Adjust oven rack to middle position and heat oven to 450 degrees.

6. Combine mozzarella and feta in bowl. Fill dough with cheese mixture, lightly compacting and mounding in center (cheese will be piled higher than edge of dough). Bake until crust is well browned and cheese is bubbly and beginning to brown in spots, 15 to 17 minutes. Transfer sheet to wire rack. Add egg yolk and butter to cheese filling and stir with fork until fully incorporated and cheese is smooth and stretchy. Lift parchment off sheet and slide bread onto serving dish. Serve immediately.

Stages of Beauty and Bliss

1. Add egg yolk and butter to molten cheese filling and stir with fork.

2. Stir until fully incorporated and cheese is smooth and stretchy.

3. Serve immediately, dipping torn crust into the melted filling.

TEXAS BREAKFAST TACOS

SERVES 4 TO 6

If you're using an electric stovetop for the eggs, heat a second burner on low and move the skillet to it when it's time to adjust the heat. You can substitute 12 (6-inch) store-bought tortillas for the homemade.

- 1 pound plum tomatoes, cored and chopped
- 2 garlic cloves, chopped
- 2 jalapeño chiles, stemmed, seeded, and chopped
- 2 tablespoons chopped fresh cilantro
- 1 tablespoon lime juice
  Salt and pepper
- ¼ teaspoon red pepper flakes
- 12 large eggs
- 6 slices thick-cut bacon, cut into ½-inch pieces
- 1 small onion, chopped fine
- 1 recipe Homemade Taco-Size Flour Tortillas (recipe follows)
  Shredded Monterey Jack cheese
  Thinly sliced scallions
  Lime wedges

1. Microwave tomatoes and garlic in bowl until liquid begins to pool in bottom of bowl, about 4 minutes; transfer to fine-mesh strainer set over bowl and let drain for 5 minutes; discard liquid.

2. Process tomato mixture, half of jalapeños, cilantro, lime juice, 1 teaspoon salt, and pepper flakes in blender until smooth, about 45 seconds. Season with salt to taste; set aside for serving. (Salsa can be refrigerated for up to 3 days.)

3. Whisk eggs, ½ teaspoon salt, and ¼ teaspoon pepper in bowl until thoroughly combined and mixture is pure yellow, about 1 minute. Set aside.

4. Cook bacon in 12-inch nonstick skillet over medium heat until crispy, 8 to 10 minutes. Pour off all but 2 tablespoons fat from skillet (leaving bacon in skillet). Add onion and remaining jalapeños and cook until vegetables are softened and lightly browned, 4 to 6 minutes.

5. Add egg mixture and, using rubber spatula, constantly and firmly scrape along bottom and sides of skillet until eggs begin to clump and spatula leaves trail on bottom of skillet, 1½ to 2½ minutes.

6. Reduce heat to low. Gently but constantly fold egg mixture until it has clumped and is still slightly wet, 30 to 60 seconds. Season with salt and pepper to taste. Fill tortillas with egg mixture and serve immediately, passing salsa, Monterey Jack, scallions, and lime wedges separately.

HOMEMADE TACO-SIZE FLOUR TORTILLAS
MAKES 12 (6-INCH) TORTILLAS
Lard can be substituted for the shortening, if desired.

- 2 cups (10 ounces) all-purpose flour
- 1¼ teaspoons salt
- 5 tablespoons vegetable shortening, cut into ½-inch chunks
- ⅔ cup warm tap water
- 1 teaspoon vegetable oil

1. Combine flour and salt in large bowl. Using your fingers, rub shortening into flour mixture until mixture resembles coarse meal. Stir in warm water until combined.

2. Turn dough out onto counter and knead briefly to form smooth, cohesive ball. Divide dough into 12 equal portions; roll each into smooth 1-inch ball between your hands. Transfer to plate, cover with plastic wrap, and refrigerate until dough is firm, at least 30 minutes or up to 2 days.

3. Cut twelve 6-inch squares of parchment paper. Roll 1 dough ball into 6-inch circle on lightly floured counter. Transfer to parchment square; set aside. Repeat with remaining dough balls, stacking tortillas with parchment squares in-between.

4. Heat oil in 12-inch nonstick skillet over medium heat until shimmering. Wipe out skillet with paper towels, leaving thin film of oil. Cook 1 tortilla until spotty brown and beginning to bubble, about 45 seconds per side, adjusting heat as needed. Transfer to plate and cover with clean dish towel. Repeat with remaining tortillas. (Cooled tortillas can be layered between parchment squares, covered, and refrigerated for up to 3 days. Before serving, discard plastic and parchment, wrap tortillas with clean dish towel, and microwave at 50 percent power until heated through, about 20 seconds.)

Why This Recipe Works We love tacos for lunch and dinner, so why not for the most important meal of the day? For our take on southern Texas egg-stuffed tacos, we made flour tortillas from scratch, which was well worth the effort. After kneading and chilling the dough, we rolled out 6-inch rounds and cooked them in a skillet. For the hearty filling, we crisped bacon, leaving some of its fat in the skillet to help soften and flavor chopped onion and minced jalapeño. We added the eggs last, scrambling them with the vegetables and bacon, and topped the tacos with Monterey Jack cheese, our cooked red salsa, and a squeeze of lime.

Why This Recipe Works Commercially made breakfast sausage always disappoints when it comes to flavor, tasting either too sweet or salty, or too bland or highly seasoned, so we decided to make our own. We started with ground pork with some fat in it (lean meat was neither fatty nor flavorful enough) and amped up its mild flavor with classic breakfast sausage flavors: garlic, sage, thyme, and cayenne pepper. A spoonful of maple syrup sweetened the patties nicely. To combine the meat mixture, we kneaded it gently with our hands, but were careful not to overmix it, which would toughen the meat.

HOMEMADE BREAKFAST SAUSAGE

MAKES 16 PATTIES

Avoid lean or extra-lean ground pork; it makes the sausage dry, crumbly, and less flavorful.

2 pounds ground pork
1 tablespoon maple syrup
1 garlic clove, minced
2 teaspoons dried sage
1½ teaspoons pepper
1 teaspoon salt
½ teaspoon dried thyme
⅛ teaspoon cayenne pepper
2 tablespoons unsalted butter

1. Combine pork, maple syrup, garlic, sage, pepper, salt, thyme, and cayenne in large bowl. Gently mix with hands until well combined. Using greased ¼-cup measure, divide mixture into 16 patties and place on rimmed baking sheet. Cover patties with plastic wrap, then gently flatten each one to ½-inch thickness.

2. Melt 1 tablespoon butter in 12-inch nonstick skillet over medium heat. Cook half of patties until well browned and cooked through, 6 to 10 minutes. Transfer to paper towel–lined plate and tent with aluminum foil. Wipe out skillet. Repeat with remaining butter and patties. Serve.

To Make Ahead Follow recipe through step 1. Refrigerate uncooked patties for up to 1 day or freeze for up to 1 month. To serve, proceed as directed in step 2, increasing cooking time to 14 to 18 minutes.

Dried Herbs

We use plenty of dried herbs in the test kitchen, but we don't use every dried herb. Delicate leafy herbs, such as basil, parsley, chives, mint, and cilantro become stale-tasting when dried. Heartier herbs, such as oregano, sage, and thyme, dry well and are good substitutes for fresh in most recipes—especially those in which the herbs will cook in liquid. We've found that tarragon and dill fall into a middle category: They do add flavor in their dried form, but that flavor is more muted than that provided by other dried herbs.

A few general rules: Use only half as much dried herbs as fresh, and add them at the same time as you would add fresh. Dried herbs lose potency 6 to 12 months after opening; you can test dried herbs for freshness by rubbing them between your fingers—if they don't smell bright, throw them away.

OREGANO
Great in tomato sauces, chili, Latin dishes, and sprinkled on pizza. Dried does not have the same sharp bite as fresh, but it does have a distinct and recognizable floral element.

SAGE
We prefer rubbed (or finely crumbled) sage to the ground or chopped kinds. Use with poultry, stuffings, pork, full-flavored vegetables (like squash), and in butter sauces.

ROSEMARY
Works well in long-cooked dishes like soups, stews, and braises. Too much dried rosemary can turn a dish bitter, so use sparingly.

THYME
Good for long-cooked soups and stews and roasted meats and poultry; pairs well with mustard and lemon flavors.

SHORT-ORDER HOME FRIES

SERVES 4

Although we prefer the sweetness of Yukon Gold potatoes, other medium-starch potatoes, such as red potatoes, can be substituted. If you want to spice things up, add a pinch of cayenne pepper.

1½ pounds Yukon Gold potatoes,
    cut into ¾-inch pieces
4 tablespoons unsalted butter
1 onion, chopped fine
½ teaspoon garlic salt
½ teaspoon salt
    Pepper

1. Place potatoes and 1 tablespoon butter in large bowl and microwave, covered, until edges of potatoes begin to soften, 5 to 7 minutes, stirring halfway through cooking.

2. Meanwhile, melt 1 tablespoon butter in 12-inch nonstick skillet over medium heat. Add onion and cook until softened and golden brown, 8 to 10 minutes. Transfer to small bowl.

3. Melt remaining 2 tablespoons butter in now-empty skillet over medium heat. Add potatoes and pack down with spatula. Cook, without moving, until bottoms of potatoes are brown, 5 to 7 minutes. Turn potatoes, pack down again, and continue to cook until well browned and crisp, 5 to 7 minutes. Reduce heat to medium-low and continue to cook until potatoes are crusty, 9 to 12 minutes, stirring occasionally. Stir in onion, garlic salt, and salt and season with pepper to taste. Serve.

GREEK DINER–STYLE HOME FRIES
Omit garlic salt and add 1 tablespoon lemon juice, 2 minced garlic cloves, and ½ teaspoon dried oregano to potatoes along with onion in step 3.

HOME FRIES WITH FRESH HERBS
Add 1 teaspoon each chopped fresh basil, parsley, thyme, and tarragon to potatoes along with onion in step 3.

The Right Spuds for Home Fries
High-starch, low-moisture potatoes, such as russets, may be great for baking and mashing, but when it comes to home fries, they are not the best choice. The fluffy flesh of these potatoes breaks down in the skillet, leaving nothing but a greasy pool of stodgy spuds. For tender tubers that retain their texture, we prefer medium-starch varieties, such as Yukon Gold and red potatoes. They hold their shape in the skillet, develop a great crust, and fry up to a beautiful golden brown.

RUSSET POTATOES
A falling-apart mess

YUKON GOLD POTATOES
Intact, crisp, and browned

Why This Recipe Works Though a commercial-grade griddle helps our local diner serve up home fries with a perfectly crispy exterior, the real secret is precooking the potatoes. Roasting or boiling our spuds took too much time for a quick breakfast side, so we turned to the microwave to jump-start their cooking before frying them in a large skillet. We found that packing the potatoes down with a spatula and cooking them a few minutes before turning them and then repeating these steps ensured they were evenly browned and extra-crunchy. Finally, we stirred in some sautéed onion and garlic salt to give our home fries a deep, savory flavor.

BETTER-THAN-THE-BOX PANCAKE MIX

MAKES ABOUT 6 CUPS; ENOUGH FOR 24 PANCAKES

Malted milk powder might seem odd here, but it gives the pancakes a deeper, more complex flavor.

- 2 cups (10 ounces) all-purpose flour
- 2 cups (8 ounces) cake flour
- 1 cup (3 ounces) nonfat dry milk powder
- ¾ cup (3⅓ ounces) malted milk powder
- ⅓ cup (2⅓ ounces) sugar
- 2 tablespoons baking powder
- 1 teaspoon baking soda
- 1 tablespoon salt
- 12 tablespoons unsalted butter, cut into ½-inch pieces

Process all ingredients in food processor until no lumps remain and mixture resembles wet sand, about 2 minutes. (Pancake mix can be frozen for up to 2 months.)

BETTER-THAN-THE-BOX PANCAKES

To make 8 pancakes, whisk 2 cups Better-Than-the-Box Pancake Mix, 2 lightly beaten large eggs, and ½ cup buttermilk in large bowl until smooth. Using ¼-cup measure, portion batter into lightly oiled 12-inch nonstick skillet or griddle in 4 places and cook over medium-low heat until golden brown, about 2 minutes per side. Repeat with remaining batter. Serve. (If you don't have buttermilk, whisk 1½ teaspoons lemon juice or white vinegar into ½ cup whole or low-fat milk and let sit until slightly thickened, about 10 minutes.)

Not Just for Milkshakes

To give our pancakes complexity and depth, we added malted milk powder to the mix. This product is made from malted barley that has been evaporated and pulverized, and sometimes includes flour or evaporated milk powder. Though it is more commonly used to make milkshakes, we found it added a sweet, nutty flavor to the pancakes made from our Better-Than-the-Box Pancake Mix.

Is the Pan Ready for Pancakes?

A properly heated pan or griddle is essential to making perfect, golden-brown, fluffy pancakes. A skillet that has not been properly heated and is too cool will produce pale, gummy pancakes. Here's a test to make sure your pan is hot enough: Drop a tablespoon of batter in its center. If, after one minute, the pancake is golden brown on the bottom, the pan is ready. If it remains blond—or is close to burning—adjust the heat accordingly.

PALE, GUMMY PANCAKE

PERFECT, FLUFFY PANCAKE

Why This Recipe Works For our take on pancake mix that delivers both store-bought ease and from-scratch taste, we combined all-purpose flour with cake flour; this duo yielded sturdy yet tender cakes. To give pancakes made from our mix complexity and depth, we added an unusual ingredient, malted milk powder, which imparted a sweet, nutty flavor. Though most mixes call for shortening, we opted for butter, which gave us moister, more flavorful pancakes. Using buttermilk instead of milk when mixing the batter gave us high-rising pancakes—the acid of the buttermilk reacts with the baking soda, causing the batter to bubble and rise.

Why This Recipe Works Getting the height and lightness of traditional pancakes with the robust flavor and texture of cornmeal pancakes is tougher than it seems. Coarsely ground cornmeal can be sandy, and it lacks the gluten necessary to support a fluffy internal structure. We found that we could use more cornmeal by heating it with some of the buttermilk to soften it first. Soaking the cornmeal also thickened the batter, helping it ride higher in the pan instead of spreading out. Letting the batter sit for a few minutes before griddling the cakes allowed the buttermilk to react with the baking soda, which resulted in fluffier, airier pancakes.

FLUFFY CORNMEAL PANCAKES

MAKES ABOUT 15 (4-INCH) PANCAKES

Our favorite cornmeal is Anson Mills Fine Yellow Cornmeal.

1¾ cups buttermilk
1¼ cups (6¼ ounces) cornmeal
2 tablespoons unsalted butter, cut into ¼-inch pieces
¾ cup (3¾ ounces) all-purpose flour
2 tablespoons sugar
1¾ teaspoons baking powder
½ teaspoon baking soda
½ teaspoon salt
2 large eggs
2½ teaspoons vegetable oil

1. Adjust oven rack to middle position and heat oven to 200 degrees. Set wire rack inside rimmed baking sheet and place in oven. Whisk 1¼ cups buttermilk and cornmeal together in medium bowl. Stir in butter, cover, and microwave until slightly thickened around edges, about 90 seconds, stirring once halfway through cooking. Let sit, covered, for 5 minutes.

2. Whisk flour, sugar, baking powder, baking soda, and salt in large bowl. Beat eggs and remaining ½ cup buttermilk together in 1-cup liquid measuring cup. Whisk egg mixture into cornmeal mixture. Whisk cornmeal mixture into flour mixture. Let sit for 10 minutes.

3. Heat ½ teaspoon oil in 12-inch nonstick skillet over medium-low heat until shimmering. Using paper towels, carefully wipe out oil, leaving thin film on bottom of pan. Using level ¼-cup measure for each pancake, drop batter for 3 pancakes into pan.

Cook until edges are set and bubbles begin to form on tops of pancakes, about 90 seconds. Flip, then cook until second side is golden brown, about 2 minutes longer. Transfer to prepared baking sheet in oven, cover loosely with aluminum foil, and repeat with remaining oil and batter. Serve.

The Virtues of Pancake Patience

For the fluffiest pancakes, let the finished batter sit for 10 minutes before griddling the cakes. The rest gives the baking soda extra time to react and form large air bubbles, lightening the batter, ergo the pancakes. With a hearty whole grain like cornmeal, you want all the lift you can get. This trick works with any pancake batter made with whole grains.

Why This Recipe Works A big, puffy pancake, a Dutch baby puffs and rises as it bakes, then falls in the center a few minutes out of the oven, resulting in a bowl-shaped breakfast treat with crisp sides and a thin, custardy bottom. For our version we started with a 12-inch skillet; its gently sloping walls promoted an even rise. Brushing the pan with oil and preheating it in the oven helped ensure the sides had the texture we wanted and jump-started the pancake's rise. Since fats tend to make baked goods tender rather than crisp, we used skim milk in our batter. For even more crispness, we replaced some of the flour with cornstarch.

DUTCH BABY

SERVES 4

You can use whole or low-fat milk instead of skim, but the texture won't be as crisp. Serve with an assortment of berries and lightly sweetened whipped cream, if desired.

- 2 tablespoons vegetable oil
- 1 cup (5 ounces) all-purpose flour
- ¼ cup cornstarch
- 2 teaspoons grated lemon zest plus 2 tablespoons juice
- 1 teaspoon salt
- 3 large eggs
- 1¼ cups skim milk
- 1 tablespoon unsalted butter, melted and cooled
- 1 teaspoon vanilla extract
- 3 tablespoons confectioners' sugar

1. Adjust oven rack to middle position and heat oven to 450 degrees. Brush bottom and sides of 12-inch skillet with oil. Heat skillet in oven until oil is shimmering, about 10 minutes.

2. Meanwhile, combine flour, cornstarch, lemon zest, and salt in large bowl. Whisk eggs in second bowl until frothy and light, about 1 minute. Whisk milk, butter, and vanilla into eggs until incorporated. Whisk one-third of milk mixture into flour mixture until no lumps remain, then slowly whisk in remaining milk mixture until smooth.

3. Carefully pour batter into skillet and bake until edges are deep golden brown and crisp, about 20 minutes. Transfer skillet to wire rack, sprinkle pancake with lemon juice and confectioners' sugar, and cut into wedges. Serve.

Easy Steps to Making a Dutch Baby

1. Brush bottom and sides of pan with vegetable oil to guarantee crisp exterior.

2. Heat greased pan before carefully pouring in batter to initiate rise.

3. Bake in 450-degree oven to ensure high rise.

4. Sprinkle deflated pancake with lemon juice and confectioners' sugar before serving.

CHEESE BLINTZES WITH RASPBERRY SAUCE

MAKES 12 BLINTZES, SERVES 4 TO 6

The batter makes about 15 crepes to account for any mistakes. When making the crepes, if the batter doesn't stick to the skillet when swirling, that means the skillet is too greased and/or not hot enough. Return the skillet to the heat and cook 10 seconds longer; then try again to swirl the batter. With the next try, use less butter to brush the skillet. If the filled and rolled blintzes split on the sides, be careful while searing them because the filling may sputter when it hits the skillet. You do not need to thaw the raspberries.

Filling

11 ounces (1¼ cups plus 2 tablespoons) whole-milk ricotta cheese
½ cup (2 ounces) confectioners' sugar
1 ounce cream cheese, softened
¼ teaspoon salt

Sauce

10 ounces (2 cups) frozen raspberries
¼ cup (1¾ ounces) granulated sugar
¼ teaspoon salt

Crepes

2 cups (10 ounces) all-purpose flour
2 teaspoons granulated sugar
½ teaspoon salt
3 cups whole milk
4 large eggs
4 tablespoons unsalted butter, melted and cooled, plus 4 tablespoons unsalted butter

1. For the Filling Whisk all ingredients in bowl until no lumps of cream cheese remain. Refrigerate until ready to use. (Filling can be refrigerated for up to 2 days.)

2. For the Sauce Combine raspberries, sugar, and salt in small saucepan. Cook over medium heat, stirring occasionally, until slightly thickened, 8 to 10 minutes. (Sauce can be refrigerated for up to 2 days.)

3. For the Crepes Whisk flour, sugar, and salt together in medium bowl. Whisk milk and eggs together in separate bowl. Add half of milk mixture to flour mixture and whisk until smooth. Whisk

in 3 tablespoons melted butter until incorporated. Whisk in remaining milk mixture until smooth. (Batter can be refrigerated for up to 2 days before cooking. It will separate; rewhisk it before using.)

4. Brush bottom of 12-inch nonstick skillet lightly with some of remaining 1 tablespoon melted butter and heat skillet over medium heat until hot, about 2 minutes. Add ⅓ cup batter to center of skillet and simultaneously lift and rotate skillet in circular motion to swirl batter, allowing batter to run and fully cover bottom of skillet. Cook crepe until edges look dry and start to curl and bottom of crepe is light golden, about 1 minute. Using rubber spatula, lift edge of crepe and slide it onto plate. Repeat with remaining batter, stacking crepes and brushing skillet with melted butter every other time. (Adjust burner between medium-low and medium heat as needed toward end of crepe-making process.)

5. Working with 1 crepe at a time, spoon 2 tablespoons filling onto crepe about 2 inches from bottom edge and spread into 4-inch line. Fold bottom edge of crepe over filling, then fold sides of crepe over filling. Gently roll crepe into tidy package about 4 inches long and 2 inches wide. Repeat with remaining crepes and filling. (Assembled blintzes can be transferred to plate, covered with plastic wrap, and refrigerated for up to 24 hours.)

6. Melt 2 tablespoons butter in now-empty skillet over medium heat. Add half of blintzes, seam sides down, and cook until golden brown, 2 to 4 minutes, gently moving blintzes in skillet as needed for even browning. Using spatula, gently flip blintzes and continue to cook until golden brown on second side, 2 to 4 minutes longer. Transfer blintzes to platter, seam sides down, and wipe skillet clean with paper towels. Repeat with remaining 2 tablespoons butter and remaining blintzes. Serve with raspberry sauce.

To Make Ahead At end of step 5, transfer blintzes to rimmed baking sheet and freeze. Transfer frozen blintzes to zipper-lock bag and freeze for up to 1 month. When ready to cook, do not thaw blintzes. Reduce heat in step 6 to medium-low and cook blintzes, covered, until golden brown, 6 to 9 minutes per side.

Why This Recipe Works We wanted to create a streamlined version of this eastern European specialty. For our filling, we replaced mild farmer's cheese with ricotta. A little cream cheese added tanginess while confectioners' sugar provided just enough sweetness and body. We found we didn't need a crepe pan; a traditional skillet worked just fine, turning out larger crepes that were easier to fill and fold. We cooked them on only one side, until they were firm enough to fill and fold. A bright quick-cooking raspberry sauce balanced the rich, lightly sweetened blintz filling.

BEIGNETS

MAKES 24 BEIGNETS

This dough is very wet and sticky, so flour the counter and baking sheet generously. Use a Dutch oven that holds 6 quarts or more for this recipe.

- 1 cup water, heated to 110 degrees
- 3 tablespoons granulated sugar
- 1 tablespoon instant or rapid-rise yeast
- 3 cups (15 ounces) all-purpose flour
- ¾ teaspoon salt
- 2 large eggs
- 2 tablespoons plus 2 quarts vegetable oil
  Confectioners' sugar

1. Combine water, 1 tablespoon granulated sugar, and yeast in large bowl and let sit until foamy, about 5 minutes. Combine flour, remaining 2 tablespoons granulated sugar, and salt in second bowl. Whisk eggs and 2 tablespoons oil into yeast mixture. Add flour mixture and stir vigorously with rubber spatula until dough comes together. Cover bowl with plastic wrap and refrigerate until nearly doubled in size, about 1 hour.

2. Set wire rack inside rimmed baking sheet. Line second sheet with parchment paper and dust generously with flour. Place half of dough on well-floured counter and pat into rough rectangle with floured hands, flipping to coat with flour. Roll dough into ¼-inch-thick rectangle (roughly 12 by 9 inches). Using pizza wheel, cut dough into twelve 3-inch squares and transfer to floured baking sheet. Repeat with remaining dough.

3. Add remaining oil to large Dutch oven until it measures about 1½ inches deep and heat over medium-high heat to 350 degrees. Fry 6 beignets, adjusting burner as necessary to maintain oil temperature between 325 and 350 degrees, until golden brown, about 3 minutes, flipping halfway through frying. Using slotted spoon or tongs, transfer beignets to prepared baking sheet. Return oil to 350 degrees and repeat with remaining beignets. Dust beignets with confectioners' sugar and serve immediately.

Forming Beignets

This dough is very wet, which allows a network of delicate holes to develop in the beignets. However, wet dough can be tricky to work with. Here's how to easily shape and cut the beignets:

1. Dust counter and rolling pin generously with flour before you roll out chilled beignet dough.

2. Cut 3-inch squares with pizza wheel.

A Faster Way to Flavor

Starting with a full tablespoon of yeast and proofing the dough in warm water jump-starts the fermentation process, giving our beignets complex flavor after just a 1-hour rise.

Why This Recipe Works To replicate the crisp, airy texture and tangy flavor of these classic New Orleans doughnuts, we began by using plenty of yeast, kick-starting it with warm water and sugar to develop its flavor. We added extra water for a super-hydrated dough, so that as soon as the wet dough hit the hot oil, it created lots of steam, giving our beignets an open, honeycombed structure. Since wet dough is tricky to roll out, we let it rise in the refrigerator to firm it up. A few minutes of frying and a shower of powdered sugar, and our beignets were ready to be enjoyed, Big Easy style.

Why This Recipe Works A good cornmeal biscuit combines the tender, fluffy crumb of a traditional biscuit with the distinct cornmeal flavor of cornbread. To make the dough, we used a food processor to cut chilled butter quickly into our dry ingredients. So our biscuits would taste like cornmeal, but wouldn't have its dry, gritty texture, we soaked the cornmeal in buttermilk; just 10 minutes was enough to soften it. A bit of honey provided a subtle sweetness that drew out the corn flavor even more. Kneading the dough briefly prior to cutting out rounds ensured evenly textured biscuits that rose to an impressive height.

CORNMEAL BISCUITS

MAKES 12 BISCUITS

If you don't have buttermilk, you can substitute clabbered milk; whisk 1 tablespoon lemon juice into 1¼ cups of milk and let the mixture sit until slightly thickened, about 10 minutes. Avoid coarsely ground cornmeal, which makes gritty biscuits.

  1 cup (5 ounces) cornmeal
1¼ cups buttermilk
  1 tablespoon honey
  2 cups (10 ounces) all-purpose flour
  1 tablespoon baking powder
 ½ teaspoon baking soda
  1 teaspoon salt
12 tablespoons unsalted butter, cut into ½-inch
     pieces and chilled

1. Adjust oven rack to middle position and heat oven to 450 degrees. Line rimmed baking sheet with parchment paper. Whisk cornmeal, buttermilk, and honey together in large bowl; let sit for 10 minutes.

2. Pulse flour, baking powder, baking soda, and salt in food processor until combined, about 3 pulses. Scatter butter evenly over top and continue to pulse until mixture resembles coarse meal, about 15 pulses. Add flour mixture to buttermilk mixture and stir until dough forms.

3. Turn dough out onto lightly floured counter and knead until smooth, 8 to 10 times. Pat dough into 9-inch circle, about ¾ inch thick. Using 2½-inch biscuit cutter dipped in flour, cut out rounds and transfer to prepared baking sheet, dipping cutter in flour after each cut. Pat remaining dough into ¾-inch-thick circle, cut rounds from dough, and transfer to baking sheet.

4. Bake until biscuits begin to rise, about 5 minutes, then reduce oven temperature to 400 degrees and bake until golden brown, 8 to 12 minutes longer, rotating baking sheet halfway through baking. Let biscuits cool on baking sheet for 5 minutes, then transfer to wire rack. Serve warm or let cool to room temperature. (Biscuits can be stored at room temperature for up to 2 days.)

Steps to Tender, Fluffy Cornmeal Biscuits

Our Cornmeal Biscuits have the moist, flavor-packed crumb of cornbread and the fluffy stature of a stamped biscuit.

1. Soak cornmeal in buttermilk for soft crumb without too much cornmeal grit before mixing with dough.

2. Transfer dough to lightly floured counter and knead briefly before patting into 9-inch circle.

3. Use biscuit cutter to cut dough into rounds, dipping cutter into flour between cuts.

CATHEAD BISCUITS

MAKES 6 BISCUITS

If you don't have buttermilk, you can substitute clabbered milk; whisk 1 tablespoon lemon juice into 1¼ cups milk and let the mixture sit until slightly thickened, about 10 minutes. The recipe will also work with 3 cups White Lily flour in place of both the all-purpose and cake flours.

1½ cups (7½ ounces) all-purpose flour
1½ cups (6 ounces) cake flour
1 tablespoon baking powder
½ teaspoon baking soda
1 teaspoon salt
8 tablespoons unsalted butter, cut into ½-inch pieces and softened
4 tablespoons vegetable shortening, cut into ½-inch pieces
1¼ cups buttermilk

1. Adjust oven rack to upper-middle position and heat oven to 425 degrees. Grease 9-inch round cake pan. Combine all-purpose flour, cake flour, baking powder, baking soda, and salt in large bowl. Using fingertips, rub butter and shortening into flour mixture until mixture resembles coarse meal. Stir in buttermilk until combined.

2. Using greased ½-cup measure or large spring-loaded ice cream scoop, transfer 6 heaping portions of dough into prepared pan, placing five around edge and one in center.

3. Bake until puffed and golden brown, 20 to 25 minutes, rotating pan halfway through baking. Let biscuits cool in pan for 10 minutes, then transfer to wire rack. Serve. (Biscuits can be stored at room temperature for up to 2 days.)

Forming Cathead Biscuits

Instead of kneading, rolling, and stamping, Cathead Biscuits are scooped.

Scoop dough and nestle biscuits in cake pan using spring-loaded ice cream scoop.

Flour Mixology

Southern bakers swear by White Lily all-purpose flour, which they say makes biscuits soft and downy, exactly the texture we sought for our Cathead Biscuits. We found we could replicate it by combining equal amounts of all-purpose flour and cake flour.

ALL-PURPOSE FLOUR
Contributes structure

CAKE FLOUR
Contributes softness

WHITE LILY
The soft and fluffy standard-bearer

Why This Recipe Works As big as a cat's head, these tender, moist biscuits that originated in the Appalachian region boast a golden-brown, craggy top and downy, soft sides. Many Southern bakers rely on White Lily flour to ensure a tender texture, but since this flour isn't readily available everywhere, we substituted an equal mix of cake flour and all-purpose flour. For biscuits with a fluffy texture, we relied on softened butter and shortening, worked in with warm hands. Scooping the dough into a round cake pan, so the mounds were touching, gave us baked biscuits with tender, soft sides.

MIXED BERRY SCONES

MAKES 8 SCONES

Work the dough as little as possible, just until it comes together. Work quickly to keep the butter and berries as cold as possible for the best results. Note that the butter is divided in this recipe. An equal amount of frozen blueberries, raspberries, blackberries, or strawberries (halved) can be used in place of the mixed berries.

Scones

1¾ cups (8¾ ounces) frozen mixed berries
3 tablespoons confectioners' sugar
3 cups (15 ounces) all-purpose flour
12 tablespoons unsalted butter, cut into ½-inch pieces, chilled
⅓ cup (2⅓ ounces) granulated sugar
1 tablespoon baking powder
1¼ teaspoons salt
¾ cup plus 2 tablespoons whole milk
1 large egg plus 1 large yolk

Glaze

2 tablespoons unsalted butter, melted
1 tablespoon honey

1. For the Scones Adjust oven rack to upper-middle position and heat oven to 425 degrees. Line rimmed baking sheet with parchment paper. (If your berry mix contains strawberries, cut them in half.) Toss berries with confectioners' sugar in bowl; freeze until needed.

2. Combine flour, 6 tablespoons butter, granulated sugar, baking powder, and salt in food processor and process until butter is fully incorporated, about 15 seconds. Add remaining 6 tablespoons butter and pulse until butter is reduced to pea-size pieces, 10 to 12 pulses. Transfer mixture to large bowl. Stir in berries.

3. Beat milk and egg and yolk together in separate bowl. Make well in center of flour mixture and pour in milk mixture. Using rubber spatula, gently stir mixture, scraping from edges of bowl and folding inward until very shaggy dough forms and some bits of flour remain. Do not overmix.

4. Turn out dough onto well-floured counter and, if necessary, knead briefly until dough just comes together, about 3 turns. Using your floured hands and bench scraper, shape dough into 12 by 4-inch rectangle, about 1½ inches tall. Using knife or bench scraper, cut dough crosswise into 4 equal rectangles. Cut each rectangle diagonally into 2 triangles (you should have 8 scones total). Transfer scones to prepared sheet. Bake until scones are lightly golden on top, 16 to 18 minutes, rotating pan halfway through baking.

5. For the Glaze While scones bake, combine melted butter and honey in small bowl.

6. Remove scones from oven and brush tops evenly with glaze mixture. Return scones to oven and continue to bake until golden brown on top, 5 to 8 minutes longer. Transfer scones to wire rack and let cool for at least 10 minutes before serving.

To Make Ahead Unbaked scones can be frozen for several weeks. After cutting scones into triangles in step 4, freeze them on baking sheet. Transfer frozen scones to zipper-lock freezer bag. When ready to bake, heat oven to 375 degrees and extend cooking time in step 4 to 23 to 26 minutes. Glaze time in step 6 will remain at 5 to 8 minutes.

Why This Recipe Works A random stop at a rural Massachusetts antique store—which had a coffee shop attached—provided the inspiration for these berry-filled scones. To re-create them, we discovered that treating the butter in two different ways was key: We processed half the cold butter to fully incorporate it into the dough, then we pulsed in the remaining butter, processing it to pea-size pieces that created pockets of steam as the scones baked. Adding confectioners' sugar to the frozen berries counteracted their tartness and helped control them from "bleeding" into the dough. A simple glaze added a nice sheen and sweet finish.

BLUEBERRY CORNBREAD

SERVES 8

We developed this recipe using commonly available Quaker Yellow Corn Meal. If you're using our favorite cornmeal, Anson Mills Fine Yellow Cornmeal, you will need to use 1¼ cups to yield 5 ounces for the batter. If you use a dark-colored cake pan, reduce the baking time in step 3 to 35 to 40 minutes. You can use frozen blueberries; if doing so, leave the berries in the freezer until the last possible moment and toss them with 2 tablespoons of all-purpose flour before stirring them into the batter. Then, increase the baking time to 45 to 50 minutes.

1½ tablespoons cornmeal, plus 1 cup (5 ounces)
1½ cups (7½ ounces) all-purpose flour
¾ cup (5¼ ounces) plus 1 tablespoon sugar
2 teaspoons baking powder
¾ teaspoon salt
1 cup whole milk
12 tablespoons unsalted butter, melted
2 large eggs
10 ounces (2 cups) blueberries

1. Adjust oven rack to middle position and heat oven to 375 degrees. Grease bottom and sides of light-colored 9-inch round cake pan, then dust pan with 1½ tablespoons cornmeal.

2. Whisk flour, ¾ cup sugar, baking powder, salt, and remaining 1 cup cornmeal together in large bowl. Whisk milk, melted butter, and eggs together in second bowl (butter may form clumps; this is OK). Stir milk mixture into flour mixture until just combined. Stir in blueberries until just incorporated. Transfer batter to prepared pan and smooth top with rubber spatula. Sprinkle remaining 1 tablespoon sugar over top.

3. Bake until golden brown and paring knife inserted in center comes out clean, 40 to 45 minutes. Let cornbread cool in pan on wire rack for 20 minutes. Run paring knife between cornbread and side of pan. Remove cornbread from pan and let cool on rack for 20 minutes. Serve warm.

HONEY BUTTER
MAKES ABOUT ⅓ CUP
This honey butter also tastes great on roasted root vegetables, boiled corn, pork chops, pancakes, muffins, biscuits, and dinner rolls.

4 tablespoons unsalted butter, softened
2 tablespoons honey
¼ teaspoon salt
Pinch cayenne pepper

Using fork, mash all ingredients in bowl until combined. Serve.

Comparing Cornmeals
Cornmeal's grind size varies from product to product. We developed this recipe using Quaker Yellow Corn Meal. If using our taste test winner, Anson Mills Fine Yellow Cornmeal, you'll need to adjust the volume (see recipe note).

QUAKER
Stick to the recipe.

ANSON MILLS
A finer grind means you
have to use more.

Why This Recipe Works A far cry from savory, dense cornbread, our rendition of blueberry cornbread is slightly sweet, moist, and studded with juicy berries. We opted for a higher ratio of flour to cornmeal, yielding a cornbread that was tender and cake-like, yet sturdy enough to keep a full two cups of blueberries from sinking. A dusting of cornmeal into the greased pan before pouring in the batter added a burst of corn flavor and crunch, and a sprinkling of sugar over the batter gave the top a golden crust. While the cornbread baked, we whipped up a honey butter that we slathered on the still-warm, blueberry-laden wedges.

Why This Recipe Works Savory skillet-baked Southern-style cornbread should boast hearty corn flavor, a sturdy, moist crumb, and a dark brown crust. For the right texture, we used finely ground cornmeal. Toasting it in the oven for a few minutes intensified the corn flavor. Buttermilk added a sharp tang that worked well with the corn, and soaking the cornmeal in the buttermilk helped to soften it so our cornbread was moist and tender. When it came to the fat, a combination of butter (for flavor) and vegetable oil (which can withstand high heat without burning) worked best, and greasing the pan with both delivered the crisp crust we were after.

SOUTHERN-STYLE SKILLET CORNBREAD

SERVES 12

If you don't have buttermilk, you can substitute clabbered milk; whisk 2 tablespoons lemon juice into 2 cups of milk and let the mixture sit until slightly thickened, about 10 minutes. We prefer a cast-iron skillet here, but any ovensafe 10-inch skillet will work fine. Avoid coarsely ground cornmeal, as it will make the cornbread gritty.

2¼ cups (11¼ ounces) cornmeal
2 cups buttermilk
¼ cup vegetable oil
4 tablespoons unsalted butter, cut into 4 pieces
2 large eggs
1 teaspoon baking powder
1 teaspoon baking soda
¾ teaspoon salt

1. Adjust oven racks to lower-middle and middle positions and heat oven to 450 degrees. Heat 10-inch cast-iron skillet on middle rack for 10 minutes. Spread cornmeal over rimmed baking sheet and bake on lower-middle rack until fragrant and color begins to deepen, about 5 minutes. Transfer hot cornmeal to large bowl and whisk in buttermilk; set aside.

2. Carefully add oil to hot skillet and continue to bake until oil is just smoking, about 5 minutes. Remove skillet from oven and add butter, carefully swirling pan until butter is melted. Pour all but 1 tablespoon oil mixture into cornmeal mixture, leaving remaining oil mixture in pan. Whisk eggs, baking powder, baking soda, and salt into cornmeal mixture.

3. Pour cornmeal mixture into hot skillet and bake until top begins to crack and sides are golden brown, 12 to 16 minutes, rotating pan halfway through baking. Let cornbread cool in pan for 5 minutes, then turn out onto wire rack. Serve.

Secrets to Savory Southern-Style Skillet Cornbread

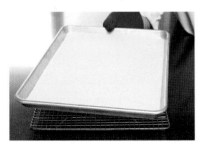

1. Toast cornmeal to give bread richer corn flavor.

2. Soak cornmeal in buttermilk to soften cornmeal and ensure tender yet sturdy crumb.

3. Grease and thoroughly heat skillet to create crisp crust.

BEER-BATTER CHEESE BREAD

SERVES 10 TO 12 (MAKES 1 LOAF)

We prefer to use a mild American lager, such as Budweiser, here; strongly flavored beers will make this bread bitter.

2½ cups (12½ ounces) all-purpose flour
½ cup minced fresh chives
2 tablespoons sugar
4 teaspoons baking powder
1 teaspoon salt
½ teaspoon pepper
8 ounces Gruyère cheese, shredded (2 cups)
1¼ cups mild lager, such as Budweiser
3 tablespoons unsalted butter, melted

1. Adjust oven rack to middle position and heat oven to 450 degrees. Grease 10-inch cast-iron skillet.

2. Whisk flour, chives, sugar, baking powder, salt, and pepper together in large bowl. Stir in 1½ cups Gruyère, breaking up any clumps, until coated with flour. Stir beer and melted butter into flour mixture until just combined. Batter will be heavy and thick; do not overmix.

3. Scrape batter into prepared skillet and smooth top. Sprinkle with remaining ½ cup Gruyère. Transfer skillet to oven and bake until loaf is golden brown and toothpick inserted into center comes out clean, 20 to 25 minutes, rotating skillet halfway through baking.

4. Using potholders, transfer skillet to wire rack and let loaf cool for 10 minutes. Being careful of hot skillet handle, remove loaf from skillet, return to rack, and let cool for at least 20 minutes before serving.

FLIPPING OUT SKILLET BREADS

Let loaf cool in skillet for 10 minutes, then gently flip loaf onto wire rack. If you try to flip loaf out of skillet before letting it cool slightly, it will crumble.

Why This Recipe Works The beauty of a quick bread is that it can be on the table in less than an hour, but that convenience is only worth it if the final product tastes good. Recipes for beer-batter cheese bread often produce loaves that taste sour or have weak cheese flavor. We wanted a lighter loaf enhanced with the yeasty flavor of beer and a rich hit of cheese—and it still had to be quick and easy. We put more than a cup of cheese into the batter itself and then sprinkled extra on top of the loaf to create a beautiful, craggy crust. Making the bread in a cast-iron skillet gave it a great bottom crust and helped it bake through quickly and evenly.

Why This Recipe Works Stella's Bakery in Madison, Wisconsin, is known for its spicy cheese bread. One challenge we had while trying to re-create this addictive bread was finding a way to incorporate the cheese without stunting the dough's rise. We found the key was to make sure the cheese cubes came to room temperature before adding them to the dough. To help keep its shape, we baked the bread in a cake pan. An egg wash and a generous sprinkle of red pepper flakes finished off the loaf. A final brush of melted butter helped the crust stay supple and gave it a nice shine.

SPICY CHEESE BREAD

MAKES 1 LOAF

Take the cheese out of the refrigerator when you start the recipe to ensure that it comes to room temperature by the time you need it. Cold cheese will retard rising. The dough needs to rise for several hours before baking.

Bread

3¼ cups (16¼ ounces) all-purpose flour
¼ cup (1¾ ounces) sugar
1 tablespoon instant or rapid-rise yeast
1½ teaspoons red pepper flakes
1¼ teaspoons salt
½ cup warm water (110 degrees)
2 large eggs plus 1 large yolk
4 tablespoons unsalted butter, melted
6 ounces Monterey Jack cheese, cut into ½-inch cubes (1½ cups), room temperature
6 ounces provolone cheese, cut into ½-inch cubes (1½ cups), room temperature

Topping

1 large egg, lightly beaten
1 teaspoon red pepper flakes
1 tablespoon unsalted butter, melted

1. For the Bread Whisk flour, sugar, yeast, pepper flakes, and salt together in bowl of stand mixer. Whisk warm water, eggs and yolk, and melted butter together in liquid measuring cup. Add egg mixture to flour mixture. Fit stand mixer with dough hook and knead on medium speed until dough clears bottom and sides of bowl, about 8 minutes.

2. Transfer dough to unfloured counter, shape into ball, and transfer to greased bowl. Cover with plastic wrap and let rise in warm place until doubled in size, 1½ to 2 hours.

3. Grease 9-inch round cake pan. Transfer dough to unfloured counter and press to deflate. Roll dough into 18 by 12-inch rectangle with long side parallel to counter's edge. Distribute Monterey Jack and provolone evenly over dough, leaving 1-inch border around edges. Starting with edge closest to you, roll dough into log. Pinch seam and ends to seal, then roll log so seam side is down. Roll log back and forth on counter, applying gentle, even pressure, until log reaches 30 inches in length. If any tears occur, pinch to seal.

4. Starting at one end, wind log into coil; tuck end underneath coil. Place loaf in prepared cake pan and cover loosely with clean dish towel. Let rise in warm place until doubled in size, 1 to 1½ hours. Adjust oven rack to lower-middle position and heat oven to 350 degrees.

5. For the Topping Brush top of loaf with egg, then sprinkle with pepper flakes. Place cake pan on rimmed baking sheet. Bake until loaf is golden brown, about 25 minutes. Rotate loaf, tent with aluminum foil, and continue to bake until loaf registers 190 degrees, 25 to 30 minutes longer.

6. Transfer pan to wire rack and brush bread with butter. Let cool for 10 minutes. Run knife around edge of pan to loosen bread. Slide bread onto wire rack, using spatula as needed for support. Let cool for 30 minutes before slicing. Serve warm.

PERFECT POPOVERS

MAKES 6 POPOVERS

Greasing the pan with shortening ensures the best release, but vegetable oil spray may be substituted; do not use butter. Bread flour makes for the highest and sturdiest popovers, but 2 cups (10 ounces) of all-purpose flour may be substituted.

- 3 large eggs
- 2 cups 1 percent or 2 percent low-fat milk, heated to 110 degrees
- 3 tablespoons unsalted butter, melted and cooled
- 2 cups (11 ounces) bread flour
- 1 teaspoon salt
- 1 teaspoon sugar

1. Adjust oven rack to lower-middle position and heat oven to 450 degrees. Grease 6-cup popover pan with shortening, then flour pan lightly. Whisk eggs until light and foamy in medium bowl. Slowly whisk in milk and butter until incorporated.

2. Combine flour, salt, and sugar in large bowl. Whisk three-quarters of milk mixture into flour mixture until no lumps remain, then whisk in remaining milk mixture. Transfer batter to 4-cup liquid measuring cup, cover with plastic wrap, and let sit at room temperature for 1 hour. (Alternatively, batter can be refrigerated for up to 24 hours. Bring to room temperature before proceeding.)

3. Whisk batter to recombine, then pour into prepared pan (batter will not reach top of cups). Bake until just beginning to brown, about 20 minutes. Without opening oven door, decrease oven temperature to 300 degrees and continue to bake until popovers are golden brown, 35 to 40 minutes longer. Poke small hole in top of each popover with skewer and continue to bake until deep golden brown, about 10 minutes longer. Transfer pan to wire rack, poke popovers again with skewer, and let cool for 2 minutes. Remove from pan and serve.

To Make Ahead Cooled popovers can be stored at room temperature for up to 2 days. To serve, adjust oven rack to middle position and heat oven to 400 degrees. Heat popovers on rimmed baking sheet until crisp and heated through, 5 to 8 minutes.

MUFFIN TIN POPOVERS

If you don't have a popover pan, you can bake the popovers in a 12-cup muffin tin—with a sacrifice in stature. To ensure even cooking, use only the outer 10 cups of the tin.

Grease and flour outer 10 cups of muffin tin, then fill ¼ inch from the top (you may have some batter left over). Reduce initial baking time in step 3 to 15 minutes, and reduce secondary baking time to 20 to 25 minutes after oven temperature has been lowered. Poke popovers as directed and continue to bake for another 10 minutes.

Popovers Gone Wrong

POP NEVER
Short, squat popovers occur when the recipe calls for cake flour, which doesn't provide enough structure to the batter. Using too little batter can also make for squat popovers, as can an oven that's not hot enough.

POP UNDER
Deflated popovers occur when they aren't baked long enough to set up properly or aren't poked during baking to allow the steam to escape.

POP UGLY
Misshapen popovers are caused by using a preheated, oiled pan. The batter that first hits the pan immediately rises up through the wet batter, resulting in an ugly shape.

Why This Recipe Works For golden-brown popovers that really popped, we used bread flour instead of all-purpose flour in the batter—the bread flour's higher protein content ensured the highest rise and crispiest crust. Resting the batter before baking prevented the popovers from setting up too quickly. We first baked our popovers at a high temperature to jump-start the initial rise, then turned the oven down so they would cook through evenly. To prevent the popovers from collapsing, we let steam escape by poking a hole in the top of each one when they were almost done baking, and then again as they cooled.

WHOLE-WHEAT BLUEBERRY MUFFINS

MAKES 12 MUFFINS

Do not overmix the batter. You can substitute frozen (unthawed) blueberries for fresh in this recipe.

Streusel

3 tablespoons granulated sugar
3 tablespoons packed brown sugar
3 tablespoons whole-wheat flour
Pinch salt
2 tablespoons unsalted butter, melted

Muffins

3 cups (16½ ounces) whole-wheat flour
2½ teaspoons baking powder
½ teaspoon baking soda
1 teaspoon salt
1 cup (7 ounces) granulated sugar
2 large eggs
4 tablespoons unsalted butter, melted
¼ cup vegetable oil
1¼ cups buttermilk
1½ teaspoons vanilla extract
7½ ounces (1½ cups) blueberries

1. For the Streusel Combine granulated sugar, brown sugar, flour, and salt in bowl. Add melted butter and toss with fork until evenly moistened and mixture forms large chunks with some pea-size pieces throughout; set aside.

2. For the Muffins Adjust oven rack to middle position and heat oven to 400 degrees. Spray 12-cup muffin tin, including top, generously with vegetable oil spray. Whisk flour, baking powder, baking soda, and salt together in large bowl. Whisk sugar, eggs, melted butter, and oil together in separate bowl until combined, about 30 seconds. Whisk buttermilk and vanilla into sugar mixture until combined.

3. Stir sugar mixture into flour mixture until just combined. Gently stir in blueberries until incorporated. Using a heaping ¼-cup dry measuring cup, divide batter evenly among prepared muffin cups (cups will be filled to rim); sprinkle evenly with streusel.

4. Bake until golden brown and toothpick inserted in center comes out with few crumbs attached, 18 to 20 minutes, rotating muffin tin halfway through baking. Let muffins cool in muffin tin on wire rack for 5 minutes. Remove muffins from muffin tin and let cool 5 minutes longer. Serve.

Don't Make this Mistake: Heavy and Dense Muffins

You can't simply swap whole-wheat flour into any muffin recipe and expect it to work. But if you know the science behind baking and account for the variables, you can make great blueberry muffins using 100 percent whole-wheat flour.

Why This Recipe Works When it comes to baking with whole wheat, the benefits—added fiber, bran, and nutty sweetness—are often trumped by the drawbacks: dense texture and squat appearance. To use one hundred percent whole wheat, we had to revise our standard blueberry muffin recipe. The resulting whole-wheat muffins were light and tender thanks to two leaveners and several high-moisture ingredients (buttermilk, eggs, blueberries, melted butter, and oil). As a final step we added a crumbly streusel topping to round out our now light and delicate muffins with hearty whole-wheat flavor.

Why This Recipe Works Created by Pam McKinstry at her café in Nantucket, morning glory muffins are chock-full of nuts, fruit, carrots, and spices. But all these tempting add-ins can make for heavy, dense muffins, so our first move was to strain the fruit and press out the extra juice to prevent our muffins from being soggy. To keep the bright, fruity flavor intact, we simply saved the released fruit juice, reduced it on the stovetop, and added the concentrated syrup back to the batter. To keep the nuts and coconut from becoming mealy or soggy in the finished muffins, we toasted and processed them. At last, our muffins were truly glorious.

MORNING GLORY MUFFINS

MAKES 12 MUFFINS

Though we prefer golden raisins here, ordinary raisins will work, too.

¾ cup (2¼ ounces) sweetened shredded coconut, toasted
½ cup walnuts, toasted
2¼ cups (11¼ ounces) all-purpose flour
¾ cup (5¼ ounces) sugar
1½ teaspoons baking soda
½ teaspoon baking powder
1 teaspoon ground cinnamon
¾ teaspoon salt
1 (8-ounce) can crushed pineapple
1 Granny Smith apple, peeled, cored, and shredded
8 tablespoons unsalted butter, melted
3 large eggs
1 teaspoon vanilla extract
1½ cups shredded carrots (2 to 3 carrots)
1 cup golden raisins

1. Adjust oven rack to middle position and heat oven to 350 degrees. Spray 12-cup muffin tin with vegetable oil spray. Process coconut and walnuts in food processor until finely ground, 20 to 30 seconds. Add flour, sugar, baking soda, baking powder, cinnamon, and salt and pulse until combined. Transfer mixture to large bowl.

2. Place pineapple and shredded apple in fine-mesh strainer set over liquid measuring cup. Press fruit dry (you should have about 1 cup juice). Bring juice to boil in 12-inch skillet over medium-high heat and cook until reduced to ¼ cup, about 5 minutes. Let cool slightly. Whisk melted butter, cooled juice, eggs, and vanilla together until smooth. Stir wet mixture into dry mixture until combined. Stir in pineapple-apple mixture, carrots, and raisins.

3. Divide batter evenly among muffin cups. Bake until toothpick inserted in center comes out clean, 24 to 28 minutes, rotating pan halfway through baking. Let muffins cool in muffin tin on wire rack for 10 minutes. Remove muffins from tin and let cool for at least 10 minutes before serving. (Muffins can be stored at room temperature for up to 3 days.)

Secrets to Glorious Morning Glory Muffins

1. Toasting the coconut and walnuts heightens their flavor, and processing them in a food processor until finely ground prevents soggy, stringy coconut and mealy nuts.

2. Pressing the juice out of the shredded apple and pineapple before stirring them into the batter keeps the muffins from being gummy and wet.

3. Reducing the released fruit juice on the stovetop (down from 1 cup to ¼ cup) and adding the syrup to the batter provides a bright, fruity flavor without adding too much moisture.

MUFFIN TIN DOUGHNUTS

MAKES 12 DOUGHNUTS

In step 3, brush the doughnuts generously, using up all the melted butter. Use your hand to press the cinnamon sugar onto the doughnuts to coat them completely.

Doughnuts
2¾ cups (13¾ ounces) all-purpose flour
1 cup (7 ounces) sugar
¼ cup cornstarch
1 tablespoon baking powder
1 teaspoon salt
½ teaspoon ground nutmeg
1 cup buttermilk
8 tablespoons unsalted butter, melted
2 large eggs plus 1 large yolk

Coating
1 cup sugar
2 teaspoons ground cinnamon
8 tablespoons unsalted butter, melted

1. For the Doughnuts Adjust oven rack to middle position and heat oven to 400 degrees. Spray 12-cup muffin tin with vegetable oil spray. Whisk flour, sugar, cornstarch, baking powder, salt, and nutmeg together in bowl. Whisk buttermilk, melted butter, and eggs and yolk together in separate bowl. Add wet ingredients to dry ingredients and stir with rubber spatula until just combined.

2. Scoop batter into prepared tin. Bake until doughnuts are lightly browned and toothpick inserted in center comes out clean, 19 to 22 minutes. Let doughnuts cool in tin for 5 minutes.

3. For the Coating Whisk sugar and cinnamon together in bowl. Remove doughnuts from tin. Working with 1 doughnut at a time, brush all over with melted butter, then roll in cinnamon sugar, pressing lightly to adhere. Transfer to wire rack and let cool for 15 minutes. Serve.

Brush with Butter

We brush the warm muffins liberally with melted butter before rolling them in the cinnamon sugar. The butter helps the coating stick and makes the muffins taste more fried.

Why This Recipe Works To capture the best of breakfast baking, we set out to create a muffin that tasted like a cake doughnut in disguise with a tender crumb, a crisp exterior, and a buttery spiced coating. Adding an extra yolk and cutting all-purpose flour with cornstarch gave the muffins a tender crumb that wouldn't break apart. To replicate a fried exterior, we turned up the oven temperature, which crisped the crust nicely. Lastly we brushed the muffins with butter and rolled them in cinnamon sugar. From coating to crumb, these doughnut muffins combined the essence of a doughnut and the ease of a muffin (without a deep fryer in sight).

ULTIMATE CINNAMON BUNS

MAKES 8 BUNS

*For smaller cinnamon buns, cut the dough into
12 pieces in step 3.*

Dough
¾ cup whole milk, heated to 110 degrees
2¼ teaspoons instant or rapid-rise yeast
3 large eggs, room temperature
4¼ cups (21¼ ounces) all-purpose flour
½ cup cornstarch
½ cup (3½ ounces) granulated sugar
1½ teaspoons salt
12 tablespoons unsalted butter,
cut into 12 pieces and softened

Filling
1½ cups packed (10½ ounces) light brown sugar
1½ tablespoons ground cinnamon
¼ teaspoon salt
4 tablespoons unsalted butter, softened

Glaze
1½ cups confectioners' sugar
4 ounces cream cheese, softened
1 tablespoon whole milk
1 teaspoon vanilla extract

1. For the Dough Make foil sling for 13 by 9-inch
baking pan by folding 2 long sheets of aluminum
foil; first sheet should be 13 inches wide and second
sheet should be 9 inches wide. Lay sheets of foil in pan
perpendicular to each other, with extra foil hanging
over edges of pan. Push foil into corners and up
sides of pan, smoothing foil flush to pan. Grease foil.
Whisk milk and yeast together in liquid measuring
cup until yeast dissolves, then whisk in eggs.

2. Adjust oven rack to middle position and place
loaf or cake pan on bottom of oven. Using stand
mixer fitted with dough hook, mix flour, cornstarch,
sugar, and salt on low speed until combined.

Add warm milk mixture in steady stream and mix
until dough comes together, about 1 minute.
Increase speed to medium and add butter, 1 piece
at a time, until incorporated. Continue to mix until
dough is smooth and comes away from sides of
bowl, about 10 minutes (if dough is still wet and
sticky, add up to ¼ cup flour, 1 tablespoon at a time,
until it releases from bowl). Turn dough out onto
counter and knead to form smooth, round ball.
Transfer dough to medium greased bowl, cover with
plastic wrap, and transfer to middle rack of oven.
Pour 3 cups boiling water into loaf pan in oven, close
oven door, and let dough rise until doubled in size,
about 2 hours.

3. For the Filling Combine sugar, cinnamon, and
salt in small bowl. Remove dough from oven and turn
out onto lightly floured counter. Roll dough into
18-inch square and, leaving ½-inch border around
edges, spread with butter, then sprinkle evenly with
sugar mixture and lightly press sugar mixture into
dough. Starting with edge closest to you, roll dough
into tight cylinder, pinch lightly to seal seam, and
cut into 8 pieces. Transfer pieces, cut side up, to
prepared pan. Cover with plastic and let rise in oven
until doubled in size, about 1 hour.

4. For the Glaze Remove buns and water pan
from oven and heat oven to 350 degrees. Whisk all
glaze ingredients together in medium bowl until
smooth. Remove plastic and bake buns until deep
golden brown and filling is melted, 35 to 40 minutes,
rotating pan halfway through baking. Transfer to
wire rack, top buns with ½ cup glaze, and let cool for
30 minutes. Using foil overhang, lift buns from pan
and top with remaining glaze. Serve.

To Make Ahead Follow recipe through step 3,
skipping step of letting buns rise. Place buns in pan,
cover with plastic wrap, and refrigerate for up to
1 day. To bake, let sit at room temperature for 1 hour.
Remove plastic and proceed with step 4.

Why This Recipe Works Gooey softball-size cinnamon buns are the ultimate breakfast treat. For the base of ours, we turned to a buttery, tender brioche dough. Adding cornstarch to the all-purpose flour in the dough made the buns especially tender. For a filling with great flavor, we combined a good amount of cinnamon—no other spices necessary—with brown sugar. Softened butter helped keep the filling from spilling out as we rolled up the dough. Baked together, the butter and cinnamon sugar turned into a rich, gooey filling. A thick, tangy glaze of cream cheese, confectioners' sugar, and milk ensured our buns really looked the part.

Why This Recipe Works Rich, gooey, homemade cinnamon buns can take upwards of 3 hours to prepare. We wanted the same tender, yeasty results in half the time. For a quicker rise, we supplemented the yeast (which we proofed in warm milk for extra speed) with baking powder. A mere 2 minutes of hand-kneading and a single 30-minute rise were enough to give us the flavor and texture we were looking for. We used a cooler-than-normal oven to give the yeast time to rise and develop flavor before the tops of the buns set. Brown sugar and butter in the filling and a touch of vanilla in our tangy cream cheese glaze made these buns ultra-rich and indulgent.

QUICKER CINNAMON BUNS

MAKES 8 BUNS

Since the filling, dough, and glaze all require melted butter, it's easier to melt all 10 tablespoons in a liquid measuring cup and divvy it up as needed. Stir the melted butter before each use to redistribute the milk solids. We developed this recipe using a dark cake pan, which produces deeply caramelized buns. If your cake pan is light-colored, adjust the oven rack to the lowest position, heat the oven to 375 degrees, and increase the baking time to 29 to 32 minutes.

Filling

- ¾ cup packed (5¼ ounces) light brown sugar
- ¼ cup (1¾ ounces) granulated sugar
- 1 tablespoon ground cinnamon
- ⅛ teaspoon salt
- 2 tablespoons unsalted butter, melted
- 1 teaspoon vanilla extract

Dough

- 1¼ cups whole milk, room temperature
- 4 teaspoons instant or rapid-rise yeast
- 2 tablespoons granulated sugar
- 2¾ cups (13¾ ounces) all-purpose flour
- 2½ teaspoons baking powder
- ¾ teaspoon salt
- 6 tablespoons unsalted butter, melted

Glaze

- 3 ounces cream cheese, softened
- 2 tablespoons unsalted butter, melted
- 2 tablespoons whole milk
- ½ teaspoon vanilla extract
- ⅛ teaspoon salt
- 1 cup (4 ounces) confectioners' sugar, sifted

1. For the Filling Combine brown sugar, granulated sugar, cinnamon, and salt in bowl. Stir in melted butter and vanilla until mixture resembles wet sand; set aside.

2. For the Dough Grease dark 9-inch round cake pan, line with parchment paper, and grease parchment. Pour ¼ cup milk in small bowl and microwave until 110 degrees, 15 to 20 seconds. Stir in yeast and 1 teaspoon sugar and let sit until mixture is bubbly, about 5 minutes.

3. Whisk flour, baking powder, salt, and remaining 5 teaspoons sugar together in large bowl. Stir in 2 tablespoons butter, yeast mixture, and remaining 1 cup milk until dough forms (dough will be sticky). Transfer dough to well-floured counter and knead until smooth ball forms, about 2 minutes.

4. Roll dough into 12 by 9-inch rectangle, with long side parallel to counter edge. Brush dough all over with 2 tablespoons butter, leaving ½-inch border on far edge. Sprinkle dough evenly with filling, then press filling firmly into dough. Using bench scraper or metal spatula, loosen dough from counter. Roll dough away from you into tight log and pinch seam to seal.

5. Roll log seam side down and cut into 8 equal pieces. Stand buns on end and gently re-form ends that were pinched during cutting. Place 1 bun in center of prepared pan and others around perimeter of pan, seam sides facing in. Brush tops of buns with remaining 2 tablespoons butter. Cover buns loosely with plastic wrap and let rise for 30 minutes. Adjust oven rack to middle position and heat oven to 350 degrees.

6. Discard plastic and bake buns until edges are well browned, 23 to 25 minutes. Loosen buns from sides of pan with paring knife and let cool for 5 minutes. Invert large plate over cake pan. Using potholders, flip plate and pan upside down; remove pan and parchment. Reinvert buns onto wire rack, set wire rack inside parchment-lined rimmed baking sheet, and let cool for 5 minutes.

7. For the Glaze Place cream cheese in large bowl and whisk in butter, milk, vanilla, and salt until smooth. Whisk in sugar until smooth. Pour glaze evenly over tops of buns, spreading with spatula to cover. Serve.

TRIPLE-CHOCOLATE STICKY BUNS

SERVES 12

Be sure to use a metal baking pan. The tackiness of the dough aids in stretching it in step 7, so resist using a lot of dusting flour. Rolling the dough cylinder too tightly in step 8 will result in misshapen rolls.

Flour Paste and Dough

⅔ cup whole milk
¼ cup (1¼ ounces) all-purpose flour
⅔ cup whole milk
1 large egg plus 1 large yolk
3¼ cups (16¼ ounces) all-purpose flour
2¼ teaspoons instant or rapid-rise yeast
3 tablespoons granulated sugar
1½ teaspoons salt
6 tablespoons unsalted butter, cut into 6 pieces and softened

Topping and Filling

¾ cup packed (5¼ ounces) brown sugar
6 tablespoons unsalted butter, melted, plus 4 tablespoons unsalted butter
¼ cup dark corn syrup
2 tablespoons water
1 tablespoon unsweetened cocoa powder
¼ teaspoon salt
4 ounces bittersweet chocolate, chopped fine
1 cup (6 ounces) milk chocolate chips

1. For the Flour Paste and Dough Whisk milk and flour in small bowl until no lumps remain. Microwave, whisking every 25 seconds, until mixture thickens to stiff paste, 50 to 75 seconds. Whisk until smooth.

2. In bowl of stand mixer, whisk flour paste and milk until smooth then whisk in egg and yolk. Add flour and yeast. Fit mixer with dough hook and mix on low speed until all flour is moistened, 1 to 2 minutes. Cover bowl and let stand for 15 minutes.

3. Add sugar and salt and mix on medium-low speed for 5 minutes. Add butter and mix until incorporated, scraping down dough hook and bowl as needed (dough will be sticky), about 5 minutes.

4. Transfer dough to lightly floured counter and knead briefly to form ball. Transfer, seam side down, to greased large bowl, cover tightly with plastic, and let rise until doubled in size, about 1 hour.

5. For the Topping and Filling Meanwhile, whisk brown sugar, melted butter, corn syrup, water, cocoa, and salt together until combined. Spray 13 by 9-inch metal baking pan with vegetable oil spray. Using rubber spatula, spread topping to edges of prepared pan; set aside.

6. About 30 minutes before dough is done rising, microwave bittersweet chocolate and remaining 4 tablespoons butter in bowl at 50 percent power, stirring occasionally, until melted, about 2 minutes. Refrigerate until matte and firm, 30 to 40 minutes.

7. Transfer dough to lightly floured counter and lightly flour top of dough. Roll and stretch dough to 18 by 15-inch rectangle with long side parallel to counter's edge. Stir bittersweet chocolate mixture with rubber spatula until smooth and spreadable (mixture should have similar texture to frosting); spread over dough, leaving 1-inch border along top edge. Sprinkle evenly with chocolate chips.

8. Beginning with long edge nearest you, loosely roll dough away from you into even log, pushing in ends to create even thickness. Pinch seam to seal. Roll log seam side down and slice into 12 equal portions. Place buns, cut side down, in prepared pan in 3 rows of four, lightly reshaping buns as needed. Cover tightly with plastic and let rise until buns are puffy and touching one another, about 1 hour.

9. Adjust oven racks to lowest and lower-middle positions and heat oven to 375 degrees. Place rimmed baking sheet on lower rack to catch any drips. Bake buns on upper rack until golden brown on top, about 20 minutes. Cover loosely with aluminum foil and continue to bake until center buns register at least 200 degrees, about 15 minutes longer.

10. Carefully remove foil from pan (steam may escape) and immediately run paring knife around edge of pan. Place large platter or second rimmed baking sheet over pan and carefully invert. Remove pan and let buns cool for 15 minutes. Serve.

To Make Ahead Follow recipe through step 8, then refrigerate buns for at least 8 hours or up to 24 hours. When ready to bake, let buns sit on counter for 30 minutes before proceeding with step 9. Increase uncovered baking time by 10 minutes.

Why This Recipe Works To take sticky buns over the top, we incorporated three types of chocolate. To ensure the buns were ultratender, we used a Japanese technique called tangzhong—microwaving a portion of the flour and milk, turning it into a gel. The gel locked in moisture so the dough was soft without becoming too sticky. For the filling, we microwaved butter and bittersweet chocolate to form a ganache to spread over the rolled-out dough. Sprinkled with milk chocolate chips and baked, these delivered just the right amount of sweetness with delightful pockets of sweet, creamy flavor. Cocoa powder added another dose of chocolate to the topping.

Why This Recipe Works Morning buns rely on a complicated croissant-like dough that requires both substantial effort and time. For an easier path, we switched to a quick dough closer to puff pastry. Instead of rolling the butter into the dry ingredients on the counter, we moved it all to a zipper-lock bag and rolled everything right in the bag. To produce multiple layers in this rich pastry, we rolled the dough into a rectangle, then into a cylinder, and gently patted it flat. A blend of brown and white sugars added a subtle molasses flavor to the filling, while orange zest instilled it with bright citrus notes.

MORNING BUNS

MAKES 12 BUNS

If the dough becomes too soft to work with at any point, refrigerate it until it's firm enough to easily handle.

Dough

  3 cups (15 ounces) all-purpose flour
  1 tablespoon sugar
2¼ teaspoons instant or rapid-rise yeast
  ¾ teaspoon salt
24 tablespoons (3 sticks) unsalted butter, cut into ¼-inch-thick slices and chilled
  1 cup sour cream, chilled
  ¼ cup orange juice, chilled
  3 tablespoons ice water
  1 large egg yolk

Filling

  ½ cup (3½ ounces) granulated sugar
  ½ cup packed (3½ ounces) light brown sugar
  1 tablespoon grated orange zest
  2 teaspoons ground cinnamon
  1 teaspoon vanilla extract

1. For the Dough Combine flour, sugar, yeast, and salt in large zipper-lock bag. Add butter to bag, seal, and shake to coat. Press air out of bag and reseal. Roll over bag several times with rolling pin, shaking bag after each roll, until butter is pressed into large flakes. Transfer mixture to large bowl and stir in sour cream, orange juice, water, and egg yolk until combined.

2. Turn dough onto floured counter and knead briefly to form smooth, cohesive ball. Roll dough into 20 by 12-inch rectangle. Starting with short edge, roll dough into tight cylinder. Pat cylinder flat to 12 by 4-inch rectangle and transfer to parchment paper–lined rimmed baking sheet. Cover with plastic wrap and freeze for 15 minutes.

3. For the Filling Line 12-cup muffin tin with paper or foil liners and spray with vegetable oil spray. Combine granulated sugar, brown sugar, orange zest, cinnamon, and vanilla in medium bowl. Remove dough from freezer and place on lightly floured counter. Roll dough into 20 by 12-inch rectangle and sprinkle evenly with filling, leaving ½-inch border

around edges. Starting at long edge, roll dough into tight cylinder and pinch lightly to seal seam. Trim ½ inch dough from each end and discard. Cut dough into 12 pieces and transfer, cut side up, to prepared tin. Cover loosely with plastic and refrigerate for at least 4 hours or up to 24 hours.

4. Adjust oven rack to middle position and place loaf or cake pan on bottom of oven. Remove plastic from buns and place in oven. Pour 3 cups boiling water into loaf pan in oven, close oven door, and let buns rise until puffed and doubled in size, 20 to 30 minutes. Remove buns and water pan from oven and heat oven to 425 degrees. Bake until buns begin to rise, about 5 minutes, then reduce oven temperature to 325 degrees. Bake until deep golden brown, 40 to 50 minutes, rotating pan halfway through baking. Let buns cool in muffin tin on wire rack for 5 minutes, then transfer to wire rack and discard liners. Serve warm.

To Make Ahead Follow recipe through step 3, skipping step of refrigerating buns. Freeze buns, in muffin tin, until firm, about 30 minutes. Transfer buns, with liners, to zipper-lock bag and freeze for up to 1 month. To bake, return buns to muffin tin, cover with plastic, and refrigerate for at least 8 hours or up to 24 hours. Proceed with step 4.

Key Steps to Flaky Pastry

1. Flatten flour-coated butter into long flakes by pressing air out of bag, sealing it, and rolling over it a few times with rolling pin.

2. Add butter-flour mixture to bowl and stir in sour cream, orange juice, water, and egg yolk. Then mix and knead briefly before rolling dough.

Why This Recipe Works For buns piled high with big crumbs the way they do in Jersey, we had to pay special attention to the types of flour and sugar we used in each layer. For a chewy texture in our cake base, we used all-purpose flour. But instead of using this same flour for the topping, we reached for cake flour, which is finer and lower in protein than all-purpose flour and gave the topping its signature soft crumbs. We used just granulated sugar to sweeten the cake layer, but found that a combination of white and brown sugars was key for the optimal flavor and texture of the crumb topping.

NEW JERSEY CRUMB BUNS

SERVES 12

Note that we call for both all-purpose and cake flours in this recipe. Do not substitute all-purpose flour for the cake flour (or vice versa), or the cake will be airy and fluffy and the topping will be tough and dry. We developed this recipe using Pillsbury Softasilk bleached cake flour; the topping will be slightly drier if you substitute unbleached cake flour. You can use either light or dark brown sugar in the topping.

Cake

2¼ cups (11¼ ounces) all-purpose flour
¾ cup milk
¼ cup (1¾ ounces) granulated sugar
1 large egg
2¼ teaspoons instant or rapid-rise yeast
¾ teaspoon salt
6 tablespoons unsalted butter, cut into 6 pieces and softened

Topping

18 tablespoons (2¼ sticks) unsalted butter, melted
¾ cup (5¼ ounces) granulated sugar
¾ cup packed (5¼ ounces) brown sugar
1½ teaspoons ground cinnamon
½ teaspoon salt
4 cups (16 ounces) cake flour
Confectioners' sugar

1. For the Cake Adjust oven rack to middle position and heat oven to 350 degrees. Grease 13 by 9-inch baking dish. In bowl of stand mixer fitted with dough hook, combine flour, milk, sugar, egg, yeast, and salt. Knead on low speed until dough comes together, about 2 minutes.

2. With mixer running, add butter 1 piece at a time, waiting until each piece is incorporated before adding next. Increase speed to medium-high and continue to knead until dough forms stretchy, web-like strands on sides of bowl, about 6 minutes longer (dough will be soft and sticky).

3. Using greased rubber spatula, transfer dough to prepared dish. Using your floured hands, press dough into even layer to edges of dish. Cover dish tightly with plastic wrap and let dough rise at room temperature until slightly puffy, about 1 hour.

4. For the Topping Ten minutes before dough has finished rising, whisk melted butter, granulated sugar, brown sugar, cinnamon, and salt together in bowl. Add flour and stir with rubber spatula or wooden spoon until mixture forms thick, cohesive dough; let sit for 10 minutes to allow flour to hydrate.

5. If dough has pulled away from sides of dish after rising, gently pat it back into place using your floured fingers. Break topping mixture into rough ½-inch pieces using your fingers and scatter in even layer over dough in dish. (Be sure to scatter all crumbs even though it may seem like too much.)

6. Bake until crumbs are golden brown, wooden skewer inserted in center of cake comes out clean, and cake portion registers about 215 degrees in center, about 35 minutes. Transfer dish to wire rack and let cake cool completely. Using spatula, transfer cake to cutting board; cut cake into 12 squares. Dust squares with confectioners' sugar and serve.

To Make Ahead Once dough has been pressed into even layer in baking dish and dish has been wrapped tightly in plastic wrap, dough can be refrigerated for at least 4 hours (to ensure proper rising) or up to 24 hours. When ready to bake, let dough sit on counter for 10 minutes before proceeding with step 4. Increase baking time to 40 minutes.

All Crumb Trails Lead to . . . Hackensack?

Since 1948, B&W Bakery in Hackensack, New Jersey, has been at the center of the crumb bun universe. At the bakery, staffers use industrial-size baking sheets to bake the cakes before sprinkling them with a thick layer of streusel (they go through 2,000 pounds of crumbs a week) and cutting them into slabs or squares, depending on your order. Fans from across northern New Jersey make it a weekly stop.

KOLACHES

MAKES 16 KOLACHES

Do not use nonfat ricotta cheese in this recipe. In step 1, if the dough hasn't cleared the sides of the bowl after 12 minutes, add more flour, 1 tablespoon at a time, up to 2 tablespoons. In step 6, to prevent sticking, reflour the bottom of the measuring cup (or drinking glass) after making each indentation.

Dough

- 1 cup whole milk
- 10 tablespoons unsalted butter, melted
- 1 large egg plus 2 large yolks
- 3½ cups (17½ ounces) all-purpose flour
- ⅓ cup (2⅓ ounces) sugar
- 2¼ teaspoons instant or rapid-rise yeast
- 1½ teaspoons salt

Cheese Filling

- 6 ounces cream cheese, softened
- 3 tablespoons sugar
- 1 tablespoon all-purpose flour
- ½ teaspoon grated lemon zest
- 6 ounces (¾ cup) whole-milk or part-skim ricotta cheese

Streusel

- 2 tablespoons plus 2 teaspoons all-purpose flour
- 2 tablespoons plus 2 teaspoons sugar
- 1 tablespoon unsalted butter, cut into 8 pieces and chilled

- 1 large egg beaten with 1 tablespoon milk

1. For the Dough Grease large bowl. Whisk milk, melted butter, and egg and yolks together in 2-cup liquid measuring cup (butter will form clumps). Whisk flour, sugar, yeast, and salt together in bowl of stand mixer. Fit stand mixer with dough hook, add milk mixture to flour mixture, and knead on low speed until no dry flour remains, about 2 minutes. Increase speed to medium and knead until dough clears sides of bowl but still sticks to bottom, 8 to 12 minutes.

2. Transfer dough to greased bowl and cover with plastic wrap. Adjust oven racks to upper-middle and lower-middle positions. Place dough on lower-middle rack and place loaf pan on bottom of oven. Pour 3 cups boiling water into loaf pan, close oven door, and let dough rise until doubled, about 1 hour.

3. For the Cheese Filling Using stand mixer fitted with paddle, beat cream cheese, sugar, flour, and lemon zest on low speed until smooth, about 1 minute. Add ricotta and beat until just combined, about 30 seconds. Transfer to bowl, cover with plastic, and refrigerate until ready to use.

4. For the Streusel Combine flour, sugar, and butter in bowl and rub between fingers until mixture resembles wet sand. Cover with plastic and refrigerate until ready to use.

5. Line 2 rimmed baking sheets with parchment paper. Punch down dough and place on lightly floured counter. Divide into quarters and cut each quarter into 4 equal pieces. Form each piece into rough ball by pulling dough edges underneath so top is smooth. On unfloured counter, cup each ball in your palm and roll into smooth, tight ball. Arrange 8 balls on each prepared sheet and cover loosely with plastic. Place sheets on oven racks. Replace water in loaf pan with 3 cups boiling water, close oven door, and let dough rise until doubled, about 90 minutes.

6. Remove sheets and loaf pan from oven. Heat oven to 350 degrees. Grease and flour bottom of ⅓-cup measuring cup (or 2¼-inch-diameter drinking glass). Make deep indentation in center of each dough ball by slowly pressing until cup touches sheet. (Perimeter of balls may deflate slightly.)

7. Gently brush kolaches all over with egg-milk mixture. Divide filling evenly among kolaches (about 1½ tablespoons per kolache) and smooth with back of spoon. Sprinkle streusel over kolaches, avoiding filling. Bake until golden brown, about 25 minutes, switching and rotating sheets halfway through baking. Let kolaches cool on pans for 20 minutes. Serve warm.

Why This Recipe Works We learned the secrets to great kolaches from Denise Mazal at Little Gretel. Brought to Texas by Czech immigrants, kolaches are palm-size rounds of sweetened bread with dollops of sweet cheese or fruit filling and a streusel topping. We discovered that long mixing with a dough hook developed plenty of stretchy gluten, making the finished pastries light and pleasantly chewy. For a Texas-style filling, a combination of tangy cream cheese and milkier, slightly salty ricotta created a perfect base, while a little sugar and lemon zest balanced the flavor. At the end of the day, our kolaches were subtly sweet, tender, buttery, and . . . gone.

MONKEY BREAD

SERVES 6 TO 8

Make sure to use light brown sugar in the coating mix; dark brown sugar has a stronger molasses flavor that can be overwhelming. After baking, don't let the bread cool in the pan for more than 5 minutes or it will stick to the pan and come out in pieces. Monkey bread is best served warm.

Dough

- 2 tablespoons unsalted butter, softened, plus 2 tablespoons melted
- 1 cup milk, heated to 110 degrees
- ⅓ cup water, heated to 110 degrees
- ¼ cup (1¾ ounces) granulated sugar
- 2¼ teaspoons instant or rapid-rise yeast
- 3¼ cups (16¼ ounces) all-purpose flour
- 2 teaspoons salt

Brown Sugar Coating

- 1 cup packed (7 ounces) light brown sugar
- 2 teaspoons ground cinnamon
- 8 tablespoons unsalted butter, melted

Glaze

- 1 cup (4 ounces) confectioners' sugar
- 2 tablespoons milk

1. For the Dough Grease 12-cup nonstick Bundt pan with softened butter; set aside. Combine milk, water, melted butter, sugar, and yeast in 2-cup liquid measuring cup.

2. Adjust oven rack to middle position and place loaf or cake pan on bottom of oven. Using stand mixer fitted with dough hook, mix flour and salt on low speed. Slowly add milk mixture and mix until dough comes together (if dough is too wet and doesn't come together, add up to 2 tablespoons more flour). Increase speed to medium and knead until dough is shiny and smooth, 6 to 7 minutes. Turn dough onto lightly floured counter and knead briefly to form smooth, round ball. Place dough in large greased bowl, coat surface with vegetable oil spray, and transfer to oven. Pour 3 cups boiling water into loaf pan in oven, close oven door, and let dough rise until doubled in size, 50 minutes to 1 hour.

3. For the Brown Sugar Coating While dough rises, combine sugar and cinnamon in small bowl. Place melted butter in second bowl. Set aside.

4. Gently remove dough from bowl and pat into rough 8-inch square. Using bench scraper or knife, cut square into quarters, then cut each quarter into 16 pieces. Roll each piece of dough into a ball. Working with one at a time, dip each ball in melted butter, allowing excess butter to drip off, then roll in sugar mixture. Layer dough balls in prepared pan, staggering seams where dough balls meet. Cover pan tightly with plastic wrap, transfer to oven, and let rest until dough balls are puffy and have risen 1 to 2 inches from top of pan, 50 minutes to 1 hour, 10 minutes.

5. Remove Bundt pan and water pan from oven; adjust oven rack to medium-low position and heat oven to 350 degrees. Remove plastic and bake until top of dough is deeply browned and caramel begins to bubble around edges, 30 to 35 minutes, rotating pan halfway through baking. Let monkey bread cool in pan for 5 minutes, then turn out on platter and let cool slightly, about 10 minutes.

6. For the Glaze Meanwhile, whisk sugar and milk together in small bowl until smooth. Using whisk, drizzle glaze over warm monkey bread, letting it run over top and sides of bread. Serve warm.

Forming Monkey Bread

After forming dough balls, dip each one in melted butter and sugar and then place in greased Bundt pan, staggering seams where dough balls meet.

Why This Recipe Works It might have a funny name, but monkey bread is a soft, sweet, sticky, ultra-cinnamony treat (its moniker probably refers to how it's pulled apart and stuffed into eager mouths). To expedite the rising and proofing of the dough, and ensure our bread had plenty of yeasty flavor, we used a good amount of instant yeast. Butter and milk helped keep the dough rich and moist, and a little sugar made the bread sweet enough to eat on its own. A dip in butter and cinnamon sugar gave the monkey bread a thick, caramel-like coating after its stint in the oven. And a drizzle of a simple glaze finished it off.

Why This Recipe Works Recipes for this "friendship bread" traditionally include two unusual ingredients: a sourdough starter shared by friends and vanilla pudding mix. We set out to develop a recipe that would capture the flavor and spirit of the original without the need for a lengthy starter. Testing revealed that there was almost no difference between breads baked with and without a starter; the bread's sweetness rendered any tang from the starter undetectable. Rather than use packaged vanilla pudding mix, we increased the sugar and added extra vanilla extract. We designed our recipe to make two soft, delicious loaves—give one to a friend.

AMISH CINNAMON BREAD

MAKES 2 LOAVES

We developed this recipe using an 8½ by 4½-inch metal loaf pan. If you use a glass loaf pan, increase the baking time in step 3 to 1¼ hours to 1 hour 20 minutes; if you use a 9 by 5-inch loaf pan, start checking for doneness 5 minutes early. If you own only one loaf pan, refrigerate half the batter and set aside half the coating so you can bake a second loaf after turning out the first onto a wire rack to cool in step 4. Be sure to clean the loaf pan and brush it with oil before baking the second loaf.

Cinnamon-Sugar Coating
½ cup (3½ ounces) sugar
1 teaspoon ground cinnamon
2 teaspoons vegetable oil

Bread
3¾ cups (18¾ ounces) all-purpose flour
3 cups (21 ounces) sugar
1 tablespoon ground cinnamon
1½ teaspoons baking powder
¾ teaspoon baking soda
¾ teaspoon salt
1¾ cups milk
1⅓ cups vegetable oil
3 large eggs, lightly beaten
2 teaspoons vanilla extract

1. For the Cinnamon-Sugar Coating Combine sugar and cinnamon in bowl. Brush 2 loaf pans evenly with oil (1 teaspoon per pan). Add 2 tablespoons cinnamon-sugar coating to each prepared pan and shake and tilt pans until bottoms and sides are evenly coated. Set aside remaining ¼ cup cinnamon-sugar coating.

2. For the Bread Adjust oven rack to middle position and heat oven to 325 degrees. Whisk flour, sugar, cinnamon, baking powder, baking soda, and salt together in large bowl. Whisk milk, oil, eggs, and vanilla together in second bowl. Stir milk mixture into flour mixture until just combined (batter will be lumpy).

3. Divide batter evenly between prepared pans (about 3¾ cups or 2¼ pounds batter per pan). Sprinkle remaining cinnamon-sugar coating evenly over top of batter (2 tablespoons per pan). Bake until paring knife inserted in centers of loaves comes out clean, 1 hour 5 minutes to 1 hour 10 minutes.

4. Let bread cool in pans on wire rack for 1 hour. Run paring knife around edges of pans to thoroughly loosen loaves. Working with 1 loaf at a time, tilt pan and gently remove bread. Serve warm or at room temperature. (Cooled bread can be wrapped in aluminum foil and stored at room temperature for up to 3 days.)

A World of Cinnamon

Vietnamese and Indonesian cinnamons are the two most commonly available varieties in U.S. markets. Our taste tests revealed that Vietnamese cinnamon is the bolder and spicier variety. Why is that?

Vietnamese cinnamon (*Cinnamomum loureiroi*) contains more spicy volatile oils than Indonesian cinnamon (*Cinnamomum burmannii*). That said, much of any cinnamon's spicy flavor dissipates with cooking.

So which of our top-rated cinnamons should you buy? If you like big, spicy flavor and frequently use cinnamon in unheated applications, we recommend **Penzey's Vietnamese Cinnamon, Ground**. But if you use cinnamon only for baking or you prefer a milder cinnamon in unheated applications, go with the cheaper **Morton & Bassett Spices Ground Cinnamon**.

Why This Recipe Works With their chewy interiors, crunchy crusts, and craggy texture, English muffins are a treat—but they're also a lot of work. For a no-fuss recipe without the kneading, rolling, cutting, or griddling, we made a simple loaf bread with the flavor and texture of English muffins. Protein-rich bread flour gave the loaf a chewy yet light consistency, and baking soda created the all-important honeycombed texture. Heating the milk before mixing the dough activated the yeast and shortened the rising time. We simply mixed the dough, let it rise, then baked it in loaf pans until the crust was well browned and the interior was perfectly craggy.

ENGLISH MUFFIN BREAD

MAKES 2 LOAVES

Serve this bread with butter and jam.

  Cornmeal
5 cups (27½ ounces) bread flour
4½ teaspoons instant or rapid-rise yeast
1 tablespoon sugar
2 teaspoons salt
1 teaspoon baking soda
3 cups whole milk, heated to 120 degrees

1. Grease two 8½ by 4½-inch loaf pans and dust with cornmeal. Combine flour, yeast, sugar, salt, and baking soda in large bowl. Stir in hot milk until combined, about 1 minute. Cover dough with greased plastic wrap and let rise in warm place for 30 minutes, or until dough is bubbly and has doubled.

2. Stir dough and divide between prepared loaf pans, pushing into corners with greased rubber spatula. (Pans should be about two-thirds full.) Cover pans with greased plastic and let dough rise in warm place until it reaches edges of pans, about 30 minutes. Adjust oven rack to middle position and heat oven to 375 degrees.

3. Discard plastic and transfer pans to oven. Bake until loaves are well browned and register 200 degrees, about 30 minutes, rotating and switching pans halfway through baking. Turn loaves out onto wire rack and let cool completely, about 1 hour. Slice, toast, and serve.

Tricks to the Right Texture

To give our English Muffin Bread the proper chew and porous texture, we needed a few tricks. High-protein bread flour allows more gluten to develop in the batter for a satisfyingly chewy loaf. Stirring baking soda in with the other dry ingredients gives the bread extra rise for an appropriately coarse, honeycombed texture.

A Well-Dressed Table

By the end of the 19th century, the English were losing their taste for English-style muffins, but in the U.S. they had become such a popular breakfast bread that the properly set breakfast table required special dishes for serving them. Victorians, of course, were ardent believers that the correct home environment shaped correct behavior; proper dining and tableware, especially, equated with proper civilization. So wealthy families had specific dishware for everything, from glass or silver vases for celery to custom dishes to hold bananas to specialized vessels and utensils for serving sardines. And don't forget asparagus forks.

Why This Recipe Works For a brown soda bread with good wheaty flavor but without a gummy, dense texture, we started by finding the right ratio of whole-wheat to all-purpose flour. Toasted wheat germ played up the sweet, nutty flavor of the whole wheat. To keep the texture light, we needed plenty of leavening; baking soda alone gave the bread a soapy taste, so we used a combination of baking soda and baking powder. Just a touch of sugar and a few tablespoons of butter kept our bread wholesome but not bland, and brushing a portion of the melted butter on the loaf after baking gave it a rich crust.

BROWN SODA BREAD

MAKES 1 LOAF

Toasted wheat germ is sold in jars at well-stocked supermarkets.

  2 cups (10 ounces) all-purpose flour
1½ cups (8¼ ounces) whole-wheat flour
  ½ cup toasted wheat germ
  3 tablespoons sugar
1½ teaspoons salt
  1 teaspoon baking powder
  1 teaspoon baking soda
1¾ cups buttermilk
  3 tablespoons unsalted butter, melted

1. Adjust oven rack to lower-middle position and heat oven to 400 degrees. Line rimmed baking sheet with parchment paper. Whisk all-purpose flour, whole-wheat flour, wheat germ, sugar, salt, baking powder, and baking soda together in large bowl. Combine buttermilk and 2 tablespoons melted butter in 2-cup liquid measuring cup.

2. Add wet ingredients to dry ingredients and stir with rubber spatula until dough just comes together. Turn out dough onto lightly floured counter and knead until cohesive mass forms, about 8 turns. Pat dough into 7-inch round and transfer to prepared baking sheet. Using sharp serrated knife, make ¼-inch-deep cross about 5 inches long on top of loaf. Bake until skewer inserted in center comes out clean and loaf registers 195 degrees, 45 to 50 minutes, rotating baking sheet halfway through baking.

3. Remove bread from oven. Brush with remaining 1 tablespoon melted butter. Transfer loaf to wire rack and let cool for at least 1 hour. Serve.

BROWN SODA BREAD WITH CURRANTS AND CARAWAY

Add 1 cup dried currants and 1 tablespoon caraway seeds to dry ingredients in step 1.

Fastest Bread Ever

No yeast, no rise time, and almost no kneading or shaping.

Measure and whisk dry ingredients	5 minutes
Measure and combine wet ingredients	2 minutes
Stir wet into dry	1 minute
Knead briefly	1 minute
Shape simply	1 minute
Total work time	10 minutes

Mimicking Whole-Meal Flour

Brown Irish soda bread boasts a delicious wheaty sweetness. Traditionally, this bread adds whole-meal flour to the all-purpose flour used in the more familiar Irish soda bread to get that uniquely wheaty flavor. Many recipes simply substitute ordinary whole-wheat flour, while others skip the white flour entirely, combining the whole-wheat flour with practically the entire contents of a natural foods store. The former produced bland loaves while the latter offered great taste but crumbly textures.

For our recipe, we tried various ratios of all-purpose and whole-wheat flours until we landed on 2 cups of white flour combined with 1½ cups of whole-wheat. To play up the toasty, nutty flavor, we tried adding by turns wheat germ, wheat bran, and oatmeal. All of them gave our loaf complex wheatiness, but the bran required a trip to a specialty store and the oats required toasting and processing. Toasted wheat germ comes in convenient jars at the supermarket, so that's what we used.

A combination of whole-wheat flour, toasted wheat germ, and all-purpose flour gives our loaf both robust flavor and tender, moist texture.

DAKOTA BREAD

MAKES ONE 10-INCH LOAF

In step 2, if the dough is still sticking to the sides of the mixing bowl after 2 minutes, add more flour 1 tablespoon at a time, up to 3 tablespoons. Be sure to use hot cereal mix, not boxed cold breakfast cereals, which may also be labeled "seven-grain."

- 2 cups warm water (110 degrees)
- 1½ cups (7½ ounces) seven-grain hot cereal mix
- 2 tablespoons honey
- 2 tablespoons vegetable oil
- 3½ cups (19¼ ounces) bread flour
- 1¾ teaspoons salt
- 1 teaspoon instant or rapid-rise yeast
- 3 tablespoons raw, unsalted pepitas
- 3 tablespoons raw, unsalted sunflower seeds
- 1 teaspoon sesame seeds
- 1 teaspoon poppy seeds
- 1 large egg, lightly beaten

1. Grease large bowl. Line rimmed baking sheet with parchment paper. In bowl of stand mixer, combine water, cereal, honey, and oil and let sit for 10 minutes.

2. Add flour, salt, and yeast to cereal mixture. Fit stand mixer with dough hook and knead on low speed until dough is smooth and elastic, 4 to 6 minutes. Add 2 tablespoons pepitas and 2 tablespoons sunflower seeds to dough and knead for 1 minute longer. Turn out dough onto lightly floured counter and knead until seeds are evenly distributed, about 2 minutes.

3. Transfer dough to greased bowl and cover with plastic wrap. Let dough rise at room temperature until almost doubled in size and fingertip depression in dough springs back slowly, 60 to 90 minutes.

4. Gently press down on center of dough to deflate. Transfer dough to lightly floured counter and shape into tight round ball. Place dough on prepared sheet. Cover dough loosely with plastic and let rise at room temperature until almost doubled in size, 60 to 90 minutes.

5. Adjust oven racks to upper-middle and lowest positions and heat oven to 425 degrees. Combine remaining 1 tablespoon pepitas, remaining 1 tablespoon sunflower seeds, sesame seeds, and poppy seeds in small bowl. Using sharp knife, make ¼-inch-deep cross, 5 inches long, on top of loaf. Brush loaf with egg and sprinkle seed mixture evenly over top.

6. Place 8½ by 4½-inch loaf pan on lowest oven rack and fill with 1 cup boiling water. Place baking sheet with dough on upper-middle rack and reduce oven to 375 degrees. Bake until crust is dark brown and bread registers 200 degrees, 40 to 50 minutes. Transfer loaf to wire rack and let cool completely, about 2 hours. Serve.

The Right Mix

Our Dakota Bread recipe calls for bread flour (for an appropriately chewy texture) supplemented with seven-grain hot cereal mix, which provides the bread with nutty depth. Don't confuse seven-grain hot cereal with seven-grain cold cereal; the latter will harm the texture of the loaf.

HOT TO TROT
Seven-grain hot cereal

Why This Recipe Works This hearty loaf from the breadbasket of America usually contains a daunting variety of flours and seeds. We shortened the ingredient list by using seven-grain cereal mix. This easy addition gave our loaf hearty texture and complex flavor. To round it out, we stirred some seeds into the batter and sprinkled more on top of the loaf. Starting the bread in a hot oven created an initial "spring," giving the loaf a lighter crumb, then lowering the temperature prevented the seeds from burning. High-protein bread flour allowed our loaf to rise high, and a pan of water in the oven prevented the crust from setting before the bread had fully risen.

great american cakes and cookies

RED VELVET CAKE

SERVES 12

This recipe must be prepared with natural cocoa powder. Dutch-processed cocoa will not yield the proper color or rise.

Cake

2¼ cups (11¼ ounces) all-purpose flour
1½ teaspoons baking soda
    Pinch salt
  1 cup buttermilk
  2 large eggs
  1 tablespoon distilled white vinegar
  1 teaspoon vanilla extract
  2 tablespoons cocoa powder
  2 tablespoons (1 ounce) red food coloring
12 tablespoons unsalted butter, softened
1½ cups (10½ ounces) granulated sugar

Frosting

16 tablespoons unsalted butter, softened
  4 cups (16 ounces) confectioners' sugar
16 ounces cream cheese, cut into 8 pieces, softened
1½ teaspoons vanilla extract
    Pinch salt

1. For the Cake Adjust oven rack to middle position and heat oven to 350 degrees. Grease two 9-inch round cake pans, line with parchment paper, grease parchment, then flour pans. Whisk flour, baking soda, and salt in medium bowl. Whisk buttermilk, eggs, vinegar, and vanilla in 4-cup liquid measuring cup. Mix cocoa with food coloring in small bowl until smooth paste forms.

2. Using stand mixer fitted with paddle, beat butter and sugar together on medium-high speed until pale and fluffy, about 3 minutes. Reduce speed to medium-low and add flour mixture in 3 additions, alternating with buttermilk mixture in 2 additions, scraping down bowl as needed. Add cocoa mixture and beat on medium speed until completely incorporated, about 30 seconds. Give batter final stir by hand. Scrape batter into prepared pans and bake until toothpick inserted in center comes out clean, about 25 minutes. Let cakes cool in pans on wire rack for 10 minutes. Remove cakes from pans, discarding parchment, and let cool completely on rack, about 2 hours. (Cooled cakes can be wrapped tightly in plastic wrap and kept at room temperature for up to 1 day.)

3. For the Frosting Using stand mixer fitted with paddle, beat butter and sugar on medium-high speed until pale and fluffy, about 2 minutes. Add cream cheese, 1 piece at a time, and beat until incorporated, about 30 seconds. Beat in vanilla and salt. Refrigerate until ready to use.

4. When cakes are cooled, cover edges of cake platter with strips of parchment. Place 1 cake layer on platter. Spread 2 cups frosting evenly over top, right to edge of cake. Top with second cake layer, press lightly to adhere, then spread remaining frosting evenly over top and sides of cake. Carefully remove parchment strips before serving. (Cake can be refrigerated for up to 3 days.)

Lost and Found

Red velvet cake fell out of fashion in the 1970s amidst health scares relating to red dye #2 (a similar fate befell red M&Ms, even though the candies never contained the dye in question). Once consumers were convinced that other red dyes were safe, red candies made it back into the M&Ms assortment (in 1987) and red velvet cakes started a comeback in bakeries.

Why This Recipe Works Although the exact origins of this cake are muddled, the appeal of a tender, shockingly bright red cake swathed in fluffy cream cheese frosting is undeniable. For a cake with an extra-tender crumb, we used two unexpected ingredients: buttermilk and vinegar. They reacted with our recipe's baking soda to create a fine, tender crumb. We also zeroed in on the perfect amount of cocoa that would add a dark hue to our cake as well as lending it a pleasant cocoa flavor.

CHOCOLATE BLACKOUT CAKE

SERVES 10 TO 12

Be sure to give the pudding and the cake enough time to cool or you'll end up with runny pudding and gummy cake.

Pudding
1¼ cups (8¾ ounces) granulated sugar
¼ cup cornstarch
½ teaspoon salt
2 cups half-and-half
1 cup whole milk
6 ounces unsweetened chocolate, chopped
2 teaspoons vanilla extract

Cake
1½ cups (7½ ounces) all-purpose flour
2 teaspoons baking powder
½ teaspoon baking soda
½ teaspoon salt
8 tablespoons unsalted butter
¾ cup (2¼ ounces) Dutch-processed cocoa powder
1 cup brewed coffee
1 cup buttermilk
1 cup packed (7 ounces) light brown sugar
1 cup (7 ounces) granulated sugar
2 large eggs
1 teaspoon vanilla extract

1. For the Pudding Whisk sugar, cornstarch, salt, half-and-half, and milk in large saucepan. Set pan over medium heat. Add chocolate and whisk constantly until chocolate melts and mixture begins to bubble, 2 to 4 minutes. Stir in vanilla and transfer pudding to large bowl. Place plastic wrap directly on surface of pudding and refrigerate until cold, at least 4 hours or up to 24 hours.

2. For the Cake Adjust oven rack to middle position and heat oven to 325 degrees. Grease two 8-inch round cake pans, line with parchment paper, grease parchment, then flour pans. Whisk flour, baking powder, baking soda, and salt in bowl.

3. Melt butter in large saucepan over medium heat. Stir in cocoa and cook until fragrant, about 1 minute.

Off heat, whisk in coffee, buttermilk, brown sugar, and granulated sugar until dissolved. Whisk in eggs and vanilla, then slowly whisk in flour mixture.

4. Divide batter evenly between prepared pans and bake until toothpick inserted in center comes out clean, 30 to 35 minutes. Let cakes cool in pans on wire rack for 15 minutes. Remove cakes from pans, discarding parchment, and let cool completely on wire rack, about 2 hours.

5. Working with 1 cake layer at a time, cut cakes horizontally into 2 layers using long, serrated knife. Crumble 1 cake layer into medium crumbs and set aside. Cover edges of cake platter with strips of parchment. Place 1 cake layer on platter. Spread 1 cup pudding over top, right to edge of cake. Top with second layer; press lightly to adhere. Repeat with 1 cup pudding and last cake layer. Spread remaining pudding evenly over top and sides of cake. Sprinkle cake crumbs evenly over top and sides of cake, pressing lightly to adhere crumbs. Carefully remove parchment strips before serving. (Cake can be refrigerated for up to 2 days.)

Lost Icon
Ebinger's Baking Company opened in 1898 on Flatbush Avenue in Brooklyn and grew into a chain of more than 60 stores before going bankrupt in 1972. Started by Arthur Ebinger, a baker who emigrated from Germany with a vast collection of recipes, the business grew to include his wife and their three sons. During its heyday, Ebinger's was a point of bragging rights for Brooklynites, as celebrities and the well-to-do from Manhattan never went to Brooklyn without taking home a cake or one of Ebinger's other specialties, which included challah, rye bread, pumpkin pie, Othellos (filled mini sponge cakes covered in chocolate), and crumb buns.

Why This Recipe Works Chocolate blackout cake, a tender chocolate layer cake sandwiched together with a puddinglike filling and covered with cake crumbs, was created by the now-shuttered Ebinger's bakery in Brooklyn. We set out to create our own version. We started by adding cocoa powder to the butter we were already melting for the cake. Heating the cocoa in the butter produced a cake that was dark and rich. And to complement the chocolate flavor of the cake, we made a chocolaty, dairy-rich pudding with a combination of milk and half-and-half, which gave it a velvety, lush quality.

Why This Recipe Works Created a century ago at Wellesley College, this fudge cake consists of an extra-fudgy frosting atop a sturdy cake. We turned to all-purpose flour to provide more structure than the original pastry flour, plus cocoa powder bloomed in hot water for deep chocolate flavor. For its signature frosting, we created a base of evaporated milk, butter, and brown sugar. Stirring in more butter and evaporated milk off the heat cooled the base and prevented the chocolate from separating. Adding sifted confectioners' sugar and cooling the mixture helped to thicken the frosting to a spreadable consistency.

WELLESLEY FUDGE CAKE

SERVES 12

We prefer the deep color and balanced flavor of Dutch-processed cocoa powder, but natural cocoa can be used. Although not traditional, two 9-inch round cake pans will also work.

Cake

2½ cups (12½ ounces) all-purpose flour
2 teaspoons baking soda
1 teaspoon baking powder
½ teaspoon salt
¾ cup hot water
½ cup Dutch-processed cocoa powder
16 tablespoons unsalted butter,
    cut into 16 pieces and softened
2 cups (14 ounces) granulated sugar
2 large eggs
1 cup buttermilk, room temperature
2 teaspoons vanilla extract

Frosting

8 tablespoons unsalted butter,
    cut in half, and softened
1½ cups packed (10½ ounces) light brown sugar
½ teaspoon salt
1 cup evaporated milk
8 ounces bittersweet chocolate, chopped
1 teaspoon vanilla extract
3 cups (12 ounces) confectioners' sugar, sifted

1. For the Cake Adjust oven rack to middle position and heat oven to 350 degrees. Grease and flour two 8-inch-square cake pans. Combine flour, baking soda, baking powder, and salt in bowl; set aside. In a small bowl, whisk hot water with cocoa powder until smooth; set aside. With electric mixer on medium-high speed, beat butter and granulated sugar until light and fluffy, about 3 minutes. Add eggs, 1 at a time, and mix until incorporated. Add flour mixture in 3 additions, alternating with 2 additions of buttermilk, until combined. Reduce speed to low and slowly add cocoa mixture and vanilla until incorporated.

2. Scrape equal amounts of batter into prepared pans and bake until toothpick inserted in center comes out with a few crumbs attached, 25 to 30 minutes. Cool cakes in pans 15 minutes, then turn out onto wire rack. Cool completely, about 1 hour. (Cooled, wrapped cakes can be stored at room temperature for 2 days.)

3. For the Frosting Heat 4 tablespoons butter, brown sugar, salt, and ½ cup evaporated milk in large saucepan over medium heat until small bubbles appear around perimeter of pan, 4 to 8 minutes. Reduce heat to low and simmer, stirring occasionally, until mixture has thickened and turned deep golden brown, about 6 minutes. Transfer to large bowl. Slice remaining butter into 4 pieces and stir in with remaining evaporated milk until mixture is slightly cool. Add chocolate and vanilla and stir until smooth. Whisk in confectioners' sugar until incorporated. Cool to room temperature, stirring occasionally, about 1 hour.

4. Place 1 cake square on serving platter. Spread 1 cup frosting over cake, then top with second cake square. Generously spread remaining frosting evenly over top and sides of cake. Refrigerate cake until frosting is set, about 1 hour. Serve. (Cake can be refrigerated, covered, for 2 days. Bring to room temperature before serving.)

Why This Recipe Works We wanted to resurrect the classic childhood favorite tunnel of fudge cake without the benefit of a prepackaged cake mix. Dutch-processed cocoa gave our cake deep chocolate flavor. Adding melted chocolate to the batter made our cake moister and contributed more chocolate punch. Slightly underbaking the cake was the first step toward achieving the ideal consistency for the tunnel. Replacing some of the granulated sugar with brown sugar and cutting back on the flour and butter provided the perfect environment for the fudgy interior to form.

TUNNEL OF FUDGE CAKE

SERVES 12 TO 14

For an accurate measurement of boiling water, bring a full kettle of water to a boil, then measure out the desired amount. Do not use a cake tester, toothpick, or skewer to test the cake—the fudgy interior won't give an accurate reading. Instead, remove the cake from the oven when the sides just begin to pull away from the pan and the surface of the cake springs back when pressed gently with your finger.

Cake

- ¾ cup (2¼ ounces) Dutch-processed cocoa powder, plus extra for dusting pan
- ½ cup boiling water
- 2 ounces bittersweet chocolate, chopped
- 2 cups (10 ounces) all-purpose flour
- 2 cups pecans or walnuts, chopped fine
- 2 cups (8 ounces) confectioners' sugar
- 1 teaspoon salt
- 5 large eggs, room temperature
- 1 tablespoon vanilla extract
- 20 tablespoons (2½ sticks) unsalted butter, softened
- 1 cup (7 ounces) granulated sugar
- ¾ cup packed (5¼ ounces) light brown sugar

Chocolate Glaze

- ¾ cup heavy cream
- ¼ cup light corn syrup
- 8 ounces bittersweet chocolate, chopped
- ½ teaspoon vanilla extract

1. For the Cake Adjust oven rack to lower-middle position and heat oven to 350 degrees. Grease 12-cup Bundt pan and dust with cocoa powder. Pour boiling water over chocolate in medium bowl and whisk until smooth. Let cool to room temperature. Whisk cocoa, flour, pecans, confectioners' sugar, and salt in large bowl. Whisk eggs and vanilla in 4-cup liquid measuring cup.

2. Using stand mixer fitted with paddle, beat butter, granulated sugar, and brown sugar on medium-high speed until light and fluffy, about 2 minutes. On low speed, add egg mixture until combined, about 30 seconds. Add chocolate mixture and beat until incorporated, about 30 seconds. Beat in flour mixture until just combined, about 30 seconds.

3. Scrape batter into prepared pan, smooth batter, and bake until edges are beginning to pull away from pan, about 45 minutes. Let cool in pan on wire rack for 1½ hours, then invert onto serving plate and let cool completely, at least 2 hours.

4. For the Chocolate Glaze Heat cream, corn syrup, and chocolate in small saucepan over medium heat, stirring constantly, until smooth. Stir in vanilla and set aside until slightly thickened, about 30 minutes. Drizzle glaze over cake and let set for at least 10 minutes. Serve. (Cake can be stored at room temperature for up to 2 days.)

Birth of the Bundt Pan

Metallurgical engineer H. David Dalquist invented the Bundt pan in 1950 at the request of bakers in Minneapolis who were using old-fashioned ceramic pans of the same design. Dalquist turned to cast aluminum to produce a pan that was much lighter and easier to use. Sales of his Bundt pan (a name he trade-marked) were underwhelming until Ella Helfrich's Tunnel of Fudge Cake made its debut in 1966. The Pillsbury Company quickly received more than 200,000 requests for the pan, and to meet demand Dalquist's company, Nordic Ware, went into 24-hour production. Over 50 million Bundt pans have been sold worldwide.

Why This Recipe Works Emma Rylander Lane of Clayton, Alabama, is credited with creating this county fair winner more than 100 years ago. Lane cake is a tall, fluffy, snow white cake filled with a rich, sweet mixture of egg whites, butter, raisins, and "a wineglass full of good whiskey." Our simplified recipe capped the number of layers at two, and using a food processor streamlined much of the tedious prep work. Replacing sugar with boiled corn syrup in our frosting quickly brought the whipped egg whites to a safe temperature without resorting to a candy thermometer or complicated (and unreliable) guesswork.

LANE CAKE

SERVES 10 TO 12

Cake

- 1 cup whole milk, room temperature
- 6 large egg whites, room temperature
- 2 teaspoons vanilla extract
- 2¼ cups (9 ounces) cake flour
- 1¾ cups (12¼ ounces) sugar
- 4 teaspoons baking powder
- 1 teaspoon salt
- 12 tablespoons unsalted butter, cut into 12 pieces and softened

Filling

- 5 tablespoons bourbon
- 1 tablespoon heavy cream
- 1 teaspoon cornstarch
- Pinch salt
- ⅓ cup sweetened shredded coconut
- ¾ cup pecans
- ¾ cup golden raisins
- 4 tablespoons unsalted butter
- ¾ cup sweetened condensed milk
- ½ teaspoon vanilla extract

Frosting

- 2 large egg whites, room temperature
- ¼ teaspoon cream of tartar
- ¼ cup (1¾ ounces) sugar
- ⅔ cup light corn syrup
- 1 teaspoon vanilla extract

1. For the Cake Adjust oven rack to middle position and heat oven to 350 degrees. Grease two 9-inch round cake pans, line with parchment paper, grease parchment, then flour pans. Whisk milk, egg whites, and vanilla in 4-cup liquid measuring cup. Using stand mixer fitted with paddle, mix flour, sugar, baking powder, and salt on low speed until combined. Add butter, 1 piece at a time, and beat until only pea-size pieces remain. Add half of milk mixture, increase speed to medium-high, and beat until light and fluffy, about 1 minute. Reduce speed to medium-low, add remaining milk mixture, and beat until incorporated, about 30 seconds. Give batter final stir by hand.

2. Scrape batter into prepared pans and bake until toothpick inserted in center comes out clean, 20 to 25 minutes. Let cakes cool in pans on wire rack for 10 minutes. Remove cakes from pans, discarding parchment, and let cool completely on racks, about 2 hours. (Cooled cakes can be tightly wrapped in plastic wrap and stored at room temperature for up to 2 days.)

3. For the Filling Whisk bourbon, cream, cornstarch, and salt in bowl until smooth. Process coconut in food processor until finely ground, about 15 seconds. Add pecans and raisins and pulse until coarsely ground, about 10 pulses. Melt butter in large skillet over medium-low heat. Add processed coconut mixture and cook, stirring occasionally, until golden brown and fragrant, about 5 minutes. Stir in bourbon mixture and bring to boil. Remove from heat and add condensed milk and vanilla. Transfer to medium bowl and let cool to room temperature, about 30 minutes. (Filling can be refrigerated for 2 days. Bring filling to room temperature before using.)

4. For the Frosting Using stand mixer fitted with whisk, whip egg whites and cream of tartar on medium-high speed until frothy, about 30 seconds. With mixer running, slowly add sugar and whip until soft peaks form, about 2 minutes; set aside. Bring corn syrup to boil in small saucepan over medium-high heat and cook until large bubbles appear around perimeter of pan, about 1 minute. With mixer running, slowly pour hot syrup into whites (avoid pouring syrup onto beaters or it will splash). Add vanilla and beat until mixture has cooled and is very thick and glossy, 3 to 5 minutes.

5. Cover edges of cake platter with strips of parchment. Place 1 cake layer on platter. Spread filling over cake, then top with second cake layer, pressing lightly to adhere. Spread remaining frosting evenly over top and sides of cake. Carefully remove parchment strips before serving. (Cake can be refrigerated for up to 2 days.)

CLEMENTINE CAKE

SERVES 8

Look for clementines that are about 2 inches in diameter (about 1¾ ounces each). We recommend using a mandoline to get consistent slices of clementine to arrange on top of the cake; you can also use a chef's knife. We found it easier to slice the clementines when they were cold. You will have a few more candied clementine slices than you will need; use the nicest-looking ones for the cake's top.

Cake
- 9 ounces clementines, unpeeled, stemmed (about 5 clementines)
- 2¼ cups (7½ ounces) sliced blanched almonds, toasted
- 1 cup (5 ounces) all-purpose flour
- 1¼ teaspoons baking powder
- ¼ teaspoon salt
- 10 tablespoons unsalted butter, cut into 10 pieces and softened
- 1½ cups (10½ ounces) granulated sugar
- 5 large eggs

Candied Clementines
- 4 clementines, unpeeled, stemmed
- 1 cup water
- 1 cup (7 ounces) granulated sugar
- ⅛ teaspoon salt

Glaze
- 2 cups (8 ounces) confectioners' sugar
- 2½ tablespoons water, plus extra as needed
- Pinch salt

1. For the Cake Adjust oven rack to middle position and heat oven to 325 degrees. Spray 9-inch springform pan with vegetable oil spray, line bottom with parchment paper, and grease parchment. Microwave clementines in covered bowl until softened and some juice is released, about 3 minutes. Discard juice and let clementines cool for 10 minutes.

2. Process almonds, flour, baking powder, and salt in food processor until almonds are finely ground, about 30 seconds; transfer to second bowl. Add clementines to now-empty processor and process until smooth, about 1 minute, scraping down sides of bowl as needed.

3. Using stand mixer fitted with paddle, beat butter and sugar on medium-high speed until pale and fluffy, about 3 minutes. Add eggs, one at a time, and beat until combined, scraping down bowl as needed. Add clementine puree and beat until incorporated, about 30 seconds.

4. Reduce speed to low and add almond mixture in 3 additions until just combined, scraping down bowl as needed. Using rubber spatula, give batter final stir by hand. Transfer batter to prepared pan and smooth top. Bake until toothpick inserted in center comes out clean, 55 minutes to 1 hour. Let cake cool completely in pan on wire rack, about 2 hours.

5. For the Candied Clementines Meanwhile, line baking sheet with triple layer of paper towels. Slice clementines ¼ inch thick perpendicular to stem; discard rounded ends. Bring water, sugar, and salt to simmer in small saucepan over medium heat and cook until sugar has dissolved, about 1 minute. Add clementines and cook until softened, about 6 minutes. Using tongs, transfer clementines to prepared sheet and let cool for at least 30 minutes, flipping halfway through cooling to blot away excess moisture.

6. For the Glaze Whisk sugar, water, and salt in bowl until smooth. Adjust consistency with extra water as needed, ½ teaspoon at a time, until glaze has consistency of thick craft glue and leaves visible trail in bowl when drizzled from whisk.

7. Carefully run paring knife around cake and remove side of pan. Using thin metal spatula, lift cake from pan bottom; discard parchment and transfer cake to serving platter. Pour glaze over cake and smooth top with offset spatula, allowing some glaze to drip down sides. Let sit for 1 hour to set.

8. Just before serving, select 8 uniform candied clementine slices (you will have more than 8 slices; reserve extra slices for another use) and blot away excess moisture with additional paper towels. Arrange slices around top edge of cake, evenly spaced. Serve. (Cake can be wrapped in plastic wrap and stored at room temperature for up to 2 days.)

Why This Recipe Works Clementine cake is a bright, delicious, citrus-kissed dessert. For maximum clementine flavor, we put clementines both inside and on top of our cake. For the batter, we used a standard creaming process and added ground whole clementines that we softened in the microwave and processed until smooth. Baking the cake in a greased springform pan allowed it to soufflé slightly, which gave us the tall cake that we wanted. While it was baking, we quickly candied sliced clementines in a sugar solution. For a showstopping finish, we topped the cake with a white glaze that accentuated the vivid orange candied fruit slices.

BLUEBERRY JAM CAKE

SERVES 10 TO 12

Having a cake stand with a turntable is a must for this cake. If your kitchen is warm, chilling the dark shades of frosting helps.

White Layer Cakes

- 1 cup whole milk, room temperature
- 6 large egg whites, room temperature
- 2 teaspoons vanilla extract
- 2¼ cups (9 ounces) bleached cake flour
- 1¾ cups (12¼ ounces) granulated sugar
- 1 tablespoon baking powder
- 1 teaspoon table salt
- 12 tablespoons unsalted butter, cut into 12 pieces and softened but still cool

Jam Filling and Frosting

- ½ cup (3½ ounces) granulated sugar
- 2 tablespoons low- or no-sugar-needed fruit pectin
-    Pinch salt
- 15 ounces (3 cups) fresh or thawed frozen blueberries
- 1 tablespoon lemon juice
- 8 tablespoons unsalted butter, softened
- 1½ cups (6 ounces) confectioners' sugar
- 8 ounces cream cheese, cut into 8 pieces and softened
- 2 teaspoons vanilla extract

1. For the White Layer Cakes Adjust oven rack to middle position and heat oven to 350 degrees. Grease three 8-inch round cake pans, line with parchment paper, grease parchment, and flour pans. Whisk milk, egg whites, and vanilla together in bowl.

2. Using stand mixer fitted with paddle, mix flour, sugar, baking powder, and salt on low speed until combined, about 5 seconds. Add butter, 1 piece at a time, until only pea-size pieces remain, about 1 minute. Add half of milk mixture, increase speed to medium-high, and beat until light and fluffy, about 30 seconds. Reduce speed to medium-low, add remaining milk mixture, and mix until incorporated, about 15 seconds (batter may look curdled). Give batter final stir by hand; do not overmix.

3. Divide batter evenly between prepared pans and smooth tops with rubber spatula. Gently tap pans on counter to settle batter. Bake until toothpick inserted in center comes out clean, 18 to 22 minutes, switching and rotating pans halfway through baking.

4. Let cakes cool in pans on wire rack for 10 minutes. Remove cakes from pans, discarding parchment, and let cool completely on rack, about 2 hours.

5. For the Jam Filling Process granulated sugar, pectin, and salt in food processor until combined, about 3 seconds. Add blueberries and pulse until chopped coarse, 6 to 8 pulses. Transfer blueberry mixture to medium saucepan and bring to simmer over medium heat, stirring occasionally, until mixture is bubbling and just starting to thicken, 6 to 8 minutes. Off heat, stir in lemon juice. Transfer 1⅓ cups jam to small bowl, cover, and refrigerate until firm, about 3 hours. Strain remaining jam through fine-mesh strainer set over bowl, cover, and set aside at room temperature. (You should have at least ¼ cup.)

6. For the Frosting Using stand mixer fitted with paddle, beat butter and confectioners' sugar on medium-high speed until light and fluffy, about 3 minutes. Add cream cheese, 1 piece at a time, and beat until no lumps remain. Add vanilla and 2 tablespoons strained jam and mix until incorporated. Transfer ⅓ cup frosting to each of 2 small bowls. Add 1 teaspoon strained jam to first bowl and 1 tablespoon strained jam to second bowl, stirring well to combine. (You should have 3 shades of frosting.)

7. Place 1 cake layer on cake turntable. Spread ⅔ cup chilled jam evenly over top. Repeat with 1 more cake layer, pressing lightly to adhere, and remaining chilled jam. Top with remaining cake layer, pressing lightly to adhere. Spread small amount of lightest-colored frosting in even layer over top and sides of cake. Using offset spatula, spread darkest-colored frosting over bottom third of sides of cake; medium-colored frosting over middle third; and remaining lightest-colored frosting over top third. While spinning cake turntable, run spatula from bottom to top of side of cake to blend frosting colors. While spinning cake turntable, run spatula over top of cake, working from outside in to create spiral. Serve.

Why This Recipe Works Blueberry shines in this stunning—but not tricky—cake, which features three layers of downy white cake, a blueberry jam filling, and tangy cream cheese frosting. To emphasize the fruit's flavor, we made our own jam—blueberries, lemon juice, pectin, and some sugar—and used it both to fill the cake layers and to color (and flavor) the frosting. To create the beautiful ombre design, we strained different amounts of jam into three bowls of frosting (the pectin prevented the frosting from thinning) to create increasingly darker hues, which we spread on the cake from light to dark, before smoothing the shades together.

STRAWBERRY DREAM CAKE

SERVES 8 TO 10

Be sure to allow the cream cheese to soften so that it blends into a smooth frosting.

Cake

- 10 ounces frozen whole strawberries (2 cups)
- ¾ cup whole milk, room temperature
- 6 large egg whites, room temperature
- 2 teaspoons vanilla extract
- 2¼ cups (9 ounces) cake flour
- 1¾ cups (12¼ ounces) granulated sugar
- 4 teaspoons baking powder
- 1 teaspoon salt
- 12 tablespoons unsalted butter, cut into 12 pieces and softened

Frosting

- 10 tablespoons unsalted butter, softened
- 2¼ cups (9 ounces) confectioners' sugar
- 12 ounces cream cheese, cut into 12 pieces and softened
  Pinch salt
- 8 ounces fresh strawberries, hulled and sliced thin (about 1½ cups)

1. For the Cake Adjust oven rack to middle position and heat oven to 350 degrees. Grease two 9-inch round cake pans, line with parchment paper, grease parchment, then flour pans.

2. Transfer strawberries to bowl, cover, and microwave until strawberries are soft and have released their juices, about 5 minutes. Place in fine-mesh strainer set over small saucepan. Firmly press fruit dry (juice should measure at least ¾ cup); reserve strawberry solids. Bring juice to boil over medium-high heat and cook, stirring occasionally, until syrupy and reduced to ¼ cup, 6 to 8 minutes. Whisk milk into juice until combined.

3. Whisk strawberry-milk mixture, egg whites, and vanilla in bowl. Using stand mixer fitted with paddle, mix flour, sugar, baking powder, and salt on low speed until combined. Add butter, 1 piece at a time, and mix until only pea-size pieces remain, about 1 minute. Add half of milk mixture, increase speed to medium-high, and beat until light and fluffy, about 1 minute. Reduce speed to medium-low, add remaining milk mixture, and beat until incorporated, about 30 seconds. Give batter final stir by hand.

4. Scrape batter into prepared pans and bake until toothpick inserted in center comes out clean, 20 to 25 minutes, rotating pans halfway through baking. Let cakes cool in pans on wire rack for 10 minutes. Remove cakes from pans, discarding parchment, and let cool completely on rack, about 2 hours. (Cooled cakes can be tightly wrapped with plastic wrap and stored at room temperature for up to 2 days.)

5. For the Frosting Using stand mixer fitted with paddle, mix butter and sugar on low speed until combined, about 30 seconds. Increase speed to medium-high and beat until pale and fluffy, about 2 minutes. Add cream cheese, 1 piece at a time, and beat until incorporated, about 1 minute. Add reserved strawberry solids and salt and mix until combined, about 30 seconds. Refrigerate until ready to use, up to 2 days.

6. Pat strawberries dry with paper towels. Cover edges of cake platter with strips of parchment. Place 1 cake layer on platter. Spread ¾ cup frosting evenly over top, right to edge of cake. Press 1 cup strawberries in even layer over frosting and cover with additional ¾ cup frosting. Top with second cake layer, press lightly to adhere, then spread remaining frosting evenly over top and sides of cake. Garnish with remaining strawberries. Carefully remove parchment strips before serving. (Cake can be refrigerated for up to 2 days.)

Why This Recipe Works Strange as it may seem, the vast majority of existing strawberry cake recipes turn to strawberry Jell-O for flavor. Hoping to avoid this artificial solution, we performed test after test to figure out the best way to flavor our cake with actual strawberries. Any strawberry solids wreaked havoc on the tender cake, but strained and reduced strawberry juices kept our cake light and packed a strawberry punch. Not to be left behind, the reserved strawberry solids enriched the frosting with more berry flavor.

Why This Recipe Works Strawberry poke cake was invented in 1969 as a way to increase Jell-O sales. It quickly became popular thanks to its festive look and easy assembly. But we encountered two problems: dull strawberry flavor and soggy box mix cake. For a sturdier cake that would hold up to hot gelatin, we opted to make our own white cake from scratch. And to improve the strawberry flavor of the Jell-O, we combined it with the juice from cooked strawberries. Making a homemade "jam" from the berry solids and spreading the mixture on top of the cake gave our cake an extra layer of flavor.

STRAWBERRY POKE CAKE

SERVES 12

The top of the cake will look slightly overbaked—this keeps the crumb from becoming too soggy after the gelatin is poured on top.

Cake
2¼ cups (11¼ ounces) all-purpose flour
4 teaspoons baking powder
1 teaspoon salt
1 cup whole milk
2 teaspoons vanilla extract
6 large egg whites
12 tablespoons unsalted butter, softened
1¾ cups (12¼ ounces) sugar

Syrup and Topping
4 cups frozen strawberries
½ cup water
6 tablespoons (2⅔ ounces) sugar
2 tablespoons orange juice
2 tablespoons strawberry-flavored gelatin
2 cups heavy cream, chilled

1. For the Cake Adjust oven rack to middle position and heat oven to 350 degrees. Grease 13 by 9-inch baking pan, line with parchment paper, grease parchment, then flour pan. Whisk flour, baking powder, and salt in bowl. Whisk milk, vanilla, and egg whites in 4-cup liquid measuring cup.

2. Using stand mixer fitted with paddle, beat butter and sugar on medium-high speed until pale and fluffy, about 2 minutes, scraping down bowl as needed. Reduce speed to low and add flour mixture in 3 additions, alternating with milk mixture in 2 additions, beating after each addition until combined, about 30 seconds each time, scraping down bowl as needed. Give batter final stir by hand. Scrape into prepared pan and bake until toothpick inserted in center comes out clean, about 35 minutes. Let cake cool completely in pan, at least 1 hour. (Once cool, cake can be wrapped in plastic wrap and kept at room temperature for up to 2 days.)

3. For the Syrup and Topping Heat 3 cups strawberries, water, 2 tablespoons sugar, and orange juice in medium saucepan over medium-low heat. Cover and cook until strawberries are softened,

about 10 minutes. Strain liquid into bowl, reserving solids, then whisk gelatin into liquid. Let cool to room temperature, at least 20 minutes.

4. Meanwhile, poke 50 deep holes all over top of cake with skewer, taking care not to poke through to dish bottom and twisting skewer to enlarge holes. Pour cooled liquid over top of cake. Wrap with plastic wrap and refrigerate until gelatin is set, at least 3 hours or up to 2 days.

5. Pulse reserved strained strawberries, 2 tablespoons sugar, and remaining 1 cup strawberries in food processor until mixture resembles strawberry jam, about 15 pulses. Spread mixture evenly over cake. Using stand mixer fitted with whisk, whip cream with remaining 2 tablespoons sugar on medium-low speed until foamy, about 1 minute. Increase speed to high and whip until soft peaks form, 1 to 3 minutes. Spread cream over strawberries. Serve. (Cake can be refrigerated for up to 2 days.)

Perfecting the Poke

Finding the right poking device wasn't as simple as you might think. Toothpicks were too small, while straws, handles of wooden spoons, pencils, and fingers were too big. A wooden skewer finally did the trick. But just poking didn't create a large enough hole for the liquid to seep into. In order to create deep lines of red color against the white crumb, we had to poke and then twist the skewer to really separate the crumb.

1. Using skewer, poke about 50 deep holes over cake, being careful not to poke through to bottom. Twist skewer to enlarge holes.

2. Slowly pour cooled gelatin mixture evenly over surface of cake and it will slowly soak into cake.

TEXAS SHEET CAKE

SERVES 24

Toast the pecans in a dry skillet over medium heat, shaking the pan occasionally, until golden and fragrant, about 5 minutes.

Cake

- 2 cups (10 ounces) all-purpose flour
- 2 cups (14 ounces) granulated sugar
- ½ teaspoon baking soda
- ½ teaspoon salt
- 2 large eggs plus 2 large yolks
- ¼ cup sour cream
- 2 teaspoons vanilla extract
- 8 ounces semisweet chocolate, chopped
- ¾ cup vegetable oil
- ¾ cup water
- ½ cup (1½ ounces) Dutch-processed cocoa powder
- 4 tablespoons unsalted butter

Chocolate Icing

- 8 tablespoons unsalted butter
- ½ cup heavy cream
- ½ cup (1½ ounces) Dutch-processed cocoa powder
- 1 tablespoon light corn syrup
- 3 cups (12 ounces) confectioners' sugar
- 1 tablespoon vanilla extract
- 1 cup pecans, toasted and chopped

1. For the Cake Adjust oven rack to middle position and heat oven to 350 degrees. Grease 18 by 13-inch rimmed baking sheet. Combine flour, sugar, baking soda, and salt in large bowl. Whisk eggs and yolks, sour cream, and vanilla in another bowl until smooth.

2. Heat chocolate, oil, water, cocoa, and butter in large saucepan over medium heat, stirring occasionally, until smooth, 3 to 5 minutes. Whisk chocolate mixture into flour mixture until incorporated. Whisk egg mixture into batter, then pour into prepared baking pan. Bake until toothpick inserted into center comes out clean, 18 to 20 minutes. Transfer to wire rack.

3. For the Chocolate Icing About 5 minutes before cake is done, heat butter, cream, cocoa, and corn syrup in large saucepan over medium heat, stirring occasionally, until smooth. Off heat, whisk in sugar and vanilla. Spread warm icing evenly over hot cake and sprinkle with pecans. Let cake cool to room temperature on wire rack, about 1 hour, then refrigerate until icing is set, about 1 hour longer. Cut into 3-inch squares. Serve. (Cake can be refrigerated for up to 2 days.)

Timing Is Everything

The key to perfectly moist Texas sheet cake is to let the warm icing soak into the hot cake. As soon as the cake comes out of the oven, pour the warm icing over the cake and use a spatula to spread the icing to the edges of the cake. This creates the fudgy layer between the icing and the cake.

Why This Recipe Works Texas sheet cake is a huge, pecan-topped chocolate-glazed cake. For the cake, we relied on a combination of butter and vegetable oil, which produced a dense, brownie-like texture. To increase the fudgy chocolate flavor, we used both cocoa powder and melted semisweet chocolate. Replacing milk with heavy cream gave the icing more body, while adding corn syrup produced a lustrous finish. The key to creating the signature fudgy layer between cake and icing was to let the warm icing soak into the hot cake. We poured the icing over the sheet cake straight out of the oven and smoothed it with a spatula.

CHOCOLATE ÉCLAIR CAKE

SERVES 15

Six ounces of finely chopped semisweet chocolate can be used in place of the chips.

1¼ cups (8¾ ounces) sugar
6 tablespoons cornstarch
1 teaspoon salt
5 cups whole milk
4 tablespoons unsalted butter, cut into 4 pieces
5 teaspoons vanilla extract
1¼ teaspoons unflavored gelatin
2 tablespoons water
2¾ cups heavy cream, chilled
14 ounces graham crackers
1 cup semisweet chocolate chips
5 tablespoons light corn syrup

1. Combine sugar, cornstarch, and salt in large saucepan. Whisk milk into sugar mixture until smooth and bring to boil, scraping bottom of pan with heatproof rubber spatula, over medium-high heat. Immediately reduce heat to medium-low and cook, continuing to scrape bottom, until thickened and large bubbles appear on surface, 4 to 6 minutes. Off heat, whisk in butter and vanilla. Transfer pudding to large bowl and place plastic wrap directly on surface of pudding. Refrigerate until cool, about 2 hours.

2. Sprinkle gelatin over water in bowl and let sit until gelatin softens, about 5 minutes. Microwave until mixture is bubbling around edges and gelatin dissolves, 15 to 30 seconds. Using stand mixer fitted with whisk, whip 2 cups cream on medium-low speed until foamy, about 1 minute. Increase speed to high and whip until soft peaks form, 1 to 3 minutes. Add gelatin mixture and whip until stiff peaks form, about 1 minute.

3. Whisk one-third of whipped cream into chilled pudding, then gently fold in remaining whipped cream, 1 scoop at a time, until combined. Cover bottom of 13 by 9-inch baking dish with layer of graham crackers, breaking crackers as necessary

to line bottom of pan. Top with half of pudding–whipped cream mixture (about 5½ cups) and another layer of graham crackers. Repeat with remaining pudding–whipped cream mixture and remaining graham crackers.

4. Microwave chocolate chips, remaining ¾ cup cream, and corn syrup in bowl, on 50 percent power, stirring occasionally, until smooth, 1 to 2 minutes. Let glaze cool to room temperature, about 10 minutes. Cover graham crackers with glaze and refrigerate cake for 6 to 24 hours. Serve. (Cake can be refrigerated for up to 2 days.)

The American Table: Worst College Food Ever

The Reverend Sylvester Graham, the inventor of the graham cracker, wasn't quite as much fun as that crisp treat might have you believe. In fact, he was a food zealot, convinced that a diet of nothing but water and graham crackers— originally a "health food" made from whole-wheat flour and honey—would turn you into a better person. Some 170 years ago, the administrators at Oberlin College, a small liberal arts school in Ohio, grew enamored of Graham's ideas and decided to feed students according to his principles. (And you think your college food was bad?) Oberlin students were encouraged to abstain from consuming meat, tea, and coffee—except for "crust coffee" made from toast and boiled water. They were discouraged from eating butter and pastries and even from seasoning their food. (As legend has it, a professor actually lost his job for bringing a pepper shaker to the dining hall.) Oberlin students complained so vociferously that the college was forced to abandon its dining plan, and the Graham diet (if not his eponymous cracker) faded into culinary history.

Why This Recipe Works This no-bake dessert is typically made by layering a mixture of instant vanilla pudding and Cool Whip between graham crackers and topping it with chocolate frosting. We loved the convenience of these store-bought items, but our enthusiasm waned when confronted by their flavor. With a couple of easy techniques (a quick stovetop pudding, whipped cream, and a microwave-and-stir glaze) and very little active time, we produced a from-scratch version that easily trumped its inspiration.

Why This Recipe Works This unique dessert combines a layer of fudgy chocolate cake and a layer of rich, caramel-coated flan that "magically" switch places as they bake. We started with an easy dump-and-stir cake recipe. The cake's flavor was great, but it was soggy due to the moisture from the flan. Cutting some of the buttermilk and sugar from the cake batter did the trick. To help our flan firm up, we swapped some of the egg yolks for whole eggs and added cream cheese. The cream cheese also lent the flan a tanginess that offset its sweetness. Convenient store-bought caramel sauce topped it all off.

MAGIC CHOCOLATE FLAN CAKE

SERVES 16

It's worth using good-quality caramel sauce, such as Fat Toad Farm Goat's Milk Caramel. If your blender doesn't hold 2 quarts, process the flan in two batches. The cake needs to chill for at least 8 hours before you can unmold it.

Cake

½ cup caramel sauce or topping
½ cup plus 2 tablespoons (3⅛ ounces) all-purpose flour
⅓ cup (1 ounce) cocoa powder
½ teaspoon baking soda
⅛ teaspoon salt
4 ounces bittersweet chocolate, chopped
6 tablespoons unsalted butter
½ cup buttermilk
½ cup (3½ ounces) sugar
2 large eggs
1 teaspoon vanilla extract

Flan

2 (14-ounce) cans sweetened condensed milk
2½ cups whole milk
6 ounces cream cheese
6 large eggs plus 4 large yolks
1 teaspoon vanilla extract

1. For the Cake Adjust oven rack to middle position and heat oven to 350 degrees. Grease 12-cup nonstick Bundt pan. Microwave caramel until easily pourable, about 30 seconds. Pour into pan to coat bottom. Combine flour, cocoa, baking soda, and salt in bowl; set aside. Combine chocolate and butter in large bowl and microwave at 50 percent power, stirring occasionally, until melted, 2 to 4 minutes. Whisk buttermilk, sugar, eggs, and vanilla into chocolate mixture until incorporated. Stir in flour mixture until just combined. Pour batter over caramel in pan.

2. For the Flan Process all ingredients in blender until smooth, about 1 minute. Gently pour flan over cake batter and place Bundt pan in large roasting pan. Place roasting pan on oven rack and pour warm water into roasting pan until it reaches halfway up side of Bundt pan. Bake until toothpick inserted in cake comes out clean and flan registers 180 degrees, 75 to 90 minutes. Transfer Bundt pan to wire rack. Let cool to room temperature, about 2 hours, then refrigerate until set, at least 8 hours. (Remove roasting pan from oven once water has cooled.)

3. Place bottom third of Bundt pan in bowl of hot tap water for 1 minute. Invert completely flat cake platter, place platter over top of pan, and gently turn platter and pan upside down. Slowly remove pan, allowing caramel to drizzle over top of cake. Serve.

Modulate the Heat

A water bath, or bain-marie, makes for a more even, temperate baking environment. Simply place your baking vessel in a larger vessel (we use a roasting pan) and partially fill the latter with water.

Why This Recipe Works A great tres leches cake—a sponge cake soaked with a mixture of "three milks" (heavy cream, evaporated milk, and sweetened condensed milk)—should be moist but not mushy and sweet but not sickeningly so. For an ideal version, we needed to make our cake sturdy enough to handle the milk mixture, so we used whipped whole eggs instead of the usual egg whites. Although some tres leches recipes use equal amounts of evaporated milk, sweetened condensed milk, and cream, we found that cutting back on the cream produced a thicker mixture that didn't oversaturate the cake.

TRES LECHES CAKE

SERVES 12

The cake is best frosted right before serving.

Milk Mixture
1 (14-ounce) can sweetened condensed milk
1 (12-ounce) can evaporated milk
1 cup heavy cream
1 teaspoon vanilla extract

Cake
2 cups (10 ounces) all-purpose flour
2 teaspoons baking powder
1 teaspoon salt
½ teaspoon ground cinnamon
8 tablespoons unsalted butter
1 cup whole milk
4 large eggs, room temperature
2 cups (14 ounces) sugar
2 teaspoons vanilla extract

Topping
1 cup heavy cream
3 tablespoons corn syrup
1 teaspoon vanilla extract

1. For the Milk Mixture Pour condensed milk into large bowl. Microwave covered at 50 percent power, stirring every 3 to 5 minutes, until slightly darkened and thickened, 9 to 15 minutes. Remove from microwave and slowly whisk in evaporated milk, cream, and vanilla. Let cool to room temperature.

2. For the Cake Adjust oven rack to middle position and heat oven to 325 degrees. Grease and flour 13 by 9-inch baking dish. Whisk flour, baking powder, salt, and cinnamon in bowl. Heat butter and milk in small saucepan over low heat until butter is melted; remove from heat and set aside.

3. Using stand mixer fitted with whisk, whip eggs on medium speed until foamy, about 30 seconds. Slowly add sugar and continue to whip until fully incorporated, 5 to 10 seconds. Increase speed to medium-high and whip until mixture is thick and glossy, 5 to 7 minutes. Reduce speed to low, add milk-butter mixture and vanilla, and mix until combined, about 15 seconds. Add flour mixture in 3 additions, mixing on medium speed after each addition and scraping down bowl as needed, until flour is fully incorporated, about 30 seconds. Using rubber spatula, scrape batter into prepared dish. Bake until toothpick inserted in center comes out clean, 30 to 35 minutes. Transfer cake to wire rack and let cool for 10 minutes.

4. Using skewer, poke holes at ½-inch intervals in top of cake. Slowly pour milk mixture over cake until completely absorbed. Let sit at room temperature for 15 minutes, then refrigerate, uncovered, for 3 hours or up to 24 hours.

5. For the Topping Remove cake from refrigerator 30 minutes before serving. Using stand mixer fitted with whisk, whip cream, corn syrup, and vanilla on medium-low speed until foamy, about 1 minute. Increase speed to high and whip until soft peaks form, 1 to 3 minutes. Spread over cake and cut into 3-inch squares. Serve.

SWISS HAZELNUT CAKE

SERVES 12 TO 16

We toast and grind the hazelnuts with their skins for better color and flavor. When working with the marsh-mallow crème, grease the inside of your measuring cup and spatula with vegetable oil spray to prevent sticking. You may use a vegetable peeler or the large holes of a box grater to shave the chocolate.

Cake

- ½ cup (2 ounces) skin-on hazelnuts, toasted and cooled
- 1¼ cups (5 ounces) cake flour
- 1 cup (7 ounces) granulated sugar
- 1½ teaspoons baking powder
- ½ teaspoon salt
- ½ cup vegetable oil
- ¼ cup water
- 3 large egg yolks, plus 5 large whites
- 2½ teaspoons vanilla extract
- ¼ teaspoon cream of tartar

Frosting

- 24 tablespoons (3 sticks) unsalted butter, softened
- ¼ teaspoon salt
- 1¾ cups (7 ounces) confectioners' sugar
- 12 ounces (2⅔ cups) Fluff brand marshmallow crème
- 2 tablespoons hazelnut liqueur
- 6 ounces bittersweet chocolate

1. For the Cake Adjust oven rack to middle position and heat oven to 350 degrees. Line the bottoms of 2 light-colored 9-inch round cake pans with parchment paper; grease parchment but not pan sides.

2. Process hazelnuts in food processor until finely ground, about 30 seconds. Whisk flour, sugar, baking powder, salt, and ground hazelnuts together in large bowl. Whisk oil, water, egg yolks, and vanilla together in separate bowl. Whisk egg yolk mixture into flour mixture until smooth batter forms.

3. Using stand mixer fitted with whisk, whip egg whites and cream of tartar on medium-low speed until foamy, about 1 minute. Increase speed to medium-high and whip until soft peaks form,

2 to 3 minutes. Gently whisk one-third of whipped egg whites into batter. Using rubber spatula, gently fold remaining egg whites into batter until incorporated.

4. Divide batter evenly between prepared pans and gently tap pans on counter to release air bubbles. Bake until tops are light golden brown and cakes spring back when pressed lightly in center, 25 to 28 minutes, rotating pans halfway through baking.

5. Let cakes cool in pans for 15 minutes. Run knife around edges of pans; invert cakes onto wire rack. Discard parchment and let cakes cool completely, at least 1 hour. (To prepare to make chocolate shavings, place food processor shredding disk and chocolate in freezer.)

6. For the Frosting Using clean stand mixer fitted with whisk, whip butter and salt on medium speed until smooth, about 1 minute. Reduce speed to low and slowly add sugar. Increase speed to medium and whip until smooth, about 2 minutes, scraping down sides of bowl as needed. Add marsh-mallow crème, increase speed to medium-high, and whip until light and fluffy, 3 to 5 minutes. Reduce speed to low, add hazelnut liqueur, return speed to medium-high, and whip to incorporate, about 30 seconds.

7. Line rimmed baking sheet with parchment paper. Fit food processor with chilled shredding disk. Turn on processor and feed chocolate through hopper. Transfer shaved chocolate to prepared baking sheet and spread into even layer. Place in freezer to harden, about 10 minutes.

8. Place 1 cake layer on cake stand. Spread 2 cups frosting evenly over top, right to edge of cake. Top with second cake layer, pressing lightly to adhere. Spread remaining 2 cups frosting evenly over top and sides of cake.

9. Fold 16 by 12-inch sheet of parchment paper into 6 by 4-inch rectangle. Using parchment rectangle, scoop up half of chocolate shavings and sprinkle over top of cake. Once top of cake is coated, scoop up remaining chocolate shavings and press gently against sides of cake to adhere, scooping and reapplying as needed. Serve.

Why This Recipe Works This sweet, nutty cake is famous in Philadelphia, but when the Swiss Haus pastry chef wouldn't disclose the recipe, we played detective. We settled on a chiffon base, knowing that the beaten egg whites would give the cake a fluffy texture. For full hazelnut flavor, we ground the nuts in a food processor, then substituted this hazelnut "flour" for a portion of the cake flour. Since meringue buttercream frosting is a project, we found an excellent shortcut using marshmallow crème. To prevent the chocolate from melting, we froze it before and after shaving and used parchment paper to gently press the curls into the frosting.

Why This Recipe Works The beauty of blitz torte is that you get five impressive layers—cake, meringue, fruit-and-cream filling, more cake, and more meringue—for about the same amount of work as a two-layer cake. That's because the recipe is incredibly clever: Each meringue layer is baked directly atop the yellow cake batter. The recipe is also pleasingly symmetrical: The egg yolks go into the cake, while the whites go into the meringue. For our filling, we mimicked the rich egginess of custard by folding store-bought lemon curd into whipped cream, stabilizing it with gelatin, and layering it with raspberries. Bliss torte is more like it!

BLITZ TORTE

SERVES 8 TO 10

If your pans are dark, reduce the baking time in step 6 to 30 to 35 minutes.

Filling
- 1 teaspoon unflavored gelatin
- 2 tablespoons water
- 1 cup heavy cream, chilled
- 1 teaspoon vanilla extract
- ½ cup lemon curd
- 10 ounces (2 cups) raspberries
- 2 tablespoons orange liqueur
- 1 tablespoon sugar

Cake
- ½ cup whole milk
- 4 large egg yolks
- 1½ teaspoons vanilla extract
- 1¼ cups (5 ounces) cake flour
- 1 cup (7 ounces) sugar
- 1½ teaspoons baking powder
- ½ teaspoon salt
- 12 tablespoons unsalted butter, cut into 12 pieces and softened

Meringue
- 4 large egg whites
- ¼ teaspoon cream of tartar
- ¾ cup (5¼ ounces) sugar
- ½ teaspoon vanilla extract
- ½ cup sliced almonds

1. For the Filling Sprinkle gelatin over water in small bowl and let sit until gelatin softens, about 5 minutes. Microwave until mixture is bubbling around edges and gelatin dissolves, 15 to 30 seconds. Using stand mixer fitted with whisk, whip cream and vanilla on medium-low speed until foamy, about 1 minute. Increase speed to medium-high and whip until soft peaks form, about 2 minutes. Add gelatin mixture and whip until firm, stiff peaks form, about 1 minute.

2. Whisk lemon curd in large metal bowl to loosen. Fold whipped cream mixture into curd. Refrigerate cream filling for 1½ to 3 hours.

3. For the Cake Meanwhile, adjust oven rack to middle position and heat oven to 325 degrees. Grease 2 light-colored 9-inch round cake pans, line with parchment paper, grease parchment, and flour pans.

4. Beat milk, yolks, and vanilla together with fork. Using stand mixer fitted with paddle, mix flour, sugar, baking powder, and salt on low speed until combined, about 5 seconds. Add butter, 1 piece at a time, and mix until only pea-size pieces remain, about 1 minute. Add half of milk mixture, increase speed to medium-high, and beat until light and fluffy, about 1 minute. Reduce speed to medium-low, add remaining milk mixture, and beat until incorporated, about 30 seconds. Give batter final stir by hand. Divide batter evenly between prepared pans and spread into even layer using small offset spatula.

5. For the Meringue Using clean, dry stand mixer fitted with a whisk, whip egg whites and cream of tartar on medium-low speed until foamy, about 1 minute. Increase speed to medium-high and whip whites to soft, billowy mounds, 1 to 3 minutes. Gradually add sugar and whip until glossy, stiff peaks form, 3 to 5 minutes. Add vanilla and whip until incorporated.

6. Divide meringue evenly between cake pans and spread evenly over cake batter to edges of pan. Use back of spoon to create peaks in meringue. Sprinkle meringue with almonds. Bake cakes until meringue is golden and has pulled away from sides of pan, 50 to 55 minutes, switching and rotating pans halfway through baking. Let cakes cool completely in pans on wire rack. (Cakes can be baked up to 24 hours in advance and stored, uncovered, in pans at room temperature.)

7. To finish filling, 10 minutes before assembling cake, combine raspberries, liqueur, and sugar in bowl.

8. Gently remove cakes from pans, discarding parchment. Place 1 cake layer on platter, meringue side up. Spread half of cream filling evenly over top. Using slotted spoon, spoon raspberries evenly over filling. Gently spread remaining cream filling over raspberries, covering raspberries completely. Top with second cake layer, meringue side up. Serve cake within 2 hours of assembly.

Why This Recipe Works The key to angel food cake is voluminous, stable egg whites. A mere speck of yolk precludes them from whipping to peaks. We had equal success with both cold and room-temperature egg whites. Cold whites achieved the same volume as room-temperature whites; they just took a few minutes longer. Cream of tartar offered some insurance against deflated whites because its acidity helped stabilize the egg whites. Cake flour was also important—all-purpose flour produced a chewy, gummy cake.

ANGEL FOOD CAKE

SERVES 10 TO 12

Do not use all-purpose flour in this recipe as it will give the cake a breadlike texture. You will need a 12-cup tube pan with a removable bottom for this recipe. If your pan has "feet" that rise above the top edge of the pan, let the cake cool upside down; otherwise, invert the tube pan over a large metal kitchen funnel or the neck of a sturdy bottle. Cake can be served plain or dusted with confectioners' sugar.

- 1 cup plus 2 tablespoons (4½ ounces) cake flour
- ¼ teaspoon salt
- 1¾ cups (12¼ ounces) sugar
- 12 large egg whites
- 1½ teaspoons cream of tartar
- 1 teaspoon vanilla extract

1. Adjust oven rack to lower-middle position and preheat oven to 325 degrees. Whisk flour and salt in bowl. Process sugar in food processor until fine, about 1 minute. Reserve half of sugar in small bowl. Add flour mixture to food processor with remaining sugar and process until aerated, about 1 minute.

2. Using stand mixer fitted with whisk, whip egg whites and cream of tartar on medium-low speed until foamy, about 1 minute. Increase speed to medium-high. Slowly add reserved sugar and whip until soft peaks form, about 6 minutes. Add vanilla and mix until incorporated.

3. Sift flour-sugar mixture over egg whites in 3 additions, folding gently with rubber spatula after each addition until incorporated. Scrape mixture into 12-cup ungreased tube pan.

4. Bake until skewer inserted into center comes out clean and cracks in cake appear dry, 40 to 45 minutes. Let cool, inverted, to room temperature, about 3 hours. To unmold, run knife along interior of pan. Turn out onto platter. Serve.

CHOCOLATE-ALMOND ANGEL FOOD CAKE

Replace ½ teaspoon vanilla extract with ½ teaspoon almond extract in step 2. Fold 2 ounces finely grated bittersweet chocolate into batter following flour in step 3.

CAFÉ AU LAIT ANGEL FOOD CAKE

Add 1 tablespoon instant coffee or espresso powder to food processor along with flour in step 1. Replace ½ teaspoon vanilla with 1 tablespoon coffee liqueur in step 2.

Key Steps to Angel Food Cake

1. Grind Sugar Process granulated sugar in food processor until powdery. It'll be fine, light, and won't deflate egg whites.

2. Stabilize Egg Whites Add cream of tartar to egg whites at start of whipping. Once whites become foamy, add half of sugar—gradually.

3. Sift Flour in Batches Gently sift flour-sugar mixture over beaten egg whites in batches to avoid deflating whites.

4. Cool Upside Down Invert cake until it is completely cool, about 3 hours. If you don't have pan with feet, invert it over neck of sturdy bottle.

CHIFFON CAKE

SERVES 10 TO 12

Separate the eggs when they're cold; it's easier. You will need a 16-cup tube pan with a removable bottom for this recipe. If your pan has "feet" that rise above the top edge of the pan, let the cake cool upside down; otherwise, invert the tube pan over a large metal kitchen funnel or the neck of a sturdy bottle.

- 5 large eggs, separated
- 1 teaspoon cream of tartar
- 1½ cups (10½ ounces) sugar
- 1⅓ cups (5⅓ ounces) cake flour
- 2 teaspoons baking powder
- ½ teaspoon salt
- ¾ cup water
- ½ cup vegetable oil
- 1 tablespoon vanilla extract

1. Adjust oven rack to lower-middle position and heat oven to 325 degrees. Using stand mixer fitted with whisk, whip egg whites and cream of tartar on medium-high speed until soft peaks form, about 2 minutes. With mixer running, slowly add 2 tablespoons sugar and whip until just stiff and glossy, about 1 minute; set aside.

2. Combine flour, remaining sugar, baking powder, and salt in large bowl. Whisk water, oil, egg yolks, and vanilla in medium bowl until smooth. Whisk wet mixture into flour mixture until smooth. Whisk one-third whipped egg whites into batter, then gently fold in remaining whites, 1 scoop at a time, until well combined. Scrape mixture into 16-cup ungreased tube pan.

3. Bake until skewer inserted into center comes out clean and cracks in cake appear dry, 55 minutes to 1 hour, 5 minutes. Let cool, inverted, to room temperature, about 3 hours. To unmold, turn pan right side up and run flexible knife around tube and outer edge. Use tube to pull cake out of pan and set it on inverted baking pan. Cut bottom free. Invert cake onto serving plate and gently twist tube to remove. Serve.

ORANGE CHIFFON CAKE

Reduce total sugar to 1¼ cups. Replace water with ¾ cup orange juice and add 1 tablespoon grated orange zest along with vanilla in step 2. For glaze, whisk 3 tablespoons orange juice, 2 tablespoons softened cream cheese, and ½ teaspoon grated orange zest in medium bowl until smooth. Add 1½ cups confectioners' sugar and whisk until smooth. Pour glaze over cooled cake. Let glaze set for 15 minutes. Serve.

Let Me Outta Here!

Like angel food cake, chiffon cake is baked in an ungreased pan. Why? The stiffly beaten egg whites need to cling to the pan to rise. If the pan were greased, they couldn't. Here's how to remove it from the pan.

1. When cake is cool, turn pan right side up and run flexible knife around tube and outer edge.

2. Use tube to pull cake out of pan and set it on inverted baking pan. Cut bottom free.

3. Invert cake onto serving plate and gently twist tube to remove.

Why This Recipe Works Chiffon cake should have the airy height of angel food cake with the richness of pound cake. For our chiffon cake recipe, we eliminated the unnecessary step of sifting the dry ingredients. We also perfected the method for beating our egg whites—slowly adding sugar once the eggs had been beaten to soft peaks and then continuing to beat them until just stiff and glossy—to avoid little pockets of cooked egg whites.

ITALIAN CREAM CAKE

SERVES 8 TO 10

Toast the coconut and nuts in a 350-degree oven until golden brown, 10 to 12 minutes. Watch carefully and stir occasionally to prevent burning.

Cake
1½ cups sweetened shredded coconut, toasted
1 cup buttermilk, room temperature
2 teaspoons vanilla extract
2½ cups (10 ounces) cake flour
2 teaspoons baking powder
¾ teaspoon salt
½ teaspoon baking soda
12 tablespoons unsalted butter, cut into 12 pieces and softened
4 tablespoons shortening, cut into 4 pieces
1¾ cups (12¼ ounces) sugar
5 large eggs, room temperature
2 cups (8 ounces) pecans, toasted and chopped

Frosting
12 tablespoons unsalted butter, softened
2¼ cups (9 ounces) confectioners' sugar
½ cup cream of coconut
½ teaspoon vanilla extract
Pinch salt
16 ounces cream cheese, cut into 8 pieces and softened

1. For the Cake Adjust oven rack to middle position and heat oven to 350 degrees. Grease two 9-inch round cake pans, line with parchment paper, grease parchment, then flour pans. Process coconut in food processor until finely ground, about 1 minute. Combine coconut, buttermilk, and vanilla in 2-cup liquid measuring cup and let sit until coconut is slightly softened, about 10 minutes; reserve.

2. Combine flour, baking powder, salt, and baking soda in bowl. Using stand mixer fitted with paddle, beat butter, shortening, and sugar on medium-high speed until pale and fluffy, about 3 minutes. Add eggs, one at a time, and beat until combined. Reduce speed to low and add flour mixture in 3 additions, alternating with 2 additions of reserved coconut-buttermilk mixture, scraping down bowl as needed. Add ¾ cup pecans and give batter final stir by hand.

3. Scrape equal amounts of batter into prepared pans and bake until toothpick inserted in center comes out clean, 28 to 32 minutes. Cool cakes in pans on wire rack for 10 minutes. Remove cakes from pans, discarding parchment, and cool completely, about 2 hours. (Cooled cakes can be wrapped with plastic wrap and stored at room temperature for up to 2 days.)

4. For the Frosting Using stand mixer fitted with paddle, mix butter and sugar on low speed until combined, about 30 seconds. Increase speed to medium-high and beat until pale and fluffy, about 2 minutes. Add cream of coconut, vanilla, and salt and beat until smooth, about 30 seconds. Add cream cheese, one piece at a time, and beat until incorporated, about 1 minute. Refrigerate until ready to use.

5. When cakes are cooled, spread 1½ cups frosting over 1 cake round. Top with second cake round and spread remaining frosting evenly over top and sides of cake. Press remaining pecans onto sides of cake. Serve. (Cake can be refrigerated for up to 2 days. Bring to room temperature before serving.)

Coconut: Toast, Grind, Soak
To bring out the flavor of the shredded coconut, we toast it in a 350-degree oven until it is golden brown (about 10 minutes). To help the coconut flavor permeate the cake, we grind it to meal in the food processor. But toasted, ground coconut is hard and dry, a real problem in such a deliciously soft, moist cake. To moisten and soften the coconut meal, we soak it in buttermilk before adding it to the cake batter.

Why This Recipe Works Although the name is a mystery (there's nothing Italian about this cake), the appeal of this Southern specialty is obvious: tender yellow cake with coconut and pecans, doused in tangy cream cheese frosting. But the recipes we found produced gummy cakes with weak coconut flavor. Cake flour made a more tender crumb, and heat-activated baking powder ensured the cake would rise evenly in the oven. To boost coconut flavor, we added it twice—pulverized, toasted coconut added flavor to the cake without drying it out, and cream of coconut amped up the frosting. Finally, we coated the sides in a blanket of toasted pecans.

Why This Recipe Works In this delicious variation on classic pound cake, we added cream cheese for richness, tangy flavor, and an especially velvety texture. We let the pure flavors of eggs, butter, and the cream cheese take center stage, adding only a few teaspoons of vanilla and a moderate amount of sugar. To achieve a tight, fine crumb and a velvety texture, we left the leavener out altogether and used lower-protein cake flour. Extra egg yolks kept the cake moist and tender. Finally, a low oven took a little longer, but it produced a perfect golden-brown crust and a moist, tender interior.

CREAM CHEESE POUND CAKE

SERVES 12 TO 14

If you do not have cake flour on hand, you can substitute ⅞ cup all-purpose flour and 2 tablespoons cornstarch for each cup of flour. Serve with Strawberry-Rhubarb Compote (recipe follows).

- 3 cups (12 ounces) cake flour
- 1 teaspoon salt
- 4 large eggs plus 2 large yolks, room temperature
- ¼ cup milk
- 2 teaspoons vanilla extract
- 3 cups (21 ounces) sugar
- 24 tablespoons (3 sticks) unsalted butter, softened
- 6 ounces cream cheese, softened

1. Adjust oven rack to middle position and heat oven to 300 degrees. Grease and flour 12-cup nonstick Bundt pan. Combine flour and salt in bowl. Whisk eggs and yolks, milk, and vanilla together in 2-cup liquid measuring cup.

2. Using stand mixer fitted with paddle, beat sugar, butter, and cream cheese on medium-high speed until pale and fluffy, about 3 minutes. Reduce speed to low and very slowly add egg mixture, mixing until incorporated (batter may look slightly curdled). Add flour mixture in 3 additions, scraping down bowl as needed. Give batter final stir by hand.

3. Scrape batter into prepared pan and gently tap pan on counter to release air bubbles. Bake until toothpick inserted in center comes out clean, 80 to 90 minutes, rotating pan halfway through baking. Cool cake in pan on wire rack for 15 minutes. Remove cake from pan and cool completely, about 2 hours. Serve. (Cake can be stored, wrapped in plastic wrap, at room temperature for 3 days.)

STRAWBERRY-RHUBARB COMPOTE
MAKES 4 CUPS

The compote can be refrigerated for up to one week. It's delicious drizzled on Cream Cheese Pound Cake or ice cream or stirred into yogurt or oatmeal.

- 1 pound strawberries, hulled and chopped (3 cups)
- 1 cup (7 ounces) sugar
- 1 tablespoon lemon juice
- 1 pound rhubarb, sliced ¼-inch thick
  Pinch salt

1. Toss strawberries with ½ cup sugar and lemon juice in medium bowl. Transfer strawberry mixture to fine-mesh strainer set over medium saucepan and let stand, stirring occasionally, for 30 minutes. Do not wash bowl.

2. Return strawberries to bowl. Add rhubarb, remaining ½ cup sugar, and salt to strawberry juices in pan and bring to boil over medium-high heat. Reduce heat to medium-low and cook, stirring occasionally, until rhubarb is soft and liquid has thickened, 6 to 8 minutes.

3. Stir strawberries into pan and remove from heat. Transfer compote to bowl and let cool to room temperature, about 45 minutes. Serve.

Preparing a Bundt Pan

To ensure a clean release, apply paste of 1 tablespoon melted butter and 1 tablespoon flour to pan using pastry brush.

COLD-OVEN POUND CAKE

SERVES 12

You'll need a 16-cup tube pan for this recipe; if not using a nonstick pan, make sure to thoroughly grease a traditional pan. In step 2, don't worry if the batter looks slightly separated.

- 3 cups (12 ounces) cake flour
- ½ teaspoon baking powder
- 1 teaspoon salt
- 1 cup whole milk
- 2 teaspoons vanilla extract
- 20 tablespoons (2½ sticks) unsalted butter, softened
- 2½ cups (17½ ounces) sugar
- 6 large eggs

1. Adjust oven rack to lower-middle position. Grease and flour 16-cup tube pan. Combine flour, baking powder, and salt in bowl. Whisk milk and vanilla in measuring cup.

2. Using stand mixer fitted with paddle, beat butter and sugar on medium-high speed until light and fluffy, about 2 minutes. Beat in eggs, one at a time, until combined. Reduce speed to low and add flour mixture in 3 additions, alternating with milk mixture in 2 additions, scraping down bowl as needed. Mix on low until smooth, about 30 seconds. Give batter final stir by hand.

3. Pour batter into prepared pan and smooth top. Place cake in cold oven. Adjust oven temperature to 325 degrees and bake, without opening oven door, until cake is golden brown and skewer inserted in center comes out clean, 1 hour 5 minutes to 1 hour 20 minutes.

4. Let cake cool in pan on wire rack for 15 minutes. Remove cake from pan and let cool completely on rack about 2 hours. Serve. (Cake can be stored at room temperature for up to 2 days.)

A Cold Oven Really Makes a Difference

Curiosity led us to try baking our Cold-Oven Pound Cake in a preheated oven. The cake baked more quickly (no surprise), but it was squat and lacked the thick crust we'd come to expect. Evidently, the hot oven stopped the small amount of leavener in our recipe before its work was done. And it turns out the crust on our Cold-Oven Pound Cake is formed by moisture in the oven reacting with starch in the batter. A hot oven is drier than a cold oven (heat evaporates moisture), so there wasn't enough moisture in the preheated oven to form a nice, thick crust.

SQUAT CAKE	PERFECT CAKE
A preheated oven produces a squat, crustless cake with this recipe.	In contrast, a cold oven produces a high rise and a thick crust.

Why Pay for Preheating?

Gas ovens became widely available in the United States during the first decades of the 20th century. Because these ovens were more expensive than their wood- and coal-fired counterparts, gas companies had to get creative in marketing them. One popular tactic was to develop and promote recipes started in a cold oven, with the hook that consumers could save money in their gas ovens by not paying for "needless" preheating. Hence: cold-oven pound cake.

Why This Recipe Works This thrifty pound cake, which was designed to save on gas by not requiring a preheated oven, is an especially tall cake and boasts a crisp crust. To create a light crumb, we used leaner whole milk instead of the heavy cream called for in most recipes. Swapping out all-purpose flour for cake flour yielded an even finer, more delicate crumb for our pound cake. We also used baking powder, which produced carbon dioxide bubbles that gave our cake its rise. Putting the pound cake into a cold oven, as is tradition, gave the carbon dioxide more time to produce greater rise.

Why This Recipe Works Packaged chocolate cream cupcakes are a childhood treat. But try one today and you're met with wan chocolate cake encasing salty whipped vegetable shortening. We knew we could do better. Blooming cocoa powder in boiling water and adding chocolate chips and espresso powder gave our cupcakes plenty of chocolate depth. Combining marshmallow crème and the right amount of gelatin gave us the perfect creamy filling. To fill our cupcakes without a pastry bag, we used a paring knife to cut inverted cones from the tops of the cupcakes, added the frosting, and plugged the holes.

CHOCOLATE CREAM CUPCAKES

MAKES 12 CUPCAKES

To ensure an appropriately thick filling, be sure to use marshmallow crème (such as Fluff), not marshmallow sauce. For an accurate measurement of boiling water, bring a full kettle of water to a boil, then measure out the desired amount.

Cupcakes

- 1 cup (5 ounces) all-purpose flour
- ½ teaspoon baking soda
- ¼ teaspoon salt
- ½ cup boiling water
- ⅓ cup (1 ounce) cocoa powder
- ⅓ cup (2 ounces) semisweet chocolate chips
- 1 tablespoon instant espresso powder
- ¾ cup (5¼ ounces) sugar
- ½ cup sour cream
- ½ cup vegetable oil
- 2 large eggs
- 1 teaspoon vanilla extract

Filling

- ¾ teaspoon unflavored gelatin
- 3 tablespoons water
- 4 tablespoons (½ stick) unsalted butter, softened
- 1 teaspoon vanilla extract
- Pinch salt
- 1¼ cups marshmallow crème

Glaze

- ½ cup semisweet chocolate chips
- 3 tablespoons unsalted butter

1. For the Cupcakes Adjust oven rack to middle position and heat oven to 325 degrees. Spray 12-cup muffin tin with vegetable oil spray and flour. Combine flour, baking soda, and salt in bowl. Whisk water, cocoa, chocolate chips, and espresso powder in large bowl until smooth. Add sugar, sour cream, oil, eggs, and vanilla and mix until combined. Whisk in flour mixture until incorporated. Divide batter evenly among muffin cups. Bake until toothpick inserted in center comes out with few dry crumbs attached, 18 to 22 minutes. Let cupcakes cool in tin on wire rack for 10 minutes, then turn out onto wire rack and let cool completely.

2. For the Filling Sprinkle gelatin over water in large bowl and let sit until gelatin softens, about 5 minutes. Microwave until mixture is bubbling around edges and gelatin dissolves, about 30 seconds. Stir in butter, vanilla, and salt until combined. Let mixture cool until just warm to touch, about 5 minutes, then whisk in marshmallow crème until smooth; refrigerate until set, about 30 minutes. Transfer ⅓ cup marshmallow mixture to pastry bag fitted with small plain tip; reserve remaining mixture for filling cupcakes.

3. For the Glaze Microwave chocolate and butter in small bowl, stirring occasionally, until smooth, about 30 seconds. Let glaze cool to room temperature, about 10 minutes.

4. Insert tip of paring knife at 45-degree angle and about ¼ inch from edge of cupcake, cut cone from top of each cupcake, and cut off all but top ¼ inch of cone, leaving circular disk of cake. Fill cupcakes with 1 tablespoon filling each. Replace tops, frost with 2 teaspoons cooled glaze, and let sit 10 minutes. Using pastry bag, pipe curlicues across glazed cupcakes. Serve. (Cupcakes can be stored at room temperature for up to 2 days.)

Filling the Cupcakes

1. Insert tip of paring knife at 45-degree angle about ¼ inch from edge of cupcake. Cut out and remove cake cone. Cut off all but top ¼ inch of cone, leaving circular disk of cake.

2. Using spoon, fill each cupcake with marshmallow mixture and then top with reserved cake "plug." The glaze and the curlicues will hide your handiwork.

Why This Recipe Works Most hot fudge pudding cakes end up looking rich and fudgy but have very little chocolate flavor. For chocolate pudding cake that tasted as good as it looked, we folded semisweet chocolate chips into the batter, which added another layer of chocolate flavor and ensured plenty of gooey pockets in the baked cake. Vegetable oil, which most recipes call for, was flavorless, and we found substituting melted butter improved our pudding cake's flavor. Using Dutch-processed cocoa, which is less acidic than natural cocoa powder, produced a richer chocolate taste.

HOT FUDGE PUDDING CAKE

SERVES 6 TO 8

For an accurate measurement of boiling water, bring a full kettle of water to a boil, then measure out the desired amount. Do not overbake this cake or the pudding sauce will burn in the pan and the cake will be dry, not fudgy. Store leftovers, covered with plastic wrap, in the refrigerator. Reheat individual servings in a microwave on high power until hot (about 1 minute).

  1 cup (7 ounces) sugar
  ½ cup (1½ ounces) Dutch-processed
    cocoa powder
  1 cup (5 ounces) all-purpose flour
  2 teaspoons baking powder
  ¼ teaspoon salt
  ½ cup milk
  4 tablespoons unsalted butter, melted
  1 large egg yolk
  2 teaspoons vanilla extract
  ½ cup semisweet chocolate chips
  1 cup boiling water
    Vanilla ice cream or whipped cream

1. Adjust oven rack to middle position and heat oven to 350 degrees. Spray 8-inch square baking pan with vegetable oil spray. Whisk ½ cup sugar with ¼ cup cocoa in small bowl.

2. Whisk flour, remaining ½ cup sugar, remaining ¼ cup cocoa, baking powder, and salt in large bowl. Whisk milk, butter, egg yolk, and vanilla in medium bowl until smooth. Stir milk mixture into flour mixture until just combined. Fold in chocolate chips (batter will be stiff).

3. Using rubber spatula, scrape batter into prepared pan and spread into corners. Sprinkle reserved cocoa mixture evenly over top. Gently pour boiling water over cocoa. Do not stir.

4. Bake until top of cake looks cracked, sauce is bubbling, and toothpick inserted into cakey area comes out with moist crumbs attached, about 25 minutes. Let cool in pan on wire rack for at least 10 minutes. To serve, scoop warm cake into individual serving bowls and top with vanilla ice cream or whipped cream.

BABY PUDDING CAKES

Put a fancy spin on this homey recipe by baking up individual pudding cakes.

Spray eight 6-ounce ovenproof ramekins or coffee cups with vegetable oil spray. Fill each with 2 tablespoons batter. Top each with 1½ tablespoons cocoa mixture, followed by 2 tablespoons boiling water. Arrange cups on rimmed baking sheet and bake until tops are just cracked, 20 to 25 minutes.

Is It Done Yet?

This highly unconventional cake breaks most of the usual rules, including how to judge when it's ready to come out of the oven.

1. Start testing for doneness when top is crackled like a brownie and sauce is bubbling up from bottom. Insert toothpick close to the edge, where the cake is firmest. (Don't insert the toothpick in center, where cake should be gooey.)

2. Toothpick should have large, moist crumbs—but no gooey batter—attached. Check at least two spots to be certain that what's sticking to toothpick isn't just melted chocolate.

LEMON PUDDING CAKE

SERVES 8

This dessert is best served warm or at room temperature the same day it is made.

- ¼ cup (1¼ ounces) all-purpose flour
- 2 teaspoons cornstarch
- 1¼ cups (8¾ ounces) sugar
- 5 tablespoons unsalted butter, softened
- 2 tablespoons grated zest and ½ cup juice from 4 lemons
- 5 large eggs, separated
- 1¼ cups whole milk, room temperature
- 2 quarts boiling water

1. Adjust oven rack to lowest position and heat oven to 325 degrees. Grease 8-inch square baking dish. Whisk flour and cornstarch in bowl. Using stand mixer fitted with paddle, beat ½ cup sugar, butter, and lemon zest on medium-high speed until light and fluffy, about 2 minutes. Beat in egg yolks, 1 at a time, until incorporated. Reduce speed to medium-low. Add flour mixture and mix until incorporated. Slowly add milk and lemon juice, mixing until just combined.

2. Using clean bowl and whisk attachment, beat egg whites on medium-high speed until soft peaks form, about 2 minutes. With mixer running, slowly add remaining ¾ cup sugar until whites are firm and glossy, about 1 minute. Whisk one-third of whites into batter, then gently fold in remaining whites, 1 scoop at a time, until well combined.

3. Place clean dish towel in bottom of roasting pan and arrange prepared baking dish on towel. Spoon batter into prepared dish. Carefully place pan on oven rack and pour boiling water into pan until water comes halfway up sides of baking dish. Bake until surface is golden brown and edges are set (center should jiggle slightly when gently shaken), about 1 hour. Transfer dish to wire rack and let cool for at least 1 hour. To serve, scoop warm cake into individual serving bowls.

Using a Water Bath

The water lowers the temperature surrounding the baking dish for gentle, even cooking.

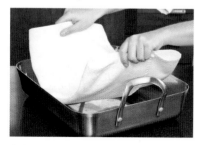

1. To prevent baking dish from sliding, line bottom of roasting pan with clean dish towel and place baking dish on top.

2. Set roasting pan on oven rack and carefully pour boiling water into pan, halfway up sides of baking dish.

3. After baking, promptly remove baking dish from water. Let water cool before moving water bath.

Why This Recipe Works For the brightest lemon flavor in our lemon pudding cake, we used a half cup of lemon juice. To coax even more flavor from the lemons, we creamed a bit of grated zest with the butter and sugar. A bit of cornstarch gently firmed the pudding layer without muddying the lemon flavor. To prevent the top layer of the cake from deflating, we beat sugar into the egg whites. This stabilized the whites and resulted in a high, golden, and fluffy cake. For the creamiest texture, it was important to bake the cake in a water bath. The hot water protected the pudding from cooking too quickly.

LEMON ICEBOX CHEESECAKE

SERVES 12 TO 16

Let the dissolved gelatin mixture cool down for a few minutes, or the gelatin will seize before combining with the filling. We tested our cheesecake with several store brands of lemon sandwich cookies; all worked well.

Crust

10 lemon sandwich cookies, broken into pieces (about 1¼ cups)
2 tablespoons unsalted butter, melted
1 teaspoon grated lemon zest

Curd

¼ cup (1¾ ounces) sugar
1 large egg plus 1 large yolk
  Pinch salt
2 tablespoons lemon juice
1 tablespoon unsalted butter
1 tablespoon heavy cream

Filling

2¾ teaspoons unflavored gelatin
¼ cup lemon juice (2 lemons)
1½ pounds cream cheese, cut into 1-inch pieces and softened
¾ cup (5¼ ounces) sugar
  Pinch salt
1¼ cups heavy cream, room temperature

1. For the Crust Adjust oven rack to middle position and heat oven to 350 degrees. Process cookies in food processor until finely ground, about 30 seconds. Add butter and zest and pulse until combined, about 10 pulses. Press mixture into bottom of 9-inch springform pan. Bake until lightly browned and set, about 10 minutes. Let cool completely on wire rack, at least 30 minutes.

2. For the Curd While crust is cooling, whisk sugar, egg and yolk, and salt together in small saucepan. Add lemon juice and cook over medium-low heat, stirring constantly, until thick and puddinglike, about 3 minutes. Remove from heat and stir in butter and cream. Press through fine-mesh strainer into small bowl and refrigerate lemon curd until needed.

3. For the Filling Sprinkle gelatin over lemon juice in small bowl and let stand until gelatin softens, about 5 minutes. Microwave until mixture is bubbling around edges and gelatin dissolves, about 30 seconds. Set aside.

4. Using stand mixer fitted with paddle beat cream cheese, sugar, and salt on medium speed until smooth and creamy, scraping down sides of bowl as needed, about 2 minutes. Slowly add cream and beat until light and fluffy, about 2 minutes. Add gelatin mixture and ¼ cup curd, increase speed to medium-high, and beat until smooth and airy, about 3 minutes.

5. Pour filling into cooled crust and smooth top. Pour thin lines of remaining curd on top of cake and lightly drag paring knife or skewer perpendicularly through lines to create marbled appearance. Refrigerate until set, at least 6 hours. Remove sides of pan. Serve. (Cheesecake can be refrigerated for up to 3 days.)

Swirl Showstopper

Making a swirl with the lemon curd on top of the cheesecake is absurdly easy and awfully impressive.

1. Use measuring cup to pour curd in 4 thin lines on top of cheesecake.

2. Drag paring knife or skewer perpendicularly through lines to create marbled design.

Why This Recipe Works In a baked cheesecake, tart lemon juice is mellowed by the heat of the oven. For our icebox version of lemon cheesecake, we needed to dial back the lemon juice to compensate for the lack of baking. Lemon curd, a rich, tangy spread made from eggs, butter, cream, sugar, and lemon juice, added crisp lemon flavor without the undesirable chewiness of zest or the processed flavor of lemon extract. Using lemon cookies instead of graham crackers for the crust created an additional layer of lemon flavor.

STRAWBERRY CHEESECAKE BARS

MAKES TWENTY-FOUR 2-INCH SQUARES

Be sure to let the crust cool completely before starting the filling.

Crust

9 whole graham crackers, broken into pieces
½ cup (3½ ounces) sugar
¾ cup (3¾ ounces) all-purpose flour
¼ teaspoon salt
8 tablespoons unsalted butter, melted

Filling

1½ pounds cream cheese
1 cup (7 ounces) sugar
3 large eggs
2 teaspoons vanilla extract

Topping

6 ounces strawberries, hulled (1 heaping cup), plus 5 hulled strawberries
½ cup (3½ ounces) plus 1 teaspoon sugar
2 cups sour cream

1. Adjust oven rack to middle position and heat oven to 300 degrees. Make foil sling for 13 by 9-inch baking pan by folding 2 long sheets of aluminum foil; first sheet should be 13 inches wide and second sheet should be 9 inches wide. Lay sheets of foil in pan perpendicular to each other, with extra foil hanging over edges of pan. Push foil into corners and up sides of pan, smoothing foil flush to pan. Spray with vegetable oil spray.

2. For the Crust Process cracker pieces and sugar in food processor until finely ground, about 30 seconds. Add flour and salt and pulse to combine, about 2 pulses. Add melted butter and pulse until crumbs are evenly moistened, about 10 pulses.

3. Using your hands, press crumb mixture evenly into bottom of prepared pan. Using bottom of dry measuring cup, firmly pack crust into pan. Bake until fragrant and beginning to brown around edges, about 20 minutes. Let cool completely.

4. For the Filling In clean, dry processor bowl, process cream cheese and sugar until smooth, about 3 minutes, scraping down sides of bowl as needed. With processor running, add eggs, one at a time, until just incorporated, about 30 seconds total. Scrape down sides of bowl. Add vanilla and process to combine, about 10 seconds. Pour cream cheese mixture over cooled crust. Bake until center is almost set but still jiggles slightly when pan is shaken, about 45 minutes.

5. For the Topping Meanwhile, in clean, dry processor bowl, process 6 ounces strawberries and ½ cup sugar until pureed, about 30 seconds. Stir strawberry puree and sour cream in bowl until combined.

6. Remove cheesecake from oven. Pour strawberry mixture over cheesecake (cheesecake layer should be completely covered). Return pan to oven and bake until topping is just set, about 15 minutes.

7. Transfer pan to wire rack and let cheesecake cool completely, about 2 hours. Refrigerate until cold and set, at least 4 hours or up to 24 hours. Slice remaining 5 strawberries thin and gently toss with remaining 1 teaspoon sugar in bowl. Using foil overhang, lift cheesecake out of pan. Cut into 24 squares. Garnish each square with 1 strawberry slice and serve.

Why This Recipe Works Bright strawberries combined with tangy, rich cheesecake make for a perfect dessert. But trying to add fresh strawberries directly to the cheesecake filling compromised its creamy texture and prevented our bars from firming up. Instead, we pureed fresh berries and stirred them into a sour cream topping that we spread over the cheesecake layer. This gave strong strawberry flavor that didn't sacrifice the signature creaminess of cheesecake. A simple graham cracker crust is a test kitchen favorite for cheesecakes, and it was supereasy to put together. A single strawberry slice on top of each bar was the perfect finishing touch.

Why This Recipe Works Too often, chocolate's bitter side can clash with the tangy flavor of cream cheese, but we were determined to create a fluffy chocolate cheese-cake without the bitterness. After making dozens of versions, we figured out that switching from dark to mild-mannered milk chocolate was the secret to a sweet, creamy cheesecake. Adding cocoa powder added depth and rounded out the choco-late flavor. Unlike traditional cheesecake that is baked in a water bath, we simplified our recipe by baking it in a low 250-degree oven. For an easy and crunchy, chocolaty crust, we used Oreo cookies processed with butter and a bit of sugar.

MILK CHOCOLATE CHEESECAKE

SERVES 12

Our favorite milk chocolate is Endangered Species Chocolate Smooth + Creamy Milk Chocolate. For the crust, use the entirety of the Oreo cookies, filling and all. The cheesecake needs to be refrigerated for at least 8 hours before serving.

16 Oreo sandwich cookies, broken into rough pieces
1 tablespoon sugar plus ½ cup (3½ ounces)
2 tablespoons unsalted butter, melted
8 ounces milk chocolate, chopped
⅓ cup heavy cream
2 tablespoons unsweetened cocoa powder
¼ teaspoon salt
1½ pounds cream cheese, softened
4 large eggs, room temperature
2 teaspoons vanilla extract

1. Adjust oven rack to middle position and heat oven to 350 degrees. Grease bottom and sides of 9-inch nonstick springform pan.

2. Process cookies and 1 tablespoon sugar in food processor until finely ground, about 30 seconds. Add melted butter and pulse until combined, about 6 pulses. Transfer crumb mixture to prepared pan and press firmly with bottom of dry measuring cup into even layer in bottom of pan. Bake until fragrant and set, about 10 minutes. Let cool completely on wire rack.

3. Reduce oven temperature to 250 degrees. Combine 6 ounces chocolate and cream in medium bowl and microwave at 50 percent power, stirring occasionally, until melted and smooth, 60 to 90 seconds. Let cool for 10 minutes. In small bowl, whisk cocoa, salt, and remaining ½ cup sugar until no lumps remain.

4. Using stand mixer fitted with paddle, beat cream cheese and cocoa mixture on medium speed until creamy and smooth, about 3 minutes, scraping down bowl as needed. Reduce speed to medium-low, add chocolate mixture, and beat until combined.

Gradually add eggs, one at a time, until incorporated, scraping down bowl as needed. Add vanilla and give batter final stir by hand until no streaks of chocolate remain.

5. Pour cheesecake mixture into cooled crust and smooth top with spatula. Tap cheesecake gently on counter to release air bubbles. Cover pan tightly with aluminum foil (taking care not to touch surface of cheesecake with foil) and place on rimmed baking sheet. Bake for 1 hour, then remove foil. Continue to bake until edges are set and center registers 150 degrees and jiggles slightly when shaken, 30 to 45 minutes. Let cool completely on wire rack, then cover with plastic wrap and refrigerate in pan until cold, about 8 hours. (Cake can be refrigerated for up to 4 days.)

6. To unmold cheesecake, remove sides of pan, slide thin metal spatula between crust and pan bottom to loosen, and slide cake onto serving platter. Microwave remaining 2 ounces chocolate in small bowl at 50 percent power, stirring occasionally, until melted, 60 to 90 seconds. Let cool for 5 minutes. Transfer to small zipper-lock bag, cut small hole in corner, and pipe chocolate in thin zigzag pattern across top of cheesecake. Let cheesecake stand at room temperature for 30 minutes. Using warm, dry knife, cut into wedges and serve.

Melt Milk Chocolate Carefully

Because milk chocolate contains milk solids, its protein content is generally higher than that of dark chocolate. The extra protein means that milk chocolate melts at a slightly lower temperature than dark; what's more, when you add heat to protein and sugar, new molecules may form, introducing unwelcome scorched or burned flavors. Microwaves are generally gentle, but notoriously inconsistent, so choose 50 percent power, keep a close eye on the chocolate, and give it a stir every 15 seconds.

Why This Recipe Works A product of 1950s nostalgia for the wild West, cowboy cookies—packed with rolled oats, chocolate chips, toasted nuts, and flakes of coconut—are perfect for tucking into your saddlebag to enjoy at high noon. When we set out to wrangle this recipe, we discovered that the mix-ins absorbed moisture in the dough, making for one tough cookie, so we melted our butter to keep the dough moist. Staggering ¼-cup portions of dough onto our baking sheets gave these oversize cookies enough room to spread, and deliberately underbaking them ensured they had a perfectly crisp exterior and soft chew once cooled.

COWBOY COOKIES

MAKES 16 COOKIES

We prefer old-fashioned rolled oats in this recipe, but you can use quick or instant oats in a pinch. Do not use thick-cut oats here; the cookies will spread too much. These cookies are big and benefit from the extra space provided by a rimless cookie sheet when baking. Our favorite cookie sheet is the Wear-Ever Cookie Sheet (Natural Finish) by Vollrath.

1¼ cups (6¼ ounces) all-purpose flour
¾ teaspoon baking powder
½ teaspoon baking soda
½ teaspoon salt
1½ cups packed (10½ ounces) light brown sugar
12 tablespoons unsalted butter, melted and cooled
1 large egg plus 1 large yolk
1 teaspoon vanilla extract
1¼ cups (3¾ ounces) old-fashioned rolled oats
1 cup pecans, toasted and chopped coarse
1 cup (3 ounces) sweetened shredded coconut
⅔ cup (4 ounces) semisweet chocolate chips

1. Adjust oven rack to middle position and heat oven to 350 degrees. Line 2 rimless cookie sheets with parchment paper. Whisk flour, baking powder, baking soda, and salt together in bowl.

2. Whisk sugar, melted butter, egg and yolk, and vanilla in large bowl until combined. Stir in flour mixture until no dry streaks remain. Stir in oats, pecans, coconut, and chocolate chips until fully combined (mixture will be sticky).

3. Lightly spray ¼-cup dry measuring cup with vegetable oil spray. Drop level ¼-cup portions of dough onto prepared sheets, staggering 8 portions per sheet and spacing them about 2½ inches apart. Divide any remaining dough among portions.

4. Bake cookies, 1 sheet at a time, until edges are browned and set and centers are puffed with pale, raw spots, 15 to 17 minutes, rotating sheet halfway through baking. Do not overbake.

5. Let cookies cool on sheet for 5 minutes, then transfer to wire rack and let cool completely before serving. (Cookies can be stored in airtight container for up to 3 days.)

To Make Ahead At end of step 3, wrap sheets tightly in plastic wrap and refrigerate for up to 2 days. When ready to bake, increase baking time to 16 to 18 minutes. To freeze, portion dough onto parchment-lined sheet and freeze until solid. Transfer frozen portions to zipper-lock bag and freeze for up to 2 months. Do not thaw before baking. Increase baking time to 17 to 19 minutes.

Don't Fence Them In
Cowboy Cookies need lots of room to expand and bake evenly. To ensure that they don't spread into each other while baking, we arrange no more than 8 portions of dough on each parchment-lined cookie sheet.

Cookie Carryover Baking
Just like meat, cookies continue to bake even after they are removed from the oven. To avoid overbaking, take the cookies out of the oven when they are slightly underdone and let them cool on the baking sheet for 5 minutes before transferring them to a wire rack.

THIN AND CRISPY CHOCOLATE CHIP COOKIES

MAKES 16 COOKIES

Note that this recipe calls for cake flour and mini (not full-size) chocolate chips.

1¼ cups (5 ounces) cake flour
¾ teaspoon table salt
¼ teaspoon baking soda
8 tablespoons unsalted butter, melted and cooled
⅓ cup (2⅓ ounces) granulated sugar
⅓ cup packed (2⅓ ounces) dark brown sugar
2 large egg yolks
1½ tablespoons whole milk
2 teaspoons vanilla extract
¾ cup (4½ ounces) mini semisweet chocolate chips

1. Adjust oven rack to middle position and heat oven to 350 degrees. Line 2 baking sheets with parchment paper. Whisk flour, salt, and baking soda together in bowl.

2. Using stand mixer fitted with paddle, mix melted butter, granulated sugar, and brown sugar on low speed until fully combined. Increase speed to medium-high and beat until mixture is lightened in color, about 1 minute. Reduce speed to low; add egg yolks, milk, and vanilla; and mix until combined. Slowly add flour mixture and mix until just combined, scraping down bowl as needed. Using rubber spatula, stir in chocolate chips.

3. Using greased 1-tablespoon measure, divide dough into 16 heaping-tablespoon portions on prepared sheets, 8 portions per sheet. Divide any remaining dough evenly among portions. Using your moistened fingers, press dough portions to ½-inch thickness. Bake cookies, 1 sheet at a time, until deep golden brown, 16 to 18 minutes, rotating sheet halfway through baking. Let cookies cool on sheet for 20 minutes. Serve. (Cookies can be stored at room temperature for up to 3 days.)

Keys to the Perfect Texture

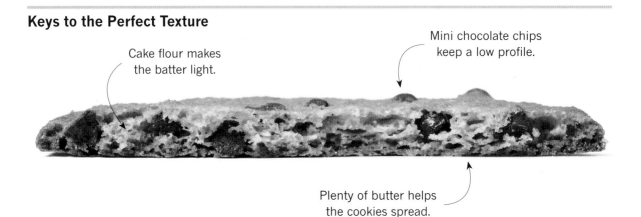

Cake flour makes the batter light.

Mini chocolate chips keep a low profile.

Plenty of butter helps the cookies spread.

Why This Recipe Works Thin and crunchy, butterschotchy chocolate chip cookies can't be beat. Melted butter helps the dough spread quickly so the cookies bake without burning. However, the batter needs more flour to keep them from spreading too much. Just ¼ cup more did the trick, but the extra flour made the cookies too chewy. Switching to a lighter cake flour, which contains less protein, made for more-tender cookies. But the cookies still weren't crisp enough. The solution was adding a bit of whole milk. The milk provided extra moisture, so the cookies didn't dry out with the additional baking time required to crisp up. Now that's the way these cookies crumble.

CHOCOLATE CHIP SKILLET COOKIE

SERVES 8

Top with ice cream for an extra-decadent treat.

12 tablespoons unsalted butter
¾ cup packed (5¼ ounces) dark brown sugar
½ cup (3½ ounces) granulated sugar
2 teaspoons vanilla extract
1 teaspoon salt
1 large egg plus 1 large yolk
1¾ cups (8¾ ounces) all-purpose flour
½ teaspoon baking soda
1 cup (6 ounces) semisweet chocolate chips

1. Adjust oven rack to upper-middle position and heat oven to 375 degrees. Melt 9 tablespoons butter in 12-inch cast-iron skillet over medium heat. Continue to cook, stirring constantly, until butter is dark golden brown, has nutty aroma, and bubbling subsides, about 5 minutes; transfer to large bowl. Stir remaining 3 tablespoons butter into hot butter until completely melted.

2. Whisk brown sugar, granulated sugar, vanilla, and salt into melted butter until smooth. Whisk in egg and yolk until smooth, about 30 seconds. Let mixture sit for 3 minutes, then whisk for 30 seconds. Repeat process of resting and whisking 2 more times until mixture is thick, smooth, and shiny.

3. Whisk flour and baking soda together in separate bowl, then stir flour mixture into butter mixture until just combined, about 1 minute. Stir in chocolate chips, making sure no flour pockets remain.

4. Wipe skillet clean with paper towels. Transfer dough to now-empty skillet and press into even layer with spatula. Transfer skillet to oven and bake until cookie is golden brown and edges are set, about 20 minutes, rotating skillet halfway through baking. Using potholders, transfer skillet to wire rack and let cookie cool for 30 minutes. Slice cookie into wedges and serve.

Making a Skillet Cookie

To ensure a uniformly baked cookie, transfer dough to skillet and press into even layer with spatula.

Seasoning Your Skillet

1. While the skillet is still warm, wipe it clean with paper towels to remove excess food bits and oil.

2. Rinse the skillet under hot running water, scrubbing with a brush or nonabrasive scrub pad to remove traces of food. Use a small amount of soap if you like, but make sure to rinse it all off.

3. Dry the skillet thoroughly (do not let it drip-dry) and put it back on the burner over medium-low heat until all traces of moisture disappear (this keeps rusting at bay). Never put a wet cast-iron skillet away or stack anything on top of a skillet that hasn't been properly dried.

4. Add ½ teaspoon of vegetable oil to the warm, dry skillet and wipe the interior with a wad of paper towels until it is lightly covered with oil.

5. Continue to rub oil into the skillet, replacing the paper towels as needed, until the skillet looks dark and shiny and does not have any remaining oil residue.

6. Turn off the heat and allow the skillet to cool completely before putting it away.

A well-seasoned skillet should have a smooth, dark black, semiglossy finish.

Why This Recipe Works A cookie in a skillet? Unlike baking a traditional batch of cookies, a skillet cookie can go straight from the oven to the table for a fun, hands-on dessert. This scaled-up cookie benefits from the hot bottom and tall sides of a well-seasoned cast-iron pan to create a great crisp crust. Reeling in the butter and chocolate chips from our usual cookie dough recipe allowed our oversized cookie to bake through in the middle while staying perfectly chewy. We increased the baking time to accommodate the giant size, but otherwise this recipe was simpler and faster than baking regular cookies.

GOOEY BUTTER CAKE BARS

SERVES 10 TO 12

A 2-pound bag of confectioners' sugar will yield enough for both the crust and filling with leftovers for dusting. Do not use a glass or ceramic baking dish here. Scrape down the sides and bottom of the mixer bowl with a rubber spatula as often as needed to make sure all the ingredients are fully combined.

Crust
2½ cups (12½ ounces) all-purpose flour
¾ cup (3 ounces) confectioners' sugar
¾ teaspoon salt
12 tablespoons unsalted butter, melted

Filling
8 ounces cream cheese, softened
8 tablespoons unsalted butter, softened
4 cups (1 pound) confectioners' sugar, plus extra for dusting
2 large eggs plus 2 large yolks
2 tablespoons vanilla extract
¼ teaspoon salt

1. Adjust oven rack to upper-middle position and heat oven to 350 degrees. Make foil sling for 13 by 9-inch baking pan by folding 2 long sheets of aluminum foil; first sheet should be 13 inches wide and second sheet should be 9 inches wide. Lay sheets of foil in pan perpendicular to each other, with extra foil hanging over edges of pan. Push foil into corners and up sides of pan, smoothing foil flush to pan. Spray foil with vegetable oil spray.

2. For the Crust Combine flour, sugar, and salt in bowl. Add melted butter and stir with rubber spatula until evenly moistened. Crumble dough over bottom of prepared pan. Using bottom of dry measuring cup, press dough into even layer. Using fork, poke dough all over, about 20 times. Bake until edges are light golden brown, about 20 minutes. Transfer pan to wire rack and let cool completely, about 30 minutes.

3. For the Filling Combine cream cheese and butter in bowl of stand mixer fitted with paddle. With mixer running on low speed, slowly add sugar and mix until fully combined, about 1 minute,

scraping down sides and bottom of bowl as needed. Increase speed to medium-high and mix until light and fluffy, about 2 minutes.

4. Reduce speed to low; add eggs and yolks, one at a time, and mix until incorporated. Add vanilla and salt and mix until incorporated, about 20 seconds, scraping down sides and bottom of bowl as needed. Increase speed to medium-high and mix until light and fluffy, about 2 minutes (mixture should have consistency of frosting). Spread filling evenly over cooled crust. Tap pan gently on counter to release air bubbles.

5. Bake until top is golden brown, edges have cracked, and center jiggles slightly when pan is gently shaken, about 30 minutes. Transfer pan to wire rack and let cool completely, at least 3 hours.

6. Using foil overhang, lift bars out of pan. Cut into 12 pieces. Dust with extra sugar and serve. (Bars can be stored in airtight container at room temperature for up to 3 days.)

A Crackly Top
The filling cracks around the edges as the bars cool and will crack even more when you cut them—and that's OK. The cracks are a natural result of the baked custard and, once dusted with confectioners' sugar, contribute to these bars' signature appearance.

Why This Recipe Works A riff on a favorite St. Louis cake, gooey butter cake bars feature three layers of goodness: an ultrabuttery crust; a custardy middle layer; and a chewy, meringue-like top. In our version, a sturdy shortbread base offers just enough salt to balance out the bar's sweetness. For our custard filling, we wanted to avoid using a double boiler, and found that swapping some butter for cream cheese prevented the eggs from curdling and yielded a filling with the ideal pudding-like consistency. Poured on top of the cooled crust and baked on the upper oven rack, this filling transformed into a gooey middle layer and a perfectly crackled top.

Why This Recipe Works These delicate butter cookies literally melt in your mouth, thanks to the generous amount of cornstarch in the dough. Unfortunately, the cornstarch leaves behind a chalky residue with each bite. After settling on the maximum amount of cornstarch we could use without detection, we scoured supermarket shelves in search of other low-protein dry ingredients to replace the remainder. We replaced all-purpose flour with cake flour and chose confectioners' sugar over granulated, but we still needed more bulk. The solution? Rice Krispies! The ground cereal added the volume we were looking for without toughening the crumb.

MELTING MOMENTS

MAKES ABOUT 70 COOKIES

If the dough gets too soft to slice, return it to the refrigerator to firm up.

½ cup Rice Krispies cereal
16 tablespoons unsalted butter, cut into 16 pieces and softened
3 tablespoons heavy cream
1 teaspoon vanilla extract
1¼ cups (5 ounces) cake flour
¼ cup (1¼ ounces) cornstarch
⅛ teaspoon salt
⅔ cup (2⅔ ounces) confectioners' sugar

1. Process Rice Krispies in blender until finely ground, about 30 seconds. Combine 4 tablespoons butter and cream in large bowl and microwave until butter is melted, about 30 seconds. Whisk in processed Rice Krispies and vanilla until combined. Let cool slightly, 5 to 7 minutes.

2. Combine flour, cornstarch, and salt in medium bowl; reserve. Whisk sugar into cooled butter mixture until incorporated. Add remaining 12 tablespoons butter, whisking until smooth. Stir in flour mixture until combined.

3. Working with half of dough at a time, dollop dough into 8-inch strip down center of 14 by 12-inch sheet of parchment paper. Fold 1 long side of parchment over dough. Using ruler, press dough into tight 1-inch-wide log. Repeat with remaining dough and another sheet of parchment. Refrigerate dough until firm, about 1 hour. (Dough can be wrapped in plastic wrap and aluminum foil and frozen for up to 1 month.)

4. Adjust oven racks to upper-middle and lower-middle positions and heat oven to 300 degrees. Line 2 baking sheets with parchment. Cut dough into ¼-inch slices and place 1 inch apart on prepared baking sheets. Bake until set but not brown, 18 to 22 minutes, switching and rotating baking sheets halfway through baking. Let cool completely on sheets, about 15 minutes. Repeat with remaining dough. Serve. (Cookies can be stored at room temperature for up to 2 days.)

CRESCENT COOKIES

After step 2, transfer dough to pastry bag fitted with ½-inch star tip. Pipe 1½-inch-long crescents onto prepared baking sheets. Refrigerate dough until firm, about 30 minutes. Bake as directed.

JAM THUMBPRINT COOKIES

After step 2, transfer dough to pastry bag fitted with ½-inch plain tip. Pipe 1-inch-wide and ½-inch-high dough rounds onto prepared baking sheets. Using back of ¼-teaspoon measuring spoon dipped in water, make indentation in center of each round. Refrigerate dough until firm, about 30 minutes. Bake until set, 18 to 20 minutes, switching and rotating sheets halfway through baking. Fill each dimple with ½ teaspoon jam and bake for 5 minutes.

ROUND SPRITZ COOKIES

After step 2, transfer dough to pastry bag fitted with ½-inch star tip. Pipe 1-inch-wide and ½-inch-high dough rounds onto prepared baking sheets. Refrigerate dough until firm, about 30 minutes. Bake as directed.

Handling Soft Dough

The high proportion of butter to flour makes the dough for these cookies very soft and challenging to handle. With this technique, you can easily roll it into a log.

1. Dollop half of dough in strip down center of sheet of parchment.

2. Pulling parchment taut, use ruler to press dough into tight log.

Why This Recipe Works We set out to create a slice-and-bake cookie recipe that would combine both crispness and rich butter and vanilla flavors—in effect, shortbread shaped into a convenient slice-and-bake log. Using both granulated sugar and light brown sugar gave the cookies a richness and complexity that tasters liked. We used the food processor to combine our recipe ingredients quickly without whipping in too much air—our cookies had the fine, shortbread-like texture we were after.

SLICE-AND-BAKE COOKIES

MAKES ABOUT 40 COOKIES

Be sure that the cookie dough is well chilled and firm so that it can be uniformly sliced.

- ⅓ cup (2⅓ ounces) granulated sugar
- 2 tablespoons packed light brown sugar
- ½ teaspoon salt
- 12 tablespoons unsalted butter, cut into pieces and softened
- 2 teaspoons vanilla extract
- 1 large egg yolk
- 1½ cups (7½ ounces) all-purpose flour

1. Process granulated sugar, brown sugar, and salt in food processor until no lumps of brown sugar remain, about 30 seconds. Add butter, vanilla, and yolk and process until smooth and creamy, about 20 seconds. Scrape down sides of bowl, add flour, and pulse until dough forms, about 15 seconds.

2. Turn out dough onto lightly floured counter and roll into 10-inch log. Wrap tightly with plastic wrap and refrigerate until firm, at least 2 hours or up to 3 days. (Dough can be wrapped in foil and frozen for up to 1 month.)

3. Adjust oven racks to upper-middle and lower-middle positions and heat oven to 350 degrees. Line 2 baking sheets with parchment paper. Slice chilled dough into ¼-inch rounds and place 1 inch apart on prepared baking sheets. Bake until edges are just golden, about 15 minutes, switching and rotating baking sheets halfway through baking. Let cool 10 minutes on sheets, then transfer to wire rack and let cool completely. Repeat with remaining dough. (Cookies can be stored at room temperature for up to 1 week.)

COCONUT-LIME COOKIES

In step 1, add 2 cups sweetened shredded coconut and 2 teaspoons grated lime zest to food processor along with sugars and salt.

WALNUT–BROWN SUGAR COOKIES

In step 1, add 2 more tablespoons brown sugar and 1 cup chopped walnuts to food processor along with sugars and salt.

ORANGE–POPPY SEED COOKIES

In step 1, add ¼ cup poppy seeds and 1 tablespoon grated orange zest to food processor along with sugars and salt.

Glaze Me

We love the simplicity of our Slice-and-Bake Cookies, but a confectioners' sugar glaze is an easy way to dress them up. If the glaze is too thick to spread, thin it with 1 tablespoon water. Each glaze makes enough for 1 recipe Slice-and-Bake Cookies.

Ginger-Lime Glaze Whisk 1 tablespoon softened cream cheese, 1 teaspoon ground ginger, and 2 tablespoons lime juice in medium bowl until combined. Whisk in 1½ cups confectioners' sugar until smooth.

Malted Milk Glaze Whisk 1 tablespoon softened cream cheese, 1 tablespoon malted milk powder, 1 teaspoon vanilla extract, and 2 tablespoons milk in medium bowl until combined. Whisk in 1½ cups confectioners' sugar until smooth.

Cappuccino Glaze Whisk 1 tablespoon softened cream cheese, 1 tablespoon instant espresso powder, and 2 tablespoons milk in medium bowl until combined. Whisk in 1½ cups confectioners' sugar until smooth.

Peanut Butter and Jelly Glaze Whisk 1 tablespoon creamy peanut butter, 2 tablespoons strawberry jelly, and 1 tablespoon water in medium bowl until combined. Whisk in 1½ cups confectioners' sugar until smooth.

FAIRY GINGERBREAD

MAKES 60 COOKIES

Use cookie or baking sheets that measure at least 15 by 12 inches. Don't be disconcerted by the scant amount of batter: You really are going to spread it very thin. Use the edges of the parchment paper as your guide, covering the entire surface thinly and evenly. For easier grating, freeze a 2-inch piece of peeled ginger for 30 minutes, then use a rasp-style grater.

1½ teaspoons ground ginger
¾ cup plus 2 tablespoons (4⅜ ounces) all-purpose flour
½ teaspoon baking soda
¼ teaspoon salt
5 tablespoons unsalted butter, softened
9 tablespoons (4 ounces) packed light brown sugar
4 teaspoons grated fresh ginger
¾ teaspoon vanilla extract
¼ cup whole milk, room temperature

1. Adjust oven racks to upper-middle and lower-middle positions and heat oven to 325 degrees. Spray 2 rimless baking sheets (or inverted rimmed baking sheets) with vegetable oil spray and cover each with 15 by 12-inch sheet parchment paper. Heat ground ginger in small skillet over medium heat until fragrant, about 1 minute. Combine flour, toasted ginger, baking soda, and salt in medium bowl.

2. Using stand mixer fitted with paddle, beat butter and sugar on medium-high speed until light and fluffy, about 2 minutes. Add fresh ginger and vanilla and mix until incorporated. Reduce speed to low and add flour mixture in 3 additions, alternating with milk in 2 additions; scrape down bowl as needed.

3. Evenly spread ¾ cup batter to cover parchment on each prepared sheet (batter will be very thin). Bake until deep golden brown, 16 to 20 minutes, switching and rotating baking sheets halfway through baking. Immediately score cookies into 3 by 2-inch rectangles. Let cool completely, about 20 minutes. Using tip of paring knife, separate cookies along score marks. (Cookies can be stored at room temperature for 3 days.)

Making Fairy Gingerbread

While making several dozen batches of Fairy Gingerbread, we had time to perfect our technique. The cookies are made with an unusual method we'd never encountered before. Here's how.

1. To form cookies of requisite thinness, use small offset spatula to spread batter to edges of 15 by 12-inch sheet of parchment paper.

2. Immediately after removing cookies from oven, use chef's knife or pizza wheel to score 3 by 2-inch rectangles. Work quickly to prevent breaking.

3. Once cookies are cool, trace over scored lines with paring knife and gently break cookies apart along lines.

Why This Recipe Works Original recipes for fairy gingerbread, a cookie popular in the 19th century, melted in our mouths but were also severely lacking in flavor. A bit of vanilla extract and salt helped boost the flavor. Doubling the ginger added a much-needed kick, but without any competing flavors it was overwhelming. We cut back a little and toasted the ground ginger to bring out its natural flavor. Grating fresh ginger straight into the batter added even more intense ginger flavor. Switching from bread flour to all-purpose flour made the batter slightly easier to spread. A little baking soda helped retain the cookies' airy crispness.

JOE FROGGERS

MAKES 24 COOKIES

Place only six cookies on each baking sheet—they will spread. If you don't own a 3½-inch cookie cutter, use a drinking glass. Use mild (not robust or blackstrap) molasses. Make sure to chill the dough for a full 8 hours or it will be too hard to roll out.

- ⅓ cup dark rum (such as Myers's)
- 1 tablespoon water
- 1½ teaspoons salt
- 3 cups (15 ounces) all-purpose flour
- ¾ teaspoon ground ginger
- ½ teaspoon ground allspice
- ¼ teaspoon ground nutmeg
- ⅛ teaspoon ground cloves
- 1 cup molasses
- 1 teaspoon baking soda
- 8 tablespoons unsalted butter, softened but still cool
- 1 cup (7 ounces) sugar

1. Stir rum, water, and salt in small bowl until salt dissolves. Whisk flour, ginger, allspice, nutmeg, and cloves in medium bowl. Stir molasses and baking soda in liquid measuring cup (mixture will begin to bubble) and let sit until doubled in volume, about 15 minutes.

2. Using stand mixer fitted with paddle, beat butter and sugar on medium-high speed until fluffy, about 2 minutes. Reduce speed to medium-low and gradually beat in rum mixture. Add flour mixture in 3 additions, beating on medium-low until just incorporated, alternating with molasses mixture in 2 additions, scraping down sides of bowl as needed. Give dough final stir by hand (dough will be extremely sticky). Cover bowl with plastic wrap and refrigerate until stiff, at least 8 hours or up to 3 days.

3. Adjust oven racks to upper-middle and lower-middle positions and heat oven to 375 degrees. Line 2 baking sheets with parchment paper. Working with half of dough at a time on heavily floured counter, roll out to ¼-inch thickness. Using 3½-inch cookie cutter, cut out 12 cookies. Transfer 6 cookies to each baking sheet, spacing cookies about 1½ inches apart. Bake until cookies are set and just beginning to crack, about 8 minutes, switching and rotating baking sheets halfway through baking time. Let cookies cool on sheets on wire rack 10 minutes, then transfer cookies to rack to cool completely. Repeat with remaining dough. (Cookies may be stored for up to 1 week.)

Salty History

Joe froggers date back more than 200 years to Black Joe's Tavern, located in Marblehead, Massachusetts, a seaside town north of Boston. A freed slave and Revolutionary War veteran, Joseph Brown, and his wife, Lucretia, opened the tavern in a part of Marblehead called Gingerbread Hill. Besides serving drinks (mostly rum), Joe and Lucretia baked cookies: large, moist molasses and rum cookies made salty by the addition of Marblehead seawater. These cookies were popular sustenance on long fishing voyages, as they had no dairy to spoil and the combination of rum, molasses, and seawater kept them chewy for weeks.

According to Samuel Roads Jr.'s *History and Traditions of Marblehead*, published in 1879, the funny name for these cookies referred to the lily pads (similar in size and shape to the cookies) and large croaking frogs that would fill the pond behind Joe's tavern. Thus the cookies became known as Joe froggers.

Why This Recipe Works Joe froggers, from a recipe that dates back more than 200 years, are incredibly moist, spicy, slightly salty cookies, found in bakeries along the North Shore of Massachusetts. We wanted to develop our own recipe. Dissolving salt into our recipe's rum and water gave the cookie its distinctive salty flavor while ginger, allspice, nutmeg, and cloves contributed warm spice flavor. Many recipes we found in our research called for lard, but we found that using butter made for a more flavorful cookie.

Why This Recipe Works These chocolate-vanilla, cakey cookies are a deli favorite in New York, but often they do not live up to the hype. To get the "cookie" just right, we made several small but high-impact adjustments. We dialed back the amount of baking soda and baking powder to get rid of unwanted air bubbles, added more vanilla extract to heighten the flavor, and used just enough sour cream to make the cookies tender but not sticky. Corn syrup made the glaze thick and shiny, while milk made it creamy and spreadable. Cocoa powder kept the chocolate glaze flavorful and simple.

BLACK AND WHITE COOKIES

MAKES 12 COOKIES

Twelve cookies doesn't sound like much, but these cookies are huge. You'll get neater cookies if you spread on the vanilla glaze first. This recipe provides a little extra glaze, just in case.

Cookies

1¾ cups (8¾ ounces) all-purpose flour
 ½ teaspoon baking powder
 ¼ teaspoon baking soda
 ⅛ teaspoon salt
10 tablespoons unsalted butter, softened
 1 cup (7 ounces) granulated sugar
 1 large egg
 2 teaspoons vanilla extract
 ⅓ cup sour cream

Glaze

 5 cups (20 ounces) confectioners' sugar, sifted
 7 tablespoons whole milk
 2 tablespoons corn syrup
 1 teaspoon vanilla extract
 ½ teaspoon salt
 3 tablespoons Dutch-processed cocoa powder, sifted

1. For the Cookies Adjust oven racks to upper-middle and lower-middle positions and heat oven to 350 degrees. Line 2 baking sheets with parchment paper. Combine flour, baking powder, baking soda, and salt in bowl.

2. Using stand mixer fitted with paddle, beat butter and sugar on medium-high speed until pale and fluffy, about 2 minutes. Add egg and vanilla and beat until combined. Reduce speed to low and add flour mixture in 3 additions, alternating with 2 additions of sour cream, scraping down bowl as needed. Give dough final stir by hand.

3. Using greased ¼-cup measure, drop cookie dough 3 inches apart onto prepared baking sheets. Bake until edges are lightly browned, 15 to 18 minutes, switching and rotating sheets halfway through baking. Let cookies cool on sheets for 5 minutes, then transfer to wire rack to cool completely, about 1 hour.

4. For the Glaze Whisk sugar, 6 tablespoons milk, corn syrup, vanilla, and salt together in bowl until smooth. Transfer 1 cup glaze to small bowl; reserve. Whisk cocoa and remaining 1 tablespoon milk into remaining glaze until combined.

5. Working with 1 cookie at a time, spread 1 tablespoon vanilla glaze over half of underside of cookie. Refrigerate until glaze is set, about 15 minutes. Cover other half of cookies with 1 tablespoon chocolate glaze and let cookies sit at room temperature until glaze is firm, at least 1 hour. Serve. (Cookies can be stored at room temperature for up to 2 days.)

Glazing Black and White Cookies

1. Using butter knife or offset mini spatula, glaze half of underside of each cookie with vanilla glaze. Chill cookies in refrigerator for 15 minutes so glaze can start to harden.

2. Glaze other half of each cookie with chocolate glaze, and let cookies sit until glaze sets, about 1 hour.

WHOOPIE PIES

MAKES 6 PIES

Don't be tempted to bake all the cakes on one baking sheet; the batter needs room to spread in the oven.

Cakes

- 2 cups (10 ounces) all-purpose flour
- ½ cup (1½ ounces) Dutch-processed cocoa powder
- 1 teaspoon baking soda
- ½ teaspoon salt
- 8 tablespoons unsalted butter, softened but still cool
- 1 cup packed (7 ounces) light brown sugar
- 1 large egg, room temperature
- 1 teaspoon vanilla extract
- 1 cup buttermilk

Filling

- 12 tablespoons unsalted butter, softened but still cool
- 1¼ cups (5 ounces) confectioners' sugar
- 1½ teaspoons vanilla extract
- ⅛ teaspoon salt
- 2½ cups marshmallow crème

1. For the Cakes Adjust oven racks to upper-middle and lower-middle positions and heat oven to 350 degrees. Line 2 baking sheets with parchment paper. Whisk flour, cocoa, baking soda, and salt in medium bowl.

2. Using stand mixer fitted with paddle, beat butter and sugar on medium-high speed until fluffy, about 4 minutes. Beat in egg until incorporated, scraping down sides of bowl as necessary, then beat in vanilla. Reduce speed to low and beat in flour mixture in 3 additions, alternating with buttermilk in 2 additions. Give batter final stir by hand.

3. Using ⅓-cup measure, scoop 6 mounds of batter onto each baking sheet, spacing mounds about 3 inches apart. Bake until cakes spring back when pressed, 15 to 18 minutes, switching and rotating baking sheets halfway through baking. Let cool completely on baking sheets, at least 1 hour.

4. For the Filling Using stand mixer fitted with paddle, beat butter and sugar on medium speed until fluffy, about 2 minutes. Beat in vanilla and salt.

Beat in marshmallow crème until incorporated, about 2 minutes. Refrigerate filling until slightly firm, about 30 minutes. (Bowl can be wrapped and refrigerated for up to 2 days.)

5. Dollop ⅓ cup filling on center of flat side of 6 cakes. Top with flat side of remaining 6 cakes and gently press until filling spreads to edges of cakes. Serve. (Whoopie pies can be refrigerated for up to 3 days.)

What's Up, Whoopie Pie?

Where did whoopie pies originate? Both Maine and Pennsylvania—the Pennsylvania Dutch of Lancaster County, to be specific—claim whoopie pies as their own. Maine's earliest claim dates back to 1925, when Labadie's Bakery in Lewiston first sold whoopie pies to the public. Some research showed that the Berwick Cake Company began manufacturing Whoopie! Pies (the exclamation point was part of the name) in 1927. These sources claim that whoopie pies were named after the musical *Whoopie*; *Whoopie* had its debut in Boston in 1927. In addition, Marshmallow Fluff, a key ingredient in many whoopie pie recipes, had been invented in nearby Lynn seven years earlier.

What about Pennsylvania's claim on whoopie pies? We found an article in a copy of the *Gettysburg Times* from 1982 that spoke of a chocolate cake sandwich with a fluffy cream center. These sandwiches were called gobs and were sold by the Dutch Maid Bakery of Geistown. While the name was different, the description (and a huge picture) showed that these were no doubt whoopie pies. The Dutch Maid Bakery purchased the rights to the gob in 1980 from the Harris and Boyer Baking Company, also of Pennsylvania, which had started manufacturing gobs in 1927. Maine might have a few years on Pennsylvania when it comes to whoopie pies, but who's to know for sure?

Why This Recipe Works We wanted a light, airy cake for our whoopie pies, so we used the creaming mixing method—blending the butter and sugar with a mixer until fluffy and nearly white in color. We also used lots of Dutch-processed cocoa powder and vanilla in our recipe for full flavor and a deep, dark-colored crumb. And for a cleaner, fuller flavor, we replaced the shortening (or lard) found in most recipes with butter.

Why This Recipe Works Chocolate truffles are often reserved for special occasions because they can be laborious to make. We wanted a streamlined, foolproof recipe, making the process as simple as possible. We utilized the microwave to melt the chocolate and cream ganache base, stirred the mixture with a rubber spatula (a whisk incorporates too much air), and chilled it. Rolling truffles can get messy, so we wore disposable gloves for easy cleanup. A dusting of cocoa powder and confectioners' sugar keeps the truffles from sticking together during chilling and storing.

BASIC CHOCOLATE TRUFFLES

MAKES 24 TRUFFLES

Wear latex gloves when forming the truffles to keep your hands clean.

- ¼ cup (¾ ounce) unsweetened cocoa powder
- 1 tablespoon confectioners' sugar
- 8 ounces bittersweet chocolate, chopped fine
- ½ cup heavy cream
  Pinch salt

1. Sift cocoa and sugar through fine-mesh strainer into pie plate. Microwave chocolate, cream, and salt in bowl at 50 percent power, stirring occasionally with rubber spatula, until melted, about 1 minute. Stir truffle mixture until fully combined; transfer to 8-inch square baking dish and refrigerate until set, about 45 minutes.

2. Using heaping teaspoon measure, scoop truffle mixture into 24 portions, transfer to large plate, and refrigerate until firm, about 30 minutes. Roll each truffle between your hands to form uniform balls (balls needn't be perfect).

3. Transfer truffles to cocoa mixture and roll to evenly coat. (Coated truffles can be refrigerated along with excess cocoa mixture for up to 1 week.) Lightly shake truffles in your hand over pie plate to remove excess coating; transfer to platter. Refrigerate for 30 minutes. Let sit at room temperature for 10 minutes before serving.

CHOCOLATE-ALMOND TRUFFLES

Substitute 1 cup sliced almonds, toasted and chopped fine, for cocoa mixture coating. Add ½ teaspoon almond extract to chocolate mixture before microwaving in step 2.

CHOCOLATE-CINNAMON TRUFFLES

Sift ¼ teaspoon ground cinnamon with cocoa powder and sugar for coating. Add 1 teaspoon ground cinnamon and ⅛ teaspoon cayenne pepper to chocolate mixture before microwaving.

CHOCOLATE-GINGER TRUFFLES

Add 2 teaspoons ground ginger to chocolate mixture before microwaving.

CHOCOLATE-LEMON TRUFFLES

Add 1 teaspoon grated lemon zest to chocolate mixture before microwaving.

No-Stick Solution

The best way to store chocolate truffles is in the cocoa mixture you dredged them in. This keeps the chocolates from sticking and avoids the need to use more cocoa to touch them up.

old-fashioned fruit desserts and puddings

Why This Recipe Works Apple dumplings are a homespun combination of warm pastry, concentrated apple flavor, raisins, butter, and cinnamon, but too often the apples turn too soft or are unevenly baked. The pastry can also turn gummy from the apples' juices. We found that biscuit dough was easier to work with than pie dough and did a great job of absorbing the liquid from the apples without getting mushy. Rather than baking the dumplings in syrup as some recipes instruct, we served our sauce on the side, which preserved the dumplings' texture.

BAKED APPLE DUMPLINGS

MAKES 8 DUMPLINGS

Use a melon baller or a metal teaspoon measure to core the apples. Serve warm, with Cider Sauce (recipe follows).

Dough

2½ cups (12½ ounces) all-purpose flour
3 tablespoons sugar
2 teaspoons baking powder
¾ teaspoon salt
10 tablespoons unsalted butter, cut into ½-inch pieces and chilled
5 tablespoons vegetable shortening, cut into ½-inch pieces and chilled
¾ cup cold buttermilk

Apple Dumplings

6 tablespoons (2⅔ ounces) sugar
1 teaspoon ground cinnamon
3 tablespoons unsalted butter, softened
3 tablespoons golden raisins, chopped
4 Golden Delicious apples
2 egg whites, lightly beaten

1. For the Dough Process flour, sugar, baking powder, and salt in food processor until combined, about 15 seconds. Scatter butter and shortening over flour mixture and pulse until mixture resembles wet sand, about 10 pulses; transfer to bowl. Stir in buttermilk until dough forms. Turn out onto lightly floured work surface and knead briefly until dough is cohesive. Press dough into 8 by 4-inch rectangle. Cut in half, wrap each half tightly in plastic wrap, and refrigerate until firm, about 1 hour.

2. For the Apple Dumplings Adjust oven rack to middle position and heat oven to 425 degrees. Combine sugar and cinnamon in small bowl. In second bowl, combine butter, raisins, and 3 tablespoons cinnamon sugar mixture. Peel apples and halve through equator. Remove core and pack butter mixture into each apple half.

3. On lightly floured counter, roll each dough half into 12-inch square. Cut each 12-inch square into four 6-inch squares. Working with one at a time, lightly brush edges of dough square with egg white and place apple, cut side up, in center of each square. Gather dough 1 corner at a time on top of apple, crimping edges to seal. Using paring knife, cut vent hole in top of each dumpling.

4. Line rimmed baking sheet with parchment paper. Arrange dumplings on prepared baking sheet, brush tops with egg white, and sprinkle with remaining cinnamon sugar. Bake until dough is golden brown and juices are bubbling, 20 to 25 minutes. Let cool on baking sheet for 10 minutes. Serve.

CIDER SAUCE
MAKES ABOUT 1½ CUPS

1 cup apple cider
1 cup water
1 cup (7 ounces) sugar
½ teaspoon ground cinnamon
2 tablespoons unsalted butter
1 tablespoon lemon juice

Bring cider, water, sugar, and cinnamon to simmer in small saucepan and cook over medium-high heat until thickened and reduced to 1½ cups, about 15 minutes. Off heat, whisk in butter and lemon juice. Drizzle over dumplings to serve.

Wrapping Dumplings

1. Fold corners of dough up to enclose apple halves, overlapping and crimping to seal.

2. Arrange dumplings on baking sheet, brush with egg white, and sprinkle with cinnamon sugar.

Why This Recipe Works Apple fritters should be crisp on the outside, moist within, and sing out apple flavor. Too often, recipes for fritters produce leaden, soggy pastries with undercooked interiors. We found that the best solution was to dry the apples with paper towels and mix them with the dry ingredients. The dry ingredients absorbed the moisture that would otherwise have leached out during frying. As for the batter, we found that replacing the milk with apple cider reinforced the sweet apple flavor. And a quick glaze, spiked with more cider and warm spices and spooned over the warm fritters, added another layer of apple flavor.

APPLE FRITTERS

MAKES 10 FRITTERS

We like Granny Smith apples in these fritters because they are tart and crisp. Apple juice doesn't have enough flavor—you really do need the cider.

Fritters

2 Granny Smith apples, peeled, cored, and cut into ¼-inch pieces
2 cups (10 ounces) all-purpose flour
⅓ cup (2⅓ ounces) granulated sugar
1 tablespoon baking powder
1 teaspoon salt
1 teaspoon ground cinnamon
¼ teaspoon ground nutmeg
¾ cup apple cider
2 large eggs, lightly beaten
2 tablespoons unsalted butter, melted
3 cups peanut or vegetable oil

Glaze

2 cups (8 ounces) confectioners' sugar
¼ cup apple cider
½ teaspoon ground cinnamon
¼ teaspoon ground nutmeg

1. For the Fritters Spread prepared apples in single layer on paper towel–lined baking sheet and pat thoroughly dry with paper towels. Combine flour, sugar, baking powder, salt, cinnamon, and nutmeg in large bowl. Whisk cider, eggs, and melted butter in medium bowl until combined. Stir apples into flour mixture. Stir in cider mixture until incorporated.

2. Set wire rack in rimmed baking sheet. Heat oil in Dutch oven over medium-high heat to 350 degrees. Use ⅓-cup measure to transfer 5 heaping portions of batter to oil. Press batter lightly with back of spoon to flatten. Fry, adjusting burner as necessary to maintain oil temperature between 325 and 350 degrees, until deep golden brown, 2 to 3 minutes per side. Transfer fritters to prepared wire rack. Bring oil back to 350 degrees and repeat with remaining batter. Let fritters cool for 5 minutes.

3. For the Glaze While fritters cool, whisk sugar, cider, cinnamon, and nutmeg in medium bowl until smooth. Top each fritter with 1 heaping tablespoon glaze. Let glaze set for 10 minutes. Serve.

Forming Fritters

1. Use ⅓-cup measure and spoon to carefully and gently portion batter into hot oil.

2. Use spoon to gently press on each fritter. Flattened shape helps interior cook through.

APPLE PANDOWDY

SERVES 6

Disturbing the crust, or "dowdying," allows juices from the filling to rise over the crust and caramelize as the dessert continues to bake. Removing the skillet from the oven allows you to properly press down on the crust. Do not use store-bought pie crust in this recipe; it yields gummy results.

Pie Dough

- 3 tablespoons ice water
- 1 tablespoon sour cream
- ⅔ cup (3⅓ ounces) all-purpose flour
- 1 teaspoon granulated sugar
- ½ teaspoon salt
- 6 tablespoons unsalted butter, cut into ¼-inch pieces and frozen for 15 minutes

Filling

- 2½ pounds Golden Delicious apples, peeled, cored, halved, and cut into ½-inch-thick wedges
- ¼ cup packed (1¾ ounces) light brown sugar
- ½ teaspoon ground cinnamon
- ¼ teaspoon salt
- 3 tablespoons unsalted butter
- ¾ cup apple cider
- 1 tablespoon cornstarch
- 2 teaspoons lemon juice

Topping

- 1 tablespoon granulated sugar
- ¼ teaspoon ground cinnamon
- 1 large egg, lightly beaten

Vanilla ice cream

1. For the Pie Dough Combine ice water and sour cream in bowl. Process flour, sugar, and salt in food processor until combined, about 3 seconds. Add butter and pulse until size of large peas, 6 to 8 pulses. Add sour cream mixture and pulse until dough forms large clumps and no dry flour remains, 3 to 6 pulses, scraping down sides of bowl as needed.

2. Form dough into 4-inch disk, wrap tightly in plastic wrap, and refrigerate for 1 hour. (Wrapped dough can be refrigerated for up to 2 days or frozen for up to 1 month. If frozen, let dough thaw completely on counter before rolling.)

3. Adjust oven rack to middle position and heat oven to 400 degrees. Let chilled dough sit on counter to soften slightly, about 5 minutes, before rolling. Roll dough into 10-inch circle on lightly floured counter. Using pizza cutter, cut dough into four 2½-inch-wide strips, then make four 2½-inch-wide perpendicular cuts to form squares. (Pieces around edges of dough will be smaller.) Transfer dough pieces to parchment paper–lined baking sheet, cover with plastic, and refrigerate until firm, at least 30 minutes.

4. For the Filling Toss apples, sugar, cinnamon, and salt together in large bowl. Melt butter in 10-inch skillet over medium heat. Add apple mixture, cover, and cook until apples become slightly pliable and release their juices, about 10 minutes, stirring occasionally.

5. Whisk cider, cornstarch, and lemon juice in bowl until no lumps remain; add to skillet. Bring to simmer and cook, uncovered, stirring occasionally, until sauce is thickened, about 2 minutes. Off heat, press lightly on apples to form even layer.

6. For the Topping Combine sugar and cinnamon in small bowl. Working quickly, shingle dough pieces over filling until mostly covered, overlapping as needed. Brush dough pieces with egg and sprinkle with cinnamon sugar.

7. Bake until crust is slightly puffed and beginning to brown, about 15 minutes. Remove skillet from oven. Using back of large spoon, press down in center of crust until juices come up over top of crust. Repeat four more times around skillet. Make sure all apples are submerged and return skillet to oven. Continue to bake until crust is golden brown, about 15 minutes longer.

8. Transfer skillet to wire rack and let cool for at least 20 minutes. Serve with ice cream, drizzling extra sauce over top.

Why This Recipe Works Unlike traditional skillet pie, apple pandowdy's crust is gently pressed into the filling (or "dowdied") during baking so the juices flood the top and caramelize in the oven. We tossed wedges of buttery Golden Delicious apples in cinnamon and brown sugar for sweet-spiced flavor and partially cooked them before simmering in an apple cider–lemon juice slurry to thicken the filling. Topping the apples with squares of dough allowed steam to escape during baking, preventing the apples from overcooking. Dowdying the crust partway through created the dessert's sweet finish.

CRANBERRY-APPLE CRISP

SERVES 8 TO 10

If you can't find Braeburn apples, Golden Delicious will work. Serve with vanilla ice cream or whipped cream.

Topping

¾ cup (3¾ ounces) all-purpose flour
½ cup packed (3½ ounces) light brown sugar
½ cup (3½ ounces) granulated sugar
1 teaspoon ground cinnamon
12 tablespoons unsalted butter, cut into ½-inch pieces and chilled
¾ cup (2¼ ounces) old-fashioned rolled oats

Filling

1 pound (4 cups) fresh or frozen cranberries
1¼ cups (8¾ ounces) granulated sugar
¼ cup water
2½ pounds Granny Smith apples, peeled, cored, halved, and cut into ½-inch pieces
2½ pounds Braeburn apples, peeled, cored, halved, and cut into ½-inch pieces
1 cup dried sweetened cranberries
3 tablespoons instant tapioca

1. For the Topping Adjust oven rack to middle position and heat oven to 400 degrees. Pulse flour, brown sugar, granulated sugar, cinnamon, and butter in food processor until mixture has texture of coarse crumbs (some pea-size pieces of butter will remain), about 12 pulses. Transfer to medium bowl, stir in oats, and use fingers to pinch topping into peanut-size clumps. Refrigerate while preparing filling.

2. For the Filling Bring fresh cranberries, ¾ cup sugar, and water to simmer in Dutch oven over medium-high heat and cook until cranberries are completely softened and mixture is jamlike, about 10 minutes. Scrape mixture into bowl. Add apples, remaining ½ cup sugar, and dried cranberries to now-empty Dutch oven and cook over medium-high heat until apples begin to release their juices, about 5 minutes.

3. Off heat, stir cranberry mixture and tapioca into apple mixture. Pour into 13 by 9-inch baking dish set in rimmed baking sheet and smooth surface evenly with spatula.

4. Mound topping over filling in center of dish, then use your fingers to rake topping out toward edges of dish and bake until juices are bubbling and topping is deep golden brown, about 30 minutes. (If topping is browning too quickly, loosely cover with piece of aluminum foil.) Let cool on wire rack for 10 minutes. Serve.

To Make Ahead After pinching topping into small clumps in step 1, transfer mixture to zipper-lock bag and refrigerate for up to 5 days or freeze for up to 1 month. The cooked filling can be refrigerated for up to 2 days. To bake, sprinkle chilled topping evenly over chilled filling, loosely cover with foil, and bake for 20 minutes. Uncover and bake until juices are bubbling and topping is deep golden brown, 15 to 20 minutes longer.

Crisp Essentials

1. Cook cranberries, sugar, and water until mixture is thick and jammy.

2. Mound topping in center of dish, then use your fingers to rake topping out toward edges of dish.

Why This Recipe Works Although it's hard to imagine that apple crisp needs much improving upon, we liked the tartness and texture that cranberries added to one of our favorite standard dessert recipes. Raw cranberries proved too bitter, but we found dried cranberries and cooked fresh berries made cranberry-apple crisp with the best taste and texture. And we used tapioca to thicken the fruit juices instead of cornstarch or flour.

Why This Recipe Works A buckle, cousin to crumble and crisp, is a classic New England dessert that consists of a thick cake batter mixed with chopped fruit or berries and baked under a crunchy streusel topping. Using peak-season berries allowed us to make the most of their sweet-tart flavor and tossing the berries with sugar helped bring out their natural sweetness while a bit of lemon zest added punch. We packed as many berries as we could into our dead-simple batter and then sprinkled the rest of the berries on top. When baked, the dense, buttery cake suspended the berries, creating a luscious, summery dessert.

MIXED BERRY BUCKLE

SERVES 8

We prefer the flavor of fresh mixed berries, but you can also use a single variety of berries as long as the total amount equals 15 ounces (3 cups). If using all fresh blueberries, omit the ¼ cup sugar for tossing the berries in step 4; blueberries are sweet on their own. You can also use 15 ounces (3 cups) of frozen mixed berries that have been thawed, drained for 30 minutes in a colander, and then patted dry.

Streusel
- 1 cup (5 ounces) all-purpose flour
- ½ cup packed (3½ ounces) light brown sugar
- 6 tablespoons unsalted butter, melted
- ½ teaspoon table salt

Cake
- ½ cup whole milk
- 2 large eggs
- 4 tablespoons unsalted butter, melted
- 1 teaspoon vanilla extract
- 1 cup (5 ounces) all-purpose flour
- ½ cup (3½ ounces) granulated sugar, divided
- 1½ teaspoons baking powder
- 1 teaspoon grated lemon zest
- ½ teaspoon table salt
- 5 ounces (1 cup) blackberries, cut in half crosswise
- 5 ounces (1 cup) blueberries
- 5 ounces (1 cup) raspberries, cut in half crosswise

1. For the Streusel Stir all ingredients in bowl until no dry spots remain and mixture forms clumps. Refrigerate until streusel is firm, at least 10 minutes. Keep refrigerated until ready to use.

2. For the Cake Adjust oven rack to middle position and heat oven to 350 degrees. Grease light-colored 9-inch round cake pan, line with parchment paper, grease parchment, and flour pan.

3. Whisk milk, eggs, melted butter, and vanilla in bowl until well combined. Whisk flour, ¼ cup sugar, baking powder, lemon zest, and salt together in large bowl. Stir milk mixture into flour mixture until just combined.

4. Toss blackberries, blueberries, and raspberries with remaining ¼ cup sugar in separate bowl until coated. Using rubber spatula, gently fold half of

berry mixture into batter until evenly distributed. Transfer batter to prepared pan and spread to edges of pan with spatula. Sprinkle remaining half of berry mixture evenly over top.

5. Break streusel into pea-size crumbs and distribute evenly over berries. Bake until top of buckle is golden brown and toothpick inserted in center comes out clean, about 50 minutes, rotating pan halfway through baking. Let buckle cool in pan on wire rack for 2 hours.

6. Run paring knife around edges of pan to release buckle from pan. Place inverted plate on top of pan (do not use plate or platter on which you intend to serve buckle). Invert buckle, remove pan, and discard parchment. Reinvert buckle onto serving platter. Cut into wedges and serve.

Berry Important Stuff
How you treat the berries can make or break your buckle.

1. Cut blackberries and raspberries in half crosswise. Toss with blueberries and sugar.

2. Fold half of sugared berries into batter.

3. Sprinkle remaining berries on top of batter before baking.

Why This Recipe Works This 19th-century fruit dessert boasts sweetened stewed berries covered with drop biscuit dough that is covered to steam and cook through. We found the idea of a simple stovetop fruit dessert appealing, but standard recipes produced washed-out fruit and a soggy topping. To improve the recipe, we cooked down half of the berries until jammy, and then stirred in the remaining berries. A bit of cornstarch further thickened the filling. For a fluffy biscuit topping, we placed a dish towel under the lid during cooking to absorb condensation. A sprinkle of cinnamon sugar over the finished dessert provided sweet crunch.

MAINE BLUEBERRY GRUNT

SERVES 12

Do not use frozen blueberries here, as they will make the filling watery. You will need a clean dish towel for this recipe.

Filling

- 2½ pounds (8 cups) blueberries
- ½ cup (3½ ounces) sugar
- ½ teaspoon ground cinnamon
- 2 tablespoons water
- 1 teaspoon grated lemon zest plus 1 tablespoon juice
- 1 teaspoon cornstarch

Topping

- ¾ cup buttermilk
- 6 tablespoons unsalted butter, melted and cooled slightly
- 1 teaspoon vanilla extract
- 2¼ cups (11¼ ounces) all-purpose flour
- 1½ teaspoons baking powder
- ½ teaspoon baking soda
- ½ teaspoon salt
- ½ cup (3½ ounces) sugar
- ½ teaspoon ground cinnamon

1. For the Filling Cook 4 cups blueberries, sugar, cinnamon, water, and lemon zest in Dutch oven over medium-high heat, stirring occasionally, until mixture is thick and jamlike, 10 to 12 minutes. Whisk lemon juice and cornstarch in small bowl, then stir into blueberry mixture. Add remaining 4 cups blueberries and cook until heated through, about 1 minute; remove pot from heat, cover, and keep warm.

2. For the Topping Combine buttermilk, butter, and vanilla in 2-cup liquid measuring cup. Whisk flour, baking powder, baking soda, salt, and 6 tablespoons sugar in large bowl. Slowly stir buttermilk mixture into flour mixture until dough forms.

3. Using small ice cream scoop or 2 large spoons, spoon golf ball–size dough pieces on top of warm berry mixture (you should have 14 pieces). Wrap lid of Dutch oven with clean dish towel (keeping towel away from heat source) and cover pot. Simmer gently until biscuits have doubled in size and toothpick inserted in center comes out clean, 16 to 22 minutes.

4. Combine remaining 2 tablespoons sugar and cinnamon in small bowl. Remove lid and sprinkle biscuit topping with cinnamon sugar. Serve immediately.

Secrets to Great Grunt

1. Use small ice cream scoop to drop evenly sized balls of biscuit dough over warm filling.

2. A clean dish towel beneath lid absorbs condensation during cooking, keeping biscuit topping light and fluffy.

3. A sprinkling of cinnamon sugar adds crunchy contrast to steamed biscuits.

SKILLET PEACH COBBLER

SERVES 6 TO 8

You can substitute 4 pounds of frozen sliced peaches for fresh; there is no need to defrost them. Start step 2 when the peaches are almost done.

Filling

- 4 tablespoons unsalted butter
- 5 pounds peaches, peeled, halved, pitted, and cut into ½-inch wedges
- 6 tablespoons (2⅔ ounces) sugar
- ⅛ teaspoon salt
- 1 tablespoon lemon juice
- 1½ teaspoons cornstarch

Topping

- 1½ cups (7½ ounces) all-purpose flour
- 6 tablespoons (2⅔ ounces) sugar
- 1½ teaspoons baking powder
- ¼ teaspoon baking soda
- ¼ teaspoon salt
- ¾ cup buttermilk
- 4 tablespoons unsalted butter, melted and cooled
- 1 teaspoon ground cinnamon

1. For the Filling Adjust oven rack to middle position and heat oven to 425 degrees. Melt butter in 12-inch ovensafe nonstick skillet over medium-high heat. Add two-thirds of peaches, sugar, and salt and cook, covered, until peaches release their juices, about 5 minutes. Remove lid and simmer until all liquid has evaporated and peaches begin to caramelize, 15 to 20 minutes. Add remaining peaches and cook until heated through, about 5 minutes. Whisk lemon juice and cornstarch in small bowl, then stir into peach mixture. Cover skillet and set aside off heat.

2. For the Topping Meanwhile, whisk flour, 5 tablespoons sugar, baking powder, baking soda, and salt in medium bowl. Stir in buttermilk and butter until dough forms. Turn dough out onto lightly floured work surface and knead briefly until smooth, about 30 seconds.

3. Combine remaining 1 tablespoon sugar and cinnamon. Break dough into rough 1-inch pieces and space them about ½ inch apart on top of hot peach mixture. Sprinkle with cinnamon sugar and bake until topping is golden brown and filling is thickened, 18 to 22 minutes. Let cool on wire rack for 10 minutes. Serve.

Peeling Peaches

1. With paring knife, score small X at base of each peach.

2. Lower peaches into boiling water and simmer until skins loosen, 30 to 60 seconds.

3. Transfer peaches immediately to ice water and let cool for about 1 minute.

4. Use paring knife to remove strips of loosened peel, starting at X on base of each peach.

Why This Recipe Works We wanted a peach cobbler that avoided a watery filling and soggy topping. To do this, we turned to a skillet and concentrated the peach flavor by first sautéing the peaches in butter and sugar to release their juices, then cooking them down until all the liquid had evaporated. To keep the filling from being too mushy, we withheld some of the peaches from sautéing, adding them just before baking. We also made the biscuits sturdy enough to stand up to the fruit by mixing melted butter rather than cold butter into the dry ingredients.

DAKOTA PEACH KUCHEN

MAKES TWO 9-INCH KUCHENS

The dough will need 2 hours to rise plus 1 hour to chill in the refrigerator. We developed this recipe using dark cake pans; if your pans are light, increase the baking time in step 7 to 55 to 60 minutes.

Crust
- ½ cup whole milk
- 2 large eggs
- 2½ cups (12½ ounces) all-purpose flour
- 1 tablespoon sugar
- 2 teaspoons instant or rapid-rise yeast
- ½ teaspoon salt
- 8 tablespoons unsalted butter, cut into 8 pieces and softened

Fruit and Custard
- 1 pound fresh peaches, peeled, halved, pitted, and cut into ½-inch wedges or 12 ounces frozen sliced peaches, thawed
- 2 tablespoons plus ¾ cup (5¼ ounces) sugar
- 1 large egg plus 1 large yolk
- ¼ teaspoon salt
- 1¼ cups heavy cream
- 4 tablespoons unsalted butter, cut into 4 pieces
- ½ teaspoon vanilla extract
- ¼ teaspoon ground cinnamon

1. For the Crust Grease large bowl. Whisk milk and eggs in 2-cup liquid measuring cup until combined. Using stand mixer fitted with dough hook, mix flour, sugar, yeast, and salt on medium-low speed until combined, about 5 seconds. With mixer running, slowly add milk mixture and knead until dough forms, about 1 minute.

2. With mixer still running, add butter 1 piece at a time until incorporated. Continue kneading until dough clears sides of bowl but still sticks to bottom, 8 to 12 minutes (dough should be soft and sticky).

3. Transfer dough to greased bowl, cover with plastic wrap, and let rise on counter until doubled in size, about 1 hour. Punch down dough and divide into 2 equal balls. Wrap each ball in plastic, transfer to refrigerator, and let rest for at least 1 hour or up to 24 hours.

4. Grease 2 dark-colored 9-inch round cake pans. Roll each chilled dough balls into a 9-inch disk on lightly floured counter. Transfer to prepared pans, pushing dough to edges of pans. Cover pans loosely with plastic and let rise on counter until puffy, about 1 hour. Adjust oven rack to middle position and heat oven to 350 degrees.

5. For the Fruit and Custard Meanwhile, toss peaches with 2 tablespoons sugar in bowl, then transfer to colander set in sink; let sit for 25 minutes. Whisk remaining ¾ cup sugar, egg and yolk, and salt in medium bowl until combined. Heat cream in medium saucepan over medium heat until just beginning to simmer.

6. Slowly whisk hot cream into egg mixture. Transfer cream mixture back to saucepan and cook over medium-low heat, stirring constantly, until mixture thickens and coats back of spoon, 3 to 5 minutes. Strain custard through fine-mesh strainer set over medium bowl. Whisk in butter and vanilla and transfer to refrigerator to cool until dough is ready. (Custard can be made up to 24 hours in advance but does not need to be fully chilled before going into crust.)

7. Leaving 1-inch border all around, press down centers of doughs with bottom of dry measuring cup to deflate and create wells for peaches and custard. Arrange peaches, evenly spaced, in circular pattern in depressed dough, avoiding border. Pour custard evenly over peaches in each pan, about 1 cup per pan (you may have a few tablespoons extra). Sprinkle with cinnamon. Bake until crusts are golden brown and centers jiggle slightly when shaken, 35 to 40 minutes, switching and rotating pans halfway through baking. Let cool completely. Remove kuchens from pans using flexible spatula. Slice and serve.

Why This Recipe Works Kuchen, the official state dessert of South Dakota, features a tender yeasted dough, peaches full of flavor, and a layer of smooth, delicately sweet custard. We created a buttery crust by slowly adding softened butter to the dough, letting the dough rise and then rest in the fridge. An extra egg yolk made our custard thick and rich, without the eggy flavor found in egg whites. Finally, to ready the peaches, we sprinkled them with sugar and let them sit in a colander to pull out their excess juice and prevent the kuchen from becoming soggy. This dessert might come from South Dakota, but it felt right at home in our kitchen.

Why This Recipe Works We wanted our banana pudding to be rich and creamy, so we opted for half-and-half instead of milk in the pudding component. Roasting the bananas intensified their flavor and helped break them down so we could incorporate them more easily into the pudding. Adding a squeeze of lemon juice to the roasted bananas prevented them from browning in the refrigerator. Even whole cookies became sodden and pasty when layered with hot pudding. We solved the problem by simply waiting for the pudding to cool a little before assembling the dessert.

BANANA PUDDING

SERVES 12

If your food processor bowl holds less than 11 cups, puree half the pudding with the roasted bananas and lemon juice in step 3, transfer it to a large bowl, and whisk in the rest of the pudding.

Pudding

- 7 slightly underripe large bananas (2½ pounds), unpeeled
- 1½ cups (10½ ounces) sugar
- 8 large egg yolks
- 6 tablespoons cornstarch
- 6 cups half-and-half
- ½ teaspoon salt
- 3 tablespoons unsalted butter
- 1 tablespoon vanilla extract
- 3 tablespoons lemon juice
- 1 (12-ounce) box vanilla wafers

Whipped Topping

- 1 cup heavy cream, chilled
- 1 tablespoon sugar
- ½ teaspoon vanilla extract

1. For the Pudding Adjust oven rack to upper-middle position and heat oven to 325 degrees. Place 3 unpeeled bananas on baking sheet and bake until skins are completely black, about 20 minutes. Let cool for 5 minutes.

2. Meanwhile, whisk ½ cup sugar, egg yolks, and cornstarch in medium bowl until smooth. Bring half-and-half, remaining 1 cup sugar, and salt to simmer over medium heat in large saucepan. Whisk ½ cup simmering half-and-half mixture into egg yolk mixture to temper. Slowly whisk tempered yolk mixture into saucepan. Cook, whisking constantly, until mixture is thick and large bubbles appear at surface, about 2 minutes. Remove from heat and stir in butter and vanilla.

3. Transfer pudding to food processor. Add warm peeled roasted bananas and 2 tablespoons lemon juice and process until smooth. Scrape into large bowl and place plastic wrap directly on surface of pudding. Refrigerate until slightly cool, about 45 minutes.

4. Peel and cut remaining bananas into ¼-inch slices and toss in bowl with remaining 1 tablespoon lemon juice. Spoon one-quarter of pudding into 3-quart trifle dish and top with layer of cookies, layer of sliced bananas, and another layer of cookies. Repeat twice, ending with pudding. Place plastic wrap directly on surface of pudding and refrigerate until wafers have softened, at least 8 hours or up to 2 days.

5. For the Whipped Topping Using stand mixer fitted with whisk, whip cream, sugar, and vanilla on medium-low speed until foamy, about 1 minute. Increase speed to high and whip until stiff peaks form, 1 to 3 minutes. (Whipped cream can be refrigerated for 4 hours.) Top banana pudding with whipped cream. Serve.

TOASTED COCONUT BANANA PUDDING

Replace 2 cups half-and-half with one 16-ounce can unsweetened coconut milk in step 2. Sprinkle ¼ cup toasted sweetened shredded coconut over whipped cream–topped pudding before serving.

PEANUT-Y BANANA PUDDING

In step 4, sandwich 2 vanilla wafers around 1 banana slice and ½ teaspoon creamy peanut butter (you'll need ½ cup total). Assemble by alternating layers of pudding and cookie-banana sandwiches, ending with pudding. Sprinkle ¼ cup chopped salted dry-roasted peanuts over whipped cream–topped pudding before serving.

Why This Recipe Works The best bourbon bread pudding is a rich, "scoopable" custard that envelops the bread with a balance of sweet spiciness and robust bourbon flavor. Tearing a crusty baguette into ragged pieces, then toasting them, gave the pudding a rustic look and kept the bread from turning soggy in the custard. We used a mixture of 3 parts cream to 1 part milk and replaced the whole eggs with yolks for a rich, creamy custard that didn't curdle. Once the custard set up in the oven, we sprinkled cinnamon, sugar, and butter on top and let it bake until the topping was caramelized.

NEW ORLEANS BOURBON BREAD PUDDING

SERVES 8 TO 10

This bread pudding is great on its own, but for a little more punch, drizzle Bourbon Sauce over individual servings (recipe follows). A bakery-quality French baguette makes this dish even better.

- 1 (18- to 20-inch) baguette, torn into 1-inch pieces (10 cups)
- 1 cup golden raisins
- ¾ cup bourbon
- 6 tablespoons unsalted butter, cut into 6 pieces and chilled, plus extra for baking dish
- 8 large egg yolks
- 1½ cups packed (10½ ounces) light brown sugar
- 3 cups heavy cream
- 1 cup whole milk
- 1 tablespoon vanilla extract
- 1½ teaspoons ground cinnamon
- ¼ teaspoon nutmeg
- ¼ teaspoon salt
- 3 tablespoons granulated sugar

1. Adjust oven rack to middle position and heat oven to 450 degrees. Arrange bread in single layer on baking sheet and bake until crisp and browned, about 12 minutes, turning pieces over and rotating sheet halfway through baking. Let bread cool. Reduce oven temperature to 300 degrees.

2. Meanwhile, heat raisins with ½ cup bourbon in small saucepan over medium-high heat until bourbon begins to simmer, 2 to 3 minutes. Strain mixture, reserving bourbon and raisins separately.

3. Butter 13 by 9-inch broiler-safe baking dish. Whisk egg yolks, brown sugar, cream, milk, vanilla, 1 teaspoon cinnamon, nutmeg, and salt together in large bowl. Whisk in reserved bourbon plus remaining ¼ cup bourbon. Add toasted bread and toss until evenly coated. Let mixture sit until bread begins to absorb custard, about 30 minutes, tossing occasionally. If majority of bread is still hard, continue to soak for 15 to 20 minutes.

4. Pour half of bread mixture into prepared baking dish and sprinkle with half of raisins. Pour remaining bread mixture into dish and sprinkle with remaining raisins. Cover with aluminum foil and bake for 45 minutes.

5. Meanwhile, mix granulated sugar and remaining ½ teaspoon cinnamon in small bowl. Using your fingers, cut 6 tablespoons butter into sugar mixture until size of small peas. Remove foil from pudding, sprinkle with butter mixture, and bake, uncovered, until custard is just set, 20 to 25 minutes. Remove pudding from oven and heat broiler.

6. Once broiler is heated, broil pudding until top forms golden crust, about 2 minutes. Transfer to wire rack and cool at least 30 minutes or up to 2 hours. Serve.

BOURBON SAUCE
MAKES ABOUT 1 CUP

- 1½ teaspoons cornstarch
- ¼ cup bourbon
- ¾ cup heavy cream
- 2 tablespoons sugar
  Pinch salt
- 2 teaspoons unsalted butter, cut into 8 pieces

Whisk cornstarch and 2 tablespoons bourbon in small bowl until well combined. Heat cream and sugar in small saucepan over medium heat until sugar dissolves. Whisk in cornstarch mixture and bring to boil. Reduce heat to low and cook until sauce thickens, 3 to 5 minutes. Off heat, stir in salt, butter, and remaining 2 tablespoons bourbon. Drizzle warm sauce over individual servings. (Sauce can be refrigerated for up to 5 days.)

SUMMER BERRY PUDDING

SERVES 6

Fill in any gaps in pudding crusts with toast trimmings.

8 (¼-inch-thick) slices challah, crusts removed
12 ounces strawberries, hulled and chopped (2 cups)
8 ounces blackberries, halved (1½ cups)
8 ounces (1½ cups) blueberries
5 ounces (1 cup) raspberries
½ cup (3½ ounces) granulated sugar
1 teaspoon unflavored gelatin
2 tablespoons cold water
½ cup (5½ ounces) apricot preserves
1 cup heavy cream, chilled
1 tablespoon confectioners' sugar

1. Adjust oven rack to middle position and heat oven to 350 degrees. Line 8½ by 4½-inch loaf pan with plastic wrap, pushing plastic into corners and up sides of pan and allowing excess to overhang long sides. Make cardboard cutout just large enough to fit inside pan.

2. Place challah on wire rack set in rimmed baking sheet. Bake until dry, about 10 minutes, flipping challah and rotating sheet halfway through baking. Let challah cool completely.

3. Combine strawberries, blackberries, blueberries, and raspberries in bowl. Transfer half of mixture to medium saucepan, add granulated sugar, and bring to simmer over medium-low heat, stirring occasionally. Reduce heat to low and continue to cook until berries release their juices and raspberries begin to break down, about 5 minutes. Off heat, stir in remaining berries. After 2 minutes, strain berries through fine-mesh strainer set over medium bowl for 10 minutes, stirring berries once halfway through straining (do not press on berries). Reserve berry juice. (You should have ¾ to 1 cup.)

4. Sprinkle gelatin over water in bowl and let sit until gelatin softens, about 5 minutes. Microwave until mixture is bubbling around edges and gelatin dissolves, about 30 seconds. Whisk preserves and gelatin mixture together in large bowl. Fold in strained berries.

5. Trim 4 slices of challah to fit snugly side by side in bottom of loaf pan (you may have extra challah). Dip slices in reserved berry juice until saturated, about 30 seconds per side, then place in bottom of pan. Spoon berry mixture over challah. Trim remaining 4 slices of challah to fit snugly side by side on top of berries (you may have extra challah). Dip slices in reserved berry juice until saturated, about 30 seconds per side, then place on top of berries. Cover pan loosely with plastic and place in 13 by 9-inch baking dish. Place cardboard cutout on top of pudding. Top with 3 soup cans to weigh down pudding. Refrigerate pudding for at least 8 hours or up to 24 hours.

6. Using stand mixer fitted with whisk, whip cream and confectioners' sugar on medium-low speed until foamy, about 1 minute. Increase speed to high and whip until soft peaks form, 1 to 3 minutes. Transfer to serving bowl. Remove cans, cardboard, and plastic from top of pudding. Loosen pudding by pulling up on edges of plastic. Place inverted platter over top of loaf pan and flip platter and pan upside down to unmold pudding. Discard plastic. Slice pudding with serrated knife and serve with whipped cream.

Constructing Summer Berry Pudding

1. Saturate dried, trimmed challah with reserved berry juices and place in bottom of plastic wrap–lined pan.

2. Spoon sweetened four-berry mixture over challah, and top with four more slices of saturated challah.

Why This Recipe Works Although our initial tests of this traditional British "pudding" were fairly disastrous, we knew that good bread and fresh summer berries could make a delicious dessert. The rectangular shape of a loaf pan proved a more stable mold than traditional round bowls. We staled challah bread (our top choice for its flavor and texture) in the oven for added support. Since the moisture content of fresh berries can vary, we strained the juice from the filling and dipped the bread in it ourselves. Cooking only half of the berries and mixing the rest in later brightened the filling, and apricot preserves and gelatin helped the pudding keep its shape.

Why This Recipe Works There's nothing like a cone of creamy frozen custard on a hot summer day—or really any day. While stores use industrial condensers to produce the consistency we know and love, we set out to find a way to achieve supersmooth custard at home without a machine. After combining our heated cream and egg yolk mixtures, we strained the custard to remove any pieces of cooked egg. To achieve the smoothest possible custard, we cooled the mixture on ice, let it chill in the refrigerator, and then whipped it in a stand mixer to add air. This prevented ice crystals from building up and made the final texture silky and creamy.

OLD-FASHIONED VANILLA FROZEN CUSTARD

MAKES ABOUT 1 QUART

One teaspoon of vanilla extract can be substituted for the vanilla bean; stir the extract into the strained custard in step 3. Use an instant-read thermometer for the best results.

6 large egg yolks
¼ cup (1¾ ounces) sugar
2 tablespoons nonfat dry milk powder
1 cup heavy cream
½ cup whole milk
⅓ cup light corn syrup
⅛ teaspoon salt
1 vanilla bean

1. Whisk egg yolks, sugar, and milk powder in bowl until smooth, about 30 seconds; set aside. Combine cream, milk, corn syrup, and salt in medium saucepan. Cut vanilla bean in half lengthwise. Using tip of paring knife, scrape out vanilla seeds and add to cream mixture, along with vanilla bean. Heat cream mixture over medium-high heat, stirring occasionally, until it steams steadily and registers 175 degrees, about 5 minutes. Remove saucepan from heat.

2. Slowly whisk heated cream mixture into yolk mixture to temper. Return cream-yolk mixture to saucepan and cook over medium-low heat, stirring constantly, until mixture thickens and registers 180 degrees, 4 to 6 minutes.

3. Immediately pour custard through fine-mesh strainer set over large bowl; discard vanilla bean. Fill slightly larger bowl with ice and set custard bowl in bowl of ice. Transfer to refrigerator and let chill until custard registers 40 degrees, 1 to 2 hours, stirring occasionally.

4. Transfer chilled custard to stand mixer fitted with whisk and whip on medium-high speed for 3 minutes, or until mixture increases in volume to about 3¾ cups. Pour custard into airtight 1-quart container. Cover and freeze until firm, at least 6 hours, before serving. (Frozen custard is best eaten within 10 days.)

OLD-FASHIONED CHOCOLATE FROZEN CUSTARD

Omit vanilla bean. Add ½ ounce finely chopped 60 percent cacao bittersweet chocolate and 1 tablespoon Dutch-processed cocoa powder to cream mixture in step 1 before cooking. Add ½ teaspoon vanilla extract to strained custard in step 3.

Steps to Smooth Frozen Custard

1. Temper Heating cream mixture before slowly adding it to cold yolk mixture prevents eggs from curdling.

2. Strain Pouring warm custard through strainer removes any pieces of cooked egg.

3. Chill Cooling custard on ice primes it for adding air.

4. Whip Whipping cooled custard adds air to make final texture especially creamy.

save room for pie

DOUBLE-CRUST PIE DOUGH

MAKES ENOUGH FOR ONE 9-INCH PIE

2½ cups (12½ ounces) all-purpose flour
2 tablespoons sugar
1 teaspoon salt
8 tablespoons vegetable shortening,
  cut into ¼-inch pieces and chilled
12 tablespoons unsalted butter,
  cut into ¼-inch pieces and chilled
6–8 tablespoons ice water

1. Process flour, sugar, and salt in food processor until combined, about 5 seconds. Scatter shortening over top and process until mixture resembles coarse cornmeal, about 10 seconds. Scatter butter over top and pulse until mixture resembles coarse crumbs, about 10 pulses. Transfer to bowl.

2. Sprinkle 6 tablespoons water over flour mixture. Using rubber spatula, stir and press dough until it sticks together. If dough does not come together, stir in remaining water, 1 tablespoon at a time, until it does.

3. Divide dough into 2 even pieces and flatten each into 4-inch disk. Wrap disks tightly in plastic wrap and refrigerate for 1 hour. Let chilled dough soften slightly on counter before rolling.

CLASSIC SINGLE-CRUST PIE DOUGH

MAKES ENOUGH FOR ONE 9-INCH PIE

1¼ cups (6¼ ounces) all-purpose flour
1 tablespoon sugar
½ teaspoon salt
4 tablespoons vegetable shortening,
  cut into ¼-inch pieces and chilled
6 tablespoons unsalted butter,
  cut into ¼-inch pieces and chilled
3–4 tablespoons ice water

1. Process flour, sugar, and salt in food processor until combined, about 5 seconds. Scatter shortening over top and process until mixture resembles coarse cornmeal, about 10 seconds. Scatter butter over top and pulse until mixture resembles coarse crumbs, about 10 pulses. Transfer to bowl.

2. Sprinkle 3 tablespoons water over flour mixture. Using rubber spatula, stir and press dough until it sticks together. If dough does not come together, add remaining 1 tablespoon water. Flatten dough into 4-inch disk, wrap tightly in plastic wrap, and refrigerate for 1 hour.

3. Let chilled dough soften slightly. Lightly flour counter, then roll dough into 12-inch circle and fit it into 9-inch pie plate. Trim, fold, and crimp edges of dough. Wrap dough-lined pie plate in plastic and place in freezer until dough is fully chilled and firm, about 30 minutes, before using.

Rolling and Fitting Pie Dough

1. Roll dough outward from its center into 12-inch circle. Between every few rolls, give dough quarter turn.

2. Toss additional flour underneath dough as needed to keep dough from sticking to counter.

3. Loosely roll dough around rolling pin, then gently unroll it over pie plate.

4. Lift dough and gently press it into pie plate, letting excess hang over plate.

NO-FEAR SINGLE-CRUST PIE DOUGH

MAKES ENOUGH FOR ONE 9-INCH PIE

Anyone can make this pat-in-the-pan pie dough—no rolling or transferring of dough to the dish required. Cream cheese helps make this dough easy to handle and helps ensure a tender crust. Make sure you press the dough evenly into a glass pie plate; if you hold the dough-lined plate up to the light, you will be able to clearly see any thick or thin spots.

1¼ cups (6¼ ounces) all-purpose flour
2 tablespoons sugar
¼ teaspoon salt
8 tablespoons unsalted butter, softened but still cool
2 ounces cream cheese, softened but still cool

1. Lightly coat 9-inch Pyrex pie plate with vegetable oil spray. Whisk flour, sugar, and salt together in bowl.

2. Using stand mixer fitted with paddle, beat butter and cream cheese on medium-high speed until completely homogeneous, about 2 minutes, stopping once or twice to scrape down beater and sides of bowl. Add flour mixture and mix on medium-low speed until mixture resembles coarse cornmeal, about 20 seconds. Scrape down sides of bowl. Increase mixer speed to medium-high and beat until dough begins to form large clumps, about 30 seconds. Reserve 3 tablespoons of dough. Turn remaining dough onto lightly floured counter, gather into ball, and flatten into 6-inch disk. Transfer disk to greased pie plate.

3. Press dough evenly over bottom of pie plate toward sides, using heel of your hand. Hold plate up to light to ensure that dough is evenly distributed. With your fingertips, continue to work dough over bottom of plate and up sides until evenly distributed.

4. On floured counter, roll reserved dough into 12-inch rope. Divide into 3 pieces and roll each piece into 8-inch rope. Arrange ropes, evenly spaced, around top of pie plate, pressing and squeezing to join them with dough in plate and form uniform edge. Use your fingers to flute edge of dough. Wrap dough-lined pie plate in plastic wrap and place in freezer until dough is fully chilled and firm, about 30 minutes, before using.

No-Fear Pie Dough

1. Hold pie plate up to light to check thickness of dough; it should be translucent, not opaque. Pay attention to curved edges.

2. Roll reserved dough into three 8-inch ropes. Arrange ropes around perimeter of pie plate, leaving small (about 1-inch) gaps between them.

3. Squeeze ropes together.

4. Create a fluted edge, dipping your fingers in flour if dough is sticky.

Why This Recipe Works Most Shaker lemon pie recipes mix lemon slices—peel and all—with sugar and eggs to form a custardy filling. But unless we macerated the lemon slices for 24 hours, the pie turned out bitter. We wanted to speed up this recipe for modern times. First, we squeezed the seeded lemon slices and reserved the juice for the filling. Then, we simmered the slices and added them to the filling with the uncooked juice for bright lemon flavor without any macerating time.

SHAKER LEMON PIE

SERVES 8

Have an extra lemon on hand in case the three sliced lemons do not yield enough juice. See page 764 for more information on rolling and fitting pie dough.

- 1 recipe Double-Crust Pie Dough (page 764)
- 3 large lemons, sliced thin and seeded
- 1¾ cups (12¼ ounces) sugar
- ⅛ teaspoon salt
- 1 tablespoon cornstarch
- 4 large eggs
- 1 tablespoon heavy cream

1. Roll 1 disk of dough into 12-inch circle on lightly floured counter, then fit it into 9-inch pie plate, letting excess dough hang over edge; cover with plastic wrap and refrigerate for 30 minutes. Roll other disk of dough into 12-inch circle on lightly floured counter, then transfer to parchment paper–lined baking sheet; cover with plastic and refrigerate for 30 minutes.

2. Adjust oven rack to lowest position and heat oven to 425 degrees. Squeeze lemon slices in fine-mesh strainer set over bowl; reserve juice (you should have 6 tablespoons). Bring drained slices and 2 cups water to boil in saucepan, then reduce heat to medium-low and simmer until slices are softened, about 5 minutes. Drain well and discard liquid. Combine softened lemon slices, sugar, salt, and ¼ cup reserved lemon juice in bowl; stir until sugar dissolves.

3. Whisk cornstarch and remaining 2 tablespoons lemon juice in large bowl. Whisk eggs into cornstarch mixture, then slowly stir in lemon slice mixture until combined. Pour into chilled pie shell. Brush edges of dough with 1 teaspoon cream. Loosely roll second piece of dough around rolling pin then gently unroll it over pie. Trim, fold, and crimp edges, and cut 4 vent holes in top. Brush top with remaining 2 teaspoons cream.

4. Bake until light golden, about 20 minutes, then decrease oven temperature to 375 degrees and continue to bake until golden brown, 20 to 25 minutes. Let pie cool on wire rack for at least 1 hour. Serve. (Pie can be refrigerated for 2 days.)

Building Bold, Not Bitter, Lemon Flavor

Using sliced whole lemons, pith and all, can produce an overwhelmingly bitter filling. We found a few tricks to create bright lemon flavor while tempering the bitterness of the pith.

1. Squeeze seeded lemon slices and reserve juice for filling.

2. Simmer slices to mellow bitterness of pith and then add them to filling with uncooked juice.

Shaker Cooking

The Shakers' food was never ornate and was always healthy and hearty enough to support their industrious, hard-working lifestyle. Shakers scrubbed—rather than peeled—their vegetables (and, in the case of Shaker Lemon Pie, their citrus fruit) to minimize waste. They were also pioneers in using exact measurements in cooking at a time when many recipes called for a "dash," "glob," or "handful" of something.

The Slice Is Right

While developing our recipe for Shaker Lemon Pie, we found that cutting the lemons into paper-thin slices was a difficult and time-consuming task. We had better results with a mandoline, which produced perfectly thin slices in no time at all. If you don't have a mandoline, another piece of kitchen equipment will make the process easier: the freezer. Freezing the lemons for about 30 minutes firms them up for better hand slicing, which is best accomplished with a serrated knife.

NORTH CAROLINA LEMON PIE

MAKES ONE 9-INCH PIE

You will need about 53 saltines, roughly one and a half sleeves, to equal 6 ounces.

Crust
- 6 ounces saltines
- ⅛ teaspoon salt
- 10 tablespoons unsalted butter, melted
- ¼ cup light corn syrup

Filling
- 1 (14-ounce) can sweetened condensed milk
- 4 large egg yolks
- ¼ cup heavy cream
- 1 tablespoon grated lemon zest plus ½ cup juice (3 lemons)
- ⅛ teaspoon salt

Topping
- ½ cup heavy cream, chilled
- 2 teaspoons sugar
- ½ teaspoon vanilla extract

1. For the Crust Adjust oven rack to middle position and heat oven to 350 degrees. Combine saltines and salt in food processor and pulse to coarse crumbs, about 15 pulses. Add melted butter and corn syrup and pulse until crumbs are broken down into oatmeal-size pieces, about 15 pulses.

2. Transfer saltine mixture to greased 9-inch pie plate. Using bottom of dry measuring cup, press crumbs into even layer on bottom and sides of plate, using your hand to keep crumbs from spilling over plate edge. Place plate on baking sheet and bake until light golden brown and fragrant, 17 to 19 minutes.

3. For the Filling Whisk condensed milk, egg yolks, cream, lemon zest, and salt in bowl until fully combined. Whisk in lemon juice until fully incorporated.

4. With pie plate still on sheet, pour filling into crust (crust needn't be cool). Bake pie until edges are beginning to set but center still jiggles when shaken, 15 to 17 minutes. Place pie on wire rack and let cool completely. Refrigerate pie until fully chilled, about 4 hours.

5. For the Topping Using stand mixer fitted with whisk, whip cream, sugar, and vanilla on medium-low speed until foamy, about 1 minute. Increase speed to high and whip until stiff peaks form, 1 to 3 minutes. Spread whipped cream over top of pie. Serve.

Why This Recipe Works This light, bright lemon pie has a perfect balance of sweet, salty, and sour. Plus, it's dead simple to make. Inspired by the North Carolina coast, its unique crust is made with saltine crackers. To keep the custard filling easy, we used both lemon zest and juice for plenty of citrus flavor, and heavy cream to soften the lemon's sharpness. Sweetened whipped cream was the perfect finishing touch.

Why This Recipe Works We wanted a lemon meringue pie with an impressively tall and fluffy topping, so we made the meringue with a hot sugar syrup and added a bit of cream of tartar to the egg whites as we beat them. This ensured that the meringue was cooked through and stable enough to be piled high on top of the filling. For our pie's bright citrus flavor, we flavored the filling with lemon zest and lemon juice and then, to ensure the filling was silky smooth, we strained out the zest.

MILE-HIGH LEMON MERINGUE PIE

SERVES 8 TO 10

*You can use Classic Single-Crust Pie Dough (page 764)
or No-Fear Single-Crust Pie Dough (page 765) for
this pie. This pie is best served on the day it's made.*

1 recipe single-crust pie dough, fitted into
9-inch pie plate and chilled

Lemon Filling
1¼ cups (8¾ ounces) sugar
1 cup lemon juice plus 2 tablespoons
grated zest (5 lemons)
½ cup water
3 tablespoons cornstarch
¼ teaspoon salt
8 large egg yolks
4 tablespoons unsalted butter,
cut into 4 pieces and softened

Meringue
1 cup (7 ounces) sugar
½ cup water
4 large egg whites
Pinch salt
½ teaspoon cream of tartar
½ teaspoon vanilla extract

1. Adjust oven rack to middle position and heat
oven to 375 degrees. Line chilled crust with double
layer of aluminum foil and fill with pie weights.
Bake until pie dough looks dry and is light in color,
25 to 30 minutes. Remove weights and foil and continue to bake crust until deep golden brown, 10 to
12 minutes longer. Let crust cool on wire rack
to room temperature.

2. For the Lemon Filling Whisk sugar, lemon juice,
water, cornstarch, and salt together in large saucepan until cornstarch is dissolved. Bring to simmer
over medium heat, whisking occasionally until mixture becomes translucent and begins to thicken,
about 5 minutes. Whisk in egg yolks until combined.
Stir in lemon zest and butter. Bring to simmer
and stir constantly until mixture is thick enough to

coat back of spoon, about 2 minutes. Strain through
fine-mesh strainer into cooled pie shell and scrape
filling off underside of strainer. Place plastic wrap
directly on surface of filling and refrigerate until set
and well chilled, at least 2 hours or up to 1 day.

3. For the Meringue Adjust oven rack to middle
position and heat oven to 400 degrees. Combine
sugar and water in small saucepan. Bring to vigorous boil over medium-high heat. Once syrup comes
to rolling boil, cook 4 minutes (mixture will become
slightly thickened and syrupy). Remove from heat
and set aside while beating whites.

4. Using stand mixer fitted with whisk, whip egg
whites in large bowl at medium-low speed until
frothy, about 1 minute. Add salt and cream of tartar
and whip, gradually increasing speed to medium-
high, until whites hold soft peaks, about 2 minutes.
With mixer running, slowly pour hot syrup into whites
(avoid pouring syrup onto whisk or it will splash).
Add vanilla and whip until meringue has cooled and
becomes very thick and shiny, 5 to 9 minutes.

5. Using rubber spatula, mound meringue over
filling, making sure meringue touches edges of crust.
Use spatula to create peaks all over meringue. Bake
until peaks turn golden brown, about 6 minutes. Let
pie cool on wire rack to room temperature. Serve.

Making a Meringue Mountain

1. Use rubber spatula to
press meringue onto
edge of pie crust. This
will keep meringue
from shrinking.

2. Use spatula to make
dramatic peaks and
swirls all over meringue.

Why This Recipe Works Think of sour orange pie as northern Florida's answer to Key lime: Its custard-like filling is made with the juice of wild sour oranges. Since fresh sour oranges are hard to source outside of Florida we re-created their ultra-sour taste with frozen orange juice concentrate, lemon juice, and orange and lemon zests. We mixed the juice with sweetened condensed milk for sweetness and egg yolks for structure. Slightly sweet animal crackers made a crunchy crust to contrast the tart filling. Chilled and topped with orange-flavored whipped cream, this sunny pie was bright and refreshing.

SOUR ORANGE PIE

MAKES ONE 9-INCH PIE

If sour oranges are available, use ¾ cup strained sour orange juice in place of the lemon juice and orange juice concentrate in the filling.

Crust
5 ounces animal crackers
3 tablespoons sugar
   Pinch salt
4 tablespoons unsalted butter, melted

Filling
1 (14-ounce) can sweetened condensed milk
6 tablespoons thawed orange juice concentrate
4 large egg yolks
2 teaspoons grated lemon zest plus 6 tablespoons juice (2 lemons)
1 teaspoon grated orange zest
   Pinch salt

Whipped Cream
¾ cup heavy cream, chilled
2 tablespoons sugar
½ teaspoon grated orange zest

1. For the Crust Adjust oven rack to middle position and heat oven to 325 degrees. Process crackers, sugar, and salt in food processor until finely ground, about 30 seconds. Add melted butter and pulse until combined, about 8 pulses. Transfer crumbs to 9-inch pie plate.

2. Using bottom of dry measuring cup, press crumbs firmly into bottom and up sides of pie plate. Bake until fragrant and beginning to brown, 12 to 14 minutes. Cool to room temperature, about 30 minutes.

3. For the Filling When crust is cool, whisk condensed milk, orange juice concentrate, egg yolks, lemon zest and juice, orange zest, and salt together in bowl until fully combined. Pour filling into cooled crust.

4. Bake until center of pie jiggles slightly when shaken, 15 to 17 minutes. Cool to room temperature, then refrigerate until fully chilled, at least 3 hours; or cover with greased plastic wrap and refrigerate for up to 24 hours.

5. For the Whipped Cream Whisk cream, sugar, and orange zest together in medium bowl until stiff peaks form, 2 to 4 minutes.

6. Slice chilled pie and serve with whipped cream.

No Sour Oranges? No Problem.

Since fresh sour oranges can be hard to come by outside of Florida, we re-created their ultrasour, slightly bitter taste by combining thawed frozen orange juice concentrate with fresh lemon juice and bolstering the mixture with lots of orange and lemon zest.

 +  =

FRESH LEMON JUICE
Provides plenty of sourness

ORANGE JUICE CONCENTRATE
Adds potent orange flavor

SOUR ORANGE
Intense tartness

ICEBOX KEY LIME PIE

SERVES 8 TO 10

Use instant pudding, which requires no stovetop cooking, for this recipe. Do not use bottled lime juice, which lacks depth of flavor.

Crust
- 8 whole graham crackers, broken into small pieces
- 2 tablespoons sugar
- 5 tablespoons unsalted butter, melted

Filling
- ¼ cup (1¾ ounces) sugar
- 1 tablespoon grated lime zest plus 1 cup juice (8 limes)
- 8 ounces cream cheese, softened
- 1 (14-ounce) can sweetened condensed milk
- ⅓ cup instant vanilla pudding mix
- 1¼ teaspoons unflavored gelatin
- 1 teaspoon vanilla extract

1. For the Crust Adjust oven rack to middle position and heat oven to 350 degrees. Process crackers and sugar in food processor until finely ground, about 30 seconds. Add melted butter in steady stream while pulsing until crumbs resemble damp sand. Sprinkle mixture into 9-inch pie plate and use bottom of dry measuring cup to press crumbs firmly into bottom and sides. Bake until fragrant and browned around edges, 12 to 14 minutes. Let cool completely.

2. For the Filling Process sugar and zest in clean food processor until sugar turns bright green, about 30 seconds. Add cream cheese and process until combined, about 30 seconds. Add condensed milk and pudding mix and process until smooth, about 30 seconds. Scrape down sides of bowl. Sprinkle gelatin over 2 tablespoons lime juice in small bowl and let sit until gelatin softens, about 5 minutes. Heat in microwave for 15 seconds; stir until dissolved. With processor running, pour in gelatin mixture, remaining lime juice, and vanilla and mix until thoroughly combined, about 30 seconds.

3. Pour filling into cooled crust, cover with plastic wrap, and refrigerate for at least 3 hours or up to 2 days. To serve, let pie sit at room temperature for 10 minutes before slicing.

Bigger Limes = Less Work
When developing our recipe for Icebox Key Lime Pie, we found the flavor of key limes and regular supermarket limes (called Persian limes) to be almost identical in our pie recipe. But there was a big difference in squeezing time.

KEY LIMES
We had to squeeze 40 key limes to yield 1 cup of juice.

PERSIAN LIMES
Just six to eight Persian limes gave us all the juice we needed.

A Mystery of Pie History
Before Gail Borden invented sweetened condensed milk in 1856, drinking milk was a health risk, as there was no pasteurization or refrigeration for fresh milk. The shelf-stability and safety of sweetened condensed milk made it especially popular in areas like the Florida Keys, where the hot climate promoted rapid spoilage of anything perishable. Like many of our iconic foods, no one knows for sure when or by whom the first key lime pie was made, but with canned milk in every pantry by the 1870s and an abundance of tiny key limes throughout the area, it was only a matter of time. Most food historians trace the history of this pie back to the 1890s, but there are those—especially in the Keys—who claim the recipe is decades older.

Why This Recipe Works Early key lime pie recipes used to be simple and uncooked—but they contained raw eggs, a no-no in modern times. We wanted to develop an eggless key lime pie recipe as bright and custardy as the original. In lieu of using egg yolks, we found the right ratio of instant vanilla pudding, gelatin, and cream cheese to thicken our Icebox Key Lime Pie's filling into a perfect, smooth consistency. A full cup of fresh lime juice produced a pie with bracing lime flavor. Lime zest added another layer of flavor, and processing the zest with a little sugar offset its sourness and eliminated the annoying chewy bits.

PEACHES AND CREAM PIE

SERVES 8

Keep an eye on the peaches at the end of their baking time to ensure that they don't scorch. You can use Classic Single-Crust Pie Dough (page 764) or No-Fear Single-Crust Pie Dough (page 765) for this pie.

- 1 recipe single-crust pie dough, fitted into 9-inch pie plate and chilled
- 2 pounds ripe but firm peaches, peeled, halved, and pitted
- 2 tablespoons plus ½ cup (4⅓ ounces) sugar
- 3 tablespoons all-purpose flour
- ¼ teaspoon salt
- ⅓ cup heavy cream
- 2 large egg yolks
- ½ teaspoon vanilla extract

1. Adjust oven racks to upper-middle and lower-middle positions and heat oven to 375 degrees. Line chilled crust with double layer of aluminum foil and fill with pie weights.

2. Place peach halves cut side up on foil-lined rimmed baking sheet and sprinkle with 2 tablespoons sugar. Bake peaches on upper-middle rack until softened and juice is released, about 30 minutes, flipping halfway through baking.

3. After 30 minutes, place crust on lower-middle rack and, while peaches continue to roast, bake until edges are lightly browned, about 15 minutes. Remove crust from oven and carefully remove foil and weights. Continue to bake until bottom of crust is light golden brown and peaches are caramelized, about 5 minutes longer. Cool crust and peaches for 15 minutes.

4. Reduce oven temperature to 325 degrees. Cut peach halves lengthwise into quarters. Arrange peaches in single layer over crust. Combine remaining ½ cup sugar, flour, and salt in bowl. Whisk in cream, egg yolks, and vanilla until smooth. Pour cream mixture over peaches. Bake until filling is light golden brown and firm in center, 45 to 55 minutes. Cool pie on wire rack for at least 3 hours. Serve.

Twice-Baked Peaches

Eat a peach out of hand, and its juiciness is no small part of what makes it so good. But cook the fruit, and that same high water content can ruin peach pie, especially when coupled with cream. To evaporate the peach juices and concentrate the peach flavor, we roasted the fruit before filling the pie. A sprinkle of sugar helps the peach halves caramelize. Plus, to save time, while you're roasting the fruit on one rack of the oven, you can prebake the crust on another.

Blind-Baking a Pie Crust

The crusts for many pies and tarts are baked before filling (this is called blind baking) so that they stay golden brown, crisp, and flaky once filled.

1. Line chilled pie crust with double layer of aluminum foil, fill crust with pie weights or pennies, and bake until lightly browned, about 15 minutes.

2. Remove pie weights and foil and continue to bake until light golden brown, about 5 minutes longer.

Why This Recipe Works Old-fashioned recipes for this pie call for simply arranging peaches in a pie crust, dousing them with fresh cream, and baking. But today's commercial cream gave us a milky, lumpy, and bland puddle rather than a rich filling. To thicken the cream, we whisked in a little flour and two egg yolks. But the juicy peaches wreaked watery havoc on our custardy pie filling. Roasting them in the oven evaporated their excess liquid, and a dusting of sugar encouraged caramelizing for even more flavor. Prebaking the crust ensured it would stay crisp and flaky after the roasted fruit and filling were added.

Why This Recipe Works These hand pies have it all: a crust that is delicate and tender but crumbly and a filling that's pure peach flavor. Starting with the filling, we cooked peeled, sliced peaches with sugar and a pinch of salt on the stovetop before gently mashing the fruit and letting it thicken. A bit of lemon juice added vibrancy. For the crust, we created a soft dough using melted butter and flour. Adding baking powder and milk created the dainty crumble we wanted. We divided, rolled out, and filled the dough, sealing in the filling before frying the pies in a Dutch oven, achieving peachy little pie perfection in minutes.

FRIED PEACH HAND PIES

MAKES 8 HAND PIES

If using frozen peaches, purchase a no-sugar-added product; we prefer Earthbound Farm or Cascadian Farm frozen peaches. There is no need to thaw the frozen peaches, but they will take longer to cook; times for both fresh and frozen are given in step 1. Use a Dutch oven that holds 6 quarts or more for frying. The assembled pies can be refrigerated for up to 24 hours before frying.

 4 ripe peaches, peeled, halved, pitted, and cut into ½-inch wedges, or 20 ounces frozen peaches
 ½ cup (3½ ounces) sugar
    Salt
 2 teaspoons lemon juice
 2 cups (10 ounces) all-purpose flour
 2 teaspoons baking powder
 6 tablespoons unsalted butter, melted and cooled
 ½ cup whole milk
 2 quarts peanut or vegetable oil

1. Combine peaches, sugar, and ⅛ teaspoon salt in medium saucepan. Cover and cook over medium heat, stirring occasionally and breaking up peaches with spoon, until tender, about 5 minutes for fresh peaches and 16 to 19 minutes for frozen peaches.

2. Uncover and continue to cook, stirring and mashing frequently with potato masher to coarse puree, until mixture is thickened and measures about 1⅔ cups, 7 to 13 minutes. Remove from heat, stir in lemon juice, and let cool completely. (Filling can be refrigerated for up to 3 days.)

3. Line rimmed baking sheet with parchment paper. Pulse flour, baking powder, and ¾ teaspoon salt in food processor until combined, about 3 pulses. Add melted butter and pulse until mixture resembles wet sand, about 8 pulses, scraping down sides of bowl as needed. Add milk and process until no floury bits remain and dough looks pebbly, about 8 seconds.

4. Turn dough onto lightly floured counter, gather into disk, and divide into 8 equal pieces. Roll each piece between your hands into ball, then press to flatten into round. Place rounds on prepared sheet, cover with plastic wrap, and refrigerate for 20 minutes.

5. Working with 1 piece of dough at a time, roll into 6- to 7-inch circle about ⅛ inch thick on lightly floured counter. Place 3 tablespoons filling in center of circle. Brush edges of dough with water and fold dough over filling to create half-moon shape, lightly pressing out air at seam. Trim any ragged edges and crimp edges with tines of fork to seal. Return pies to prepared sheet, cover with plastic, and refrigerate until ready to fry, up to 24 hours.

6. Line platter with triple layer of paper towels. Add oil to large Dutch oven until it measures about 1½ inches deep and heat over medium-high heat to 375 degrees. Gently place 4 pies in hot oil and fry until golden brown, about 1½ minutes per side, using slotted spatula or spider to flip. Adjust burner, if necessary, to maintain oil temperature between 350 and 375 degrees. Transfer to prepared platter. Return oil to 375 degrees and repeat with remaining 4 pies. Let cool for 10 minutes before serving.

On the Road: Peach Park

The massive, peach-shaped water tower looming over Clanton, Alabama, heralds Peach Park, a roadside retail attraction and restaurant that serves as the spiritual center of Alabama's peach-producing region. Out front, an open-air market sells fresh produce (peaches, mostly) and peach-based pantry products; inside, a long cafeteria case houses meat-and-three fare (preludes, perhaps, to peach ice cream and peach cobbler). Portraits of the reigning Miss Peach and her younger counterparts Junior Miss Peach, Young Miss Peach, and Little Miss Peach honor their regal stone-fruit court.

But the best reason to visit Peach Park is the fried peach hand pies. Rumor has it these sweet, warm pies were created as a way to use up overripe peaches, too soft and ugly to sell as is but still full of peach flavor. At Peach Park, we left no leftovers.

OREGON BLACKBERRY PIE

SERVES 8

Do not substitute frozen berries. Freezing the butter for the dough before processing it in step 1 is crucial to the flaky texture of this crust. Plan ahead: The pie dough needs to chill for at least an hour before rolling. When brushing the lattice strips with egg wash, be sure to leave the ends of each strip unbrushed so the wash doesn't impede the crimping process.

Pie Dough

⅓ cup ice water, plus extra as needed
3 tablespoons sour cream
2½ cups (12½ ounces) all-purpose flour
1 tablespoon sugar
1 teaspoon salt
16 tablespoons unsalted butter, cut into ¼-inch pieces and frozen for 15 minutes

Filling

¾ cup (5¼ ounces) sugar, plus 1 teaspoon for topping
5 tablespoons (1¼ ounces) cornstarch
¼ teaspoon salt
20 ounces (4 cups) blackberries, rinsed and dried
2 tablespoons lemon juice
2 tablespoons unsalted butter, cut into ½-inch pieces

1 large egg, lightly beaten

1. For the Pie Dough Mix ice water and sour cream in bowl. Process flour, sugar, and salt in food processor until combined, about 5 seconds. Scatter butter over top and pulse until butter is size of large peas, about 10 pulses.

2. Pour half of sour cream mixture into bowl with flour mixture and pulse until incorporated, about 3 pulses. Scrape down bowl and repeat with remaining sour cream mixture. Pinch dough with your fingers; if dough feels dry and does not hold together, sprinkle 1 to 2 tablespoons extra ice water over mixture and pulse until dough forms large clumps and no dry flour remains, 3 to 5 pulses.

3. Transfer dough to lightly floured counter. Divide dough in half and form each half into 4-inch disk. Wrap disks tightly in plastic wrap and refrigerate for 1 hour. (Wrapped dough can be refrigerated for up to 2 days or frozen for up to 1 month. If frozen, let dough thaw completely on counter before rolling.)

4. Adjust oven rack to lower-middle position and heat oven to 400 degrees. Let chilled dough sit on counter to soften slightly, about 10 minutes, before rolling. Roll 1 disk of dough into 12-inch circle on lightly floured counter. Loosely roll dough around rolling pin and gently unroll it onto 9-inch pie plate, letting excess dough hang over edge. Ease dough into plate by gently lifting edge of dough with your hand while pressing into plate bottom with your other hand.

5. Wrap dough-lined plate loosely in plastic and refrigerate until dough is firm, about 30 minutes. Roll other disk of dough into 12-inch circle on lightly floured counter, then transfer to parchment paper–lined baking sheet. Using pizza cutter, cut dough into twelve 1-inch strips. Discard 4 short end pieces, then cover remaining 8 long strips with plastic and refrigerate for 30 minutes.

6. For the Filling Whisk sugar, cornstarch, and salt together in large bowl. Add blackberries and toss gently to coat. Add lemon juice and toss until no dry sugar mixture remains. (Blackberries will start to exude some juice.)

7. Transfer blackberry mixture to dough-lined pie plate and dot with butter. Lay 4 dough strips parallel to each other across pie, about 1 inch apart. Brush strips with egg, leaving ½ inch at ends unbrushed. Lay remaining 4 strips perpendicular to first layer of strips, about 1 inch apart.

8. Pinch edges of lattice strips and bottom crust firmly together. Trim overhang to ½ inch beyond lip of plate. Tuck overhang under itself; folded edge should be flush with edge of plate. Crimp dough evenly around edge of plate using your fingers.

9. Brush lattice top and crimped edge with egg and sprinkle with remaining 1 teaspoon sugar. Set pie on parchment-lined baking sheet. Bake until golden brown and juices bubble evenly along surface, 45 to 50 minutes, rotating sheet halfway through baking. Let cool on wire rack for at least 4 hours before serving.

Why This Recipe Works The hallmark of Oregon blackberry pie is its thick, fruity filling that retains its shape after slicing instead of oozing into a mess. Re-creating that perfect texture required trying a number of different thickeners. We ultimately landed on cornstarch, which provided the best texture and didn't impact the flavor. Tossing the blackberries in sugar, cornstarch, salt, and lemon juice kept the focus on the fruit. Adding a bit of sour cream to the pie dough inhibited gluten development, preventing the dough from becoming tough. An attractive faux lattice top allowed steam to escape, preventing a soggy crust.

Why This Recipe Works The hallmark of Dutch apple pie is its creamy apple and vanilla-flavored filling, but we didn't rely on cream to achieve it. Instead we added melted vanilla ice cream to the apple filling for extra creaminess and rich flavor that complemented the apples. We let sliced apples sit in the melted ice cream along with cinnamon, sugar, and lemon juice until they were soft and pliable. Before baking, we sprinkled a mixture of melted butter, flour, brown sugar, and salt over the top of the pie for a supremely buttery crumble topping. Letting the pie cool completely before slicing into it allowed it to firm up so that we could produce beautifully clean wedges.

PENNSYLVANIA DUTCH APPLE PIE

SERVES 8 TO 10

We prefer Golden Delicious or Gala apples here, but Fuji, Braeburn, or Granny Smith varieties also work well. You may substitute ½ cup of heavy cream for the melted ice cream, if desired. This pie is best when baked a day ahead of time and allowed to rest overnight. Serve with vanilla ice cream.

Crust

- ¼ cup ice water
- 4 teaspoons sour cream
- 1¼ cups (6¼ ounces) all-purpose flour
- 1½ teaspoons granulated sugar
- ½ teaspoon salt
- 8 tablespoons unsalted butter, cut into ¼-inch pieces and frozen for 15 minutes

Filling

- 2½ pounds apples, peeled, cored, halved, and sliced ¼ inch thick
- ½ cup melted vanilla ice cream
- ½ cup raisins (optional)
- ½ cup (3 ½ ounces) granulated sugar
- 1 tablespoon lemon juice
- 1 teaspoon vanilla extract
- 1 teaspoon ground cinnamon
- ½ teaspoon salt

Topping

- 1 cup (5 ounces) all-purpose flour
- ½ cup packed (3½ ounces) light brown sugar
- 6 tablespoons unsalted butter, melted
- ½ teaspoon salt

1. For the Crust Combine water and sour cream in bowl. Process flour, sugar, and salt in food processor until combined, about 5 seconds. Scatter butter over top and pulse until butter is size of large peas, about 10 pulses. Add sour cream mixture and pulse until dough forms clumps and no dry flour remains, about 12 pulses, scraping down sides of bowl as needed.

2. Turn dough onto sheet of plastic wrap and form into 4-inch disk. Wrap tightly in plastic and refrigerate for 1 hour. (Wrapped dough can be refrigerated for up to 2 days or frozen for up to 1 month. If frozen, let dough thaw completely on counter before rolling.)

3. For the Filling Toss all ingredients in large bowl until apples are evenly coated. Let sit at room temperature for at least 1 hour or up to 2 hours.

4. Adjust oven rack to lower-middle position and heat oven to 350 degrees. Let chilled dough sit on counter to soften slightly, about 10 minutes, before rolling. Roll dough into 12-inch circle on lightly floured counter. Loosely roll dough around rolling pin and gently unroll it onto 9-inch pie plate, letting excess dough hang over edge. Ease dough into plate by gently lifting edge of dough with your hand while pressing into plate bottom with your other hand.

5. Trim overhang to ½ inch beyond lip of plate. Tuck overhang under itself; folded edge should be flush with edge of plate. Crimp dough evenly around edge of plate using your fingers. Wrap dough-lined plate loosely in plastic and refrigerate until dough is firm, at least 30 minutes.

6. For the Topping Stir all ingredients in bowl until no dry spots remain and mixture forms clumps. Refrigerate until ready to use.

7. Place dough-lined plate on parchment paper–lined rimmed baking sheet. Working with 1 large handful at a time, distribute apple mixture in plate, pressing into even layer and filling in gaps before adding more. Take care not to mound apple mixture in center of plate. Pour any remaining liquid from bowl into pie. Break topping (it will harden in refrigerator) into pea-size crumbs and distribute evenly over apple mixture. Pat topping lightly to adhere.

8. Bake pie on sheet until top is golden brown and paring knife inserted in center meets no resistance, about 1 hour 10 minutes, rotating sheet halfway through baking. Let pie cool on wire rack for at least 4 hours or preferably overnight. Serve.

Why This Recipe Works Apple pie and cheddar cheese share a history, and we wanted to incorporate this sweet-savory pairing into a single recipe. For a flaky crust infused with cheesy flavor, extra-sharp cheddar and a teaspoon of dry mustard amped up the crust's savory qualities. Traditional apple filling got a kick from some cayenne, and precooking the filling allowed us to cram in twice as many apples. Starting with a hotter oven browned the bottom crust, and then reducing the heat kept the top from burning. The result: a moist, sweet-tart filling that perfectly complemented our flaky, cheesy crust.

APPLE PIE WITH CHEDDAR CRUST

SERVES 8

For the best flavor, be sure to use extra-sharp cheddar here. Freezing the butter for 15 minutes promotes flakiness in the crust—do not skip this step.

Crust

2½ cups (12½ ounces) all-purpose flour
1 tablespoon granulated sugar
1 teaspoon salt
1 teaspoon dry mustard
⅛ teaspoon cayenne pepper
8 ounces extra-sharp cheddar cheese, shredded (2 cups)
8 tablespoons unsalted butter, cut into ¼-inch pieces and frozen for 15 minutes
⅓ cup ice water, plus extra as needed

Filling

2 pounds Granny Smith, Empire, or Cortland apples, peeled, cored, halved, and sliced ¼-inch thick
2 pounds Golden Delicious, Jonagold, or Braeburn apples, peeled, cored, halved, and sliced ¼-inch thick
6 tablespoons (2⅔ ounces) granulated sugar
¼ cup packed (1¾ ounces) light brown sugar
½ teaspoon grated lemon zest plus 1 tablespoon juice
¼ teaspoon salt
⅛ teaspoon ground cinnamon

1. For the Crust Process flour, sugar, salt, mustard, and cayenne in food processor until combined, about 5 seconds. Scatter cheddar and butter over top and pulse until butter is size of large peas, about 10 pulses.

2. Pour half of ice water over flour mixture and pulse until incorporated, about 3 pulses. Repeat with remaining ice water. Pinch dough with your fingers; if dough feels dry and does not hold together, sprinkle 1 to 2 tablespoons extra ice water over mixture and pulse until dough forms large clumps and no dry flour remains, 3 to 5 pulses.

3. Divide dough in half and form each half into 4-inch disk. Wrap disks tightly in plastic wrap and refrigerate for 1 hour. Let chilled dough sit on counter to soften slightly, about 10 minutes, before rolling. (Wrapped dough can be refrigerated for up to 2 days or frozen for up to 1 month. If frozen, let dough thaw completely on counter before rolling.)

4. For the Filling Stir apples, granulated sugar, brown sugar, lemon zest, salt, and cinnamon together in Dutch oven. Cover and cook over medium heat, stirring frequently, until apples are just tender but still hold their shape, 10 to 15 minutes. Off heat, stir in lemon juice. Spread apple mixture on rimmed baking sheet and let cool completely, about 30 minutes. (Filling can be refrigerated for up to 24 hours.)

5. Roll 1 disk of dough into 12-inch circle between 2 sheets of parchment paper or plastic. Loosely roll dough around rolling pin and gently unroll it onto 9-inch pie plate, letting excess dough hang over edge. Ease dough into plate by gently lifting edge of dough with your hand while pressing into plate bottom with your other hand. Trim overhang to ½ inch beyond lip of pie plate. Wrap dough-lined pie plate loosely in plastic and refrigerate until dough is firm, about 15 minutes.

6. Adjust oven rack to lowest position and heat oven to 425 degrees. Fill pie shell with apple mixture. Roll other disk of dough into 12-inch circle between 2 sheets of parchment or plastic. Loosely roll dough around rolling pin and gently unroll it onto filling.

7. Trim overhang to ½ inch beyond lip of pie plate. Pinch edges of top and bottom crusts firmly together. Tuck overhang under itself; folded edge should be flush with edge of pie plate. Crimp dough around edge of pie plate using your fingers. Cut four 2-inch slits in top of dough.

8. Set pie on foil or parchment-lined baking sheet and bake for 20 minutes. Reduce oven temperature to 375 degrees and continue to bake until crust is deep golden brown and filling is bubbling, 35 to 45 minutes. Transfer pie to wire rack and let cool for at least 1½ hours. Serve.

APPLE SLAB PIE

SERVES 18 TO 20

We prefer an 18 by 13-inch nonstick rimmed baking sheet for this pie. If using a conventional baking sheet, coat it lightly with vegetable oil spray.

Pie

3½ pounds Granny Smith apples, peeled, cored, halved, and sliced thin
3½ pounds Golden Delicious apples, peeled, cored, halved, and sliced thin
1½ cups (10½ ounces) granulated sugar
½ teaspoon salt
1½ cups (4 ounces) animal crackers
2 (16-ounce) boxes refrigerated pie dough
4 tablespoons unsalted butter, melted and cooled
6 tablespoons instant tapioca
2 teaspoons ground cinnamon
3 tablespoons lemon juice

Glaze

2 tablespoons lemon juice
1 tablespoon unsalted butter, softened
1¼ cups (5 ounces) confectioners' sugar

1. For the Pie Combine apples, 1 cup sugar, and salt in colander set over large bowl. Let sit, tossing occasionally, until apples release their juices, about 30 minutes. Press gently on apples to extract liquid and reserve ¾ cup juice. Adjust oven rack to lower-middle position and heat oven to 350 degrees.

2. Pulse crackers and remaining ½ cup sugar in food processor until finely ground, about 20 pulses. Dust counter with cracker mixture, brush half of 1 pie round with water, overlap with second pie round, and dust top with cracker mixture. Roll out dough to 19 by 14 inches and transfer to rimmed baking sheet. Brush dough with butter, cover loosely with plastic wrap and refrigerate.

3. Roll remaining 2 dough rounds together with remaining cracker mixture to a 19 by 14-inch rectangle.

4. Toss drained apples with tapioca, cinnamon, and lemon juice and arrange evenly over bottom crust, pressing lightly to flatten. Brush edges of bottom crust with water and arrange top crust on pie. Press crusts together. Use paring knife to trim any excess dough. Use fork to crimp and seal outside edge of pie and then pierce top of pie at 2-inch intervals. Bake until pie is golden brown and juices are bubbling, about 1 hour. Let pie cool on wire rack for 1 hour.

5. For the Glaze While pie is cooling, simmer reserved apple juice in saucepan over medium heat until syrupy and reduced to ¼ cup, about 6 minutes. Stir in lemon juice and butter and let cool to room temperature. Whisk in sugar and brush glaze evenly over warm pie. Let pie cool completely, at least 1 hour longer. Serve. (Pie can be refrigerated for up to 24 hours.)

How to Make Apple Slab Pie

1. Use water to "glue" together 2 store-bought pie crusts.

2. Add flavor to the bottom crust by rolling it out in mixture of crushed cookie crumbs and sugar.

3. After transferring bottom crust to baking dish, brush with melted butter for extra richness.

4. Top filled pie with second "double" crust and use fork to tightly seal edges of crust.

Why This Recipe Works Unlike a traditional apple pie, a slab pie is prepared in a baking sheet and can feed up to 20 people. Its filling is thickened to ensure neat slicing, and its crust is topped with a sugary glaze. But rolling out the dough for this mammoth pie proved problematic, as did making the filling thick enough to hold up to slicing. Gluing two sturdy store-bought crusts together with water and then rolling the dough into a large rectangle allowed us to get the crust into the large pan without a tear. To give the crust a sweet, buttery flavor, we rolled it in crushed animal crackers. Tapioca thickened the filling well without making it starchy.

OLD-FASHIONED PECAN PIE

SERVES 8 TO 10

Serve with Bourbon Whipped Cream (recipe follows), if desired. You can use Classic Single-Crust Pie Dough (page 764) or No-Fear Single-Crust Pie Dough (page 765) for this pie.

  1 cup maple syrup
  1 cup packed (7 ounces) light brown sugar
 ½ cup heavy cream
  1 tablespoon molasses
  4 tablespoons unsalted butter, cut into
    ½-inch pieces
 ½ teaspoon salt
  6 large egg yolks, lightly beaten
1½ cups (6 ounces) pecans, toasted and chopped
  1 recipe single-crust pie dough, fitted into 9-inch pie plate and chilled

1. Adjust oven rack to lowest position and heat oven to 450 degrees. Heat syrup, sugar, cream, and molasses in saucepan over medium heat, stirring occasionally, until sugar dissolves, about 3 minutes. Remove from heat and let cool for 5 minutes. Whisk butter and salt into syrup mixture until combined. Whisk in egg yolks until incorporated.

2. Scatter pecans in pie shell. Carefully pour filling over. Place pie in oven and immediately reduce oven temperature to 325 degrees. Bake until filling is set and center jiggles slightly when pie is gently shaken, 45 minutes to 1 hour. Let pie cool on rack for 1 hour, then refrigerate until set, about 3 hours or up to 24 hours. Bring to room temperature before serving.

BOURBON WHIPPED CREAM
MAKES ABOUT 2 CUPS
Although any style of whiskey will work here, we like the smokiness of bourbon.

  1 cup heavy cream
  2 tablespoons bourbon
1½ tablespoons packed light brown sugar
 ½ teaspoon vanilla extract

Using stand mixer fitted with whisk, whip cream, bourbon, sugar, and vanilla on medium-low speed until foamy, about 1 minute. Increase speed to high and whip until stiff peaks form, about 2 minutes. (Whipped cream can be refrigerated for 4 hours.)

Move Over, Karo
Before cloying Karo syrup monopolized the market, pies were made with many other, less processed types of syrup, including sorghum (made from a cereal grass) and cane (made from the boiled-down juice of the sugarcane plant). These syrups still exist, and you can mail-order them or travel to places such as Louisiana or Kentucky to find them. We tasted a range of such syrups, including Steen's 100% Pure Cane Syrup and Townsend's Sweet Sorghum, then tried to duplicate their complex flavors with products we could buy at the supermarket. In the end, a combination of three ordinary sweeteners created an old-fashioned flavor that easily bested Karo.

| Molasses brings a robust, slightly bitter quality. | Light brown sugar adds warmth and caramel tones. | Maple syrup adds delicate complexity. |

Why This Recipe Works The pecan pies of today bear little resemblance to their 19th-century inspiration. Could we re-create old-fashioned pecan pie without using modern-day processed corn syrup? Many traditional syrups (cane, sorghum) produced a great pie, but we had to mail away for those ingredients. In the end, combining maple syrup with brown sugar and molasses replicated the old-fashioned versions perfectly. We started the pie at a high oven temperature to ensure the bottom crust was crisp and golden brown and then dropped the temperature to finish baking.

Why This Recipe Works Hoping to streamline this holiday dessert, we started by "baking" whole sweet potatoes in the microwave. A food processor made quick work of pureeing the flesh and lent a super-smooth texture. Sour cream added subtle tang while smoothing out the custard even more, and supplementing whole eggs with extra yolks added richness and helped with sliceability. We heated the spices in butter to intensify (or bloom) their flavor before adding them, along with some bourbon and vanilla, to the filling. First we sprinkled brown sugar onto the crust, which melted into a gooey faux caramel and took this pie to the next level.

SWEET POTATO PIE

SERVES 8

The best pies use homemade crust. You can use Classic Single-Crust Pie Dough (page 764) or No-Fear Single-Crust Pie Dough (page 765) for this pie. If you're pressed for time, try our favorite store-bought crust, Pillsbury Refrigerated Pie Crusts. Choose sweet potatoes that are about the same size so that they'll cook evenly. Serve with Bourbon Whipped Cream (page 788), if desired.

1   (9-inch) single-crust pie dough
1¼ cups packed (8¾ ounces) light brown sugar
1¾ pounds sweet potatoes, unpeeled
½   teaspoon salt
4   tablespoons unsalted butter
½   teaspoon ground cinnamon
¼   teaspoon ground nutmeg
1   cup sour cream
3   large eggs plus 2 large yolks
2   tablespoons bourbon (optional)
1   teaspoon vanilla extract

1. Adjust oven rack to middle position and heat oven to 375 degrees. Roll dough into 12-inch circle on lightly floured counter. Loosely roll dough around rolling pin and gently unroll it onto 9-inch pie plate, letting excess dough hang over edge. Ease dough into plate by gently lifting edge of dough with your hand while pressing into plate bottom with your other hand. Trim overhang to ½ inch beyond lip of pie plate. Tuck overhang under itself; folded edge should be flush with edge of pie plate. Crimp dough evenly around edge of pie using your fingers. Wrap dough-lined pie plate loosely in plastic and freeze until dough is firm, about 15 minutes.

2. Line chilled pie shell with two 12-inch squares of parchment paper, letting parchment lie over edges of dough, and fill with pie weights. Bake until lightly golden around edges, 18 to 25 minutes. Carefully remove parchment and weights, rotate crust, and continue to bake until center begins to look opaque and slightly drier, 3 to 6 minutes. Remove from oven. Let crust cool completely. Sprinkle ¼ cup sugar over bottom of crust; set aside. Reduce oven temperature to 350 degrees.

3. Meanwhile, prick potatoes all over with fork. Microwave on large plate until potatoes are very soft and surface is slightly wet, 15 to 20 minutes, flipping every 5 minutes. Immediately slice potatoes in half to release steam. When cool enough to handle, scoop flesh into bowl of food processor. Add salt and remaining 1 cup sugar and process until smooth, about 60 seconds, scraping down sides of bowl as needed. Melt butter with cinnamon and nutmeg in microwave, 15 to 30 seconds; stir to combine. Add spiced butter, sour cream, eggs and yolks, bourbon, if using, and vanilla to potatoes and process until incorporated, about 10 seconds, scraping down sides of bowl as needed.

4. Pour potato mixture into prepared pie shell. Bake until filling is set around edges but center registers 165 degrees and jiggles slightly when pie is shaken, 35 to 40 minutes. Let pie cool completely on wire rack, about 2 hours. Serve.

Why This Recipe Works French coconut pie, a Southern favorite, is a coconut-custard pie that is often too eggy, too sweet, or lacking in coconut flavor. We set out to tackle all of these issues. First, we found that two whole eggs plus one extra yolk provided just the right amount of richness. To better control the sweetness, we tried unsweetened shredded coconut, which also intensified the coconut flavor. Since the dried coconut was not fully softening as the pie baked, we soaked it in buttermilk and vanilla before adding it to the filling. The finished pie was golden brown—from the pie crust to the lovely sugar crust that formed on top of the custard.

FRENCH COCONUT PIE

SERVES 8 TO 10

Look for shredded unsweetened coconut, about ¼ inch in length, in the natural foods section of the supermarket. It sometimes goes by the name "coconut flakes." Do not use large flaked coconut in this recipe. Our favorite shredded unsweetened coconut is Now Real Food Organic Unsweetened Coconut, Shredded.

- 1 (9-inch) store-bought pie dough round
- 1¼ cups (3¾ ounces) unsweetened shredded coconut
- ½ cup buttermilk
- 1 teaspoon vanilla extract
- 1 cup (7 ounces) sugar
- 8 tablespoons unsalted butter, melted and cooled
- 2 large eggs plus 1 large yolk
- 2 tablespoons all-purpose flour
- ¼ teaspoon salt

1. Adjust oven rack to lower-middle position and heat oven to 325 degrees. Roll dough into 12-inch circle on lightly floured counter. Loosely roll dough around rolling pin and gently unroll it onto 9-inch pie plate, letting excess dough hang over edge. Ease dough into plate by gently lifting edge of dough with your hand while pressing into plate bottom with your other hand.

2. Trim overhang to ½ inch beyond lip of plate. Tuck overhang under itself; folded edge should be flush with edge of plate. Crimp dough evenly around edge of plate using your fingers. Wrap dough-lined plate loosely in plastic wrap and freeze until dough is firm, about 15 minutes.

3. Discard plastic wrap and line chilled pie shell with two 12-inch squares of parchment paper, letting parchment lie over edges of dough, and fill with pie weights. Bake until lightly golden around edges, 18 to 25 minutes. Transfer to wire rack and carefully remove parchment and weights. (Pie shell needn't cool completely before proceeding.)

4. Meanwhile, combine coconut, buttermilk, and vanilla in bowl. Cover with plastic and let sit for 15 minutes.

5. Whisk sugar, butter, eggs and yolk, flour, and salt together in large bowl. Stir in coconut mixture until fully incorporated. Pour filling into warm pie shell. Bake until custard is set and golden-brown crust forms on top of pie, 40 to 55 minutes.

6. Transfer pie to wire rack and let cool completely, about 4 hours. Serve at room temperature. (Cooled pie can be covered with plastic and refrigerated for up to 2 days. Let come to room temperature before serving.)

Crimping a Single-Crust Pie Shell
Our easy crimping technique makes a decorative, sturdy edge.

1. Use scissors to trim overhanging dough to uniform ½ inch.

2. Tuck dough under to form thick, even edge on lip of pie plate.

3. Use both hands to pinch dough into ridges, working around perimeter.

Why This Recipe Works To do justice to this retro classic—the star of the diner dessert case with its lofty profile and shaggy coconut garnish—we packed each component with coconutty goodness. We ground sweetened shredded coconut together with Nilla Wafers and melted butter for a snappy cookie crust (a hit with tasters) and prebaked it until it was golden brown and aromatic. More sweetened shredded coconut added tropical flavor to our custard filling, which we spooned into our cooled crust. After a three-hour rest in the refrigerator, we piled the pie high with whipped cream, and dressed it up with a sprinkling of toasted coconut.

COCONUT CREAM PIE

SERVES 8 TO 10

Be sure to let the cookie crust cool completely before you begin making the filling—at least 30 minutes. Plan ahead: For the filling to set completely, this pie needs to be refrigerated for at least 3 hours or up to 24 hours before serving.

Crust

- 2 cups (4½ ounces) Nilla Wafer cookies (34 cookies)
- ½ cup (1½ ounces) sweetened shredded coconut
- 2 tablespoons sugar
- 1 tablespoon all-purpose flour
- ¼ teaspoon salt
- 4 tablespoons unsalted butter, melted

Filling

- 3 cups whole milk
- 5 large egg yolks
- 5 tablespoons cornstarch
- ¼ teaspoon salt
- ½ cup (3½ ounces) sugar
- ½ cup (1½ ounces) sweetened shredded coconut
- ½ teaspoon vanilla extract

Topping

- 1½ cups heavy cream, chilled
- 3 tablespoons sugar
- 1 teaspoon vanilla extract
- ¼ cup (¾ ounce) sweetened shredded coconut, toasted

1. For the Crust Adjust oven rack to middle position and heat oven to 325 degrees. Process cookies, coconut, sugar, flour, and salt in food processor until finely ground, about 30 seconds. Add melted butter and pulse until combined, about 6 pulses. Transfer mixture to 9-inch pie plate. Using bottom of dry measuring cup, press crumbs firmly into bottom and up sides of plate. Bake until fragrant and set, 18 to 22 minutes. Transfer plate to wire rack and let crust cool completely.

2. For the Filling Whisk ¼ cup milk, egg yolks, cornstarch, and salt together in large bowl. Bring sugar and remaining 2¾ cups milk to simmer in large saucepan over medium heat. Slowly whisk half of hot milk mixture into yolk mixture to temper.

3. Return milk-yolk mixture to remaining milk mixture in saucepan. Whisking constantly, cook over medium heat until custard is thickened and registers 180 degrees, 30 to 90 seconds. Remove from heat and stir in coconut and vanilla. Pour filling into cooled crust and spread into even layer.

4. Spray piece of parchment paper with vegetable oil spray and press flush onto surface of custard to cover completely and prevent skin from forming. Refrigerate until cold and set, at least 3 hours or up to 24 hours.

5. For the Topping Using stand mixer fitted with whisk attachment, whip cream, sugar, and vanilla on medium-low speed until foamy, about 1 minute. Increase speed to high and whip until stiff peaks form, 1 to 3 minutes. Spread whipped cream evenly over pie. Sprinkle coconut over top. Serve.

Backstory

After auditioning traditional graham cracker and pastry crusts for our coconut cream pie recipe, we came upon an even better option: a Nilla Wafer crumb crust. With their crunchy yet lightly cakey texture and vanilla-forward flavor, these slender, airy cookies turned out to be a terrific choice. When ground with sweetened shredded coconut and mixed with a little flour, sugar, and melted butter, they produced an ideal tropical base for our pie.

The original recipe for the cookies was cooked up by German-born inventor and confectioner Gustave Mayer in Staten Island, New York. Mayer sold his recipe to Nabisco in 1929. At the time, Nabisco marketed the cookies as Vanilla Wafers; they shortened the name to Nilla Wafers in 1967. Since their introduction, the cookies have been eaten straight from the box as well as used as an ingredient in many desserts.

RASPBERRY CHIFFON PIE

SERVES 8 TO 10

You can use Classic Single-Crust Pie Dough (page 764) or No-Fear Single-Crust Pie Dough (page 765) for this pie. The raspberry-flavored gelatin is important for the color and flavor of the chiffon layer; do not substitute unflavored gelatin. For an accurate measurement of boiling water, bring a full kettle of water to a boil, then measure out the desired amount.

1 recipe single-crust pie dough, fitted into 9-inch pie plate and chilled

Fruit
12 ounces (2½ cups) frozen raspberries
3 tablespoons pectin (Sure-Jell)
1½ cups (10½ ounces) sugar
Pinch salt
5 ounces (1 cup) fresh raspberries

Chiffon
3 tablespoons raspberry-flavored gelatin
3 tablespoons boiling water
3 ounces cream cheese, softened
1 cup heavy cream, chilled

Topping
1¼ cups heavy cream, chilled
2 tablespoons sugar

1. Adjust oven rack to middle position and heat oven to 375 degrees. Line chilled crust with double layer of aluminum foil and fill with pie weights. Bake until pie dough looks dry and is light in color, 25 to 30 minutes. Remove weights and foil and continue to bake crust until deep golden brown, 10 to 12 minutes longer. Let crust cool on wire rack to room temperature.

2. For the Fruit Cook frozen berries in medium saucepan over medium-high heat, stirring occasionally, until berries begin to give up their juices, about 3 minutes. Stir in pectin and bring to full boil, stirring constantly. Stir in sugar and salt and return to full boil. Cook, stirring constantly, until slightly thickened, about 2 minutes. Pour through fine-mesh strainer into medium bowl, pressing on solids to extract as much puree as possible. Scrape puree off underside of strainer into bowl.

3. Transfer ⅓ cup raspberry puree to small bowl and let cool to room temperature. Gently fold fresh raspberries into remaining puree. Spread fruit mixture evenly over bottom of cooled pie shell and set aside.

4. For the Chiffon Dissolve gelatin in boiling water in bowl of stand mixer. Fit stand mixer with paddle, add cream cheese and reserved ⅓ cup raspberry puree, and beat on high speed, scraping down bowl once or twice, until smooth, about 2 minutes. Add cream and beat on medium-low speed until incorporated, about 30 seconds. Scrape down bowl. Increase speed to high and beat until cream holds stiff peaks, 1 to 2 minutes. Spread evenly over fruit in pie shell. Cover pie with plastic wrap. Refrigerate until set, at least 3 hours or up to 2 days.

5. For the Topping When ready to serve, fit stand mixer with whisk and whip cream and sugar on medium-low speed until foamy, about 1 minute. Increase speed to high and whip until stiff peaks form, 1 to 3 minutes. Spread or pipe over chilled filling. Serve.

Two Layers, Two Thickeners

For the Fruit Layer
For the bottom layer, we used Sure-Jell (pectin) to achieve a concentrated raspberry flavor and texture. There are two formulations of Sure-Jell. We found that the original formula made the smoothest, thickest bottom layer of fruit.

For the Chiffon Layer
A few tablespoons of raspberry gelatin made for great stability and color in the creamy chiffon layer and reinforced the berry flavor.

Why This Recipe Works Raspberry chiffon pie can often be weak on berry flavor. We wanted to produce an intensely flavored pie, so we included a layer of sweetened, thickened fruit on the crust and beneath the chiffon. We also stiffened our recipe's chiffon filling by using extra gelatin and a little cream cheese, which enabled it to hold additional raspberry puree for even more flavor.

ICEBOX STRAWBERRY PIE

SERVES 8

You can use Classic Single-Crust Pie Dough (page 764) or No-Fear Single-Crust Pie Dough (page 765) for this pie. In step 2, it is imperative that the cooked strawberry mixture measures 2 cups; any more and the filling will be loose. If your fresh berries aren't fully ripe, you may want to add extra sugar to taste in step 3.

1 recipe single-crust pie dough, fitted into 9-inch pie plate and chilled

Filling
2 pounds (7 cups) frozen strawberries
1 tablespoon unflavored gelatin
2 tablespoons lemon juice
2 tablespoons water
1 cup (7 ounces) sugar
  Pinch salt
1 pound fresh strawberries, hulled and sliced thin

Topping
4 ounces cream cheese, softened
3 tablespoons sugar
½ teaspoon vanilla extract
1 cup heavy cream

1. Adjust oven rack to middle position and heat oven to 375 degrees. Line chilled crust with double layer of aluminum foil and fill with pie weights. Bake until pie dough looks dry and is light in color, 25 to 30 minutes. Remove weights and foil and continue to bake crust until deep golden brown, 10 to 12 minutes longer. Let crust cool to room temperature on wire rack.

2. For the Filling Cook frozen berries in large saucepan over medium-low heat until berries begin to release juice, about 3 minutes. Increase heat to medium-high and cook, stirring frequently, until thick and jamlike, about 25 minutes (mixture should measure 2 cups).

3. Sprinkle gelatin over lemon juice and water in small bowl. Let stand until gelatin is softened and mixture has thickened, about 5 minutes. Stir gelatin mixture, sugar, and salt into cooked berry mixture and return to simmer, about 2 minutes. Transfer to bowl and cool to room temperature, about 30 minutes.

4. Fold fresh berries into filling. Spread evenly in pie shell and refrigerate until set, about 4 hours. (Filled pie can be refrigerated for 24 hours.)

5. For the Topping Using stand mixer fitted with whisk, beat cream cheese, sugar, and vanilla on medium speed until smooth, about 30 seconds. With mixer running, add cream and whip until stiff peaks form, about 2 minutes. Dollop individual slices of pie with topping and serve.

Don't Make This Mistake

In step 2, be sure to accurately measure the reduced strawberry mixture: You'll need exactly 2 cups. Scrape the strawberry mixture into a large liquid measuring cup. If it measures more than 2 cups, return it to the pan to cook down. It may seem fussy to stop to measure, but the pie will not set or slice properly if you have more than 2 cups of the strawberry mixture.

Why This Recipe Works Frozen strawberries, which are great for cooking, form the base of our strawberry pie. We cooked them down in a dry saucepan until they released their juice and the mixture was thick, concentrated, and flavorful. Because strawberries are low in pectin, the natural thickener found in citrus fruits and many other plants, we added some lemon juice, which perked up the flavor and tightened the texture of the filling a little. To thicken the filling further, we added a bit of unflavored gelatin. Then we mixed in fresh strawberries for a fresh finish with big berry flavor.

Why This Recipe Works This prize-winning icebox pie with a sophisticated name originally called for raw eggs. Testing showed that we could cook the eggs with sugar on the stovetop, almost like making a custard. Once the egg and sugar mixture was light and thick, we removed it from the heat and continued whipping it until it was fully cooled. Bittersweet chocolate folded into the cooled egg and sugar mixture made for a pie with more intense chocolate flavor. And to lighten the filling's texture, we incorporated whipped cream.

FRENCH SILK CHOCOLATE PIE

SERVES 8 TO 10

You can use Classic Single-Crust Pie Dough (page 764) or No-Fear Single-Crust Pie Dough (page 765) for this pie. Serve with lightly sweetened whipped cream.

1 recipe single-crust pie dough, fitted into 9-inch pie plate and chilled
1 cup heavy cream, chilled
3 large eggs
¾ cup (5¼ ounces) sugar
2 tablespoons water
8 ounces bittersweet chocolate, melted and cooled
1 tablespoon vanilla extract
8 tablespoons unsalted butter, cut into ½-inch pieces and softened

1. Adjust oven rack to middle position and heat oven to 375 degrees. Line chilled crust with double layer of aluminum foil and fill with pie weights. Bake until pie dough looks dry and is light in color, 25 to 30 minutes. Remove weights and foil and continue to bake crust until deep golden brown, 10 to 12 minutes longer. Let crust cool on wire rack to room temperature.

2. Using stand mixer fitted with whisk, whip cream on medium-low speed until foamy, about 1 minute. Increase speed to high and whip until stiff peaks form, 1 to 3 minutes. Transfer whipped cream to small bowl and refrigerate.

3. Combine eggs, sugar, and water in large heat-proof bowl set over medium saucepan filled with ½ inch barely simmering water (don't let bowl touch water). Using hand-held mixer set at medium speed, beat egg mixture until thickened and registers 160 degrees, 7 to 10 minutes. Remove bowl from heat and continue to beat egg mixture until fluffy and cooled to room temperature, about 8 minutes.

4. Add chocolate and vanilla to cooled egg mixture and beat until incorporated. Beat in butter, few pieces at a time, until well combined. Using spatula, fold in whipped cream until no streaks of white remain. Scrape filling into pie shell and refrigerate until set, at least 3 hours or up to 24 hours. Serve.

Whisking Chocolate into Silk

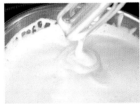 

1. Beat eggs and sugar together in double boiler to incorporate air for filling with light, ethereal texture. Remove from heat when egg mixture reaches 160 degrees; it will be very thick.

2. Continue beating egg mixture until fluffy and cool. Add melted chocolate and beat in softened butter for rich flavor and silky-smooth texture.

The Pillsbury Bake-Off

In 1949, General Mills launched the "Grand National Recipe and Baking Contest" (later known as the Pillsbury Bake-Off). It was held at the posh Waldorf-Astoria Hotel in New York. The grand-prize winner (for No-Knead Water Rising Twists) brought home $50,000; Eleanor Roosevelt was one of the luminaries on hand to present the awards. Since then, many prize-winning Pillsbury recipes have become part of our culinary heritage, among them French Silk Chocolate Pie (the name reflects the international curiosity of postwar America), Open Sesame Pie (which caused a run on sesame seeds nationwide), and Peanut Blossom Cookies (with a Hershey's Kiss in the middle).

CHOCOLATE ANGEL PIE

SERVES 8 TO 10

Serve the assembled pie within 3 hours of chilling.

Filling
9 ounces milk chocolate, chopped fine
5 ounces bittersweet chocolate, chopped fine
3 large egg yolks
1½ tablespoons granulated sugar
½ teaspoon salt
½ cup half-and-half
1¼ cups heavy cream, chilled

Meringue Crust
1 tablespoon cornstarch, plus extra for pie plate
½ cup (3½ ounces) granulated sugar
3 large egg whites
Pinch cream of tartar
½ teaspoon vanilla extract

Topping
1⅓ cups heavy cream, chilled
2 tablespoons confectioners' sugar
Unsweetened cocoa powder

1. For the Filling Microwave milk chocolate and bittersweet chocolate in large bowl at 50 percent power, stirring occasionally, until melted, 2 to 4 minutes. Whisk egg yolks, sugar, and salt together in medium bowl until combined, about 1 minute. Bring half-and-half to simmer in small saucepan over medium heat. Whisking constantly, slowly add hot half-and-half to egg yolk mixture in 2 additions until incorporated. Return half-and-half mixture to now-empty saucepan and cook over low heat, whisking constantly, until thickened slightly, 30 seconds to 1 minute. Stir half-and-half mixture into melted chocolate until combined. Let cool slightly, about 8 minutes.

2. Using stand mixer fitted with whisk, whip cream on medium-low speed until foamy, about 1 minute. Increase speed to high and whip until soft peaks form, 1 to 3 minutes. Gently whisk one-third of whipped cream into cooled chocolate mixture. Fold in remaining whipped cream until no white streaks remain. Cover and refrigerate for at least 3 hours, or until ready to assemble pie. (Filling can be made up to 24 hours in advance.)

3. For the Meringue Crust Adjust oven rack to lower-middle position and heat oven to 275 degrees. Grease 9-inch pie plate and dust well with extra cornstarch, using pastry brush to distribute evenly. Combine sugar and 1 tablespoon cornstarch in bowl. Using stand mixer fitted with whisk, whip egg whites and cream of tartar on medium-low speed until foamy, about 1 minute. Increase speed to medium-high and whip whites to soft, billowy mounds, 1 to 3 minutes. Gradually add sugar mixture and whip until glossy, stiff peaks form, 3 to 5 minutes. Add vanilla to meringue and whip until incorporated.

4. Spread meringue into prepared pie plate, following contours of plate to cover bottom, sides, and edges. Bake for 1½ hours. Rotate pie plate, reduce oven temperature to 200 degrees, and bake until completely dried out, about 1 hour longer. (Shell will rise above rim of pie plate; some cracking is OK.) Let cool completely, about 30 minutes.

5. For the Topping Spoon cooled chocolate filling into cavity of pie shell, distributing evenly. Using stand mixer fitted with whisk, whip cream and sugar on medium-low speed until foamy, about 1 minute. Increase speed to high and whip until stiff peaks form, 1 to 3 minutes. Spread whipped cream evenly over chocolate. Refrigerate until filling is set, about 1 hour. Dust with cocoa. Slice with sharp knife and serve.

Busted Crust
The egg white crust is part of what distinguishes angel pie. To avoid a sticky, broken meringue shell, we added cornstarch to the whites, and we greased the pie plate and dusted it with more cornstarch.

MERINGUE MESS
Don't let this happen to you.

Why This Recipe Works Chocolate angel pie is a lavish version of chocolate cream pie with creamy chocolate mousse, fluffy whipped cream, and an airy meringue crust. For a light, crisp crust, 2½ hours in a low oven was necessary. To prevent the crust from sticking to the pan, we relied on cornstarch, both in the egg whites and dusted over the pie plate. We loaded nearly a pound of chocolate into the filling by making a cooked custard. Using two kinds of chocolate lent depth and complexity. To finish, we topped the pie with lightly sweetened whipped cream and a sprinkling of cocoa powder for a decadent, supremely chocolaty dessert.

MISSISSIPPI MUD PIE

SERVES 8 TO 12

This recipe takes at least 5 hours from start to finish. We used Nabisco Famous Chocolate Wafers in this recipe. Be sure to use milk chocolate in the mousse, as bittersweet chocolate will make the mousse too firm. Do not begin making the mousse until the brownie layer is fully chilled.

Crust
25 chocolate wafer cookies (5½ ounces), broken into coarse pieces
4 tablespoons unsalted butter, melted

Brownie Layer
4 ounces bittersweet chocolate, chopped fine
3 tablespoons unsalted butter
3 tablespoons vegetable oil
1½ tablespoons Dutch-processed cocoa powder
⅔ cup packed (4⅔ ounces) dark brown sugar
2 large eggs
2 teaspoons vanilla extract
¼ teaspoon salt
3 tablespoons all-purpose flour

Topping
10 chocolate wafer cookies (2 ounces)
2 tablespoons confectioners' sugar
1 tablespoon Dutch-processed cocoa powder
⅛ teaspoon salt
2 tablespoons unsalted butter, melted

Mousse
6 ounces milk chocolate, chopped fine
1 cup heavy cream, chilled
2 tablespoons Dutch-processed cocoa powder
2 tablespoons confectioners' sugar
⅛ teaspoon salt

1. For the Crust Adjust oven rack to middle position and heat oven to 325 degrees. Process cookie pieces in food processor until finely ground, about 30 seconds. Add melted butter and pulse until combined, about 6 pulses. Using bottom of dry measuring cup, press crumbs firmly into bottom and up sides of 9-inch pie plate. Bake until fragrant and set, about 15 minutes. Transfer to wire rack.

2. For the Brownie Layer Combine chocolate, butter, oil, and cocoa in bowl and microwave at 50 percent power, stirring often, until melted, about 1½ minutes. In separate bowl, whisk sugar, eggs, vanilla, and salt until smooth. Whisk in chocolate mixture until incorporated. Whisk in flour until just combined.

3. Pour brownie batter into crust (crust needn't be cool at this point). Bake pie until edges begin to set and toothpick inserted in center comes out with thin coating of batter attached, about 15 minutes. Transfer to wire rack and let cool for 1 hour, then refrigerate until fully chilled, about 1 hour longer.

4. For the Topping Meanwhile, line rimmed baking sheet with parchment paper. Place cookies in zipper-lock bag, press out air, and seal bag. Using rolling pin, crush cookies into ½- to ¾-inch pieces. Combine sugar, cocoa, salt, and crushed cookies in bowl. Stir in melted butter until mixture is moistened and clumps begin to form. Spread crumbs in even layer on prepared sheet and bake until fragrant, about 10 minutes, shaking sheet to break up crumbs halfway through baking. Transfer sheet to wire rack and let cool completely.

5. For the Mousse Once brownie layer has fully chilled, microwave chocolate in large bowl at 50 percent power, stirring often, until melted, 1½ to 2 minutes. Let cool until just barely warm and registers between 90 and 100 degrees, about 10 minutes.

6. Microwave 3 tablespoons cream in small bowl until it registers 105 to 110 degrees, about 15 seconds. Whisk in cocoa until homogeneous. Combine cocoa-cream mixture, sugar, salt, and remaining cream in bowl of stand mixer. Fit mixer with whisk and whip cream mixture on medium speed until beginning to thicken, about 30 seconds, scraping down bowl as needed. Increase speed to high and whip until soft peaks form, 30 to 60 seconds.

7. Using whisk, fold one-third of whipped cream mixture into melted chocolate to lighten. Using rubber spatula, fold in remaining whipped cream mixture until no dark streaks remain. Spoon mousse into chilled pie and spread evenly from edge to edge. Sprinkle with cooled topping and refrigerate for at least 3 hours or overnight. Serve.

Why This Recipe Works This pie is so named because its chocolate layers are reminiscent of the Mississippi River's silty bottom, but there's nothing muddy about its flavor. To simplify each layer of the pie, we started with a press-in chocolate wafer cookie crust. For a perfectly soft, chewy middle layer, we created a brownie-like batter and underbaked it slightly. Once this layer was fully chilled, we spread on a simple milk chocolate mousse and sprinkled on a crunchy chocolate cookie topping to finish off our striated chocolate showstopper.

SHOPPING FOR EQUIPMENT

With a well-stocked kitchen, you'll be able to take on any recipe. But there's so much equipment out there on the market, how do you figure out what's what? Price often correlates with design, not performance. Over the years, our test kitchen has evaluated thousands of products. We've gone through copious rounds of testing and have identified the most important attributes in every piece of equipment, so when you go shopping you'll know what to look for. And because our test kitchen accepts no support from product manufacturers, you can trust our ratings. Prices in this chart are based on shopping at online retailers and will vary. See AmericasTestKitchen.com for updates to these testings.

KNIVES AND MORE	ITEM	WHAT TO LOOK FOR	TEST KITCHEN FAVORITES
MUST-HAVE ITEMS	CHEF'S KNIFE	• High-carbon stainless steel knife • Thin, curved 8-inch blade • Lightweight • Comfortable grip and nonslip handle	**Victorinox Swiss Army Fibrox Pro 8" Chef's Knife** $39.95
	PARING KNIFE	• 3- to 3½-inch blade • Thin, flexible blade with pointed tip • Comfortable grip	**Victorinox Swiss Army 3¼-Inch Spear Point Paring Knife** $7.51
	SERRATED KNIFE	• 10-inch blade • Fewer broader, deeper, pointed serrations • Thinner blade angle • Comfortable, grippy handle • Medium weight	**Mercer Culinary Millenia 10" Wide Bread Knife** $22.10
	SLICING/CARVING KNIFE	• Tapered 12-inch blade for slicing large cuts of meat • Oval scallops (called a granton edge) carved into blade • Fairly rigid blade with rounded tip	**Victorinox Swiss Army 12" Granton Slicing Knife** $54.65
	STEAK KNIVES	• Supersharp, straight-edged blade • Sturdy, not wobbly, blade	**Victorinox Swiss Army 6-Piece Rosewood Steak Set, Spear Point, Straight Edge** $170.74 for a set of six Best Buy: **Chicago Cutlery Walnut Tradition 4-Piece Steak Knife Set** $17.95 for a set of four

KNIVES AND MORE	ITEM	WHAT TO LOOK FOR	TEST KITCHEN FAVORITES
	SANTOKU KNIFE	• Narrow, curved, and short blade • Comfortable grip	**Misono UX10** **Santoku 7.0"** $179.50
	BIRD'S BEAK PARING KNIFE	• Narrow tip makes near-surgical incisions • Lightweight with a relatively grippy wood veneer handle • Comfortable to hold for long periods	**MAC Paring Knife,** **Bird's Beak, 2½"** $29.95
	BONING KNIFE	• 5.5-inch blade • Ultrasharp, moderately flexible blade • Slightly shorter length gives more control • Slim plastic handle easy to grip in different ways	**Zwilling Pro 5.5" Flexible** **Boning Knife** $99.95 Best Buy: **Victorinox Swiss** **Army Fibrox Pro 6"** **Flexible Boning Knife** $26.95
	MEAT CLEAVER	• Razor-sharp blade • Balanced weight between handle and blade • Comfortable grip	**Shun Classic Meat Cleaver** $149 Best Buy: **Lamson** **Products 7.25" Walnut** **Handle Meat Cleaver** $59.95
	GYUTOU	• High-carbon stainless steel knife • Lightweight • Thin blade that tapers from spine to cutting edge and from handle to tip	**Masamoto VG-10** **Gyutou, 8.2"** $136.50
	ELECTRIC KNIFE	• Good slicing ability • Low noise level • Comfortable rounded handle with start button located conveniently underneath	**Black + Decker** **ComfortGrip 9"** **Electric Knife** $19.92
	MANDOLINE	• Razor-sharp blade(s) • No fixed thickness settings for customization with slicing • Simple plank shape can be used vertically or hooked over a bowl	Co-winner: **Super Benriner** **Mandoline Slicer** $50.99
		• Clearly marked, accurate dial allows thickness adjustments in both ¹⁄₁₆-inch and 1-millimeter increments • Rubber-coated kickstand • Spring-loaded food pusher helps protect hands	Co-winner: **OXO Good** **Grips Chef's Mandoline** **Slicer 2.0** $84.99

KNIVES AND MORE	ITEM	WHAT TO LOOK FOR	TEST KITCHEN FAVORITES
	CARVING BOARD	• Trenches can contain ½ cup of liquid • Large and stable enough to hold large roasts • Midweight for easy carrying, carving, and cleaning	**J.K. Adams Maple Reversible Carving Board** $69.95
MUST-HAVE ITEM	CUTTING BOARD	• Roomy work surface at least 20 by 15 inches • Teak board for minimal maintenance • Durable edge-grain construction (wood grain runs parallel to surface of board)	**Teakhaus by Proteak Edge Grain Cutting Board** $104.95
MUST-HAVE ITEM	KNIFE SHARPENER	• Diamond abrasives and a spring-loaded chamber to precisely guide blade • Quickly removes nicks in blades • Can convert a 20-degree edge to a sharper 15 degrees	Electric: **Chef'sChoice Trizor XV Knife Sharpener** $139.99 Electric, Best Buy: **Chef'sChoice 315XV Knife Sharpener** $109.99 Manual: **Chef'sChoice Pronto Manual Diamond Hone Asian Knife Sharpener** $49.99

POTS AND PANS	ITEM	WHAT TO LOOK FOR	TEST KITCHEN FAVORITES
	TRADITIONAL SKILLET	• Stainless-steel interior and fully clad for even heat distribution • 12-inch diameter and flared sides • Comfortable, ovensafe handle • Tight-fitting lid included	**All-Clad D3 Stainless Steel 12" Fry Pan with Lid** $119.95
MUST-HAVE ITEMS	NONSTICK SKILLET	• Dark, nonstick surface • 12- or 12½-inch diameter, thick bottom • Cooking surface of at least 9 inches • Lightweight, easy to lift	12-inch: **OXO Good Grips Non-Stick Pro 12" Open Frypan** $42.49 10-inch: **OXO Good Grips Non-Stick Pro 10" Open Frypan** $39.95 8-inch: **OXO Good Grips Hard Anodized Pro Nonstick 8-Inch Fry Pan** $29.95

POTS AND PANS	ITEM	WHAT TO LOOK FOR	TEST KITCHEN FAVORITES
	CAST-IRON SKILLET	• Thick bottom and straight sides • Roomy interior (cooking surface of 9¼ inches or more) • Preseasoned	Co-winner: **Lodge Classic Cast Iron Skillet, 12"** $33.31
		• Flaring sides, an oversize helper handle, and wide pour spouts • Enameled exterior and satiny interior with balanced weight	Co-winner: **Le Creuset Signature 11¾" Iron Handle Skillet** $204.95 Best Buy: **Lodge Enamel Coated Cast Iron Skillet, 11"** $48.90
	BRAISER	• Comes in 5 quart, 3.5 quart, and 2.25 quart sizes • Light interior makes it easy to monitor browning and a moderately thick bottom ensures good heat retention • Large, comfortable looped handles and a stainless-steel lid knob provides secure grip	**Le Creuset Signature Enameled Cast-Iron 3.5-Quart Braiser** $299.95
	DUTCH OVEN	• Enameled cast iron or stainless steel • Capacity of at least 6 quarts • Diameter of at least 9 inches • Tight-fitting lid • Wide, sturdy handles	**Le Creuset 7¼ Quart Round Dutch Oven** $367.99 Best Buy: **Cuisinart Chef's Classic Enameled Cast Iron Covered Casserole** $83.70
	SAUCEPAN	• Large saucepan with 3- to 4-quart capacity and small nonstick saucepan with 2- to 2½-quart capacity • Tight-fitting lids • Pans with rounded corners that a whisk can reach into • Long, comfortable handles that are angled for even weight distribution	Large: **All-Clad Stainless 4-Qt Sauce Pan** $211.13 Best Buy: **Tramontina Gourmet Tri-Ply Clad 4 Qt. Covered Sauce Pan** $89.95 Small Nonstick: **Calphalon Contemporary Nonstick 2½ Quart Shallow Saucepan with Cover** $39.95
	RIMMED BAKING SHEET	• Light-colored surface (heats and browns evenly) • Thick, sturdy pan • Dimensions of 18 by 13 inches • Good to have at least two	**Nordic Ware Baker's Half Sheet** $14.97

MUST-HAVE ITEMS

POTS AND PANS	ITEM	WHAT TO LOOK FOR	TEST KITCHEN FAVORITES
	SAUTÉ PAN	• Aluminum core surrounded by layers of stainless-steel • Hefty but well-balanced pan • 9½- to 10-inch diameter • Helper handle and tight-fitting lid	**All-Clad Stainless 3-Quart Tri-Ply Sauté Pan** $244.95 Best Buy: **Cuisinart MultiClad Pro Stainless 3½-Quart Sauté Pan with Helper and Cover** $78.13
	STOCKPOT	• Lightweight • Stainless-steel interior • Lid that easily slides into place • Comfortable handles with rubber grips	**Cook N Home Stainless Steel Stockpot with Lid 12 Quart** $28.42
	ROASTING PAN WITH RACK	• At least 15 by 11 inches • Stainless-steel interior with aluminum core for even heat distribution • Upright handles for easy gripping • Light interior for better food monitoring	**Calphalon Contemporary Stainless Roasting Pan with Rack** $99.99 Best Buy: **Cuisinart MultiClad Pro Stainless 16" Roasting Pan with Rack** $72.22
	ROASTING RACK	• Fixed, not adjustable, to provide sturdiness • Tall, vertical handles positioned on long side of rack	**All-Clad Nonstick Large Rack** $24.95
	COOKWARE SET	• Fully clad stainless steel with aluminum core for even heat distribution • Moderately heavy, durable construction • Lids included • Ideal mix of pans includes 12-inch skillet, 10-inch skillet, 2-quart saucepan, 4-quart saucepan, 8-quart stockpot	**All-Clad D3 Tri-Ply Bonded Cookware Set, 10 Piece** $559.94 Best Buy: **Potluck Cookware Set** $160

MUST-HAVE ITEM

HANDY TOOLS	ITEM	WHAT TO LOOK FOR	TEST KITCHEN FAVORITES
	KITCHEN SHEARS	• Take-apart scissors (for easy cleaning) • Supersharp blades • Sturdy construction • Work for both right- and left-handed users	**Kershaw Taskmaster Shears/Shun Multi-Purpose Shears** $26.30 Best Buy: **J.A. Henckels International Take-Apart Kitchen Shears** $14.95
	KITCHEN TONGS	• Scalloped edges • Slightly concave pincers • Length of 12 inches (to keep your hand far from the heat) • Open and close easily	**OXO Good Grips 12-Inch Tongs** $12.95
	SLOTTED SPOON	• Wide, shallow, thin bowl • Long, hollow, comfortable handle • Steep, ladle-like angle between handle and bowl	**Cuisinart Stainless Steel Slotted Spoon** $9.12
	ALL-AROUND SPATULA	• Head about 3 inches wide and 5½ inches long • 11 inches in length (tip to handle) • Long, vertical slots • Good to have a metal spatula to use with traditional cookware and plastic for nonstick cookware	Metal: **Wüsthof Slotted Fish Spatula** $49.95 Nonstick-Safe: **Matfer Bourgeat Exoglass Pelton Spatula** $13.25
	SILICONE SPATULA	• Firm, wide blade ideal for efficient scraping and scooping • All-silicone design for easy cleanup	**Di Oro Living Seamless Silicone Spatula—Large** $10.97
	WOODEN SPOON (CO-WINNER)	• "Spootle" (a combination spoon and spatula) has slim, long scraping edge and rounded bowl for scooping food • Cherry wood has a smooth texture and resists becoming overly dried out and rough • Available in right- or left-handed versions	**Jonathan's Spoons Spootle** $28
		• Light, long, and maneuverable—keeps hands far from the heat • Rounded, tapered handle is comfortable and easy to grip in a variety of ways • Wood resists staining or drying out, retains its color, and resists becoming rough to touch	Best Buy: **FAAY 13.5" Teak Cooking Spoon** $10.99

MUST-HAVE ITEMS

HANDY TOOLS	ITEM	WHAT TO LOOK FOR	TEST KITCHEN FAVORITES
	OFFSET SPATULA	• Flexible blade offset to a roughly 30-degree angle • Enough usable surface area to frost the radius of a 9-inch cake • Comfortable handle	Large: **OXO Good Grips Bent Icing Knife** $9.99 Mini: **Wilton 9-inch Angled Spatula** $4.79
	PIE SERVER	• Comfortable, balanced, and rubbery grip • Slides neatly under pie wedges for easy removal • Sharp serrated blade slices pie effortlessly	**OXO SteeL Pie Server** $9.99
	COMPACT SPATULA	• Generous handle • Flexible silicone head	**OXO Good Grips Silicone Cookie Spatula** $7.99
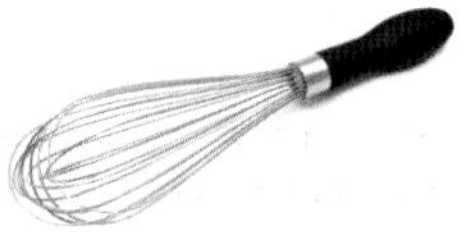	ALL-PURPOSE WHISK	• At least 10 wires • Wires of moderate thickness • Comfortable rubber handle • Balanced, lightweight feel	**OXO Good Grips 11" Balloon Whisk** $9.99
	PEPPER MILL	• Easy-to-adjust, clearly marked grind settings • Efficient, comfortable grinding mechanism • Generous capacity	**Cole & Mason Derwent Pepper Mill** $49.99
	CONFECTIONERS' SUGAR SHAKER	• Mesh head that produces a fine, even dusting • Narrow cylinder that fits comfortably in your hand	**Ateco Stainless Steel Fine Mesh Shaker** $3.88
	LADLE	• Stainless steel • Hook handle • Pouring rim to prevent dripping • Handle 9 to 10 inches in length	**Rösle Hook Ladle with Pouring Rim** $34 Best Buy: **OXO Good Grips Brushed Stainless Steel Ladle** $9.99

MUST-HAVE ITEMS

MUST-HAVE ITEM

HANDY TOOLS	ITEM	WHAT TO LOOK FOR	TEST KITCHEN FAVORITES
MUST-HAVE ITEM	CAN OPENER	• 3½-inch driving handle makes it easy and comfortable to rotate • Can opening is smooth and effortless	**EZ-DUZ IT Can Opener** $10
	JAR OPENER	• Strong, sturdy clamp grip • Adjusts quickly to any size jar	**Amco Swing-A-Way Jar Opener** $5.99
MUST-HAVE ITEM	GARLIC PRESS	• Conical holes that press garlic through efficiently • Solid, stainless-steel construction • Comfortable handle • Easy to clean	**Kuhn Rikon Epicurean Garlic Press** $44.95
	GARLIC PEELER	• Thick, comfortable silicone sleeve • Removes skins without bruising • Easy to wash	**Zak! Designs E-Z Rol Garlic Peeler** $8.79
	SERRATED FRUIT/ VEGETABLE PEELER	• Comfortable grip and nonslip handle • Sharp blade	**Messermeister Serrated Swivel Peeler** $5.50
MUST-HAVE ITEM	VEGETABLE PEELER	• Sharp, carbon-steel blade • 1-inch space between blade and peeler to prevent jamming • Lightweight and comfortable	**Kuhn Rikon Original Swiss Peeler** $3.50
	RASP-STYLE GRATER	• Sharp teeth (require little effort or pressure when grating) • Maneuverable over round shapes • Soft, grippy, secure handle	**Microplane Premium Classic Zester/Grater** $14.95
MUST-HAVE ITEM	GRATER	• Flat, easy to store • Large surface area • Solid, rigid frame that fits over bowls • Grippy rubber feet prevent slipping	**Rösle Coarse Grater** $35.93
	ROTARY GRATER	• Drum and handle separate for easy interior cleaning • Classic turn-crank design • Comfortable handle • Crank can switch sides for left-or right-handed use	**Zyliss Classic Cheese Grater** $11.49

HANDY TOOLS	ITEM	WHAT TO LOOK FOR	TEST KITCHEN FAVORITES
	MANUAL JUICER	• Directs juice in a steady stream with no splattering or overflowing • Large, rounded handles that are easy to squeeze	**Chef'n FreshForce Citrus Juicer** $23.04
	ICE CREAM SCOOP	• Forms perfectly round orbs that release easily • Wide, comfortable handle contains heat-conductive fluid that warms up instantly when a hand grips the exterior and also warms the bowl, making scooping easy	**Zeroll Original Ice Cream Scoop** $18.44
	MEAT POUNDER	• At least 1½ pounds in weight • Vertical handle for better leverage and control	**Norpro GRIP EZ Meat Pounder** $19.99
	BENCH SCRAPER	• Sturdy blade • Beveled edge for easy cutting and scraping • Comfortable handle with plastic, rubber, or nylon grip	**Dexter-Russell 6" Dough Cutter/Scraper** $7.01
	ROLLING PIN	• Moderate weight (1 to 1½ pounds) • 19-inch straight barrel • Slightly textured wooden surface to grip dough for easy rolling	**J.K. Adams Plain Maple Rolling Dowel** $13.95
	MIXING BOWLS	• Good to have both stainless steel and glass (for mixing, microwaving, and holding prepped ingredients) • Sets of 3 to 4 nesting bowls ranging in capacity from about 1 quart to 4 quarts (for glass) and 1½ quarts to 5 quarts (for stainless steel)	Stainless Steel: **Vollrath Economy Stainless Steel Mixing Bowls** $2.90–$6.90 per bowl Glass: **Pyrex Smart Essentials Mixing Bowl Set with Colored Lids** $13.19 for 4-bowl set
	MINI PREP BOWLS	• Wide, shallow bowls • Easy to hold, fill, empty, and clean • Microwave-safe and ovensafe	**Anchor Hocking 6-Piece Nesting Prep Bowl Set** $11

MUST-HAVE ITEMS

HANDY TOOLS	ITEM	WHAT TO LOOK FOR	TEST KITCHEN FAVORITES
MUST-HAVE ITEM	OVEN MITT	• Silicone is heavily textured for better grip • Flexed with hands, making it easy to pinch cookie sheets and small handles or knobs • Machine-washable	**OXO Silicone Oven Mitt** $14.99 each
	PASTRY BRUSH	• Bristles of moderate length and density • Grippy handle • Loses few bristles	**Winco Flat Pastry and Basting Brush, 1½ inch** $6.93
	CHINOIS SIEVE	• Conical shape • Depth of 7 to 8 inches • At least one hook on rim for stability	**Winco Reinforced Extra Fine Mesh Bouillon Strainer** $33.78
MUST-HAVE ITEMS	COLANDER	• 4- to 7-quart capacity • Metal ring attached to bottom for stability • Many holes for quick draining • Small holes so pasta doesn't slip through	**RSVP International Endurance Precision Pierced 5 Qt. Colander** $25.60
	FINE-MESH STRAINER	• Stiff, tightly woven mesh • Capacity of at least 5 cups with large, durable hooks for support over bowls and pots	**Rösle Fine Mesh Strainer, Round Handle, 7.9 inches** $45
	SPIDER SKIMMER	• Long handle is easy to maneuver and clean • Capable of handling fragile items like ravioli with care	**Rösle Wire Skimmer** $41.68 Best Buy: **WMF Profi Plus Spider Strainer 14" (5" dia.)** $19.95

HANDY TOOLS	ITEM	WHAT TO LOOK FOR	TEST KITCHEN FAVORITES
	FOOD MILL	• Good at straining out seeds from coulis and sauces • Quick and efficient	**Küchenprofi Vegetable Sieve/Food Mill** $57.12
	FAT SEPARATOR	• Bottom-draining model • Detachable bowl for easy cleaning • Strainer for catching solids	**Cuisipro Fat Separator** $33.95
	SPLATTER SCREEN	• Perches securely on skillet • Easy to clean	**Frywall Stovetop Splatter Guard** $28.95
	POTATO MASHER	• Solid mashing disk with many small holes • Comfortable grip • Long handle	**Zyliss Stainless Steel Potato Masher** $12.99
	SALAD SPINNER	• Ergonomic and easy-to-operate hand pump • Wide base for stability • Flat lid for easy cleaning and storage	**OXO Good Grips Salad Spinner** $29.99
	STEAMER BASKET	• Collapsible stainless-steel basket with feet • Adjustable and removable center rod for easy removal from pot and easy storage	**OXO Good Grips Stainless Steel Steamer with Handle** $17.95
	MORTAR AND PESTLE	• Heavy, stable base keeps it firmly on counter while in use • Rough interior to help grip and grind ingredients • Comfortable, heavy pestle	**Frieling Goliath Natural Stone Mortar & Pestle** $57.95

MUST-HAVE ITEMS

MEASURING EQUIPMENT	ITEM	WHAT TO LOOK FOR	TEST KITCHEN FAVORITES
MUST-HAVE ITEMS	DRY MEASURING CUPS	• Accurate measurements • Easy-to-read measurement markings • Durable measurement markings • Strong and durable design • Handles perfectly flush with cups • Stacks and stores neatly	**OXO Good Grips Stainless Steel Measuring Cups** $19.99
	LIQUID MEASURING CUP (GLASS)	• Bold, easy-to-read measurement lines that clearly correspond to specific numbers • Heatproof and durable glass resists staining	**Pyrex 1 Cup Measuring Cup** $10.05
	LIQUID MEASURING CUP (PLASTIC)	• Lightweight cup has a secondary set of measurements located on a U-shaped strip set in the cup so it can be read from above • Dishwasher safe	**OXO Good Grips 1 Cup Angled Measuring Cup** $6.99
	ADJUSTABLE MEASURING CUP	• Plungerlike bottom (with a tight seal between plunger and tube) that you can set to correct measurement, then push up to cleanly extract sticky ingredients (such as shortening or peanut butter) • 1- or 2-cup capacity • Dishwasher-safe	**KitchenArt Pro 2 Cup Adjust-A-Cup Satin** $23.81
MUST-HAVE ITEMS	MEASURING SPOONS	• Metal construction is remarkably sturdy • Ingredients don't cling to the stainless steel • Simple design allows for a continuous, bump-free sweep, with a ball-chain connector that is easy to open and close	**Cuisipro Stainless Steel 5-Piece Measuring Spoons** $12.33
	KITCHEN RULER	• Stainless steel and easy to clean • 18 inches in length • Large, easy-to-read markings	**Empire 18-inch Stainless Steel Ruler** $8.49
	DIGITAL SCALE	• Easy-to-read display not blocked by weighing platform • At least 7-pound capacity • Accessible buttons • Gram-to-ounce conversion feature • Roomy platform	**OXO Good Grips 11 lb Food Scale with Pull Out Display** $49.99 Best Buy: **Ozeri Pronto Digital Multifunction Kitchen and Food Scale** $11.79

THERMOMETERS AND TIMERS	ITEM	WHAT TO LOOK FOR	TEST KITCHEN FAVORITES
MUST-HAVE ITEMS	INSTANT-READ THERMOMETER	• Display auto-rotates • Lights up in low light • Wakes up when unit is picked up • Takes a single AAA alkaline battery • Water resistant	**ThermoWorks Thermapen Mk4** $99 Best Inexpensive Option: **ThermoWorks ThermoPop** $29 Best Midpriced: **Lavatools Javelin PRO Duo** $49.99
	OVEN THERMOMETER	• Wide, sturdy base • Clear temperature markings • Fairly easy to read	**CDN Pro Accurate Oven Thermometer** $8.70
	MEAT/CANDY/ DEEP-FRY PROBE THERMOMETER	• Digital model • Easy-to-read console • Mounting clip (to attach probe to the pan)	**ThermoWorks ChefAlarm** $59 Best Buy: **Polder Classic Digital Thermometer/ Timer** $24.99
	BARBECUE THERMOMETER	• Simultaneously checks food and grill temperature • Easy to read • Heatproof finger-grip	**Polder Dual Sensor Meat and Oven Thermometer** $10
	REFRIGERATOR/ FREEZER THERMOMETER	• Large, easy-to-read display • Accurate, and carefully monitors fluctuations in temperature	**ThermoWorks Fridge/ Freezer Alarm** $22

THERMOMETERS AND TIMERS	ITEM	WHAT TO LOOK FOR	TEST KITCHEN FAVORITES
	KITCHEN TIMER	• Lengthy time range (1 second to at least 10 hours) • Able to count up after alarm goes off • Easy to use and read • Able to track multiple events	**OXO Good Grips Triple Timer** $19.99
	WEARABLE TIMER	• Combines a clock, timer, and stopwatch • Vertical orientation fits comfortably in hand and pockets • 38-inch lanyard is comfortable and long enough to slip over head	**ThermoWorks TimeStick** $25

BAKEWARE	ITEM	WHAT TO LOOK FOR	TEST KITCHEN FAVORITES
MUST-HAVE ITEM	GLASS BAKING DISH	• Dimensions of 13 by 9 inches • Lightweight with large handles for easy grip and maneuvering	**Pyrex Easy Grab 3-Quart Oblong Baking Dish** $7.29
	13 BY 9-INCH BROILER-SAFE BAKING DISH	• Dish has looped handles that are easy to grab • Capacity of 14.25 cups • Easy cleanup whether by hand or in the dishwasher	**Mrs. Anderson's Baking Lasagna Pan with Handle (Rose)** $60.99
MUST-HAVE ITEMS	METAL BAKING PAN	• Dimensions of 13 by 9 inches • Straight sides • Nonstick surface for even browning and easy release of cakes and bar cookies	**Williams Sonoma Goldtouch Nonstick Rectangular Cake Pan, 9" x 13"** $32.95
	8-INCH SQUARE BAKING PAN	• Straight sides • Durable • Flattened lip that made it easy to hold • Seamless interior that is easy to clean	**Fat Daddio's ProSeries Square Cake Pan** $13.48

BAKEWARE	ITEM	WHAT TO LOOK FOR	TEST KITCHEN FAVORITES
MUST-HAVE ITEMS	ROUND CAKE PAN	• Best for cake • Straight sides • Light finish for tall, even baking • Nonstick surface for easy release	Best All-Around: **Nordic Ware Naturals Nonstick 9-Inch Round Cake Pan** $14.32
		• Dark finish is ideal for pizza and cinnamon buns • Nonstick	Best for Browning: **Chicago Metallic Non-Stick 9" Round Cake Pan** $10.97
	PIE PLATE	• Golden-hued metal plate bakes crusts without overbrowning • Produces crisp and flaky bottom crusts • Nonfluted lip allows for maximum crust-crimping flexibility • Good to have two • Ceramic nonstick coating	**Williams Sonoma Goldtouch Nonstick Pie Dish** $18.95
	LOAF PAN	• Folded loaf pan • Produces tall, picture-perfect pound cake • Corrugated pattern on the metal doesn't affect the appearance of baked goods	Best Results: **USA Pan Loaf Pan, 1 lb Volume** $14.95 Best for Cleanup: **OXO Good Grips Non-Stick Pro 1 Lb Loaf Pan** $16.95
	SPRINGFORM PAN	• Tall sides make for an easy grip • Gold-toned pan produces evenly baked crusts • Wide, 9-inch raised base provides support	**Williams Sonoma Goldtouch Leakproof Springform Pan** $49.95 Best Buy: **Nordic Ware 9" Leakproof Springform Pan** $16.22
	COOKIE SHEET	• Thick aluminum heats and browns evenly • Won't warp with repeated use • Raised edges for easy maneuvering • Nonstick, spacious surface	**Vollrath Wear-Ever Cookie Sheet (Natural Finish)** $15.99

BAKEWARE	ITEM	WHAT TO LOOK FOR	TEST KITCHEN FAVORITES
MUFFIN TIN	• Gold nonstick surface for perfect browning and easy release • Wide, extended rims and raised lip for easy handling	**OXO Good Grips Non-Stick Pro 12-Cup Muffin Pan** $24.99
WIRE RACK	• Reinforced with extra support bar • Fits inside a standard 18 by 13-inch rimmed baking sheet • Dishwasher-safe	**Checkered Chef Cooling Rack** $12.95
BAKER'S COOLING RACK	• Sturdy rack • Four collapsible shelves • Unit folds down for easy storage	**Linden Sweden Baker's Cooling Rack** $17.99
BISCUIT CUTTERS	• Sharp edges • A set with a variety of sizes	**Ateco 5357 11-Piece Plain Round Cutter Set** $14.95
BUNDT PAN	• Heavyweight cast aluminum • Thick, easy-to-grip handles • Clearly defined ridges for elegant cakes • 15-cup capacity	**Nordic Ware Anniversary Bundt Pan** $30.99
TART PAN	• Nonstick mold released tarts more readily than traditional finish • Deep grooves for impressive edges • Dark surface for deeply, evenly browned edges	**Matfer Steel Non-stick Tart Mold with Removable Bottom 9½"** $27
TUBE PAN	• Heavy pan (at least 1 pound) • Heavy bottom for leak-free seal • Dark nonstick surface for even browning and easy release • 16-cup capacity • Feet on rim	**Chicago Metallic 2-Piece Angel Food Cake Pan with Feet** $17.99
PULLMAN LOAF PAN	• Squared-off pan (4 by 4 inches) • Nonstick aluminized steel for easy cleanup • Light surface for even browning	**USA Pan 13 by 4-inch Pullman Loaf Pan & Cover** $33.95

MUST-HAVE ITEMS

BAKEWARE	ITEM	WHAT TO LOOK FOR	TEST KITCHEN FAVORITES
	BAKER'S EDGE PAN	• Dark nonstick surface for easy release	**Baker's Edge Brownie Pan** $34.95
	RAMEKIN	• Heavy, sturdy ceramic • Thick walls for gentle insulation • Straight sides • Stack securely for easy storage	**Le Creuset Stackable Ramekin** $16 for 1 ramekin Best Buy: **Mrs. Anderson's Baking Souffle** $22.52 for set of 6
	BAKING STONE	• Absolutely flat with no handholds or cutouts that waste space • Easy cleanup	Co-winner: **The Original Baking Steel** $99
		• Tough, unbreakable steel is a great choice for home pizza making or bread baking	Co-winner: **Nerd Chef Steel Stone, Standard ¼"** $74.99 Best Buy: **Pizzacraft All-Purpose Baking Stone** $28.99

SMALL APPLIANCES	ITEM	WHAT TO LOOK FOR	TEST KITCHEN FAVORITES
MUST-HAVE ITEM	FOOD PROCESSOR	• 14-cup capacity • Sharp and sturdy blades • Wide feed tube • Should come with basic blades and discs: steel blade, dough blade, shredding/slicing disc	**Cuisinart Custom 14 Cup Food Processor** $229.95 Small Food Processor: **Cuisinart Elite Collection 4-Cup Chopper/Grinder** $59.95
	STAND MIXER (HIGH-END)	• Planetary action (stationary bowl and single mixing arm) • Powerful motor • Bowl size of at least 4½ quarts • Slightly squat bowl to keep ingredients in beater's range • Should come with basic attachments: paddle, dough hook, metal whisk	**KitchenAid Pro Line Series 7 Quart Bowl-Lift Stand Mixer** $549.95

SMALL APPLIANCES	ITEM	WHAT TO LOOK FOR	TEST KITCHEN FAVORITES
	STAND MIXER (INEXPENSIVE)	• Fits all KitchenAid attachments, from meat grinder to ice cream maker (sold separately), so it could stand in for several other appliances • Highly efficient and powerful mixing action	**KitchenAid KSM75WH Classic Plus Series 4.5-Quart Tilt-Head Stand Mixer** $207.99
	HANDHELD MIXER	• Lightweight model • Slim wire beaters without central post • Variety of speeds	**KitchenAid 5-Speed Ultra Power Hand Mixer** $49.99 Best Buy: **Cuisinart PowerSelect 3-Speed Hand Mixer** $26.77
	BLENDER	• Mix of straight and serrated blades at different angles • Jar with curved base • At least 44-ounce capacity • Heavy base for stability	High-End: **Vitamix 5200** $449 Midpriced: **Breville Fresh & Furious** $199.95 Inexpensive: **NutriBullet Full Size Blender** $99.99
	IMMERSION BLENDER	• Easy to maneuver and lightweight with a slim, grippy body • Well-designed blade and cage • Detachable handle for easy cleanup	**Braun MultiQuick 5 Hand Blender** $59.99
	ELECTRIC GRIDDLE	• Large cooking area (about 20 by 12 inches) • Attached pull-out grease trap (won't tip over) • Nonstick surface for easy cleanup	**BroilKing Professional Griddle with Backsplash** $99
	ELECTRIC JUICER	• Ideal for making a large amount of fruit or vegetable juice • Centrifugal, not masticating, model for fresher-tasting juice • 3-inch-wide feed tube • Easy to assemble and clean	**Breville Juice Fountain Cold** $178

MUST-HAVE ITEMS

SMALL APPLIANCES	ITEM	WHAT TO LOOK FOR	TEST KITCHEN FAVORITES
	ELECTRIC KETTLE	• Heats water rapidly • Secure base and wide comfortable handle • Removable filter in spout	**OXO Brew Cordless Glass Electric Kettle** $79.95 Best Buy: **Capresso Silver H2O Electric Kettle** $55.69
	COFFEE MAKER (AUTOMATIC DRIP)	• Thermal carafe that keeps coffee hot and fresh with capacity of at least 10 cups • Short brewing time (6 minutes is ideal) • Copper, not aluminum, heating element • Easy-to-fill water tank • Clear, intuitive controls	**Technivorm Moccamaster 10-Cup Coffee Maker** $299 Best Buy: **Bonavita 8-Cup Coffee Maker with Thermal Carafe** $121.80
	MEAT GRINDER	• Grinds pounds of meat easily, even on older KitchenAid stand mixers • Mostly dishwasher-safe	**KitchenAid Food Grinder Attachment** $48.74
	ICE CREAM MAKER	• Simple to use and very compact • Modestly priced • Made ice cream that rivaled the smooth texture of our favorite store-bought ice creams	**Cuisinart Frozen Yogurt, Ice Cream & Sorbet Maker** $53.99
	STOVETOP PRESSURE COOKER	• Stainless steel rather than aluminum for more durable construction that doesn't react to acidic foods • Stovetop model with low sides and wide base for easy access and better browning and heat retention • Pressure indicator that is easy to see and interpret at a glance	**Fissler Vitaquick 8½-Quart Pressure Cooker** $219.95 Best Buy: **Zavor Duo 8.4 Quart Pressure Cooker** $119.95

SMALL APPLIANCES	ITEM	WHAT TO LOOK FOR	TEST KITCHEN FAVORITES
	SLOW COOKER	• At least 6-quart capacity (4-quart capacity for small slow cookers) • Insert handles • Clear lid to see progress of food • Dishwasher-safe insert • Intuitive controls with programmable timer and warming mode	**KitchenAid 6-Quart Slow Cooker with Solid Glass Lid** $99.99
	ELECTRIC DEEP FRYER	• Large basket holds lots of food and is easy to lower and lift during use • High walls and lid contains messes • Built-in filter and handy oil storage container	**T-Fal Ultimate EZ-Clean Fryer** $114.35
	LONG-SLOT TOASTER	• Produced crisp, uniform, golden toast every time • Helpful features like "A Bit More" button	**Breville A Bit More Toaster** $79.95 Best Buy: **Dash Clear View Toaster** $36.03
	TOASTER OVEN	• Quartz heating elements for steady, controlled heat • Roomy but compact interior • Simple to use	**Breville Smart Oven** $219.95
	WAFFLE IRON	• Indicator lights and audible alert • Makes two waffles at a time • Six-point dial for customizing waffle doneness	**Cuisinart Double Belgian Waffle Maker** $99.95

	GAS GRILL	• Large main grate • Built-in thermometer • Two burners for varying heat levels (three is even better) • Made of thick, heat-retaining materials such as cast aluminum and enameled steel	**Weber Spirit II E-310 Gas Grill** $479
	CHARCOAL GRILL	• Sturdy construction to efficiently maintain heat • Well-designed cooking grate, handles, lids, and wheels • Generous cooking surface • Large charcoal capacity • Well-positioned air vents • Gas ignition to instantly and easily light coals • Ash catcher for easy cleanup	**Weber Performer Deluxe Charcoal Grill** $439 Best Buy: **Weber Original Kettle Premium Charcoal Grill, 22-Inch** $149
	PORTABLE CHARCOAL GRILL	• Ample cooking surface with raised lip • Cover that can be secured for travel • Lightweight but durable	**Weber Smokey Joe Premium** $34.70
	SMOKER	• Large cooking area • Water pan • Multiple vents for precise temperature control	**Weber Smokey Mountain Cooker Smoker 18"** $329
	CHIMNEY STARTER	• 6-quart capacity • Holes in canister so air can circulate around coals • Sturdy construction • Heat-resistant handle • Dual handle for easy control	**Weber Rapidfire Chimney Starter** $14.99

GRILLING EQUIPMENT	ITEM	WHAT TO LOOK FOR	TEST KITCHEN FAVORITES
	GRILL TONGS	• 16 inches in length • Scalloped, not sharp and serrated, edges • Open and close easily • Lightweight • Moderate amount of springy tension	**OXO Good Grips 16" Locking Tongs** $14.93
	GRILL BRUSH	• Short metal bristles and triangular head shape easily cleans grill grates by sweeping the top or by wedging it between the bars • Shorter handle gives good leverage	**Weber 12-Inch Grill Brush** $7.99
	GRILL SPATULA	• Front edge is 3 inches across • Head flares out toward the handle to support wider items • Rounded handle with silicone grip	**Char-Boil Comfort-Grip Grill Spatula** $14.94
	BARBECUE BASTING BRUSH	• Silicone bristles • Handle between 8 and 13 inches • Heat-resistant	**OXO Good Grips Large Silicone Basting Brush** $11.95
	GRILL GLOVES	• Excellent heat protection • Gloves, rather than mitts, for dexterity • Long sleeves to protect forearms	**Steven Raichlen Ultimate Suede Grilling Gloves** $29.99 per pair
	SKEWERS	• Flat and metal • $3/16$ inch thick	**Norpro 12-Inch Stainless Steel Skewers** $6.85 for a set of 6
	RIB RACK	• Sturdily supports six racks of ribs • Doubles as roasting rack (when flipped upside down) • Nonstick coating for easy cleanup	**Charcoal Companion Reversible Rib Rack** $14.95
	GRILL LIGHTER	• Flexible neck • Refillable chamber with large, easy-to-read fuel window • Comfortable grip	**Zippo Flexible Neck Utility Lighter** $18.35

GRILLING EQUIPMENT	ITEM	WHAT TO LOOK FOR	TEST KITCHEN FAVORITES
	OUTDOOR GRILL PAN	• Narrow slits and raised sides so food can't fall through or off • Sturdy construction with handles	**Weber Professional-Grade Grill Pan** $19.99
	SMOKER BOX	• Cast iron for slow heating and steady smoke • Easy to fill, empty, and clean	**GrillPro Cast Iron Smoker Box made by Onward Manufacturing Company** $12.79
	VERTICAL ROASTER	• Helps poultry cook evenly • 8-inch shaft keeps chicken above fat and drippings in pan • Attached basin catches drippings for pan sauce • Sturdy construction	**Vertical Roaster with Infuser by Norpro** $22.11 Best Buy: **Elizabeth Karmel's Grill Friends Porcelain Chicken Sitter** $11.99
	PROPANE INDICATOR	• Easy-to-read dial • Accurately measures propane by weight	**Original Grill Gauge** $13.99
	GRILL LIGHT	• Durable and waterproof • Sturdy, simple clamp • Can be configured to stand freely on a side table for grills without handles	**Blackfire Clamplight Waterproof** $24.95

SPECIALTY PIECES	ITEM	WHAT TO LOOK FOR	TEST KITCHEN FAVORITES
	APPLE CORER	• Comfortable grip with offset handle • Sharp teeth • Wide blade diameter	**Cuisipro Apple Corer** $9.95
	CORN STRIPPER	• Two sets of plastic prongs helped center the corn for more efficient cutting • Contained mess well	**RSVP International Deluxe Corn Stripper** $23.30
	TOMATO CORER	• Sharp teeth make easy, clean cuts • Lightweight, rounded-off plastic handle • Comfortable head-handle combination	**Norpro Tomato Core It** $2.99
	NUT CHOPPER	• Sharp, sturdy stainless steel chopping tines • Dishwasher-safe	**Prepworks from Progressive Nut Chopper with Non-Skid Base** $11.70
	GRILL PAN	• Well-seasoned surface releases food and cleans up easily • Tall, well-defined ridges produce excellent grill marks	**Lodge Chef Collection 11" Cast Iron Square Grill Pan** $35.99
	STOVETOP GRIDDLE	• Nonstick • Upright handles make it easy to pick up griddle • Wider models are better for cooking large batches • Sits over two burners	**Calphalon Classic Nonstick Double Griddle Pan** $54.99
	OYSTER KNIFE	• Sturdy, flat blade with slightly curved tip for easy penetration • Slim, nonstick handle for secure, comfortable grip	**R. Murphy New Haven Oyster Knife with Stainless Steel Blade** $16.65
	SEAFOOD SCISSORS	• Curved blade neatly snips off shells • Tidy removal of shrimp vein	**RSVP International Endurance Seafood Scissors** $14.99

SPECIALTY PIECES	ITEM	WHAT TO LOOK FOR	TEST KITCHEN FAVORITES
	SILICONE MICROWAVE LID	• Thin, silicone round to cover splatter-prone food during microwave heating • Easy to clean • Doubles as jar opener	**Piggy Steamer** $18
	PIPING SET	• Contains all of the essentials: twelve 16-inch pastry bags; four plastic couplers; and the following Wilton tips: #4 round, #12 round, #70 leaf, #103 petal, #2D large closed star, #1M open star • All parts available at most crafts stores	**Test Kitchen Self-Assembled à La Carte Decorating Set** $15.32
	CHEESE WIRE	• Comfortable plastic handles • Narrow wire	**Fante's Handled Cheese Wire** $2.99
	PIZZA CUTTER	• Clear plastic wheel to prevent damage to pans • Comfortable, soft-grip handle	**OXO Good Grips 4" Pizza Wheel** $12.99
	POTATO RICER	• Large hopper that can hold 1¼ cups sliced potatoes • Interchangeable fine and coarse disks • Sturdy, ergonomic handles	**RSVP International Potato Ricer** $13.95
	TORTILLA WARMER	• Triple-layered sides with two layers of fabric around sheet of insulating plastic • 12-inch diameter to fit large wraps	**IMUSA 12" Cloth Tortilla Warmer** $19.99
	INSULATED FOOD CARRIER	• Keeps food piping hot for over 3 hours • Fits two 13 by 9-inch baking dishes • Handy zippered pocket holds serving utensils	**Rachael Ray Expandable Lasagna Lugger** $34.99

SPECIALTY PIECES	ITEM	WHAT TO LOOK FOR	TEST KITCHEN FAVORITES
	CUPCAKE AND CAKE CARRIER	• Fits both round and square cakes and cupcakes • Snap locks • Nonskid base • Collapses for easy storage	**Progressive Collapsible Cupcake and Cake Carrier** $29.95
	CAKE LIFTER	• Sturdy but small and slightly flexible • Rounded corners for visibility • Comfortable offset handle	**Fat Daddio's Cake Lifter** $11.88
	CAKE STAND	• Elevated rotating stand so you can hold the spatula steady for easy frosting • Solid, light construction	**Winco Revolving Cake Decorating Stand** $49.87
	CREAM WHIPPER	• Responsive lever for better control and easy piping • Grips on handle and neck for easy refilling and cleanup	**iSi Gourmet Whip** $99.27
	BLADE GRINDER	• Electric, not manual, grinders • Deep bowl to hold ample amount of coffee beans • Good to have two, one each for coffee grinding and spice grinding	**Krups Coffee and Spice Grinder** $17.99
	INNOVATIVE TEAPOT	• Contained ultrafine-mesh strainer keeps tea leaf dregs separate • One-piece design for easy cleaning	**IngenuiTEA by Adagio Teas** $14.95

SPECIALTY PIECES	ITEM	WHAT TO LOOK FOR	TEST KITCHEN FAVORITES
	TRAVEL MUG	• Simple, leakproof lid design • Good heat retention • Easy to clean and dishwasher-safe	**Zojirushi Stainless Mug (SM-SE)** $29.97
	WATER BOTTLE	• Clear plastic sides makes it easy to fill • Bi-level twist-on lid for easy sipping • Handy carrying loop	Plastic: **Nathan LittleShot** $11.99 Glass: **Lifefactory 22 Oz Glass Bottle with Classic Cap-Orange** $22.99
	WINE OPENER	• Durable design • Teflon-coated worm	**Pulltap's Classic Evolution Corkscrew by Pulltex** $39.95 Best Buy: **Trudeau Double Lever Corkscrew** $12.99
	ELECTRIC WINE OPENER	• Sturdy, quiet corkscrew • Broad base that rests firmly on bottle	**Cuisinart Cordless Wine Opener with Vacuum Sealer** $39.95
	WINE AERATOR	• Long, tubelike design that exposes wine to air as it is being poured • Neat, hands-free aerating	**Nuance Wine Finer** $19.95
	COCKTAIL SHAKER	• Holds at least 18 ounces to make one or two cocktails at once • Comfortable carafe-like shape • Wide mouth for easy filling, muddling, and cleaning	Cobbler Style: **Tovolo Stainless Steel 4-in-1 Cocktail Shaker** $27.50 Boston Style: **The Boston Shaker Professional Boston Shaker, Weighted** $14.50

SPECIALTY PIECES	ITEM	WHAT TO LOOK FOR	TEST KITCHEN FAVORITES
	BEER SAVERS	• Fits both glass and plastic bottles • Preserves carbonation for up to 2 days	**SaveBrands Beer Savers** $6.99 for six-pack
	COOLER	• Ice lasted 7 days, and soda stayed at 50 degrees for five days • Durable construction	**Yeti Tundra 45** $299.99 Best Buy: **Coleman 50 QT Xtreme Wheeled Cooler** $45.99
	ICE PACK	• Convenient handle for easy transporting • No bulges formed upon freezing • Remained cold for almost 14 hours when sitting at room temperature	**Arctic Ice Alaskan Series, X-Large** $20.99
	SELTZER MAKER	• Machine is sturdy and fairly compact • Easy to use, large button on the top • Internal mechanism latches on to the water bottle and releases it gently	**SodaStream Fizzi Classic** $82.43
	COUNTERTOP VACUUM SEALER	• Digital screen tracks the machine's progress • Intuitive control panel • Gentle setting for vacuum sealing fragile foods • Built-in storage for plastic roll	**Nesco Deluxe Vacuum Sealer** $99.02
	COMPOST BUCKET	• Plastic pail to collect food scraps for composter • Carbon filter prevents odors from escaping and allows oxygen to enter so decomposition can occur • Easy to open lid that latches securely in place • 2.4-gallon capacity	**Exaco Trading Kitchen Compost Waste Collector** $19.98

SPECIALTY PIECES	ITEM	WHAT TO LOOK FOR	TEST KITCHEN FAVORITES
MUST-HAVE ITEM	FIRE EXTINGUISHER	• Fast and effective • Intuitive to use and easy to figure out • Powerful spray worked well on grease fire and burning fabric	**Kidde ABC Multipurpose Home Fire Extinguisher** $19.99

KITCHEN SUPPLIES	ITEM	WHAT TO LOOK FOR	TEST KITCHEN FAVORITES
MUST-HAVE ITEMS	PARCHMENT PAPER	• Sturdy paper for heavy doughs • Easy release of baked goods • 12 by 16 inches fits in standard rimmed baking sheets	**King Arthur Flour Parchment Paper 100 Half-Sheets** $19.95
	PLASTIC WRAP	• Clings to vessels of different materials • Dispenses easily • Resilient and strong over long periods of time	**Freeze-Tite Clear High Cling Freezer Wrap** $13.21 for 315 square feet
	BUTTER SAVER	• Fits the end of standard-size stick of butter • Kept butter from picking up off-flavors for more than a week • Measures 1 tablespoon	**SaveBrands Butter Saver** $4.99
	HERB KEEPER	• Adjustable height makes it easy to add or remove herbs • Vented lid prevents condensation from building up • Internal dividers keep things nice and tidy	**Cole & Mason Fresh Herb Keeper** $17.31
	PLASTIC FOOD STORAGE CONTAINER	• Clear, lightweight material stays as stain-free as glass • Snug seal doesn't leak • Flat top makes for secure, compact stacking	**Rubbermaid Brilliance Food Storage Container, Large, 9.6 Cup** $12.99
	DISH TOWEL	• Thin cotton for absorbency and flexibility • Dries glassware without streaks • Washes clean without shrinking	**Williams Sonoma Striped Towels, Set of 4** $19.95

KITCHEN SUPPLIES	ITEM	WHAT TO LOOK FOR	TEST KITCHEN FAVORITES
	DISPOSABLE PLATES	• Roomy eating surface with steep lip • Thick paper holds up to 2 pounds of food	**Hefty Super Strong Paper Plates** $2.99 for 16 plates
	PAPER TOWELS	• Thick, soft, sturdy sheets • Single full-size sheet holds nearly ¼ cup of water • Double-ply construction	**Bounty Paper Towels** $2.49 for 1 roll (full sheet, regular and Select-A-Size, regular)
	APRON	• Adjustable neck strap and long strings • Full coverage; chest area reinforced with extra layer of fabric • Stains wash out completely	**Bragard Travail Bib Apron** $27.95
	LIQUID DISH SOAP	• High concentration of surfactants to wash away oil • Clean scent	**Mrs. Meyer's Clean Day Liquid Dish Soap, Lavender** $3.99 for 16 fluid ounces
	DISH DRYING RACK	• Two roomy utensil holders • Seven-slot knife block • Ledge that can hang four wineglasses upside down for spot-free drying • Raised feet to hold it up off the counter	Innovative, Large: **simplehuman Steel Frame Dishrack** $78.93
		• Readily fits smaller items • Folds flat for easy storage • Best choice for small spaces or light loads	Innovative, Small: **Progressive Prepworks Collapsible Over-The-Sink Dish Drainer** $24.99
		• Fits dishes for a family of four • Angled mat tidily drains off water	Traditional/Best Buy: **Rubbermaid Antimicrobial Sink Drainer, Large and Antimicrobial Drain Board, Large** $10.99 for basket, $7.38 for mat

STOCKING YOUR PANTRY

Using the best ingredients is one way to guarantee success in the kitchen. But how do you know what to buy? Shelves are filled with a dizzying array of choices—and price does not equal quality. Over the years, the test kitchen's blind-tasting panels have evaluated thousands of ingredients, brand by brand, side by side, plain and in prepared applications, to determine which brands you can trust and which brands to avoid. In the chart that follows, we share the results, revealing our top-rated choices and the attributes that made them stand out among the competition. And because our test kitchen accepts no support from product manufacturers, you can trust our ratings. See AmericasTestKitchen.com for updates to these tastings.

	TEST KITCHEN FAVORITE	WHY WE LIKE IT	RUNNERS-UP
	ANCHOVIES **King Oscar Flat Fillets in Olive Oil**	• Right amount of salt • Savory without being fishy • Firm, meaty texture • Minimal bones • Aged 4 to 6 months	Ortiz in Olive Oil, Crown Prince in Olive Oil
	APPLESAUCE **Musselman's Lite**	• An unusual ingredient, sucralose, sweetens this applesauce without overpowering its fresh, bright apple flavor • Pinch of salt boosts flavor above weak, bland, and too-sweet competitors • Coarse, almost chunky texture, not slimy like applesauces sweetened with corn syrup	Musselman's Home Style, Santa Cruz Organic
	BACON, SUPERMARKET **Oscar Mayer Naturally Hardwood Smoked**	• Good balance of chew and crispness • Not too smoky, with a mildly meaty flavor	Smithfield Hometown Original, Hormel Black Label Original
	BACON, ARTISANAL **Vande Rose Applewood Smoked Artisan Dry Cured**	• Perfectly balanced salt, sugar, and smoke levels • Substantial, thick and chewy texture	Burger's Smokehouse Original Country
	BAKING POWDER **Argo Double Acting**	• Easy-to-use plastic tub • Makes chewy cookies, fluffy biscuits, and moist but airy cakes	Bob's Red Mill, Calumet, Clabber Girl

	TEST KITCHEN FAVORITE	WHY WE LIKE IT	RUNNERS-UP
	BARBECUE SAUCE **Bull's-Eye Original**	• Fresh tomato taste • Good balance of tanginess, smokiness, and sweetness • Robust flavor	Heinz Classic Sweet & Thick, Sweet Baby Ray's
	BEANS, CANNED BAKED **B&M Vegetarian**	• Firm and pleasant texture with some bite • Sweetened with molasses for complexity and depth	Bush's Best Original, Van Camp's Original
	BEANS, CANNED BLACK **Bush's Best**	• Clean, mild, and slightly earthy flavor • Firm, almost al dente texture, not mushy or pasty • Good amount of salt	Goya, Progresso
	BEANS, CANNED CHICKPEAS **Goya**	• Nutty flavor • Plump, buttery • Nicely seasoned with just enough salt	Pastene, Bush's
	BEANS, CANNED WHITE **Goya**	• Clean, earthy flavor • Smooth, creamy interior with tender skins and a nice, firm bite • Not full of broken beans like some competitors	Bush's Best
	BREAD, MULTIGRAIN **Nature's Own Specialty 12 Grain**	• Substantial, chewy slices • Nutty, hearty seeds throughout and topped with rolled oats • Uses no white flour	Arnold 12 Grain, Pepperidge Farm 15 Grain
	BREAD, WHITE SANDWICH **Arnold Country White**	• Subtle sweetness, not tasteless or sour • Perfect structure, not too dry or too soft	Pepperidge Farm Farmhouse Hearty White
	BREAD, WHOLE-WHEAT SANDWICH **Arnold Whole Grains 100% Whole Wheat**	• Mild nuttiness with clean wheat flavor and a touch of sweetness • Tender and chewy with crunchy flecks of bulgur on the crust	Pepperidge Farm Farmhouse 100% Whole Wheat

	TEST KITCHEN FAVORITE	WHY WE LIKE IT	RUNNERS-UP
	BREAD CRUMBS, PANKO **Kikkoman Panko** **Japanese Style**	• Crisp, with a substantial crunch • Not too delicate, stale, sandy, or gritty	Progresso, 4C

	BROTH, BEEF
	Better Than Bouillon
	Roasted Beef Base
		• Contains good amount of salt and
		  multiple powerful flavor enhancers
		• Paste is economical, stores easily,
		  and dissolves quickly in hot water	

	BROTH, CHICKEN
	Swanson Chicken Stock
		• Rich and meaty flavor
		• Hearty and pleasant aroma
		• Not sour, rancid, or salty like some
		  competitors
		• Flavor-boosting ingredients include
		  carrots, celery, and onions
			Better Than Bouillon
			Chicken Base

	BROTH, VEGETARIAN **Orrington Farms Vegan** **Chicken Flavored Broth** **Base & Seasoning**	• Savory depth without off-tasting vegetable undertones • Easy to store • Yeast extract adds depth and richness	Better Than Bouillon Vegetable Base, Reduced Sodium

	BROWNIE MIX
	Ghirardelli Chocolate
	Supreme
		• Rich, balanced chocolate flavor from
		  both natural and Dutch-processed
		  cocoa powders
		• Moist and chewy with perfect texture	

	BUNS, HAMBURGER
	Martin's Sandwich Potato
	Rolls
		• Potato starch provides soft, moist crumb
		• Tender, fluffy texture
		• Rich sweetness complements saltiness
		  of burgers
		• Primarily available in East Coast grocery
		  stores or online
			Pepperidge Farm,
			Arnold's

	BUTTER, UNSALTED
	Challenge
		• Clean, strong dairy flavor
		• Sticks are wrapped in aluminum foil,
		  which may protect them from picking up
		  off-flavors during shipping and storage
			Kate's Creamery, Land
			O'Lakes

	BUTTER, SALTED **Lurpak Slightly Salted**	• Made with cultured cream • Rich, creamy texture	Kate's Homemade, Plugrá European-Style, Land O'Lakes

	TEST KITCHEN FAVORITE	WHY WE LIKE IT	RUNNERS-UP
	CHEESE, AMERICAN, **Boar's Head**	• Strong cheesy flavor, unlike some competitors • Higher content of cheese culture contributes to better flavor	Kraft Deli Deluxe, Land O'Lakes
	CHEESE, BLUE, CRUMBLED **Roth Buttermilk Blue Crumbles**	• Assertive, clean, well-balanced flavor • Lush, creamy crumbles cooked and uncooked	Boar's Head, Athenos
	CHEESE, CHEDDAR, SHARP **Cabot Vermont Sharp Cheddar**	• Buttery, creamy texture • Nutty, complex sharpness	Tillamook, Cracker Barrel
	CHEESE, CHEDDAR, EXTRA-SHARP **Cracker Barrel Extra Sharp White**	• Perfect balance of tang • Moderate amounts of fat and moisture ensure toothsome, crumbly texture when eaten plain and melty, creamy texture when cooked	Cabot Vermont Extra-Sharp, Kerrygold Reserve
	CHEESE, CHEDDAR, ARTISANAL **Milton Creamery Prairie Breeze**	• Earthy complexity with nutty, buttery, and fruity flavors • Dry and crumbly, not rubbery or overly moist • Aged no more than 12 months to prevent overly sharp flavor	Cabot Cellars at Jasper Hill Cheddar Clothbound
	CHEESE, CHEDDAR, LOW-FAT **Cracker Barrel Reduced Fat Sharp**	• Ample creaminess • Strong cheesy flavor • Good for cooking	Cabot 50% Light Sharp
	CHEESE, COTTAGE **Daisy 4%**	• Large, uniform curds • Thick, creamy consistency • Clean, tart flavor	Good Culture, Breakstone's 4%
	CHEESE, CREAM **Philadelphia Brick Original**	• Rich, tangy, and milky flavor • Thick, creamy texture, not pasty, waxy, or chalky	Philadelphia Cream Cheese Spreads Original, Organic Valley
	CHEESE, FETA Block: **Real Greek**	• Silky, luxurious texture • Savory, complex flavor	Dodoni, Boar's Head
	Crumbled: **Athenos Crumbled**	• High fat and relatively moderate sodium levels • Nice big chunks that keep their shape	Boar's Head Creamy Feta Cheese Crumbles

	TEST KITCHEN FAVORITE	WHY WE LIKE IT	RUNNERS-UP
	CHEESE, FONTINA Real deal: **Mitica Fontina Val d'Aosta**	• Impressively complex: savory and earthy, with a nutty sweetness • Aged in caves for at least 80 days • Melts well	Zerto Fontal, Carr Valley, Fontina
	Supermarket winner: **Boar's Head Fontina Cheese**	• Soft, creamy texture and a buttery, tangy flavor • Blends well with other ingredients	
	CHEESE, GOAT **Pure Goat Milk Cheese** **Original Log**	• Rich-tasting, grassy, tangy flavor • Smooth and creamy both unheated and baked • High salt content	Vermont Creamery, Chevrion
	CHEESE, GRUYÈRE **1655 Le Gruyère AOP**	• Aged between 12 and 14 months • Crystalline structure with dense, fudgy texture • Deeply aged, caramelized, grassy flavors shine through even when cooked	Mifroma Le Gruyère Cavern AOP, Emmi Roth Grand Cru Surchoix
	CHEESE, MOZZARELLA Block: **Polly-O Whole Milk**	• Creamy, rich flavor with a hint of salt reminiscent of fresh mozzarella • Elastic but not gooey when melted	Galbani Whole Milk, Boar's Head Whole Milk Low Moisture
	Shredded: **Sargento Off the Block** **Shredded Low Moisture** **Part-Skim**	• Short strands easily spreadable over pizza dough • Classic creamy milkiness and slight tang	Kraft Low-Moisture Part-Skim
	CHEESE, PARMESAN, **SUPERMARKET** **Boar's Head** **Parmigiano-Reggiano**	• Rich and complex flavor balances tanginess and nuttiness • Dry, crumbly texture yet creamy with a crystalline crunch, not rubbery or dense • Aged for 24 months for better flavor and texture	Il Villagio Parmigiano-Reggiano 18 Month, Sarvecchio
	CHEESE, PARMESAN, **SHREDDED** **Sargento Artisan Blends**	• Mix of small and large shreds • Blend of 10- and 18-month-aged Parmesan • Rich, nutty flavor	Kraft Natural Cheese
	CHEESE, PEPPER JACK **Boar's Head Monterey Jack** **with Jalapeño**	• Buttery, tangy cheese • Clean, balanced flavor with assertive spice	Tillamook

	TEST KITCHEN FAVORITE	WHY WE LIKE IT	RUNNERS-UP
	CHEESE, AMERICAN PROVOLONE **Organic Valley Cheese Slices**	• Pleasantly tangy with subtle sharpness • High salt content intensifies flavor	Kraft Sliced Provolone Cheese, Applegate Naturals
	CHEESE, RICOTTA **Belgioioso Ricotta Con Latte Whole Milk**	• Rich, dense consistency • Slight sweetness thanks to sweet whey and small amount of milk	Galbani Whole Milk, Calabro Whole Milk
	CHEESE, SWISS For eating out of hand: **Edelweiss Creamery Emmentaler Switzerland**	• Produced using traditional Swiss methods, including copper vats for flavor development • Grassy, nutty notes	Emmi Kaltbach Cave-Aged Emmentaler Switzerland AOC
	For cooking: **Boar's Head Gold Label Switzerland**	• Mildly nutty flavor • Smooth texture when melted	
	For eating out of hand or cooking: **Emmi Emmentaler Cheese AOC**	• Pleasantly pungent • Creamy texture preferable for grilled cheese sandwiches	
	CHICKEN, WHOLE **Mary's Free Range Air Chilled (also sold as Pitman's)**	• Great, savory chicken flavor • Very tender • Air-chilled for minimum water retention and cleaner flavor	Bell & Evans Air Chilled Premium Fresh
	CHICKEN, BREASTS, BONELESS, SKINLESS **Bell & Evans Air Chilled**	• Juicy and tender with clean chicken flavor • Not salted or brined • Air-chilled • Aged on bone for at least six hours for significantly more tender meat	
	CHILI POWDER **Morton & Bassett**	• Bold, full-flavored heat • Multidimensional flavor • Spices that complement but don't overwhelm the chiles	Penzeys Spices Medium Hot

	TEST KITCHEN FAVORITE	WHY WE LIKE IT	RUNNERS-UP
	CHOCOLATE, DARK **Ghirardelli 60% Cacao Bittersweet Chocolate Premium Baking Bar**	• Creamy texture • Complex flavor with notes of cherry and wine with slight smokiness	Callebaut Intense Dark L-60-40NV
	CHOCOLATE, MILK **Endangered Species Chocolate Smooth + Creamy Milk Chocolate**	• Rich and intense with a balanced sweetness thanks to its high cacao percentage • Smooth and snappy texture	Scharffen Berger Extra Rich Milk Chocolate
	CHOCOLATE, DARK CHIPS **Ghirardelli 60% Premium Baking Chips**	• Rich, chocolate flavor • Higher cacao and fat percentages	Guittard Extra Dark Chocolate Chips 63%
	CHOCOLATE, MILK CHIPS **Hershey's Kitchens**	• Bold chocolate flavor outshines too-sweet, weak chocolate flavor of other chips • Deep cocoa flavor and creamy texture	Guittard, Ghirardelli
	CHOCOLATE, UNSWEETENED **Baker's Baking Chocolate Bar 100% Cacao**	• Familiar, classic flavor • Makes a rich and caramel-y hot fudge sauce, and brownies with a deep cocoa flavor	Hershey's Kitchens Baking Bar
	CHOCOLATE, WHITE CHIPS **Ghirardelli Classic White Baking Chips**	• Milky flavor with hints of vanilla, caramel, and butterscotch • Pleasantly creamy when eaten plain	Ghirardelli White Melting Wafers
	CIDER, HARD APPLE **Angry Orchard Crisp**	• Crisp and refreshing • Strong apple flavor	Strongbow Gold Apple, Woodchuck Amber
	CINNAMON **Morton & Bassett**	• The perfect balance of sweet and spicy • Mellow in baked applications	Penzeys Vietnamese, McCormick

	TEST KITCHEN FAVORITE	WHY WE LIKE IT	RUNNERS-UP
	COCOA POWDER **Droste Cacao**	• Earthy and woodsy deep chocolate flavor • High fat content and less starch yields perfectly chewy, rich, and moist baked goods	Guittard Cocoa Rouge, Valrhona
	COCONUT MILK **Aroy-D**	• Velvety, luxurious, and not overly thick texture • Balanced, clean coconut flavor	Roland, Goya
	COCONUT, UNSWEETENED SHREDDED **Now Real Food Organic**	• Nutty, tropical flavor • Fluffy, crisp texture	Woodstock Foods Organic
	COFFEE, SUPERMARKET MEDIUM-ROAST **Peet's Coffee** **Café Domingo**	• Extremely smooth but bold-tasting with a strong finish • Rich chocolate and toast flavors • Few defective beans, low acidity, and optimal moisture	
	COFFEE, DECAFFEINATED **Maxwell House Decaf** **Original Roast**	• Smooth, mellow flavor without being acidic or harsh • Complex, with a slightly nutty aftertaste • Made with only flavorful Arabica beans	Peet's Decaf House Blend Ground, Starbucks Coffee Decaf House Blend
	CORNMEAL **Anson Mills Fine Yellow**	• Slightly muted flavor, less corn forward and more buttery • Cornbread made with this cornmeal was soft and tender, with a smooth, cakey texture	Goya Fine Yellow Corn Meal
	CREOLE SEASONING **Tony Chachere's** **Original Creole** **Seasoning**	• Strong garlic and red pepper notes • Vibrant and zesty with a punch of heat	McCormick Perfect Pinch Cajun Seasoning

	TEST KITCHEN FAVORITE	WHY WE LIKE IT	RUNNERS-UP
	CUMIN **Simply Organic**	• Ground, flavorful, and robust with earthiness and warmth • Bright, with a touch of sweetness	Spice Islands Ground Cumin Seed
	CURRY POWDER **Penzeys Sweet**	• Balanced, neither too sweet nor too hot • Complex and vivid earthy flavor, not thin, bland, or one-dimensional NOTE: Available at penzeys.com, or on Amazon	Durkee
	DINNER ROLLS, FROZEN **Pepperidge Farm Stone Baked Artisan French**	• Tender on the inside with crispy crust • Has only seven ingredients • Tastes homemade, with a hint of salt	Rhodes Warm-N-Serv French Crusty Rolls
	EGG WHITES, PROCESSED **Eggology 100% Egg Whites**	• Work well in egg white omelets • Pasteurized; safe for use in uncooked applications • Make satisfactory baked goods	
	FIVE-SPICE POWDER **Frontier Natural Products Co-op**	• Nice depth, not one-dimensional • Balanced heat and sweetness	Dynasty Chinese, McCormick Gourmet Collection Chinese
	FLOUR, WHOLE-WHEAT **King Arthur Premium**	• Finely ground for hearty but not overly coarse texture in bread and pancakes • Sweet, nutty flavor	Bob's Red Mill Organic
	FRENCH FRIES, FROZEN **Alexia Organic Yukon Select**	• Crispy exteriors with fluffy, creamy interiors • Earthy, potato-y flavor	Ore-Ida Golden

	TEST KITCHEN FAVORITE	WHY WE LIKE IT	RUNNERS-UP
	GARLIC SUBSTITUTES **Spice World Fresh Peeled** **Organic Garlic**	• Tastes practically identical to freshly peeled cloves • Great shortcut to avoid fussing with papery skins	Dorot Gardens Crushed Garlic
	GIARDINIERA **Pastene**	• Sharp, vinegary tang • Crunchy mix of vegetables • Mellow heat that's potent but not overpowering	Scala Hot
	GRITS **Anson Mills Pencil Cob**	• Full, ripe, fresh corn flavor • Nice chew while still thick and creamy	Arrowhead Mills Organic Yellow, Bob's Red Mill
	HAM, BLACK **FOREST DELI** **Dietz & Watson Smoked** **with Natural Juices**	• Good texture • Nice ham flavor	
	HAM, COUNTRY **Burgers' Smokehouse** **Ready to Cook**	• Balanced, nuanced, and rich and fatty ham flavor • Slices are silky, tender, and slightly dry	Tripp Country Hams Whole, Edwards Virginia Traditions Uncooked Virginia
	HAM, SPIRAL-SLICED, **BONE-IN** **Burgers' Smokehouse** **Spiral-Sliced City**	• Very smoky flavor that was assertive but not over the top • Texture was moist and tender	Applewood Farms
	HOISIN SAUCE **Kikkoman**	• Balances sweet, salty, pungent, and spicy flavors • Initial burn mellows into harmonious and aromatic blend without bitterness	

	TEST KITCHEN FAVORITE	WHY WE LIKE IT	RUNNERS-UP
	HONEY **Nature Nate's 100% Pure Raw and Unfiltered**	• Bold notes of citrus, clover, and anise • Mild sweetness and slight acidity	Aunt Sue's Raw-Wild, Sue Bee Clover
	HORSERADISH **Woeber's Pure**	• Pleasant, slow burn was strong but not overwhelming • Distinct shreds of grated horseradish mixed together with a little vinegar	Silver Springs Prepared
	Inglehoffer Cream Style (also sold as Beaver Brand Grandma Rose's Hot Cream Horseradish)	• Lots of heat up front and a mustardy burn that lingered	
	HOT DOGS **Nathan's Famous Skinless Beef Franks**	• Meaty, robust, and hearty flavor, not sweet, sour, or too salty • Juicy but not greasy • Firm, craggy texture, not rubbery, mushy, or chewy	Kayem Skinless Beef
	HOT FUDGE SAUCE **Hershey's**	• True fudge flavor, not weak or overly sweet • Thick, smooth, and buttery texture	
	HOT SAUCE **Frank's RedHot Original Cayenne Pepper Sauce**	• Complex flavor • Aged peppers as first ingredient • 190–200mg sodium	Original Louisiana Brand, Tapatío
	ICE CREAM BARS **Dove Bar Vanilla Ice Cream with Milk Chocolate**	• Rich, prominent chocolate flavor • Thick, crunchy chocolate coating • Dense, creamy ice cream with pure vanilla flavor • Milk chocolate, not coconut oil, listed first in coating ingredients	Häagen-Dazs Vanilla Milk Chocolate All Natural, Blue Bunny Big Alaska
	ICE CREAM CONES **Joy Waffle**	• Lightly sweet, with vanilla, toasty, and nutty flavors • Crunchy and crisp but not overly hard • Individual paper jackets keep things neat	Joy Sugar, Keebler Waffle

	TEST KITCHEN FAVORITE	WHY WE LIKE IT	RUNNERS-UP
	ICE CREAM, CHOCOLATE **Turkey Hill Premium Dutch**	• Ultra-creamy, smooth texture • Milk chocolate taste	Breyers, Edy's (known as Dreyer's in the Western United States and Texas)
	ICE CREAM, VANILLA **Turkey Hill Original Premium**	• Silky and creamy with a rich vanilla flavor • Spoonable and airy, but still velvety from the use of viscous corn syrup	Ben & Jerry's
	ICED TEA, LOOSE LEAF **Tazo**	• Distinctive flavor with floral notes • Balanced level of strength and astringency	Luzianne, Tetley Premium Blend
	ICED TEA, BOTTLED, WITH LEMON **Lipton PureLeaf Black Tea with Lemon**	• Bright, balanced, and natural tea and lemon flavors • Uses concentrated tea leaves to extract flavor	Gold Peak
	JUICE, GRAPEFRUIT **Natalie's 100% Florida**	• Balanced and bright flavor, not too sweet • Clean and refreshing crispness	Florida's Natural Ruby Red
	JUICE, ORANGE **Natalie's 100% Florida Orange Juice, Gourmet Pasteurized**	• Fresh, sweet, and fruity flavor without overly acidic, sour, or from-concentrate taste • Gentler pasteurization helps retain fresh-squeezed flavor • Pleasant amount of light pulp	Simply Orange Not from Concentrate 100% Pure Squeezed Pasteurized, Medium Pulp
	JUICE, FROZEN ORANGE CONCENTRATE **Minute Maid Original**	• Full-bodied orange flavor • Good texture, includes some pulp	Tropicana 100% Juice
	KETCHUP **Heinz Organic**	• Smooth, viscous consistency • Bold, harmonious punch of saltiness, sweetness, tang, and tomato flavor • Classic, familiar flavor	Heinz Tomato Ketchup
	KING CAKE **Joe Gambino's Bakery**	• Moist, with a light and fluffy texture • Buttery, vanilla flavor with mellow cinnamon notes • DIY frosting keeps the cake from getting messy in transit	Poupart Bakery Incorporated – Cinnamon, Haydel's Bakery "Piece of Cake" Package – Traditional

	TEST KITCHEN FAVORITE	WHY WE LIKE IT	RUNNERS-UP
	LARD, ARTISANAL **U.S. Dreams**	• Preservative-free, nonhydrogenated lard • Clean and rich flavor while remaining light	
	LARD, SUPERMARKET **John Morrell Snow Cap**	• Partial hydrogenation helps ensure firmness • Neutral flavor leaves food very tasty	
	LEMONADE **Natalie's Natural**	• Supertart, fresh lemon flavor from 20 percent real lemon juice, without artificial flavors or off-notes • Perfect balance of tartness and sweetness, unlike many overly sweet competitors	Simply Lemonade, Minute Maid Premium Frozen Concentrate
	MACARONI & CHEESE **Kraft Velveeta Original Shells & Cheese**	• Strong and rich cheese flavor • Thick liquid sauce made from real cheese and milk • Dry shell pasta, instead of frozen, gives substantial texture	
	MAPLE SYRUP **Uncle Luke's, Grade A Dark Amber**	• Inexpensive • Dark, molasses-y color • Rich caramel flavor that tastes pleasantly toasty in pie	Highland Sugarworks, Coombs Family Farms, Anderson's
	MAYONNAISE **Blue Plate**	• Great balance of taste and texture • Tastes close to homemade NOTE: While it's one of the top-selling brands in the country, you'll have to mail-order it unless you live in the South or Southeast	Hellmann's Real, Hellmann's Light
	MAYONNAISE, LIGHT **Hellmann's Light**	• Bright, balanced flavor close to full-fat counterpart, not overly sweet • Not as creamy as full-fat but passable texture NOTE: Hellmann's is known as Best Foods west of the Rocky Mountains	

	TEST KITCHEN FAVORITE	WHY WE LIKE IT	RUNNERS-UP
	MOLASSES **Brer Rabbit All Natural Unsulphured Mild Flavor**	• Acidic yet balanced • Strong and straightforward raisin-y taste • Pleasantly bitter bite	Plantation Barbados Unsulphured, Grandma's Unsulphured Original
	MUSTARD, BROWN **Gulden's Spicy**	• Complex flavor with both heat and gentle tang • Smooth, creamy texture that goes perfectly with hot dogs	French's, Beaver Deli
	MUSTARD, COARSE-GRAIN **Grey Poupon Harvest Coarse Ground** and **Grey Poupon Country Dijon**	• Spicy, tangy burst of mustard flavor • High salt content amplifies flavor • Contains no superfluous ingredients that mask mustard flavor • Big, round seeds add pleasant crunch • Just enough vinegar, not too sour or thin	Woeber's Reserve Whole Grain
	MUSTARD, DIJON **Trois Petits Cochons Moutarde de Dijon**	• Potent, bold, and very hot, not weak or mild • Good balance of sweetness, tanginess, and sharpness • Not overly acidic, sweet, or one-dimensional like competitors	Maille Dijon Originale, Roland Extra Strong
	MUSTARD, YELLOW **Heinz**	• Moderate acidity • Mild sweetness • Smooth texture	French's Classic, Koops' Original
	OATS, ROLLED **Bob's Red Mill Old Fashioned**	• Toasty flavor, even in cookies • Tender texture with just the right amount of chew • Hearty, tender texture and nutty flavor in oatmeal	Bob's Red Mill Extra Thick, Quaker Old Fashioned
	OATS, STEEL-CUT **Bob's Red Mill Organic**	• Rich and complex oat flavor with buttery, earthy, nutty, and whole-grain notes • Creamy yet toothsome texture • Moist but not sticky NOTE: Not recommended for baking	Arrowhead Mills Organic Hot Cereal, Country Choice Organic

	TEST KITCHEN FAVORITE	WHY WE LIKE IT	RUNNERS-UP
	OLIVE OIL, EXTRA-VIRGIN **Bertolli Extra Virgin, Original, Rich Taste**	• Brings a balanced taste to dishes • Very green, very grassy	Filippo Berio Robusto
	California Olive Ranch Global Blend Medium Extra Virgin	• Rich, fruity, and delicious with a very olive-forward flavor • Tastes fresh and bright	
	OLIVE OIL, EXTRA-VIRGIN, PREMIUM **Gaea Fresh Extra Virgin**	• Smooth, buttery, and balanced flavor • Sweet olive fruitiness with peppery aftertaste	Casa de Santo Amaro Selection Extra Virgin
	PANCAKE MIX **Hungry Jack Buttermilk**	• Flavorful balance of sweetness and tang well-seasoned with sugar and salt • Light, extra fluffy texture • Requires vegetable oil (along with milk and egg) to reconstitute the batter	Aunt Jemima Original Pancake and Waffle
	PAPRIKA, SWEET **The Spice House Hungarian Sweet**	• Complex flavor with earthy, fruity notes • Bright and bold, not bland and boring • Rich, toasty aroma NOTE: Available only through mail order, 312-274-0378 or thespicehouse.com	Penzeys Hungarian Sweet Kulonleges NOTE: Available at penzeys.com, or on Amazon
	PASTA, CHEESE RAVIOLI **Rosetto**	• Creamy, plush, and rich blend of ricotta, Romano, and Parmesan cheeses • Pasta with nice, springy bite • Perfect dough-to-filling ratio	Celentano
	PASTA, CHEESE TORTELLINI **Barilla Three Cheese**	• Robustly flavored filling from combination of ricotta, Emmentaler, and Grana Padano cheeses • Tender pasta that's sturdy enough to withstand boiling but not so thick that it becomes doughy	Seviroli, Buitoni Three Cheese

	TEST KITCHEN FAVORITE	WHY WE LIKE IT	RUNNERS-UP
	PASTA, EGG NOODLES **Pennsylvania Dutch Wide**	• Balanced, buttery flavor with no off-flavors • Light and fluffy texture, not gummy or starchy	Manischewitz Wide, Manischewitz Yolk Free Wide
	PASTA, ELBOW MACARONI **Creamette**	• Buttery flavor • Firm but slightly tender texture • Longer noodles, close to 1 inch in length	De Cecco
	PASTA, FETTUCCINE **Garofalo**	• Wide, thick noodles that cook up plump and springy with mild, clean flavor • Retained perfect chew when tossed with sauce	De Cecco, Barilla Classic Blue Box
	PASTA, LASAGNA NOODLES No-boil: **Barilla**	• Taste and texture of fresh pasta • Delicate, flat noodles	Ronzoni Oven Ready, Pasta DeFino
	Whole-wheat: **Bionaturae Organic 100% Whole Wheat**	• Complex nutty, rich wheat flavor • Substantial chewy texture without any grittiness	DeLallo 100% Organic Whole Wheat, Ronzoni Healthy Harvest
	PASTA, PENNE **Mueller's Penne Rigate**	• Hearty texture, not insubstantial or gummy • Wheaty, slightly sweet flavor, not bland	Benedetto Cavalieri Penne Rigate, De Cecco
	PASTA, SPAGHETTI **De Cecco Spaghetti No. 12**	• Rich, nutty, wheaty flavor • Firm, ropy strands with good chew, not mushy, gummy, or mealy	Rustichella D'Abruzzo Pasta Abruzzese di Semola di Grano Duro, Garofalo
	PASTA, SPAGHETTI, GLUTEN-FREE **Jovial Organic Gluten-Free Brown Rice**	• High in fiber and protein • No gumminess or off-flavors as experienced with other brands • Delicate and thin strands	Barilla Gluten Free Spaghetti
	PASTA, SPAGHETTI, WHOLE-WHEAT **Bionaturae Organic 100% Whole Wheat**	• Chewy and firm, not mushy or rubbery • Full and nutty wheat flavor	Barilla PLUS Multigrain

	TEST KITCHEN FAVORITE	WHY WE LIKE IT	RUNNERS-UP
	PASTA SAUCE, JARRED **Rao's Homemade Marinara**	• Vibrant, bright, aromatic sauce • Adds buttery, creamy richness to dishes • Uses imported whole tomatoes	Victoria Fine Foods Premium Marinara
	PEANUT BUTTER, CREAMY **Skippy**	• Smooth, creamy, and spreadable • Good balance of sweet and salty flavors	Jif, Peter Pan Natural
	PEPPERCORNS, BLACK **Tone's Whole Black Peppercorns**	• Whole peppercorns (not preground) • Moderate, balanced heat with subtle floral and smoky notes • No overpowering or off-flavors	Penzeys Whole Telicherry Indian Peppercorns
	PEPPERONI, SLICED **Margherita Italian Style**	• Nice balance of meatiness and spice • Tangy, fresh flavor with hints of fruity licorice and peppery fennel • Thin slices with the right amount of chew	Boar's Head
	PEPPERS, ROASTED RED **Dunbars Sweet**	• Balance of smokiness and sweetness • Mild, sweet, and earthy red pepper flavor • Firm texture, not slimy or mushy • Packed in simple yet strong brine of salt and water without distraction of other strongly flavored ingredients	Cento
	PICKLES, BREAD-AND-BUTTER **Bubbies Chips**	• Subtle, briny tang • All-natural solution that uses real sugar, not high-fructose corn syrup	

	TEST KITCHEN FAVORITE	WHY WE LIKE IT	RUNNERS-UP
	PICKLES, WHOLE KOSHER DILL **Boar's Head**	• Pleasantly crisp with a great snap • Slightly spicy and very garlicky, has a homemade pickle flavor	Mt. Olive Kosher Dills
	PIE CRUST, READY-MADE **Pillsbury Refrigerated**	• Flaky, buttery texture • Fits in standard pie plate • Enough overhang to crimp edges nicely	
	PIZZA, PEPPERONI, FROZEN **Pizzeria! by DiGiorno Primo Pepperoni**	• Thick, crisp, and airy crust with a browned and charred bottom • Herby, zesty sauce • Very meaty pepperoni	Freschetta Brick Oven Crust Pepperoni and Italian Style Cheese, Red Baron Fire Baked
	POPCORN, BAGGED **Smartfood Smart50 Sea Salt**	• Subtle saltiness and nice toasty flavor • Round, fluffy kernels that are crunchy on the outside with a tender interior	Kettle Sea Salt, Popcorn Indiana Sea Salt
	PORK, PREMIUM **Snake River Farms American Kurobuta (Berkshire)**	• Deep pink tint, which indicates higher pH level and more flavorful meat • Tender texture and juicy, intensely pork-y flavor	D'Artagnan Berkshire Chops (Milanese-Style Cut)
	POTATO CHIPS Kettle Style: **Utz's Kettle Classics, Original**	• Perfectly salted, flavorful chips • Slightly thick chips that are crunchy • Not too greasy	
	Regular: **Herr's Crisp 'N Tasty**	• Thin and crispy without being flimsy	
	PRESERVES, PEACH **American Spoon Red Haven**	• Bold, ripe peach taste and balanced sweetness • Loose and spreadable texture, similar to homemade preserves	Bonne Maman, Smucker's

	TEST KITCHEN FAVORITE	WHY WE LIKE IT	RUNNERS-UP
	PRESERVES, RASPBERRY **Smucker's**	• Clean, strong raspberry flavor, not too tart or sweet • Not overly seedy • Ideal, spreadable texture, not too thick, artificial, or overprocessed	Trappist
	RICE, ARBORIO **RiceSelect**	• Creamier than competitors • Smooth grains • Characteristic good bite of Arborio rice in risotto where al dente is ideal	Riso Baricella Superfino, Rienzi Premium Gourmet
	RICE, BASMATI **Daawat**	• Pleasantly chewy, long, intact, fluffy grains • Fragrant, aromatic flavor • Aged 18 to 24 months • Imported from India	Goya, Royal
	RICE, BROWN **Lundberg Organic Long Grain**	• Firm yet tender grains • Bold, toasty, nutty flavor • Works with a range of cooking methods • Includes the best instructions	Riceland Extra Long Grain Natural, Carolina Whole Grain (also sold as Mahatma)
	RICE, LONG-GRAIN WHITE **Lundberg Organic Long Grain**	• Nutty, buttery, and toasty flavor • Distinct, smooth grains that offer some chew without being overly chewy	Carolina Enriched Extra-Long-Grain
	RICE, READY **Minute Ready to Serve**	• Parboiled long-grain white rice that is ready in less than 2 minutes • Toasted, buttery flavor • Firm grains with al dente bite	
	SALSA, JARRED GREEN **Frontera Tomatillo**	• Sweet and nuanced flavor with a roasted, smoky taste from charred tomatillo skins • A good amount of heat • Has no preservatives or stabilizers	
	SALSA, JARRED HOT **Pace Hot Chunky**	• Good balance of bright tomato, chile, and vegetal flavors • Chunky, almost crunchy texture, not mushy or thin • Spicy and fiery but not overpowering	Frontera Hot Habanero with Roasted Tomatoes and Cilantro, Newman's Own All Natural Chunky

	TEST KITCHEN FAVORITE	WHY WE LIKE IT	RUNNERS-UP
	SALSA, JARRED, MILD **Chi-Chi's Mild** **Thick & Chunky**	• Hint of heat with good balance and sweet, satisfying tomato flavor • Thick, smooth base fortified with concentrated crushed tomatoes and chunks of vegetables	
	SALT, KOSHER **Diamond Crystal**	• Flakes have a soft, delicate texture that is easy to crush between your fingers • Contains no anticaking agents • Dissolves rapidly	Morton Kosher Salt
	SAUERKRAUT **Eden Organic**	• Slight sweetness and subtle zing, bright tanginess • Small, soft shreds with just enough chew	Libby's
	SAUSAGE, BREAKFAST **Jimmy Dean Fully** **Cooked Original Pork Links**	• Meaty chew and a crisp golden crust • Balance of sweet and spicy for a rich pork taste	
	SOUP, CANNED CHICKEN NOODLE **Muir Glen Organic**	• Organic chicken and vegetables and plenty of seasonings give it a fresh taste and spicy kick • Firm, not mushy, vegetables and noodles • No off-flavors	Progresso Traditional
	SOUP, TOMATO **Progresso Vegetable** **Classics Hearty**	• Includes fresh, unprocessed tomatoes, not just tomato puree like some competitors • Tangy, slightly herbaceous flavor • Balanced seasoning and natural sweetness • Medium body and slightly chunky texture	Imagine Organic Vine Ripened
	SOY SAUCE **Kikkoman Soy Sauce**	• Good salty-sweet balance • Long fermentation (6 to 8 months) • Simple ingredient list (wheat, soybeans, water, and salt) with no added sugar or flavor enhancers	Lee Kum Kee Table Top Premium, Kikkoman Gluten-Free Tamari

	TEST KITCHEN FAVORITE	WHY WE LIKE IT	RUNNERS-UP
	SPREAD, STRAWBERRY **Smucker's Preserves**	• Robust, natural strawberry flavor without any added flavoring • Pleasing consistency, it is neither too runny nor too thick	Welch's Natural Strawberry Spread, Crofter's Organic Strawberry Just Fruit Spread
	STEAK SAUCE **Heinz 57 Sauce**	• Mellow, restrained flavor that doesn't overpower the meat • Fruity, sweet, and tangy flavor with hints of heat and smoke • Smooth texture with enough body to cling to steak without being gluey	Lea & Perrins Traditional
	SWEETENED CONDENSED MILK **Borden Eagle Brand** and **Nestlé Carnation**	• Made with whole milk • Thick, smooth, velvety	
	TARTAR SAUCE **McCormick Original**	• Rich and eggy sauce with good acidity • Abundance of sweet pickle bits	
	TEA, BLACK For plain tea: **Twinings English Breakfast**	• Bright, bold, and flavorful yet not too strong • Fruity, floral, and fragrant • Smooth, slightly astringent profile preferred for tea without milk	Lipton Black Tea, Bigelow English Teatime
	With milk and sugar: **Tetley British Blend**	• Boasts caramel notes and full, deep, smoky flavors • Bold, fruity flavor	Celestial Seasonings English Breakfast Estate Tea
	TERIYAKI SAUCE **Soy Vay Veri Veri Teriyaki Marinade & Sauce**	• Contains sesame seeds and small chunks of onion • Strong garlic flavor	
	TOMATOES, CANNED CRUSHED **SMT**	• Bright, clear tomato flavor • Crushed tomatoes in liquid contribute thick, hearty texture	Red Pack Crushed Tomatoes in Puree (also sold as Red Gold), Pastene Kitchen Ready Chunky Style Ground Peeled Tomatoes

	TEST KITCHEN FAVORITE	WHY WE LIKE IT	RUNNERS-UP
	TOMATOES, CANNED DICED **Hunt's**	• Bright, fresh tomato flavor that balances sweet and tart • Firm yet tender texture	Muir Glen Organic
	TOMATOES, CANNED WHOLE **Muir Glen Organic Whole Peeled**	• Pleasing balance of bold acidity and fruity sweetness • Firm yet tender texture, even after hours of simmering	Hunt's
	TOMATO PASTE, CANNED **Cento Tomato Paste**	• Savory, with good fruity flavors • Bright and acidic but not bitter or harsh	Contadina Tomato Paste
	TOMATO PASTE, TUBED **Cento Double Concentrated Tomato Paste**	• Intense, robust tomato flavors • Balance of sweet and tart flavors	Mutti Double Concentrated Tomato Paste
	TORTILLA CHIPS **On the Border Café Style**	• Traditional, buttery sweetness and bright corn flavor • The perfect counterpart to salsa • Light, crisp exterior	Tostitos Original Restaurant Style, Santitas White Corn
	TORTILLAS, CORN **Maria and Ricardo's Handmade Style Soft Corn Tortillas, Yellow** **Guerrero White Corn Tortillas**	• Subtle corn flavor and slight nuttiness • Pleasantly chewy • Soft and pliable, thin but not frail • Tender with some chew	
	TORTILLAS, FLOUR **Old El Paso Flour Tortillas for Soft Tacos & Fajitas**	• Thin, flaky, tender tortilla • Made with plenty of fat and salt	Guerrero Tortillas de Harina Caseras

	TEST KITCHEN FAVORITE	WHY WE LIKE IT	RUNNERS-UP
	TOSTADAS, CORN **Mission Tostadas** **Estilo Casero**	• Crisp, crunchy texture • Good corn flavor • Flavor and texture that are substantial enough to stand up to hearty toppings	Charras
	TUNA PACKED IN OIL **Tonnino Tuna Fillets in** **Olive Oil**	• Meaty yellowfin tuna that has a clean and bright taste • Large, lovely flakes	
	Ortiz Bonito del Norte **Albacore White Tuna in** **Olive Oil**	• Firm but with delicate layers • Very well seasoned	
	TUNA PACKED IN WATER **American Tuna Pole** **Caught Wild Albacore**	• Seasoned well with lots of flavor • Moist but not mushy • Creamy texture	
	TURKEY, WHOLE **Mary's Free-Range** **Non-GMO Verified**	• Turkey flavor that is rich and robust • Tender and juicy meat • Untreated vegetarian-fed turkeys have clean turkey flavor	Plainville Farms Young, Diestel Turkey Ranch Non-GMO Verified
	TURKEY, WHOLE HERITAGE **Mary's Free-Range** **Heritage Turkey**	• Richly flavored • Great texture and moisture • Exquisitely crisp skin	Elmwood Stock Farm Organic, Good Sherpherd Poultry Ranch

	TEST KITCHEN FAVORITE	WHY WE LIKE IT	RUNNERS-UP
	VANILLA BEANS **McCormick** **Madagascar**	• Moist, seed-filled pods • Complex, robust flavor with caramel notes	Spice Islands Bourbon, Nielsen-Massey Madagascar Bourbon Gourmet
	VANILLA PURE EXTRACT **Simply Organic** Imitation: **Baker's Imitation Vanilla Flavor**	• Good vanilla presence • Complex flavor	
	VEGETABLE OIL, ALL-PURPOSE **Crisco Blends**	• Unobtrusive, mild flavor for stir-frying and sautéing and for use in baked goods and in uncooked applications such as mayonnaise and vinaigrette • Neutral taste and absence of fishy or metallic flavors when used for frying	Mazola Canola Oil, Crisco Pure (Soybean)
	VINEGAR, APPLE CIDER **Heinz Filtered**	• Right amount of acidity • Distinct apple flavor with a floral aroma and assertive, tangy qualities • Sharp and punchy	White House, Bragg Organic
	VINEGAR, BALSAMIC **Bertolli of Modena**	• Tastes of dried fruit like figs, raisins, and prunes • Tastes pleasantly sweet once reduced or whisked into vinaigrette	Monari Federzoni of Modena, Colavita of Modena

	TEST KITCHEN FAVORITE	WHY WE LIKE IT	RUNNERS-UP
	VINEGAR, RED WINE **Laurent du Clos**	• Crisp red wine flavor balanced by stronger than average acidity and subtle sweetness • Complex yet pleasing taste from multiple varieties of grapes	Pompeian Gourmet
	VINEGAR, WHITE WINE **Napa Valley Naturals Organic**	• Balanced sweetness and acidity • Fruity and vibrant in vinaigrettes • Floral and aromatic notes with robust acidity in pickled vegetables	Star, Colavita Aged
	WHIPPED TOPPING **Cool Whip Extra Creamy**	• Thick, silky, and luscious • Excellent, fresh cream flavor and just enough sweetness	Land O'Lakes Whipped Heavy Cream
	WORCESTERSHIRE SAUCE **Lea & Perrins Original**	• Balanced notes of vinegar, pepper, and tamarind • Distinctly punchy, bright tanginess in marinades	French's, Annie's Organic Vegan
	YOGURT, GREEK WHOLE MILK **Fage Total Classic**	• High in protein with no added stabilizers or thickeners • Rich, creamy, dense, faintly sweet flavor • Holds its own against garlicky sharpness of tzatziki sauce	Dannon Oikos Traditional Plain 4%, Wallaby Organic Plain
	YOGURT, WHOLE-MILK **Brown Cow Cream Top Plain**	• Rich, well-rounded flavor, not sour or bland • Especially creamy, smooth texture, not thin or watery • Higher fat content contributes to flavor and texture	Stonyfield Farm Organic Plain

EPISODE DIRECTORY

2008
season one

episode 101
Forgotten Cakes
Strawberry Poke Cake 679
Chocolate Blackout Cake 664

episode 102
Sunday Dinner
Sunday-Best Garlic Roast Beef 273
Mashed Potato Casserole 331

episode 103
Feeding a Crowd, Italian-Style
Slow-Cooker Italian Sunday
Gravy 397
Meatballs and Marinara 412

episode 104
Southern Regional Recipes
Lexington-Style Pulled Pork 513
Memphis Chopped Coleslaw 571

episode 105
Autumn Supper
Old-Fashioned Roast Pork 301
Cranberry-Apple Crisp 744

episode 106
All-American Picnic
Extra-Crunchy Fried Chicken 72
All-American Potato Salad 572

episode 107
Easy as Pie
Raspberry Chiffon Pie 796
No-Fear Single-Crust Pie Dough 765

episode 108
Steakhouse Favorites
Broiled Steaks 196
Super-Stuffed Baked Potatoes 235

episode 109
Barbecued Chicken
Classic Barbecued Chicken 459
Best Potluck Macaroni and Cheese 10

episode 110
Regional Chops
Tennessee Whiskey Pork Chops 141
Smoked Double-Thick Pork Chops 526

episode 111
Midwestern Favorites
Chicago-Style Barbecued Ribs 506
Cincinnati Chili 151

episode 112
California Grilling
California Barbecued Tri-Tip 495
California Barbecued Beans 560
Santa Maria Salsa 495

episode 113
Diner Favorites
Fluffy Diner-Style Cheese Omelet 593
Short-Order Home Fries 604

2009
season two

episode 201
Old-Fashioned Roast Beef Dinner
Classic Roast Beef and Gravy 275
Perfect Popovers 630

episode 202
Pucker-Up Pies
Mile-High Lemon Meringue Pie 771
Icebox Key Lime Pie 774

episode 203
Rise and Shine
Ultimate Cinnamon Buns 638
Better-Than-the-Box Pancake
Mix 606

episode 204
Surefire Seafood
Wood-Grilled Salmon 544
Baked Stuffed Shrimp 210
Grilled Jalapeño and Lime
Shrimp Skewers 553

episode 205
Fudgy Cakes
Tunnel of Fudge Cake 669
Hot Fudge Pudding Cake 705

episode 206
Texas Chili
Easy Chili con Carne 385
Southern-Style Skillet
Cornbread 625

2010
season three

2017
season ten

episode 1001
Pork and Pierogi
Cider-Braised Pork Roast 304
Potato-Cheddar Pierogi 166

episode 1002
Arroz con Pollo and Sour Orange Pie
Arroz con Pollo 352
Sour Orange Pie 773

episode 1003
Smoky Barbecue Favorites
Texas Thick-Cut Smoked Pork
Chops 525
Backyard Barbecue Beans 559

episode 1004
Smothered and Dowdied
Southern-Style Smothered
Chicken 31
Apple Pandowdy 742

episode 1005
BBQ Thighs and Fried Peach Pies
BBQ Chicken Thighs 474
Fried Peach Hand Pies 779

episode 1006
Ribs and Mashed Potatoes Revisited
Slow-Cooker Memphis-Style
Wet Ribs 144
Mashed Potato Cakes 216

episode 1007
Bourbon and Broccoli Hit the Grill
Grilled Bourbon Steaks 486
Grilled Broccoli with Lemon
and Parmesan 565

episode 1008
Pork Tacos and Churros
Citrus-Braised Pork Tacos 367
So-Cal Churros 388

episode 1009
Southern Discoveries
South Carolina Smoked Fresh
Ham 511
Smashed Potato Salad 584

episode 1010
Cast-Iron Comforts
Cast Iron Skillet Pizza 435
Chocolate Chip Skillet Cookie 718

episode 1011
Plenty of Garlic and Parm
Garlic Fried Chicken 79
Crispy Parmesan Potatoes 231

episode 1012
When Only Chocolate Will Do
Mississippi Mud Pie 804
Whoopie Pies 732

episode 1013
The Italian-American Kitchen
Pasta with Sausage Ragu 401
Fluffy Baked Polenta with Red
Sauce 409

2018
season eleven

episode 1101
Ultimate Comfort Foods
Wellesley Fudge Cake 667
Chicken and Pastry 7

episode 1102
Ballpark Classics
Grilled Sausages with Bell Peppers
and Onions 522
Ballpark Pretzels 184

episode 1103
A Trip to Tarheel Country
North Carolina Dipped Fried
Chicken 81
North Carolina Lemon Pie 768

episode 1104
New Recipes for the Grill
Grill-Fried Chicken Wings 469
Grilled Pork Burgers 521

episode 1105
Spaghetti House Classics
Hearty Beef Lasagna 422
Chicken Scarpariello 441

2019
season twelve

2020
season thirteen

2021
season fourteen

CONVERSIONS AND EQUIVALENTS

SOME SAY COOKING IS A SCIENCE AND AN ART. WE would say that geography has a hand in it, too. Flour milled in the United Kingdom and elsewhere will feel and taste different from flour milled in the United States. So we cannot promise that the loaf of bread you bake in Canada or England will taste the same as a loaf baked in the States, but we can offer guidelines for converting weights and measures. We also recommend that you rely on your instincts when making our recipes. Refer to the visual cues provided. If the bread dough hasn't "come together in a ball," as described, you may need to add more flour—even if the recipe doesn't tell you to. You be the judge.

The recipes in this book were developed using standard U.S. measures following U.S. government guidelines. The charts below offer equivalents for U.S., metric, and imperial (U.K.) measures. All conversions are approximate and have been rounded up or down to the nearest whole number.

EXAMPLE:

| 1 teaspoon | = | 4.9292 milliliters, rounded up to 5 milliliters |
| 1 ounce | = | 28.3495 grams, rounded down to 28 grams |

VOLUME CONVERSIONS

U.S.	METRIC
1 teaspoon	5 milliliters
2 teaspoons	10 milliliters
1 tablespoon	15 milliliters
2 tablespoons	30 milliliters
¼ cup	59 milliliters
⅓ cup	79 milliliters
½ cup	118 milliliters
¾ cup	177 milliliters
1 cup	237 milliliters
1¼ cups	296 milliliters
1½ cups	355 milliliters
2 cups (1 pint)	473 milliliters
2½ cups	591 milliliters
3 cups	710 milliliters
4 cups (1 quart)	0.946 liter
1.06 quarts	1 liter
4 quarts (1 gallon)	3.8 liters

WEIGHT CONVERSIONS

OUNCES	GRAMS
½	14
¾	21
1	28
1½	43
2	57
2½	71
3	85
3½	99
4	113
4½	128
5	142
6	170
7	198
8	227
9	255
10	283
12	340
16 (1 pound)	454

CONVERSIONS FOR INGREDIENTS COMMONLY USED IN BAKING

Baking is an exacting science. Because measuring by weight is far more accurate than measuring by volume, and thus more likely to achieve reliable results, in our recipes we provide ounce measures in addition to cup measures for many ingredients. Refer to the chart below to convert these measures into grams.

INGREDIENT	OUNCES	GRAMS
1 cup all-purpose flour*	5	142
1 cup whole-wheat flour	5½	156
1 cup granulated (white) sugar	7	198
1 cup packed brown sugar (light or dark)	7	198
1 cup confectioners' sugar	4	113
1 cup cocoa powder	3	85
4 tablespoons butter† (½ stick or ¼ cup)	2	57
8 tablespoons butter† (1 stick or ½ cup)	4	113
16 tablespoons butter† (2 sticks or 1 cup)	8	227

* U.S. all-purpose flour, the most frequently used flour in this book, does not contain leaveners, as some European flours do. These leavened flours are called self-rising or self-raising. If you are using self-rising flour, take this into consideration before adding leavening to a recipe.

† In the United States, butter is sold both salted and unsalted. We generally recommend unsalted butter. If you are using salted butter, take this into consideration before adding salt to a recipe.

OVEN TEMPERATURES

FAHRENHEIT	CELSIUS	GAS MARK (IMPERIAL)
225	105	¼
250	120	½
275	135	1
300	150	2
325	165	3
350	180	4
375	190	5
400	200	6
425	220	7
450	230	8
475	245	9

CONVERTING TEMPERATURES FROM AN INSTANT-READ THERMOMETER

We include doneness temperatures in many of the recipes in this book. We recommend an instant-read thermometer for the job. Refer to the above table to convert Fahrenheit degrees to Celsius. Or, for temperatures not represented in the chart, use this simple formula:

Subtract 32 degrees from the Fahrenheit reading, then divide the result by 1.8 to find the Celsius reading.

EXAMPLE:

"Roast chicken until thighs register 175 degrees."
To convert:

175°F − 32 = 143°
143° ÷ 1.8 = 79.44°C, rounded down to 79°C

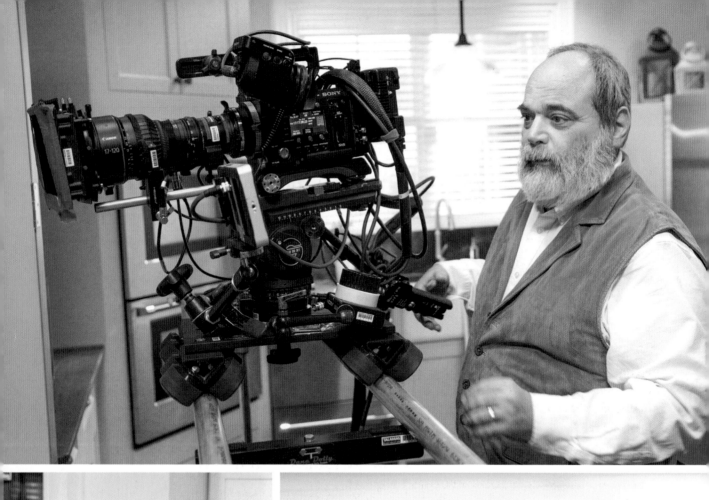

index

Note: Page references in *italics* indicate photographs.

Butter, flavored

Barbecue-Scallion, 557

Basil Pesto, 557

Brown Sugar–Cayenne, 554

Chesapeake Bay, 557

Cilantro-Chipotle, 557

Cilantro-Lime, 554

Honey, 622, *623*

Mustard-Paprika, 554

Rosemary-Pepper, 554

C

Cabbage

Apple Slaw, Tangy, *568*, 569

California-Style Fish Tacos, *356*, 357

Chinese Chicken Salad, 114, *115*

chopping, 571

Memphis Chopped Coleslaw, *570*, 571

Milk-Can Supper, 56, *57*

Caesar Green Bean Salad, 238, *239*

Caesar Salad, Grilled, 566, *567*

Café au Lait Angel Food Cake, 693

Cakes

Angel Food, *692*, 693

Café au Lait, 693

Chocolate-Almond, 693

Baby Pudding, 705

Blitz Torte, *690*, 691

Blueberry Jam, 674, *675*

Chiffon, 694, *695*

Chiffon, Orange, 694

Chocolate Blackout, 664, *665*

Chocolate Cream Cupcakes, *702*, 703

Chocolate Éclair, *682*, *683*

Clementine, 672, *673*

Hot Fudge Pudding, *704*, 705

Italian Cream, 696, *697*

Lane, *670*, 671

Cakes *(cont.)*

Lemon Icebox Cheesecake, 708, *709*

Lemon Pudding, 706, *707*

Magic Chocolate Flan, *684*, 685

Milk Chocolate Cheesecake, *712*, 713

Mixed Berry Buckle, *746*, 747

New Jersey Crumb Buns, *646*, 647

Pound, Cold-Oven, 700, *701*

Pound, Cream Cheese, *698*, 699

Red Velvet, 662, *663*

Strawberry Dream, 676, *677*

Strawberry Poke, *678*, 679

Swiss Hazelnut, 688, *689*

Texas Sheet, 680, *681*

Tres Leches, *686*, 687

Tunnel of Fudge, *668*, 669

Wellesley Fudge, *666*, 667

Whoopie Pies, 732, *733*

California Barbecued Beans, 560, *561*

California Barbecued Tri-Tip, *494*, 495

Canadian whisky, about, 486

Caper(s)

about, 586

Hard-Cooked Eggs, and Radishes, Tuna Salad with, 20

-Lemon Sauce, Grilled Salmon Steaks with, *548*, 549

and Oregano, Crushed Red Potatoes with, 227

and Pine Nuts, Stuffed Tomatoes with, 240

Cappuccino Glaze, 725

Carrots

buying and storing, 5

Chuck Roast in Foil, *294*, 295

Guinness Beef Stew, *268*, 269

Milk-Can Supper, 56, *57*

Morning Glory Muffins, *634*, 635

One-Pan Prime Rib and Roasted Vegetables, 290, *291*

One-Pan Roast Chicken with Root Vegetables, *256*, 257

D

Dakota Bread, 658, *659*
Dakota Peach Kuchen, 752, *753*
Delmonico Potato Casserole, *220,* 221
Delta Hot Tamales, 156, *157*
Desserts
    Apple Fritters, *740,* 741
    Apple Pandowdy, *742,* 743
    Baked Apple Dumplings, *738,* 739
    Banana Pudding, *754,* 755
    Chocolate Truffles, Basic, *734,* 735
        -Almond, 735
        -Cinnamon, 735
        -Ginger, 735
        -Lemon, 735
    Cranberry-Apple Crisp, 744, *745*
    Dakota Peach Kuchen, 752, *753*
    Gooey Butter Cake Bars, 720, *721*
    Maine Blueberry Grunt, *748,* 749
    Mixed Berry Buckle, *746,* 747
    New Orleans Bourbon Bread Pudding, *756,* 757
    Old-Fashioned Chocolate Frozen Custard, 761
    Old-Fashioned Vanilla Frozen Custard, *760,* 761
    Peanut-y Banana Pudding, 755
    Skillet Peach Cobbler, 750, *751*
    So-Cal Churros, 388, *389*
    Strawberry Cheesecake Bars, 710, *711*
    Summer Berry Pudding, 758, *759*
    Toasted-Coconut Banana Pudding, 755
    Zeppoles, *448,* 449
    see also Cakes; Cookies; Pies (sweet)
Detroit-Style Pizza, *164,* 165
Deviled Beef Short Ribs, 286, *287*
Dill
    and Garlic, Slow-Roasted Salmon with, 314
    Potato Salad, *580,* 581
Dips
    Buffalo Blue Cheese Sauce, 171
    Chive Sour Cream, *230,* 231
    Chunky Guacamole, 348, *349*

Dips *(cont.)*
    Creamy BBQ Sauce, 171
    Curried Chutney Sauce, 171
    Honey-Mustard Sauce, 87
    One-Minute Salsa, 345
    Santa Maria Salsa, 495
    Seven-Layer, Ultimate, *346,* 347
    Seven-Layer, Ultimate Smoky, 347
    Smoky Salsa Verde, 372, *373*
    Sweet and Sour Sauce, 87
Double-Crust Chicken Pot Pie, *40,* 41
Double-Crust Pie Dough, 764
Doughnuts
    Beignets, 614, *615*
    Muffin Tin, 636, *637*
Dressing, Green Goddess, *22,* 23
Drop Meatballs, 410, *411*
Duchess Potatoes, *328,* 329
Dumplings
    Baked Apple, *738,* 739
    Potato-Cheddar Pierogi, 166, *167*
Dutch Baby, *610,* 611

E

Easier Chicken Chimichangas, 370, *371*
Eastern North Carolina Fish Stew, 96, *97*
Easy Chicken Tacos, 360, *361*
Easy Chili con Carne, *384,* 385
Easy Green Chile Chicken Enchiladas, 376, *377*
Easy Steak Frites, 202, *203*
Easy Sweet Italian Sausage, *162,* 163
Eggplant Pecorino, 426, *427*
Eggs
    Adjaruli Khachapuri, *598,* 599
    Breakfast Pizza, 596, *597*
    Chorizo and Manchego Breakfast Pizza, 596
    Croque Madame, 126
    Eastern North Carolina Fish Stew, 96, *97*
    Fluffy Diner-Style Cheese Omelet, *592,* 593

F

I

K

Kitchen supplies, ratings of, 834–35
Knives and more, ratings of, 806–8
Kolaches, 648, *649*

L

Lamb, Crumb-Crusted Rack of, *312*, 313
Lane Cake, *670*, 671
Lard, cooking with, 368
Lasagna
    Beef, Hearty, 422, *423*
    Skillet, 420, *421*
    Skillet, with Sausage and Peppers, 420
    Spinach and Tomato, *424*, 425
Lemon(s)
    -Caper Sauce, Grilled Salmon Steaks with,
        548, 549
    Chicken, Grilled Butterflied, 464, *465*
    Chicken, Roast, 252, *253*
    and Chives, Slow-Roasted Salmon with,
        314, *315*
    -Chocolate Truffles, 735
    Greek Chicken, 90, *91*
    and Herb Red Potato Salad, 586, *587*
    Icebox Cheesecake, 708, *709*
    juicing, 23
    Meringue Pie, Mile-High, *770*, 771
    Pie, North Carolina, 768, *769*
    Pie, Shaker, *766*, 767
    Pudding Cake, 706, *707*
    Salsa Verde, 283
    -Thyme Wood-Grilled Salmon, 544
Lettuce
    Almond Boneless Chicken, *118*, 119
    Chinese Chicken Salad, 114, *115*
    Grilled Caesar Salad, 566, *567*

Lexington Barbecue Sauce, 513
Lexington-Style Pulled Pork, *512*, 513
Lighthouse Inn Potatoes, *222*, 223
Lime
    -Coconut Cookies, 725
    -Garlic Fried Chicken, 354, *355*
    -Ginger Glaze, 725
    Key, Pie, Icebox, 774, *775*
Loaded Baked Potato Omelet Filling, 593
Louisiana Seasoning, 92
Lyonnaise Potatoes, *218*, 219

M

Macaroni
    and Cheese, Best Potluck, 10, *11*
    and Cheese with Tomatoes, *12*, 13
    Salad, Hawaiian, 182, *183*
Magic Chocolate Flan Cake, 684, 685
Maine Blueberry Grunt, *748*, 749
Malted Milk Glaze, 725
Manchego and Chorizo Breakfast Pizza, 596
Manicotti, Baked, with Meat Sauce, *428*, 429
Marshmallow crème
    Chocolate Cream Cupcakes, *702*, 703
    Swiss Hazelnut Cake, 688, *689*
    Whoopie Pies, 732, *733*
Masa harina
    Puffy Tacos, *364*, 365
Mashed Potato Cakes, 216, *217*
Mashed Potato Casserole, *330*, 331
Measuring equipment, ratings of, 817
Meat
    scoring fat on, 543
    see also Beef; Lamb; Pork
Meatballs
    Drop, 410, *411*
    and Marinara, 412, *413*
    and Marinara, Slow-Cooker, *414*, 415

N

O

Q

R

Radish(es)
Hard-Cooked Eggs, and Capers, Tuna Salad with, 20
and Sweet Potato, Chicken Baked in Foil with, *262, 263*

Raisins
Classic Steak Sauce, 199
Lane Cake, *670,* 671
Morning Glory Muffins, *634,* 635
New Orleans Bourbon Bread Pudding, *756,* 757
Steak Sauce, 206

Ranch Fried Chicken, *84,* 85

Ranch Potato Salad, 578, *579*

Raspberry(ies)
Blitz Torte, *690,* 691
Chiffon Pie, 796, *797*
Mixed Berry Buckle, *746,* 747
Sauce, Cheese Blintzes with, 612, *613*
Summer Berry Pudding, 758, *759*

Recipe and culinary history
Basque cooking in California, 79
Bastien's Restaurant, 195
beef Stroganoff, 50
Big Bob Gibson's restaurant, 456
Bundt pans, 669
B&W Bakery crumb buns, 647
Campbell's Noodle with Chicken Soup, 2
chicken Divan, 35
chicken Florentine, 36
chuck roast in foil, 295
cold-oven recipes, 700
Colonel Sanders, 28
cooking with lard, 368
Cornell chicken, 454
cowboy food lingo, 56
Delmonico potatoes, 221
Delmonico's restaurant, 221

Recipe and culinary history *(cont.)*
Detroit-style pizza, 165
Divan Parisien restaurant, 35, 36
Ebinger's Baking Company, 664
first American restaurant, 202
frozen fish sticks, 64
gelatin-based salads, 16
grandma pizza, 432
green goddess dressing, 25
Heinz ketchup, 42
Hidden Valley Ranch Dressing, 578
honeybees in America, 77
Horn and Hardart's automats, 13
"huli"-ed chicken, 453
innovative sandwiches, 130
Joe froggers, 728
Jucy Lucy burgers, 500
Kentucky barbecue, 530
macaroni and cheese, 13
meatloaf, 42, 44
New Orleans Vietnamese community, 101
Nilla Wafers, 795
North Carolina barbecue, 513
North Carolina fish stews, 96
Oberlin College dining plan, 682
Papa Kay Joe's, 519
Peach Park, 779
Pillsbury Bake-Off, 801
po' boy sandwiches, 111
popcorn chicken, 88
proper dining and tableware, 655
Salisbury steak, 53
Shaker Lemon Pie, 767
smothered pork chops, 61
St. Louis–Style pizza, 158
St. Paul sandwich, 122
Sunbeam Mixmaster, 327
sweet-and-sour flavors, 577
sweetened condensed milk, 774

2/2022
$34.99

WITHDRAWN